philosophical guidelines for counseling

second edition

philosophical
guidelines
for counseling

CARLTON E. BECK

UNIVERSITY OF WISCONSIN — MILWAUKEE

WM. C. BROWN COMPANY PUBLISHERS
Dubuque, Iowa

EDUCATION SERIES

Consulting Editor in Counseling
and Guidance
Joseph C. Bentley
University of Utah

Copyright ©1966 by Carlton E. Beck

Copyright ©1971 by Wm. C. Brown Company Publishers

Library of Congress Catalog Card Number: 72-142228

ISBN 0-697-06099-3

Printed in the United States of America

To my father and mother,
Mr. and Mrs. S. C. Beck

Contents

Foreword

The field of guidance and counseling is undergoing a critical degree of expansion. It is critical in that it represents both special opportunities and special dangers. The expansion can be seen especially in the United States, but there are also interesting auguries from abroad. In England, which has been slow to recognize the necessity for special training in this field, there have now been instituted courses for school counselors at Keele and Reading Universities and at Edgehill Training College.

It is especially at such a time of critical expansion that there is a need for careful, rigorous, and fundamental examination of the directions and assumptions that prevail in the field. There is a dangerous temptation for workers in an expanding field to concentrate upon satisfying exigent, practical needs and to neglect the less immediately rewarding and more difficult and demanding tasks of philosophical clarification. Moreover, it is in exactly such a developing field that rigorous philosophical investigation will bear greatest fruit, for careful thinking now will produce multiplied benefits in the expanded conditions of the future.

The present volume therefore is particularly timely. There are signs that the prevailing momentum of the field is less frequently being regarded as self-justifying. An increasing number of thoughtful scholars and practitioners are engaging in a healthy process of self-examination and self-criticism.

This tendency is to be welcomed wholeheartedly, but there arises the antithetical danger that immoderate or unbalanced self-criticism may produce discouragement or despair, especially among the young and inexperienced. There is an acute need, therefore, for a well-balanced and selective presentation of some of the more thoughtful and seminal contributions to this process of critical self-appraisal.

The editor has collected here the thinking of some of the key writers who have given consideration to this issue. The volume should provide invaluable material for critical discussion among those entering the field of guidance and those more experienced workers who are preparing counselors, as well as those for whom long familiarity with practical problems may have dulled the habit of questioning basic assumptions.

It is not too much to claim that the person who masters the material in this volume will have gained an epitomized view of what the major scholars in the field consider to be the principal philosophical issues that deserve our attention in the coming decades. There is little doubt that the intellectual sophistication attendant upon familiarity with this material would contribute significantly to raising the critical standards of those entering the field of guidance and counseling at this crucial time.

In particular, it draws attention to the excellent treatment of the relationship between existentialism and counseling. One could argue that American philosophical thinking, which has been much influenced by pragmatism and more recently by linguistic analysis, stands in need of correction by the particular emphases and concerns brought by the existential philosopher. However this may be, the present volume is strengthened significantly by its inclusion of some of the most profound and searching recent contributions to the examination of the implications of existentialism for counseling.

Boston University   Paul Nash

Preface

This book is a revision of *Guidelines for Guidance* which originally appeared in 1966. The change of title of this version indicates clearly that the emphasis has changed. This edition concentrates chiefly upon the philosophical bases of *counseling*. Much has happened since the first edition, and the selections in this edition reflect those changes. The whole human potential movement (sensitivity training, encounter groups, and related activities) is now widely discussed and debated. Behavioral counseling, including especially the behavior modification approach, is a subject of great interest among counselors. The existentialist approaches to counseling which were deemed promising in the early 1960s, but were also then criticized for being "too poetic," "too subjective," and "lacking specific techniques," have begun to consolidate and to answer some of these criticisms.

The Woodstock phenomenon, the campus strikes and other great unrest of 1970, the drug subcultures, the hardhat versus hippies confrontations—all of these and more have so changed the arena of human problems and value decisions that any counselor who is not aware of them is at best irrelevant and at worst dangerous to his clients. The revision of human priorities and human concerns is reflected in the revision of this book. We are still too close to these pressing issues and problems to know their ultimate effects on man, but we must somehow take them into account.

Other issues remain, despite changes in the outward trappings, and knowledge of these issues and viewpoints are still essential for both novice counselors and those who wish to remain professionally alive. We have retained many of the key essays from the original edition. Professors and students who have used the first edition have commented often that these articles represent the underlying assumptions and patterns of thinking which are perennially important in counseling. This edition, following the general design of the first edition, is composed of key philosophically-oriented articles which have appeared in journals and of new articles written especially for this edition by both well-established professionals and by promising younger authors whose insights even at this stage augur well for the field. My sincere thanks to these perceptive men and women and to the publishers who have so kindly allowed the reprinting of articles first appearing in their journals. In all, the

new edition has retained twenty-eight articles from the original collection of
fifty-two items; it includes four new essays written especially for this edition;
it contains reprints of seventeen key philosophically-oriented articles written
after the original edition went to press, largely in 1969-70, and revisions of
two articles from the original collection. This mix would seem in my judgment
to be a healthy, stimulating updating of the philosophical concerns currently
besetting counseling, plus the needed balance of the perennial concerns of
the field.

One of the most rewarding developments I have observed since the publication of my own *Philosophical Foundations of Guidance* (Prentice-Hall,
1963) has been the greatly increased amount of attention and publication
space given to philosophical articles. A field such as counseling must constantly take stock of itself and its directions. As each new development takes
place, it must be carefully examined and evaluated. This book is dedicated
to the presentation of recent developments which are only now beginning
to be analyzed and to the analysis of other issues and ideas which have been
with us comparatively longer. Our hope is that professors, students, and
others involved in counseling will use our book as a starting point in understanding better and in helping to examine the basic assumptions, movements,
issues, and ideas involved in counseling.

Many of the articles will raise hackles and eyebrows as well as questions.
This has been built into the book deliberately. I can assume no responsibility
nor can I assume any credit for the views expressed by the writers of the
articles, but I do assume gladly the responsibility for presenting their thinking
to a wider readership.

One will note that there are some key omissions. There are, for example,
no articles from Carl Rogers, Gilbert Wrenn, or E. G. Williamson, although
there are articles by some of their staunchest followers. Their work has been
among the most significant and most often reprinted in the field of counseling. Their omission here does not indicate a lack of respect for their work;
quite the opposite. I feel that instead of presenting bits and pieces it would
be far better to encourage counselors to read the major works of these men
in their entirety, so important and so widely discussed have their contributions
been.

Throughout the book there appears a common thread: concern for man
as he seeks meaning in his life. The thinking of the thoughtful men and
women who have contributed to *Philosophical Guidelines for Counseling* provides aid to those who are helping in the search for meaning. In the words
of Seneca, "God divided man into men that they might help one another."

                                                                              C. E. B.

Acknowledgments

As is obvious in any collection of readings, the major contribution has been the permission and cooperation of the many journals and authors to allow the reprinting of their materials. Sincere gratitude, also, is in order to those men and women who created new materials especially for this book in order that important gaps might be filled in places where the literature had been silent to date.

I am sure I speak for all members of our writing team when I say that we owe far more to our students than we can ever express as, with so much patience and forbearance, they listen, respond, and suggest alternatives in our lectures and seminars.

I am grateful to the many readers of the first version of this book (then entitled *Guidelines for Guidance*) for their suggestions which I have tried to incorporate into this revision. Their kind words and suggestions cannot be repaid by me, but I hope that the book itself makes partial repayment for their time and efforts.

Thanks, too, is in order to the cooperative staff of the Wm. C. Brown Company Publishers and Professor Shirley Kersey, my efficient colleague, whose suggestions and assistance contributed greatly to production of the manuscript.

Chapter

1

Important Issues

It has been said that "*Issues* never change; only our *views* of them change." Whether we choose to agree with this or not, it is apparent that views on issues — like all views — can be narrow or wide, nearsighted or clearly discerned. It is and must be the task of the sincere counselor candidate to wipe the steam from his lenses, examine his vision periodically, and keep his eyes open. His continued effectiveness as a counselor depends upon his vision.

The issues dealt with in this chapter are recurring ones in the fields of guidance, counseling, and related helping relationships. They focus on scope, utilization of available resources, value problems related to practice, and common assumptions which have recently been called to question. Some of the central questions running through the whole chapter are those which call upon the reader to ask himself, "Within what limits shall I operate? In what phase of helping relationships have I the most to offer to my fellow man? How well do I really understand the social context in which counseling and guidance takes place? What old ways of viewing issues must I re-examine immediately? What issues must be studied at length and over an extended period of time?"

The essays in this chapter, of course, are not all-inclusive. They raise *some* of the vital issues in counseling and guidance. As our views of issues become clearer, other issues will come into focus. Issues emerge to our view as research is forthcoming, as men think through the assumptions under which they have been operating, and as life in the larger society changes because of far-reaching technological and human development. The counselor must never fall victim to what I have termed elsewhere "completism" (the feeling that "Now at last I am a counselor, certified and educated, once and for all")! To do so would be tantamount to stating that people and societies are static, not dynamic. A counselor must attune to the nuances of the total society in which he functions and must think of himself as always "in process" of becoming an effective counselor. His commitments, hopefully, will grow with him and aid him in seeing the commitments and meanings of others.

ISSUES IN COUNSELING: ELUSIVE AND ILLUSIONAL

Donald H. Blocher
University of Minnesota

An examination of the questions which continue to command attention in most discussions of counseling theory, practice, and research seems to reveal an interesting dichotomy. The first set of these questions comprises a group that are frequently discussed, often elicit considerable emotion, and are generally quite unproductive in terms of the consequences which they generate. These questions can well be called illusions in counseling. The second set of issues are frequently avoided in discussions; they are extremely difficult to frame clearly but have very important consequences. They are indeed elusive in character.

ILLUSIONS IN COUNSELING

It is perhaps easier to begin by demolishing illusions than by attempting to trap the elusive. One of the foremost illusions in counseling concerns the old question of should counseling be "directive" or "non-directive." This is one of the oldest, most decrepit, and least productive arguments in the field of counseling. Part of its feebleness is drawn from the fact that as an issue it is not even clear in meaning. Two kinds of questions are involved. The first concerns whether or not the counselor influences his client. The answer to this question is really no longer at issue. Writers as different in orientation as Williamson (16) and Patterson (10) agree that counselors do, should, and cannot avoid influencing clients. The relevant questions which survive around this part of the issue concern only directions and degrees of influence.

The second aspect of this sterile controversy over "directive vs. non-directive counseling" concerns the distribution of responsibility for the content of the interview or the nature of the counseling process as apart from its outcomes. Research by Robinson (13) and others of the so-called "communications" school of counseling has indicated rather clearly that division of responsibility for the content of the counseling interview is one and only one of a number of relevant dimensions in the counseling process. This research suggests that virtually all counselors vary their behavior along this continuum from client to client or from one point to another in the counseling process. No counselors completely abdicate responsibility for the nature of the interview. For example, many so-called non-directive counselors use formal structuring techniques at the beginning of counseling which are quite "directive" in one sense. Decisions to respond to affect or content, to clarify, to accept, all require some degree of responsibility on the part of the counselor.

Reprinted by permission of the author and the *Personnel and Guidance Journal*, Vol. XLIII, April 1965, 796-800.

Again, the relevant questions which survive in this issue are merely how much and in what directions should counselor responsibility be exerted.

A second rather moribund question is whether or not counselors should diagnose. This is illusion number two. The term diagnosis has been an emotionally loaded word in the counseling vocabulary for some years. Two basic reasons seem to account for this fact. First, the term diagnosis was largely borrowed from medicine, and to many counselors it carries a strong flavor of telling clients what is wrong with them. This connation does violence to values which many counselors hold concerning building on the assets of clients, distinguishing between counseling and psychotherapy, and so forth.

A second reason for this emotional reaction is the connection which many counselors see between diagnosis and the use of tests. Many counselors apparently feel that if they do not use tests, they also do not diagnose.

Most of the thinking surrounding both of these reactions to diagnose is fallacious. The only philosophical assumption which really affects the question of diagnostic activity is whether or not the counselor views one of his tasks in the counseling process as that of understanding the counselee. Diagnostic activities are merely those activities which have as one of their purposes helping the counselor understand his client. Research on the nature of this kind of activity by Koester (5), McArthur (7), and Parker (9) has indicated that for many counselors this activity resembles a hypothesis-testing process. The Pepinskys (11) have called attention to the counselor as a scientist-practicioner and have described the process of observation and inference by which the counselor builds a hypothetical model through which to understand his client.

The question again is not whether or not to diagnose. All counselors who attempt to understand their clients are engaged in diagnosis. The degree to which a particular counselor is committed to differential treatment for different clients may influence the nature and extent of his diagnostic activities. The counselor with a strong client-centered approach may not vary treatment processes from one client to another to as great a degree as one who considers himself eclectic. The difference in diagnostic activity between the two refers to differential diagnosis rather than to the process of diagnosis itself, however.

Diagnosis also has nothing to do with the use of tests. Tests are merely samples of behavior from which other behavior is inferred. The moment that the counselor makes inferences about behavior from any source, he is diagnosing.

From what we know about diagnostic processes now, we must conclude that all counselors do diagnose but that diagnostic activities contribute most when they are *continuous, tentative,* and *testable.* Diagnosis in this sense is a continuous process which is integrated into the total counseling. It is always tentative and subject to revision as further behavior samples become available. Finally, it is testable in the sense that diagnostic constructs or hypotheses are rooted in behavior and are operationally defined so that they may be confirmed or rejected through prediction.

A third illusion revolves around the question of whether counseling is personal-emotional or informational-didactic in nature. This question is another which has generated more heat than light in recent years. When either side of this issue is explored thoroughly, it can be reduced to a set of patent absurdities.

First, examine the didactic-informational side. The logical extensions of this position are:

1. Counseling is impersonal.
2. Counseling is teaching occupational information to a class of one.
3. Only sick people have emotions.
4. The affective and intellectual functions of human beings can be separated and treated as self-contained entities.

These are obvious absurdities. A look at the opposite side of the coin, however, reveals some equally indefensible propositions.

1. Human behavior is not mediated by rational-intellectual problem-solving processes. (How did the client get to the counselor in the first place?)
2. The counseling interview is characterized by primarily verbal communication processes, but it is still an entirely emotional rather than an intellectual exchange.
3. All problems arise out of emotional conflicts rather than vice versa.
4. Personal problem-solving is not an important matter for counseling. People can solve all personal problems readily once their deep-seated emotional conflicts are removed.

These propositions seem equally absurd. If counseling is a process which helps whole human beings cope with total life situations, it seems clear that both affective and intellectual aspects of life will have to be considered.

Three illusions in counseling which have commanded research time and energy from counselors have been discussed and hopefully disposed of.

ELUSIVE ISSUES

The second set of issues which are dubbed elusive in character are naturally more difficult to discuss than those mentioned previously. These issues are important, have vital consequences, and are exceedingly difficult to resolve. The first of these is set up in terms of the following question, "Is counseling developmental-educative-preventive, or is it remediating-adjustive-therapeutic?"

It seems better to deal with this issue in terms of goals rather than in terms of methodologies. Efforts to distinguish between counseling and psychotherapy have dealt largely with methodologies and their applications. The intensity of the process, its level of impact upon the client or patient, the setting in which it is done all have been used as distinguishing criteria. Writers such as Perry (12) and Brammer and Shostrom (4) have characterized human personality in terms of a sort of onionskin analogy, with the counselor busy peeling away the outer layers of skin while the therapist penetrates to the inner and apparently more pungent layers of the onion core. Presumably, every counselor should stop at whatever point his eyes begin to water.

None of these kinds of distinctions seem particularly useful. Counseling and psychotherapy are processes which are aimed at changing human behavior. If any real differences exist between the two processes, they must involve the kinds of outcomes which are specified for each, and possibly with the underlying assumptions which translate such outcomes into goals.

It seems to this writer that when the usual outcomes for counseling and psychotherapy are pooled and an impromptu factor analysis performed, two rather dominant clusters of goals appear. These can be characterized as (1) developmental-educative-preventive goals, and (2) remediating-adjustive-therapeutic outcomes.

It may be worthwhile examining these two clusters for a moment. One part of the first cluster deals with developmental goals. An underlying assumption here is that human personality grows or unfolds in terms of a largely healthy interaction between the growing organism itself and the culture or environment. From this point of view, development is seen as a reasonably ordered and patterned process of change moving in directions which are typically desirable for both the individual and society. The function of counseling in such a framework is to facilitate normal development. The outcomes may be stated in terms of mastering developmental tasks or moving from one stage of development to another.

The whole concept of development is closely tied to education, obviously. As part of this cluster, one may then include understanding of self, understanding of environment (world of work, for example), development of problem-solving skills, etc. Also associated with this cluster are preventive mental hygiene outcomes such as preventing too great frustrations, anxieties, or stresses; avoiding unhealthy relationships or experiences; etc.

The second cluster of outcomes can be described by labels such as remediative, adjustive, and therapeutic. These outcomes are generally characterized by goals that involve breaking down and replacing defenses; learning new adjustments to particular situations which may be family, institutional, or societal; and removing conflicts in personality organization. These goals cluster around concepts of removing pathological components, adjusting people to environmental demands, and restoring mental health.

When the processes which are familiarly called counseling and psychotherapy are examined in the light of these two presumed clusters of outcomes, reasons for confusion in terms become apparent. Much of what is attempted in the name of counseling has been as remediative and adjustive in purpose as anything attempted in the name of psychotherapy. Counselors have attempted to "adjust" youngsters to the demands of schools and teachers. They have attempted to remediate and remove presumed pathological elements, for example, "laziness," "negativism," "aggression," and so forth.

One important issue facing counseling is whether distinctions on the basis of the kinds of clustering which have been described will be strengthened or whether they will be further broken down and no valid differences will exist between counseling and therapy. Perhaps, of course, writers such as Rogers (14) and Arbuckle (2) believe this has already happened.

A second elusive issue which faces counseling today is not unrelated to the first. It can be stated in its strongest terms in this question: Is counseling liberating or conditioning in nature? Modern psychology has generally tended to look upon man, as Allport (1) says, as a reactive being or at best a reactive being in depth. Personality or learning theories based upon such a view tend to search for a set of uniform variables to which all behavior is subject. In a sense, such a system is closed. It tends to produce models based upon homeostatic principles and to view the human being functioning in a mechanistic-deterministic environment. Changing behavior in terms of this model, whether in counseling, therapy, or whatever, involves primarily identifying and controlling these variables.

The philosophical background from which counseling and guidance has emerged is not one in which formulations of this kind are comfortable. Instead, as Beck (3) points out, these philosophical antecedents place great emphasis upon terms like individualism, responsibility, independence, personal freedom, etc. The philosophical frame of reference and American behavioristic *Zeitgeist* have now collided. This collision has become disturbingly clear in the controversies between those who term themselves existential psychologists such as May (6), Rogers (14), Maslow (6), and Allport (1), and the radical behaviorists best exemplified by Skinner (15) and represented in the guidance literature by writers such as Michael and Meyerson (8).

Two rather distinctly alternative directions seem to open before counseling. The existentialist position seems a philosophically attractive but scientifically unclear path. The Skinnerian-behavioristic road is scientifically rigorous, but philosophically frightening. Can or should counselors specify the outcomes of counseling in rigorous behavioral terms and proceed to shape them by conditioning processes? Do they instead deal in such quasi-behavioral commodities as self-awareness, immediate experience, and self-actualization? If counseling takes the latter course, what is its eventual relationship to a behaviorist psychology? If counseling takes the path of conditioning, what becomes its commitment in a philosophical sense?

These issues are elusive but vital in terms of their consequences. Counselors above all need to spend less time and energy tilting at the illusional windmills of the past and more time in resolving the elusive but inescapable issues which will shape the future.

BIBLIOGRAPHY

1. Allport, G. W. Psychological models for guidance. *Harvard educ. Rev.*, 1962, 32, 4, 373-381.
2. Arbuckle, D. S. *Counseling: an introduction*. Boston: Allyn and Bacon, 1961.
3. Beck, C. *Philosophical foundations of guidance*. Englewood Cliffs, New Jersey: Prentice-Hall, 1963.
4. Brammer, L. & Shostrom, E. *Therapeutic psychology: fundamentals of counseling and psychotherapy*. Englewood Cliffs, New Jersey: Prentice-Hall, 1960.
5. Koester, G. A. A study of the diagnostic process. *Educ. psychol. Measmt.*, 1954, 14, 473-486.
6. May, R. (ed.) *Existential psychology*. New York: Random House, 1961.
7. McArthur, C. Analyzing the clinical process. *J. counsel. Psychol.*, 1954, 1, 203-208.
8. Michael, J. & Meyerson, L. A behavioral approach to counseling and guidance. *Harvard educ. Rev.*, 1962, 32, 4, 382-401.
9. Parker, C. As a clinician thinks. *J. counsel. Psychol.*, 1958, 5, 4, 253-262.
10. Patterson, C. H. The place of values in counseling and psychotherapy. *J. counsel. Psychol.*, 1958, 5, 216-233.
11. Pepinsky & Pepinsky. *Counseling: theory and practice*. New York: Ronald Press, 1954.
12. Perry, W. G. On the relation of psychotherapy and counseling. *Annals of the New York Academy of Sciences*, 1955, 63, 396-407.

13. Robinson, F. P. *Principles and procedures in student counseling*. New York: Harper and Brothers, 1950.
14. Rogers, C. R. *Client-centered therapy*. Boston: Houghton-Mifflin Co., 1957.
15. Skinner, B. F. *Verbal behavior*. New York: Appleton-Century-Crofts, 1957.
16. Williamson, E. G. Value orientation in counseling. *Personnel guid. J.*, 1958, 36, 520-528.

ON THE PHILOSOPHICAL NEUTRALITY OF COUNSELORS

Robert L. Browning
Methodist Theological School, Ohio (Delaware)

Herman J. Peters
The Ohio State University, Columbus, Ohio

THERE APPEARS TO BE AN URGENT DEMAND AMONG GUID-
ANCE COUNSELORS FOR A CLARIFICATION OF THE RELATION-
SHIP BETWEEN THE COUNSELOR'S BASIC PHILOSOPHY AND HIS
COUNSELING PROCEDURES. *Can* a counselor remain philosophically
neutral, on the one hand, and *should* the counselor do so, on the other hand.
Is Vordenberg's dictum true that "Regardless of the *kind* of personal philoso-
phy evolved by the counselor, it must surely affect the techniques he uses
and the evaluation of the effectiveness of his work"? (16:440)

I. DEMANDS FOR THE CONSIDERATION OF THE INFLUENCE OF PHILOSOPHY OF COUNSELING

After giving a survey of the inadequacies of the current attempts to develop a philosophical foundation and direction for guidance, Donald Walker
and Herbert Peiffer issue a call to action. They say, ". . . we would urge
close and careful attention to the problems of the goals of counseling, both
at the general theoretical level and as they affect the progress of the individual counseling case. . . . We are handicapped by the fact that in psychotherapy we are, to some extent, the victims of our disease orientation, our
bias against value judgments and our contradictory cultural goals." (17:209)
Mathewson says that the old myth of economic man is inadequate. He says,
"A new myth may be forming; we cannot tell what it may be and perhaps
we cannot hasten its formation, or even consciously affect its form. But unless
we wish to take a completely passive position in the determination of our
national destiny, it seems necessary to think about and to choose between
alternative sets of social and moral values, especially in the education and
guidance of our youth." (9:26)

Arbuckle compares the counselor and the surgeon, saying that the philosophy of the surgeon may have very little effect on the recovery or death of a

Reprinted by permission of the authors and *Educational Theory*, Vol. X, April
1960, 142-147.

patient. "The attitude and the philosophy of the counselor, however, are all important and in any research it is difficult to keep such an inconsistent factor consistent." (2) In Arbuckle's thinking the personnel point of view must include a consideration of every aspect in the development of the student — ". . . his intellect, his emotions, his physical being, his moral values, his skills and aptitudes, his means of recreation, his esthetic and religious values, his social adjustment, and his environmental situation. (3:3) This is a big order! The fulfillment of such a goal in guidance is greatly complicated by the fact that the counselor, in dealing with the counselee's development along such broad lines, is confused about whether or not his own loyalties, his own philosophy of life, should be shared, or whether, in fact, he can keep himself from sharing it!

> Counseling involves the interaction of two personalities through the medium of speech and other symbolic behavior. It is reasonable to suppose, therefore, that the structure of each of these personalities will have a marked influence on the interaction. It may be hypothesized further that the ways in which the personality structure of each of the counseling participants is symbolized in the speech of the interview will also have a marked effect upon the interaction.

> If it is true that the counselor's personality influences the direction, course, and outcome of the counseling interaction, it might be profitable to speculate about the kinds of counselor personality traits which are likely to facilitate counseling and those which are not.

Strang states,

> The counselor should be himself but not impose himself. He should be genuine and sincere. He is likely to fail if he tries to play a role that is not natural for him. If a person cannot risk being himself in the counseling relationship, he should not try to be a counselor. Moreover, he is consciously or unconsciously influenced by his theory of counseling; his attitude toward school policies, his outlook on life, his attitude toward people. In short, his counseling is an expression of his personality, not merely a technic applied at will. (14:   )

Pepinsky and Pepinsky, writing in 1954, state,

> There is no denying that the counselor's behavior, also, is subject to change as a function of his experience in working with clients." (11:173)

A little later under this same topic, "The Primary Function of Interaction," they go on to say,

> Indeed, the more closely we examine the counselor's motives, the more they become suspect! It appears to be, at best, nonsense and, at worst, a delusion to try to maintain that the counselor does or ought to leave his own needs parked outside the door while he interviews a client. We can state only that the explicit function of the counseling relationship — to help the client to change — should not be interfered with or destroyed. (11:174)

Perhaps the greatest single influence on counselors to be philosophically neutral has come from the work of Carl Rogers. His non-directive theory of psychotherapy was built on the belief that man could be trusted to work his way through to insights and new orientation if he could have a genuinely permissive relationship with the counselor in which he could open his inner life to himself and the helping person. Early research by Rogers led him to state that, "One can read through a complete recorded case or listen to it, without finding more than a half dozen instances in which the therapist's views on any point are evident. . . . One could not determine his diagnostic views, his standards of behavior, his social class." (12:358) Rogers did not, at that time, comment on the effect of the half dozen times and the absolute inevitability of such sharing of values. More recently, but only after a number of years of general confusion about the issue, has he addressed himself more directly to this pressing concern. In 1957, he said, in answer to certain articles challenging his position, that, "One cannot engage in psychotherapy without giving operational evidence of an underlying value orientation and view of human nature. It is definitely preferable, in my opinion, that such underlying views may be open and explicit, rather than covert and implicit." (13:199) Rogers' insistence upon as much neutrality as possible has been a helpful technique and allowed him and his associates to see deeply into the inner dynamics of the self. From his research there is ample evidence that the self, when free from threat or attack, is able to consider "hitherto rejected perceptions, to make new differentiations and to reintegrate the self in such a way as to include them." (12:365) Rogers' method seems honestly to help the person change. ". . . as changes occur in the perception of self and in the perception of reality, changes occur in the behavior." (12:363) The fact that persons often integrate their lives on levels that are not ultimately satisfactory but which only give the illusion of well-being must now be faced by Rogers and others.

II. ATTEMPTS TO CLARIFY THE RELATIONSHIP OF BASIC PHILOSOPHY TO COUNSELING

One of the most powerful attempts to do away with philosophical relativism has been made by the humanistic psychotherapist and author, Erich Fromm, in his several writings, especially in *The Sane Society*. Fromm seeks to establish a solid foundation for the development of mental health for all men in whatever society. He observes that man has not only physiological and anatomical commonalities but that he is governed universally by certain basic psychic factors as well. His system of right and wrong is therefore built squarely upon whether or not man as man, in his essential being, is having his basic human needs fulfilled.

Fromm's inclusion in his list of basic needs the necessity for a "frame of orientation and devotion" has led him to be most sympathetic toward the insights of the great religions and philosophies of the past and present. He is sensitive also to the moral standards propagated in our varying societies, because he believes that whole culture can become full of *defects* which can and do tend to make men mentally ill. Societal arrangements, therefore, often must be changed before man's needs can be met. This observation forces counselors to be concerned with social, political, and religious philosophies which have created and are sustaining, often, such unhealthy social structures.

Fromm's theory is an attempt to build on what man's needs are *objectively* and not on what man *feels* his needs to be. This concept challenges in many ways the goal of non-directive counseling which tends to center on the process of man's expression of his inner feelings of need without reference to the fact that such needs are often a result of cultural defects which will not and cannot bring ultimate health to the client. This is true because of the very nature of his human condition, and the breadth of his needs which are in the area of ultimate loyalties and basic, undergirding frames of orientation, about which most counselors feel insecure and from which discussions they tend to steer clear!

A similar trend to that of Fromm's can be seen in the writings of Kurt Lewin. He stated as far back as 1935 that, "The individual psychical experiences, the actions and emotions, purposes, wishes and hopes, are rather embedded in quite definite psychical structures, spheres of the personality, and whole process." (8:54)

Also to be found in Fromm and Lewin thought is an emphasis on man's freedom and the necessity to broaden the range of that freedom in psychotherapy as well as in intelligent political action. Lewin observed that often the individual area of freedom is very small due to the vectors and forces in his field of psychic experience, built on past identifications, inhibitions and loyalties. Yet, this freedom existed. Man as man had qualities beyond the realm of the animal. Therapy should help man use his freedom to find the paths to growth, and to overcome the psychic barriers.

One of the most dramatic and controversial attempts to deal with the question of philosophy in psychotherapy has been made by Dr. Viktor E. Frankl, the Director of the Neurological Polyclinic in Vienna and a Professor of Psychiatry at the University of Vienna. Frankl's point of view grows out of the emphasis in existentialist philosophy on man's actual conditions of existence. Man in his essence is endowed with certain capacities for freedom, for decision making, for determining his destiny. Man is a responsible being with the power to transcend his own situation and to prophesy the results of his decisions. His intellectual powers and his psychic powers are qualitatively different than other animals. Frankl joins Fromm, at this point, in that he is seeking to analyze man's basic need for a value system on which he will increase his freedom and his meaning.

He recognizes the significance of both individual psychology, stemming from Adler, and psychoanalysis, stemming from Freud. He maintains, however, that psychotherapy will be incomplete until man has a "psychotherapy of the mind" which deals with philosophical issues. Differing with Freud and others, he says, "The individual's philosophical attitude is part and parcel of his psychological one and emerges in every case." (6:34) He also believes, against the stream of thought in psychotherapy, that, "In no case should the intellectual problems of a person be written off as a 'symptom.'" (6:33)

Frankl honestly discusses the many profound problems related to his point of view, and pushes ahead, along with Fromm, to establish certain fundamental values inherent in man's situation. And yet, he maintains that existential analysis must not interfere with the ranking of values. ". . . what values he elects is and remains the patient's own affair. Existential analysis must not be concerned with what the patient decides for, what goals he sets himself, but only that he decides at all. . . The physician should never be allowed to take over the patient's responsibility; he must never permit that responsibility to be shifted to himself; he must never anticipate decisions or impose them upon the patient. His job is to make it possible for the patient to reach decisions; he must endow the patient with the capacity for deciding." (6:270)

Such a view has been given great impetus by the philosophical writings of Martin Buber. Buber's philosophy urges man to relationships of trust with other men — very much like that between the counselor and the client in a permissive setting; and yet, he believes that real trust must allow and encourage honest *dialogue* between both parties. When there is a real meeting of persons (Buber describes this meeting in terms of an I — Thou relationship — very similar to Schweitzer's "reverence for life" concept) each person is bringing his full self to the dialogue. He must "be willing . . . to say what is really in his mind about the subject of conversation. And that means further that on each occasion he makes the contribution of his spirit without reduction and without shifting ground." (4:112)

Dialogue on a philosophical level, on the level of the quest for ultimate meaning is a basic need for every human being. The counselor must be sensitive, nevertheless, to the existential situation in which the client finds himself at any given time.

Gordon Allport emphasizes the profundity of this renewed interest in studying the basic conditions of man's existence. He says, "Existentialism calls for a doctrine of an active intellect, for more emphasis upon propriate functions, including self-objectification and oriented becoming. In particular it calls for a wider and fresher view of anxiety, of courage, and of freedom. (1:80) Allport stresses the fact that Freud and his followers have dealt mostly with the anxiety in man aroused by feelings of guilt and fear of punishment and not at all the anxiety which comes from a fear of *nonbeing* (death — either actual or psychological, in the Buber sense of being not in relation; not affirmed and confirmed by others).

Allport believes that the consideration of philosophical matters has been greatly de-emphasized in counseling, to the detriment of our whole concept of personality structure. Philosophic and religious decisions have to do with what he terms *Intentional Characteristics* which become a part of the personality. He believes that, "Intentional characteristics represent above all else the individual's primary modes of addressing himself to the future. As such they select stimuli, guide inhibitions and choices, and have much to do with the process of adult becoming. Relatively few theories of personality recognize the pre-emptive importance of intentional characteristics." (1:89)

So, we are seeing a powerful movement within the guidance field, psychotherapy, philosophy, theology, and psychology for a deeper view of man's problems of existence, his wide and deep needs, his essential freedom of being, and his finite situation which forces him to go beyond knowledge to an ultimate devotion — built on faith (not an irrational faith, but faith, nonetheless).

Buber, in his William Alanson White Lectures given at the Washington School of Psychiatry, says that the counselor or educator "cannot wish to impose himself, for he believes in the effect of the actualizing forces. . . . The propagandist who imposes himself, does not really believe even in his own cause, for he does not trust it to attain the effect of its own power, without his special methods." (4:111) While Buber believes so strongly in the power of honest meeting between persons in an I — Thou relationship of mutual trust and confirmation, even with differences of loyalties, he is very *cautious about the right of the psychotherapist* to embark upon a 'treatment of the essential in man.' He agrees with the late Viktor von Weizsaecker who said that it is not the privilege of the therapist or counselor to deal with the final destiny of man.

Returning to the area of guidance and student personnel services, it is becoming equally well established that basic educational philosophy does inevitably influence the procedures of the guidance counselor. If he is thoroughly pragmatic in his orientation he will probably be inclined to play down or ignore the importance of religious or metaphysical beliefs that the student brings to the counseling situation. He may feel that value judgments must be left out of the considerations. Of course, with this Pragmatic Philosophy which seems on the surface to be a neutral position, goes a basic commitment just as much so as the student may have, with his religious commitment. It seems to us that considerations of ultimate values cannot be avoided by the counselor as a person, and that he must operate from some philosophical point of view — some form of Idealism, Realism (Christian or otherwise), Pragmatism, Naturalism, or Existentialism (again religious or otherwise).

It seems imperative that guidance counselors and educators must join other leaders in education, psychology, psychotherapy, philosophy and religion in doing basic research in this field.

In this spirit of scientific inquiry (even with its obvious limitations in the area of ultimate values) and also in the spirit of dialogue (with free discussion of important questions related to man's basic needs and his basic conditions of existence) we should proceed to clarify and come to decisions about the foundation and goals of counseling.

Recently, Williamson has stated that, "I have further argued for making explicit our own value orientations as individual counselors, not in order that we may adopt a counselor's orthodox creed, but rather that we may responsibly give societal and moral direction to our individual work in terms of the explicitly desired goals chosen by our student clients." (19:528)

When guidance counselors, psychotherapists, or religious counselors admit that they are not philosophically neutral, then we will be able to study more systematically the effect of our philosophical loyalties upon our counseling.

BIBLIOGRAPHY

1. Allport, Gordon W. *Becoming: Basic Considerations For a Psychology of Personality.* Yale University Press, 1955.
2. Arbuckle, Dugald S. *Student Personnel Services in Higher Education.* McGraw-Hill. N.Y. 1953.
3. Arbuckle, Dugald S. *Teacher Counseling.* Addison-Wesley Press. Cambridge, Mass.
4. Buber, Martin. "William Alanson White Memorial Lectures." *Psychiatry* No. 20, No. 2, May 1957.
5. Buber, Martin. "The Teacher and Teaching" — compiled by Dr. Ross Snyder, Univ. of Chicago. Unpublished form.
6. Frankl, Viktor E. *The Doctor and the Soul.* Alfred Knopf. N.Y. 1955.
7. Fromm, Erich. *The Sane Society.* Rinehart & Co. N.Y. 1955.

8. Lewin, Kurt. *A Dynamic Theory of Personality.* McGraw-Hill Co. New York. 1935.
9. Mathewson, Robert H. *Guidance Policy and Practice.* Harper and Bros. New York. 1955.
10. Oates, Wayne E. *The Religious Dimensions of Personality.* Assoc. Press. N.Y. 1957.
11. Pepinsky, Harold B. and Pepinsky, Pauline N. *Counseling: Theory and Practice.* New York: The Ronald Press Company. 1954.
12. Rogers, Carl. "Some Observations on the Organization of Personality." *The American Psychologist.* Vol. 2. 1947.
13. Rogers, Carl. "A Note on the Nature of Man." *Journal of Counseling Psychology.* Vol. 4. No. 3. 1957.
14. Strang, Ruth. *The Role of the Teacher in Personnel Work.* 4th ed. 1953.
15. Tillich, Paul. *Systematic Theology.* Vol. 1. University of Chicago Press. 1952.
16. Vordenberg, Wesley. "The Impact of Personal Philosophies on Counseling." *The Personnel and Guidance Journal.* XXXI. April 1953.
17. Walker, Donald and Peiffer, Herbert. "The Goals of Counseling." *Journal of Counseling Psychology.* Vol. 4. No. 3. 1957.
18. Weitz, Henry. "Counseling as a Function of the Counselor's Personality." *The Personnel and Guidance Journal.* Vol. XXXV. No. 5 January 1957.
19. Williamson, Edmond G. "Value Orientation in Counseling." *The Personnel and Guidance Journal.* XXXVI. April 1958.

FIVE PHILOSOPHICAL ISSUES IN COUNSELING[1]

Dugald S. Arbuckle

Boston University

Philosophy should probably be discussed in philosophical terms, but many of the philosophical issues in counseling are of a realistic and down-to-earth nature. This paper is an attempt to look realistically at some of these issues.

THE SELF CONCEPT

1. The first issue has to do with the relationship between the self concept, the goals and objectives of the counselor, and the techniques and methods that he may use to achieve these objectives. What the counselor does during the counseling process is not only a measure of his techniques and methods, but it is also a measure of his self concept, which in turn, is surely related to his goals and objectives as a counselor. Goals and purposes may be thought of as having a philosophical orientation, but the more pragmatic techniques and methods are merely the tools which are used to implement these objectives and to achieve these goals.

Reprinted by permission of the author and *Journal of Counseling Psychology,* Vol. V, No. 3, 1958, 211-215.

[1]A paper presented at the Fall meeting of the New England Personnel and Guidance Conference, at Hartford, Connecticut.

The counselor's techniques, for example, are reflections of his attitude that the client must be directed, since he does not have the capacity for growth; that the client needs little or no direction, since he is capable of self determination; that the client must be told what is good and what is bad for him, since he is incapable of determining right from wrong; that respect for the integrity of the individual implies respect for the right of the individual to make his own decisions as to what might be good and what might be bad for him; that the client cannot be trusted to take positive action; the client can be trusted to take action that is generally socially acceptable. These counselor attitudes are reflected in the counselor's counseling, and they tend to be a portrait of the individual's concept of his self.

The discrepancy then, between what the counselor verbalizes he *should* do, what he actually *feels* that he should do, and what he actually *does* in an operational situation would appear to be a measure of the individual's total personality, rather than something that he has learned in his professional preparation at Chicago, or Boston, or New York. A study of Arbuckle and Wicas (2) tends to indicate that counselors receiving their doctorate education from one institution appear to differ in their attitudes and their techniques of counseling in just as many ways as those receiving their professional preparation in different institutions. One does not become a "Rogerian" by attending Chicago, or, more recently, Wisconsin, nor does one become a "Superian" or "Williamsonian" by attending Columbia or Minnesota. There would seem to be some evidence to indicate that the counselor, as he actually works, is giving a display of his philosophy of life rather than showing how well he has learned certain techniques and procedures in a graduate school.

Thus a real problem for the counselor is that ancient and honorable, although by now, well-worn phrase, "Know Thyself." As one listens to counselors describe first their concept of their' role, and then what they do, he is struck by the discrepancy between their concept and their operation, and also by the frequency with which he hears the statement, "I know I shouldn't do this, and I don't particularly like what I am doing, but you know how it is . . . I just have to do it . . ." Such a statement is surely a rather unhappy expression of the counselor's real concept of his role, and of the counselor himself. He would sometimes appear to see himself as the echoer of his superior officer, as one who has no responsibility other than to do as he is told, and one who recognizes no professional responsibility whatsoever. Again, here, the counselor would appear to be expressing his personal concept of himself, and his attitudes toward his fellow man.

An article by Walker and Peiffer (6), while aimed at raising serious questions as to the validity of some of the goals of counseling, also tends to imply that the counselor, in what he does, is primarily displaying his self concept and his value system.

RELIGION

2. Another somewhat allied problem, very much related to the counselor's self concept, is his religious orientation, or lack of it. A case in point on this item is a fairly recent publication called "The Catholic Counselor"; another is the fact that the author of this present article, in writing a paper for a

religious group, was criticized gently because his paper described the "secular" counselor, rather than the "Christian" counselor. Some counselors would feel that anything that is of importance to the Catholic counselor, *as a professional counselor,* is of equal importance to every other counselor, and vice versa; some would also feel that one cannot talk about the "Christian way" of counseling any more than one can talk about the Christian way of removing one's appendix, the Jewish way of teaching reading, and the Moslem way of solving a problem in mathematics.

To what extent, then, does one's religious philosophy, orientation or bias act as a controlling agent, and affect the counselor's relationship with the client? Does the fact that the readers of this article represent a number of different religious denominations mean that they function in a different manner, as counselors, because of this religious difference? If we assume that there is such a thing as a "Catholic counselor," or a "Methodist counselor," or a "Baptist counselor," then this would also seem to assume that there must be something different about a Catholic counselor when compared with a Seventh Day Adventist counselor or a Southern Baptist counselor. Is this so? If it is, it would seem necessary to readjust our concepts of the goals and the objectives of the counseling process, since they would apparently vary according to the religious concepts of the counselor.

This also tends to imply that one's professional preparation can be effective only to a point, but from that point on there can be no change or growth. Does the Mormon counselor operate in a different manner with a Mormon client who talks about his heavy drinking than he would with a similar client who was a Methodist? Is there any difference in the relationship between an Orthodox Jewish counselor and a Jewish client who describes his feelings about the foolishness of the acceptance of the use of Kosher foods, and the relationship between a similar client and a Presbyterian counselor? One may say, offhand, that there will be no difference in the *actions* of the counselors toward the clients although there will be differences in the *attitudes* of the counselors toward the clients. And yet, if this is so, is it possible to operate in the same way with a client, regardless of one's attitudes? Can counseling be a professional task, then, if the goals as well as the methods to be used by the counselor are to be affected by his religious orientation, first, and secondly, by his professional preparation!

THE NATURE OF MAN

3. Related to the counselor's religious concepts will be his concept of the nature of man. This again raises some interesting questions. The *Journal of Counseling Psychology* carried an article by Walker (5) on this subject. In later issues there were several "letters" on this article, and more recently Rogers (3) has written on this subject. The counselor's philosophical concept of the nature of man is, probably, more than anything else, an indication of the extent to which he holds to a client-centered concept of counseling. It is difficult to see how one can accept the Freudian view of man as being basically hostile and carnal and still describe himself as a client-centered counselor. If one is oriented to a client-centered philosophy he has a more Rousseau-ian and optimistic picture of man as being basically a perfect creature who may

have been corrupted and injured by numerous pressures. Rogers raises the intriguing question as to how the counselor can have a deep feeling of caring for the client if his own basic and innate tendency is to destroy! He also postulates the theory that the fact that Freud in his self-analysis was denied a warmly acceptant relationship may have meant that although he came to know the denied and hidden aspects of himself, he could never really come to accept them as a part of himself. One's concept of the nature of man, then, must surely affect his operation as a counselor since it means that the counselor must see both himself and the client in a different light. A basic measure of the extent to which one is Freudian or client-centered would appear to be related to his concept of the nature of man. Is he Freudian and pessimistic à la Karl Menninger, or is he client-centered and optimistic a la Carl Rogers?

COUNSELOR RESPONSIBILITY

4. Another somewhat obvious problem is the counselor's concept of his role in his society, and the question of the confidentiality of the information the client may receive. Does the counselor think of his sole responsibility as being the client and will he therefore never divulge information of a confidential nature? We can then push this to an extreme case and say if the client, in talking about his hatred for society and particularly for those who are the rulers, describes in some detail his elaborate plot to assassinate the President of the United States, would the counselor maintain the client's confidence? We might ask the same question of the Catholic Priest who hears the same thing in the confessional, or we might ask the same question of the defense lawyer who has just heard his client describe in detail the manner in which he raped and murdered a little girl. Does the counselor, does the priest, does the defense lawyer remain silent? There is much argument for saying that surely they would not remain silent, and yet, once one enters into the realm of the relative, one becomes the judge (even the Rogerian) who determines when the price that society may have to pay for counselor silence is too great. It would also be safe to say that there are very few school counselors who err on the side of maintaining confidence too much, and there are many who maintain confidences practically not at all.

The author recently read a paper on personnel work and counseling before a group of top administrators of teacher preparation institutions in Massachusetts. It was interesting to note that a significant number of them apparently felt that a counselor should be expected to reveal any information that he might have on a student to a dean or other administrative officer. This question is also related to the first one, since if the counselor himself does not have any concept of his role he will probably see no reason why he should not tell the principal about Mary's plans to run away, about Bobby's sexual deviations, about John's cheating in class. It is likely also, of course, that the number of his clients will rapidly decline and all those who do come in will be extremely wary and come forth with safe and innocuous statements.

This also raises the question of the counselor as a source of references. It is unfortunate that counselors are used for references since even a statement to the effect that one has a policy of not giving references on students who have been clients implies that the student in question was a client, and to some employers this can mean only something bad. A client recently commented to the author that a neutral statement by a former employer or teacher was almost always interpreted as being a negative statement.

COUNSELOR EDUCATION

5. Finally, these philosophical issues raise questions on the whole problem of counselor education. Can we educate counselor-trainees regarding the use of certain techniques or methods? How does one educate a counselor-trainee to be acceptant (inside as well as outside) of hostility as expressed by the client? How does one educate a counselor-trainee to be unaffected and acceptant as the client describes some extremely deviate behavior? How does one educate the counselor-trainee to see his own hostility, to realize that his narrowness of procedure might be because of his own insecurity? How does one educate the counselor-trainee so that he may develop a self-understanding of who he is and what he is trying to achieve as a counselor, and as a result, possibly leave counseling and go into another occupation where he will be less dangerous to himself and to others. How does the formal education of the counselor-trainee help him to perform the tasks described by Tooker (4), Wrenn (7), and a host of others. How, indeed, can we "educate" the counselor-trainee to be the sort of person described in an earlier article by this author (1).

Certainly it would seem that the education of the counselor cannot be at a remote academic and intellectual level. One must become involved in hostility before one can come to see where he stands on the acceptance of hostility; one must hear highly risqué stories from the lips of a handsome woman before he knows how he will react to such stories when he hears them from such a source; one must, indeed, become accustomed to the psychological equivalent of the bloody and gory wound before one can even come close to understanding the degree of his capacity to accept, let alone to understand. In this last comparison, however, there is one important difference. The surgeon can become accustomed to the gory wound, but he can also become a relatively unfeeling individual, intrigued by physical wounds and defects. In fact, he might even be a somewhat sadistic individual, and still win high regard for his capacities as a surgeon. The counselor, however, cannot accept the deviation of behavior as described by the client if he does not accept the client. The education of the counselor-trainee must change him, it would seem, rather than increase his store of knowledge. The more basic question for the counselor-educator is not what does the student know, but rather what can he do with what he knows?

Thus counselor education should probably be primarily centered on self-evaluation, self-measurement, and, might we dare to say, self-analysis. It might well be that the counselor-educator should be more of a counselor than an educator.

EXPERIENCE NEEDED

A final problem on this question has to do with the need for and the extent of the counseling experience that the counselor should have, as a client.

The American Academy of Psychotherapists requires personal counseling for admittance to the Academy so that "there may be an evaluation of the applicant by his personal therapist." If a counselor-trainee feels no particular pressures, issues or problems, however, what sort of client will he be when the purpose of the counseling would then appear to become an evaluation of him by the counselor? This is a particular problem in client-centered counseling. If the student gives every appearance of being a sound person, in class work, in practicum, in small group sessions, in the regard he appears to have for himself and for others, must the counselor-educator say, in effect, "You must come in to us as a client, even though you feel that you have no particular pressures and have no evidence that you have any problems that you cannot work out effectively yourself."? This would appear to place the client-centered counselor-educator in a rather contradictory and even Freudian position!

REFERENCES

1. Arbuckle, D. S. Client perception of counselor personality. *J. counsel. Psychol.*, 1956, 3, 93-96.
2. Arbuckle, D. S. & Wicas, E. The development of a counseling perception instrument. *J. counsel. Psychol.*, 1957, 4, 304-312.
3. Rogers, C. R. A note on the nature of man. *J. counsel. Psychol.*, 1957, 4, 199-204.
4. Tooker, E. D. Counselor role: counselor training. *Personnel guid. J.*, 1957, 36, 263-268.
5. Walker, D. E. Carl Rogers and the nature of man. *J. counsel. Psychol.*, 1956, 3, 89-92.
6. Walker, D. E. & Peiffer, H. C., Jr. The goals of counseling. *J. counsel. Psychol.*, 1957, 4, 204-210.
7. Wrenn, C. G. Status and role of the school counselor. *Personnel guid. J.*, 1957, 36, 175-184.

THE UTILIZATION OF CREATIVE POTENTIAL IN OUR SOCIETY

Walter Gruen

VA Hospital, Canandaigua, N.Y.

The title of this paper was also the title of a symposium at the 1960 APA Convention in Chicago. My purpose here is to examine the reasons for scheduling such a discussion in the first place, and to report some of the conclusions emanating from the meeting.

The question is raised with increasing insistence whether everyone in our society is living up to his own maximum potentials, and one is apt to ask quickly: "Why not?" if one encounters people who are somehow found wanting. We even have ready-made and sometimes quasi-scientific labels for such people. The terms "underachievers" in the schools and "beatniks" and "non-

Reprinted by permission of the author and the *Journal of Counseling Psychology*, Vol. 9, No. 1, 1962, 79-83.

conformists" in the adult world attest to the increasing tendency to spotlight the offender and to advertise our concern with keeping everyone at top effficiency.

There are three reasons why the concern is so much greater and more acute today.

1. We are engaged in a critical examination and reaffirmation of the basic democratic ideal, the worth of the individual. The Bill of Rights has been interpreted as proclaiming the right of the individual to develop himself to the full extent of his capacity. Not only should he be free from adverse pressures and from countercoercive forces, but he should be encouraged at every step to fulfill this destiny.

2. The second reason rests with the soul-searching into the mental health of the individual in our increasingly complex society. This concern has been partially influenced by the social problems of our time, such as delinquency, mental illness, alcoholism, including changes in social organization brought about by urbanization, mechanization, increase in leisure time, the growing influence of the mass media of entertainment, and others. The concern has also been partially fanned by some of our social scientists and by the "social prophets" of our time. The latter especially have warned us of the handwriting on the wall, by depicting the "organization man," the "marketing personality," the "suburban conformist," the "apathy of the voter," as setbacks in the development and in the progress of western man.

3. The final reason is tied up with our not-so-peaceful rivalry with Russia. We are suddenly awakened to the possibility that Russian society and Russian education may utilize the existing talents of their population more effectively, while we may keep talent dormant or siphon it off into other less socially creative channels. I need not remind anyone that the philosophical and practical issues as to where we should go as a society of humans is involved in the third reason but also in the other two.

Hence the concern with utilization of the creative potential rests on ethical considerations, on developmental theories about man, and on national objectives in a world where rival social systems compete strenuously for attention and for hegemony over the globe.

A DEFINITION OF CREATIVITY

The very moment that anyone, including the writer, takes up an examination of creativity and its socio-cultural underpinnings, it becomes necessary to define and limit the terms. Hence a creative act designates the making of something new or different out of existing objects, the reorganization or reorientation of given elements, or the utilization of existing objects and ideas in a different way. The use of a round wooden block as a wheel, the combination of wood and wire for a mouse trap, the discovery of a new principle for the organization of colors into a pattern pleasing to a number of others, are all examples. However, the creative act need not be defined by popular acclaim, nor by the label of greatness tagged on by a large number of people. The person with limited abilities and below average intelligence is "creative," if he utilizes his native and acquired skills to bring about a reorganization of words and symbols. The creative act is thereby distinguished from the habitual reaction to given elements and objects; and the latter reaction is usually known as adaptation or adjustment.

The creative act may further be a discovery of a relationship that is already known to others, but new to the individual. The discoveries of children and of culturally or socially more isolated individuals are often expressed by an idea which is new in the life space of the person, even if it is already known to adults or to other cultural groups.

Of course, the dividing line between creativity and habitual behavior is not easy to make. When is the constantly changing pattern of words in ordinary speech just adaptation and when does it become a poem or an essay? While disclaiming above the judgment of many others about the creative value of an act in the popular sense, we have to bring a consensus of some people back into play at this point. Just as some philosophers remind us that statements about truth must be statements of probability depending on some consensus of relevant individuals, the judgment of creative behavior must in the final analysis rest with a consensus or with a judgment.

The creative act can be defined by a consensus of experts or by a jury of trained peers. While we must reject the acclaim by even a majority as a criterion, we are not taking refuge into scientific double-talk when we propose the reliable judgment of more than one person as a measuring device. The experts would look into the antecedents in a given person's training and experience and judge an act as creative on the basis of past accomplishments and its different use of given elements of experience.

The Person and the State

Most of us make the implicit assumption that everyone in a democracy *should* be able to utilize all of his potentials for creative purposes for his own and society's good. This assumption is a value judgment and is one of the very cornerstones of our western choice of social organization. We do not pay only lip service to it, but we make many provisions for it and encourage it with many different institutions. Scholarships, endowments, grants-in-aid, self-development courses and workshops, are all relevant examples.

When we introduce national concern for creativity and also remember our third reason for concern, namely world competition of social systems for the attention of man, we are talking about a different meaning of the term. It is then defined as the development of talent for the production of new ventures in the fields of art and science for the advancement of society, and changes are hopefully evaluated as progress. It is worthwhile to distinguish clearly between the two meanings of creativity, because our first and primary focus here is taken to be a stage in the development of a person and may not necessarily be related to the greatness of a society. We should therefore distinguish the concern for developing "inner" creativity as a target of the ethical principles of a democracy which wants man to develop to his fullest measure from the concern for developing "popular" creativity for the sake of social progress and world competition. Of course a good case can and has been made that the full development of inner creative potential is the necessary prerequisite of a rich harvest of useful ideas for the advance of society.

THE FOUR PAPERS

Pepinsky and Productive Nonconformity

The contributions of the four papers in the symposium perhaps shed some new light on the development of creativity. Pepinsky (1960) is concerned with it by contrasting nonconformity with conformity. She examines some of the conditions under which creativity emerges in contrast to those conditions where it is inhibited. She attempts a definition of nonconformity involving both statistical and psychological criteria by distinguishing a creative from a habitual act. She distinguishes productive nonconformity as behavior contributing to task accomplishment of a group or of a society or of an individual, and shows how it differs from mere conformity to another set of values. She accomplishes this by contrasting it clearly with nonproductive nonconformity of — for instance — the persistent rebel. Her points are illustrated by finding different antecedents for each type of nonconformity in three different settings, where she carefully studied the people and the environment. The antecedents are not merely concerned with personality attributes, but also with social conditions which allow productive nonconformity as behavior to emerge.

She asks an important question which she wisely does not answer, and which we can pass on to the reader to ponder. She mentioned that we have studied people in extreme social disorganization and trained them to cope with it from what we have learned. However we do not train people to cope with the extreme social organization which she found to be a pre-disposing social milieu factor for conformity and which also has been found to be prevalent in many urbanized and highly routinized sections of our western world. The question arises here whether we can train people to cope with such conditions without killing their potential for productive nonconformity and their desire to change the social conditions toward a more fertile climate. One of the important issues implied in her paper concerns the nature and locale of such a training program.

Another very important point of issue concerns our and Pepinsky's implication that productive nonconformity is an important prerequisite for the health and progress for human society. If we equate productive nonconformity with certain aspects of Maslow's self-actualization and Erikson's generativity, we find that in such theories creative behavior becomes an important criterion of the mental health of the individual and constitutes the apex of human development. Fromm and others have felt that the accumulation of healthy individuals in these terms insures a healthy society. The fact that the questions have been answered in the affirmative by certain thinkers and scientists still does not put an end to speculation. The answer, as Smith (1961) and others have pointed out, may well depend in the final analysis on one's own goals and values so that we are faced with the need for a consensus, which we raised in the process of justifying a definition.

Fiedler and the Group Climate

Fiedler (1960) investigates some of the social conditions under which members of a discussion group become more creative. While antecedents in both inner man and in his social organization with others were investigated

by Pepinsky, Fiedler concentrated on structural antecedents of group productivity under carefully measured conditions. He concentrated on the
variables of formality of leadership, homogeneity of group composition, and
psychological distance of leaders from members. Starting from the same definition of creativity as we have used, he devised a task for group creative action
of very high reliability. His findings suggest that creative group action may
require different group structure than those found beneficial in task-oriented
groups. His paper represents a contribution to our knowledge of group structure and group practices, especially in the light of some of the wild claims
for greater group creativity that are made by the inventors of new gimmicks
in group discussion techniques.

It also suggests strongly that a group climate that is task and efficiency
oriented may breed social conditions which inhibit creative behavior. We can
see all kinds of implications here for work groups, research teams and even
educational settings, where choices about individual creativity versus getting
something accomplished are involved. Since two of the papers have studied
and identified some of the antecedents for creativity, we can ask whether
we now have a recipe for unfolding the creative behavior in a large number
of individuals. A catalogue of these findings suggests creativity and the unfolding of potentials in an individual if we provide a family structure which
contains independence-training and lack of conflict between members, the
experience of unpopularity with the social leaders and with the majority of
teachers while the child is in school, securing a sponsor for him outside his
family and circle of friends. We must allow for diversity of expression in the
groups he will enter as an adolescent and as an adult, but the groups themselves should be homogeneous in composition. I suspect that the problem is
less simple, especially in view of the discussion by Bronfenbrenner (1960), who
investigated the effects of parental discipline, social class, sex of child, dominance of father or mother, and social setting of father's job on initiative and
independence in the child. Nevertheless the recipe coming from the symposium sounds like an intriguing hypothesis for a future action research study.

The prescriptions suggested by our research studies are too simple precisely because they leave out a consideration of the values already encountered
in trying to arrive at a definition. What is a good society for human beings
and what is a productive and creative individual are two important value
questions which must be decided before we can answer on more empirical
grounds which of several training methods are more effective.

Gruen and Attitudes toward Creativity

Gruen's (1960) study addressed itself to values by probing for attitudes
toward creativity as defined here. It was found that preferences for unfolding
of potentials and for creative activity are gratifyingly very wide-spread in a
sample of upper-middle class adults. The findings here tie in with Riesman's
(1960) observation that there are a good many private Utopias among contemporary Americans but no public movement or program for a better world.
That is, people have visions among themselves and within their family and
friendship circles, but on the national and public scene there seems to be a
void. Similarly, Gruen's adults professed both private feelings of inspiration
and application on one questionnaire but adhered on another to publicly pro-

claimed values of upward mobility for higher status, of emotional control and of devitalization in some areas of living.

One wonders how such findings contrast with some of the conclusions drawn by Gurin, Veroff, & Feld in *Americans View Their Mental Health* (1960). In this recent study many respondents seemed to function with little zest and joy, but stressed effortlessness and comfort as goals.

Drews on Creativity in the Schools

Drews' (1960) study showed that intellectual and creative activity is de-emphasized in the public schools. The alternate preference for status and popularity has often been identified as components of the accepted official "American core culture," which the second of Gruen's questionnaires attempted to measure. It has also been mentioned by some as a possible inhibitor of the creativity we are investigating here. The question therefore arises whether the social atmosphere in the schools described by Drews is correlated with lack of creativity later on in the lives of the children as adults. Since we find both informally and by our researches a good number of creative adults in our society, we may wonder if they went through the same schooling and social climate so eloquently described by Drews and emerged despite it, or whether their schooling was different in the past. There is encouraging evidence that dormant intellectual ability can be encouraged in adult years. I am thinking here of the Bell Telephone Middle Management Program in which executives are placed into a humanistic university program for one year. It has been amazing to competent observers how much stimulation this program produces and how much unfolding goes on in the "students" as they read and study various ideas and sources.

CONCLUSIONS

Evident in the four papers is our tendency to study the emergence and the nature of creative behavior in so-called elite groups. In these groups our findings are somewhat encouraging of favorable results but we still have not investigated creativity in lower class groups. I suspect that our concentration "above the belt" represents an implicit acceptance of the doctrine of natural selection. It does not answer the question whether or not the development and use of creativity in lower class groups is also a criterion for a healthy society, or for a healthy climate in which man can develop. Just as Terman's gifted children did not all become creative adults, it may be just as reasonable to assume that the ungifted or the unprivileged children will not always remain unproductive. However, someone should find out if this is so.

Obviously we need to know a lot more. We have not decided whether creativity is the ultimate pinnacle of development of all men, as postulated by some of our cross-cultural theories of personality, or is a typical American ideal and not exportable as a goal for man in other societies. Undoubtedly we are committed to a search for the factors that will facilitate or impede our western type of creativity. We have also become detectives searching for the forces in our society that will guarantee the use of all the human and psychic resources contained therein. This issue was not raised fifty years ago. A complex society and the peculiar requirements of increased interdependence in the urbanized life of today and in the One World of the future have molded this issue into a new frontier. We are increasingly examining our values, our institutions, our training and personality shaping techniques for this purpose. We also compare ourselves with other contemporary cultures to see how they may have solved the common human problems. Whatever our findings, we are now convinced that it is later than we think.

REFERENCES

Bronfenbrenner, U. The changing American child — a speculative analysis. Paper read at American Psychol. Assn., Chicago, September, 1960.

Drews, Elizabeth. Aspirations and achievement motives in gifted adolescents. Paper read at American Psychol. Assn., Chicago, September, 1960.

Fiedler, F. E. Leadership, group composition, and group creativity. Paper read at American Psychol. Assn., Chicago, September, 1960.

Gruen, W. So-called core culture attitudes and the belief in one's own creative potential. Paper read at American Psychol. Assn., Chicago, September, 1960.

Gurin, G., Veroff, J., & Feld, Sheila. *Americans view their mental health.* New York: Basic Books, 1960.

Pepinsky, Pauline N. The social dialectic of productive non-conformity. Paper read at American Psychol. Assn., Chicago, September, 1960.

Riesman, D. The search for challenge. *New university thought.* Spring, 1960, 3-15.

Smith, M. B. Mental health reconsidered: A special case of the problem of values in psychology. *Amer. Psychol.,* 1961, 16, 299-306.

NON-SEQUITURS IN THE LITERATURE OF COUNSELING

Robert B. Nordberg
Marquette University

When we of the middle-aged set studied behavioral science, we were sternly warned that philosophy should stay in its own back yard. Today, we get mixtures of Zen Buddhism and clinical psychology and other blends that could never have been foreseen. It is good that more literature is appearing on philosophical aspects of counseling, but some of it is poor philosophy. It is often unclear, self-contradictory, or does not meet the conditions for valid inference.

This chapter is concerned with *non-sequiturs* in counseling literature. These are arguments in which the conclusion does not follow from the premises. We shall also be somewhat concerned with other types of logical fallacies: the fallacy of accident (failure to distinguish what is essential from what is not); arguments *ad hominem, ad populum, ad baculum,* and *ad verecundium;* begging the question; arguing from a consequent to its antecedent; *post hoc ergo propter hoc* reasoning; and lumping several questions as one. If counselors are going to be philosophers, it is time we learned the tricks of the trade! This presentation will sample a variety of logical fallacies rather than

An original article for this book.

develop one or two exhaustively, the purpose being to stimulate the reader to go forth and find other such examples himself.

Epistemology figures prominently in philosophy of counseling. The old rationalist-empiricist debate is bound to be relevant, and today's far-flung empiricism is bound to be felt. One of its fruits runs like this: No one can understand what he has not experienced. Most counselors have not experienced life in the slums, poverty, psychedelic drugs, and so on. Therefore, most counselors cannot understand the problems of the poor, the drug addict, and others whose dilemmas they have not lived through. The argument is not without merit. Certainly it is easier to have an "I-thou" relationship with someone whose sufferings parallel one's own, other factors equal. *Understanding*, however, is an intellectual function. One need not have lived through everything that he presumes to comprehend.

A counselor must also be concerned with what we are doing when we "know." The Idealist-Realist-Instrumentalist debate thus becomes relevant. For example, F. R. Styles argues that he is a directivist in counseling *because* he is an objectivist in epistemology. Carl Rogers basically gives us two reasons for being nondirective: (1) The client is ego-involved with his problem. (2) There is no objective truth, anyway, so why should a counselor foist his "truth" upon a client? If one rejects the second reason, there can still remain the first. Thus, one can be an objectivist and yet avoid advice-giving and opinion-expressing in counseling on grounds of the client's ego-involvement. Styles speaks of a real world and his ability to comprehend "it," but this is not a claim to omniscience! Besides the question of *whether* man can know there is the question of *how much* he can know. From the premise that truth is objective, it in no way follows that a given counselor possesses all the truth on any given subject. It is a safe assumption that he does not!

There is also the problem of where directiveness starts. Styles states, "I do not determine which decision the student is to reach." This is really an analytic proposition. That is, it is true by definition. Nobody can make a decision which yet remains somebody else's decision. But, one can push and coerce. Even for Realists, among whom I stand, there are plenty of psychological reasons to avoid doing that.[1]

The relationship of knowledge to action must concern counselors, especially in view of the widespread assumption that our purpose is to change people's behavior. Arbuckle typifies one common viewpoint in writing, "The education of the counselor-trainee must change him, it would seem, rather than increase his store of knowledge."[2] Is this a plausible dichotomy? Can one imagine a signifcant, sustained behavioral change which does not entail new understandings, new ways of thinking? Again, is it likely that such new understandings would have no behavioral consequences?

Dreikurs illustrates the view of knowledge as a univocal rather than an analogical notion: "Truth is merely a statistical phenomenon." Quantum theory,

---

[1]F. R. Styles, "Guidance Counseling from the Right," *Personnel and Guidance Journal* 48 (January, 1970), 349-352. Commentary: R. B. Nordberg, *Personnel and Guidance Journal* 48 (May, 1970), 703.

[2]Dugald S. Arbuckle, "Five Philosophical Issues in Counseling," *Journal of Counseling Psychology* 5 (1958), 211-215.

he says, "spells the end of the Aristotelian logic."[3] Two misunderstandings
are involved here. It is generally agreed that scientific work presupposes some
uniformity of nature, some "laws" that might eventually be discovered in
their exact form. If each event were a random freak, there would be no point
in observations and experiments and theories. Experimentation cannot establish what it presupposes without begging the question. Similarly, the scientist
must presuppose that perception, given certain technical safeguards, correlates
with what is. If the investigator were merely studying his own mental processes, the scientific scheme would be nonsense. Quantum theory presupposes
these points about perception and causality and therefore can neither verify
nor negate them. Neither physics nor any other science has demonstrated or
could demonstrate that truth is "merely" statistical. (If it were, incidentally,
the "merely" could be dropped as meaningless.) Rather, there are some situations in which we cannot observe what we are concerned with directly and
must settle for accounts of how it behaves in the mass.

As for Dreikurs' comment on Aristotelian logic, this rests on a serious misunderstanding begun by Alfred Korzybski and continued by other general
semanticists.[4] Korzybski felt that most human mixups are abetted by an Aristotelian way of thinking. The Aristotle at whom he threw rocks never existed.
For example, Korzybski misunderstood Aristotle's law of contradiction and
the law of the excluded middle, turning them into the idea that a thing must
be one way or the opposite way—black or white. Aristotle never had any such
notion. As for the " 'is' of identity" which Korzybski called Aristotelian, Aristotle was at pains to deny it—pointing out, for example, that subjects and
predicates are not interchangeable.[5] The two-valued orientation which Korzybski disapproved (as did Aristotle) is what Dreikurs here associates with
Aristotelian logic.

Some of the *non-sequiturs* in counseling theory have come from identifying causality with one kind of causality: mechanical. Causation is a complicated subject. Various thinkers have posited primary and secondary causality,
principal and instrumental, and have stressed the forces acting in a situation,
the purposes sought by an entity, the composition of a thing, functions, and
so on. To repudiate any one of these views is not to commit oneself to total
anarchy. Yet, we are frequently confronted in effect with the propositon that
those who reject a given view of cause-effect relations must believe in a
world where things happen for no reasons whatever. Behaviorists, especially,
seem prone to saying, "Behavior has causes, you know," as if to imply that
non-Behaviorists take a contrary view.

This puzzle of causality relates directly to that of free will. Carl Rogers
has written with admirable candor about the paradoxes between the freedom of

---

[3]Rudolf Dreikurs, "The Scientific Revolution," in *Foundations of Guidance and
Counseling: Multi-Disciplinary Readings*, edited by C. E. Smith and O. G. Mink
(Philadelphia: J. B. Lippincott, 1969), pp. 59-69. Reprinted from *The Humanist*.

[4]Alfred Korzybski, *Science and Sanity*, 3d ed. (Lakeville, Conn.: International
Non-Aristotelian Pub. Co., 1948). An excellent analysis: 'The Educational Implications of the Theory of Meaning and Symbolism of General Semantics," by Margaret Gorman, *Educational Research Monographs* 21 (April, 1958) (Washington:
Catholic University Press, 1958).

[5]Aristotle, *The Basic Works of Aristotle*, edited by Richard McKeon (New York:
Random House, 1941).

choice that he sees in persons as a clinician and the pan-determinism he accepts as a scientist. Rogers seems to equate assertion of free will with denial of causality.[6] "Science, to be sure, rests on the assumption that behavior is caused —that a specified event is followed by a consequent event. Hence all is determined, nothing is free, choice is impossible." If choices were indeed uncaused, "out of the blue," there would be scant logic to rewarding and punishing them! To call a choice free means it is the product of conscious deliberation of options. Thomas Aquinas held that man has free choice on the grounds that "man acts from judgment" and that "this judgment in the case of some particular act is not from a natural instinct but from some act of comparison in the reason. . . ."[7] Thus the dilemma of choice between scientific determinism and acceptance of free will has no proper basis. The question is not whether decisions are caused but whether a rational, unmechanical process can be part of that causality. The issue of free choice is also occasionally confused with whether our actions make any difference. Astor, suggesting a reconciliation between determinism and free willism, writes, "Since man is able to control some things and other things are determined for him, is it not possible to consider both aspects of responsibility as part of the same problem?"[8] The fate of inanimate objects, however, depends alike on what they do and what happens to them, if one wishes to make the distinction, and nobody says *they* have free will.[9]

Still another confusion on free choice is illustrated by Williamson. He writes of freedom of choice as a "lovely ideal" which "is not yet available to many, many individuals, even in this latter half of the twentieth century," because they have no real opportunity to have the kinds of careers they want.[10] Williamson certainly makes a valid point in saying that equal opportunity is a myth. The concept of freedom of choice, though, as it has been traditionally discussed and as Williamson apparently intends to discuss it here, has never been taken to refer to whether one can do or have whatever he wants. Choice is always among viable options.

The nature of intellect is another theoretical problem in which necessary distinctions are often overlooked. Among the common errors here is that of confounding a power to know with the fruits of that power. McCully, for example, writes that "The mind is of social origin. This postulate would challenge the assumption that human intelligence is fixed by genetic inheritance."[11] Whether it would or not depends on what is meant by "mind." The *contents*

[6]Carl R. Rogers, "The Place of the Person in the New World of the Behavioral Sciences," *Personnel and Guidance Journal* 39 (February, 1961), 442-451. Commentary: R. B. Nordberg, *Personnel and Guidance Journal* 40 (September, 1961), 58-59.

[7]Anton C. Pegis, *Introduction to Saint Thomas Aquinas* (New York: Modern Library, Inc.), pp. 368-370.

[8]Martin H. Astor, "Counselors Seek to Understand Themselves: A Philosophical Inquiry," *Personnel and Guidance Journal* 43 (June, 1965), 1029-1033.

[9]Robert B. Nordberg, *Guidance: A Systematic Introduction* (New York: Random House, Inc., 1970), pp. 104-106.

[10]E. G. Williamson, *Vocational Counseling* (New York: McGraw-Hill, Inc., 1965), p. 8.

[11]C. Harold McCully, "Conceptions of Man and the Helping Professions," *Personnel and Guidance Journal* 44 (May, 1966), 911-917.

of the mind are social in that we learn our beliefs, interests, and attitudes, and do so largely in social settings. That we *have* minds need not be regarded in the same light. Put a flea or a horse in the same social settings and each will not acquire the same mental contents. Indeed, it is most unlikely that men would have the kinds of social organizations they have except that their mental capacities make them possible.

One of the most frequent *non-sequiturs* concerns a counselor's values and his expression of them. Again and again we hear that a counselor cannot avoid expressing his values by the clothing he wears, the way his office is arranged, his habitual vocabulary, and in other ways. Samler comments, ". . . to say that the counselor manifests no values is to require that he have no feelings . . ."[12] This is very questionable. It implies that whoever has feelings will express them whether he intends to or not. It seems to be the case that many people (including many clinicians) are highly skilled at hiding their feelings when they deem it appropriate. Further, even if a counselor cannot help communicating something of his values, it does not follow (although it may on other grounds be the case) that he should express his values to his client openly and explicitly. A colleague to whom I criticized a news magazine for chronically slanted coverage commented, "Oh, well, objectivity is impossible, anyway." The magazine in question has always officially excused its slanted coverage on exactly that basis. If complete objectivity is unattainable, it does not follow that complete subjectivity is to be desired! Similarly, if a clinician cannot help occasionally revealing something of his ideas of right and wrong, important and unimportant, true and false, tasteful and banal, it does not follow that he should inject as much of such matters as he can into his counseling. This is surely a feeble rationalization for self-centered counseling.

The last example to be considered is the idea that counseling has failed unless it changes behavior. Eysenck's celebrated conclusion was that, when neurotics are treated by psychoanalysis, two-thirds of them are basically cured; when they are treated by client-centered counseling, the proportion is the same; and, when nothing at all is done, the proportion is the same.[13] This conclusion, based on a review of numerous research projects and clinical findings of others, has been subjected to various criticisms, but the most fundamental one is often missed: The criterion used throughout is behavioral change. But what if that is not the *purpose* of counseling and psychotherapy? Many counselors hold that their aim is to help the client understand himself better, turn his emotional conflicts into conscious, intellectual conflicts by articulating them. The client can then do what he chooses with this understanding. If his behavior did not change, or if it changed in subtle, unmeasurable ways, it would not follow that the counseling had failed.

At this point an urge to qualify and soften pops up. To be sure, it is easier to punch holes in the other fellow's logic than to build a case of one's own. To this, I would plead that I have built my cases in other places. Again, there is always the chance of taking someone else's point "out of context," which is almost true by definition when one quotes someone. Sometimes the

---

[12]Joseph Samler, "Change in Values: A Goal in Counseling," *Journal of Counseling Psychology* 7 (1960), 32-39.

[13]H. J. Eysenck and S. Rackman, *The Causes and Cures of Neuroses* (San Diego, Calif.: Knapp, 1965).

phrase means to take unfair advantage of the isolation of what is quoted. Thus Alexander Woollcott once found himself cited as evaluating a certain dramatic production as "a perfect play," whereas, what Woollcott had said was "a perfect play for an idiot." I have tried to avoid playing that game and do not believe that anyone's position has been misrepresented.

Again, some positions which have come under fire here may be correct. The present concern has been less with their *validity* than with the *arguments by which* they are supported. Deduction as an art form is not in much favor among scientists. Nevertheless, the separation of induction and deduction has always proved impossible. There is an element of each in the other. This essay has been concerned with conclusions presented in partly or wholly deduced ways in the literature.

Despite these qualifications, it remains my thesis that there are too many *non-sequiturs* and other logical fallacies in counseling literature. Having occasionally committed some myself, perhaps I should not object to the fault in others. On second thought, that is another one!

COUNSELING IN THE PUBLIC SCHOOLS — SOME LEGAL CONSIDERATIONS

Henry E. Butler, Jr.
University of Rochester

This essay is concerned with some of the more obvious legal considerations that should be kept in mind by guidance counselors in the public schools. It is general in nature, and in large measure nontechnical. For the most part, it is exploratory and speculative rather than expository, and it is selective rather than comprehensive in its approach.[1] Attention is focused more on problems involving the exercise of judgment than on questions that are resolved by judicial or legislative mandate, because it seems to the writer that such an emphasis is more likely to provoke fruitful discussion than a more "cut and dried" presentation. Finally, this essay reflects the writer's point of view on a number of matters about which there is, admittedly, a legitimate difference of opinion. At the outset, the setting in which guidance activities take place needs to be defined as clearly as possible.

THE SETTING

Guidance counselors in the public schools are, legally, specialized teachers, whose function is performed for the most part outside the classroom. They are employees of a public agency, and as such are charged primarily with a public, not a private, responsibility. They share with classroom teachers, administrators, and other specialists, including noncertified employees, respon-

---

An original article for this book.

[1]For a detailed treatment of the topic see Martha L. Ware (Editor), *Law of Guidance and Counseling* (Cincinnati: The W. H. Anderson Company, 1964).

sibility for providing and maintaining an educational program that is as effective as it can be for each pupil enrolled in the public schools.

It should be noted that the guidance counselor performs his specialized functions in a system that is controlled externally by relevant provisions of the United States Constitution and by the constitutions, statutes, and administrative regulations of the respective states. Furthermore, and perhaps equally important here, his activities take place in an organizational structure that is still characterized predominantly by line-staff relationships. While it is frequently difficult to identify a function that is purely "line" or purely "staff," it seems evident that insofar as internal controls are concerned the guidance counselor, as the teacher, occupies a subordinate position and is subject to policies legally adopted by a local board of education and to administrative rules, and decisions which implement these policies, whether made arbitrarily or on a consultative basis.

Many guidance activities concern individual pupils, unemancipated minors, whose parents have a substantial legal right to control the education of their children, and who themselves have legal rights that will be protected by the courts if suit is instituted by the parents. Inasmuch as it is doubtful that such minor pupils can waive any of these rights without the agreement of the parents, the guidance counselor, in dealing with individual pupils, needs to be aware of the legal presence of the parent in the background.

The setting in which the guidance counselor conducts his activities involves the relationship between ethical and legal standards. A code of ethics, rooted in "professional" consensus but lacking legal acceptance or sanction, may have little relevance to the outcome of litigation.[2]

Finally, the role and function of the guidance counselor in the public educational system have not been clearly defined. As specialists, guidance counselors are expected to provide educational and vocational guidance and counseling of an informative nature. In some school systems they are assigned disciplinary functions. Increasingly, it appears, guidance counselors are undertaking, and are being permitted to undertake, a conscious therapeutic function in relation to individual students. If a more favorable student-counselors ratio results as greater numbers of guidance counselors are trained and placed in the public schools, this trend can be expected to accelerate in response to the need of young people "for someone to talk to."

Acceptance of the concept of psychotherapy and recognition of the widespread need for therapeutic services leave unanswered two questions: (1) Are guidance counselors appropriately trained to provide such services? and (2) Should such services be provided by guidance counselors in the public schools? Whatever answer one may give to these questions, as of this writing guidance counselors have the general legal status of teachers, not of psychologists or psychiatrists. The point is, of course, that in the absence of a clear legal definition of his specialized role and function, the guidance counselor faces uncertainty insofar as his legal rights and responsibilities are concerned. This uncertainty increases the farther he departs from the specialized teaching role and undertakes a consciously therapeutic function.

---

[2]The Board of Trustees of the Lassen Union High School District v. Jack Owens, 23 Cal. Rptr. 710 (1962).

POTENTIAL AREAS OF LEGAL INVOLVEMENT

As guidance counselors engage in their daily routine, some of their activities hold a potential for legal involvement that warrant identification here.

Cumulative records for individual students are frequently maintained by the guidance counseling department of a school district. These records may be transferred from one school district to another as students change their residence, and are an important source of information for members of the school staff whose function relates to the instruction of individual students. They may contain derogatory data or information which, if disclosed without the protection of qualified privilege, would indefensibly embarrass the student concerned and could lead to legal complications for the individual who disseminated the information improperly. The parents of a particular student have a right, in the absence of a controlling statute or state regulation, to consult the school records that pertain to their children.[3] Similarly, those members of a school staff who work directly with a particular student may properly have access to his records. Beyond this, great care should be exercised in general not to release information contained in a student's records without parental permission or a parental request in writing. In situations where the authorization of a parent or guardian cannot be obtained because his whereabouts are unknown, the written authorization of the student concerned should be obtained.

In this regard, it is highly desirable that administrative rules implementing locally adopted school board policy be formulated to protect the privacy of such records and to enjoin silence with respect to the data included in them on members of the clerical and secretarial staff who may assist in posting information in individual student's records. Unless such measures are taken and enforced, a violation of the security of information by a member of the secretarial staff might be legally imputed to the professional member of the staff charged with responsibility for maintaining the records or to the school district itself.

Information obtained from a student during an interview should be treated in a similar fashion. The problem here is likely to arise when a student reveals information about himself or other students that makes it impossible to base a decision on whether to report the information (orally or in writing) to the building principal or other responsible administrator or to the parents of a student, solely on a consideration of the "confidential relationship" with the student who provided the information. If a guidance counselor receives information which implies harm or danger to the counselee or others, his failure to report this information, even at the risk of revealing the identity of the counselee supplying the information, could constitute the basis for a successful negligence action. Under some conditions, it is conceivable that it might also expose the guidance counselor to a criminal prosecution. For example, if a counselee reveals to a guidance counselor an intention to participate in a criminal act, this information should be reported to the responsible superior in the school system or to the parent in such a way that the guidance counselor has a record of the fact that the report has been made. Failure to make such a report would leave the counselor in the position of possibly being

---

[3]Van Allen v. McCleary, 211 N.Y.S. 2d 501 (1961).

involved legally in any criminal act committed in fulfillment of the expressed intention, or of being unable to establish the fact that he had made an appropriate report.

Tests and questionnaires that seek directly or indirectly to elicit information of an intimate nature relating to conditions in the homes of student-respondents and their feelings about themselves in the home environment present another source of potential conflict. It may well be that the relevance of such tests and questionnaires to educational and vocational decisions affecting a particular student make it desirable to use them. The fact remains, however, that the administration of such instruments may, in effect, invade the privacy of the home through the participation of a minor child. If such tests are administered without parental permission as part of a testing program approved by a local board of education, presumably the board of education, not the guidance counselor, would be answerable to complaining parents. On the other hand, if a guidance counselor administers such tests without parental permission that are not part of the approved district testing program or have not otherwise been approved by the governing board of the district, he would be answerable as an individual to complaining parents.

BASIC GUIDELINES

The sparsity of cases involving guidance counselors suggests that statistically the specialized activities of guidance counselors involve but slight exposure to legal liability.[4] This exposure can be minimized if the guidance counselor exercises sound judgment based on an understanding of the legal principles that apply to his activities. These principles have been discussed comprehensively elsewhere and are not repeated here. It does seem appropriate, however, to suggest a number of operational guidelines calculated to help guidance counselors avoid potential legal pitfalls.

1. Guidance counselors should seek a definition in writing of the functions they are expected to perform consistent with the policies of the specific school district that employs them. Particular attention should be given to the procedures to be followed in maintaining the security of information contained in student records, and in releasing such information to parents and to others in the school system and to prospective employers and institutions of further education upon request. In addition, the administrator to whom guidance counselors should report information which implies harm or danger to a counselor or to others should be identified, and the procedure for making referrals for diagnosis and possible therapeutic treatment should be clearly defined, consistent with parental rights in such matters.
2. Guidance counselors should make as clear as possible to counselees that while they have an obligation to exercise good faith toward the counselee and generally to maintain in confidence information provided by a coun-

---

[4]For a significant, related discussion see Reynolds C. Seitz, "The Law of Privileged Communications As It Affects The Work and Responsibility Of The Principal" in *Law and the School Principal* (Reynolds C. Seitz, Editor, Cincinnati: The W. H. Anderson Company, 1961).

selee, they also have an obligation to a counselee's parents, other students, and to the employing school system, and under some circumstances might have to divulge to others information which the counselee would prefer not to have reported. Unless a forthright position is taken in this matter, a guidance counselor may readily find himself torn between what he perceives to be his ethical obligation to a counselee and his legal responsibility as a professional employee of a school district.

3. Guidance counselors should limit their activities to their specialized area of competence and should not become involved with the diagnosis and alleviation of emotional problems. If doubtful as to whether such problems exist, the guidance counselor should resolve such doubt by a referral in accordance with approved procedures.

4. Guidance counselors should conduct their activities in a manner consistent with the substantial right of parents to control the education of their children. Providing opportunities for parent-student conferences and parent participation in reaching decisions growing out of educational and vocational guidance activities appears to be the most effective way to make allowance for the legitimate interest of parents in educational decisions affecting their children.

Guidance counselors have an assured future in the public schools. They cannot capitalize on this future if they walk in fear and trembling. Neither can they realize their potential if they plunge ahead blindly without regard to the possible legal consequences of their actions. They are likely to function best if they educate themselves carefully concerning their legal responsibilities, and exercise educational discretion in the light of this knowledge.

THE PHILOSOPHY-THEORY-PRACTICE CONTINUUM
A POINT OF VIEW

Ben Strickland
Texas Christian University

During the past decade more and more attention has been directed to counseling theory and philosophy in the guidance literature. The result of this attention has been at least three-fold: (a) to distinguish among, yet to articulate, philosophy, theory, and practice; (b) to draw attention to the need for additional clarification of philosophy, or philosophies; and (c) to challenge counselors with the realization that their own philosophical orientations are sources of their own counseling guidelines. Despite the availability of literature on philosophy, theory, and practice, however, there still exists much confusion and ambiguity on the part of counselor education students as to the meaning and relationship of these terms or concepts. The significance of this confusion, and the necessity for reducing it, seems readily appar-

Reprinted by permission of the author and *Counselor Education and Supervision,* Vol. 8, No. 9, Spring 1969, 165-175.

ent when we realize that these counselor education students will become counselors in a few years and will be asked to produce innovations, implement change, and create the kinds of productive counseling environments projected in current literature. All of these accomplishments seem to be predicated upon the counselor's ability to develop productive communications with professional colleagues (administrators, teachers, supervisors, etc.), parents, and community personnel. One important prerequisite for productive communications would seem to be clarity rather than ambiguity. It seems apparent then that some communicable understanding of philosophy, theory, and practice would enhance the counselor's ability to communicate effectively counseling goals, counselor commitments, and the guidance program in total.

The point of view presented herein is one which has been evolving for some time through the writer's experience in a counselor education setting. The purpose of the present paper is to present this point of view rather than to provide a review of available literature. More extensive formulations are readily available, e.g., in the contributions of Arbuckle (1965, 1967), Beck (1963, 1966), Blocher (1966), and Shoben (1962).

IMPLICATIONS

Why bother with all this? The answer to this question would seem to be that if philosophy, theory, and practice (techniques) are important to teach in a counselor education program, then it is important to present these in some kind of context that can be understood and which will have some residual effect. The following implications seem apparent in teaching from the point of view described herein.

1. *Improved communication.* Although the importance of effective communication has already been mentioned, the practical significance of improved communication seems worthy of reinforcement. Recently the writer read of the discontinuance of a major portion of guidance services in a school system which has had a guidance program for some time. Lack of funds was given as the reason for the reduction. Everyone who has been employed in a school system must contend with the shortage of funds. The interesting thing is, however, that schools can usually find a source of funds for programs which are considered vital to the educational program. The vitality of a program seems strongly related to the degree to which it is understood by those involved with it. From a practical, economic viewpoint it seems that counselor education institutions should be quite concerned with the ability of their graduates to communicate effectively about guidance.

2. *Increased commitment.* It is sometimes embarrassing to conduct a follow-up study of counselor education graduates to determine the extent to which they are putting into effect the "teachings" they have "acquired." Although several reasons might be presented to account for this lack of application, the lack of personal commitment to guidance certainly must be high on the list. One important factor in commitment is understanding. Another important factor is action. It seems that we must have some understanding of possibilities before we really get involved or take a stand. One possible reason for lack of implementation of guidance philosophy is that philosophy is frequently taught from an academic point of view and as such

is not related to theory and practice. Not only is this a seemingly sterile approach but a nonproductive one as well. Commitment seems to imply action. Productive action evolves from some sort of plan which is understandable and acceptable by those involved.

3. *Decreased "gaming."* Because of certification requirements most counselors come from the teaching ranks. Teachers are constantly searching for techniques, methods, or approaches which seem to be effective, or which "work." While the continuing search for techniques is a desirable activity, it can be a very frustrating "game" if counselors are concerned only with what "works," simply because few techniques work in all situations. Furthermore, unless we have some idea of our goals we might not be able to distinguish between factors which keep an individual busy and those which really assist him in adjusting to his environment. Someone has said that any road will do just fine if you don't care where you are going. Counselors who have no idea as to why a technique works will probably be hard put to use any technique with consistent effectiveness. Furthermore, when we feel that a technique works it seems that we are saying that it helps to attain the goals which are important. Since counseling goals are a function of philosophy, it seems that techniques are implementations of philosophy. From this point of view, effective techniques evolve from a philosophy which is understandable to the degree that it can be implemented.

4. *Better understanding of literature.* Much emphasis is currently being directed to counseling research and particularly to research which is experimentally oriented. While most of us would agree to the appropriateness of such research, we sometimes find it difficult to understand the implications of some studies. For example, many of us who are interested in group counseling and think it an effective technique are sometimes confused, even annoyed, by research which indicates that no improvement in self-concept results from group counseling. Studies which utilize group counseling in short-term research and which employ self-report instruments to evaluate change seem to produce particularly ambiguous results. One of the difficulties in this approach seems to be that many self-report instruments equate improvement in self-concept with positive statements concerning self which, of course, reveals something of one's philosophy. Not all practitioners, however, have the same philosophy concerning change. Some feel that growth in self-concept can be indicated by more honest self-reports wherein individuals can recognize and admit limitations. From this it seems apparent that two counselors might evaluate identical data differently because of their own philosophies. A counselor, not realizing this, would seem to be in for some confusing reading experiences as he attempts to understand current counseling literature.

These are but a few of what would appear to be the most important implications. Other more specific implications could be drawn for instructional purposes.

THE MODEL

The plan proposed herein is not presented as a panacea, but rather as a point of view. Its purpose is that of attempting to provide some kind of organization for an area of counselor preparation in which confusion and misunderstanding seem most common.

The continuum model seems appropriate here since there appears to be a necessary and direct relationship between techniques, theory, and philosophy. If these elements can be seen in relationship to each other, some confusion might be eliminated. Furthermore, if any of the three are considered in isolation, unfortunate consequences seem probable since counseling goals and techniques must contain some consistency. The continuum model necessitates a consideration of elements in context and in relation to other factors and might appear as follows:

Philosophy ←——→ Theory ←——→ Practice

PHILOSOPHY, THEORY, AND PRACTICE

Perhaps it would be appropriate initially to propose tentative definitions or descriptions of the terms, *philosophy, theory,* and *practice,* particularly from the viewpoint of the counselor. *Philosophy* can be considered, for the purposes of this paper, the counselor's frame of reference: his attitudes, values and feelings concerning himself and others. This is not to ignore the fields of philosophical inquiry such as metaphysics, epistemology, axiology, and possibly logic, but rather to develop a dialogue in terms more common to counselors. Regardless of the terminology, the focus of the dialogue will be upon reality, truth, values, and reason as these relate to counseling. *Theory* consists of behavioral guidelines which emerge from and are consistent with philosophy. Practice consists of the operational approaches, methods, and the techniques which achieve the goals of philosophy through the design or guidelines of theory.

Webster has defined philosophy as "the sum of the ideas and convictions of an individual or group." The existentialist might define philosophy as those beliefs to which an individual is unconditionally committed. No matter who is defining the term, however, the intangible, subjective nature of the term is always present. The personal nature of philosophy is, in fact, its essential ingredient.

To a counselor, the personal nature of his philosophy can have both advantages and disadvantages, however. If, for example, his beliefs are too personal to allow careful examination by himself and others, then his philosophy might be obstructive to his personal growth. His mind is made up and he wants not to be confused with facts. Rigidity would hardly seem characteristic of creative counselors. On the other hand, if the counselor's beliefs are well formulated but flexible and subject to continuing evaluation, then the personal nature of his beliefs can be advantageous because his own professional and personal pride should encourage him to continually improve where possible.

What are the components of a counselor's philosophy? Arbuckle (1958) has listed the self concept, religious orientation, counselor responsibility, and the nature of man as issues which must be considered in relation to the counselor's philosophy. The possible scope of these four areas, or issues, is certainly sufficient to include most items worthy of consideration under the classification of philosophy. Examples of philosophical positions expressed by counselors might be as follows:

1. I am/am not a person of worth. Other people are/are not persons of worth.
2. I am/am not basically good, altruistic. Other people are/are not basically good.
3. I am/am not fearful of my basic needs and behavior. Other people should/should not be feared.
4. I believe that helping is/is not important. Other people are/are not deserving of help.
5. I believe that people have/have not an inward source of self-direction and therefore should/should not be coerced by others.
6. I feel that the belief in a supreme being is/is not important for individual growth.

From these philosophical positions might evolve a variety of theoretical positions. In fact, some might feel that these are theoretical positions since the distinction between philosophy and theory is not always apparent. Some theorists make no distinction between the two. The two concepts are being considered herein as distinct but related entities in order to make certain points pertaining to each.

Brammer (1966) has defined theory as "a collection of assumptions, interpretations, and hypotheses which help to explain what is happening in counseling." Hall and Lindzey (1957) have described a theory as a cluster of relevant assumptions systematically related to each other and related to a set of empirical definitions. McCabe (1958) has suggested that a theory is a device explaining the relationships between events or facts. A term now commonly used synonymously with theory is "model." Theories are behavioral models. Whether a theory is called a collection, cluster, device, or model, however, need not greatly concern the counselor as long as its importance is understood and it evolves from and is consistent with his own philosophical orientation.

What are the components of a theory? Patterson (1966) has suggested four components: (a) related and internally consistent assumptions, (b) definitions relating elements of the theory to observable data, (c) hypotheses which predict what should result from theory utilization, and (d) meaningful organization of what is known. Stefflre (1965) has broadened the components of theory to include some elements listed previously under the heading of philosophy, suggesting an inseparable relationship between the two. He has listed the following components of a theory:

1. Assumptions regarding the nature of man.
2. Beliefs regarding learning theory and changes in behavior.
3. A commitment to certain goals in counseling.
4. A definition of the role of the counselor.
5. Research evidence supporting the theory. (p. 26)

From the foregoing it seems apparent that the development of a theory to meet the criteria of Patterson and Stefflre is a formidable task. It might also explain the limited number of theories which have stood the test of time, research, and validation. The difficulty in constructing a sophisticated theory should not overwhelm counselors who are beginning to formulate their own theories, however, because few theories were refined in first draft. The important thing for counselors is to organize and develop their own theories and refine these with experience. It might help to begin this theorizing with the consideration of several questions which need answering somewhere in the theoretical structure. Some possible questions, in keeping with previous suggestions, are as follows:

1. How can counseling be defined?
2. What are the objectives (general or specific) of counseling?
3. How and when do changes in behavior occur?
4. What is the counselor's role and responsibility in changing behavior?
5. How can behavioral changes be facilitated?
6. How can behavioral changes be identified and evaluated?
7. What are the stages, steps, or processes in counseling?

Answers to questions such as these should provide guidelines consistent with the philosophy of the counselor since these answers must come from basic beliefs. Without this consistency the development of techniques will probably be difficult. As these guidelines are established, at least tentatively, the development of practice or methodology can also occur.

The close relationship between theory and practice can be seen in the previous questions. Implicit in each guideline should be some indication of methodology. The counselor should consider, for example, techniques which encourage behavioral changes consistent with his beliefs as he considers how he can facilitate change in his role as a counselor. The importance of consistency, not rigidity, between technique and philosophy cannot be overly stressed. Without this consistency, the counselor will probably experience some discomfort between his "means" and "ends." His techniques may take him where his philosophy would fear to tread. He may profess to be client-centered, for example, and in fact, be behavioristic, or vice versa. This can, of course, be somewhat embarrassing, particularly to counselor educators whose frames of reference might not yet be well organized and whose students are perceptive.

The client-centered theory of counseling provides a possible example for the philosophy-theory-practice continuum. Briefly it might possibly be stated as follows:

Philosophy—The individual has within himself the capacity for positive self-direction. His impulses are not basically evil. He is not bent upon destroying society.

Theory—If the individual is provided a climate which is non-threatening and which encourages self-evaluation, his capacity for self-direction can become effective. If given an opportunity to utilize his potential, he will do so.

Practice—The counselor can best create the optimum counseling relationship with a warm, understanding, non-coercive approach. He should use techniques such as reflection and clarification which are not overly threatening and which encourage the client to reevaluate himself and seek appropriate solutions or direction.

Frequently, counselors complete the process from philosophy to theory to practice in reverse. This occurs when a counselor searches for a technique which will "work" without considering its theoretical or philosophical base. Little prediction seems probable in such a situation because the counselor may have little understanding of why the technique worked. He may use it again until it doesn't work and then search for a new "panacea." If the counselor has adequately formulated his beliefs, the articulation between philosophy, theory, and practice should be apparent.

If the foregoing has been presented in such a manner as to suggest a lock-step sequence in the philosophy-theory-practice development, nothing could be farther from the truth. As previously suggested, the development might be viewed as a continuum or possibly as a cycle. Each element should provide a continuing contribution to the expansion and refinement of the others. In this context the continuum might be a real force for effective counseling. Philosophical re-evaluation, for example, should provide additional possibilities in theory and practice. By the same token, continuing experimentation with technique should provide an expansion of the philosophical base as new evidence is found.

CLARIFICATION OF PHILOSOPHY(IES)

How long has it been since you were asked, "What's your philosophy on . . . ?" Since the terms theory and philosophy are often used interchangeably, you may have been asked your theory concerning a particular topic. A more common method of asking the same thing is merely, "What do you think about . . . ?" In any of the three cases, if we respond sincerely, we will reveal how we feel about the topic, what factors have accounted for our feelings, and what should be done about the situation. In revealing the feelings we are, in fact, revealing something of our philosophy, our theory, and our practice.

In academic circles it is common for people to accept elements of established philosophies such as realism, idealism, pragmatism, or existentialism. Statements such as, "I consider myself a pragmatist," are not uncommon among counselors and counselor educators. This can be a very positive identification, or it can be quite superficial. If, after careful examination of his philosophical structure, a counselor recognizes elements in his philosophy which are similar to those of an established philosophy, it would seem only natural for him to accept this similarity for the present, while ever seeking to attain additional clarification and understanding. An understanding of the implications of established philosophies would assist the counselor in understanding the possible impact which his own philosophy or theory would have on the development of his techniques and, ultimately, the impact upon those with whom he works.

A non-productive development can occur when a counselor identifies superficially with a philosophy which seems to be in vogue, or one which seems to provide an easy way out. An example of this is the growing acceptance on the part of counselors of the philosophy of existentialism. To many counselors, the philosophy of existentialism holds many exciting challenges since it encourages, among other things, the development of individuality, and the realization of freedom. If the counselor chooses to accept only the existential concepts which are enticing such—as freedom without its counterpart, responsibility—he probably does not understand the existential meaning of freedom. Unfortunate consequences for both counselor and client seem possible from such a situation.

Summarily stated, if a counselor, after careful self-evaluation, can accept an established philosophy, or parts thereof, and recognizes the implications of such an acceptance for himself and his clients, then he might well use this knowledge as a *force* for improving his counseling effectiveness. If, on the other hand, a counselor merely accepts a philosophy or parts thereof because it is the easy way out or because it is the popular thing to do, he may have, in fact, the ingredients for an ineffective *facade*.

It should be mentioned at this point that there is nothing innately constructive or obstructive from a functional viewpoint in any established philosophy. The constructive or obstructive aspects develop through the counselor's understanding and use of a philosophy. The obstructive utilization of popular philosophies occurs when a counselor accepts a philosophy superficially. Sooner or later he gives himself enough philosophical rope to hang himself, philosophically.

The moral to this story is that counselors should utilize all available philosophical data in the organization and development of their own personalized philosophies. Philosophical eclecticism seems inevitable because the experiences and values of each counselor are unique. After all, it seems probable that only Carl Rogers can truly be "client-centered," since only he has the experiences, values, attitudes, beliefs, etc., necessary to be totally committed to the client-centered point of view.

PHILOSOPHY AND COUNSELING EFFECTIVENESS

The philosophy which is the real force in determining the effectiveness of the counselor is probably his own personalized philosophy, whether it be totally original or totally eclectic. As previously suggested, it would seem much more productive for a counselor to have an unsophisticated philosophical development which is his own than to adopt unquestioningly the sophisticated philosophy of another person or persons. The only philosophy to which a counselor can be totally committed is one which he understands and can accept, at least tentatively.

It should be remembered that a counselor's philosophy is never static. It is always changing as new data are received and evaluated. The mistake that counselor candidates often make is that they spend much time in developing verbally what they believe to be their philosophy and feel that this is "it," the finished product. This can be unfortunate because a philosophy is not like vintage wine. It does not improve undisturbed with time. A philosophy, if it is vital counseling force, is dynamic, always changing, even if ever so slightly. An interesting parallel to the counselor's philosophy is that of the philosophy of a school or school system. Frequently, philosophies of education are developed by faculties and then filed, never to be re-evaluated and updated. In this case, the philosophy is just a formality; it will probably have little impact upon the education of children. The school may *have* a philosophy, but it may not project that philosophy.

The development of individual counselor philosophies is not always an easy task. Considerable time and effort are usually required initially, and continually. Perhaps this raises a question or two. Is it really worth it? Why bother? What can I show for all the efforts expended? Will it make me a better counselor?

The answers to these questions must be found by each counselor, individually. Obviously, a highly organized and systematized theory would not make the poor counselor into a master counselor. One reason for the master counselor's being so, however, is probably his understanding of and commitment to his own philosophical, theoretical, and methodological orientation.

This is not to suggest that it is impossible for a counselor to be effective until he can articulately verbalize all the elements of his philosophy or theory. Some people are interpersonally effective with little or no orientation to counseling philosophy or theory. The inability of a person to verbalize his counseling theory, however, should not be equated with theoretical sterility. The experience of most counselors whom the writer has known has been that increased understanding of philosophical, theoretical, and methodological orientations also provides greater understanding of counseling relationships. The counselor who understands himself, his subjective and objective elements, can probably more adequately understand why he is effective when he is effective, and why he is not effective when he is not effective. He should also be in a better position to predict how he will react to another person and what will be the impact of that reaction on the person.

This leads to one final question. Is one philosophical orientation better than another? That is, is there a philosophy from which could be developed superior theoretical positions and better techniques or practices? Obviously there would be some disagreement concerning this question also. Furthermore, research provides no clear-cut answers. The counselor from each philosophical orientation probably believes that his is the best, and for him, it probably is, if he is effective in his counseling relationships. Furthermore, he can probably produce some kind of research evidence to substantiate his belief.

The difficulty in ascertaining which counseling orientation is most appropriate for certain kinds of client problems stems from the fact that experience level of the counselor or therapist must be considered as another factor relating to counseling effectiveness. In other words, the effectiveness of counselors with rational, client-centered, behavioral, existential, and psychoanalytic orientations may well be the result of their experience levels rather than just their counseling orientations. The frequently-quoted study of Fiedler (1950), for example, identified a greater similarity between experienced therapists from different schools than between experienced and unexperienced therapists from the same schools regarding their concept of the therapeutic relationships. His study further suggested that theoretical differences in therapists might be the result of poor communication between therapists of different schools. It seems possible that generalizations from Fiedler's study might be made to counselors as well as therapists. The only conclusions which seem appropriate at this point is that more research is needed before any "best" counseling theory can be identified.

It remains the professional responsibility of each counselor to continually assess his beliefs, attitudes, values, techniques, etc., for the purpose of improving consistency and effectiveness. Through personal commitments to individual growth, the possibility of continuing growth of the counseling profession would seem to be enhanced. With the challenges of the 20th century, certainly the premium on individual and collective professional growth must be at an all-time high. Increased emphasis on the part of each counselor toward increased understanding of his own philosophical, theoretical, and methodological positions might well be the force which makes counseling a stable "blue chip stock" in an increasingly unstable society.

REFERENCES

Arbuckle, D. S. *Counseling and psychotherapy: An overview.* New York: McGraw-Hill, 1967.

Arbuckle, D. S. *Counseling: Philosophy, theory and practice.* Boston: Allyn and Bacon, 1965.

Arbuckle, D. S. Five philosophical issues in counseling, *Journal of Counseling Psychology,* Fall, 1958, 5, 211-15.

Beck, C. E. (Ed.) *Guidelines for guidance.* Dubuque, Iowa: Wm. C. Brown Company, 1966.

Beck, C. E. *Philosophical foundations of guidance.* Englewood Cliffs, New Jersey: Prentice-Hall, 1963.

Blocher, D. H. *Developmental counseling.* New York: The Roland Press, 1966.

Brammer, L. M. Teaching counseling theory: Some issues and points of view, *Counselor Education and Supervision,* Spring, 1966, 5, 120-30.

Fiedler, F. E. A comparison of psychoanalytic, non-directive, and Adlerian therapeutic relationships, *Journal of Consulting Psychology,* 1950, *14,* 436-45.

Hall, C. S. & Lindzey, G. *Theories of personality.* New York: Wiley, 1957.

McCabe, G. E. When is a good theory practical? *Personnel and Guidance Journal,* September, 1958, 37, 47-52.

Patterson, C. H. *Theories of counseling and psychotherapy.* New York: Harper & Row, 1966.

Shoben, E. J. The counselor's theory as personal trait, *Personnel and Guidance Journal,* March, 1962, 40, 617-21.

Stefflre, B. (Ed.) *Theories of counseling.* New York: McGraw-Hill, 1965.

THE SENSITIVITY TRAINING MOVEMENT—PROFESSIONAL IMPLICATIONS FOR ELEMENTARY AND SECONDARY SCHOOL COUNSELING AND TEACHING

Eugene D. Koplitz

University of Northern Colorado, Greeley

The Sensitivity Training Movement: Professional Implications for Elementary and Secondary School Counseling and Teaching was a challenging topic to pursue. Time does not permit me to react to all of the issues, problems, and complexities that confront counselors and teachers when consideration is being made for the utilization of this group process, but I will touch upon a number of concerns and discuss others in greater detail.

The intent of this paper is (1) to present a few historical facts which are basic to understanding more fully the present-day scene regarding sensitivity

This paper was presented at the American Personnel and Guidance Association National Convention in New Orleans, La., March 25, 1970. Reprinted by permission of the author.

training, (2) to discuss some of the concerns expressed by key professionals in the field of the behavioral sciences, (3) to describe various facets of sensitivity training institutes as they exist today, and (4) to discuss some implications the movement has for counseling and teaching in elementary and secondary schools.

THE SENSITIVITY TRAINING MOVEMENT: AN OVERVIEW

Sensitivity training, in its various forms, has grown tremendously in popularity in recent years. The increasing number of certain people who express enthusiasm for this group process greatly surpasses the objective research reports that might support it. There appears to be a gulf between the on-going activities and the failure of the facilitator (or agent of charge) to interpret for himself and others the psychological-sociological base for sensitivity-encounter sessions.

Historically, human relations training was started over two decades ago. Among the persons who established the first training center in Bethel, Maine (National Training Laboratory—Institute for Applied Behavioral Sciences) were Leland Bradford, Ronald Lippitt, and Kenneth Benne. Basically, these men were influenced by the work of Kurt Lewin, internationally known social psychologist. The fertile ideas germinated during the summer months of 1946-48. Focus was on a new method of training people for communities in the process of democratic group formation. This new dynamic procedure was to be a laboratory for self-examination of group process. The original intent of these innovators was to explore the roles and functions of the leadership and membership rather than the individual personality and development of personality. The major focus at this time was on structural group task exercises including the development of techniques to be used by the participants when they returned to their organizations.

About the mid 1950s the activities at the National Training Laboratory (NTL) came under the influence of persons who represented the developing field of humanistic and existential psychology. It was around this time that the original ideas fostered by NTL began to take on many different forms. New procedures and techniques were developed for the group process now called marathon groups, sensitivity groups, encounter groups, and personal growth laboratories.

As one surveys the literature of the human laboratory movement, a trend can be observed. In the 1940s the emphasis was placed on certain methods for use in teaching American communities how to participate in a democracy. This was the period of group process and task-oriented group function. By the early 1950s the shift was from task orientation to individual growth, to self-knowledge, actualization, and motivation. Then by the sixties a rather abrupt change occurred when the emphasis shifted from an educative to a therapeutic orientation. Weschler, Massarik, and Tannenbaum (1962) in an article entitled "The Self in Process: A Sensitivity Training Emphasis" stated, "By now it should be quite clear that major similarities exist between this type of sensitivity training and some forms of group psychotherapy. The rather distinctive difference between training and therapy . . . appears to be coming more and more blurred. . . . Today it is difficult to talk about what sensitivity training or what psychotherapy is and should be. Nor is it necessary to draw a clear distinction between them."

BEHAVIORAL SCIENTISTS EXPRESS CONCERNS

The position held in this statement is, however, being challenged as we enter a new decade. After I had sifted and winnowed the literature on the subject, it was interesting to note that a number of key persons who have been involved in small groups from its beginnings are now looking at the entire scenario from a critical and analytical perspective. Just recently these people have expressed themselves in writing, pointing out their concerns and suggesting caution in the use of certain small group procedures and techniques.

In his book *A Time to Speak Out—On Human Values and Social Research,* Dr. Herbert C. Kelman (1968), Professor of Psychology and Social Research at Harvard University, addresses himself to the topic "Manipulation of Human Behavior: An Ethical Dilemma." Professor Kelman raises some penetrating questions—questions that have emerged out of his experiences in T-groups, encounters, and sensitivity training sessions.

Dr. Martin Lakin, Department of Psychology, Duke University, has expressed himself in a very articulate manner in an article for the *American Psychologist,* October, 1969, entitled "Ethical Issues in Sensitivity Training." His observations and perceptive analysis of the situation that presently exists throughout the country is well taken. He devotes his paper to five major topics: (1) Pre-group Concerns, (2) Ethical Questions Related to the Processes of Training Groups, (3) Learning and Experiential Focuses, (4) Ethical Issues and Evaluations, and (5) Post-training Ethical Issues. For all who work in the field of the helping professions, those who train persons for various positions in psychology, counseling, and guidance, and in teacher education, this paper should be required reading.

In the November 15, 1969, issue of *Saturday Review,* an article appeared entitled "Sense and Non-Sense about Sensitivity Training," written by Dr. Max Birnbaum, Associate Professor of Human Relations and Director of Boston University Human Relations Laboratory. He states: "The most serious threat to sensitivity training comes first from its enthusiastic but frequently unsophisticated supporters, and second from a host of newly hatched trainers, long on enthusiasm or entrepreneural expertise, but short on professional experience, skill, and wisdom."

Each of these three men has expressed his concerns in a somewhat similar but yet in a slightly different way. All, however, have one thing in common. Each has participated in the activities of the National Training Laboratory in Bethel, Maine. In 1948 Professor Kelman spent the summer at the National Training Laboratory for Group Development; in 1949 he spent the summer at the Survey Research Center, University of Michigan, working on a study of human relations in industry. Throughout his graduate studies at Yale he devoted much time to study of attitude change with Carl Hovland. Professors Martin Lakin and Max Birnbaum also participated in the activities of the National Training Laboratory and in 1964 became associates of the organization.

Focusing our attention on the history and development of this group dynamic theory and relating it to what is actually occurring in the field would seem to be an important obligation for school counselors, counselor-educators, and those whose main responsibility is to train teachers of youth.

THE SENSITIVITY TRAINING SCENE TODAY

What is the present status of sensitivity training throughout the country? Observations suggest that the original intent of the group dynamics processes has become distorted by some extreme methods and procedures. The intent of this portion of the paper is to describe, comment on, and point out some issues regarding certain activities on the present scene.

Probably the most dramatic development that has occurred over the past three or four years is the creation of Sensitivity Training Institutes described as nonprofit corporations. These corporations are usually formed by a few people whose general concern is to help other human beings to develop and utilize their human potentialities for a more fulfilling life experience. Brochure material of one particular institute states: "This undertaking is entirely humanistic in concept. In order to remain effective it must also be humanistic in structure and operation. It has, therefore, been resolved that this endeavor shall be professional in creativeness, aggressive in purpose, and nonprofit in operation." You can make what you will of that statement.

Brochures used to advertise the institute programs are usually attractive in design, clear in stating tuition fees, somewhat vague in the discussion of purposes, goals, and functions. The novice, one who has little knowledge of the behavioral sciences, will find it difficult to understand just what the program is precisely all about. As indicated in a number of articles, persons from industry and business, especially, find the initial stages of the training period incomprehensible. A front-page news release in the *Wall Street Journal,* July 14, 1969, reported that management of certain industries are now retreating from participation in this group dynamics activity. Some companies see more harm than good in sensitivity training sessions. It has been stated that frank exchanges sometimes have hampered work and sessions have produced psychological breakdowns.

Dr. George Odiorne (1969), Dean of University of Utah's College of Business, stated, "If there is one thing we cannot stand in this world it is the business called 'leveling.' Often we can't bear to find out what everybody thinks of us. If you want to work with a group, there are some things you just don't say to them. Frankness that is not work-oriented should go on in the bedroom, not in the boardroom." He concluded: "Members of a group should not be allowed to probe the very depths of a person's soul."

Among industrial firms who have withdrawn from sensitivity training sessions are Humble Oil and Refining, Honeywell, Inc., U. S. Plywood—Champion Papers, Inc., Aerojet and General Corp., Northrop Corp., and others.

Marvin Dunnette and John Campbell (1969) of the University of Minnesota have supported industry's decision to terminate such training as presently being conducted on grounds that little to no evidence exists to support the contention that T-group sessions will change the work behavior of most trainees.

The costs involved in attending a sensitivity-encounter institute are not to be overlooked. Tuition fees vary from $35-$100 for a weekend session to $300-$350 for a three-week session. Food and lodging is an added expenditure. In some areas where the public can carry a heavier financial burden, the institute fees can run as high as $1,000-$1,500 for a one-week session. As stated in Bradford's original thinking, meetings are to be held in a residential setting, away from one's home and employment. This usually means a "posh" lodge or resort by the ocean, a lake, or in the mountains.

The major emphasis of the program of the institutes that have sprung up like mushrooms across the country is on directly experiencing the kind of group that is suggested by Carl Rogers (1966) when he writes:

> It usually consists of ten to fifteen persons and a facilitator or leader. It is relatively unstructured, providing a climate of maximum freedom for personal communication. Emphasis is upon the interactions among the group members, in an atmosphere which encourages each to drop his defenses and facades and thus enables him to relate directly and openly to other members of the group—the basic encounter. Individuals come to know themselves and each other more fully than is possible in the usual social or working relationships; the climate of openness, risk-taking, and honesty generates trust, which enables the person to recognize and change self-defeating attitudes, test out and adopt more innovative and constructive behaviors, and subsequently to relate more adequately and effectively to others in his everyday life situation.

This is the stated premise that is generally used by encounter-sensitivity training leaders. In actuality the observed behavior of participants does not always coincide with the kinds of outcomes hoped for and as stated above. The assumption made is that persons will relate better in their everyday life as a result of group training. This still remains as an assumption which needs to be researched objectively. Some of my personal observations of certain individuals who have experienced a number of encounter-sensitivity training sessions indicate they do not relate more adequately and effectively to others in their everyday life situation. In fact, some become extremely insensitive. In small groups, a person might develop warm and open relationships with strangers—only to return home unable to use his so-called innovative, constructive behaviors with his wife, children, and colleagues.

This position is also held by Dr. Robert W. Resnick (1970) in a recent article when he stated: "Even when a person breaks through his own shackles as often happens in encounter groups, sensitivity groups, nude groups, marathon groups and drug groups, he typically has great difficulty in integrating his behavior and experiences into his everyday life. I'm convinced that his freedom to *be* was given him by the situation, the group, the leader, fatigue or drugs."

The above statement expresses clearly my observations and analysis of several persons who have participated in groups. I have in the past raised a number of situational questions regarding a person's future behavior as a result of his experience in an institute which offers training in assisting persons to become more sensitive, honest, and open in relationships with others. Will a person develop a high level of integrity in a small group situation but in the real world not practice integrity? Will a person develop close intimate relationships in the small group, discuss his experiences with friends back home but conclude his story by saying—"but—oh don't tell my wife!" Is this person who shouts "It was great! fantastic! It was a beautiful experience!" really as open, honest, and sensitive as he claims? Or did this situation give him the opportunity to experience a catharsis only? Will a facilitator of groups use the group situation as an opportunity to unload his frustrations and problems on members of the group and thereby experience a type of therapy at the expense of the others?

What kind of professional guidelines and controls have been established for the institute where it has been estimated that between one and two million people have experienced their offerings? Will a participant, through the group experience, find *true* perceptual answers to such questions as—What is it that I do that turns other people off? Why am I not getting through to those for whom I care most? How do others see me? Does the encounter group really facilitate the individual to unlock his true feelings and communicate them to others? Or are these expressed feelings his feelings of the moment which were aroused by the group which may or may not be the person's real continuing feelings regarding himself and others?

Letting the group members see the true *me* seems to be very important to the underlying assumptions held by persons directing institute activities. The question raised is—is this the *true me* as expressed by the participant? Is it possible that his expressed feelings at that moment in time were influenced by the group and do not represent the me that exists in his life space while on the job, in the home, and during his socializing hours?

A number of institutes state in their brochures that college credit can be earned by participating in the program. In some instances nine to fifteen hours can be earned by paying an additional fee to the college or university. I have contacted the academic deans in institutions of higher education in the State of Colorado. To my present knowledge none of the state-supported colleges and universities in Colorado grant academic credit to students for participating in privately sponsored sensitivity-encounter sessions. Something needs to be done about this kind of subtle generalized implication.

What are the professional qualifications of the persons who establish and run sensitivity training institutes? What quality of training have the facilitators had? Where might an interested potential participant learn about the quality of the staff members of a particular institute? These questions should be answered so no doubt is left in the minds of the reader. It is not uncommon to read in their literature that the same directors and consultants serve several geographical regions. How much time and effort is devoted to each organization by these persons? Does the end justify the means?

What are the selection criteria for admission to the sensitivity-encounter training institutes? Is the assumption made that this process is good for all who pay the fee? Is it possible that such training will attract the psychologically unsound? If this did occur, is the group facilitator professionally qualified to deal with the kind of behavior that could develop during sessions? Or will he not take on such responsibility and state—"people will do what they need to do."

These are just a few of the major questions that have come to my mind in the use of the laboratory method in this kind of situation. In a few instances these problems have not escaped the attention of professional educators and lay people. In some rare cases, careful measures have been taken to deal with these problems. In other instances such problems are almost totally unobserved or ignored.

IMPLICATIONS FOR COUNSELING AND TEACHING IN ELEMENTARY AND SECONDARY SCHOOL

It is quite evident that much confusion exists among directors and facilitators of sensitivity training institutes. The purposes, goals and processes for developing positive self-concepts and behavior patterns are not spelled out. Many of the so-called growth processes to which reference is made are seldom articulated. In my own experience in a training laboratory, I found that the participants were not interested in engaging in an intellectual discussion for purposes of relating the affective learning to the cognitive. Instead, response to issues I thought important to explore were met with nonverbal response— the shrug of the shoulder, raising an eyebrow, or some other facial contortion coupled with a few vocal inflections. As one group leader told me at the beginning of the sessions, "Go through the experience first, then we'll talk theory." For some reason we never did get together to do just that! A review of the literature also indicates there is a lack of agreement on the definitions of terms, purposes, goals, and procedures of group work.

What implications does all of this have for sensitivity-encounter sessions for elementary and secondary school children? I believe there are a number of concerns which deserve serious analysis and evaluation by counselors, teachers, administrators, and parents.

Before counselors and teachers introduce this group process into the lives of young children and adolescents, a number of issues and problems need to be explored. What solid objective evidence do we have that suggests these procedures are of significant value for adults? What objective follow-up studies might be referred to for bona fide knowledge that people, in fact, benefit by such experiences and are able to apply their so-called newly acquired skills to everyday life situations? What evidence do we have that encounter-sensitivity group sessions are beneficial for the elementary and secondary school child? What objective evidence do we have that so-called "Teenage Awareness Workshops" develop positive, wholesome concepts about self and others?

There is absolutely no respectable objective evidence that sensitivity training sessions for young children and adolescents have fostered the kind of changes in behavior the enthusiasts purport. Proponents of sensitivity training programs keep saying, "We've got to change!" The question I raise is "Change for what?" Why is there a need for a person to change his life style if it works well for him and does not infringe on another? Are we to facilitate change just for the sake of change? If a child comes from a home where the value system has in fact fostered good and wholesome family, school, and community relations, what need is there for change? Might not the attacks leveled at children from such an environment cause a child to develop some ambivalent and even false feelings about himself and his home situation? I am reminded of a counselor who in a sensitivity training session asked a twelve-year-old boy if he really felt his parents planned for him and wanted him. This, I suppose, was to cause the child to explore himself in depth and breadth which would result in giving him a new and full dimension to his life space. However, this incident resulted in the need for psychiatric help lasting for over a year. All this following a weekend encounter? What were the purposes, the goals, the rationale for this particular group session?

Too frequently educators hear of new ideas, grab them, and put them into operation before little or any pretesting has been conducted and no controlled plans for evaluation established. At present the whole concept of group dynamics appears to be distorted. What one person perceives as appropriate another may not, and yet neither has evidence to justify his operation. What is needed, it seems to me, are established models for these activities with complete and clear explanations. Of course this will force those involved in these activities to incorporate his affective insights together with cognitive descriptions. This is a necessary step and it must be done if proponents of this movement intend to use these procedures in the elementary and secondary schools.

The child, parents, teachers and administrators must have a clear understanding of what the school counselor and the teacher are doing in group work. The counselor and/or teacher should be able to articulate the rationale behind his activities orally and in writing. He should allow teachers and parents to observe and participate if they wish. The purposes and goals must be spelled out. The young, more so than adults, must have a clear understanding of what they are getting into. This activity cannot be passed off as fun and games. It is not ethical to seduce pupils in getting them to respond emotionally toward one another in a manner which could develop into a hate session.

Young children are usually very open and honest—so much so they can hurt one another deeply. The expressed feeling of certain group members leveled at a particular child could result from long-felt feelings, or they could be feelings of the moment stimulated by the situation. Might not the attacker be wrong? Is it not possible that certain children will experience an emotional, freeing experience at the expense of another child? Will children really benefit from such group work? What are the purposes, goals, and processes?

As professional counselor-educators, counselors, and teachers, it behooves us to pause and take a good look at what is happening. For some people this is "the thing to do." It has become a fetish or cult verging on mysticism. Statements have been made by some enthusiasts that anyone can conduct group sessions and that all will benefit from experiences in group process. I wish I could point to some highly controlled objective research findings which would bear this out. There are so many questions yet to be answered before encounter-sensitivity training sessions are incorporated into the guidance and counseling programs in the elementary and secondary schools. I fear that counselors and teachers could create serious problems rather than alleviating them. Certainly without thorough training unfortunate outcomes could result. Up to this time many persons have been interested in the techniques for conducting group sessions—but not in evaluation of outcomes. This appears to be one of the more serious shortcomings of those persons who conduct group sessions.

Truly professional people in the field of psychology, counseling, and guidance know the theory which undergirds their practice. I am convinced that many who are sold on sensitivity training know very little of the origin and development of the present group dynamic activities. There seems to be an anti-intellectual position developing in counselor and teacher education. Focus on the affective domain of the learning process devoid of the cognitive seems to be in vogue. To me this is irresponsible education. Counselor and teacher educators must combine the two—feelings and thinking need to be interrelated, forming a meaningful whole.

SUMMARY AND CONCLUDING STATEMENTS

My attempt in this paper was fourfold: (1) to present some historical facts regarding sensitivity training, (2) to discuss concerns of some key professionals in the field, (3) to describe some facets of sensitivity training programs, and finally (4) to note implications of this movement for counseling and teaching in elementary and secondary schools.

The laboratory movement has developed some powerful procedures for facilitating human change. To date, some of the problems in the use of these techniques and processes have not been clearly specified and dealt with. The many issues and problems related to this movement should be analyzed and evaluated. Any positive results from a program of systematic evaluation could form the basis for firmly developed institutional and professionalized position for the implementation of the laboratory method. Until this is done, I shall continue to hold serious reservations regarding the use of sensitivity group sessions with young children, adolescents, and adults.

BIBLIOGRAPHY

1. Benne, K. D. "History of the T-Group in the Laboratory Setting." In *T-Group Theory and Laboratory Method: Innovation in Re-Education*, edited by L. P. Bradford, T. R. Gibb, and K. D. Benne. New York: John Wiley & Sons, Inc., 1964, chap. 4.
2. Birnbaum, Max. "Sense and Non-Sense about Sensitivity Training." *Saturday Review*, November 15, 1969, pp. 82-83, 96-98.
3. Dunnette, M., and Campbell, J. *Wall Street Journal*, July 14, 1969, p. 14.
4. Kelman, Herbert C. *A Time to Speak—On Human Values and Social Research*. San Francisco: Jossey-Bass, 1968.
5. Lakin, Martin. "Some Issues in Sensitivity Training." *American Psychologist*, Vol. 24, No. 10, October 1969, pp. 923-928.
6. Odiorne, George. *Wall Street Journal*, July 14, 1969, p. 14.
7. Resnick, Robert, W. "Chicken Soup Is Poison." Mimeographed. 435 North Bedford Drive, Beverly Hills, California, 1970. Received 1970.
8. Rogers, Carl R. *A Plan for Self-Directed Change in an Educational System*. Mimeographed. Western Behavioral Sciences Institute, LaJolla, California, 1966.
9. Schein, E. H., and Bennis, W. B. *Personal and Organizational Change through Group Methods: The Laboratory Approach*. 3rd printing. New York: John Wiley & Sons, Inc., 1967.
10. Wall Street Journal. *"The Truth Hurts, Some Companies See More Harm than Good in Sensitivity Training,"* July 14, 1969, pp. 1, 14.
11. Weschler, I. R., Massarik, F., and Tannebaum, R. "The Self in Process: A Sensitivity Training Emphasis." In *Issues in Human Relations Training*, edited by I. R. Weschler, Vol. 5 of National Training Laboratories Selected Reading Series, Washington, D. C., National Training Laboratories and National Education Association, 1962, pp. 33-46.

$$\boxed{9}$$

GUIDING THE EDUCATIONALLY DISADVANTAGED

Martin Haberman
University of Wisconsin—Milwaukee

By using data from the 1960 decennial census, one can calculate the dropout rate for the United States as a whole; these data show that approximately 60 percent of twenty-year-old youths were high school graduates in 1960, and therefore the dropout rate for the country was 40 percent before 1960.[1] But those who argue that the dropout is a major national educational problem are neglecting the question of absolute numbers; that is, although the high school population expanded by 500 percent between 1920 and 1960 and will probably increase by another 400 percent between 1960 and 1975, the number of high school dropouts has remained relatively constant. From 1900 to 1930 there were about 500 thousand dropouts annually; from 1930 to 1950 this number increased to 600 thousand; and since 1950 there have been about 650 thousand dropouts annually.[2] Whereas the large number of former dropouts could be absorbed by an economy in need of unskilled labor, the present group are just added to the ranks of the unemployed. Whether the absolute number of dropouts has actually increased therefore is a less important concern than what kind of life opportunities await those unprepared for work in a technical society.

The popular conclusion that if there were enough guidance counselors to work with these youngsters then the dropout problem could be ameliorated is not borne out by the research evidence. A six-year study has found that individual counseling of potentially delinquent high school girls is ineffective in improving their school behavior or in reducing the number of dropouts.[3] The investigators concluded that persons suffering from poverty, discrimination or a disorganized family life could not be expected to respond to individual therapy with any major character change.

The study, involving 400 fourteen-year-old high school girls who entered a Manhattan central vocational high school eight years ago, is the first long-term experimental study of its kind to be made. The girls were identified as potentially delinquent on the basis of their junior high school records and divided into two groups of 200 each. One group received individual attention and group therapy while the control group received no special attention. The experimental group included 54 percent Negroes and 18 percent Puerto Ricans.

An original article for this book.

[1] R. J. Havighurst. *The Public Schools of Chicago*. The Board of Education of the City of Chicago. Chicago, 1964. p. 274.

[2] R. A. Dentler. "Dropouts, Automation and the Cities." A paper delivered to Third Work Conference on Curriculum and Teaching in Depressed Urban Areas. Teachers College, Columbia University. June 22-July 3, 1964.

[3] E. F. Borgatta, H. J. Meyer and W. C. Jones. Interim Report of a Study sponsored by the Russell Sage Foundation and presented to the Eastern Regional Conference of the Child Welfare League of America. (Reported by the New York Times News Service, Sunday, February 21, 1965.)

At the completion of the study it was found that the same number of girls in each group graduated from high school and that there were no statistical differences in their grades, truancy, tardiness, school service, pregnancy or performance of psychological tests. Although many of the girls who received therapy felt they had been helped in their general attitudes, there was no real effect on any form of their measurable behavior. The researchers recommend that an attack on changing the whole community would be more effective than counseling which attempts to solve individual emotional problems.

But the number of physical dropouts is easy to calculate in comparison to the number of intellectual and emotional dropouts. How many of the 60 percent who complete high school by age twenty are never really affected in any important ways by the process of schooling? How many youngsters merely live through their school experiences without any real intellectual and emotional involvement? The development of more effective guidance principles will invariably improve the services offered to emotional dropouts who continue to attend, as well as those who remove themselves physically.

The discussion which follows will attempt to (1) describe the approaches used to define the disadvantaged; (2) suggest the characteristics of the disadvantaged which are most relevant to the process of schooling; (3) draw implications from these characteristics relevant to the work of the school guidance counselor; and (4) recommend fruitful areas of future study and development.

WHO ARE THE EDUCATIONALLY DISADVANTAGED?

Researchers and writers define the disadvantaged using a variety of conceptual schemes. Sociologists concerned with group behavior and interaction tend to use concepts related to the process of alienation. The means by which selected individuals become detached from their primary groups and the processes by which subgroups become disaffected and move into conflict with the majority group are a major emphasis of those who study alienation. Psychologists and others whose major unit of study is the individual rather than the group are more likely to utilize the concept of dependency than alienation in delimiting the disadvantaged. Educators, forced to focus on symptoms rather than causes, will more likely use a term like "nonachieving."

But the matter of delimiting the disadvantaged has become more complex than merely designating those who are alienated, dependent and nonachieving as disadvantaged. Figure 1 is a brief attempt to indicate how various realms of knowledge are led to concentrate on different human processes, analyze different orders of behavior and arrive at different terminology of symptoms by which to identify the disadvantaged.

The one generalization that can be made about all of these approaches is that the disadvantaged are conceived of as individuals who lack, miss or never develop attributes and characteristics considered to be necessary and positive. Very few social scientists stress the positive qualities and strengths among those designated as culturally deprived, since to recognize strengths among the disadvantaged would require rejecting many of the norms which structure middle-class society. Frank Riessman is an outstanding spokesman for those who, seeing more personal congruence in the lives of lower-class individuals than among members of the middle-class, stress the term culturally different rather than culturally deprived.[4]

In response to the naive term "cultural deprivation" which was popular a few years ago, scholars raise the simple objection that no one can lack culture any more than he can lack personality and that what was really needed was a specification of cultural differences rather than a definition of deprivation. It was not long, however, before the question was raised, "Different from whom?" and the term difference took on a value connotation which clearly implied that those who were different were missing elements of culture they should have. In most conceptualizations, whether they are termed deprivations or differences, it is crucial to recognize three facts: (1) that some individual with a particular frame of reference is deciding who is deprived; (2) that with some notable exceptions these definitions will focus on elements of personality or culture which are considered to be underdeveloped or missing; and (3) that there is an assumption that these gaps or inadequacies *should* be made up or rectified.

But who will decide when a cultural difference is no longer a disadvantage? What criteria will be used to make this determination? Does the middle class furnish so adequate a milieu for the development of individual potential that non-middle-class views must be eliminated?

There is no way to resolve the issue of whether the middle-class or the lower-class person is more mentally healthy, more congruent in his responses to life, or more satisfied in meeting his basic needs. The lives of members of the lower class are generally more open to inspection than the lives of middle-class individuals. Welfare workers, social workers, doctors, nurses, building inspectors, landloards, school representatives, policemen and even salesmen gain entry into the homes of poor people more frequently than they visit middle-class individuals' homes. Lower-class homes are more open to inspection and as a result social scientists have a greater amount of data about the poor and their life styles than they have about others. Middle-class problems frequently tend to be smoothed over and confined to the immediate family and the physical limits of the home. This basic difference in available data is one reason that individuals of various class groups cannot be adequately compared.

Although lower-class life is more public and middle-class life more private, the lower-class person is no longer a complete outsider to the affluent society. Through mass media — particularly television — he is vulnerable to all the lures and attractions of the good life. Whereas he formerly was ignorant of a middle-class orientation, he must now suffer the dilemma of having his expectations raised while he is kept from acquiring the means for realizing them. Riessman may be right about the strengths in the lives of lower-class individuals which are overlooked in designating them as deprived or disadvantaged. At the same time conditions of poverty, ignorance and disease in a society of plenty must be regarded as absolute disadvantages. In response to a psychologist's presentation which emphasized the more emotionally stable life led by members of the lower-classes in comparison to the striving and straining of middle-class persons, a well-known educator was heard to remark,

---

[4]F. Riessman. *The Culturally Deprived Child.* (New York: Harpers, 1962).

Discipline	Major Area of Study	Examples of Behaviors and Responses Analyzed	Terminology
Linguistics[1]	Communi-cation	-The process of learning to speak -Verbal interaction with mother -Speech patterns -Responses and interpretations to language -Linguistic interactions	1. Nonverbal 2. Illiterate 3. Nonfunctional reader 4. Inarticulate 5. Uncommunicative
Psychology[2]	Perception	-Self-concept -Identification with significant others -Motivation -Habits, responses, behavior patterns -Stages of conceptual develop-ment	1. Unmotivated 2. Unaspiring 3. Experience-poor 4. Perceptually-blocked 5. Dependency-prone
Sociology[3]	Values	-Child-rearing practices -Ethnic influences in sociali-zation process -Status, role in early family life -Race, religion, class influ-ences on child's values -Migration	1. In-migrant 2. Mobile 3. Lower class member 4. Member of minor-ity ethnic groups 5. Alienated
Psychiatry[4]	Needs and Drives	-Sexual role definitions -Masculine-feminine learning -Corporal punishment -The role of love in the home -Physiological need satisfaction	1. Prone to seek out immediate gratifi-cation 2. Physically oriented 3. Lacking successful adult models 4. Unloved 5. Unattended
Education[5]	Knowledge	-Interest in school -Ability to learn school behaviors -Achievement -I.Q. -Academic motivation	1. Educationally disadvantaged 2. Remedial reader 3. Underachiever 4. Hard-to-reach 5. Difficult-to-serve 6. Disaffected
Economics[6]	Resources	-Consumption -Distribution -Production -Money and banking -Employment	1. Underdeveloped 2. Unskilled 3. Nonproductive 4. Unemployed 5. Consumer

Figure 1

Conceptual Schemes for Studying the Nature of Culturally Different Children and Youth

Social Work[7]	Human Welfare	-Family breakdown -Delinquency -Individual adjustment to social conditions -Providing for basic human needs	1. Antisocial 2. Maladjusted 3. Neglected 4. Unprovided for 5. Poor

[1]B. Bernstein. "Some Sociological Determinants of Perception: An Inquiry into Sub-Cultural Differences." The British Journal of Sociology. June, 1958.
[2]M. Deutsch. "The Disadvantaged Child and the Learning Process." An unpublished paper. New York Medical College, July, 1962.
[3]A. Davis and R. J. Havighurst. "Social Class and Color Differences in Child Rearing." American Sociological Review, April, 1953.
[4]D. R. Miller and G. E. Swanson. Inner Conflict and Defense. New York, 1960.
[5]H. H. Davidson, (et al.). "Characteristics of Successful School Achievers from a Severely Deprived Environment." Unpublished Report. Department of Education, The City University of New York. October, 1962.
[6]O. Hamlin. The Uprooted, Boston: Little, Brown and Co., 1951.
————, The Newcomers: Negroes and Puerto Ricans in Changing Metropolis. Garden City, New York, 1962.
[7]S. and E. Glueck. Family Environment and Delinquency. Boston: Houghton Mifflin Co., 1962.

Figure 1 (continued)

"Anytime you want to give up your place in the middle class, just say so. I know a couple of people who would be happy to take your place."

It is no longer useful for educators to pursue the academic discussions related to terminology alone. It is necessary only to admit that because of the nature of the *forces* controlling the schools, there are large populations of youngsters who are not being offered equal opportunity to develop their potentialities. The term educationally disadvantaged is used not only to indicate lacks or failures in the personalities or backgrounds of the youngsters, but also to recognize that the perceptions of the middle-class persons who run our schools are a self-fulfilling prophecy: those whom they perceive as educationally disadvantaged become so.

Contrary to popular notions, lower-class people place a high value on education, but lack the confidence and know-how to realize their goal.[5] Even the process of schooling — which is a negative experience for many of them — still does not undermine their belief in the value of education.

Recent research is placing more and more emphasis on the actual learning disadvantages suffered by the non-middle-class children because of differences in their home environments. Benjamin Bloom lists four specific factors which handicap children in a deprived environment compared with what he calls children in an "abundant environment."[6]

1. Poor speech habits and language patterns in the home discourage language development and restrict the number and variety of words which

[5]F. Riessman. "Workers' Attitudes Towards Participation and Leadership." Unpublished Ph.D. dissertation, Columbia University, 1955.
[6]B. S. Bloom. Stability and Change in Human Characteristics, (New York: John Wiley and Sons, Inc., 1964), p. 77.

the child recognizes; this contributes to lower scores on I.Q. tests and lower school achievement, especially in reading.

2. Families have less time, opportunity, or know-how to take their children on expeditions to the zoo, museums, stores, or different neighborhoods; the children also have fewer indirect experiences with the world around them through books, pictures, films, etc. Such experiences not only increase verbal facility but help in making distinctions, comparing objects, ideas, etc. — all important not only for I.Q. tests but for learning itself.

3. Children in these disadvantaged homes have fewer opportunities for solving problems or for thinking about a variety of issues, as compared with children in more abundant environments. The former's parents do not have the habit of encouraging children to ask questions or to think things out for themselves.

4. There is less interaction between adults and children. Discipline tends to be authoritarian and the "good" child is quiet and out of the way. This, too, limits the background of experience and language which the child brings to school.

The term "disadvantaged" is useful to educators because it can be used to designate the populations of youngsters who are not making the desired responses to the process of schooling. Rather than seeking out the conceptualization of various social scientists trying to define deprivation or cultural differences, educators can begin by focusing on the real problem presented by the large number of physical and emotional dropouts who do not achieve according to their capabilities. From this orientation of underachievement, the condition of educational disadvantagement can be considered as being fed by four basic sources: (1) the innate disabilities which can prevent an individual from achieving in school situations; (2) the preschool family conditions which would socialize a youngster in such a manner that he is not predisposed to realize his potentialities in subsequent school situations; (3) the process of schooling itself (particularly the teachers under whose aegis the youngster is placed) which may be of a debilitating rather than an enhancing nature; and (4) the self-concept or educational aspirations which a youngster develops by the later stages of his elementary school experience that may have a negative or deprecating effect.[7]

These four kinds of elements must be viewed as interrelated; for example, a child's preschool and family life experiences can affect the development of his innate abilities, and the quality of his school experiences will markedly influence the self-concept and aspirations which he develops.

Through consideration of the factors of inheritance, the conditions of preschool family living, early school experiences and the self-concept, youngsters can be accurately designated as educationally disadvantaged; that is, they will not experience equal educational opportunities in our schools as these institutions are presently constituted. Before drawing implications for the role of the guidance worker, it would be useful to consider the behavioral characteristics of youngsters who are educationally disadvantaged.

---

[7]R. J. Havighurst. *op. cit.* p. 33.

CHARACTERISTICS OF THE EDUCATIONALLY DISADVANTGED

In order to provide clues that may help to explain differences in school performance, one group of researchers conducted a pilot study of disadvantaged pupils in a New York City elementary school. In comparing good achievers, these researchers came up with the following hypotheses:[8]

1. Good achievers are more controlled, cautious and constructed than poor achievers.
2. Good achievers exhibit a greater "need to know" and more of them show a "need for achievement"; they are also more work oriented and less concerned with immediate gratification than poor achievers.
3. Good achievers have a more positive attitude toward authority figures than poor achievers and see the world as less threatening.
4. Good achievers are more accepting of adult standards and expectations than poor achievers.
5. Good achievers have a more positive self-image and greater self-confidence.
6. Good achievers are less anxious and fearful than poor achievers.
7. Good achievers show greater ability to view themselves and the world about them objectively, accurately and critically.
8. Good achievers are superior to poor achievers in general verbal behavior; they do not excel, however, in divergent production.
9. Good achievers are superior to poor achievers in memory and attention.
10. Good achievers show better analyzing, organizing, elaborating and generalizing abilities than poor achievers.

There did not seem to be any consistent differences between good and poor achievers with respect to such factors as willingness to cooperate and eagerness to do well. From the findings of this study, the hypothetical good achiever from an underprivileged environment emerges as:

. . . . . a child who is relatively controlled and cautious, often stereotyped and constricted, but who still retains a degree of originality and creativity. He seems more willing than his less successful classmates to conform to adult demands, has a more positive view of authority figures and greater self-confidence. In cognitive functioning he excels chiefly in tasks requiring memory, attention and verbal abilities. He is also superior in analytical and organizational abilities and generally in processes that require convergent thinking.

In contrast, the composite picture of the poor achiever is that of a child burdened by anxiety, fearful of the world and authority figures and lacking in self-confidence. He is more apt to be impulsive and labile with relatively poor controlling mechanisms. His defenses against anxiety and feelings of inadequacy may be expressed in excessive talking and in uncritically favorable surface attitudes toward self and others. Nevertheless the poor achiever still seems to have sufficient potential for adaptive behavior which the school could build upon. His cognitive activities are often quite similar in content

[8]H. H. Davidson, J. W. Greenberg, J. M. Garver. "Characteristics of Successful School Achievers from a Severely Deprived Environment." School of Education, The City University of New York, Mimeograph, October, 1962. (Reported at the American Educational Research Association, Chicago, February, 1963.)

approach and process to those of a good achiever and in fact, he demonstrates greater facility in divergent production. Many of his reactions give evidence of creative capacity which might be directed and controlled. From this behavior in the testing situations and in tasks requiring social comprehension, the poor achiever seems to possess substantial understanding of the world around him although he seems less able to act upon this understanding than the good achiever.

It must be remembered in considering results like these that the "good achievers" would be just average in terms of national norms. Yet it seems clear that disadvantaged youngsters who are most successful are most like middle-class youngsters.

There are indications from recent research that the disadvantaged youngster needs a structured classroom environment and much help in order to learn to control his impulses and to cope with a freer learning situation.[9] In addition, he seems to need help in developing the cognitive bases for improving his memory and attention levels, as well as his listening, speaking and verbal abilities. In response to the frequently cited need to raise self-confidence and expectations, it must be emphasized that continued success is not enough; youngsters don't need easy success but do need learning activities that stimulate and challenge them. Classrooms and teaching must be deliberately organized to provide initial and continued success in worthwhile and challenging activities.

Thus far there has been a deliberate attempt to avoid a discussion of the social class and ethnic differences between lower-class and middle-class individuals and to focus on the differences which appear in the process of schooling. As educators it is important that we develop means for dealing with factors which block learning and do not become embroiled in the fruitless debate over lower-class characteristics vis-à-vis middle-class characteristics. It may very well be that in spite of the monumental accumulation of sociological literature on the subject of social class differences, such differences are merely after-the-fact descriptions and not the designation of characteristics or values which would allow us to predict how an individual will behave in subsequent situations. Perhaps the catalog of differences which have been attributed to social class and ethnic differences are merely the differences in response to different life situations, and changes in the conditions of existence will lead to changes in behavior which we have heretofore regarded as the reflection of deep-seated, permanent value systems. The implication of this assumption that changing conditions will change behavior offers educators the basis for believing that changes in curriculum teachers, procedures and materials will effect changes among the disadvantaged. But what characteristics of the disadvantaged should guidance workers seek to change? And what can they do to effect these changes?

---

[9]J. H. Jackson. "The Relationship Between Psychological Climate and the Quality of Learning Outcomes Among Lower Status Pupils." Unpublished Ph.D. thesis. University of Chicago, 1957.

THE GUIDANCE FUNCTION IN SCHOOLS SERVING
THE EDUCATIONALLY DISADVANTAGED

The nature of a youngster's inheritance and his early family experiences are the two most critical factors for predicting the degree of his educational disadvantages. The power of environmental factors to compensate for inherited deficiencies is greatest in the early years. Bloom summarizes the research which indicates the degree to which early family life can compensate for inheritance and states:

> A conservative estimate of the effect of extreme environments on intelligence is about 20 I.Q. points. This could mean the difference between a life in an institution for the feeble-minded or a productive life in society. It could mean the difference between a professional career and an occupation which is at the semi-skilled or unskilled level. . . . . The implications for public education and social policy are fairly clear. Where significantly lower intelligence can be attributed to the effects of environmental deprivations, steps must be taken to ameliorate these conditions as early in the individual's development as education and other social forces can be utilized.[10]

It is necessary to recognize, therefore, that the most powerful factors for determining those who will be educationally disadvantaged are in large measure beyond the aegis of the school and the guidance counselor. Somewhat less powerful but nevertheless important contributing factors for determining who will be disadvantaged are events which occur in later stages of childhood; the nature of school experiences and the self-image and aspirations which these experiences engender have the most far-reaching influence. The guidance worker has some possibility for professional service in these areas but even here his influence is often indirect and minimal in comparison to the impact of the teachers, the curriculum and the total school setting.

The guidance counselor faced with the challenge of service to a disadvantaged population can maximize his effectiveness by utilizing principles which take account of the nature of the youngsters and the nature of the process of schooling, that is, operational principles which have as their goal the equalization of educational opportunities and the unblocking of human potentialities. Four principles which can give such direction relate to the need for affecting parents and community wherever possible, directing choices for those who lack the experiences on which to make them, building aspirations and counseling with teachers.

1. *Effective school guidance programs for the disadvantaged include goals of parent education and community change.* As children move from elementary to secondary schools, contact with parents is usually diminished. Unfortunately the number of important educational choices which must be made increase as a youngster advances. In essence, we have a system which fosters greatest parental involvement at a time when their advice about educational choices is least useful.

Civil rights groups, community associations, religious organizations and special governmental crash programs are all attempting to influence parents

---

[10]B. Bloom. *op. cit.,* p. 89.

and the community regarding the equalization of educational opportunities. This is particularly true in large urban areas. It is important that professional guidance people also reach parents. While parental attitudes are a powerful influence on their children's choice of program, the currently aroused community interest in educational programs will be an even greater pressure on schools in the future.

One critical example of the need for guidance programs in schools serving the disadvantaged to effect change in parents and community attitudes is in the area of school integration. Many well-meaning but uninformed civil rights and community leaders are creating the impression that all efforts at compensatory education and guidance are attempts to prevent integration or preserve inequities. In such situations any effort to give added services or courses — even on a temporary basis — is rejected. Equal educational opportunity becomes defined as the *same* educational opportunity. It is the role of guidance workers serving the disadvantaged youngsters to help them, their parents and the community understand that while good education has the same long-term purposes for all, there are different means for reaching them. In a slum high school where youngsters may be an average of two years behind in reading and study skills and where there is a poor general science program, it is just as dangerous for a local civil rights leader to demand an advanced placement physics class as it is for the school principal to dismiss such a demand as ridiculous. By procedures of special help, special materials and special effort such a goal may be realized. But this means treating some youngsters differently for temporary periods. It is a major responsibility of all guidance workers to help teachers, youngsters, parents and the community to understand that truly equal educational opportunity is individualized and that there is a significant educational distinction between differentiation of instruction based on need and that on planned segregation.

In addition to seeking to inform and work directly with parents, the guidance program can be most effective by working indirectly through teachers, principals, nurses, school secretaries, janitors, attendance officers and the other personnel with whom parents come into contact. As experts in the way people relate to one another, the guidance counselors in schools serving the educationally disadvantaged should have time built into their work loads which will enable them to help to improve any contacts parents have with school personnel. Disadvantaged parents may understandably regard any person employed by the school as representative of the "school's opinion." Since it is well known that a callous school secretary or a bigoted custodian can be detrimental to school-community relations and the educational program, there should be planned, organized effort by guidance personnel to work with all those who are part of the school setting.

A third way of affecting parents and community is to serve as a clearing house for information which can upgrade the parents themselves. There must be better coordination and greater effectiveness in informing parents of opportunities related to literacy programs, adult education, vocational training, consumer education and health services. Improving these efforts will not only upgrade the quality of parental influence on youngsters now in school but may make parents better models for their preschool youngsters on whom their influences are currently even greater.

This description of responsibilities of guidance personnel is not an attempt to make them individually responsible for effecting marked changes in parents and communities. It is instead a recognition that parents are the greatest environmental determinant of who will be educationally disadvantaged and that early, minimal efforts with parents will have an intense and pervasive effect on the youngsters.

2. *Disadvantaged children and youth should be directed to make decisions which will give them the widest choices in future.* The outstanding characteristics of the American educational system are threefold: it is universal, diverse and lifelong. The system intends that everyone have the opportunity to develop in the direction of his abilities and interests and that his opportunity for extended and adult education always be kept open. These basic beliefs should guide school counselors into helping youngsters make choices which will not channel them into specializations at an early age. The longer youngsters can be kept in general studies the greater the possibility for mature choice-making on their part. This means that rather than taking a nondirective or laissez-faire role the guidance counselor serving disadvantaged youngsters must often be quite directive. His experience enables him to predict that if he can keep a youngster from limiting himself to some narrow specialization too early the youngster's future choices will be broader.

It is common to hear the rationalization that the need for a job and skills which are marketable should take precedence over programs of general studies; "If he had a job and some pocket money, he wouldn't have any problem." But the purposes of American education are not to "get a job and stay out of jail" — even for the disadvantaged. The real goals involve participation as a citizen and the individual fulfillment which can come only through participation in a wide sampling of the fields of human knowledge and endeavor.

Narrow specialization begun too early inevitably fails youngsters in two basic ways: it does not provide the general education required by most post-secondary education programs nor does it develop the level of skills needed for securing technical employment. Such specializations are effective preparation for personal disaster.

It is unfortunate for the guidance counselor serving a disadvantaged population if his preparation has led him to believe that nondirective methods are always "good" and directive ones always "bad," since he must not hesitate to authoritatively make those decisions which he knows will provide youngsters with the greatest number of alternative courses of action at some future time.

3. *The major goal of counseling disadvantaged children and youth is the development of a positive self-image and high educational and life aspirations.* Poverty, parental neglect and related social conditions impose certain stresses on youngsters which frequently cause negative perceptions of self. Unfortunately, effective school learning can take place only if children view themselves as important and valuable people. The normal universal need of all children for feelings of self-esteem becomes accentuated in disadvantaged youngsters who more frequently face unsuccessful experiences in the process of schooling. Beginning with experiential handicaps, the school program itself is often the cause of developing strong negative self-images among disadvantaged populations. Some experts place the age at which these negative

self-perceptions are conceptualized at age 10.[11] It is very likely, however, that the process of schooling has reinforced enough unsuccessful attempts at learning so many youngsters are educationally disadvantaged by age 7. It is often possible to predict who will drop out or be generally unsuccessful in subsequent school situations by the completion of third grade. We have this ability to predict not because youngsters will not change but because most school situations do not adapt to fit the students; more frequently students are expected to adjust to rigid, unchanging conditions of mass education.

Disadvantaged youngsters often overcompensate for these feelings of inadequacy by assuming superficially high aspirations. It is not uncommon to hear nonreaders in eighth and ninth grade respond to questions regarding their future occupational goals with choices such as "brain surgeon," "astronaut," or "banker." It is not the role of guidance counselors to discourage even apparently unrealistic aspirations. This recommendation is in direct conflict with more usual guidance positions.

> One might well imagine a present-day counselor exhorting Columbus to give up this mad confusion of sailing westward to find the East and to settle down quietly in a pleasant villa on the outskirts of Genoa. This advice would not be completely foolish; on the contrary, it would be sound practical counseling from the advisor's point of view, because while he could not help the adventurer at all on his proposed journey, he could be of great assistance in helping him choose a pleasant villa. . . . .[12]

Such an approach, although popular, would be disastrous in guiding the disadvantaged. There are no villas along the Mediterranean or anywhere else for one who is educationally disadvantaged. His best chance for an existence which will enable him to realize his potentialities is to break from the stereotyped but safe ideas of his ghetto, his family or his ethnic group. In the absence of a villa, his choice is to be Columbus or no one.

But high aspirations are not merely the fostering of daydreams. The implications for guidance personnel are clear: they must encourage youngsters to develop, keep and expand all their aspirations, and at the same time help to effect the changes in curriculum and teaching which will afford youngsters real success experiences on which to grow. Healthy aspirations derive from some form of success experience in the real world. In addition to working directly with youngsters, guidance personnel who wish to affect the education of the disadvantaged therefore must become involved in curriculum development and in-service teacher education.

4. *The most effective means of implementing the school guidance program for disadvantaged children and youth requires direct work with teachers and principals.* There will never be enough guidance personnel to work with the school age youngsters who could use their services. Evidence cited earlier indicates that even if there were sufficient personnel, such services would have minimal effect in the absence of simultaneous changes in the community and in school programs. Given the present limited supply of guidance counselors and the fact that others (e.g. teachers, principals, nonprofessional staff,

---

[11]R. J. Havighurst. *op. cit.* p. 34.
[12]R. Mammarella and J. Crescimbeni. *"Guidance Problems: Cultural or Cosmic?"* *Saturday Review,* Nov. 21, 1964, p. 76.

etc.) have more consistent influence on youngsters' self-concepts, guidance personnel in all schools should spend more time working directly with teachers and principals than with children or youth. This is not to imply that teachers and principals are emotionally disturbed to a greater degree than any other group in the general population, but to recognize the need for extending the influence of guidance personnel as broadly as possible. By effecting change in teachers' self-concepts, attitudes and values, it is likely that almost all disadvantaged children and youth can be influenced to some degree.

One teacher who believes "these children can't be expected to learn" may influence from 30 to 150 youngsters on a daily basis. Consider how much more effective it would be to work with Miss Jones rather than the large number of pupils she regularly sends out of class as behavior problems. In some instances the guidance counselor may just serve as a nonjudgmental, nonthreatening listener with whom teachers would be free to share their complaints and problems.

Organizational procedures should be created which would open regular channels of communication between counselors and teachers. It is necessary to recognize that even the most successful teacher working with disadvantaged youth is engaged in a physically taxing, emotionally stressful situation. Such a teacher needs to be recognized as having the professional right to have his problems and concerns listened to and receiving the counsel of an experienced guide in working out ways of handling his own and his youngsters' problems. Principals and supervisors have similar needs. It is unrealistic to believe that individuals with great professional responsibility, engaged in human relations which are often tense and highly emotional for long periods of time, should not be helped by accepted procedures of guidance and counseling. Given the tremendous influence of teachers' attitudes on youngsters' self-concepts, it seems sensible that limited guidance resources be devoted to helping professional personnel.

RECOMMENDATIONS FOR FUTURE STUDY

What kinds of information are needed to implement the suggestions implied in the preceding discussion? Rather than await well-controlled research it is necessary to begin on the action level utilizing the most efficient means of evaluation available. Following are some of the questions which, when answered, will help establish more effective guidance programs for serving the disadvantaged.

1. How should guidance personnel be selected? (Can we assume that successful classroom teaching and college course work is the only appropriate basis, or are there other criteria of selection?)

2. How should guidance personnel be supervised? (Can we assume that these individuals can function best in complete professional isolation, or do they need closer association with colleagues performing comparable roles?)

3. What criteria should be used to evaluate guidance personnel? (Can we assume that the work is so complex and long-term that it is beyond evaluation, or that observable, behavioral objectives can be specified?)

4. What are some effective ways of reaching parents and effecting changes in the community? (Can we assume a narrow role for the school, or is the school serving the disadvantaged a community school?)

5. What are the results of follow-up studies which compare disadvantaged youth given directive guidance with those given indirect counseling? (Can we assume that nondirective methods are best for everyone in all situations, or does effective guidance involve the selection of various procedures for realizing different purposes?)

6. What are some effective means of working directly with youngsters to build their self-concepts and aspirations? (Can we assume that only pre-school and early elementary children are susceptible to emotional growth, or are there procedures which are equally effective with adolescents?)

7. What methods have been used to work with teachers, principals and nonprofessional staff? (Can we assume that guidance counselors will be most effective working only with youngsters, or that they would be most useful working predominantly with teachers?)

8. What means have guidance counselors used for effecting curriculum change? (Can we assume that the basic purpose of the counselor is pupil — or even teacher — adjustment, or that he has a concomitant responsibility for trying to induce change in the system?)

Before summing up, it would be useful to note the numerous items which have been omitted from this discussion. Nothing has been said about the physical facilities in which the counselor operates or the clerical help he is provided. Neither has there been an emphasis on issues such as the purposes of elementary guidance as opposed to secondary guidance, or whether the functions of vocational, educational and emotional guidance should be performed by separate individuals or the same person. Nothing has been said about the problems of testing and those measures which can most effectively assess disadvantaged children and youth. All of these, as well as other items, are important concerns for describing the work of the counselor. In order to limit this discussion, however, the issues and problems selected for analysis are those considered to be the most crucial for guiding the disadvantaged.

SUMMARY

There are a variety of approaches used for studying the problems of the educationally disadvantaged. It is suggested that studying the nature of children's inheritance, early family life and school experiences, with particular reference to the self-concept engendered by these experiences, is the most fruitful approach. Selected characteristics of the educationally disadvantaged are presented which indicate the nature of the difference between high and low school achievers. On the basis of these characteristics four action principles are presented for guidance counselors serving disadvantaged youngsters. These guidelines emphasize working with parents, community, curriculum and teachers, in addition to working directly with youngsters. Recommendations are made which attempt to outline the basic questions about which more information is needed before the work of the guidance counselor serving the educationally disadvantaged can be specified in further detail.

BIBLIOGRAPHY

Bloom, B. S. *Stability and Change in Human Characteristics*, (New York: John Wiley and Sons, Inc., 1964).

Borgatta, E. F., Meyer, J. H., and Jones, W. C. Interim Report of a study sponsored by the Russell Sage Foundation and presented to the Eastern Regional Conference of the Child Welfare League of America. (Reported by the New York Times News Service, Sunday, February 21, 1965.)

Davidson, H. H., Greenberg, J. W., and Garver, J. M. "Characteristics of Successful School Achievers from a Severely Deprived Environment." School of Education, The City University of New York, Mimeograph, October, 1962. (Reported at the American Educational Research Association, Chicago, February, 1963.)

Dentler, R. A. "Dropouts, Automation and the Cities." A paper delivered to Third Work Conference on Curriculum and Teaching in Depressed Urban Areas. Teachers College, Columbia University. June 22-July 3, 1964.

Havighurst, R. J. *The Public Schools of Chicago.* The Board of Education of the City of Chicago. Chicago, 1964.

Jackson, J. H. "The Relationship Between Psychological Climate and the Quality of Learning Outcomes Among Lower Status Pupils." Unpublished Ph.D. thesis. University of Chicago, 1957.

Mammarella, R., and Crescimbeni, J. "Guidance Problems: Cultural or Cosmic?" *Saturday Review,* Nov. 21, 1964, p. 76.

Riessman, F. *The Culturally Deprived Child.* New York: Harpers, 1962.

Riessman, F. "Workers' Attitudes Towards Participation and Leadership." Unpublished Ph.D. dissertation, Columbia University, 1955.

PARABLE OF THE GOOD COUNSELOR

John D. Krumboltz
Stanford University

Merely responding to client feelings may be a grossly inadequate counselor response with many clients' problems. The counselor has available a variety of techniques by which he can help his client learn to consider all relevant facts before making a crucial decision. In a behavioral approach to counseling, the counselor would (a) help each client define his goals in specific terms, (b) provide resources and encouragement in helping the client move toward his goals, and (c) experiment with a variety of techniques for helping clients with different problems.

And who is my neighbour?
(Luke 10: 25-37)

CASE 1: MR. LEVITEN

"I've just been offered the chance of a lifetime!" exclaimed Marsha bursting into the counselor's office. Marsha was 16, mature for her years, and unusually attractive in spite of the little money she could spend for clothes.

"Tell me more," said Mr. Leviten. Mr. Leviten had counseled with Marsha many times before and knew of the alcoholic fights between her parents and

Reprinted by permission of the author and *Personnel and Guidance Journal,* Vol. 43, No. 2, October 1964, 118-124.

of the impending return of her embittered brother from the Youth Authority Camp.

"Well, last night, while I was waiting for the bus, this man in a convertible pulled up and introduced himself. He showed me his business card and talked nice, so it seemed OK. Really, I never talk to strangers usually."

Co: You felt this time it would be all right.

Cl: Yes, and so we talked for a long time and I told him all my troubles with my family and how I hated the whole situation.

Co: Um-hmm.

Cl: So eventually he told me about this job he could fix up for me in New York. It just sounds so terrific and fun and so different from the miserable life I lead here.

Co: You feel this job could take you away from the unhappiness you've had here.

Cl: Oh yes, Mr. Leviten, you said it exactly. And all I would have to do on this job is have dates with rich businessmen, go to parties and fancy restaurants, and on top of all that I would get paid too—sometimes as much as $100 for going to just one party.

Co: You see the adventures and profits of this job as quite a contrast to your present life, and you feel attracted by the possibilities.

Cl: You always seem to know exactly how I feel, Mr. Leviten, and that's why it's always so easy to talk with you. What would you advise me to do?

Co: You feel a need to get someone's opinion about the wisdom of your choice.

Cl: I guess so, although really it is my own decision, and as you say, this job would take me away from all the unhappiness I've had here. Besides, as you put it so well, I'd have adventure and profits too. That settles it. I'm going. And thanks so much for your help.

Mr. Leviten leaned back as Marsha bounced out of his office. He was pleased that he had empathically reflected Marsha's feelings without imposing his own values, thus freeing his client for self-direction.

CASE 2: MR. SAMARSKY

"I've just been offered the chance of a lifetime!" exclaimed Marsha bursting into the counselor's office. Marsha was 16, mature for her years, and unusually attractive in spite of the little money she could spend for clothes.

"Tell me more," said Mr. Samarsky. Mr. Samarsky had counseled with Marsha many times before and knew of the alcoholic fights between her parents and of the impending return of her embittered brother from the Youth Authority Camp.

Cl: Well, last night, while I was waiting for the bus, this man in a convertible pulled up and introduced himself. He showed me his business card and talked nice, so it seemed OK. Really, I never talk to strangers usually.

Co: You find it's better not to talk to strangers as a general rule.

Cl: Yes, I know what happens to girls who aren't careful. But anyway he seemed respectable and all, so we talked for a long time and I told him all my troubles with my family and how I hated the situation.

Co: Um-hmm.

Cl: So eventually he told me about this job he could fix up for me in New York. It just sounds so terrifc and fun and so different from the miserable life I lead here.

[*Pause*]

And all I would have to do on this job is have dates with rich businessmen, go to parties and fancy restaurants, and on top of all that I would get paid too—sometimes as much as $100 for going to just one party.

[*Longer pause*]

Why are you so quiet, Mr. Samarsky? Doesn't this sound like a great thing?

Co: I was wondering if there were some other facts you should think through before you make a decision about this job.

Cl: That's why I wanted to talk with you. I'll bet you're wondering why this man is offering the job to me.

Co: That seems like a good question to ask.

Cl: I sort of wondered about that too. He said he just wanted to do me a favor, but he just kind of casually mentioned in passing that we might share the commissions since he was making all the contacts.

Co: And have you also wondered exactly what kind of service you would be expected to perform for all this money?

Cl: Just be friendly, I guess. But that doesn't make sense. There was some talk about how lonely and affectionate some of these guys were and how I should humor them.

[*Pause*]

Say, you don't suppose . . .

Co: Now you sound more skeptical.

Ci: Yes, why didn't I see it before? Now I know what that slick character wanted! And to think I nearly fell for it! I think this is something the police should investigate.

Co: Would you like to use my telephone?

Mr. Samarsky leaned back as Marsha left his office after reporting the details to the police. He was pleased that his questions and selective reinforcement had helped Marsha to consider more relevant facts in reaching her own decision.

Which now of these, thinkest thou, was neighbour unto him that fell among the thieves?

*   *   *   *   *

This brief and oversimplified parable has been constructed to dramatize some fundamental questions in the nature of counseling.

1. What is the purpose of counseling?
2. Who determines the purpose of counseling?
3. What counselor activities promote the attainment of counseling purposes?
4. What are the dangers of different counseling approaches?
5. Where should we direct our search for new knowledge?

These questions were raised in my mind by Patterson (1963) in contrasting two approaches to counseling—the "understanding" approach and the "manipulative" approach. Unfortunately, the use of such emotionally toned words tends to detract from a rational discussion of the issues involved. Hence more descriptive words with fewer emotional connotations are needed.

While no single term is fully adequate to summarize the complexities of each approach, I should like to use the terms "client-centered" and "behavioral" to designate the two approaches. The term "client-centered" is preferred by Rogers over "non-directive" and is clearly what Patterson refers to in advocating the "understanding" approach. "Behavioral" has been used by Michael and Meyerson (1962). It is probably as good a term as "reinforcement," "learning," or "re-educative," and is definitely superior to such adrenalin-arousers and cortex-inhibitors as "conditioning" and "manipulative."

GOALS OF COUNSELING

What is the purpose of counseling? Proponents of both the client-centered approach and the behavioral approach would agree that the purpose of counseling is to change behavior. Patterson very frankly states, "The counselor is attempting to influence the behavior of the client—this is obvious; otherwise he wouldn't be engaged in counseling" (1963, p. 683). The difference in the two approaches seems to be in their degree of willingness to state different objectives for different clients. The client-centered proponents have the same goal for all clients—specifically, "less dependence upon others, an increase of expressiveness as a person, an increase in variability, flexibility, and effectiveness of adaptation, an increase in self-responsibility and self-direction" (Rogers, 1961, p. 398).

In behavioral counseling, on the other hand, the goal of counseling may be defined differently by each client. One client may wish to learn how to become more aggressive, another one how to become less aggressive; one might desire to become less fearful about speaking in class, another might wish to learn how to reduce excessive verbalization; one may need to learn how to become more responsible, another to learn to delegate responsibility to others. In the parable, Mr. Samarsky determined that Marsha came to see him because she wanted to think through all the relevant facts before making a decision. Since Marsha's goal was consistent with Mr. Samarsky's own values, he acted in a way that led Marsha to consider several additional factors.

Thus, while both approaches advocate helping others to make behavior changes, the client-centered approach is more likely to define the same abstract goals for all clients, whereas the behavioral approach is more likely to define specific goals for specific clients.

WHO SELECTS GOALS

Who determines the purpose of counseling? Patterson criticizes the behavioral approach because he claims a behavioral counselor determines the goal for the client and hence controls the client's behavior. He puts the issue this way, "The difference, then, is one of directly conditioning behavior which is desired by the manipulator on the one hand, and on the other, providing the conditions under which the individual is enabled to make his own choices and decisions regarding his specific behavior." And yet he goes on, "We freely admit that the latter is the *choice of the counselor* as the goal of counseling, and thus represents his values and philosophy" (italics added) (1963, p. 684). Similarly, Rogers states, "In client-centered therapy, we are deeply engaged in the prediction and influencing of behavior. As therapists we institute certain attitudinal conditions, and the client has relatively little voice in the establishment of these conditions" (1961, p. 397). Thus, it is clear that in client-centered counseling it is the counselor, not the client, who determines the goal of counseling.

Does the behavioral counselor also determine the goal of counseling? Not necessarily. While not relinquishing his ethical responsibility for helping the client define worthwhile goals, the behavioral counselor is primarily interested in helping the client change whichever behavior the client desires to change. If the client wishes to overcome an overpowering fear of taking tests, then the counselor endeavors to structure a situation where this fear can become extinguished. He makes no pretense of working toward high-sounding and elaborate goals which involve a whole restructuring of the client's personality. He is only interested in helping the client make the particular change that the client himself desires. Therefore, the behavioral counselor would actually play a smaller part in determining the goals of counseling than would the client-centered counselor.

Certainly every counselor has values which determine what he will and will not do, but it is totally unrealistic to assume that the behavioral counselor imposes his values while the client-centered counselor does not. To some extent, both do—the client-centered counselor perhaps more than most people realize.

ATTAINING GOALS

What counselor activities promote the attainment of counseling purposes? Patterson has admirably summarized the evidence on the effectiveness of reinforcement in changing behavior. The basic principle is well established and has been known for years: Those responses followed by a "satisfying" state of affairs tend to be repeated, whereas those responses not followed by "satisfying" situations tend to be eliminated. As Patterson points out, the verbal behavior of a client may be influenced in accordance with this principle. The counselor can provide "satisfying" conditions by paying attention to and responding to certain words of the counselee, thus reinforcing the client for these responses. Certain kinds of content would then tend to be discussed more than others. Such a fact is important in counseling because it means the counselor can and does influence a great deal of what the counselee says by the way in which he reinforces certain statements of the client. Bandura (1961) has provided a lucid description of the process.

In the parable, certain words of both Mr. Leviten and Mr. Samarsky were probably acting as reinforcers. Mr. Leviten, by communicating his understanding of the feelings expressed by Marsha, was reinforcing the expression of these feelings. Since Marsha had expressed only positive feelings toward her job offer, Mr. Leviten could only reinforce positive feelings. This led Marsha to use the words of the counselor as further confirmation of her predisposition to accept the offer. Mr. Samarsky, on the other hand, noted early in the interview that Marsha had considered only the desirable aspects of her decision and asked whether Marsha wanted to consider all factors. Since she did, he reinforced more skeptical question-asking by saying, for example, "That seems like a good question to ask." Both counselors reinforced further talk from Marsha by saying, "Tell me more" and "Um-hmm." Both counselors selected certain aspects of Marsha's story to reinforce with real concern for Marsha's welfare, but they differed in the specific types of responses they chose to reinforce.

Thus the behavioral approach and the client-centered approach are not essentially different in their basic operations. Although the evidence is far from complete, there seems to be at least three points on which both client-centered and behavioral counselors would agree at the present time:

a. Both agree that the counselor's words or actions can change the behavior of the client. Both seem to agree that the counselor's words may act as reinforcers for the client. That is, certain counselor words will tend to increase the probability that certain types of client statements or actions will occur in the future. As Patterson puts it, "We must recognize that anything we do, in or out of counseling, has some influence on others, that it is not possible, in this sense, to avoid some control or manipulation of the behavior of others . . . everyone, including the client-centered counselor, manipulates" (1963, p. 683).

b. Both behavioral proponents and client-centered proponents would agree that it is necessary for the counselor to make some selection of the statements, parts of statements, or inferred statements to which he will respond or which he will ignore. In the case of the client-centered counselor, for example, "The counselor encourages the client to talk about himself and his relations with others, about his feelings and attitudes toward himself and others, by responding to self-statements and feelings, and by not responding to comments or statements about the weather, current events, or other impersonal material" (Patterson, 1963, p. 684).

The behavioral counselor also selects which statements he will reinforce, though not necessarily the same statements that would be reinforced by the client-centered counselor. The parable illustrates how different aspects of the interview are selected for reinforcement while others are ignored, hence influencing further responses of the client.

c. Proponents of both approaches would agree that a counselor who responds in a warm, human way, communicating verbally and non-verbally his sincere concern for a client's welfare, will probably be more effective in producing client behavior changes than a counselor who responds in a cold, detached, objective manner. The studies on this point cited by Patterson are in agreement with still other studies that point in the same direction (Binder, McConnell, & Sjoholm, 1957; Ferguson & Buss, 1960). Behavioral counselors who respond in a cold and detached manner are probably just as ineffective as client-centered counselors who respond in a cold and detached manner.

Some clients wish only that someone will listen to their problems and try to understand them. Such clients already have all the necessary facts and skills at their command, and need only a genuinely interested listener to help them put the pieces together.

But other clients are not so fortunate. Like Marsha, many are trying to reach serious decisions in their lives in the absence of relevant information or with gross misinformation. Not only do they not know the answers to some vital questions; they do not even know what questions to ask. With such clients, a counselor's understanding is not sufficient. The counselor has an obligation to act in such a way that the client will wish to seek out the information he needs in order to arrive at a wise decision. In the parable, Mr. Leviten communicated his understanding of Marsha's feelings, but Mr. Samarsky acted in a manner which encouraged Marsha to consider some additional evidence. Marsha wanted more than understanding alone. She wanted to consider all the important facts and opinions relevant to her decision.

POTENTIAL DANGERS

What are the dangers inherent in different counseling approaches? The primary bugaboo expressed by Patterson is that a behavioral approach will result in the loss of a client's freedom. Of course the degree to which any of us is "free" is a debatable point and rests upon the particular definition of freedom used. It is difficult, however, to see what can be feared if the behavioral counselor allows the client to define the problem with which he wishes help, if the counselor seeks to help him solve this problem and none other, and if the primary techniques involve verbal encouragement and resource provision. On the basis of preliminary knowledge it seems likely that verbal reinforcement may produce some desired results. Thus it may be a powerful technique. In the wrong hands it could be used to the disservice of humanity. But do we deny the surgeon use of a scalpel because in the wrong hands it could be dangerous? Any powerful technique can be used for good or evil purposes. We do not deny ourselves use of a powerful technique simply because it could be misused. We use it wisely and set up safeguards against its abuse.

The amount of "freedom" a client has in counseling can be assessed by determining the number of alternatives open to him. Accordingly, a client would be more free if he came to a behavioral counselor than to a client-centered counselor. What would the client-centered counselor do if the client asked for help in making one particular behavior change? Suppose the client said, "I don't want to be more expressive. I don't want to be more flexible and more adaptive, and I don't want to increase my self-responsibility. All I want to do is to get rid of my fear of giving speeches in class." Would the client-centered counselor change his goals and change his techniques? Would he be willing to set up an active program for extinguishing this fear consistent with well-known learning principles?

To turn the problem around, what if a client came to a behaviorally oriented counselor and stated client-centered goals? Suppose he said, "I would like to become more self-actualizing; I would like to develop greater expressiveness as a person, a greater effectiveness of adaptation and become more self-directing." In my opinion, the behavioral counselor would first attempt to understand more precisely the exact kinds of behavioral changes the client desired, and then use whatever ethical techniques were known to work. He would not hesitate to use non-directive reflection if he had evidence that such a technique did indeed produce the changes desired by the client. In short, the client would have more alternative degrees of freedom open if he went to a behaviorally oriented counselor because the behavioral counselor would be more flexible in modifying his procedures to adapt to the problem defined by the client.

Clients want to be influenced by counselors. Their freedom is not increased by the failure of counselors to influence them. Quite the contrary. Their freedom is restricted if the counselor is not willing to use whatever procedures give his clients a better opportunity of achieving their goals.

NEW DIRECTIONS

Where should we direct our search for new knowledge? A variety of avenues are open:

a. Most behavioral counselors would agree with Patterson's statement that "The techniques which the counselor uses may be considered as the operant conditioning of the client's behavior in the interview" (1963, p. 684). The unresolved question is this: Which types of counselee statements need to be reinforced in order to help the client attain which types of behavior change? Finding answers to this one question would provide a profitable use of doctoral dissertations for years to come. The parable illustrates how the presentation of reinforcing words and the withholding of reinforcing words at certain times make a large difference in the probability that a client would consider all relevant facts before making a decision. Other patterns of reinforcement might result in different outcomes.

b. We need to explore other techniques besides interview reinforcement that may help clients attain the behavior changes they desire. Robinson (1963) has called attention to the wide variety of activities that are open for the counselor to use. It is far too early to restrict the definition of counselor activities.

c. The powerful effect of providing models of desired behavior is a procedure which is just now beginning to be explored. The work of Bandura (1962) is particularly significant in suggesting characteristics of models that enable them to be imitated by students. The studies by Krumboltz and

Schroeder (in press) and Krumboltz and Thoresen (in press) have also demonstrated a procedure by which a tape-recorded model interview could be influential in encouraging students to seek relevant occupational and educational information.

d. Once the counselor becomes aware that his behavior and the behavior of other persons at home and at school may be reinforcing certain behaviors of his client, the question of scheduling these reinforcers becomes important. Various schedules of reinforcement have remarkably different consequences on "persistent" behavior. For example, it is quite likely that many students who complain of an inability to concentrate on their studies may find that such behavior is the result of an inappropriate schedule of reinforcement. If the counselor can work with parents, teachers, and curriculum experts to help restructure the schedule of reinforcements for different youngsters, tremendous progress might be made in the motivation which youngsters might display in accomplishing their educational objectives.

The unanswered questions crying for research are unlimited. Our present knowledge barely scratches the surface. An open mind and an experimental orientation may enable us to discover many new ways in which we can be of service to mankind.

SUMMARY

Behavioral and client-centered approaches to counseling are similar in that (a) both endeavor to change a client's behavior, (b) both accept some responsibility for defining the goals of counseling, (c) both acknowledge that the words of the counselor may reinforce certain response classes of the client, (d) both select certain types of client responses to reinforce, and (e) both believe that a counselor will be more effective if he responds with a genuine warmth and feeling of concern for the welfare of the client.

The two approaches differ in that (a) the behavioral counselor helps each client to define the specific behavior changes the client desires, while the client-centered counselor tends to define the same set of more abstract goals for all, (b) the behavioral counselor chooses to reinforce only those responses which seem to move the client toward the client's goal, while the client-centered counselor chooses to reinforce any expression of feeling, (c) the behavioral counselor would be flexible in using whatever ethical procedures seemed most likely to help solve the particular problem while the client-centered counselor would tend to use the same basic procedures for every problem.

Since most of the unresolved questions are subject to empirical test, we may wish to reinforce the research efforts of others as well as to heed the advice: "Go and do thou likewise."

REFERENCES

Bandura, Albert. Psychotherapy as a learning process. *Psychol. Bull.*, 1961, *58*, 143-159.

Bandura, Albert. Social learning through imitation. In Marshall Jones (Ed.), *Nebraska symposium on motivation, 1962.* Lincoln: Univ. Nebraska Press, 1962.

Binder, A., McConnell, D., & Sjoholm, Nancy A. Verbal conditioning as a function
    of experimenter characteristics. *J. abnorm. soc. Psychol.*, 1957, 55, 309-314.
Ferguson, D. D., & Buss, A. H. Operant conditioning of hostile verbs in relation
    to experimenter and subject characteristics. *J. consult. Psychol.*, 1960, 24, 324-327.
Krumboltz, John D., & Schroeder, Wade W. Promoting career planning through
    reinforcement and models. *Personnel guid. J.*, in press.
Krumboltz, John D. & Thoresen, Carl E. The effect of behavioral counseling in
    group and individual settings on information-seeking behavior. *J. counsel.
    Psychol.*, in press.
Michael, Jack, & Meyerson, Lee. A behavioral approach to counseling and guidance.
    Harvard educ. Rev., 1962, 32, 382-402.
Patterson, C. H. Control, conditioning, and counseling. *Personnel guid. J.*, 1963,
    41, 680-686.
Robinson, Frances P. A cubist approach to the art of counseling. *Personnel guid. J.*,
    1963, 41, 670-676.
Rogers, Carl R. *On becoming a person.* Boston: Houghton Mifflin, 1961.

SENSITIVITY TRAINING, ENCOUNTER GROUPS, LABORATORY LEARNING—IMPLICATIONS FOR COUNSELORS

Joseph C. Bentley
University of Utah

Mother, to five-year-old son as he prepares to leave for his first day in
school: "You'll love kindergarten, Darling. It's just like your group therapy!"
While this cartoon which appeared recently in a national magazine represents
an exaggeration of sorts, nevertheless it seems that everyone these days has
attended a group session, or is attending one, or will be attending one within
two weeks or so. There is no question that we are in the middle of a cultural
and social revolution. The primary purpose of this essay is not to trace the
history and development of this movement, not to attempt an analysis of the
values or the dangers associated with group learning or, as I prefer to call it,
laboratory learning, except where applicable. My purpose here is to consider
the usefulness of T-groups, sensitivity groups, laboratory learning groups,
encounter groups (there are dozens of names used freely) as additional tools
which, when understood and used wisely, can help counselors reach their
objectives in helping others.

ON THE NATURE OF OUR SOCIETY

While we live in the most affluent and productive society the world has
ever known, we have created within this society forces which have produced
what Archibald McLeish (1969) has called the "diminished man" or what
has been described by Louis Mumford (1964) as the "automatic man." These
forces are many, complex, and often mentioned: industrialization, mechaniza-

An original article for this book.

tion and its attendant depersonalization; rapid social and cultural change; increasing materialism; loss of old values and absence of new ones; widespread mobility; increasing tension and anxiety, brought about by many causes such as the ever-present bomb, the unpopular wars, and the Women's Liberation movement; uncertainty of the future, and so on. There is no question in my mind that these and other societal forces, out of control in the sense that very little can be done about them, have resulted in a widespread loneliness, alienation, and despair.

The "group movement" with its emphasis upon genuineness, honesty, intimacy, and caring has touched the loneliness and despair of many and has provided a way out of a modern and genuine human dilemma: "No one cares for me"; "No one appreciates me"; "I have no real friends"; "I don't think I can talk to my wife, and she doesn't listen anyway." Regardless of how it is phrased, the message remains the same: "I am lonely and afraid. I don't have much self-confidence. When I look for someone to help me, no one cares."

As has been the case with most social revolutions that have touched human problems at the center (and thereby have become immensely popular), this movement has become corrupted by con artists, quacks, and seekers of the fast buck. Even more frightening, perhaps, has been the infiltration by those well-meaning persons (including some counselors), poorly prepared both intellectually and emotionally, who seek to solve their own personal problems through "turning-on" others. As a result, suddenly people, any people, can attend nude groups or experience the sensation of touching all parts of another person's body in order to help him to learn to "trust," or learn to be hostile, or participate in any number of unusual "learning" experiences. While there may be learning derived from these and similar activities, the applicability of such extreme activities to the work of most counselors seems dubious. Yet this does not mean that no laboratory learning experiences are useful and appropriate. My strong conviction is that as *a philosophy of learning* and as a *set of appropriate procedures,* laboratory learning is useful and, when used well, will result in significant personal growth and change.

ON THE NATURE OF OUR EDUCATIONAL SYSTEM

As a nation we have committed ourselves to education for all. We have not yet reached that goal, although we have made more progress than any other nation in history. Yet what we have accomplished is so inadequate compared to what we could do. Today we have the knowledge to develop an educational system that will surpass even our most enthusiastic dreams. Yet we seem unable to use this knowledge effectively. Consider what some perceptive observers have said about education in our time:

> . . . students who endure it (the old education) come out as passive, acquiescent, dogmatic, intolerant, authoritarian, inflexible, conservative personalities who desperately need to resist change in an effort to keep their illusions of certainty intact. (Postman and Weingartner, 1969, p. 217)

> Most schools, in spite of their good intentions, do untold harm to most children. This is a sad and difficult thing to have to say. But I have seen and known a lot of children *before* they went to school, and a lot of children

after they were in school. There is no doubt in my mind that before he gets to school, virtually every child is an eager, curious, confident, competent learner. It is *in* school that he gets turned off. (Holt, 1969)

Teachers tend to assume more and more responsibility for deciding what is to be learned, how the child shall be motivated, and the way he shall learn. Less attention is given to what children think and feel and believe. . . . (ASCD, 1962)

I could go on and on. Consider the titles of recent books about education: *How Children Fail, Compulsory Mis-Education, The Classroom Disaster, Death at an Early Age, The University Game, Where Colleges Fail, The Necessary Revolution in Education, Reforming American Education*. It should be clear by now that I have purposefully selected book titles critical of our educational system. Yet most competent observers would agree, I believe, that there is much to be done.

One of the institutional settings where counselors have found a home is in education. Yet we have contributed little to revising the system that is being maintained. Our focus traditionally has been toward helping individuals change their behavior rather than providing assistance in changing total systems. Perhaps this is where our focus ought to have been. One wonders, however, whether we have been as successful as we could have been. To attempt to change behavior without actively changing the system that produced that behavior may not be of much value.

Those counselors who work outside of institutional settings have had their time consumed by the daily crises of keeping sick people from withdrawing completely. They have exerted little influence toward improving the larger problem: that of helping people face and overcome the daily destruction of living in a society that is no longer interested in them as individuals.

TWO LEARNING SYSTEMS COMPARED

There are other ways of living and learning. There are other ways of developing and maintaining institutions to carry the work of society that do not by their nature destroy the humanness of man. It is possible to conceive of an educational system that meets the needs of its members rather than suppressing them. South (1969) has compared the traditional system of learning with what he calls a process model:

TRADITIONAL MODEL	PROCESS MODEL
1. Educator knows proper definition or function of manager, student, etc., and of a person.	1. Definition of manager, student, person, etc., is something to be worked on by both educator and learner.
2. Educator is authority and controls power; learning is enhanced when learners defer to authority.	2. Power is shared; learning is enhanced when all have access to equal power and influence.
3. Members are placed in a structure in which role is precisely de-	3. Members are placed in a network of relationships in which role be-

(Continued)

TRADITIONAL MODEL	PROCESS MODEL
fined, i.e., teachers are teachers and learners are students.	comes a function of interaction and involvement. Teachers can be learners, and learners teachers.
4. Educator formulates problems, identifies relevant information and relevant resources.	4. Learners formulate problems, identify relevant information and resources. Educator can aid but does not control.
5. Educator provides technique for problem-solving and standards for solutions.	5. Learner develops technique for problem-solving, and standards for solutions.
6. Learners work with what is external and abstract to them.	6. Learners work with what is external and internal, and distinctions between the two tend to disappear; what is immediate is the focus for learning.
7. Educator continuously defines what learner needs to learn next, educator tries to be aware of learner's learning process.	7. Learner defines his own learning needs, and develops ways to see his own learning process.
8. Individual seeks to know himself through measuring himself against an ideal type (i.e., man, woman, manager, teacher, etc.)	8. Individual seeks to know himself through the choices he makes, the relationships he enters into, and knowledge he seeks.
9. Major learning problems are efficiency (are standardized bits of information accumulated rapidly and in proper quantity), and motivation (keeping learners devoted to task).	9. Major learning problems are communication (increasing understanding), involvement (finding a satisfactory level of participation), and risk taking (being self-directed).

The Process Model as outlined by South need not be a narrow one, restricted only to schools. It can serve to guide the major learning activities associated with creative and abundant living. The essential skills needed for the Process Model are—

> Understanding and accepting personal power
> Learning to become involved
> Effective interpersonal interaction
> Formulating problems
> Identifying relevant information and resources
> Solving problems
> Immediate, here-and-now focus for learning
> Learner defining his own needs
> Increasing self-knowledge
> Finding satisfying levels of participation
> Taking appropriate risks

Two general conclusions seem warranted: one, that it is specifically in helping students acquire such learning and living skills as these that our educational systems have failed; and two, there is no reason to believe that what counselors typically do with clients has much relationship with this kind of learning. Does the counselor himself have such skills? If not, how is he going to acquire them? Can he help others to acquire them? How is he going to do it?

ON THE NATURE OF LABORATORY LEARNING

As so often happens with controversial issues, there is a great deal of misunderstanding over encounter groups, sensitivity training, and laboratory learning. There are those who see the group movement as the salvation of all the nations; there are those who see it as the Devil's own curse. Obviously, neither of these extremes can be true. Sensitivity training, encounter groups, and so forth, are tools for learning, nothing more. As is the case with any tool, the effectiveness depends upon the skill of those who are handling it. As is the case with any set of tools, there are appropriate situations when they should be used, and there are inappropriate situations when they should not be used.

Laboratory learning is experience-based. The personal, subjective experience of the learner becomes his reality for understanding himself and the world. (In this sense, the learning approximates living.) In order to avoid the dangers of solipsism, conditions are created in laboratory learning which permit him, even encourage him, to compare his perceptions of himself and of the world with those of others, thus providing him with a test of his own reality. In addition, he can come to understand better his own learning style, management style, prejudices, and attitudes by comparing his experience with those of others. Coercion and manipulation are avoided. An attempt is made to permit maximum freedom in order to continue to behave in old ways or to consider and plan for new ways. If a person decides that he would like to change his behavior in certain ways (ways which have been identified by others in the group in addition to ways which have been selected by himself), he has opportunities to practice new behavior in a relatively safe setting. Above all, two major themes exist: that the individual has value, that his differences are important and merit acceptance and respect, and that an individual must accept responsibility for his own behavior. If, for example, he learns that he deals with others in an overly hostile, aggressive manner, and, after having learned this, he decides to continue, then he must accept the consequences of such psychonoxious behavior.

Because the learning is experienced-based, people find it very difficult to communicate to others what they have learned. Two examples of laboratory learning may help at this point.

Thomas (1969) described an experience he had as a consultant to a counseling center staff. The purpose of his visit was to deal with interpersonal problems in the hope of improving staff effectiveness. After the day had passed, with relatively little progress, Thomas expressed his own feelings, "What does one do at times like these? I feel as though I have nothing to offer." An attractive young woman, obviously angry, responded:

"Well, if *you* don't know, then who does? I had heard a lot about you, and I'm really disappointed. I came here expecting you to turn us on, and you haven't done a damn thing! Where's your act?"

"This *is* my act," Thomas replied. "I have no suggestions to make, I can only be what I am." The young lady began to weep and, looking at Thomas and then to her supervisor with whom she had had great difficulty relating, explained with intense emotion: "Now I really understand. You are people, too! Here I've had you up on a high pedestal, fearing you, both admiring and hating you, but I couldn't get close to you. I also expected you to have the answers for me." She looked around at the others in the room and exclaimed, "My God, we're all just human beings and that's great!"

An example from my own experience may provide another perspective. I was working with a group of junior high school teachers whose school was being transformed into a community school the following year. The purpose of the eight-week workshop (meeting once a week) was to help the teachers gain more effective human relations skills. The theme for one session was giving and receiving help. I divided the group of thirty into three teams: those with a problem (A), the helpers (B), and the observers (C). Groups A and B were given forty minutes to accomplish the following: Group A was to select and define a problem, Group B was to develop a strategy for helping, Group C observed both groups. After the forty minutes the first two groups came together—the group with a problem to receive help from the helping group. The observers continued their observation.

Within minutes the groups were sharply divided, angry, and shouting at each other. What had happened? The spokesman for Group A began to explain the problems. Before he had explained the first part of a rather complicated problem, the spokesman for the helping group said, "I don't think you've defined the problem very well. In fact, it isn't even a good problem."

In the planning period, Group A had decided to explain clearly the problem, then leave Group B to come up with solutions. At the same time, Group B had decided to emphasize that it could not solve the problem for Group A, only listen, reflect, and facilitate.

Chaos resulted. The teams began first by arguing with each other. Before long, they were arguing among themselves. Group B had decided that only one member of the team would speak. This lasted less than two minutes. Suggestions, comments, and criticism soon came from all sides.

I stopped the exercise after twenty minutes or so and asked the observers to report. We then began a gradual and systematic conceptual analysis of the behaviors of the groups in the context of giving and receiving help. This lasted over an hour. I then had each member write down the one most important thing he learned from the experience. Here are some random observations:

When people state problems, they must be sure to communicate completely how much and what kind of help they need and what action they expect of those who are to help.

Neither group really listened. Neither group was willing to really give.

A helper must be truly sincere with a positive attitude if he is going to give the other person any help.

It is essential to communicate the feeling that you are earnestly trying to help.

Set an atmosphere that welcomes solutions and ideas.

To this day, those people talk about that experience. I am convinced that they gained much more understanding of giving and receiving help than they would had I lectured to them.

In my opinion, both of these incidents, as well as the better known T-group or encounter group, are examples of laboratory learning. They share two sets of conditions which are basic to the concept of laboratory learning: certain specific values and goals; and the development of effective interpersonal skills.

Values and Goals of Laboratory Learning

The central values which underlie laboratory learning have been outlined by Schein and Bennis (1965). The first value they call *the spirit of inquiry*. In this phrase they include two elements: "The hypothetical spirit, the feeling for tentativeness and caution, and the respect for probable error" (p. 31). The second major element of the spirit of inquiry is an experimentation, a willingness to expose ideas and beliefs to scrutiny and analysis, a willingness to try new ways of listening, of responding, of behavior, and then analyzing the consequences of the experimentation.

A second major value grows out of this willingness to risk, to experiment: *expanded consciousness and choice*. In order to choose wisely one must have at his command as much information as he can acquire. By experimenting with his own behavior in a psychologically safe environment, one can come to know more about himself, thus providing him with more freedom to choose. He is able to test, to determine, and to decide.

A third major value is *authenticity in interpersonal relationships*. When a person is able to be himself *with himself*, that is, to feel no need, conscious or unconscious, to distort or deny his own experiences or perceptions, then he comes to be more nearly authentic, more nearly congruent, more nearly able to make useful choices, more accepting of himself.

When a person is able to be himself with *others*, keeping in mind the complexities of motive and needs in interpersonal relationships and focusing upon being helpful rather than destructive with the other,[1] then he will not expend his creative energies trying to impress, to convince, to influence: in short, trying to be something that he is not. Those energies can be better used elsewhere. The individual is more free, more capable of choosing.

---

[1]The line between helpful relationships and destructive relationships is a difficult one to find. If I truly report to you your impact upon me, and if in that reporting I am not meeting some neurotic need of my own to control, to dominate or to hurt, then, even if my observations are hurtful, they may also be helpful. You now know something you did not know. Whether my observation is "true" is, in this case, irrelevant. It is true for me. You now have increased opportunities to consider yourself as I see you. You can also check out my perception with others. And, if I do not place a condition of rejection if you do not change upon my observation, you are free to change or not to change and not lose my respect. However, you must be willing to live with the consequences if you do not change: i.e., I may not choose to be around you very much since I do not enjoy being with you when you act in that certain way.

This ideal relationship—open, helpful, sharing with no danger of diminished respect and value—is extremely difficult to achieve fully. Perhaps we can only approximate it and, by understanding how we fail, continue to move toward the ideal.

Argyris (1962) has defined authentic relationships as those in which an individual enhances his sense of self-awareness and self-worth and his sense of other-awareness and other-worth in such a way that others can do the same. In this sense, then, authenticity is entirely interpersonal. As Argyris states, "An individual cannot be authentic independent of the relationship he has with others. His feelings of authenticity will depend as much upon the capacity of others to create authentic relationships as well as upon his own" (p. 21).

A fourth central value in laboratory learning is *collaboration*. The traditional power hierarchy found so frequently in education is, insofar as possible, done away with. Individuals are encouraged to challenge, to ask questions, to disagree, but also encouraged to provide alternate solutions to the element being challenged. An attempt is made to create psychological conditions which foster trust, openness, and sharing. Within this climate, a person can more effectively find his own preferred style of participation and involvement and, more importantly perhaps, feel that he can contribute in his own way and be valued for it.

Finally, Schein and Bennis (1965) list as their last central value, *conflict resolution through rational means*. Conflict, which seems to be inevitable in human affairs, is traditionally dealt with by denial, suppression, or compromise. There is a better, more productive way. Conflict can lead to more effective decisions and more useful solutions to problems if it is seen as a positive sign that people are different and feel free to express those differences. The *way* conflict is dealt with becomes the critical factor. If it can first be recognized and confronted, then managed and resolved by seeking to understand its causes and consequences by consulting those who are involved, encouraging them to be open and frank without fear or penalty, then conflict can result in a greater sense of fairness, in an increased commitment to the individual or the organization.

The goals of laboratory learning have typically been identified as the following: (1) self-insight; (2) understanding the conditions which inhibit or facilitate group functioning; (3) understanding interpersonal operations in groups; and (4) developing skills for diagnosing individual, group, and organizational behavior (Schein and Bennis, 1965).

An outline of these goals follows:

SELF

1. Our feelings and motivations
2. Consequences of behavior in others.
3. Hearing others, accepting feedback, and communicating with other persons.
4. Skills of appropriate interactions with other persons

1. Finding our place in a group
   a. Reduction of anxieties
   b. Finding need satisfactions
   c. Finding place in influence structure
   d. Meeting (or not meeting) expectation of others

1. Finding our place in the organization
2. Diagnosing social organizational problems
3. Inventing, constructing and adapting group norms, standards, laws.
4. Diagnosing problems between and among units in the organization.

(Continued)

5. Skills for continuous learning.

2. Gaining understanding of group behavior.
3. Giving diagnostic skills.
4. Gaining skills of appropriate member action on
   a. Task problems
   b. Maintenance problems

5. Working as a member in the organization:
   a. Finding and filling appropriate roles.
   b. Applying problem-solving methods.
   c. Maintaining oneself as a constructive member of the organization

(Adapted from Schein and Bennis, 1965, p. 36.)

Increased Interpersonal Competence

The psychological meaning of our lives comes from the quality of our relationships with others. We cannot be fully human without significant human relationships. Many of the symptoms of modern neurosis—alienation, valueless-ness, loneliness, anguish—grow out of inappropriate or inadequate relation-ships with others. It may be said that the key to successful living in our modern era lies in the area of effective and appropriate human encounters and relationships: those relationships which enhance our sense of individuality and personal worth and do the same for the other person.

Earlier I listed those skills needed for a Process Model of learning and growing. They were—

> Understanding and accepting personal power
> Learning to become involved
> Effective interpersonal interaction
> Formulating problems
> Identifying relevant information and resources
> Solving problems
> Immediate, here-and-now focus for learning
> Learner defining his own needs
> Increasing self-knowledge
> Finding satisfying levels of participation
> Taking appropriate risks

A more specific, yet highly related, statement defining interpersonal com-petence is provided by Argyris (1962):

a. Giving and receiving non-evaluative, descriptive feedback.
b. Owning and helping others to own to their values, attitudes, ideas, and feelings.
c. Openness to new values, attitudes and feelings as well as helping others to develop their degree of openness.
d. Experimenting (and helping others to do the same) with new values, attitudes, ideas, and feelings.
e. Taking risks with new values, attitudes, ideas, and feelings.

Given the values of inquiry, expanded consciousness and choice, authen-ticity in interpersonal relationships, collaboration, conflict resolution through rational means, and given the desired interpersonal competencies of giving and receiving nonevaluative, descriptive feedback, owning values, attitudes, ideas and feelings, openness to new values, experimentation and risk-taking, where does one turn for help in designing an educational program, or counseling strategy, which will result in such learning? In my opinion, our traditional educational and counseling programs are sadly deficient in designing learning activities which will prepare us to live abundantly in the twentieth century. In my opinion, educators and counselors who can develop developmental learning programs based upon laboratory methods will provide the best possible solution to the problems I have raised in the paper. Such learning programs may contain regular T-groups with the here-and-now emphasis, modified T-groups, structured learning exercises, simulations, problem-solving practice, role-playing, and so forth. They would provide experience and practice in the general and specific skills discussed so far in this paper.

ON EVALUATION AND RESEARCH
IN LABORATORY LEARNING

There is a need for research and evaluation in laboratory learning. However, this statement could be applied indiscriminately to any area in the social and behavioral sciences. Such a plea for research should not blind us to the fact that a great deal of research has been done. Schein and Bennis (1965) report a selected bibliography of over 180 studies. Campbell and Dunnette, in a review restricted to an analysis of the effectiveness of T-group experiences in the training of managers, report 90 studies related to their topic.

As in most areas of applied psychology, studies can be found which both support and do not support conclusions about the effectiveness of laboratory learning. In general, however, there seems to be significant agreement on the following:

1. People who attend sensitivity training programs are more likely to improve their managerial skills than those who do not (as reported by their peers, superiors, and subordinates).
2. Everyone does not benefit equally. Roughly two-thirds of the participants are seen as increasing their skills after attendance at laboratories. This figure represents an average across a number of studies.
3. Many individuals report extremely significant changes and impact on their lives as workers, family members, and citizens. This kind of anecdotal report should be viewed cautiously in terms of direct application to job settings, but it is consistent enough that it is clear that T-group experiences can have a powerful and positive impact on individuals.
4. The incidence of serious stress and mental disturbance during training is difficult to measure, but it is estimated to be less than one per cent of participants and in almost all cases occurs in persons with a history of prior disturbances. (NTL News, 1968)

Without entering into the argument over the validity of anecdotal and subjective evidence versus objective, controlled research, I should like only to mention the fact that most people who participate in laboratory learning are enthusiastic and are convinced that they have been helped. Here is an excerpt from the diary of a student of mine who participated in a thirty-five-hour sensitivity group designed to increase self-awareness and to provide more knowledge about the dynamics of groups:

It has been a long, tired, and somewhat sad day, this day following the final meeting. The feelings are many—and to say that some moments of the day did not have bits and pieces of deep feeling would be to skirt the fact. On my way to school there were very strange feelings circulating in my mind. One passed that although the members of the group may never be seen again, they will always be with me in memory for although they are going, they have left tools behind with me to better my relationships in the future. Each tool seems to picture their warmth.

I have carried a piece of note paper with me all day to try to make clear all the events that were significant to me from the group meetings. I think last night's meeting was the culmination of all those thoughts that were expressed. On that paper I also noted things that I had done that day that were the direct or indirect result of the group. The results were overwhelmingly successful, in fact, frightening to know that just a small bit of that which was learned is so very powerful and unbelievably comfortable to use.

I have come away from the meetings not with words, but tools. I made a mental note today to purchase a small book and jot down in it key words or phrases which trigger the mind to bring back the interaction of the wonderful people in that group.

My one regret in this last meeting was that I did not interact more—it was as if to say I had learned but wasn't going to apply it. That's not true. This day I have applied some of the learning and my desire to look at group meetings as an opportunity and not a fearful thing as I have done in the past, is all the more intense now than at any time in my life. I have realized for the first time that I am far too quiet. I hid my life, my feelings too long now. Just today, in the office, I shared experiences that I would have never shared before without fear. Just at noon, I stopped to talk to a person that I had sort of had to drag myself to talk to. The relationship was so successful that I received more in return than I really ever gave. It is still confusing and makes tears come into my eyes when I think of these things. I felt like leveling with people for the first time. I had nothing really to hide now. I felt strength and power.

I must keep some reminder above my desk as a reminder—already I have copied the poem and stuck it on file right in front of me on the desk. Each reminder will bring back memories to better the relationships around me.

"NOW" is a very important word to me. It means that feelings fleet away far faster than you think. What you feel now is important and it must be expressed, now.

"A situation not tried cannot be judged." That was very important to me. It simply means that to hide, fear, or otherwise suppress your feelings, impulses, ideas, is to invite destruction or decay. Each thing must be tried, then judged. Prejudging is withdrawal.

Honesty in what you say seems to be the real key to the comfortable feeling of expressing feelings. You *know* what you say is true. It is as if to say, I like you and this is why I'm telling you this; or I don't like what you're doing and it makes me feel uncomfortable. It allows me to be free from anxiety which only builds if truth is not presented honestly.

It's what we do for ourselves that counts. We can't expect to receive for very long without all resources running out very rapidly. The "magic dust" is in ourselves and cannot be applied without first a giving from within. No one can really give us anything unless we give part of ourselves.

We cannot stand alone like a pillar. This is something which is hard for me but is part of the puzzle which has been a barrier to my relationships.

Dependency upon others is not to be feared. It is warmth of the two-way expression that people must share.

Physical contact has been very hard for me. (Seems like I have all the symptoms.) But, today, I made physical contact with our former secretary—a solid but friendly grab of the arm. It was a feeling that was far better than I expected it to be. It may have been the best communication I have expressed to her.

I have sincere thanks to a fellow co-worker—something I have wanted to do but never really have done—at least in this way. Appreciation not expressed is to ignore and alienate friendship.

I am listing here some of the things I am jotting in my book which will remind me to clarify my life:

(1) Be more initiative in responses.
(2) Don't be afraid to say what's on your mind—for better or for worse. The risk is unavoidable if you are to succeed.
(3) Be honest with other people—really say what you mean.
(4) To participate in a group is an honor and most important an opportunity and not a fearful thing to resist.
(5) Be in the "now"—Don't wait for your responses to "develop."
(6) Learn to identify certain specific feelings with certain individuals. This will help me elicit response.
(7) I must learn to take compliments. I must learn to listen for the meanings that people direct toward me. I must learn to recognize the gift when it comes—even though it may react as a hurt within me at the time.
(8) I must be able to see the light from the negative. It always follows. If it is ignored, I have learned nothing. If I don't hear it right I am confused and again learn nothing. It is the firing back and forth that clarifies meaning . . . then gives body to what is said.
(9) Don't be embarrassed, worried, or hung up on trying something really different and new. "The hills are green this morning and there is new life in everything" describes my feeling when the cloud clears away.

There have been moments in this day when I can't stand to be without people. It hurt when I was alone. I'm very tired tonight and I look forward to a new adventure tomorrow.

I have never received anything like this from students who have been involved in conventional, traditional learning activities. Have you?

APPLICATION TO COUNSELING AND GUIDANCE

Counseling has come to be seen as a semitherapeutic process to help those who have problems. Thus, the population from which clients would come has been made up of people in difficulty; not as much difficulty as those who should be treated by a clinical or school psychologist, but those who were having "personal" problems. Recently, however, it has become evident that all of us have personal problems and that all of us could benefit from help.

More pertinent to the subject of this essay, rather than help people who are in trouble, perhaps we as counselors should be working with larger groups in order to help them develop their own personal learning and problem-solving skills. Then, when they are faced with a critical personal situation, they themselves will have the resources with which to deal with the problem, or they will understand and have confidence in a process orientation to learning and problem solving which will permit them to search for appropriate resources outside of themselves. In short, they will have "learned how to learn" in the sense that they will be able to initiate positive, constructive action toward realizing their potential. Thus, the emphasis should be upon development and growth rather than upon remedial procedures or treatment. Wrenn (1962) emphasized this point when he stated the following:

> . . . Primary emphasis in counseling should be placed upon the developmental needs and decision points in the lives of the total range of students rather than upon the remedial needs and the crisis points in the lives of a few students, with the major goal of counseling being that of increased self-responsibility and an increased motivity in decision-making upon the part of the student. (p. 109)

The implications for this point of view for counseling programs in schools and elsewhere are important. First, it suggests small groups as the setting for much of the learning. There are not enough counselors nor enough time to help "normal people" develop their potential.

Second, it implies that the learning emphasis should be upon self-awareness and interpersonal competence.

Third, it is clear to me that the counselor will have to learn new attitudes, new roles, and new skills. He cannot assume that because he has taken courses in counseling, he can then do all things.

Fourth, if he is to be successful, the counselor will not be able to retain the mantle of "expert." Gibbs' (1968) concept of the "role-free" counselor, while somewhat confusing in terms of role-theory (How can anyone be role-free? To be "role-free" is to play a role of having no role to play), suggests the idea that the counselor can be most helpful by being the person he is and nothing more.

Fifth, the counselor must be able to provide a variety of appropriate learning activities for the client group. Appropriate as used here means learning experiences which show promise of developing specific interpersonal skills needed to function outside of the learning group. In addition, it implies that the activities will need to be modified depending upon the age and learning needs of the group.

For example, in my experience, an unstructured T-group with its attendant ambiguity and anxiety is not too helpful for youngsters from fourteen to eighteen years of age. Typically, there are too many critical identity issues with which this group is struggling. A more structured learning activity is called for, but one which will involve the students in the planning and implementing of their own learning.

The fifth point requires that the counselor be flexible and creative enough to create effective learning conditions for the client group. Old ways may not be sufficient. He will need to become a learner himself—an attitude that may be difficult for some—and adopt a process orientation to counseling itself.

CAUTIONS AND RESERVATIONS

Earlier in this chapter, I discussed the infiltration into the human potential movement by a number of quacks and con artists. In addition, there are those who are intrigued by the promise of easy money. I do not plan to examine in great detail this problem. It seems that in the United States you can find someone who will do anything at any time, and often do it in the name of health, well-being, or happiness, either for themselves or others. People who pay money for this kind of "help" without checking carefully into the qualifications of the helper deserve what they get.

My more immediate concern has to do with counselors in schools, clinics, and other institutional settings. During the past four or five years, I have witnessed a development that has caused me worry. On all sides there are springing up "experts" who can direct encounter groups, sensitivity groups, and other types of laboratory learning experiences. For example, I have been both amazed and discouraged at the workshops that have attached themselves to national conventions of professional organizations. I ask myself, where did they get special training and preparation to do this? It has been my experience that most training programs for counselors are barely acceptable in preparing a person to counsel on a one-to-one basis. Most provide one or two courses in group guidance, or group counseling. Many do not provide a supervised practicum or internship especially in the area of groups. This is particularly true at the master's level. The area of group counseling and laboratory learning is, in my opinion, a specialized skill area requiring its own preparation and supervision. Being a counselor is not enough. In my own case, several years after the Ph.D. degree in counseling psychology from a respectable university (University of Minnesota), I entered into a year-long internship with the NTL Institute for Applied Behavioral Science, which included a full summer at Bethel, Maine, followed by supervised learning experiences during the remainder of the year. And I am very aware that I am still learning.

Another concern I have is related to my belief that this kind of learning is not appropriate for everyone. There needs to be research into the interaction between the outcomes of such learning and the kind of people that participate in it.

And this point leads us to another one, already mentioned. We do need research. Yet the fact that we need it should not blind us to the fact that we know a great deal already. Perhaps we are faced with the problem of applying what we know. For example, if we wish to change a person's behavior, we cannot only help him to see himself differently, to develop new skills, and so forth. We must also pay attention to the significant environments which provide him with information and support for specific behavior. Unless we become specialists in changing the environment *as well* as helping the person change, we will have little success.

We have known this for years. Yet we continue, with some notable exceptions, in our same person-centered process of counseling.

SUMMARY

What I have tried to say in this essay can be summarized in several statements:

1. Educators and counselors have been captives of a traditional learning model which has emphasized such elements as role position, authority, structure, and "expert"-centered intervention, leading to irrelevance of learning experience.

2. This traditional model is giving way to a process model emphasizing shared definitions of roles and positions, shared power, flexibility, problem identification by both teachers and learners, individual initiative in learning, self-knowledge, focus upon such learning problems as communication in order to increase understanding, involvement, and risk-taking.
3. Most counselors have little experience or skill in a process-centered model for learning.
4. Laboratory learning, including T-groups, encounter groups, role-playing, skill development sessions, structured simulations, provides the most hopeful direction for process-centered learning.
5. Laboratory learning is based upon the values of inquiry, expanded consciousness and choice, authenticity in interpersonal relationships, collaboration, and constructive use of conflict.
6. Laboratory learning emphasizes the development of interpersonal competence including such skills as giving and receiving nonevaluative, descriptive feedback; owning and helping others to own their own feelings, attitudes, and ideas; openness to new values, attitudes and feelings, experimenting, and taking risks.
7. Research has demonstrated that laboratory learning is a powerful method for behavior change. Research is needed (it always is) in order to learn more about appropriate interventions and populations.
8. Counselors need specifc preparation, including supervision, in the practice of laboratory learning skills. Having a master's degree in counseling (even a doctorate from most places) is not enough.
9. In order to be truly helpful, counselors will need to modify many of their attitudes and practices. For example, seeing students one-at-a-time in an office in order to interpret test results to them probably is not an effective way to influence behavior.

BIBLIOGRAPHY

American Association for Supervision and Curriculum Development. *Perceiving, Behaving, Becoming: A New Focus for Education.* Washington, D. C.: NEA, 1962.
Argyris, C. *Interpersonal Competence and Organizational Effectiveness.* Homewood, Ill.: Irwin-Dorsey, 1962.
Gibbs, Jack. "The Counselor as a Role-Free Person." In *Counseling Theories and Counselor Education,* edited by C. Parker. Boston: Houghton-Mifflin, 1968.
Holt, J. *How Children Fail.* New York: Pitman Publishing Corp., 1964.
McLeish, A. "Revolt of the Divided Man." *Saturday Review,* June 7, 1969.
Mumford, L. "The Automation of Knowledge." *Vital Speech of the Day* 30 (1964): 441-446.
NTL Institute for Applied Behavior Science, *NTL Institute News and Reports* (1968): 2.
Postman, N., and Weingartner, C. *Teaching as a Subversive Activity.* New York: The Delacorte Press, 1969.
Schein, E., and Bennis, W. *Personal and Organizational Change Through Group Methods.* New York: John Wiley & Sons, Inc., 1965.
South, O. *Observation Guide: On Hearing, Seeing, Hearing and Feeling.* Mimeographed. Washington: NTL Institute for Applied Behavioral Science, 1969.
Thomas, H. "Encounter—The Game of No Game." In *Encounter,* edited by A. Burton. San Francisco: Jossey-Bass, 1967.
Wrenn, C. *The Counselor in a Changing World.* Washington, D. C.: APGA, 1962.

CHAPTER 1: QUESTIONS FOR DISCUSSION

1. What are the major difficulties generated by what Blocher terms "elusive issues" in counseling? What ethical issues arise from each of them?
2. What are some of the advantages and disadvantages of "trying to remain as philosophically neutral" as possible in counseling? To you, do the advantages outweigh the disadvantages, or vice versa? Why?
3. Consider the five philosophical issues raised by Arbuckle. Might you add a sixth category which you feel is of equal importance? Which of Arbuckle's five issues interests you most? What pertinent comments have you read about that issue in the literature?
4. What recent developments in our schools and in the larger society have hindered effective use of creative potential? What recent developments have furthered it? Which of Gruen's points seems most meaningful on college campuses today?
5. What does each of the "logical errors" referred to by Nordberg mean? What example for each can you give either from counseling or education?
6. What in Strickland's presentation seems to contradict present views about counseling? What to you seems to be the strength of his presentation?
7. What arguments by Koplitz seem strongest to you? What questions do you have concerning any of his basic assumptions?
8. Haberman presents a number of recommendations for working with the "educationally disadvantaged." What are the largest obstacles which interfere with counselor effectiveness in dealing with the sorts of youngsters he describes?
9. Krumboltz states that in some ways the behavioral counselor is more flexible than the client-centered counselor. Do you agree? What problems seem paramount in the two approaches?
10. Comparing Bentley's views on sensitivity training and encounter groups with those of Koplitz, what questions would you like to ask each man? Would you like that type of training to be part of your own preparation? Why or why not?

Chapter

2

Changing Views

This chapter presents some significant changes and trends in the field of guidance and counseling, and calls to question some long-held beliefs about the goals, operations, and responsibilities of the counselor. As Lord Tennyson once put it, "Our little systems have their day; they have their day, and cease to be. . . ." While the poet was not speaking about counseling, the message is clear. "The old order changeth, and giveth place the new" — but only reluctantly. The weight of tradition is heavy in any field of endeavor, and many assumptions often go unexamined all too long. Bold thinking, insightful syntheses, and serious philosophical critiques are at a premium. The articles in this chapter present interesting ways of viewing the important trends and problems in the field.

The concept of self and the ultimate objectives of counseling, guidance, and therapy are the central focus of these essays. There emerges from the aggregate of these ideas a far different picture of man from that which our textbooks presented at earlier stages in the development of the fields.

Of significance to the counselor is the ever-present self-question, "What ways of viewing my client and my position as counselor will raise the probabilities of my being able to help him?" Subsidiary, yet vital, considerations are "What alternative ways of viewing society and social problems will aid me in understanding my clients and their meaning-structures?" "What unanswered questions from older theories now demand intensive attention?" "What trends are visible in my field, as research and theory add to our store of knowledge?"

The counselor must be alert constantly to "related" articles, i.e., articles about therapy, when the reader deals almost exclusively with the so-called "normal range" of students in school; he must decide what he can sift and winnow from these before they can be applied in his daily work. He must not dismiss them because they are "not in my field." This has been a fundamental weakness, fully as much as applying "borrowed" concepts blindly. This form of "professional myopia" must be avoided in all human helping relationships.

(12)

THE BEHAVIORAL GOALS OF GUIDANCE

Edward C. Glanz

Provost, Southampton College, New York

The free and responsible person strives to solve problems of life as they are encountered; he also is able to reflect upon himself and his life. He uses his total capacity to know and to understand himself as he seeks to integrate education with his concept of self to create a life.

He chooses among available alternatives. He recognizes that his freedom is limited by his nature as a person and the culture that gives meaning to his life. He learns to be free and responsible, progressively building upon past experience to face the present and future.

He recognizes that he is cumulatively a product of his physical, emotional and psychological nature as he learns from experiences. The values he learns and accredits are determining forces in the establishment of life objectives and life purposes.

He understands that freedom is the opportunity to solve problems with the total capacity present within himself. He views his freedom to create his own life as his most precious possession. He knows he is constantly in the process of becoming.

He defends and attempts to extend the freedom of others to live their lives with a dignity and integrity that are extensions of his respect for his own dignity and integrity as a person. He respects and is responsible to his own free, open society and culture as a surrounding and supporting force that permits him to be free to choose and to value.

The free person accepts the responsibility for his decisions. He is free to seek aid and counsel from others in resolving any issue, but accepts the implications and consequences of his actions.

He accepts youthful dependence while striving for mature independence. He attempts to understand the irrational and the rational in life. He seeks security, acceptance, and self-esteem in psychologically healthful ways. He is capable of loving and being loved.

He values education as an opportunity to learn creatively about life while preparing himself to live a fuller life. Educational decisions become related to step-by-step formulations of career concepts. He views work and career development as expressions of his own relations to the world.

The free and responsible person views life as an opportunity to realize his own potential as an individual while demonstrating by each act of life that he knows self-realization is at the same time social self-realization.

$$\boxed{13}$$

GUIDELINES FOR CAREER DEVELOPMENT COUNSELING

Lawrence P. Blum
University of Wisconsin—Milwaukee

MODERN GUIDANCE BEGAN AS VOCATIONAL GUIDANCE

Concern for vocational guidance, vocational adjustment, and career development has always been a major aspect of guidance services. The guidance movement had its roots in the vocational concerns of individuals. Frank Parsons, a public-spirited and versatile social scientist and social worker, established the Vocation Bureau in Boston in 1908 as part of the Civic Service House of that city. In this agency he established the spirit and pattern of vocational counseling with sufficient soundness to cause it to be influential to the present time. His philosophy of guidance and methods for implementing vocational guidance are set forth in *Choosing a Vocation,* published in 1909 shortly after his death. He states the essentials of vocational guidance as follows: "There are three broad factors: (1) a clear understanding of yourself, your aptitudes, abilities, interests, ambitions, resources, limitations, and their causes; (2) a knowledge of the requirements and conditions of success, advantages and disadvantages, compensation, opportunities, and prospects in different lines of work; (3) true reasoning on the relations of these two groups of facts."[1] It is worthy of note that Parsons attempted the difficult task of individual assessment long before systematic procedures for analysis of the details of the world of work became available.

Further evidence of the vocational emphasis in early guidance activities is seen in the fact that the first professional organization of guidance workers, established in 1913, bore the name National Occupational Conference, was financed by the Carnegie Corporation, and published *Occupations,* a journal dedicated to publicizing techniques and content relevant to vocational guidance. These and many other phases of the history of guidance provide sufficient documentation of the large place that vocational guidance has in the development of the guidance movement.

GUIDANCE NOW IS VOCATIONAL
PLUS MANY ADDITIONAL AREAS

With the passage of time many additional responsibilities were crowded into the guidance field. To accommodate this broadened range of activity the National Vocational Guidance Association banded with other groups functioning in guidance to become the American Personnel and Guidance Asso-

---

An original article for this book.
[1]Frank Parsons, *Choosing a Vocation* (Boston: Houghton Mifflin Co., 1909), p. 5.

ciation, and its publication, *Occupations,* for many years the key publication in the guidance field, became the *Personnel and Guidance Journal.*

The interests and duties of counselors have likewise broadened and, in the process, vocational counseling and guidance have not received the attention they once had. This reduction of emphasis on vocational counseling is summarized by Wrenn in his review of the findings of Project TALENT, one phase of which surveyed the status of counseling in American secondary schools. Project TALENT was a project concerning identification, development, and utilization of human talents, conducted by the American Institute for Research, under sponsorship of the U. S. Office of Education. In analyzing the findings, Wrenn notes that of counseling duties reported by counselors, "counseling for college" and "counseling for high school" were cited with greatest frequency. Also frequently cited were "counseling for developing for potential" and "counseling for inadequate achievement." All of these rank higher in frequency than did "counseling for occupations." As Wrenn states, "The interpretation of what is meant by an item may vary, but the low ranking of vocational counseling suggests a disturbing absence of what many assume to be a vital counseling area for adolescents." He goes on to state that "counseling for occupations" ranks much lower than other counseling emphases in the three- to four-year senior high school."[2]

THERE SEEMS TO BE A RESURGENCE OF INTEREST
IN VOCATIONAL GUIDANCE AND COUNSELING

Several factors account for the renewed interest which has become apparent in vocational guidance and counseling. One such factor has been the emergence of thoughtful theories concerning the process of decision-making in vocational and career areas. Hoppock reports and discusses no fewer than seventeen of these,[3] and his list is being added to each year. They do, however, provide vocational counselors with hypothetical explanations about the way in which occupational plans are developed. Another factor responsible for renewed interest in vocational guidance involves concern over the influence of technological change upon the career possibilities of youth.

THE IMPACT OF AUTOMATION
ON CAREER DEVELOPMENT

The increased mechanization and instrumentation of activities related to the production of goods often has been regarded as a blessing for a Frankenstein. Those who regard it as a blessing point to the tremendous possibility of producing consumer and luxury goods in such quantity and so inexpensively that they can be available to all at low cost. The net result, they feel, is a heightened living standard and a better life for all.

The fact that fewer people can produce vastly more goods is certain to affect the kinds of opportunities awaiting young people. The "viewers with

[2]G. C. Wrenn, *The Counselor in a Changing World* (Washington, D.C.: American Personnel and Guidance Association, 1962), p. 115.
[3]R. Hoppock, *Occupational Information* (New York: McGraw-Hill, 1967), ch. 7.

alarm" feel that substantially increased unemployment will accompany technological change. Others take a more moderate view that unemployment need
not necessarily follow, but that employment displacement is most likely.

Specific activities related to careers are to have at least the following
effects:

1. There will be a higher premium on training and skill. The technical demands of the mechanical era are such that the training for them cannot be
   completed within a conventional period of schooling. Any young man or
   woman who does not contemplate continuing his education or training
   beyond high school can be regarded as a dropout from educational experience and be subject to all the disadvantages of those who drop out before
   high school graduation.
2. Business, industry; and other employers generally must assume greater
   responsibility for education and training.

   The expectation that many candidates for careers on the automated scene
   will not have the requisite skills makes it imperative that employers pay
   more attention to training and selective placement of these people. Much
   recent research regarding the ways and rates of learning among adults
   can be applied in business and industry. It is incumbent also upon school
   guidance personnel to establish such relationships and communication with
   employers that the employers have a clear picture of how their training
   and educational efforts can supplement those of the school.
3. School guidance people must continually reappraise their career information.

   The changing employment picture has resulted in an accelerated rate of
   obsolescence of occupational information. It is probable that the total
   supply of occupational information in the files of school guidance personnel will be obsolete and nearly useless within five years. In some career
   areas items of information acquired as recently as one or two years ago
   have greatly reduced utility. The rapid decline of assembly and production line opportunities, the replacement of middle-management executive
   personnel with computer apparatus for decision-making, and the increased
   demands for skilled workers are in a constant state of flux, and school
   guidance personnel need constantly replenished information. Career information of the future must include more detailed attention to the psycho-
   social aspects of work. When individuals establish patterns of relationship
   to machines more than to people, there are implications for morale and
   for the kinds of people most likely to be successful employees.

THEORIES OF CAREER DEVELOPMENT HAVE INFLUENCED VOCATIONAL GUIDANCE

The reports of numerous theories of career development in recent years
have been influential in focusing attention upon the role of the curriculum,
teaching staff, and guidance personnel in shaping career plans. One conclusion
deriving from these theories is that the term *choice* regarding the selection
of an occupation or career is a misnomer. This is true because there is, in
reality, no point in time when an individual makes a "decision" to be this or
that. A more accurate way of describing the selection and entering upon an

occupation is as a *process* to which many forces have contributed. In a real sense a person "becomes" something vocationally rather than "decides" to be something.

After examining numerous reports of investigations of the influence on vocational development, Miller prepared the following summary of the most influential forces.

1. The most frequently given reason for choice is liking for or attraction to the occupation. This is true of both high school and college students.
2. The second most frequently given reason for choice is a belief in fitness or qualification for the occupation.
3. A considerable proportion of both high school and college students feel that they have been influenced in their occupational choices by parents.
4. Other persons significant in the student's life—teachers or professors, friends, and relatives other than parents—are regarded as being influential in choice, but their influence is reported somewhat less frequently than is the influence of parents.
5. Of the influences felt to be important by both high school and college students, the hope of financial reward is yet to be among the four or five most frequently mentioned reasons.[4]

Among the earliest of the theories of vocational development was that of Ginzberg which is summarized as follows:

The basic elements in the theory which we developed were three: Occupational choice is a process; the process is largely irreversible; compromise is an aspect of every choice. We found that the process of occupational decision making could be analyzed in terms of three periods—fantasy choice (before 11); tentative choices (between 11 and 17); and realistic choices (between 17 and young adulthood when a person finally determines his choice). The child, in the fantasy period, believes that he can become whatever he wants to become. He makes an arbitrary translation of his impulses and needs into an occupational choice. During the tentative period, his translation is almost exclusively in terms of such subjective factors as his interests, capacities, and values. Adolescents consider their choices tentative, because they sense that they have not effectively incorporated the reality factors into their considerations. They are able to do this during the realistic period, when they seek to work out a compromise between their interests, capacities, and values, and the opportunities and limitations of the environment.[5]

The ideas embodied in Ginzberg's theories have become basic to career-development thought since they were first presented. In some instances extensions and minor alterations of the basic concept have occurred. For example, Super and his students see career development as a process extending throughout the entire lifetime of the individual. He states,

Just as general development can be broken down into major life stages placed sequentially on a continuum, each stage having characteristics which are peculiar to it and which justify singling it out, so the continuum of vocational development can be broken down into vocational life stages, each defined by its peculiar characteristics. We have seen that the major voca-

---

[4]Miller, *Foundations of Guidance* (New York: Harper & Row, Publishers, 1961), p. 251.
[5]E. Ginzberg, "Toward a Theory of Occupational Choice," *Occupations* (December 1951), p. 492.

tional life stages may be classified as the Exploratory, Establishment, Maintenance, and Decline stages.[6]

Super also refines the theory by his view that career development is a mode of implementing a self concept. Total personal development and career development are thus seen to accompany each other.

It can be seen that achievement of the three basic stages varies from individual to individual. However, the following characteristics seem to prevail:

a. The three stages are developmental and follow one another chronologically.
b. Considerable overlap occurs as the transition is made from one stage to another.
c. The number of occupations considered becomes progressively fewer during the tentative and realistic choice stages until one occupation is selected.

A theory which is not clearly consistent with the developmental stages concept of Ginzberg, but which has proved influential, is that of Hoppock. Hoppock feels that individual needs, and the way in which they are met, constitute the basis of career development. His theory consists of the following steps:

1. Occupations are chosen to meet needs.
2. The occupation that we choose is the one that we believe will best meet the needs that most concern us.
3. Needs may be intellectually perceived or they may be only vaguely felt as attractions which draw us in certain directions. In either case, they may influence choices.
4. Vocational development begins when we first become aware that an occupation can help to meet our needs.
5. Vocational development progress and occupational choice improves as we become better able to anticipate how well a prospective occupation will meet our needs. Our capacity to anticipate thus depends upon our knowledge of ourselves, our knowledge of occupations, and our ability to think clearly.
6. Information about ourselves affects occupational choice by helping us recognize what we want, and to anticipate whether or not we will be successful in collecting what the contemplated occupation offers to us.
7. Information about occupations affects occupational choice by helping us to discover the occupations that may meet our needs, and to anticipate how well satisfied we may hope to be in one occupation as compared with another.
8. Job satisfaction depends upon the extent to which the job that we hold meets the needs that we feel it should meet. The degree of satisfaction is determined by the ratio between what we have and what we want.
9. Satisfaction can result from a job which meets our needs today or from a job which promises to meet them in the future.
10. Occupational choice is always subject to change when we believe that a change will better our needs.[7]

The idea that vocational development follows a sequence beginning with indefinite, probably fantasy-based, choices, continuing with a period of tenta-

---

[6]D. E. Super, *Psychology of Careers* (New York: Harper & Row, Publishers, 1957), p. 185.
[7]Hoppock, *op. cit.*, pp. 111-112.

tive choices, and terminating with reality-based decisions has implications for the kinds of vocational guidance and educational experience which are provided.

It can be noted immediately that the period of indefinite, fantasy-based vocational experience coincides with the elementary school years. The implication for teachers and elementary school guidance personnel are several:

1. The normal fantasy life of the young child provides opportunity to determine "how it feels" to play vocational roles. He can be a cowboy, locomotive engineer, spaceman, teacher, etc., with no risk and with no need for consideration of reality factors.
2. In the later elementary school years he can be introduced to occupations which are close to the experience of the group. For example, the occupations of the fathers and/or mothers of the class members can be discussed and a bit of role-playing of these careers can be engaged in.
3. Attention can be devoted to subject-matter content of a vocational nature. Biographies, for example, can be read with a view to discovering how people earned their living and possibly the factors which caused them to enter upon those particular careers. In arithmetic and science an opportunity exists to discuss careers and even role-play some of the activities related to those areas.

The school experience coinciding with the period of tentative choices includes the junior high school years. The goal of school experience in this period is to provide sufficient knowledge in vocational areas so that valid attitudes toward specific careers can be developed. This experience necessarily is vicarious. It can consist of vocational reading, visits, interviews with professional people, tours of work settings, and career films. It makes little difference whether this experience is provided as part of a formal course in occupations or as an incidental part of other courses. The important factor is that opportunity be provided for discussion and evaluation. It is important also to remember that the attitudes which are being developed at this stage are strictly tentative and are not to be regarded as career decisions or binding vocational plans. It is true that some individuals make a vocational choice while still rather young, but the majority do not arrive at firm plans during the junior high school years. The tentative nature of plans at this age is reported by Super and Overstreet who state that

> Preferences expressed at the ninth-grade level should not be viewed as definite vocational objectives. . . . The task of the vocational counselor in the ninth grade is essentially a matter of furthering vocational development rather than of fostering specific vocational choices.[8]

At the level of the senior high school the narrowing of possibilities as a result of considering reality factors can take place. It is the responsibility of instruction and counseling at the senior high school level to facilitate this narrowing of the field. This will necessitate identifying students in terms of their immediate plans. These plans may include withdrawing from school prior to

---

[8]D. E. Super, and P. L. Overstreet, "The Vocational Maturity of Ninth Grade Boys," *Career Pattern Study Monograph 2* (New York: Bureau of Publications, Teachers College, Columbia University, 1960).

graduation, entering the world of work immediately upon graduation, or continuing education and training beyond the high school. Each of these groups will require guidance of a special type at the time when it will be most beneficial to the recipient. Since it is true that people are most motivated to learn content which is to be used in the immediate future, it is sensible to provide the specialized guidance immediately prior to his need for it. It thus is probable that concentrated occupational guidance should occur in the ninth or tenth grade for those pupils who may drop out of school at that time. This guidance should be directed at the identification and development of abilities and skills which will be immediately useful in the labor market. Much as dropping out of school is deplored, those who do it should have minimum handicap on entering the job market.

Those pupils who plan to complete high school, but not continue their education or training, need a program of guidance and instruction similar to that for dropouts. These people also have a real need for immediately available skills which are usable by employers. Detailed consideration needs to be given to identification of abilities, interests, and needs of individuals and the reality factors which are going to be influential in narrowing the range of possibilities and ultimately in arriving at a suitable entry job in the world of work. It is probable that the school agency should be more directly involved in the placement function than it customarily has been. This involvement can mean more cooperative relationships with the state employment service, and it also can mean continued contact with the new employee as he goes through his first employment experience. At present it is relatively rare for a school to continue the availability of its guidance services for postgraduates. Since career adjustment for the high school graduate may mean trying several jobs, however, it is important that counseling be available so he can evaluate systematically his experience with each.

For the pupil who plans to continue education and training beyond high school, the urgency for decision is somewhat reduced and the period for exploration and tentative choices extended. In fact it may be desirable to deliberately avoid early decision in order to gain breadth and depth in high school education. Counseling and guidance for these people consists of helping them to understand their abilities, interests, and needs, and to explore with them their in- and out-of-school experiences. The aim is to arrive at eventual long-range career objectives for which education and training beyond high school are necessary.

THE ROLE OF OCCUPATIONAL INFORMATION
IN CAREER DEVELOPMENT

The maintenance of supplies of recent and accurate occupational information in useful form is indeed a responsible guidance function. As was mentioned earlier, our technology, as far as vocation and careers are concerned, is changing so rapidly that keeping up to date on developments is a major challenge. Since many young people will secure their first jobs in their home communities, it is important for guidance people to be familiar with opportunities in their community. This means getting out of the school and getting acquainted with potential employers in offices, shops, and business places. It also involves careful noting of help-wanted ads in the newspaper and keeping in close touch with public employment service personnel. These latter people can be a source for the numerous government publications which cover the national scene as well.

A well-planned program of follow-up on recent graduates and those who leave can also be a worthwhile source of local occupational information. Present students are well informed on what became of (vocationally) people they knew from preceding classes.

Numerous sources of occupational information are available on the national level, and some of this is quite worthwhile. As a rule, that which is compiled by a nationally known publisher and disseminator of occupational information is satisfactory. Information which is supplied free from trade associations, professional societies, or training institutions may be very attractively presented but may suffer from serious defect as bona fide occupational information. One defect involves its tendency to be "recruiting literature" with a selective presentation of the facts regarding the area it represents. Some information from such private sources may be useful, but all of it must be read by the counselor before it is accepted as part of his selection of occupational information.

Probably the most serious deficiency of occupational information is its rapid obsolescence. The speed of change in the work world necessitates the constant removal of outmoded information. Any item in the file which has copyright or acquisition date prior to the past two years in all probability contains enough obsolete information to warrant its replacement.

The question is sometimes raised as to when occupational information should be introduced into the counseling process. No definite answer can be given, but it can be assumed that the introduction of factual information is premature if the counselee has matters of a more personal, intimate, or emotional nature on his mind. The vocational indecision problem and the request for information may be a facade or an opening for a relationship with the counselor as a prelude to discussion of other matters. Little is gained by exposing a person to occupational information when his mind and emotions are preoccupied with other matters.

Recent applications of learning theory based upon behavior modification and reinforcement have also been influential on career information usage and career development. It has long been recognized that effective exploration of career information, however presented, is dependent on the level of motivation to do it. An approach to increasing such exploratory behavior is described by Krumboltz and Thoresen[9] who employed three counseling procedures with 192 eleventh-graders. One group received strong reinforcement of verbal information-seeking behavior; another group was exposed to a tape recording of a model who was actively seeking occupational information. This was followed by counseling. A third group viewed a film which was followed by group discussion. It was concluded that the reinforcement of information-seeking behavior produced a significant increase in that behavior.

---

[9] J. D. Krumboltz and C. E. Thoresen, "The Effects of Behavioral Counseling in Group and Individual Settings on Information Seeking Behavior," *Journal of Counseling Psychology*, Vol. 11 (1964), pp. 325-333.

COMPUTER-BASED VOCATIONAL AND CAREER
GUIDANCE SYSTEMS

The complexity of career opportunity and the difficulty of relating individual characteristics to the infinite variety of career opportunities have led to experimentation with computers as an important aid in vocational and career counseling. For several years the systems approach has been used as a management tool for the orderly solution of complex problems. Since 1966 efforts have been made in various locations to apply the systems approach to problems of career choice and development. These attempts are well summarized in the report of the Fourth Symposium for Systems Under Development for Vocational Guidance entitled *Computer-Based Vocational Guidance Systems*.[10] One such system is the *Information System for Vocational Decisions* developed by the Harvard University Graduate School, New England Education Data Systems, and Newton, Massachusetts, Public Schools which attempts to improve decision-making by providing supervised experience in relating accurate and comprehensive data about careers to information about one's personal characteristics.[11] *The Experimental Education and Career Exploration System*, a computer-based system developed by International Business Machines Corporation, provides opportunity to enter data such as grades, interests, ratings of intellectual strengths and weaknesses, and prediction of level of attainment. The system then retrieves career goals which are compatible with this data as well as educational and training institutions which can facilitate entry upon these careers.[12]

The American Institutes for Research is developing a system which is closely related to Project TALENT appraisal data. Abilities and interests based upon this data can be entered into the system and the retrieval will consist of guidance-learning units for areas in which preference is expressed and for which high probability of success is indicated.[13]

Another system, that of Systems Development Corporation, specifically attempts to increase counselor efficiency in the career information and exploration phases and allows concentration more fully on those aspects of counseling which require effective interpersonal relationships, group and individual. Basically it stores a large amount and variety of information about students which counselors can retrieve at will. It also allows for retrieval of career information regarding career levels, families of occupations, and educational and training opportunities for specific careers.[14]

At Willowbrook High School, Villa Park, Illinois, a vocational guidance system is being developed into which interest data from the Kuder Preference Record, achievement data, and aptitudes are entered. The retrieval consists of descriptive data on numerous occupations classified according to the system of Dr. Ann Roe.[15]

---

[10]*Computer-Based Vocational Guidance Systems*, U. S. Department of Health, Education, and Welfare, Office of Education, Washington, D. C., Superintendent of Documents, 1969.
 [11]*Ibid*. 124-129.
 [12]*Ibid*. 130-134.
 [13]*Ibid*. 135-138.
 [14]*Ibid*. 139-143.
 [15]*Ibid*. 158-161.

It should be emphasized that all present systems are experimental, and several types of problems are inherent in their use. These include (a) the factor of cost for data entry and storage in a central data bank, transmission line costs, and console equipment for use at the counseling location, (b) counselor resistance based on the apparent inconsistency between the depersonalization of the systems approach and the traditional emphasis on the values of an interpersonal relationship, (c) lack of counselor training in and apprehension regarding learning a new set of technical skills. It is probable that in the near future the element of cost will be reduced, as systems become perfected, for data storage, transmission services, and computer equipment. Continued research will be employed to demonstrate if the systems approach to counseling via computer is enhancing to career development counseling or is, in effect, inhibiting. It is apparent, however, that counselor training in the last quarter of the twentieth century must take account of computer technology as a valuable adjunct to the counseling process.

THE ROLE OF TESTING IN CAREER DEVELOPMENT

Tests have long been used as aids in the process of decision-making in career areas. Ability and achievement tests are employed when predicting suitability for certain educational or vocational opportunities is desired. Interest measures have been used to evaluate motivation factors and personality measuring devices to determine the personal suitability or adaptability of a person. In vocational guidance, as in many other areas, administrators of tests should allow for the factors which have been demonstrated to reduce the tests' utility. These include inadequate reliability and validity for the purposes for which they are being used. This is not to say that tests have little value in vocational guidance—because they do have value—but rather to suggest that their main value is supplementary rather than primary. As a rule, the more one knows about a person, the more supplementary test results become. If an individual is known in a primary sense by means of interviews, work samples, observations, and similar devices, less reliance is necessary on test results. On the other hand if little is known in a primary sense, extensive reliance upon test results is essential. It can thus be seen that tests do have a value in supplementing what is known about people.

SUMMARY

It is the writer's contention that the vocational phases of guidance deserve reexamination and reemphasis. This is true because of the social, educational, and technical changes which are occurring in the world of careers. These changes are rapidly making current information and assumptions about occupations progressively more obsolete. Current theories of vocational development stress the vital role of appropriate educational experience at every level. They also underline the importance of vocational guidance and the appropriate role of testing. New technologies, now emerging, will need to become a part of the vocational counseling of the future.

(14)

TECHNIQUES FOR ASSISTING LIFE-STAGE VOCATIONAL DEVELOPMENT

David B. Hershenson
Illinois Institute of Technology

Since vocational development processes are not synonymous with psychopathology, the techniques for assisting vocational development must be conceptualized as distinct from psychotherapy. Two levels of assistance are suggested: facilitation (promoting normal development) and remediation (actively removing serious blocks to development). Utilizing the author's earlier formulation of five vocational development life stages, four transitions exist: (a) social amniotic to self-differentiation; (b) self-differentiation to competence; (c) competence to independence; and (d) independence to commitment. Procedures required for making these transitions involve, respectively: (a) determining the program; (b) information in-put; (c) information processing; and (d) information utilization. Techniques for assisting these procedures involve, respectively: (a) facilitation—life style analysis, remediation—environmental manipulation and psychotherapy; (b) facilitation—guidance, remediation—skill training; (c) for content—client-centered approach, for process—training in decision-making; and (d) for intrapsychic difficulties—existential approaches, for situational difficulties—job matching. For c and d, facilitation and remediation differ in degree, not in kind.

In an earlier paper (Hershenson, 1968), the author suggested that the vocational development process could be conceptualized as occurring in a five-stage process. Each successive stage is defined by the principal use of energy which it requires. The stages, with type of energy utilization for each one, given in parentheses, are: (a) social-amniotic (awareness); (b) self-differentiation (control); (c) competence (directed); (d) independence (goal-directed); and (e) commitment (invested). The vocational modes related respectively to these stages are being, play, work, occupation, and vocation. The measurement constructs related to these modes are, respectively: socioeconomic status and family atmosphere; affective self-concept, attitudes, and values; abilities; interests; and satisfaction. Within this conceptual framework there are, consequently, four transitions: from the social-amniotic to the self-differentiation stage; from the self-differentiation to the competence stage; from the competence to the independence stage; and from the independence to the commitment stage. It is the purpose of this paper to suggest certain techniques which, at least in theory, may assist each of these transitions, thereby promoting vocational development.

THE INTEGRITY OF VOCATIONAL ASSISTANCE

Before suggesting these techniques, it would be appropriate to make explicit the orientation underlying the formulation presented here. While the author by no means wishes to give the impression that the view is original

Reprinted by permission of the author and *Personnel and Guidance Journal,* April 1969, 776-780.

or unique to him (see, for example, Samler, 1966), he wishes to assert the premise employed here that a distinction exists between problems in vocational development and psychopathology and that, consequently, a distinction must be drawn between vocational development assistance and psychotherapy. Thus, a vocational problem may exist without the presence of emotional illness (for example, a lack of certain occupational information or a temporary work lay-off due to a production cut-back), or an emotional problem may exist without the presence of a vocational problem (for example, working psychotics or the "Sunday neurosis" syndrome). Likewise, naturally, an emotional disturbance may run concomitantly with or impinge upon or create a vocational problem, in which case the emotional disturbance should be treated by a psychotherapist. However, to the extent that a vocational problem exists (either on its own or as a by-product of some other condition), it must be viewed in its own right and treated by techniques specifically appropriate to it. This is not to imply that the processes of psychotherapy and vocational assistance have nothing to contribute to each other, but rather to indicate that each should be viewed as having its own independent methodology. In its push to utilize the dynamic insights of psychotherapy, vocational counseling has, to some measure, lost sight of the fact that vocational problems have other unique aspects which require the use of different sorts of remediation techniques. This paper seeks to suggest techniques which are specifically relevant to vocational assistance and is concerned with the psychotherapeutic process only insofar as it has something to contribute to this conceptually distinct area of professional practice.

It may be pointed out that evidence of the distinctive nature of vocational functioning has existed in the literature for over a decade, since Neff (1955, p. 210) reported, "Vocational rehabilitation apparently takes place without any alteration of the basic personality structure of the individual involved." Likewise, as yet unpublished work by several students of the author lend support to the view of vocational functioning expressed here. Bennett (1968) found a non-linear relationship between a self-report measure of vocational maturity and diagnosed level of emotional maturity in a sample of college students. Further, Glass, in a master's project currently in progress, has found no linear relationship between a scale (drawn from the MMPI item pool) she has constructed to predict work performance of mental patients in a sheltered workshop setting and any of the MMPI scales of psychopathology.

LEVELS OF VOCATIONAL ASSISTANCE

The term "assistance," which has been used above, was selected for its value as a generic concept, covering two levels of intervention. One level of assistance, concerned with promoting normal development in the absence of severe vocational development pathology, may be termed facilitation. The other level of assistance, concerned with actively removing serious blocks to normal vocational development, may be termed remediation. The difference between the two usages is fairly well reflected in the difference between the French (assister) and English (assist) verbs, the former meaning "to be present at" and the latter meaning "to help." Stated in other words, the difference may be likened to that between a midwife at a normal delivery and an obstetrical surgeon at a caesarean section. However, in both this analogy and in vocational assistance, it must be kept in mind that the clients must conceive and give birth to their own products.

TRANSITIONAL PROCEDURES AND ASSISTANCE TECHNIQUES

As may be seen in TABLE 1, five categories of data are suggested as relevant to the conceptualization and modification of vocational life-stage transitions. The first of these categories, Transitional Procedure, is obviously derived from a data processing model. This is not meant to imply that the author views the decisional process models (e.g., Hershenson & Roth, 1966; Hilton, 1962; Tiedeman, 1961) as sufficient in themselves to conceptualize the process of vocational development. Rather, this model is suggested as a convenient frame of reference for this context. Associated with each of these categories is a Transitional Concept, that is, the basic concept which must be defined and spelled out to allow attainment of the succeeding stage. The three right-hand columns suggest techniques which appear specific to facilitating and remediating each of these successive transitional concept attainments and individuals or schools peculiarly associated with or exemplary of these techniques.

As was indicated in the author's earlier paper, the social-amniotic stage is primarily concerned with soaking up inputs from the environment, out of which, in turn, the self is differentiated. Which inputs are accepted and integrated toward this end and which are rejected is a function of the individual's set. Without a set, the individual would produce internal chaos and no possibility for a consistent self to develop (see Lecky, 1945). Sullivan's (1953) formulation of "the good me," "the bad me," and "the not me" is an excellent way of conceptualizing this process of self-definition by consistent inclusion and exclusion, as is Mead's (1934) "social self." However, presumably the individual coming for vocational assistance who is caught at this stage of development is more mature and verbally adept than Sullivan's infant, and hence more verbal techniques might be more appropriate in defining the "me." Of all therapeutic formulations considered, Adler's (1927) life-style analysis seemed to offer the most in the way of constructs relevant to the issues involved here. It is doubtless not an accident that Adler wrote in greater detail about work adjustment than did almost all other major therapeutic theorists. This is not to suggest that Adlerian therapy is the only one that is valid for resolving problems with self-definition and self-differentiation, but rather that whatever approach is employed, utilization of Adlerian constructs will provide a most relevant frame of reference for conceptualizing the tasks of assistance at this level. Thus, a client's attainment of a functioning awareness of his life style might be taken as an appropriate index of his having defined the transitional concept of "me" and hence having attained the mechanism for self-differentiation. While the Adlerian approach is clearly the most explicit way of gaining awareness of one's life style, the outcomes of almost any other approach can, with relatively little difficulty, be conceptualized and assessed in these terms. Although a life-style formulation should prove adequate in facilitating the first transition of an individual within the normal range of vocational development, further remediation techniques may be required in the case of severe intrapsychic or situational blocks. For example, a culturally different ghetto resident may have developed a life style

TABLE 1
Techniques for Assisting Vocational Life-Stage Transitions

Stages	Transitional Procedure	Transitional Concept	Assistance Techniques		Prototype Theorist or School
			Facilitation	Remediation	
Social amniotic	Determining program (set)	"me"	Life style analysis	Environmental manipulation; psychotherapy	Adler
Self-differentiation	Information input	"go-versus-no-go"	Guidance	Skill training	Trait-and-factor
Competence	Information processing	"go-versus-go"	{ Content: Process:	Client-centered Training in decision-making	Rogers Tiedeman Krumboltz
Independence	Information utilization	"application"	{ Intrapsychic: Situational:	Existential Job matching	Frankl Beck Herzberg
Commitment					

which is adaptive to his environment but yet vocationally maladaptive. Without environmental manipulation, there is no basis for him to modify his life style to a more vocationally adaptive one. Similarly, an emotionally disturbed individual must be freed of his thought distortion before a meaningful, vocationally relevant life-style analysis can be made.

Once the individual has determined a program (or set) through which inputs are to be processed, the next step involves feeding in information for processing. That is, what "works" and what doesn't for his program of "me" must be ascertained. Decisions are of a "go-versus-no-go" variety, with the "go" being retained to form his realm of competence. The technique of greatest relevance here may be called "guidance," as defined by the practices of the trait-and-factor approach (Williamson, 1965). Thus, for the client who comes for vocational assistance with an attained self-differentiation but with a problem in defining his competencies, the techniques of guidance (ability and aptitude tests, work samples and structured feed-back of performance) appear to be most appropriate in providing information of the go-no-go type. IQ, manual dexterity, form perception, critical thinking, and other capacities and limitations can be assessed and made explicit for the client. Naturally, this does not mean that one should overlook the possibility that measured levels of functioning may be inaccurate or depressed by situational or personal problems. As was indicated earlier, where an emotional or situational problem causes vocational difficulties, the underlying problem must be treated by techniques appropriate to it. Insofar as a vocational deficit is thereby created, it must be treated by vocationally relevant techniques. Thus, while guidance techniques (revealing skills and assets) may be sufficient to facilitate relatively normal transition at this point, a remediation technique of training (producing skills) may be required in a severe vocational problem (for example, a physically, mentally, or socially handicapped individual).

Once the no-go's are eliminated, the individual must decide among the go's; that is, the information which was retained must be processed. Of particular relevance to this occupational choice process is Rogers' (1951) formulation that to be utilized toward growth, choices must be (a) clearly perceived and (b) adequately symbolized. This offers criteria for assessing the adequacy of the content material at this stage, but the process of utilizing this content may also be a problem. For clients who have solved the earlier issues and present themselves for assistance in attaining independence, the techniques for training in decision-making appear relevant. These techniques include (a) non-directive counseling, (b) decision-making behavior models, and (c) programmed learning of decision-making. It may be argued that non-directive counseling, by allowing the client to gain the satisfaction of reaching his own conclusions, reinforces the attainment of decision-making skills. Similarly, Krumboltz's (Krumboltz & Schroeder, 1965) behavioral models and Tiedeman's (Ellis & Wetherell, 1966; Tiedeman, 1967; Wilson, 1967) concept of occupational fact mediation via programmed dialogue offer approaches to learning decision-making skills in an occupationally relevant context. Although some proponents of each of these approaches would doubtless disagree, it appears possible to utilize a combination of these three techniques to facilitate the development of decision-making: Krumboltz and Tiedeman for skill training in decision-making, and Rogers and Tiedeman for integrative use of these skills. At this transition and the following one, the difference between facilitation and remediation seems to be one of degree more than of kind.

Having gained decision-making skills and having formulated the choices among go's to be made, the individual should be able to apply these skills to these choices and attain independence. Having done so, the individual should be motivated to move on to the commitment stage, in which his energy is invested in the choices he has made. In the transition to commitment, two sorts of difficulties may arise to hinder the individual in the application of his choices: intrapsychic and situational. At this level of development, intrapsychic blocks probably revolve around difficulties in involving oneself. This issue has been focused on most thoroughly by the existentialist writers such as Frankl (1955) and Beck (1963), who suggest a personalized search for subjective meaning with the client as the treatment of choice for such problems. However, the problem with application may also lie in the lack of an appropriate setting in which the individual can exercise his already available capacity to invest. Thus, a routine job may be given up for a creative one in the same field, or a field which fails to offer certain opportunities for the expression of the choices made at the prior stage may be given up for one which does offer these opportunities. In exploring the opportunity structure of a client's selected job, Herzberg's (1959) formulations of motivational factors may be useful. The decision as to whether the problem in making this transition is an intrapsychic or a situational one would have to be based on a differential diagnosis.

ISSUES FOR RESEARCH

This paper and the earlier formulation to which it is related (Hershenson, 1968) suggest two major research questions. First, can successive vocational life stages be empirically defined and ordered in the manner suggested in the earlier paper? If these stages can be so defined (even if their sequential order does not conform to the system proposed here), are the techniques of assistance suggested as specifically stage-relevant in this paper empirically more effective than other approaches? Measurement techniques relevant to the five stages were suggested in the author's earlier paper, so that progress effected by the use of various assistance approaches can be assessed by pre- and post-testing.

REFERENCES

Adler, A. *The practice and theory of individual psychology.* New York: Harcourt, 1927.

Beck, C. E. *Philosophical foundations of guidance.* Englewood Cliffs, N. J.: Prentice-Hall, 1963.

Bennett, B. E. Perceived occupational fit, diagnostic category, and academic achievement. Unpublished master's thesis, Illinois Institute of Technology, 1968.

Ellis, A. B., & Wetherell, C. S. *The computer and career decisions, Technical Memorandum I.* Cambridge, Mass.: Harvard-NEEDS-Newton Information System for Vocational Decisions, September, 1966.

Frankl, V. *The doctor and the soul: An introduction to logotherapy.* New York: Knopf, 1955.

Hershenson, D. B., & Roth, R. M. A decisional process model of vocational development. *Journal of Counseling Psychology,* 1966, *13,* 368-370.

Hershenson, D. B. Life-stage vocational development system. *Journal of Counseling Psychology,* 1968, *15,* 23-30.

Herzberg, F., Mausner, B., & Snyderman, B. B. *The motivation to work.* (2nd ed.) New York: Wiley, 1959.

Hilton, T. L. Career decision-making. *Journal of Counseling Psychology,* 1962, *9,* 291-298.

Krumboltz, J. D., & Schroeder, W. W. Promoting career exploration through reinforcement. *Personnel and Guidance Journal,* 1965, *44,* 19-26.

Lecky, P. *Self-consistency.* New York: Island Press, 1945.

Mead, G. H. *Mind, self, and society.* Chicago: University of Chicago Press, 1934.

Neff, W. S. The use of the Rorschach in distinguishing vocationally rehabilitable groups. *Journal of Counseling Psychology,* 1955, *2,* 207-211.

Rogers, C. R. *Client-centered therapy: Its current practice, implications, and theory.* Boston: Houghton Mifflin, 1951.

Samler, J. A new psychological specialty: Vocational counseling. *Vocational Guidance Quarterly,* 1966, *15,* 82-89.

Sullivan, H. S. *The interpersonal theory of psychiatry.* New York: Norton, 1953.

Tiedeman, D. V. Recent developments and current prospects in occupational fact mediation. Presentation to Institute on the Implications of Career Development Theory and Research for Counselor Education, Columbia University, New York, June, 1967.

Williamson, E. G. Vocational counseling: Trait-factor theory. In B. Stefflre (Ed.), *Theories of counseling.* New York: McGraw-Hill, 1965. Pp. 193-214.

Wilson, E. H. *A task-oriented course in decision-making. Project report No. 7.* Cambridge, Mass.: Information System for Vocational Decisions, 1967.

EMERGING CONCEPTS AND PATTERNS OF GUIDANCE IN AMERICAN EDUCATION

Edward C. Glanz

Provost, Southampton College, New York

Guidance, counseling, and personnel work have recently been cast into a significant new role in American education. Congressional action has helped to focus attention upon this area of America's educational program. The increased concern for guidance by accrediting agencies, the changing patterns of teacher training, the spurt in post World War II training in guidance, these factors, among many other similar forces, have provided a background against which national legislation served as a catalytic agent to bring about the heightened concern for guidance in American education.

Public school administrators on all educational levels, college presidents, deans, faculty members and parents, as well as guidance personnel themselves, now need to face an increased responsibility for providing effective and adequate guidance for America's youth. Guidance, as an emerging force in education, has largely been accepted as a valuable and required factor in the total educational process. The major question which must now be faced by all concerned with education is: *"How and in what patterns may guidance best be integrated into the total educational process?"*

The patterns of "Topsy-like" growth in guidance services and programs need now to be changed into mature conceptual designs or constructs for

Reprinted by permission of the author and the *Personnel and Guidance Journal,* November 1961, 259-265.

educators to utilize in educational institutions. A brief examination of the historical perspectives within the guidance field and a review of present structures may provide a basis for the projection of emerging concepts and patterns of guidance for the future.

PERSPECTIVE

Counseling, guidance, and an increased concern for the individual student and his welfare is largely a development of the early twentieth century in American education. The vocational guidance movement, child guidance clinics, and the mental health emphasis in clinics and hospitals, as well as early personnel services for women on the college campuses were all early signals of the significant change to occur in the American educational pattern in the years to follow. The American Personnel and Guidance Association now has approximately fourteen thousand members in six divisions. Thousands more devote part time to counseling, guidance, and related efforts. New training institutes, financed by the federal government, are supplying thousands of new guidance personnel for American schools.

The counseling and guidance movement in the first part of the century was spurred on by an identification with reform and revolt. Education had to be "humanized"; the individual student needed to be recognized and aided; individual differences and intelligence variables needed to be identified; different counseling methods were developed; these and many more approaches were re-emphasized or brought into American education by counselors, guidance workers, and other school personnel.

The zeal arising out of the reform spirit and the "revolt character" of the personnel and guidance movement led to a patch-work pattern of organization and chance-determined character in schools and colleges. The recent past and the present have, however, begun to cast definite shadows for the future.

THE RECENT PAST AND THE PRESENT

Lloyd-Jones [45], described general education programs in education as being divided into three major patterns: classical, neo-classical, and instrumental. A similar characterization can conveniently be utilized with education as a whole and to the development of guidance in personnel services and counseling in education. Counseling and guidance, or its absence, were related and patterned after the basic structure of the schools or colleges serving as models. The classical or traditional point of view in education generally has refused to recognize counseling and guidance as a professional specialty. These institutions have preferred to assign any or all of these so-called "personnel duties" to academic faculty members. The neo-classical or more modern institutions, usually with varied curricula, have generally accepted counseling and guidance. Varied patterns of organization have emerged as philosophy and/or budget have dictated or allowed. Instrumental (or progressive?) institutions have not only accepted counseling and guidance, but have provided the environment for experimental and highly individualized programs.

Patterns of guidance and counseling in all types of institutions have continued to develop within the presently recognized twofold pattern of "specialist" and "generalist" as characterized by Lloyd-Jones [45], and Barry and Wolf [42]. Highly organized patterns of bureaus, centers, and clinically oriented specialists have compartmentalized personnel services into smaller and more compact units. At the same time, guidance personnel have begun to recognize the essential weakness of a specialized approach and an interest in the guidance efforts of the teacher or faculty member has grown stronger. The defenders of the classroom teacher or professor as the primary guidance agent have in turn recognized the contributions of the specialist and have moved toward a position reflecting the combined efforts of both. Also, new approaches paralleling the older "specialist-generalist" dichotomy are now appearing as guidance continues to grow and develop.

Guidance is a virile force and is now becoming an entrenched feature of American education. The integration of guidance into education as a mature professional discipline as described by Wrenn [47, 48] is a direct concern of administrators, budget makers, taxpayers, parents, and ultimately students. Prediction is always dangerous but virtually 50 years are now in the past of counseling and guidance. It is time to seek generalizations, constructs, and patterns which will serve to make problem-solving in counseling, guidance, and personnel work an easier task tomorrow than it is today.

MODELS FROM THE PRESENT AND FOR THE FUTURE

The practices of the past are becoming channeled into major trends and it appears that at least four basic structural or organizational patterns are emerging. Other emphases are present but appear to be below the surface of widespread present attention. Four major models of counseling and guidance seem to be:

1. Centralized Specialism
2. Decentralized Generalism
3. Curricular Counseling and Guidance (Group Guidance)
4. Human Relations and Group Work (Mental Health)

These four trends may be labelled differently or be recognizable in other ways; however, they seem to be basic to the many present approaches to the guidance problem in schools and colleges.

1. Centralized Specialism

The skilled techniques of clinical counselors, reading consultants, test administrators, school social workers, and many other specialists offer highly qualified aid to students of all ages and in all types of school programs. Coordination and administration needs in such programs have demanded a strong administrator or coordinator. The classroom teacher or faculty member, in the beginning, was usually encouraged to "leave it to the specialists"; in recent years, the significant contribution which can be made by faculty members as cooperating partners in guidance has been recognized. Somewhat reluctantly the teacher and non-specialist have been urged to consider a small contribution to the program.

Strengths. Many strengths are inherent in this view of guidance, personnel services and counseling. These strengths include:

1. *highly qualified personnel* in specific positions to solve difficult problems;
2. *coordinated services* through centralized control and administration;
3. *referral resources.*

Weaknesses. Certain problems or weaknesses are basic to this construct of guidance. These weaknesses include:

1. *cost and supply* — specially trained personnel are expensive and often difficult to find;
2. *centrifugal tendencies,* bureaus, clinics, and even individual specialists often tend to seek independence and separation. Such action sometimes strengthens individual units, but weakens the total program.
3. *de-emphasis of teachers'* role, classroom personnel often feel to be unimportant and unneeded in personnel and guidance work;
4. *compartmentalization of students,* particular problems of students are often treated and the *whole* student is forgotten or ignored.

Examples. College programs are usually coordinated by deans of students (student personnel, personnel services) or even vice-presidents. Public school programs are administered by directors of pupil personnel or assistant superintendents. *Services* is an important word and concept in this approach. Areas of action usually include: psychological counseling, reading clinics, school social workers, testing specialists, speech and/or hearing centers, and activities or student life. Discipline is usually handled by administrative deans (of men, boys, girls, women). Large city school systems, many elementary schools, state universities, and urban universities are frequent examples of this model of a guidance system in action.

Variations. Certain programs of this type have developed from one clinic or bureau within the system. Chronologically, this approach may be recognized by an examination of how services have been added and where the control is (or will be). Services are often "tacked on" and variations of this approach are as widespread as are new ideas, services, equality in an administrative view, and the *presence* or *need* for a purely administrative control center.

2. Decentralized Generalism

The importance of a guidance or personnel point of view in all areas of education has led to a movement designed to involve all educative personnel in the guidance or counseling process. All areas and levels of education have been affected by this view. Single coordinators or directors have attempted to involve faculty members, administrators, students, and others in the guidance program. Specialists were avoided at an early time, but have been sought in recent years to serve in a buttressing or supportive role. "Every teacher a better counselor" has often been the watchword of adherents to this view of the program.

Strengths. A concern for the total learning atmosphere and the appreciation of the contributions of every person within an educational program has
been a major pillar in the approach of this group. Other strengths include:

1. support for the contributions of the classroom teacher;
2. a concern for the process and climate for learning and growth;
3. identification with classroom learning experiences.

Weaknesses. The broadness of this approach has bred inherent weakness
which must be faced when it is adopted or implemented. Among these weaknesses are:

1. poorly trained practitioners in some problem areas of guidance (testing,
   clinical services, etc.);
2. vitiated efforts because of trying to do (and to be) all things to all people;
3. a depreciation of the value or merit of guidance through the belief that
   everyone should get into "the act";
4. poor practices in areas where standards should be tenaciously upheld.

Examples. A broad philosophical view of guidance and education is basic
to those who profess to support this approach to guidance. Single units
(schools, colleges) of city systems or universities; small public school systems;
small and medium sized colleges; and junior colleges offer examples of programs adopting this position.

High schools and colleges with a restricted budget and the services only
of a single guidance person often have adopted this approach toward a
particular view of guidance and education. Similar kinds of institutions have
expanded funds to hire guidance leaders and to develop and train faculty
members in order to implement a freely selected concept of guidance. The
latter examples are more truly representative of a conceived and chosen position rather than an imposed or financially dictated position.

Variations. Recent innovations in "generalist" programs have included the
integration of specialized or service units within the total program; clinics,
clinicians, and even psychiatrists have been added and used to strengthen
a given concept of guidance, counseling, and personnel work. The essential
feature, recognizable within any variation of this approach, is a stress upon
philosophy, program, and *integration of effort* rather than upon the "services
concept." Specially trained guidance or personnel workers may not even be
on the staff or a school or college in certain variations of this pattern. The
rationale or perspective or the faculty, administration, and even staff are the
key factors to seek in recognizing variations.

3. Curricular Counseling and Guidance

The integration of guidance and counseling into the academic curriculum
of the schools and colleges was a flirtatious affair for many years. Educators,
counselors, and guidance workers hoped for this pattern but were unable
to evolve a model capable of successful implementation. Experimentation in
group guidance, vocations courses, life adjustment courses, as well as social
planning and orientation courses were the forerunners of this third major pat-

tern in guidance. The general education movement [46] with its roots in the past and its forward view of the educational process frequently provided a sensitive and nurturing environment for the growth of such programs on the college level. Foundation support for experimental programs has, at the same time, made it possible for such patterns to be constructed on the junior high and senior high school levels.

Curricular approaches have been characterized by the offering of guidance and counseling preparation within a classroom setting through a course in psychology or life adjustment. The early lack of meaningful subject matter for such courses was a deterring factor in its growth. Group Guidance became almost a "dirty word" in high schools. Content study areas of self-concept study, self-analysis, vocational and educational planning, values, and the increasingly varied aspects of individual psychology have overcome this problem for classroom activity.

Strengths.
1. parallel structure with other academic courses in high schools and colleges;
2. use of psychological content to aid in individual counseling and guidance;
3. placement of counselors, guidance workers, etc., within the framework of academic teacher rather than in the role of administrators and coordinators;
4. realistic emphasis of guidance as a continuing process rather than a "one shot cure."

Weaknesses.
1. group guidance offered as a shallow, superficial, and meaningless time-filler;
2. pressure for dual qualifications as effective classroom teacher *and* counselor;
3. inflexibility demanded by classroom contact and scheduling;
4. need for a larger number of well-qualified personnel to implement the goals of program;
5. high cost (compared to 1-300/500-counselor-student ratio).

Examples. College and high school programs have predominated thus far in the implementation of this approach. Occupation courses, [24] and curricular approaches to guidance [18, 19] have often provided the subject-matter foundation for these courses. Private and public junior colleges have also experimented in this area. Junior high schools and senior high schools across the country have been involved through foundation support and the efforts of the Educational Testing Service [25]. Recent developments in the program of text materials spurred this pattern of guidance [20, 26].

Variations. Curricular patterns are a recent product of earlier experimentation in the previously cited areas of group guidance, occupations, orientation, and life adjustment courses. These programs pre-date the curricular pattern but are still technically variations on a theme.

The significant factor in this guidance concept is the *classroom contact with meaningful subject matter content.* Elements of the first two major patterns of centralized specialism and decentralized generalism can be seen in variations of the curricular pattern, but the broad concept of guidance and counseling necessary for successful teaching and counseling activities has tended to bring the generalist view rather than the specialist view into the curriculum and the classroom.

4. Human Relations and Group Work

A fourth pattern of guidance has recently emerged as a method of providing guidance for youth. Human relations centers, mental health programs, group work activities, and related inter-personal approaches have crystallized into programs designed to promote student growth. These programs have not been narrowly focused on such topics as vocational and educational counseling or psychological testing but have tended to strive for the broad general outcomes of adjustment, mature thinking, effective inter-personal skills, and mental health.

The "group dynamicists" and "human relations" specialists, with the help of Naval research funds, began a national training laboratory program at Bethel, Maine, shortly after World War II. Since the beginning of the training concept, this group has published a tremendous number of skill manuals and integrative, cross-disciplinary approaches to education and guidance. Guidance workers have often viewed with suspicion the emergence of this force within a school or college. Somewhat belatedly many guidance workers have realized that the goals of this human relations-group work approach were almost identical to those of guidance.

Specialized programs for maladjusted children, school-wide programs of mental health, and developmental programs on skill training have all demonstrated the techniques of this varied approach and its application.

Strengths.
1. a broad concept of guidance and education which stresses adjustment and maturity;
2. a special tool of group work — highly developed and utilizable by all workers in guidance;
3. a desire to cooperate (and to effect better total programs) with any existing program of guidance;
4. a cross-disciplinary approach with strong roots in the social sciences;
5. a stress on the importance of all personnel (teachers, *et al.*) in working for common goals.

Weaknesses.
1. the lack of specificity in the major tools of guidance, viz. counseling, testing, occupational techniques, etc.;
2. the need for recognition as a "guidance pattern" since many guidance personnel are provincial and often chauvinistic in their own techniques and tools;
3. the tendency for some workers trained in human relations and group work to lack thorough or even minimal training in one of the major disciplines upon which guidance rests — (psychology, sociology, education.)

Examples. Human relations and group work specialists have entered high school and college programs as catalysts in aiding others. Such personnel aid in the development of a focus on helping students and faculty alike in identifying common goals in education, guidance, and personal growth. Such programs were then allied with specialized or clinical programs, curricular, generalists or faculty-advisor programs. As catalysts, these personnel tend to lose their own identity occasionally and to serve as strengthening units in existing programs. As such, this pattern may be denied as a pure model, and yet it has been an increasingly effective and practical method of reaching guidance goals. Samler and others [40] have described several variations on this basic theme.

SUMMARY AND CONCLUSION

Guidance has become a significant force in American education in the recent past. Guidance traces its roots to the early part of this century but has thus far been unable to identify basic patterns or constructs for its functioning. Because of the need to strengthen the entire guidance movement in view of the focus of national, regional, and local scrutiny, four patterns or models of guidance organizational structures have been offered. The four patterns were identified as:

1. Centralized Specialism
2. Decentralized Generalism
3. Curricular Counseling and Guidance
4. Human Relations and Group Work

Many strengths can accrue to a coordinated and clear concept of guidance programming on any educational level. Inconsistent organizational patterns can vitiate the inherent strengths of any single approach. Educational standards of policy and practice demand excellence in any guidance pattern. Future research designs will need to test the relative effectiveness of each approach. Beginning research designs [43-44] show only indications rather than clearly demonstrable results.

The future basic questions which must be answered by administrators on all school and college levels as well as guidance personnel, are three:

1. Do different patterns of guidance actually exist?
2. What is the relative effectiveness of each pattern?
3. Can and should American education accept a pluralistic philosophy of guidance?

ILLUSTRATIVE REFERENCES[1]

[1]Listings are more detailed in patterns III and IV, since these aproaches are less well known than patterns I and II.

I.   *Centralized Specialism*
1. Arbuckle, Dugald S. *Student personnel services in higher education.* New York: McGraw-Hill, 1953.
2. Blum, Milton I., & Balinsky, Benjamin. *Counseling and psychology.* Englewood Cliffs, N. J.: Prentice-Hall, 1951.
3. Callis, Robert, Polmantier, Paul C., & Roeber, Edward C. *A casebook of counseling.* New York: Appleton-Century-Crofts, 1955.

4. Froehlich, Clifford P. *Guidance services in schools.* (2nd. ed.) New York: McGraw-Hill, 1958.
5. Hahn, Milton E., & MacLeon, M. S. *Counseling psychology.* New York: McGraw-Hill, 1955.
6. Hatch, Raymond H., & Stefflre, Buford. *Administration of guidance services.* Englewood Cliffs, N. J.: Prentice-Hall, 1958.
7. Traxler, Arthur E. *Techniques of guidance.* (Rev. Ed.) New York: Harper & Bros., 1957.

II. *Decentralized Generalism*

8. Arbuckle, Dugald S. *Counseling and guidance in the classroom.* Boston: Allyn and Bacon, 1957.
9. Arbuckle, Dugald S. *Teacher counseling.* Cambridge, Mass.: Addison, Wesley, 1950.
10. Cantor, Nathaniel. *The teaching-learning process.* New York: The Dryden Press, 1951.
11. Gordon, Ira. *The teacher as a guidance worker.* New York: Harper & Bros., 1956.
12. Gordon, Ira. The class as a group: the teacher as a leader — some comments and questions. *Educ. Admin. Superv.,* 1951, 37, 108-118.
13. Johnston, Edgar G., Peters, Mildred, & Evraiff, William. *The role of the teacher in guidance.* Englewod Cliffs, N. J.: Prentice-Hall, 1959.
14. Lloyd-Jones, Esther, & Smith, Margaret Ruth (eds.) *Student personnel work as deeper teaching.* New York: Harper & Bros., 1954.
15. Strang, Ruth. *The role of the teacher in personnel work* (4th ed.) New York: Bureau of Publications, Teachers College, Columbia University, 1953.

III. *Curricular Counseling and Guidance*

16. Anthony, V. A., *et al.* The team approach to general education. *Junior Coll. J.* 1956, *26,* Part I, 319-327, Part II, 405-410.
17. Bernard, Harold W. *Toward better personal adjustment.* New York: McGraw-Hill, 1951.
18. Borow, Henry. Curricular approaches to personal development: some problems of research. *J. counsel. Psychol.,* 1958, 5, 63-69.
19. Borow, Henry, & Lindsey, Robert V. *Vocational planning for college students.* Englewood Cliffs, N. J.: Prentice Hall, 1959.
20. Glanz, Edward C., & Walston, E. B. *An introduction to personnel adjustment.* Boston: Allyn and Bacon, 1958.
21. Glanz, Edward C. Personnel and guidance work in a new era. *Junior coll. J.,* 1958, *24,* 141-145.
22. Glanz, Edward C. *Groups in guidance.* Boston: Allyn and Bacon, 1962.
23. Glanz, Edward C. The faculty team in general education. *J. Higher Educ.,* 1956, *26,* 389-392.
24. Hoppock, Robert. Group guidance. New York: McGraw-Hill, 1949.
25. Katz, Martin. *You: today and tomorrow.* (3rd. ed.) Princeton, N. J.: Educational Testing Service, 1959.
26. Mahoney, Harold, & Engle, R. *Points for decision.* (Rev.). Yonkers-on-Hudson, New York: World Book Co., 1961.
27. Richardson, Harold, & Borow, Henry. Evaluation of a technique of group orientation for vocational counseling. *Educ. psychol. Measmt.,* 1952, *12,* 587-597.
28. Warters, Jane. *Guidance in groups.* New York: McGraw-Hill, 1959.

IV. *Group Work and Human Relations*

29. American Council on Education. *Helping teachers understand children.* Washington, D. C.: American Council on Education, 1945.

30. Association for Supervision and Curriculum Development. *Fostering mental health in our schools*. Washington, D. C.: National Education Association, 1950.
31. Association for Supervision and Curriculum Development. *Guidance in the curriculum*. Washington, D. C.: National Education Association, 1955.
32. Benne, K., & Muntyan, N. *Human relations in curriculum change*. New York: The Dryden Press, 1951.
33. Cartwright, Darwin, & Zander, Alvin. (eds.) *Group dynamics: research and theory*. Evanston, Ill.: Row Peterson & Company, 1953.
34. Founce, Roland C., & Bossing, Nelson L. *Developing the core curriculum*. Englewood Cliffs, N. J.: Prentice-Hall, 1952.
35. Kolinsky, Ruth, & Witmer, Helen I. *Community programs for mental health*. Cambridge, Mass.: Harvard University Press, 1955.
36. National Society for the Study of Education. *Mental health in modern education*, Fifty-fourth Yearbook. Chicago: University of Chicago Press, 1955, part 2.
37. Hymes, James L., Jr. *A child development point of view*. Englewood Cliffs, N. J.: Prentice-Hall, 1955.
38. Prescott, Daniel A. *The child in the educative process*. New York: McGraw-Hill, 1957.
39. Redl, Fritz, & Wattenberg, William W. *Mental hygiene in teaching*. (Rev. ed.) New York: Harcourt Brace and Company, 1959.
40. Samler, Joseph, *et al. Basic approaches to mental health in the schools*. Washington, D. C.: American Personnel and Guidance Association, 1959. (Reprint series of seven articles from the *Personnel and Guidance Journal*, 1958-1959.)
41. Thelen, Herbert A. *Dynamics of groups at work*. Chicago: University of Chicago Press, 1954.

V. *General Sources*

42. Barry, Ruth, & Wolf, Beverly. *Modern issues in guidance-personnel work*. New York: Bureau of Publications, Teachers College, Columbia University, 1957.
43. Glanz, Edward C., & Penney, James F. Developing a cooperative research design for curriculum validation. *J. Higher Educ., 39*, 39-44.
44. Ivy, Allan F. A study of two types of guidance staff organizations and their relationship to student perception and use of college guidance services. Unpublished Ed.D. dissertation, Harvard University, 1959.
45. Lloyd-Jones, Esther M. Personnel work and general education, in National Society for the Study of Education, *General education*, Fifty-first Yearbook. Chicago: University of Chicago Press, 1952. Part I, 214-229.
46. National Society for the Study of Education. *General education*, Fifty-first Yearbook. Chicago: University of Chicago Press, 1952.
47. Wrenn, C. Gilbert. Professions and professional membership. *Occupations*, 1951, *30*, 24-29.
48. Wrenn, C. Gilbert. Status and role of the school counselor. *Personnel guid. J.*, 1957, *36*, 175-183.

SOME ASPECTS OF DEVELOPMENTAL GUIDANCE WITHIN AN EXISTENTIAL CONTEXT

Joseph S. Zaccaria
University of Illinois

In this paper developmental guidance and existentialism are viewed as parallel but relatively independent modes of thought. The major theoretical dimensions of developmental guidance are summarized and a brief comparison between developmental guidance and existentialism is made. Certain aspects of existential thought are related to some principles of developmental guidance. Existentialism can provide an idiographic dimension to the fundamentally nomoethetic theoretical orientation of developmental guidance by complementing an objective understanding of the individual with a subjective understanding.

In its quest for a more adequate conceptual framework, the field of counseling and guidance has increasingly drawn concepts and principles from that broad sector of thought in the behavioral sciences known as developmentalism. There has been a trend in both the literature and research in the counseling field toward viewing the individual in a process of change and development over a considerable period of time, the change leading to progressive stages of differentiation and complexity. Developmentalism as it relates to humans encompasses a number of basic concepts which, when systematically incorporated into guidance thought and practice, has contributed to that mode of thought known as the developmental approach to guidance. Developmental guidance has been described both in the form of major publications (Farwell & Peters, 1959; Little & Chapman, 1953; Mathewson, 1962) and in synoptic form (Tyler, 1961; Zaccaria, 1966).

NATURE OF DEVELOPMENTAL GUIDANCE

Because human development is continuous and the individual must approach and master a lifelong series of societal demands (developmental tasks) if he is to achieve optimum development (self-actualization), developmental guidance is generally envisioned as a relatively long-term endeavor. The extension of counseling and guidance into the elementary school setting reflects the influence of developmentalism coupled with a growing belief that our society should provide the individual with help throughout the entire span of his education if the goals of education and guidance are to become more than empty platitudes or hollow objectives.

Developmental guidance is cumulative, with the guidance process at one level of education building upon the guidance prior levels of education and articulating with the counseling and guidance that will follow. Developmental

Reprinted by permission of the author and *Personnel and Guidance Journal,* January 1969, 440-445.

guidance is also multiphasic, concentrating on the total development of the individual rather than on a few areas of problems, crises, choices, or adjustment. The needs of the individual are considered within the context of his sociocultural milieu. The twin emphases of problem prevention and remediation are superseded by the more dominant concern for fostering the positive development of all aspects of the individual's life.

As new dimensions of thought have become part of its theoretical fabric and as it has begun to become operational in the school setting, developmental guidance has been described as a concept in transition (Zaccaria, 1966). Thus, developmental guidance has been defined as

> the systematic, professional process of helping the individual through educative and interpretive procedures to gain a better understanding of his own characteristics and potentialities and to relate himself more satisfactorily to social requirements and opportunities, in accord with social and moral values [Mathewson, 1962, p. 141].

Operationally, the developmental approach to guidance emphasizes individual casework, consultation, coordination, programming, counseling, and related group work among the wide range of functions for realizing its goals.

DEVELOPMENTAL GUIDANCE AND EXISTENTIALISM

Paralleling the emergence of developmental guidance, but evolving independently from it, has been the existential movement. In actuality it would be more accurate to speak in terms of existential modes of thought, rather than an existential movement as such. Existential thought is a dynamic and vital force in the helping professions. To date, the greatest impact of existentialism has been felt in the areas of counseling and psychotherapy. Recently, however, existentialism has been explored as a backdrop for contemporary theories of vocational development (Simon, 1966), as a philosophical foundation for the guidance program (Beck, 1963), and as a theoretical stance for the entire educational process (Kneller, 1958).

There are a number of barriers to overcome in relating existentialism to developmental guidance. Historically, for example, existentialism has evolved from 19th century European philosophical inquiry, while developmental guidance has emerged within the context of 20th century American behavioral sciences. While developmental guidance thought clearly flows from the findings of scientific investigations concerning the nature and dynamics of human development, existential thinking is clearly *a*scientific. The terminology of developmental guidance has been quite explicit, couched in terms well understood by behavioral scientists, the general educators, and guidance personnel. Existential concepts, on the other hand, have remained somewhat esoteric and ill-defined. Indeed, the existentialists feel that the real meaning of a concept is lost in the process of definition. Viewing existentialism from a scientific frame of reference, Landsman (1965) notes the lack of empirical basis, public definition, and rigorous methodology in existential thought and literature.

Both developmental guidance and existentialism are emergent modes of thought. Yet, while the developmental approach to guidance has continued to remain well-articulated in terms of general theoretical orientation, presuppositions, goals, etc., there can be seen within the broad spectrum of existentialism some profound differences and cleavages of thought. Concepts have no inherent meanings in and of themselves, but derive their meanings from the contexts in which they are used. There is a distinct danger that an attempt to relate the fluid and multifaceted dimensions of existential thought with an emerging developmental approach to guidance may result in a poorly articulated and possibly incongruous amalgamation. While it may be the case that differences in general orientation, foci, and contexts may, in the long run, render developmental guidance and existential thought mutually exclusive and, therefore, theoretically incompatible, a preliminary exploration within an articulative context may prove to be meaningful to subsequent thought and practice.

A CONTEXT FOR COMPARISON

To date, the theoretical frame of reference for developmental guidance has emerged largely within a nomothetic rather than an idiographic context. The constructs utilized from the behavioral sciences have been those which have attempted to describe the dynamics of development of the typical person or of groups of typical individuals. These constructs are broad and encompassing in an attempt to describe typical patterns of growth and maturation in our culture. While there has been a passing nod to the consideration of the development of the individual as a unique person, the general theoretical focus of developmental guidance has continued to stress the general similarities resulting from constitutional factors (genetic makeup), the common effects of socialization, and the molding effect of the entire sociocultural milieu. Thus, the major unifying theoretical constructs for developmental guidance have been developmental stages, developmental tasks, vocational developmental tasks, psychosocial crises, etc.

Mathewson (1962) has warned about the use of developmental tasks and related concepts, noting that stereotypes of nomothetic behavior may or may not apply to a particular individual. Beck is also concerned about nomothetic approaches to studying individuals, noting that the newer thinking, i.e., existentialism, is an attempt to see the individual man as a meaningful whole, not as the product of our preconceptions, as a system-fitting mosaic piece, or as a statistical probability" (1963, p. 108). It is in the context of the uniqueness of the individual and his subjective world of meaning that existential thought can make a contribution to developmental guidance, and it is within this context that some principles of developmental guidance are stated below and amplified within an existential frame of reference.

Principle 1. Developmental guidance is a systematic professional process which utilizes literature and research in various source fields as the bases for theory and practice.

To date, developmental guidance has drawn concepts from the behavioral sciences and as noted above, its theoretical constructs have remained largely nomothetic. The role of the guidance worker has been viewed in terms of a human development consultant or an applied behavioral scientist. The existentialist adds that each person has two selves. One self (the empirical self) is historically conditioned and is responsive to the demands of the world around him. The empirical self is predictable and can be studied by the traditional methods of psychology and the other behavioral sciences. Developmental psychology, for example, has studied the empirical self and has described the course of human development in terms of common learnings (developmental tasks) and the societal forces (socialization and cultural patterning) which act on individuals resulting in similar courses of development (developmental stages) among members of a given society.

There is also, however, a second and more important dimension to the self. This, the existentialists note, is the "transcendent self" or the "authentic self" which is the source of meaning for the individual. This self is beyond the scope of empirical methods and procedures. The authentic self or the transcendent self refers to those aspects of the self-concept in which the individual is unique as a person. Thus, there is a scientific understanding *about* an individual and existential understanding of the individual.

The existentialist would hope to complement the systematic nomothetic view of the person from an external frame of reference with an idiographic view of the individual within an internal existential frame of reference. A distinction is therefore necessary first between the guidance worker attempting to understand the dynamics of the individual's personality functioning within an objective theoretical context and second, the guidance worker as a human being in a personal encounter with another human being, attempting to enter into that person's subjective world. Existentialism does not suggest an entirely new approach to the helping relationship, nor does it offer a new set of techniques. Rather, it adds a new modality of thought to the guidance worker's theory and suggests an additional dimension to the helping relationship. May notes, "The grasping of the being of the other person occurs on quite a different level from our knowledge of scientific things about him" (1958, p. 38). In the broadest sense, therefore, existentialism constitutes a source field for additional dimensions to the theory and practice of developmental guidance.

Principle 2.   The prime goal of developmental guidance is to foster the worth and dignity of the individual by promoting his maximum development.

The preceding statement has become an implicit axiom for all approaches to guidance. It is the developmental orientation, however, that stresses facilitating human development in both a remedial, preventive, and positive growth context. An existential orientation can help to convert the above humanistic axiom to a realistic objective and can contribute meaning to this often quoted objective which in some other contexts may be, in reality, mere empty words. The existentialist feels that the worth and dignity of the individual is best fostered by facilitating within him responsible independence through meaningful choice. In a sense, anyone who chooses to evaluate and determine his destiny through responsible choice is operating within an implicitly existential framework. It is when the existential dimension becomes both explicit and well-integrated with the other aspects of guidance that the practice of the guidance worker can take on the rich dimension of meaning that existentialism offers.

Principle 3.   Developmental guidance attempts to foster self-understanding within the individual in order that he might use this self-understanding to make the most adequate choices and decisions from among the alternative courses of action available to him.

The existentialist holds that while much of the natural world operates within a deterministic framework, man has freedom of choice. Indeed, man *must* make choices. With freedom of choice, however, goes the responsibility for having made a choice. Like developmental guidance, existentialism emphasizes that the first step toward responsible choice is for the individual to begin to become aware of who he is (meaning) and subsequently to be fully responsible for his own existence (responsible independence). The importance of self-understanding is emphasized by Allport when he says, "The process of becoming is largely a matter of organizing transitory impulses into a pattern of striving and interest in which the element of self-awareness plays a large part" (1955, p. 29).

In fostering self-understanding, developmental guidance helps the individual to find meaning for himself and subsequently to begin to realize his potential, i.e., to become that self which the individual really is, by implementing his self-concept through choice and action. Thus it is through an adequate implementation of the self-concept that the individual relates himself satisfactorily with social requirements and opportunities. But the self-concepts must be developed before it can be implemented. An existential focus upon meaning, choice, responsibility, etc., would appear to assist the guidance worker in helping the individual to develop the subjective dimension of his meaning of life as it relates to his self-concept.

Principle 4. Human development is relatively continuous and can be understood and facilitated by focusing upon the individual's approach to societal demands (developmental tasks) and his subsequent mastery or lack of mastery of these tasks.

For the purposes of description, the behavioral sciences have abstracted the course of human development into a series of developmental stages, viz., infancy, babyhood, childhood, preadolescence, adolescence, adulthood, etc., each of which is characterized by a set of common demands made upon the individual. Having completed successfully one stage of development the individual is then "free to abandon the habits appropriate to this stage and to enter the mature reaches of becoming" (Allport, 1955, p. 32). Affecting the individual's becoming are two sets of forces which can be described in terms of the nomothetic-idiographic continuum described above. One set of forces (socialization, patterning, and conformity) tend to influence the individual's becoming by attempting to make him similar to other members of the society of which he is a part. The limiting forces are necessary and legitimate, operating through the family, secondary institutions, cultural symbols, social values, etc. In a sense they define the limits of acceptable behavior within the culture. The existential protest against these forces is a reaction against the growing sense of alienation, rootlessness, fragmentization, and meaninglessness of much of life resulting in part from an overemphasis upon the conforming nomothetic dimension of development.

The second set of forces have their origin within the individual and emphasize self-expression through uniqueness and individuality. It is the latter dimension of existence that the existentialist stresses. Realizing the importance of societal norms, the existentialist emphasizes that the primary vehicle for becoming one's self is the realization of one's potential for individuality. Thus, to become one's self is to develop responsible independence and individuality within societal limits. Individuality does not develop in a vacuum but in the crucible of societal living and against the backdrop of cultural life. Although the individual is a part of a culture and a member of society, his being is separate from them.

Principle 5. Developmental guidance attempts to facilitate the individual's growth and development by helping him to approach and master developmental tasks.

Human development, i.e., the process of an individual's becoming, consists largely of his decisions and subsequent courses of action. Man is what he does and man is fashioned by his acts, i.e., existence precedes essence. While it is true that the individual lives within a cultural milieu and while it is also true that the culture delimits a range of sanctioned behavior for its members, nomothetic concepts such as basic personality, modal personality, class-linked behavior, etc., are of secondary importance in understanding and helping individuals. Allport, for example, says:

> While we accept certain cultural values as appropriate, as important for our own course of becoming, it is especially true that we are all rebels, deviants, and individualists. Some elements in our culture we reject altogether; many we adopt as mere opportunistic habits, and even those elements that we genuinely appropriate we refashion to fit our own personal style of life. Culture is a condition of becoming but is not itself the full stencil [1955, p. 82].

Therefore, developmental guidance can help the individual more effectively by complementing the decision-making process and the mastery of developmental tasks in the nomothetic context with a consideration of the implementation of the individual's unique meaning structure.

A PERSPECTIVE

The arena of controversy in the field of counseling and guidance is filled with both pseudo and real issues. The field appears to be moving toward a pattern similar to those in other fields in which extreme either/or positions are being mediated by continua of thought and by syntheses of related ideas. The history of guidance reveals a number of conceptual views of man as practitioners have attempted to provide individuals with help. The early decades of the guidance movement seemed to be dominated by a view of "economic man" as the individual was viewed as a worker, an earner, and an economic producer. More recently man has been viewed as "democratic man," "psychological man," and "man as a social unit" (Mathewson, 1962). An emerging view of man is that of "existential man," i.e., man in a process of becoming. It appears that the maturity of the field of counseling and guidance is beginning to enable it to function satisfactorily within emerging theoretical contexts with a growing assurance that future theory-building will supplant contemporary thought with more adequate conceptual frameworks.

A preliminary exploration of some aspects of developmental guidance within an existential context suggests that the existential mode of thought can add significant dimensions to this approach. The inherent danger in attempting to relate broad and diversified emerging constructs is that the resultant end product may represent a superficial eclecticism rather than a meaningful creative integration of related modes of thought.

REFERENCES

Allport, G. W. *Becoming.* New Haven, Connecticut: Yale University Press, 1955.

Beck, C. E. *Philosophical foundations of guidance.* Englewood Cliffs, New Jersey: Prentice-Hall, 1963.

Farwell, G., & Peters, H. J. *Guidance: a developmental approach.* Chicago: Rand McNally, 1959.

Kneller, G. F. *Existentialism and education.* New York: Wiley, 1958.

Landsman, T. Existentialism in counseling: the scientific view. *Personnel and Guidance Journal,* 1965, *43,* 568-573.

Little, W., & Chapman, A. L. *Developmental guidance in the secondary school.* New York: McGraw-Hill, 1953.

Mathewson, R. H. *Guidance policy and practice.* New York: Harper and Row, 1962.

May, R. *Existence.* New York: Basic Books, 1958.

Simon, J. An existential view of vocational development. *Personnel and Guidance Journal,* 1966, *44,* 604-610.

Tyler, L. E. *The work of the counselor.* New York: Appleton-Century-Crofts, 1961.

Zaccaria, J. S. Developmental guidance: Past, present and future. *School Counselor,* 1966, *13,* 226-229.

SOME PHILOSOPHICAL PROBLEMS IN MENTAL DISORDER AND ITS TREATMENT[1]

O. Hobart Mowrer
University of Illinois

In this provocative article, the author discusses some of the scientific and philosophical implications of Freudian theory, and takes the position that certain aspects of the Freudian view must be revised if we are to have a valid conception of neurosis and reliable methods for its alleviation and prevention. Whereas the Freudian view considers neurosis a disease, the causative factors of which lie *outside* the individual, Dr. Mowrer contends that neurosis is a *way of life* which is largely determined by the individual himself. An individual's neurosis, one may say, is his "own idea."

The root cause of neurosis is the denial, repression and repudiation of guilt; and the aim of therapy, therefore, should be to help the patient allow

Reprinted by permission of the author and the *Harvard Educational Review,* Vol. 23, No. 2, Spring 1953, 117-127.

[1]This article is based upon a lecture delivered in the Great Hall of the Cooper Union in New York on January 16, 1953, as part of a lecture series entitled "Our Search for Mental Health."

this repressed guilt to return to consciousness, thereby enabling him to reassume the responsibility he has been trying to avoid. The re-acknowledgment of guilt and self-criticism is essential if the neurotic is to achieve mental health.

In the final section of the paper, Dr. Mowrer presents a critique of Freud's views on religion and metaphysics.

Dr. Mowrer is Research Professor in Psychology at the University of Illinois. He is President-elect of the American Psychological Association, and is currently President of the Division of Clinical and Abnormal Psychology and the Division of Personality and Social Psychology of that organization.

Asked if psychoanalysis gives us any particular philosophy of life, Freud characteristically replied that the only philosophy to which psychoanalysis leads is that of science in general. And this he vigorously contrasted with the *Weltanschauung*, the "world view" or philosophy, of religion. The possession of the kind of *Weltanschauung* that religion provides is, said Freud, "one of the ideal wishes of mankind. When one believes in such a thing, one feels secure in life, one knows what one ought to strive after, and how one ought to organize one's emotions and interests to the best purpose" (1, p. 216).

But "if this is what is meant by *Weltanschauung*," Freud continued, "then the question is an easy one for psychoanalysis to answer. As a specialized science, a branch of psychology — 'depth-psychology' or psychology of the unconscious — [psychoanalysis] is quite unsuited to form a *Weltanschauung* of its own; it must accept that of science in general" (1, p. 217).

The sentences just quoted are from the last chapter, entitled "A Philosophy of Life," of Freud's book, *New Introductory Lectures on Psychoanalysis* (1). In this chapter Freud develops at length his conception of the scientific outlook for man, its limitations and its possibilities. "It asserts," he says, "that there is no other source of knowledge of the universe, but the intellectual manipulation of carefully verified observations, in fact, what is called research, and that no knowledge can be obtained from revelation, intuition or inspiration" (1, p. 217). And "intuition and inspiration," Freud tells us, "can safely be counted as illusions, as fulfilments of wishes, [having] a purely emotional basis" (1, p. 218).

It will be the first task of this paper to show that one of the principal reasons why Freudian psychoanalysis has had such a widespread appeal in our time is that it, itself, generates or implies a *Weltanschauung* with some of the very qualities that its founder regarded as so objectionable and so contrary to the procedures and values of science. Indeed, as will be indicated a little later, many of the things which Freud said about the religious orientation apply much more aptly and specifically to his own position — or at least what most people regard as his position — than to the one he was criticizing.

I. THE FREUDIAN CONCEPTION OF NEUROSIS

Freud's theory concerning the causation and treatment of those personality difficulties which we commonly call neurosis can be most quickly summarized by means of a simple diagram. This theory starts (Figure 1) with some "instinctual force" or drive, D_1, demanding gratification in the form of some action or response, R_1. However, the resulting behavior, particularly if it is motivated by sex or hostility, is likely to be socially disapproved and to bring down upon the individual (represented by the circle in the diagram) something called punishment. This is represented here as a second drive, D_2, which commonly takes the form of pain of some sort. And pain, as we well know, produces, among other effects, an emotional reaction of *fear*. This we have labeled, R_2.

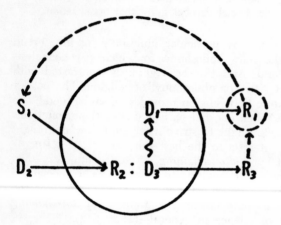

Figure 1

The Freudian conception of neurosis represented diagrammatically.

What has been said thus far will have been easy enough to follow, but what comes next will require closer attention. It will be noted that there is a broken line extending from the forbidden behavior, R_1, over to something labeled S_1. S_1 is simply a designation for the incidental stimulation which accompanies the performance of R_1, the stimulation, the happenings, the sensations that make us aware that we are performing, have just performed, or are *about* to perform the response, R_1. If, now, R_1 is punished, if, that is to say, the occurrence of R_1 is followed by D_2, then we see that S_1 will be, as we say, "associated" with D_2, with the result that the fear reaction, R_2, that is produced by the punishment tends to get connected, by a form of learning which we call *conditioning*, to S_1. This means, quite simply, that when the individual later starts to gratify D_1 by making response R_1, he will, by virtue of the occurrence of S_1, be reminded of the punishment and will experience anticipatory fear. That is to say, the performance or contemplation of R_1 will arouse S_1, and S_1 will now produce the fear reaction R_2.

If the reader has followed the discussion thus far, he will readily see how it will continue, in terms of Freud's theory. The fear response R_2, aroused by the contemplated performance of the socially disapproved response, R_1, will create a third drive, D_3, and the individual will be prompted, if this fear drive is at all powerful, to do whatever he or she can to diminish it. The solution, at least in principle, is perfectly straightforward. Since R_1, through the mediation of S_1, is arousing the fear drive D_3, all the individual has to do is to make an incompatible response, R_3 — some response that will *stop*, or "inhibit," R_1. One might say that the fear drive, D_3, thus *blocks*, by a form of "feedback," the intended gratification of D_1.

But this is not quite the end of the story. Obviously when one experiences desire and fear simultaneously, there is conflict; and conflict, as we all well know, is painful. In most instances we manage sooner or later, to resolve conflicts realistically, integratively; but as Freud has repeatedly emphasized, for the child there is likely to be no integrative, no realistic solution to either his sexual or aggressive needs. And every expression of these impulses is regarded as "bad"; and all such behavior is so persistently and so severely punished that, finally, in many instances the individual resorts to a desperate expedient. The impulse or desire, D_1, proves to be so painfully irreconcilable with the fear drive, D_3 that the individual begins, according to Freud, to do a very remarkable thing: he begins to *repress* D_1 to refuse to access to consciousness, to deny its very existence, as indicated in the diagram by the wavy arrow. When thus finally excluded from consciousness, D_1 produces no temptation and no fear, and intrapsychic peace is once again restored. The conflict is ended, and the individual is enormously relieved.

Sometimes, says Freud, these repressive solutions to conflicts prove enduringly satisfactory; indeed, he even thought that civilization itself is, in part, built upon the capacity of human beings to disown and deny certain brutish impulses more or less permanently. In other instances, however, this strategy meets with very imperfect success. Some impulses — and here Freud pointed particularly to sex, though to some extent also to aggression — these impulses, though they lose the struggle for conscious acknowledgment and direct gratification, continue to assert themselves but now "unconsciously," "neurotically." With the return or, rather, threatened return of repressed impulses to awareness, old conflicts are partially reactivated and the individual experiences the peculiar form of dread or panic known as neurotic anxiety. The resulting actions which we call *symptoms* are, said Freud, a compromise formation which serves the double purpose of (a) controlling the neurotic anxiety, so that it is not so unbearable as it otherwise would be and at the same time (b) allowing the imprisoned, repudiated impulses which lie behind the anxiety to achieve at least a partial, surreptitious satisfaction.

II. THE PHILOSOPHY IMPLICIT IN FREUDIANISM

In the interest of brevity we have had to be highly synoptic here, but the foregoing is neither unfair nor inaccurate as a summary of the Freudian position. And this position, we must agree, is not an unreasonable one. It could be well that this is the way neurosis develops and manifests itself. But more to the point is the question: Is the position, or theory, the *true* one? Does it conform to the clinical facts? Growing evidence indicates that in one important respect it does not.

It will presently be indicated wherein the Freudian view has to be drastically revised if we are to have a really sound conception of neurosis and reliable procedures for its alleviation and prevention. For the moment, however, let us examine the Freudian view of neurosis in the context of Freud's remarks, quoted at the outset, concerning psychoanalysis and the philosophical views one espouses. Despite Freud's assertions to the contrary, there can be no doubt that psychoanalysis does generate some very specific and — one may add — rather singular philosophical implications, implications which laymen have been quick to sense — and either eagerly embrace or emphatically reject!

Traditionally, it was the individual's "own fault" if he got something wrong with him mentally. He was, in some sense, "responsible." Perhaps the alleged causal sequence was a little obscure or hard to trace, but the disturbance was always, in principle, due to something which the individual had himself *done*. Neurosis was, in short, either a natural or supernatural retribution for misconduct.

How very different is the Freudian position. Immediately we note that in this frame of reference neurosis is a result of something that has been *done to* the individual. He has been punished so severely, we are told, for attempting to gratify natural, biologically given needs that he is thrown into conflicts that can be resolved only by repression — and this predisposes the individual to neurosis. Mental disease is thus not a disgrace, not a stigma, not something to feel guilty or ashamed of; it is something that "might happen to anybody."

What a relief it is to discover that it is one's parents, and behind them the irrationality of "society," itself, that have caused one's neurotic suffering! And how comforting to learn, if one is oneself a parent, that it is the very excess of moral zeal on the part of parents that causes neurosis and that one may, indeed *should*, be less concerned about the moral training of one's children and *more* interested in seeing that their instinctual outlets do not become obstructed!

Surely it is not hard to see how profound and how primordial an appeal this kind of theorizing or, may we say, philosophizing must have to many rebellious, immature persons and, in some degree, to all of us. Freud was himself very active in pointing out the ambivalence, or mixed feelings, which every human being has toward the regulations and restraints which are necessarily imposed by the conditions of social life. Yet psychoanalysis fans the hope that we can, and for our own psychological health *should*, take these restraints and regulations somewhat less seriously than we have traditionally thought we should.

In the same chapter from which the earlier quotations are taken one finds Freud making statements such as the following one:

> The same father (the parental function) who gave the child his life and preserved it from the dangers which that life involves, also taught it what it may or may not do, made it accept certain limitations of its instinctual wishes, and told it what consideration it would be expected to show towards its parents and brothers and sisters, if it wanted to be tolerated and liked as a member of the family circle, and later on of more extensive groups (1, p. 224).

This universal dependence upon the father, says Freud, has caused mankind to create the notion of a Heavenly Father and the attendant conceptions of salvation and damnation which are part and parcel of religious ideology. Then there follows this remarkable passage:

> . . . the ban which religion has imposed upon thought in the interests of its own preservation is by no means without danger both for the individual and for society. Analytic experience has taught us that such prohibi-

tions, even though they were originally confined to some particular field, have a tendency to spread, and then become the cause of severe inhibitions in people's lives. In women a process of this sort can be observed to follow from the prohibition against their occupying themselves, even in thought, with the sexual side of their nature. The biographies of almost all eminent people of past times show the disastrous results of the inhibition of thought by religion (1, p. 234).

Yet this is the author who in the same context condemns the religious *Weltanschauung* as based upon illusions, "as fulfilments of wishes," with a "purely emotional basis." In all soberness we must ask ourselves: Which is likely to have the more profound "emotional" appeal, a philosophy which calls for restraint and sacrifice, or one which ridicules and promises to deliver us from such limitations? If at this point one becomes confused by Freud's arguments, it is scarcely surprising. Traditionally religion, more than any other great social institution, has been concerned with ethics, with morality, with the planned, organized, integrated style of life, with, that is to say, the attainment of satisfactions and happiness through the strategy of postponement, saving, sacrifice, and labor. Yet we are now asked to believe that the motives for such a regulated, controlled existence are unrealistic, illusory, emotionally biased! Surely it is psychoanalysis that enflames and appeals to the more primitively emotional side of our natures; and contemporary clinical researches are showing that psychoanalysis also has more than its fair share of that which is unrealistic and illusory.

III. A MORE DEFENSIBLE VIEW OF NEUROSIS

Let us now sketch another way of looking at neurosis and the therapeutic challenge it offers to us. Here (see Figure 2) we start, as does Freud, with some drive or desire, D_1, instigating some form of gratification, R_1. Again, with Freud, we assume that this behavior elicits punishment, D_2, and that

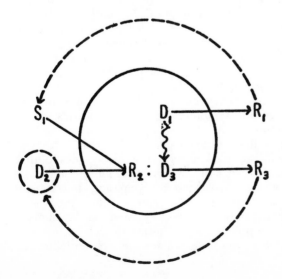

Figure 2

A modified conception of neurosis which eliminates the difficulties inherent in Freudian theory.

the fear $(R_2:D_3)$ produced by this punishment becomes connected, through conditioning, to the incidental stimulation, S_1, which R_1 produces.

But at this point our views diverge sharply from those of Freud. We assume that the individual headed for neurotic troubles is one who, when impulse and fear are in conflict, tries to resolve this conflict, not by controlling the impulse, but instead by *evasion and deception*. The fear we assume, results in behavior, R_3, which instead of blocking R_1 tries to prevent punishment, D_2 from occurring; and this strategy commonly involves secrecy and falsehood.

Some individuals have had so little moral training that, as long as they can avoid actual social chastisement, their actions, however deviant, bother them very little — and the deception involved in protecting these actions, even less. These are the characterless individuals known as psychopaths: the dead-beats, swindlers, confirmed liars and criminals. But for most persons who attempt to avoid punishment for disapproved action, the picture is very different. Even though they succeed in averting *external* punishment, their conscience "*hurts*" them — not only because of having engaged in behavior R_1, but also because of the duplicity. R_3, involved in concealing R_1.

Finally the fear, the guilt, the bad conscience which such an individual thus experiences will drive him to one of two things: he will either (a) confess and, as we say, "take his punishment," or (b) begin to *repress* (see wavy line in Figure 2) these emotions. If a person can, by repression, keep his conscience from "bothering" him, he will have achieved a kind of peace and freedom; he can engage in forbidden behavior R_1 without the occurrence of the complex of fear and guilt here labeled $R_2:D_3$.

But repression, as we have already seen, is likely to be imperfect, with the result that the forces which are thus excluded from direct awareness eventually express themselves in a very troublesome way, that is to say, as neurotic anxiety, depression, and inferiority feeling. And these painful emotions cause the afflicted individual to try to reduce or avoid them by whatever means he can discover, thus giving rise to those forms of behavior which we know as neurotic symptoms.

In the beginning and in the end, our theory is thus very similar to that of Freud. We assume, with him, that neurosis originates in a conflict between biological impulses and social fears, between forces of the *id* and those of the *superego;* and we assume that in the person destined to be neurotic such a conflict is resolved by the process known as repression. We further assume with Freud that repression is likely to be only partially effective and that the repressed forces, in attempting to get back into consciousness, will periodically besiege the ego in such a way as to produce neurotic anxiety, panic, or depression, and that neurotic symptoms are the individual's efforts to control these disagreeable experiences.

But in one respect there is a basic disagreement with Freud. He held that in the conflict between desire and conscience it is always desire that suffers and falls under repression, and that the energies thus imprisoned make themselves felt as neurotic emotions, which lead to symptoms. But it now appears that it is conscience, not desire, which is repressed and imprisoned in neurosis, and neurotic emotions and symptoms represent an involuntary — and often very alarming — outcropping, not of "instincts" such as lust and hostility, but of one's own denied sense of shame and self-criticism. In numerous technical publications the author has elaborated upon this distinction and given both logical and empirical support for it (3, 4, 5, 6). This conception of neurosis has far less appeal to neurotics and other immature persons than does the strictly Freudian conception. And it is, rather obviously, related to the traditional religious view in such matters, which is epitomized by the familiar adage: Be good and you will be happy, i.e., normal, non-neurotic. In contrast, the Freudian position says, in essence: Be happy (have pleasure) and you will be good. However much this point of view appeals to neurotic individuals, we are still very far from having seen it clinically confirmed.

IV. MENTAL HEALTH AND THE CAPACITY TO BE GUILTY, RESPONSIBLE

There is, moreover, another problem which we must face in this connection. In addition to appealing to the undisciplined, the rebellious, instinctual side of human personality, Freud's theory is likely to receive quite a different type of support. Note how very "scientific" it sounds. It does not talk about individual choice or responsibility: it puts everything in a strictly cause-and-effect framework, and all of the "causes," very conveniently, are placed *outside* the individual himself.

By contrast, the view of neurosis which has just been sketched focuses the spotlight, in a quite uncomfortable but often highly productive way, directly upon the individual himself. Discerning critics of this position have been quick to cry: "But you seem to be saying that if a person becomes neurotic, it is his own fault. Surely you cannot mean this and at the same time claim to take a scientific view of human nature." How often we have been told in recent decades that all behavior is "caused" and that the individual is not responsible, is not to blame or in any way at fault if he develops a neurosis! It is not surprising, therefore, if our position is quickly challenged on this score.

In replay we may say two things. First, it must be admitted that, according to this view, the neurotic individual *is* responsible in the sense that his neurosis is, one may say, his "own idea." Who urged him to meet the threat of punishment for socially disapproved behavior by deception and evasion? Who told or required him to turn against his conscience and repress it when it bothered him in connection with his various misdeeds? The Freudian view makes neurosis an illness which is created by others. Is it not rather an *invention*, a creation of the individual himself? It has been impressed upon us all too often that neurosis is a disease. This is wholly misleading. Neurosis is a *way of life*, and to liken it to a disease, however comforting for the moment, can only lead us into frustration and despair in the long run.

We need not become involved here in the subtleties of free-will vs. determinism. There is an eminently satisfactory scientific solution to this problem, but we cannot pursue it at this time (2). All that needs saying here is that neurosis, as a way of behaving, as a life style, is probably just as much the choice of the individual himself, just as much determined by himself as is any other form of conduct. If a person is responsible for *any* action, then he is neither more nor less responsible for the steps that lead to neurosis.

But there is an important sense in which the neurotic is *not* responsible. He is not responsible precisely in the sense that he *ought* to be. He tries to have his cake and eat it too; he tries to engage in certain forbidden actions and at the same time avoid the normal consequences of such actions. Irresponsibility is thus perhaps the neurotic's greatest offense; and one of the main objectives of therapy is to get the patient, little by little, to reverse this trend and become increasingly willing to *be* responsible, to take rather than evade consequences, and in this way to be changed by reality instead of trying to live on in a false world of his own creation. Personal freedom and psychological health imply, not an absence of guilt, but a lively capacity for it; and it is the very fact that the neurotic is denying, repressing, repudiating his guilt that is the root cause of his difficulties. In therapy we feel a distinct advance has been made when the patient begins to reacknowledge his guilts and moral fears and self-criticisms, for then, and then only, is he in a position to take realistic measures, as opposed to neurotic ones, for coping with his problems.

What has just been said may, in its brevity, sound very arbitrary. One of the difficulties in clinical writing is that so little of the evidence on which one's inferences are based can be readily conveyed to others. But perhaps a fragment of clinical material will illustrate the kind of observation which constantly intrudes itself upon our attention. A colleague recently gave the author the following excerpt from the opening remarks of a young man who had just reached a turning point in his treatment. The patient began as follows:

> I've been in a mood all week, and I'm just beginning to come to my senses. (Pause.) Talking about that, I, my wife, when she was commenting upon how lousy I've been feeling — she was a little mad at me yesterday — she said, "That's all you're interested in. You're just plain narcissistic — just interested in yourself and your school and so forth." And that's been pretty true, I guess.
>
> In fact, when I first read a little bit of Mowrer, when I was reading about the neurotic, the neurotic not being so far from the psychopath as we think, uh, this was completely foreign to me. (A little laugh.) Since the psychopath is, is completely rejected by society inasmuch as he just destroys, and is anti-, or a-social, is just, most of his behavior is just motivated against society when he does behave, uh, I couldn't place myself in the same boat. But I think recently, oh several weeks ago, I started seeing some of the same — in the same direction, I should say. When you have neurotic problems, you have enough conscience to work on that and develop it, but there is a lot of the same things. That is what I just saw.
>
> And that — I don't know — I didn't like the way Dorothy (his wife) said it about me, but, uh, it contained a large element of truth.

In this context the patient did not specify some of the more serious forms which his immaturities and deviations had taken, but the passage quoted serves well enough to illustrate the principle that re-acknowledgment of guilt and self-criticism is an essential and significant step along the road which the neurotic has to follow if he is to recover, if he is to leave his fool's paradise and return to responsibility and mental and moral health.

It would be possible to give many other clinical excerpts indicating that the neurotic, far from having *too* much guilt, as the Freudian position implies, has *too little*, too little in the sense of not letting it enter consciousness and participate in the control of his decisions and actions. The rightful aim of therapy, of a rational, *effective* therapy is, therefore, to help the patient allow his repressed guilt to return to consciousness and thereby enable him to re-assume the responsibility — and realistic learning — he has been trying to avoid.

V. ETHICS AND METAPHYSICS NOT INSEPARABLY LINKED

Finally, let us return to some of the other philosophical issues raised at the outset of this paper. The chapter by Freud on "A Philosophy of Life" from which the earlier quotations were taken contains one or two additional points which we must examine. In this chapter Freud goes on to attack religion most vigorously. He says:

> The truth could have been seen at any time, but it was long before anyone dared to say it aloud: the assertions made by religion that it could give protection and happiness to men, if they would only fulfil certain ethical obligations, were unworthy of belief. It seems not to be true that there is a power in the universe, which watches over the well-being of every individual with parental care and brings all his concerns to a happy ending (1 p. 229).
>
> . . . in our view the truth of religion may be altogether disregarded (1, p. 229).
>
> No attempt to minimize the importance of science can alter the fact that it attempts to take into account our dependence on the real external world, while religion is illusion, and it derives its strength from the fact that it falls in with our instinctual desires (1, p. 239).

As already indicated, there is another way of viewing the situation. But it will be more persuasive, perhaps, if another presents the argument. Dr. Jacob H. Conn, Assistant Professor of Psychiatry at Johns Hopkins University, has recently written to the author as follows:

> You may be interested in George Bernard Shaw's opinion as expressed in the speech which Don Juan makes in *Man and Superman*. The Devil has referred to Man as being an "engine of destruction," as the inventor of the rack, stake, gallows . . . gun, poison gas, and the "isms" by which men are "persuaded to become the most destructive of all the destroyers." Don Juan replies: "You take Man at his own opinion . . . . He loves to think of himself as bold and bad. He is neither one nor the other; he is only a coward. Call him tyrant, murderer, pirate, bully; and he will adore you and swagger about with the consciousness of having the blood of the old sea kings in his veins . . . . But call him coward and he will go mad with rage; he will face death to outface that stinging truth. Man gives every reason for his conduct save one, every excuse for his crimes save one; that is his cowardice.

To this Dr. Conn adds the following terse comment: "I believe Shaw was a better *Menschen Kenner* [student of man] than Freud. . . . Man would rather admit incest and hostility than inadequacy." With this thought in mind, we may ask once again whether religion, with its ethical goals, is more or less irrational, emotional, "instinctual" in its appeal than is Freudian psychoanalysis!

But in questioning and opposing the Freudian position on this score, one is likely to be misunderstood. It is easy to assume that if one agrees with some of the moral and social teachings of religion one is committed to the supernatural trappings of religion as well. This is not in the least true. One can substitute the scientific world view for the speculative one of religion without having to infer that *everything* religion has stood for is bogus. The primary, the socially and historically most important concern of religion has been the *moral* concern, and metaphysics has been introduced simply as a means of trying to make moral principles more impressive and to insure obedience to them. While this tactic may have seemed justifiable in the past, it has historically backfired: Many modern men and women look with suspicion and contempt upon any enterprise that would enforce morality with a myth, that would try to teach honesty with a dishonesty, with what many regard as a cosmic lie.

This is the error, the immorality of which traditional religion today stands accused, and it is not yet certain how it will acquit itself. In the meantime, it remains for those persons devoted to the scientific *Weltanschauung*, with its emphasis upon empirical truth, to make sure that they do as good a job with the ethical and moral issue, as religion has done, with its metaphysics. And here, it seems, psychotherapists have a unique opportunity and obligation. In the intimacy and deep sincerity of the psychological consulting room, we have the immortal lessons of personal and interpersonal morality continually reimpressed upon us. And we must not be so energetic and overdetermined in our rejection of religious mythology that we become obdurate to the great ethical principles for which religion has also stood. These are man's psychological and social salvation, today as well as in the past.

In his calmer moments Freud acknowledged much of what we have here been saying. In fact, in the same chapter from which we have previously quoted, we find statements such as the following:

> It is true that from the applications of science, rules and recommendations for behavior may be deduced. In certain circumstances they may be the same as those which are laid down by religion . . . . (1, p. 219).
> The ethical commands, to which religion seeks to lend its weight, require some other foundations instead, for human society cannot do without them, and it is dangerous to link up obedience to them with religious belief (1, p. 230).

But Freud was not as explicit about all this as he might have been; and his teachings, transformed by his less prudent followers into what is popularly known as "Freudianism," have fostered the error — may we not say "illusion"? — of supposing that the *scientific* view of human nature and neurosis is one that repudiates ethics and ethical responsibility almost as completely as it does metaphysics. This is a confused point of view, and the issue involved is one that modern man, in his quest for a new, naturalistic view of himself and his universe, cannot afford to be confused about. I believe we may now be on our way to reducing and correcting the confusion which Freudianism, in both its popular and professional version, has unfortunately contributed in this connection, while at the same time preserving all therein that is technically sound and valid. The challenge of a new era of psychological understanding and achievement lies before us.

BIBLIOGRAPHY

1. Freud, Sigmund. *New Introductory Lectures on Psychoanalysis*. New York: W. W. Norton and Co., 1933.
2. Mowrer, O. Hobart. "Freedom and Responsibility — A Psychological Analysis." *J. of Legal Education*, (in press).
3. Mowrer, O. Hobart. "Learning Theory and the Neurotic Fallacy." *Amer. J. Orthopsychiatry*, 1952, 22, #4, 679-689.
4. Mowrer, O. Hobart. *Learning Theory and Personality Dynamics*. New York: Ronald Press Co., 1950.
5. Mowrer, O. Hobart. "Pain, Punishment, Guilt and Anxiety." In Hoch, Paul H. and Zubin, Joseph (Eds.) *Anxiety*. New York: Grune and Stratton, 1950. Pp 27-40.
6. Mowrer, O. Hobart. *Psychotherapy — Theory and Research*. New York: Ronald Press Co., 1953.

A CRITIQUE OF THE PHILOSOPHY OF MODERN GUIDANCE

James J. Cribbin

New York University

One of the most successful methods of stirring up low moans and muffled mutterings, particularly in a Catholic graduate school, is to embark upon a discussion of either "principles" or "philosophy." This is especially true of guidance courses in which the students are enrolled not to organize their ideas but to organize a program, not to take counsel within themselves as to the role of modern guidance in traditional education but to learn how to counsel others. Yet, the importance of both "principles" and "philosophy" is brought home in a striking manner when one reads:

At the beginning of this study we were primarily concerned with personnel practices and techniques. We had no clearly defined principles by which to proceed nor did we, at that time, feel any need for them. We were interested chiefly in introducing better guidance practices and were scarcely aware of the fact that such practices must ultimately be based upon sound psychological theory.[1]

If this happened in the green wood of experienced and sophisticated educators, one wonders what marvels take place daily in the dry of the ordinary school program.

Reprinted by permission of the author and *The Catholic Educational Review*, Vol. 53, No. 2, February 1955, 73-91.

[1]Sister Annette, "Psychological Principles," *Student Personnel Services in General Education*, edited by Paul J. Brouwer (Washington, D. C.: American Council on Education, 1949), p. 225. [Emphasis added.]

So far as guidance has reference to theoretical considerations, three procedural alternatives are open to every personnel worker. He may temporize, meeting each emergency and contingency on a catch-as-catch-can basis, a process which makes Jack an erratic if not dull counselor. On the other hand, like the educators referred to in the quotation above, he can cope with the complexities of guidance on a trial and error basis until he develops a "felt need" for some frame of reference which will afford him consistency in action. Or, finally, he can formulate a system of ideas and ideals to guide his efforts to assist students, conscious of the need to implement these ideas in a practical way yet convinced of the primacy of principles over procedures. If one may take for granted the superiority of this third approach, it should be evident that a critique of the philosophy of guidance may serve some useful, if perhaps minor, purpose. Moreover, it is equally clear that such an analysis should consider at least three factors: (1) the principles which are fundamental to the movement, (2) the nature of the guidance process, and (3) the objectives which it seeks to attain. It is the purpose of this paper, therefore, to examine modern guidance from these three points of view.[2]

THE TERM "PRINCIPLE" IN MODERN GUIDANCE

After examining more than forty-five definitions, descriptions and definitional distortions of the term *principle,* the writer abandoned hope of finding any univocal interpretation of the word. Most frequently it was either confused with, or employed as a synonym for, *assumption.* Less often it was used interchangeably with such concepts as: *major postulates, hypotheses, basic concepts, general statements, conclusions, aims, premises, propositions, basic connections, characteristics, accepted bases, generalizations* and so on.

1. Principle Identified With Assumption

The most common element of these wrestlings with the idea of a *principle* was to identify it with *assumption.* Thus, the first sentence in Little and Chapman's work reads, "Implicit in this book are certain fundamental assumptions."[3] Wrenn, in a similar vein, writes of the college personnel program. "This educational philosophy (the student personnel point of view) is based upon three assumptions."[4] Finally, Froehlich, who writes for the small secondary school, has as his first subheading of his initial chapter "*Basic Assumption of This Book.*"[5] The copyright dates of all three works are 1950 or later, but

---

[2]Certain limitations of this paper are obvious. It is concerned with ideas as presented in standard, general texts in guidance rather than with those which deal with a specific area of the personnel program, such as counseling. It is oriented about the secondary school, although much of what is presented applies equally well to the college level.

[3]Wilson Little and A. L. Chapman, *Development Guidance in Secondary School* (New York: McGraw-Hill Book Company, Inc., 1953), p. vii.

[4]C. Gilbert Wrenn, *Student Personnel Work in College* (New York: The Ronald Press Company, 1951), p. 4.

[5]Clifford P. Froehlich, *Guidance in Smaller Schools* (New York: McGraw-Hill Book Company, Inc., 1950), p. 7.

it would make little difference if one were to consult the first (1930) edition of Jones' standard work in which a similar identification is made.[6]

2. Principle Not Unrestricted

A second characteristic of guidance literature is a tendency to deny that a principle, once established, need be accepted. Smith maintains that ". . . even principles must not be accepted as inviolable."[7] Chisholm declares that ". . . . the following principles might be developed or accepted by the faculty."[8] Hamrin avers that ". . . it is not necessary for every teacher to believe each of these aspects of basic philosophy."[9] On the other hand, several authorities have approached the essential idea of a principle, even though they may have in other sections of their works contradicted themselves. For instance, Lefever, Turrell, and Weitzel insist that "the only way in which this ideal can be accomplished is to start with a body of principles upon which all reasonable people can agree."[10] But perhaps Erickson and Smith best illustrate the general tenor of intellectual vagueness when they hold that certain "basic assumptions" (sic) apply to all schools without regard to the factors which serve to condition the character of the techniques and practices employed.[11]

THREE REASONS FOR CONFUSION

1. Metaphysical Reason

The reasons for this situation are three in number, metaphysical, historical and logical. For the first, one must look to those who teach the teachers. Rather than dredge up worn out quotations from Dewey, it might be better to look to Childs, the disciple on whom perhaps more than on any other Dewey laid his experimentalist hands. In his most recent work, Childs makes the following points: (1) all principles may be revised or even discarded; (2) all "truths" are subject to correction; (3) all values have a natural basis and origin; (4) principles do not give security; (5) the criterion of truth is not first principles but consequences.[12] He then adds: "It (the experimental method) lodges the authority of a principle, a value, or a belief not in the nature of the originating source — be it supernatural revelation, hallowed institution, mystical experience, the so-called laws of mind, the intuitions of the heart, necessary axioms, or common sense — but rather in its actual working, that is, in its observable outcome or consequence."[13]

---

[6]Arthur J. Jones, *Principles of Guidance* (New York: McGraw-Hill Book Company, Inc., 1930), p. 33.

[7]Glenn E. Smith, *Principles and Practices of the Guidance Program* (New York: The Macmillan Company, 1951), p. 2.

[8]Leslie L. Chisholm, *Guiding Youth in the Secondary School* (New York: American Book Company, 1945), p. 70.

[9]Shirley A. Hamrin, *Guidance Talks to Teachers* (Bloomington, Illinois: McKnight and McKnight, 1947), p. 18.

[10]D. Welty Lefever, Archie M. Turrell, and Henry I. Weitzel, *Principles and Techniques of Guidance* (New York: The Ronald Press Company, 1941), pp. 30-31.

[11]Clifford E. Erickson and Glenn E. Smith, *Organization and Administration of Guidance Services* (New York: McGraw-Hill Company, Inc., 1947), p. vii.

[12]John L. Childs, *Education and Morals* (New York: Appleton-Century-Crofts, 1950), pp. 20, 30, 166, 174.

[13]*Ibid.*, p. 173.

2. Historical Reason

The second reason is largely historical in nature. Guidance has always been something of an educational tourniquet, seeking to staunch the loss of human potentialities for good caused by an educational system which at times cannot seem to make up its mind whether it is physician or butcher. Even as the charitable bystander has little time for pondering Harvey's theory as he seeks desperately to stop the blood gushing from the severed artery, so guidance workers have been so beset by the pressing need to minister to those requiring immediate attention that they have had little time for the reflective mediations so dear, in theory at least, to the heart of the metaphysician. On the other hand, it would be unfair to imply that personnel workers have been unaware of the need for serious consideration of the nature, scope, content, ends, and means of guidance. Young social movements develop through a process of idea conflict. Guidance is young and has had more than its share of discussion and debate.[14]

3. Logical Reason

The final reason for confusion with reference to the meaning of principle is logical, namely, a failure to distinguish clearly between such terms as *principle, policy, rule,* and *practice.* Strictly speaking, a principle refers to a universal judgment or truth which, because it takes into account only essential factors, applies to every person, problem, or situation. *Policy,* on the other hand, has reference to all cases within a particular class, taking into account the pattern of generalized circumstances which apply to a general class of person, problem, or situation. Thus, *policy* and *rule* refer to basically the same idea, the former being a general guide for action which allows for individual discretion within broad limits, while the latter is a mandatory prescription of procedure. *Practice,* of course, has to do with the "here and now," a procedure to meet the particular circumstances of a specific person, problem, or situation.[15] Thus, it is a *principle* that one can not teach without a clear understanding of the nature of the educand. It is the *policy* of schools to employ tests in an effort to gain a clearer understanding of the student. It is the *practice* in this school to administer this or that test. The principal may make it a *rule* that no test is to be administered after 2 P.M., or on the day preceding or following a holiday.

Although the distinctions made may appear to be "much ado about nothing," the fact remains that the guidance of youth is far too important a task to be founded on the mere "takings for granted" which are assump-

---

[14]Cf. Jane Warters, *High-School Personnel Work Today* (New York: McGraw-Hill Book Company, Inc., 1946), chap. ii. Critics of guidance have stressed the inability of authorities to formulate a definition of guidance which will be acceptable to all. Cf. Nelson L. Bossing, *Principles of Secondary Education* (New York: Prentice-Hall, Inc., 1949), pp. 405-13, especially footnote 20, p. 408. On the other hand, the needs to be met and the services to be rendered in the guidance program are quite clearly defined. Moreover, there is at least as much uniformity in content and emphasis in recent guidance texts as is to be found in similar works in the fields of educational psychology, personality, and many other disciplines.

[15]Mortimer J. Adler, "In Defense of the Philosophy of Education," *Philosophies of Education* (Forty-First Yearbook of the University of Chicago Press, 1942), pp. 224 ff.

tions, or on the temporary working bases of crystallized experience and custom. The guidance worker can not be ever mindful of these distinctions but their validity may well serve to help him discriminate between the essential and accidental aspects of the process.

FIFTEEN PRINCIPLES OF GUIDANCE

After examining some two hundred and more expositions of the principles of guidance and pupil personnel, as presented in texts and journal articles, the writer came to the weary conclusion that many authors seemed to be engaged in a merry game of saying the same thing according to the apostle, the while making sedulous use of their Roget's so as not to say it in the same way as the apostle. The following fifteen principles, however, were proposed by a majority of those who, because of their long-time association with and prominence in the field, qualify as genuine leaders in guidance and student personnel.[16]

1. Guidance is based on the recognition of the dignity and worth of the individual and on his right to personal assistance in time of need.

2. Guidance is student-centered, being concerned for the optimum development of the whole student and the fullest realization of his potentialities for individual and social ends.

3. Guidance, as a point of view, is as old as good education. It is modern with reference to (1) the areas of the student's life which are considered to be the responsibility of the school, (2) the services which it offers students, and (3) the techniques employed to attain its objectives.

4. Guidance is a continuous, sequential, educational process. Hence, it is an integral part of education and not a mere peripheral adjunct.

5. Guidance has a responsibility to society as well as to the individual.

6. Guidance must respect the right of every student to the help and services it offers.

7. Guidance is oriented about co-operation not compulsion. Hence, it is monitory in character with no place for coercion.

8. Guidance implies assistance given students in making wise choices, plans, interpretations, and adjustments in the critical situations of life.

9. Guidance demands a comprehensive study of the student in his cultural setting by the use of every scientific technique available. Student understanding must precede student assistance.

10. Guidance should be entrusted to those only who are naturally endowed for the task and have the necessary training and experience.

11. Guidance is the prerogative of no special clique of specialists. It requires the co-operation of all, each working within his own area of responsibility and at the level of his own competence.

12. The focus of guidance is on helping the student realize and actualize his best self rather than on solving isolated problems, be they those of the individual or the school.

13. Guidance is the mediating agency between the student and a mass system of education.

---

[16]Only those principles which might properly be termed "philosophical" have been considered here.

14. Guidance is the individualizing, the personalizing, and the socializing element in education.

15. The guidance program must be under constant, scientific evaluation in terms of its effectiveness.

An examination of these fifteen principles indicates that those listed in numbers 2, 3, 5, 7, 13, and 14 are only partially true. Guidance is not primarily student-centered (Principle 2) but God-centered, and so the eternal element in guidance can not be ignored, as it is in Principles 2 and 5. The first sentence in Principle 3 is true but the remainder is an accidental characteristic of American education. Much the same comment may be made with reference to Principles 13 and 14. Principle 7 introduces a dichotomy which does not always exist. With respect to Principle 10, the personnel worker must first have the right to guide and only then do his training and personality become important. It would appear that the remaining principles are valid and might well be mulled over by Catholic guidance personnel for the truth they contain.

TEN MAJOR CONCEPTS OF GUIDANCE

A survey of the literature, much of it largely historical in nature at this date, indicates no fewer than ten different concepts of guidance. Naturally, in such a discussion the ideas of different authorities can not be subsumed under mutually exclusive categories, since many have at one time or another touched upon all of these different approaches to guidance. However, as symphonies differ chiefly because of their central themes, so also authorities have tended to stress certain ideas while devoting only minor attention to others. It is this phenomenon which has constituted the basis for classification. No conscious effort, however, has been made to force conformity to a given category.

1. Guidance as a "Racket" or Meaningless Term

Surprisingly enough, although probably hordes of non-guidance personnel have at one time or other entertained the idea, this accusation was made by one of the most respected pioneers in the field, Anna Y. Reed. In 1938 she declared, "Guidance has become a meaningless term — a commercialized racket."[17] Insofar as this represented a petulant protest against shoddy training of personnel and shabby performance of guidance functions, it contained a germ of truth. However, if it purported to be anything else, in the absence of proof it may simply be denied. It is one thing to admit that guidance is subject to human foibles; it is quite another to stigmatize the sincere, if not always successful, efforts of personal workers as a racket.

Other authorities have become dissatisfied with the term because it lacks a hard core of meaning. Thus, Wrenn rejects it because it savors overmuch

---

[17]Anna Y. Reed, "Is Guidance A Racket?" *The National Education Association Proceedings,* LXXVI (June, 1938), 628.

of paternalistic advice-giving and because it has lost its usefulness through excessive use.[18] Moreover, Kitson considers it as a useless abstraction,[19] while Williamson and Darley jettison it because of its pollyanna connotation.[20] This position is much more tenable than the shrill accusation of Reed. "Guidance," like the Bible, has suffered overmuch from individual interpretation. The continued use of the term to mean, Alice-in-Wonderlandwise, precisely what the speaker wishes it to mean at the moment of speaking has at times created a situation in which some programs represent the nearest approximation of *nihil creatum ex nihilo* to be found in education today.

2. Guidance as Self-analysis and Self-direction

This approach of Parsons to the guidance process, oldest in point of time, had three essential elements (1) self-understanding on the part of the client, (2) knowledge of the requirements and conditions of success, and (3) true reasoning concerning the relationships between the two.[21] At times, unfortunately, some counselors have interpreted these ideas so mechanically that the student has felt as though he were being put through an electronic sorter. However, if the corrective perspective of the findings of cultural anthropology, sociology, psychoanalysis, and the various branches of psychology be utilized in considering the aspects of guidance, the basic validity of Parson's analysis remains.

3. Guidance as Restricted to Its Vocational Aspects

A much more formidable theory of guidance would restrict the use of the term to its vocational phase. Traditionally the strongest of the personnel organizations, the National Vocational Guidance Association, has been primarily concerned with problems of vocational guidance and occupational adjustment. Since its founding in 1913 it has grown until, as of 1952, it numbered some 6,460 members in 86 branches.[22] Despite this growth, however, a division of thought developed as to the wisdom of restricting the major emphasis to vocational problems.[23] One section favored the traditional position for the following reasons: (1) it represented the origin of organized guidance

---

[18]C. Gilbert Wrenn, "The Evaluation of Student Personnel Work: A Critique of the Guidance Movement," *School and Society*, LII (November 2, 1940), 409; "The Guidance Movement," *The Measurement of Student Adjustment and Achievement*, ed. by Wilma T. Donahue and others (Ann Arbor: University of Michigan Press, 1949), pp. 3-4.

[19]Harry D. Kitson, "Getting Rid of a Piece of Educational Rubbish," *Teachers College Record*, XXVI (October, 1934), 31.

[20]E. G. Williamson and J. G. Darley, *Student Personnel Work* (New York: McGraw-Hill Book Company, Inc., 1937), p. 28, footnote 1.

[21]Frank Parsons, *Choosing a Vocation* (Boston: Houghton-Mifflin Company, 1909), pp. 4-5.

[22]Willa Norris, "Highlights in the History of the National Vocational Guidance Association," *The Personnel and Guidance Journal*, XXXIII (December, 1954), 205-208.

[23]"A Symposium Regarding Change of Name and Statement of Purpose of the National Vocational Guidance Association," *Occupations*, XX (October, 1941), 27-44.

in the United States; (2) it had a clear meaning, aims, principles, and techniques which all could understand; (3) it had a record of achievement in developing standards for improving training procedures, for composing and evaluating vocational literature, for the evaluation of vocational counseling agencies and the practice of vocational guidance; (4) it was feared that the uncritical acceptance of other so-called kinds of guidance might undo much of the valuable work which had already been accomplished. The opposing group, however, felt that the organization should emphasize the broader functions of guidance. The upshot of this disagreement was that in 1951 the NVGA joined with other guidance and personnel groups to form the American Personnel and Guidance Association, the while retaining unaltered its own organization and pattern of functions.

However much one may sympathize with the efforts of those who seek to prevent guidance from becoming so overextended as to be ineffectively superficial and amorphous, the fact remains that this position tends to ignore three facts: (1) "guidance" though vague, has kept constantly before the personnel worker the truth that the whole child is affected by any problem and by its solution; (2) student problems ignore semantic distinctions; and (3) at least logically, this stand tends to confine one's study of the individual to a few seemingly pertinent disciplines instead of seeking to understand him by a multidisciplinary approach.

4. Guidance as Identical With Education

This interpretation of guidance has persistently been attributed to Brewer,[24] despite the objections of Super[25] and some others. Whatever may have been Brewer's precise position in this matter, certain it is that this position has been advanced by some leaders in the field. Thus, Hawkes stated ". . . that education is guidance and guidance is education";[26] while Keller maintained, "I have a notion that guidance . . . in all its implications is education,"[27] and Hildreth contended that no valid distinction was possible between education and guidance in purpose, methods, or results.[28]

It is true that the spirit of the so-called "new" philosophy of education, in which an individual has a right to his own individuality and to an education suited to his real needs, is also the spirit of guidance and pupil personnel. This, however, is a far cry from making the two simply convertible. Bluntly, guidance is but one ingredient in the educational cake; by no means can it be taken for the entire pedagogical pastry.

---

[24]John M. Brewer, *Education as Guidance* (New York: The Macmillan Company, 1932).

[25]Donald E. Super, *The Dynamics of Vocational Adjustment* (New York: Harper and Brothers, 1942), p. 5.

[26]Herbert E. Hawkes and Anna L. Rose Hawkes, *Through a Dean's Open Door* (New York: McGraw-Hill Book Company, Inc., 1945), p. 37.

[27]Franklin J. Keller, "Same Door Wherein I Went, A Confession of Faith in Guidance As Education," *Occupations*, XIII (May, 1935), 689.

[28]Gertrude H. Hildreth, "Guidance in the Lincoln School," *Teachers College Record*, XXXVII (February, 1936), 432.

5. Guidance as a Mediating Agency and as a Series of Supplementary Services

This concept was proposed by both Proctor[29] and Reed.[30] According to the latter — and, in view of her pioneering efforts in behalf of the movement, it would be grossly unfair to give the impression that her contributions were negligible — guidance is of two kinds: (1) inherent, or the kind of help every conscientious teacher seeks to give his students, and (2) purposeful, or organized guidance, which endeavors to facilitate the student's progress along the educational highway. This concept of guidance as a series of supplementary services is one of the strongest trends in modern guidance.

6. Guidance as Distribution and Adjustment

Although throughout the twelve-year period, 1925-1937, Proctor altered his emphasis in guidance from one of a co-ordinating agency to one chiefly oriented about the processes of distribution and adjustment,[31] this approach to guidance is generally associated with the names of Koos, Kefauver, and H. C. Hand.[32] According to these authorities, ". . . the concept of guidance has two main phases: (1) distributive and (2) adjustive." The former phase has to do with the distribution of students in the most effective manner possible to suitable educational and vocational opportunities, whereas the latter aspect seeks to help the individual to adjust to his educational and vocational situations.

7. Guidance as Assistance in Making Choices

Two authorities have stressed the element of choice in guidance perhaps more than any others. The major theme of all four editions of Jones' work in the field, covering a period of time from 1930 to 1951, has been this problem of choice-making.[33] In fact, for Jones the guidance situation exists only when the student needs help in making choices, interpretations, or adjustments. Myers, the other authority who has emphasized the element of choice, holds that a guidance situation is had only when two sets of differences are involved, namely, differences among individuals and differences among possible choices.[34] With this as his criterion, Myers excludes from

---

[29]William Martin Proctor, *Educational and Vocational Guidance* (Boston: Houghton-Mifflin Company, 1925), p. 13.

[30]Anna Y. Reed, "If Guidance Is Inherent in Education, Who Shall Guide?" *Association of American Colleges Bulletin*, XXI (March, 1935), 121. Reed has also published two outstanding works in the field: *Guidance and Personnel Services in Education* (Ithaca: Cornell University Press, 1944), and *Occupational Placement* (Ithaca: Cornell University Press, 1946).

[31]William M. Proctor, "The Task of Guidance in a Modern School," *California Journal of Secondary Education*, XII (March, 1937), 142.

[32]Leonard V. Koos, "The Interpretation of Guidance," *The Clearing House*, VIII (September, 1933), 8; Leonard V. Koos and Grayson N. Kefauver, *Guidance in Secondary Schools* (New York: The Macmillan Company, 1932), pp. 15-17, 439, 609; and "The Concept of Guidance," *The School Review*, XL (March, 1932), 204.

[33]Arthur J. Jones, *Principles of Guidance* (4th ed.; New York: McGraw-Hill Book Company, Inc., 1951), pp. 78-79, 95, etc.

[34]George E. Myers, *Principles and Techniques of Vocational Guidance* (New York: McGraw-Hill Book Company, Inc., 1941), pp. 15-16.

the purview of guidance all such concepts as "civic guidance," "social guidance," "health guidance," and most of the other "57 varieties" which used to wander in and out of the literature in the field. It is Myers' contention that, since all are expected to be as civic-minded, as socially-mature, and as healthy as possible, these are matters for instruction not guidance.[35] Thus, for Myers, the fundamental guidance areas are educational, vocational, recreational and community service. The difference, then between Jones and Myers lies principally in this, namely, that for the former a guidance situation exists whenever there is an element of choice regarding either means or ends, whereas for the latter there must be simultaneously multiple possibilities for choosing within the individual and multiplicity of choice possibilities in the environment.

8. Guidance as a Clincial Process

First introduced by Viteles, but developed chiefly by Paterson, Williamson, and their students at Minnesota, the clinical approach to guidance has been characterized by the following: (1) it represents a protest against shoddy methods which so frequently masquerade as guidance; (2) it seeks to develop techniques whereby a comprehensive analysis of the individual may be made; (3) it is considered a method by which educators' professed interest in individualizing education may be translated into practice; (4) it seeks to introduce order by subdivision of labor among instructional, advisory, administrative and clinical groups, all of whom work co-ordinately for the benefit of the student, each, however, retaining his own sphere of independent action; (5) it stresses the role of the professionally trained counselor, whose task it is to help students with their more difficult problems of adjustment;[36] (6) it follows an orderly — but not necessarily mechanical — procedure in terms of analysis, synthesis, diagnosis, prognosis, counseling, and follow-up.[37] Since its inception certain shifts in emphasis have taken place, due largely to the attacks of the Rogerians on directive methods of counseling. A second major change has been the recognition of the need for gearing guidance to the attainment of the objectives of a democratic society. Williamson states that he was made conscious of this need by his experiences in post-war Germany, which "awoke him from his clinic ivory-tower dogmatic slumber."[38]

---

[35]The reader may, in using Myers' criterion, wish to determine just what is involved in moral guidance, what in moral instruction, or whether any distinction should be made between them.

[36]The terms "clinical" and "clinician" should not be confused with "counseling psychologist" or "clinical psychologist," although one may very well be the other. The whole matter of terminology for the different levels of competence in counseling is something of a *bête noire*, ranging from teacher-counselor to part-time counselor to faculty adviser, to faculty counselor, to professional counselor, therapeutic counselor, clinical psychologist, counseling psychologist, and psychiatrist.

[37]Donald G. Paterson, "The Genesis of Modern Guidance," *The Educational Record*, XVI (January, 1938), 41; E. G. Williamson and J. G. Darley, *op. cit.*, pp. 28, 37-39; E. G. Williamson and M. E. Hahn, *Introduction to High School Counseling* (New York: McGraw-Hill Book Company, Inc., 1940), pp. 18-19, 74-80; E. G. Williamson, *How to Counsel Students* (New York: McGraw-Hill Book Company, Inc., 1939), p. 57.

[38]E. G. Williamson, *Counseling Adolescents* (New York: McGraw-Hill Book Company, Inc., 1950), p. vii.

9. Guidance as an Eclectic System

In guidance, as in other fields, there have been more practitioners than theorists. Hence, the vast majority of leaders have been content to combine into a workable system those elements, from whatever source, which have proved their usefulness. Accordingly, it was not possible to subsume under any of the above categories such authors as Erickson, Hamrin, Traxler, Germane and Germane, Davis, Warters, Allen, Dunsmoor and Miller, Chisholm, and a host of others of equal stature.

One authority, Strang, deserves particular mention because her prolific and her lucidly clear pen has done much to clarify the nature and purposes of guidance. Among her contributions, although perhaps none of these are solely hers, might be numbered: (1) her insistence on the need for understanding the student in terms of his developmental history and in his cultural setting; (2) her stress on "wholeness" in guidance which has enabled her, better than most, to integrate it with the total school program; and (3) her organismic interpretation of guidance as basically a process of self-realization and self-actualization.

Furthermore, Strang's explanation of the relationships existing between such concepts as education, personnel work, and guidance, although not completely satisfactory, are surely the easiest to grasp. For Strang, the broadest term of all is education. A basic aspect of education is personnel work, which can be subdivided into the personnel point of view and the personnel services. The former of these is identical with the guidance point of view and the spirit of all true education, since it is naught but the personal interest of the educator in the welfare of his students. The latter has three distinct aspects: the *consultant*, which is concerned with the formulation of school policies which will create an environment that is conducive to the best development of the individual; the *administrative*, which seeks representation for the personnel point of view in the business routine of the school; and, *guidance*, the central service of personnel work. Guidance, dealing directly with students, helps them to profit optimally from their school experiences. As such, it includes two distinct processes: *appraisal*, which embraces all efforts to understand the student; *adjustment*, which seeks to make available to him those experiences, information, and counsel that the process of appraisal has indicated to be necessary or desirable.[39]

10. Student and Pupil Personnel Work

This brief overview of the major interpretations of guidance gives no hint of the incessant beating of the hammers and the constant ringing of the anvil that have taken place as concepts have been submitted to intellectual trial by fire of those most interested in the best growth of the guidance movement. Certain it is, however, that from this matrix of idea conflict and experience has come a better comprehension of the nature, scope, objectives, and methodology of the process.

At the college level, although here too there has at times been generated a maximum of heat with the usual minimum of light, there has ever been a

---

[39]Ruth Strang, *Pupil Personnel and Guidance* (New York: The Macmillan Company, 1940), p. 25.

clearer understanding of the nature of student personnel work (the term "guidance" is rarely if ever employed at this level of education) if for no other reason than the fact that an official publication of the American Council on Education has its specific definition.[40] As has already been stated, the student personnel point of view is an attitude of mind which seeks the well-rounded development of the whole student through the acquisition of a pattern of knowledge, skill, and attitudes consistent with his abilities, aptitudes, and interests. Implementing this philosophy of education in a practical manner are seventeen personnel services organized to meet some fifteen major student needs.[41]

At the secondary level, too, the passage of time has brought clarification of understanding, despite the fact that as late as 1951 the U. S. Commissioner of Education could say, "The lack of an adequate understanding of what should constitute pupil personnel services . . . has been a matter of deep concern to me and my associates in the Office of Education."[42] In the first place, although the two terms, historically, have had different connotations, it is generally agreed that the terms "guidance services" and "pupil personnel services" refer to the same functions and so can be used interchangeably. Secondly, and far more significantly, there is a large measure of agreement as to just what constitutes the core of such services. At the Office of Education conference just referred to it was agreed that the basic services included the following: child accounting, orientation, individual analysis, health, information, counseling, clinical, placement and follow-up, and home-school-community. Interestingly enough four of the most recent works in the field, Froehlich (1950),[43] Smith (1951),[44] Hatch and Dressel (1953),[45] and Hamrin (1953),[46] are all organized in terms of some or all of these services.

What does all this mean for Catholic education? The first noteworthy fact is that, although Catholic educators have been interested in the problems of guidance since the turn of the century, they have not played a role in the evolution of pupil and student personnel work proportionate to their strength in American education.[47] In fact, it has only been in the relatively recent past, excluding such remarkable individual efforts as those of Sheehy and many others, that Catholic educators have given serious and energetic attention to guidance problems in a practical way. More important, however, is the fact that now that the essential personnel services have been defined with a moderate degree of exactness, thanks to our peers in public education,

---

[40]*The Student Personnel Point of View* (rev. ed.; Washington, D.C.: American Council on Education, 1949).

[41]*Ibid.*

[42]*Pupil Personnel Services in Elementary and Secondary Schools* (Washington, D.C.: Federal Security Agency, Office of Education, Circular No. 325, 1951).

[43]Froehlich, *op. cit.*

[44]Smith, *op. cit.*

[45]Raymond N. Hatch and Paul L. Dressel, *Guidance Services in the Secondary School* (Dubuque: Wm. C. Brown, 1953).

[46]S. A. Hamrin, *Initiating and Administering Guidance Services* (Bloomington, Ill.: McKnight and McKnight, 1953).

[47]The writer has just completed some minor research which indicates this. See also Sr. T. G. Murray, O.S.B., *Vocational Guidance in Catholic Secondary Schools* (Teachers College Contributions to Education, No. 754. New York: Teachers College, Columbia University, 1938), pp. 15-38.

it is needful that we do something complete and efficient in this area. Certainly, it is inexcusable either for the individual guidance worker to be unaware of these services, or for the individual institution, within the unalterable limitations of its resources, to fail to provide them for those students who stand in need of help. Thanks to our confreres in public education, we have a funded capital of experience and concepts which we can make our own, a gift for which we may well feel grateful.

AIMS AND OBJECTIVES OF GUIDANCE

After examining over 120 different expressions of ends in guidance, the writer concluded that the scholastic distinction between ultimate aims and proximate objectives was one which concerned few guidance authorities. For this reason, it seemed prudent to restrict the first part of this section to a discussion of those authors who employed such terms as the following to indicate that they were thinking in terms of ultimate aims: basic aim, major end-goal, central task, primary purpose, crux of the matter, desired end, consummation of guidance, primary objective, supreme end, primary aim, central goal, final purpose, chief aim, final aim, chief interest and ultimate goal.

1. Ultimate Aims

The most frequently expressed ultimate aim of guidance was found to be that of the "best development of the individual." Although it was expressed in a host of ways, it was perhaps most eloquently phrased in *The Student Personnel Point of View* in such terms as "well-rounded," "optimum," "full and balanced" and "broad gauged" development of the individual, physically, intellectually, socially, emotionally and spiritually.[48] The second major point of emphasis centered on the need for helping the student grow in self-guidance and individual maturity. Miller has perhaps expressed the consensus in this matter in declaring that the goal is ". . . to make students self-supporting, self-contained, self-directing and replete with inner resourcefulness."[49] The third category of final ends was oriented about the need for maximizing the students' satisfactions and their social productivity, as Mathewson would have it.[50] Finally, and all too rarely, there were found authors who, like Neuberg, made the distinction between the specific aims of individual and social efficiency and the ultimate aim of individual happiness,[51] or who,

---

[48]*Student Personnel Point of View, op. cit.,* pp. 1-4. The writer realizes that these divisions are hardly mutually exclusive. Thus, this work stresses greatly the need for individual maturity and social effectiveness and nods in the direction of value systems and a philosophy of life.

[49]J. Hillis Miller, "The Need for Personnel Services in a Smaller College," *Student Personnel Services in Colleges and Universities,* ed. by John Dale Russell (Chicago: The University of Chicago Press, 1941), p. 20.

[50]Robert Hendry Mathewson, *Guidance Policy and Practice* (New York: Harper and Brothers, 1949), p. 12.

[51]Maurice J. Neuberg, *Principles and Methods of Vocational Choice* (New York: Prentice-Hall, Inc., 1934), pp. 70-72, 80.

like Brewer, emphasized that ". . . the purpose of it all is simply that students may learn to live better lives. This is essentially the guidance aim."[52]

2. Proximate Objectives

The variety of ways in which the proximate objectives of guidance were expressed in the guidance field was a function of the rhetorical resources of the individual author. However, it was possible to classify the objectives proposed under twelve general classifications with a minimum amount of overlapping.

These objectives were the following: (1) to develop student initiative, responsibility, self-direction, and self-guidance; (2) to develop in the student the ability to choose his own goals wisely; (3) to know one's self, to know the school and to be known by the school; (4) to anticipate, avoid and prevent crises from arising in the lives of the student; (5) to help the student adjust satisfactorily to school and to life; (6) to help the student to recognize, understand, meet and solve his problems; (7) to assist the student in making wise choices, plans, and interpretations at critical points in his life; (8) to help the students acquire the insights and techniques necessary to enable him to solve his own future problems; (9) to assist teachers to teach more effectively; (10) to help administrators to administer more efficiently by making a maximum contribution to the total school program; (11) to develop citizens who will participate in and contribute to the democratic way of life; (12) miscellaneous objectives: included under this category were such ideas as assisting the home, helping the community, building ethical character, and fostering better human relations and international understanding.

SUMMARY AND CONCLUSIONS

This paper has sought to analyze the philosophy of guidance, as revealed in standard texts covering the field, from three points of view: (1) the principles basic to the movement; (2) the nature of the guidance process; (3) the aims and objectives of the process. With reference to the meaning of the term *principle*, no consistent interpretation was found, due largely to the naturalistic and experimentalist influences in American education. The majority of authorities employed the word as a synonym for assumption or else used it in the sense of crystallized custom to be employed as a basis for the mechanics of guidance. The chief defect of the guidance principles proposed, as might be expected, was the disregard for God's rights (and this should be distinguished from the rights of any sectarian religion) in the matter. Apart from this, the principles of guidance presented are not easily distinguishable from those of true education; as such they are worthy of the consideration of Catholic educators.

Regarding the nature of guidance, it was found that some ten different foci of emphasis were evident in the literature. What was more significant, however, is the fact that with time has come clarification of understanding with respect to the number, nature, and content of those services which are essential to a comprehensive guidance or pupil personnel program. Lastly, as

---

[52]Brewer, *op. cit.*, pp. vii-viii.

in the case of the principles, the chief difficulty with the statements of aims was the omission of God's rights. The proximate objectives, on the other hand, are cogent and valid. In fact, the school personnel worker might very quickly make a rough evaluation of the efficacy of his efforts by examining what he does in the light of these dozen objectives.

RAPPORT AS MUTUAL RESPECT

Constance T. Fischer
Duquesne University, Pittsburgh

Rapport in testing and counseling contexts is usually described by a listing of conditions said to produce optimal performance through eliciting or inhibiting certain behaviors and traits. In this article, the traditional conditions are criticized as grounded in a combination of inadequate faculty-trait and behavioristic theories. "Mutual respect" is proposed as a more accurate and practical alternative, one that is explicitly grounded in a conception of the person as always involved with his total situation and acting in accordance with his experience of it. Rapport, then, exists when each person recognizes and respects the reality of the other's experience.

Dictionary references to *harmonious relations* are an imprecise definition of *rapport* for testing and counseling. In the absence of a more relevant and explicit definition, rapport is customarily described in terms of the conditions which facilitate the tester's or counselor's purpose.

Specifically, in abilities-testing the traditional goal of establishing rapport is to elicit the individual's best performance within the limits of the test situation. With projective testing and in counseling settings, the usual purpose is to elicit optimal spontaneity, candor, and receptivity. Hence, the tester or counselor is supposed to ensure that the person is motivated but not anxious, interested but not engrossed to the point of inefficiency, comfortable but not overly relaxed, and confident in but not dependent on the tester or counselor.

In practice, rapport is often assumed through the absence of negative variables, such as anxiety, blocking, inattention, inefficiency, and derogation. The professional has been trained in techniques for preventing and controlling these events; he has been taught how to reassure the person, how to encourage him, and how to be sympathetic while remaining clear about his own purposes.

INADEQUACIES OF THE CURRENT CONCEPT

The inadequacy of the current concept of rapport can be outlined in four related points. First, in practice it is difficult to assess and control all the rapport-related conditions simultaneously. To do so requires that the tester or counselor identify and manipulate optimal levels and combinations of these

Reprinted by permission of the author and *Personnel and Guidance Journal,* Vol. 48, No. 3, November 1969, 201-204.

conditions, while at the same time he must remain attuned to the continuing relationship.

Second, despite all the lip service that has been paid to a holistic view of man as integrated and purposeful, we behave as though we believe that people are composed of actually existing, mechanically mobilized traits. Through repeated references to such terms as anxiety, motivation, and ability, these abstractions become reified traits—things in themselves—despite the historical rejection of faculty psychology and the cogent criticism of mechanistic theories of behavior (Lyons, 1963). Moreover, we behave as though it is only the client, the "subject," whose characteristics are relevant. The person in the role of the professional is assumed to be objective, meaning that he is a standardized constant, a nonparticipant—indeed, a nonperson. Hence, given a client who is allegedly composed of mechanical traits, and a tester or counselor thought to be a nonperson, there seems to be denial of the existence of an interpersonal relationship.

From this disregard of man's nature as an intentional being, the third point follows: Since we behave as though traits exist and must be identified or measured, it becomes the task of the tester or counselor to do things *to* the person in order to insure optimal emergence of the relevant trait (e.g., intelligence, spelling achievement, frank personal opinion). For instance, he motivates the person, makes him feel comfortable, and eases his anxieties so that the central stimulus (a test item or counselor's statement) can activate the relevant trait. Hence, despite recognition of rapport as interpersonal, we nevertheless regard it in practice as something the tester or counselor establishes and sustains unilaterally. A dangerous consequence could be that the client will in fact experience himself precisely as this manipulated object whose reality is determined by the professional. To the extent that he does experience himself in this way, his possibilities for taking responsible initiative are reduced, both in and beyond his role as a client.

Fourth, since the techniques of manipulation are based on the mechanistic, trait framework, they fail to allow for the unity and integrity of the person. Each related variable is manipulated in turn, in the hope of eliciting the desired trait. For example: "A friendly, cheerful, casual manner helps to relax the client"; "Explanation of the use of scores will imply the seriousness of the test"; "Intermittent approval and encouragement maintain motivation." Some manuals for individual intelligence tests explicitly recommend that children be instructed that they are going to play games with the tester. Presumably, these instructions ensure the child's interest and cooperation, which, in turn, allow his intelligence to emerge in response to the test items.

The main limitation of such an approach is that it neglects the child's total, on-going involvement in the testing situation. If the child experiences himself as in a playful relationship, then optimal achievement is not his goal. And when he finds that the examiner does not want to play after all, but is intent on completing the test instead, the child is likely to be resentful and suspicious—hardly a condition of rapport. Moreover, the tester's limited focus on eliciting interest and cooperation has probably precluded any effort to find out what the child thinks about the testing. The tester does not know the context of the child's responses, but instead assumes that, given the stimulus of the test, the relevant abilities will be elicited for measurement. Thus, we see that in the absence of an explicit alternative, a tacitly accepted mechanistic theory of behavior has served as our model of human nature.

THE ALTERNATIVE

Improvement of the current, but inadequate, conception of rapport requires an explicit alternative view of human nature. The view proposed here is that man is an integrated unity. That is, rather than being a collection of traits, he is a unity, always in continuing relationship or interaction with people, events, and objects. His behavior is necessarily in accordance with *his* experience in these relationships (Binswanger, 1963; Boss, 1963). He does not behave in terms of "rapport variables" and a central stimulus defined by a tester or counselor, but rather in terms of what the situation means to him. Thus, within this context, the testing or counseling situation is necessarily an interpersonal one, one in which two persons are *with* each other. Each interacts through his perception of the situation (which is not necessarily a reflected or cognitive one). Since the client behaves in accordance with his involvement, rather than from the tester's or counselor's perspective, his own experience cannot be reduced to constructs imposed from the professional's preexisting theory (Fischer, 1969).

Ideally, then, the testing or counseling situation should be one in which both participants grasp at least partially the other's perspectives. They should be aware that a person can act only in terms of the meanings a situation holds for him. In other words, each person must in some way understand the other's frames of reference, his modes of relating. From this understanding, there arises a recognition of the worth of the other's real and meaningful concerns. This interpersonal relationship is one of *mutual respect*; it is proposed here as a sound theoretical and pragmatic conception of rapport.

This version of rapport does not demand agreement with the other person's perspectives. Rather, it calls for respect for his perspectives as powerful limiters or facilitators of possible experience and action. For example, the hypothetical child referred to earlier is limited to a playful approach to the intelligence test as long as he believes the examiner's presentation of the test as a game. Another example: If a person views his counselor as attempting to change him into somebody he does not want to be, then there are severe limits on what the counselee can share of himself and listen to openly. The counselor must broaden the individual's outlook and contribute to a change in the meaning of the counseling relationship if they are both to make progress. To do so, the counselor must at some level recognize that outlooks come into being through the interpersonal situation; they are not merely responses elicited from one person by another.

THE EFFECTS OF RAPPORT

The Client's Perspectives

Now, we can go beyond the traditional view of rapport as a precondition for testing and counseling. We can see that rapport is essential for the testing or counseling to influence the client's life. For example, if a client is to integrate test results into his own world effectively, the tester must discuss them from the client's point of view. If the tester is to communicate clearly to a person about his performance on an intelligence test, he must know what that person thinks intelligence is. Starting there, they can then discuss their notions until common understanding is reached.

Similarly, if the counselor is to help a person broaden his perspectives, and hence his possibilities of action, he must first discuss those present perspectives. Suppose a young man views most of life in terms of his emerging manhood. Efforts to cajole, reason with, or threaten him into ceasing delinquent activities will be of little avail if he feels these activities are essential to his manhood. The counselor will have to accept the power of the manhood perspective and work within it. Perhaps from there he can help the young man discover that such things as good school grades and tenderness can also be characteristic of manhood. Again, it is a matter of two people together founding their interpersonal experience; a conception of the tester or counselor doing things unilaterally is inaccurate and unfruitful.

The Professional's Perspectives

So far, we have spoken only about the professional's respect for the power of his client's perspectives. However, the discussion applies in much the same way for the other half of the mutual respect relationship. For a person to enter a constructive relationship with the tester or counselor, he must know something of that individual's purposes and feel that they are consonant with his own, at least at a pragmatic level. In addition, the client must sense that the particular tester or counselor sees things in his own way, and hence will be limited in how much *he* can understand and help. In other words, rapport necessarily includes the client's recognition of his positive worth in relation to the professional; the client senses that what is said and done to him is necessarily open to question, interpretation, and dialogue. To put it still another way, the client's respect for the professional acknowledges the limited scope of his experience and views; the client recognizes that he is obliged to interpret what is said to him and judge its applicability, in dialogue with the professional where possible.

Awareness of the role of the professional's perspectives is important not only for the client, but for the professional as well. He, too, can broaden his outlooks, his ways of experiencing, and his behaviors through involvement with the client. Especially if the counselor is aware of the powerful role of perspectives, he will seek to understand his client's world as the client experiences it. And he will try to discover his own perspectives, and his modes of expressing them, and he will see how they help or hinder himself and his client. In so doing, he will expand and enrich his own world, and become a fuller person and a better professional.

On the other hand, if he fails to acknowledge the significance of his own perspectives, and does not respect (the power of) the client's understandings, then he will instead interpret in terms of predetermined, theoretical traits and dynamics. Accordingly, he will seriously limit his own growth and that of the other person.

In summary, the proposed concept of rapport as two-way respect for the reality and power of the other's perspectives efficiently captures all the elements of the multiple-list approach to rapport. And it does so without reifying rapport's various aspects. Neither does the proposed concept reduce rapport to prepersonal abstractions to be utilized according to a mechanistic model. Rather, it allows the interpersonal nature of the relationship to serve as the focus not only for the immediate testing or interview situation but also for the continuing personal growth of both the professional and the client.

REFERENCES

Binswanger, L. *Being-in-the-world.* New York: Basic Books, 1963.

Boss, M. *Psychoanalysis and daseinanalysis.* New York: Basic Books, 1963.

Fischer, C. T. Intelligence defined as effectiveness of approaches. *Journal of Consulting and Clinical Psychology,* 1969.

Lyons, J. *Psychology and the measure of man: a phenomenological approach.* New York: Free Press, 1963.

PHILOSOPHIC ASPECTS OF COUNSELING COMMUNICATION

Herbert Stroup
Brooklyn College of the City University of New York

The continuing engagement between counseling and philosophy leads to the examination of three basic aspects of counseling communication from the perspective of philosophic understanding. These are: private *versus* public; present *versus* past; and content *versus* structure. An examination of these three aspects indicates that counselors may well benefit from increased knowledge of the manner in which philosophers are currently dealing with matters that relate to counseling communication.

It was a philosopher, George Berkeley, who lamented that philosophers "have first raised a dust, and then complained we cannot see" (Berkeley, 1955). But, unfortunately there are times when the dust has settled and still one cannot see. This state may be as true of the counselor as of the philosopher. In fact, the common task of both counselor and philosopher, as well as others, is both to raise the dust and to see through it.

Counseling and philosophy are not unconversant allies on the current intellectual scene. Thus, in the spirit of their interdependence, three philosophic aspects of counseling communication will be explored briefly: (1) private *versus* public; (2) present *versus* past; and (3) content *versus* structure. These three themes are arranged in antithetical relations in order to heighten their philosophic complications.

PRIVATE VERSUS PUBLIC

The counselor regularly distinguishes between private *versus* public knowledge concerning his client. The client who says "I feel generally unhappy"

Reprinted by permission of the author and *Personnel and Guidance Journal,* Vol. 44, June 1966, 1020-1024.

is expressing private knowledge. His expression may be termed "subjective." But the client who says "I got all B's in my courses" is expressing public knowledge or what is commonly called "objective" knowledge.

Another aspect of the private knowledge of the client is the psychoanalytic expression, the "unconscious." The unconscious, however, is a more delimited word than private. But, according to Freud the unconscious and the conscious are both relatively undependable sources of knowledge. Thus, he writes: "The unconscious is the true psychic reality; *in its inner nature it is just as much unknown to us as the reality of the external world, and it is just as imperfectly communicated to us by the data of consciousness as is the external world by the reports of our sense-organs*" (Brill, 1938b).

Private expressions appear to depend upon inner states of being concerning which there is admittedly no externally dependable way of providing certification. Yet counselors and others place considerable reliance upon such utterances. By definition, however, private experiences are accessible only to those who have them. Attempts may be made to communicate them to others, but the experiences themselves cannot be transferred from one person to others; it is merely information regarding the experiences that can be conveyed. (The Vienna circle of philosophers at one time argued that experiences as such are incommunicable; see, for example, Schlick (1918) and Carnap (1928).

In fact some philosophers have gone so far as to undermine firm belief in any kind of permanent and self-identifying self, as seemingly did David Hume when he spoke of the self as a "bundle of perceptions" (Hume, 1951). It was Hume who said that when he looked for an impression of his self, he failed to find one and that he always found instead some particular perception of himself (Hume, 1951).

Descartes (1955) thought that it might be possible for an evil force to deceive him even with regard to those matters of which he was most certain. All communicable meaning of private experience was thus incapable of validation, according to Descartes. But he went on in his reasoning to claim that there was one proposition that can be asserted that necessarily is beyond the reach of any demon or any other limiting power. That proposition is the famous *cogito ergo sum:* I think, therefore I am (Descartes, 1955). So, in Descartes' reasoning that which appears to be the least reliable, verifiable, and communicable, namely private experience, is in actuality self-evident and, therefore, in need of no proof.

Public knowledge at first blush seems to be on a different ground. Being "objective," this kind of knowledge seems not to require extensive validation. If the client relates that he is one of five members of a family or describes the day-by-day itinerary of last summer's trip he is communicating regarding what most people would consider to be objectively verifiable experiences. Such statements are in the realm of public knowledge.

Yet, in this connection, it is significant to note that oftentimes public knowledge is the least significant knowledge pertaining to a client. Thus, for a client to refer to his space occupancy by saying "I was in the gym at one o'clock" may in itself be highly unimportant. Mere space occupancy is like that. Similarly a person's fingerprints, social security number, army number, and similar objective means of personal identification are for most counseling relationships relatively unimportant. Even the proper names of persons, that are used so widely in human communication as Mill (1930) noted, carry no particular connotations in themselves of an objective reality. He called them "unmeaning marks."

Public knowledge, moreover, is dependent usually and to some degree upon private knowledge. Public knowledge seldom is as "hard" or "objective" as it appears to be. It too is "accepted" in the form in which it is presented or else one would need to be like the man who bought several copies of a newspaper in order to assure himself that what one said was also said by the others. This degree of skepticism would lead one to buy or view every copy of a newspaper's printing (Wittgenstein, 1958).

Carnap (1934) dealt at length with private *versus* public knowledge. Carnap used the term "protocol language" to designate that class of statements which ostensibly refer to one's private experiences and "physical language" to designate that class of statements that ostensibly refer to physical objects or occurrences. While Carnap appreciates the distinction between private and public knowledge, he maintains that these languages are interrelated. He believes that any use of physical language requires that protocol language be included in it. Carnap reasons that protocol statements are necessarily bound up in physical statements, otherwise "physical statements would float in a void disconnected, in principle, from all experience." Carnap may not be sufficiently aware of the contradictions that are involved in any effort to merge the two kinds of languages but he is clear in wanting to interrelate the two. The counselor can do no less.

PRESENT VERSUS PAST

Both the counselor and the client tend to intermingle the present and the past in the counseling process without a critical appraisal of what the "present" and the "past" should properly mean. Ayer illustrates the complexity of this philosophic dilemma in a non-counseling context:

> It was one and the same man, Napoleon Bonaparte, who won the battle of Austerlitz and lost the battle of Waterloo, but in what sense was he the same? What is it that makes a set of descriptions, which are logically independent of one another, into descriptions of the same person? (Ayer, 1956).

The problem of present and past experience is even more complicated, in reference to the above quotation, if one were to ask for a report by Napoleon himself in contrast to a report on Napoleon by an observer. Present experience seems to be "objective," while past experience seems to be "subjective."

The client who says "I feel a headache now" implies that he has had headaches before with which he is able in the present to make comparisons. His statement about the present is open to some degree of confirmation. But what can one say with certainty about his inference from the past? Admittedly one can be in different places at different times, but the idea of being at different times at the same time is illogical. There appears to be no known way by which past experience can be reclaimed with anything like the objectivity of present experience. Does this fact, then, invalidate past experience? Does it place past experience into a secondary or inferior realm of knowledge regarding the client's experience of himself?

The relation of the present to the past raises, of course, the question of causation. Is the present directly and necessarily related causally to the past? If so, in what way is the relation determinative? Can the counselor draw a direct line, so to speak, between any particular instance of the present and any particular instance of the past? If he cannot, should he claim that he is scientific in any significant sense of that term? If he cannot, what does such a conclusion mean for his dependence upon client content derived from the past?

Surely the question of the relation of the present to the past in counseling communication is related to that which is assumed to exist in the physical sciences. There the notion of "functional dependence" is widely held, especially among modern physicists. This view holds that phenomena are so correlated in nature that, "when one measurable quantity, characterizing a certain physical state (say, the Earth's distance from the sun) varies, this corresponds to a change of another (say, the Earth's acceleration towards the sun) according to a simple mathematical rule" (Waismann, 1961).

Yet, the fact that there is a "functional dependence" evident in physics does not necessarily mean that it is apparent in counseling. The "functional dependence" of present and past, in parts and in whole, is not fully understood for counseling communication.

The knowledge of such relationships in physical nature leads to the possibility of prediction, securing the future from the present. It suggests that the unknown can be known from the known. But, it also provides the physicist with an ability to understand the past through an understanding of the present. Thus, information about the present state of the solar system can be used to calculate the condition in which it was at any past moment of its history. The reason for this is that the equations of dynamics are insensitive to a change in the direction of time. But, the question remains: Does the counselor have the same or anything like the same method of apprehending the past through an understanding of the present? Does the present in itself provide the counselor with an adequate means for appropriating the factual nature of the past? The answer seemingly is negative.

Russell (1921) claims that an image is a *memory* insofar as it is accompanied simply by a feeling of familiarity. But "familiarity" is not a sufficient validation of past experiences. I may be able to recall an image from childhood, but mere recall or familiarity with the image gives me no assurance that my present impression of the image is identical with or even similar to the one I held in childhood.

But there can be no denying that whatever memory image a person may have of past experience is for him in the present the only image that he has available to him and to others. Alexander (1920) puts it: "the pastness of [a remembered] object is a datum of experience, directly apprehended." Alexander means, of course, that no one can experience a past event, since experience is necessarily confined to the present. But one can remember a past experience and by the reconstitution of the past experience in memory possess a present experience. Thus, the seeming antithesis between present and past knowledge is lessened to some degree.

Philosophers also may be helpful to counselors by their recognition of two classes of memory: (1) "habit-memory," and (2) "factual-memory." By habit-memory philosophers generally refer to those instances of knowing how to do things in which it is not necessary that the performer should know that anything is the case. Factual-memory refers to those instances of knowing in which the knowledge displayed is classified as knowledge of fact. If I write a letter, walk on the sidewalk, fine-tune my television set, I am involved in habit-memory. But when I tell when Columbus discovered America, relate the proof of the existence of irrational numbers, or recall that the Republican party was founded in Ripon, Wisconsin, I am engaged in factual-memory. Habit-memory (knowing how) calls for direct past participation, while factual-memory (knowing that) obviously in many cases cannot even permit past participation in what is recalled. So, for the counselor as well as for the philosopher, a different sort of knowledge is secured according to the class of memory assertion involved in declarations regarding the present and the past. "How-to-do memory" (habit-memory) commonly involves no sense-data or images for present communication, but "I-recall-that memory" (factual-memory) depends essentially upon sense-data and images that are much more readily communicable.

CONTENT VERSUS STRUCTURE

The contrast between "content" and "structure" in counseling communication refers philosophically to the two principles which Hume (1951) admitted that he could neither renounce nor reconcile. He states "all our distinct perceptions are distinct existences." In contrast he also stated "the mind never perceives any real connection among distinct existences." For the counselor the contrast may be stated in a somewhat different language. The counselor, like others, is intent on acknowledging the face-value of direct and verbal communication. This is the "content" of counseling communication. On the other hand, the counselor also recognizes the validity of the organized forms by which the content in counseling communication is expressed. This is "structure."

Freud (Brill, 1938a) had to face this dilemma in his efforts to account for the various forms of mistakes in speech, memory, erroneously carried-out actions, and so forth, in his account of the psychopathology of everyday life. But, necessarily he faced the problem of dealing with the philosophic implications of "chance" and "determinism." As a stimulant he received a criticism of his version of name-forgetting by "a colleague of a philosophical turn of mind." Freud asked himself the question: "Does the solution given for faulty and chance actions apply in general or only in specific cases, and if only in the latter, what are the conditions under which it may also be employed in the explanation of the other phenomena?" Interestingly for a person of the intellectual scope of Freud, he commented upon his own question, saying: "In answer to this question, my experiences leave me in the lurch..." (Brill, 1938a). Apparently Freud could not solve the dilemma of content *versus* structure, at least for the phenomena under review.

The client regularly infers or states that he "knows." Yet knowing takes many forms. It may involve, as Locke (1959) stated, both "simple" and "complex" ideas. Locke believed that the mind is capable of "simple ideas" among which are its ideas of the qualities of objects. The mind, however, constructs "complex ideas" from these "simple ideas." Complex ideas are ideas of the objects which possess qualities. The objects in Locke's view are "substances." The traditional language of "perception" and "conception" also expresses the contrast between the two kinds of knowing.

The counselor then must distinguish, in Locke's terms, whether a client is expressing a simple or a complex idea and he must be in a position to evaluate the significance of each. It is not sufficient for him to rely in the spirit of empiricism upon the sheer words which are communicated by a client. He also must take into account the relationship of the client's communication of simple ideas to the client's assumptions regarding the nature of complex ideas.

This means, furthermore, that no person is capable of restricting himself only to expression derived from the empirical sphere. Every person who makes sense in his communication rests his declarations upon assumptions regarding reality that the rational enterprise makes available. The role of reason may be inadequate for the transfer of valid information from one person to another, but its existence and importance cannot be denied. Simple ideas secure their meaning within the shared context of complex ideas, or as Ryle (1954) says: "There can be false coins only where there are coins made of the proper materials by the proper authorities." Thus, a perception that is not consonant with conceptions that are veridical is by nature illusory. Content, both for the counselor and his client, must be related to structure if reliability and meaningfulness are to be achieved.

In summary, it is apparent that counseling communication involves philosophic implications that are worthy both of exploration and of the development of precise understanding. Three such elements have been described briefly to illustrate the task: (1) private *versus* public; (2) present *versus* past; and (3) content *versus* structure. Arranging the three as "contraries" illustrates the complexity of the philosophic aspects of communication in counseling.

REFERENCES

Alexander, S. *Space time & deity*. London: Macmillan, 1920, Vol. 1, 113.

Ayer, A. J. *The problem of knowledge*. Baltimore: Penguin Books, 1956, 187.

Berkeley, G. *The principles of human knowledge*. Chicago: Encyclopaedia Britannica, 1955, Introd. Sect. III, 405.

Brill, A. A. Psychopathology of everyday life. In *Basic writings of S. Freud*. New York: The Modern Library, 1938, 171. (a)

Brill, A. A. The interpretation of dreams. In *Basic writings of S. Freud*. New York: The Modern Library, 1938, 542. (b)

Carnap, R. *Der logische aubau der welt*. Berlin, 1928.

Carnap, R. *The unity of science*. London: K. Paul, Trench, Trubner, 1934, 82.

Descartes, R. *Meditations on the first philosophy*. Chicago: Encyclopaedia Britannica, 1955, Meditation II, 1952.

Hume, D. *A treatise of human nature*. Oxford: Clarendon Press, 1951, Book I, Sect. VI, 252, App. 636.

Locke, J. *An essay concerning human understanding*. New York: Dover, 1959.

Mill, J. S. *A system of logic*. London: Longman, Green & Co., 1930, Chap. 2, Sect. V, 20.

Russell, B. *The analysis of mind*. London: G. Allen & Unwin, 1921, Lect. IX.

Ryle, G. *Dilemmas*. Cambridge: University Press, 1954, 95.

Schlick, M. *Allegemeine erkenntnislehre*. Berlin, 1918.

Waismann, F. The decline and fall of causality. In *Turning points in physics*. New York: Harper Torchbook, 1961, 86-87.

Wittgenstein, L. *Philosophical investigations*. Oxford: Blackwell, 1958, I, 265, 93.

(21)

HUMAN FREEDOM AND THE COUNSELOR

Wayne R. Maes
Arizona State University

The nature and the source of human freedom have prompted considerable
discourse and controversy among behavioral scientists and practitioners.
Some believe that man's behavior results from a series of free choices while
others contend that all behavior is determined and is therefore not free. This
apparent dilemma often leads to the erroneous conclusion that we must either
see man as determined and treat personal experiences of freedom as illusory,
or preserve the existential experience of being free by denying prior causes
for behavior. But there is no essential inconsistency in viewing all behavior
as caused while also accepting and valuing the existential experience of being
free. Counselors who acknowledge the causes of free experiences are in a
position to establish the conditions necessary for such experiences for their
clients.

Men have fought and died for their freedom. The fetters of political,
religious, and social orders repeatedly have been torn loose and cast aside
through the forces of rebellion, of legislation, or of passive resistance. Orthodox religion, and more recently counseling and psychotherapy, have repeatedly
claimed one of their major goals to be the freeing of man from the crippling
restraints of guilt, anxiety, and fear. Man values psychological and political
freedom. He wants to be able personally to make decisions and to act upon
them.

There are those who contend that men can be the authors of their acts,
while others hold all behavior to be determined by prior biological, psychological, and environmental conditions.

Prior to discussing the relative merits of these two positions, some attention should be given to describing the behavioral and experiential referent
that the word "freedom" symbolizes.

When we use this word in a political sense we usually mean the scope
of behaviors in which an individual can engage without social restraint or
punishment. When we use the word "freedom" in a psychological sense we
are usually referring to a certain kind of personal experience. We who are
interested in human behavior change are especially interested in this latter
kind of freedom, and it is often our wish to assist clients to change in the
direction of more frequently experiencing what they conceive to be "free"
behavior. These personal experiences that are designated as free have certain
features that are unique to each individual but there are also generally
shared experiences commonly acknowledged as free.

There are at least two kinds of personal experiences commonly considered
to be free. (1) Facility in action. Performing with the "ease and grace of a
gazelle"; free of tension and flowing naturally. This experience of freedom
may be characterized by euphoria, ecstasy, or serenity. Its major feature is

Reprinted by permission of the author and *Personnel and Guidance Journal,* Vol.
46, No. 8, April 1968, 777-781.

an absence of self-consciousness and of concern over the way the organism is functioning. The experience is often reported as "feeling natural." It may occur while lying in the lush green grass looking at the sky, while suspended in the cool waters of a pool or lake, sailing into the windblown ocean spray, listening to music, looking at a painting, caressing or being caressed by a loved person, or while lying on the warm sands of the ocean shore. This sort of experience of freedom has been most effectively expressed by the poets and the masters of prose.

The antithesis of this experience is being aware of inner tension, feeling conspicuous, being aware of one's gait or body positioning and deliberately planning the next body movement so that it will conform to external expectations rather than to what is natural or comfortable.

(2) A second kind of experience commonly called "free" is the awareness of alternative courses of action in a problem situation, and the ability to act upon the one that is judged best. We describe this variously as problem solving, critical thinking, or inquiry.

Observing, wondering why, trying out possible answers conceptually or actually, narrowing alternatives and proceeding with a course of action, are all elements in a free problem-solving process. The freedom in such a process is characterized first by the individual's knowledge of various alternatives and their consequences, and second, the ability to weigh them in the absence of internal anxiety and external threat which narrow and distort thought and perception. A child sits on the floor with a piece of jigsaw puzzle in his hand, observes the color and shape, glances at the partially completed profile of a horse before him, glances back at the piece in his hand, rotates it a half turn and attempts to place it on the mane. It doesn't fit. He glances back at the partial profile . . . rotates the piece a quarter turn . . . looks again at the profile, and contentedly places the piece neatly in a space in the horse's forelock. This we would be inclined to call a free choice.

This relatively free problem-solving pursuit can be contrasted to the following brief vignette. A child picks up a piece of jigsaw puzzle and an adult peering over his shoulder says, "That's not the piece that goes next." The piece is discarded and another picked up, followed by, "No, not that one either. Now, you know better than that, this is the third puzzle you've worked on since your birthday." The piece is dropped uncertainly. After a questioning glance at the adult a piece is touched, followed by a backward glance . . . a shake of the head . . . the child turns his attention again to the array of pieces on the floor . . . three more false starts . . . the adult nods approvingly and the child picks up a piece of puzzle . . . intermittent glances at the piece of puzzle, the adult, the partial profile, the adult . . . several faulty attempts, and the piece is correctly inserted. The child says he is tired and would like to go outside and play. We would not be inclined to call this a free choice.

THE SOURCE OF FREEDOM

What are the necessary conditions for "free acts" such as those mentioned above? Are we to believe Sartre's conviction that "we are our choices," that in Rogers' terms we are "the architect of self"? Or are we to believe that free choice is an illusion that we perpetuate because of our oblivion to the predisposing causes for all of our acts.

BEHAVIOR IS CAUSED

Progressively throughout his history, man has learned more about himself and his world. He has found it to be, in many ways, a lawful, organized, predictable world. The Newtonian universe is a universe of predictable cause-and-effect relationships. A common belief today is that the unpredictable aspects of the universe remain so only because of our incomplete knowledge or insufficient sensory modalities. It is commonly assumed that a lawful cause-and-effect world exists that is continuously more explicable and predictable.

The Darwinian theory of the natural selective process, through which man is presumed to have originated, attributed the same sort of lawful order to biological phenomena as Newton found existed in the physical universe. More recently, numerous psychological theorists have ventured to explain the lawful biological, psychological, and environmental determinants of behavior. It is commonly agreed today that behavior is caused.

Someone says, "I chose to join the Democratic Party." A careful examination of the individual's past experiences, his attitudinal make-up, and his current group associations would undoubtedly provide an adequate account of why he became a member of this party. Each human event theoretically can lend itself to the same kind of analysis. Our logic and empirical tests tell us that all behavior is caused. Based upon the given biological equipment and the past experiences, the individual could not have done other than consider the alternatives present for him in the situation with a substantial probability that he would choose the one that he did. What he called choice is a response that was caused by the conditions that existed at the time of the "choice."

MAN ATTESTS TO FREEDOM

The personal reaction to a causal approach to behavior is frequently one of alarm and defensiveness. We resist the logical identification of the causes of behavior with their implied reduction of the will and the autonomy of the individual much as man resisted the Copernican shift from a geocentric to a heliocentric solar system. One of the usual reactions is to resort to intellectual gymnastics in an effort to isolate an "uncaused" act that we can own as uniquely ours. This aversive reaction to specifying the causes of behavior cannot be completely explained by the influences of our jurisprudence, which holds men accountable, to notions concerning inalienable rights to choose, or to our Judaeo-Christian heritage. The opposition to giving up the concept of freedom is, at least in part, because men attest that they *are* free and that they greatly value the experience of being free.

It is this personal experience of freedom that Rogers (1962) describes in his clients in the following manner:

> The client begins to realize, "I am not compelled to be simply the creation of others, molded by their expectancies, shaped by their demands. I am not compelled to be a victim of unknown forces in myself. I am less a creature

of influences in myself which operate beyond my ken in the realms of the unconscious. I am increasingly the architect of self. I am free to will and choose."

To say that this experience does not exist is to deny experience, the only reality that exists for the individual. To say that the individual and personal experience of freedom is a mystical event disengaged from the natural chain of cause-and-effect events is to deny empirical evidence and our own sense of logic which says all behavior is caused. The individual can experience being the "architect of himself." However, observation of behavior tells us that the experience of being free, of willing and of choosing, is the product of predisposing events, an orderly sequence that necessitated the "choice" of one alternative rather than another. On the surface the existential and logical approaches to human freedom are irreconcilable. The existentialist can say, "I chose." The experience of choosing has sufficient potency for him to accept it as more nearly the nature of reality than the logical machinations that would deny this potent, immediate experience. The logical positivist can look at the existentialist's purported choice, recognize the causal elements, and disdain the living of an illusion.

Logic and empirical evidence demand the acceptance of causes for all behavior lest ours be a senseless, capricious universe. However, we have more alternatives open than to assume that notions of human freedom and a potent human will are stupid illusions. The most frequent error in our thinking is to conclude that if the determinants of behavior can be identified, we must therefore deny the existential experience of being free. When we discover causes for electricity we are not prompted to deny the experience of being shocked. Why should we deny experiences that we call free simply because we become progressively more aware of their determinants? Maybe our alarm and subsequent flight or fatalism is related to an egoistic wish to be the first cause of something, but isn't this one of the attributes of God and not man?

A further error in our thinking is to conclude that, if an act is caused, man cannot be creative in that act and bring something new into the universe. Eiseley (1966) regards the universe (not only man) as being creative:

> If it were not for the fact that familiarity leads to assumed knowledge we would have to admit that the earth's atmosphere of oxygen appears to be the product of a biological invention, photosynthesis, another random event that took place in archeozoic times. That single "invention," for such it was, determined the entire nature of life on this planet and there is no possibility at present of calling it preordained. Similarly the stepped-up manipulation of chance, in the shape of both mutation and recombination of genetic factors, which is one result of the sexual mechanism, would have been unprophesiable.

This does not suggest that events in the universe are not caused but that they are *unpredictable, creative inventions* and that our discovery of the causes is after the fact.

Dewey (1922) treats the free, creative human act in much the same way that Eiseley regards creation in the physical and biological universe at large:

> To foresee future objective alternatives and to be able by deliberation to choose one of them and thereby weigh its chances in the struggle for future existence, measures our freedom. . . . It is assumed sometimes that if it can be shown that deliberation determines choice and deliberation is deter-

mined by character and conditions, there is no freedom. This is like saying that because a flower comes from root and stem it cannot bear fruit. The question is not what are the antecedents of deliberation and choice, but what are their consequences? What do they do that is distinctive?

Like Eiseley's notion of a creative, unexpected universe, Dewey sees causes existing for all human behavior but sees man as creative and capable of doing the unexpected, the causes of which may be explained only after the fact. Such a position bears a striking similarity to Adler's "creative self" principle, Jung's "teleological" principle, and Allport's "propriate striving," none of which deny causes for behavior but all of which attribute a creative potential and an unpredictability to man.

Photosynthesis was caused but at the same time it was novel. *Man was caused and all that he does is caused, but he can invent novel elements in the universe.* First causes lie obscured in the phylogenetic past and attempts to isolate them lead to infinite regress.

WHAT ARE THE CAUSES OF HUMAN BEHAVIOR?

The recent debate between Rogers and Skinner concerning the problem of human freedom does not really have to do with whether behavior is caused, but with *what* causes behavior. Skinner, in the tradition of Locke, considers the organism to be essentially a *tabula rasa* that is written on by the environment. (However, the initial causes of operant behavior exist within the organism and are laid down genetically.) Rogers sees the human, as did Leibnitz, as organizing sensory data according to its own inherent nature. From birth the infant is not completely at the mercy of the cause-and-effect relationships in the world about it, but is actively creating itself and its world.

To say that man is completely the architect of himself seems just as absurd as to venture that man is completely at the mercy of the environment for what he becomes. How we feel, think, and behave is greatly influenced by our environmental milieu. The cultural relativism of values, attitudes, and mores is clearly demonstrated in cross-cultural anthropological studies such as those of Margaret Mead (1953). On the other hand, evidence of an innate structuring, an a priori in man, comes from various sources. Malinowski (1944) contends that while there are many cross-cultural differences in man, there are threads of communality that seem to run through all cultures. The need to survive is the major universal in Malinowski's theory. The need for self-esteem, for a sense of personal adequacy, and for relative freedom from stress are examples of other apparent cross-cultural threads. The smile reflex has often been cited as an example of behavior that is not learned but that supports the notion of inborn tendencies to develop in a direction specified by the structure of the organism. In *The Structure of Behavior*, Merleau-Ponty (1963) corroborates the notion of an inborn structure in speaking of the nature of the conscious processes of the infant:

> Consciousness is not comparable to a plastic material which would receive its privileged structure from the outside by the action of a sociological or physiological causality. . . . In other words, it cannot be in virtue of the fact that it exists around the child that the human world can immediately acquire a privileged importance in infantile consciousness; it is in virtue of the fact

that the consciousness of the child, who sees human objects used and begins to use them in turn, is capable of discovering immediately in these objects the intention of which they are the visible testimony.

To say that man is not by nature directional, and that he is *only* what he is reinforced to become, denies to man that structure and creativity which seems to characterize the entire universe.

Equally apparent is the broad-reaching effect on human behavior of external social determinants. Within the broad structure laid down by the nature of the species, the social learnings write extremely varied narratives on the individual human tablets of men. Much study is being devoted today to understanding further the genetic and environmental factors that determine behavior. As such studies are successful, we will learn more about the components that predispose one man to frequent experiences of freedom and another to infrequent, or virtual absence of, free experiences.

It is an error, then, to conclude that the free human act is distinguished by its capricious genesis without historical antecedents. It is equally erroneous to react to an awareness of the determinants of behavior with a reconciled fatalism. While the genetic determinants of behavior are laid down by the phylogenetic characteristics of the species, the ontogenetic development of an individual is in part a product of his creative, choicemaking expression of the creative, choicemaking capacity of the species *homo sapiens*. It is more human to say "I can" and "I will" than to say "I can't" and "It makes no difference." We are born saying "I can"; we learn to say "It makes no difference." To say "I will" is to assert our nature and this is a part of the measure of our freedom.

IMPLICATIONS FOR COUNSELING

In recent years the controversy over the issue of human freedom has revolved, to a large extent, around the operant conditioning and client-centered explanations of learning. However, little is to be served by signal reactions to such symbols as "successive approximation" and "self-actualization," "control," and "freedom." The one does not represent control and the other freedom. Both are attempts at explaining the causes of behavior and, to the extent that they do so, both hold promise that we can more effectively establish the necessary conditions for more universal experiences of human freedom.

Our society values psychological freedom and we as counselors are called upon to devote our energies to establishing the conditions necessary to facilitate the individual psychological experience of freedom in ourselves and our clients.

Existential, client-centered, and other therapeutic techniques hold promise of increasing human freedom. Likewise, reinforcement schedules hold a similar promise. Both desensitization techniques and unconditional positive regard, genuineness, and so on, if appropriately employed, can expand human freedom and creativity.

REFERENCES

Dewey, J. *Human nature and conduct: an introduction to social psychology.* New York: Holt, 1922.

Eiseley, L. Science and the unexpected universe. *American Scholar,* 1966, *35*(3), 415-429.

Malinowski, B. *A scientific theory of culture, and other essays.* Chapel Hill, N. C.: University of North Carolina Press, 1944.

Mead, M. National character. In A. L. Kroeber (Ed.), *Anthropology today.* Chicago: University of Chicago Press, 1953.

Merleau-Ponty, M. *The structure of behavior.* Boston: Beacon Press, 1963.

Rogers, C. R. Learning to be free. Paper given to a session on "Conformity and Diversity" in the conference on "Man and Civilization" sponsored by the University of California School of Medicine, San Francisco, January 28, 1962.

EXISTENTIALISM, SELF THEORY
AND THE EXISTENTIAL SELF

Ernest L. Johnson
Mississippi State College for Women

Self theory is reductionistic: it brackets off "real" reality and leaves it in metaphysical realms. Existentialism views both subjective and external reality as contained in existence. Rogers' theory is deterministic to the extent that it is built on causal constructs. The non-deterministic, holistic, and teleological assumptions of the existentialists may help strengthen self theories. For example the term *existential self* would combine self-as-doer and self-as-object, making such constructs as self-concept, self structure, individual, and organism unnecessary. The individual's experience or perception would not have to be *caused by* a self-definition, but would be for the *purpose of* something, i.e., his intentions or goals.

Several investigators have observed connections between Rogers' self theory and existentialist concept (Arbuckle, 1965; Landsman, 1961; Maslow, 1961; Pervin, 1960). In this study an attempt is made to identify some similarities and differences and suggest areas where a synthesis is indicated. Client-centered theory and the existential psychotherapies have evolved independently and simultaneously, are among the most recent developments in psychotherapy on two continents, and are characterized by their tentative and unfinished state of development. Their similarities should suggest confirmation, their differences may identify weaknesses, and a unification could result in the emergence of a better model of the individual.

Rogers' theory is itself a synthesis of several American personality theories —that stress self-processes, phenomenology, holistic and organismic processes (see Rogers, 1951, p. 482). Rogers draws directly from Maslow, Angyal, Snygg and Combs, Raimy, Lecky, Goldstein, Allport, Stagner, and others. Rogers begins with the *individual,* or *organism,* in his private world of experience. The individual differentiates and selects experience, hence he helps to make his own world (phenomenal field). The individual, or organism, as used by

Reprinted by permission of the author and *Personnel and Guidance Journal,* Vol. 48, No. 3, November 1969, 201-204.

Rogers, describes what is known in personality theory as the self-as-process, or the self-as-doer (Hall & Lindzey, 1957, p. 468).

The *self* in Rogers' theory is differentiated out of the other perceptual objects of the phenomenal field and refers to the "I" or "me." The *self-concept* refers to all the self-definitions and descriptions that the individual holds about himself. The *self structure* includes the self, self-concept, and the values that are attached to them. All these terms refer to "objects" and are governed by the same organizational principles that govern other perceptual objects. Although the self structure (self-as-object) is differentiated and defined by the individual, it finally appears to become rather organized, structured and autonomous in governing the experience of the individual.

Rogers believes that much of the self structure consists of values introjected or taken over from other people. The child may deny his real feelings because they contradict the picture that others appear to have of him, which is later assimilated by the child himself. Therefore, the "objective self," which may be the introjected values of other people or society at large, may determine the behavior or even the perceptions of the "subjective self."

Maladjustment, as viewed by Rogers, "exists when the organism denies to awareness significant sensory and visceral experiences, which consequently are not symbolized and organized into the gestalt of the self-structure" (1951, p. 510). In psychotherapy, Rogers seeks a congruence between the experience of the organism and the conceptual structure of self.

SOME EXISTENTIAL CONCEPTS

Existentialism also is often regarded as a synthesis. Heidegger combined Husserl's phenomenology, Nietzsche and Kierkegaard's expressions of individuality, and his own creative thinking to lay the cornerstone of the modern movement. The writings of Jaspers and Sartre helped propel it into the limelight.

Existentialism has been known as a philosophy that is concerned with the search for identity in times when selfhood is threatened by theoretical systems, mass reactions, mechanistic and technological production, exploitive mass media, and industrial and governmental hierarchical organizations. The philosophy is usually defined by several themes that permeate certain modern European philosophies, themes such as alienation and self-estrangement, transcendence, self-assertion, meaning in life, authentic living, existence in the face of death, and many others.

The philosophy places existence prior to essence. "Essence," which refers to the substance of things that is permanent and unchangeable, has been sought by the natural sciences. "Existence" on the other hand refers merely to the apparent fact of "being there." Existence, according to Sartre (1947), is just plain, absolute "to be." This existence is neither created by man, nor can he analyze it through his logical systems of thinking. Thus, his thinking does not create his existence, as Descartes would have it. According to existentialists, man exists first and then he speculates and contemplates it.

By stressing existence, existentialism undercuts the dichotomy between subject and object. Man is not a subject who perceives an object, but he exists with his objects. Subject and object become one in being-in-the-world. Man is with and a part of every object he encounters. Existentialism is said to be anti-scientific because science seeks essence and is concerned with the objects impersonally. But every object is a personal object, and according to the existentialists the individual must be fitted into every scientific observation and equation.

The individual's existence is the central factor in the analysis of things, because he creates his world and gives meaning to phenomena. He creates the objects of his experience through his *intentions* and goals. Man is viewed as being on his way toward his essence, as bridging the gap between the finite and infinite. There is nobody or no system outside of man that can affect his existence. Sartre states that "man is that which he makes himself," and therefore is responsible for what he is. If essence, what a man consists of, preceded existence, the fact that man is, then man would be determined. However, since man does not have a previously given essence, he is free, and he himself must take the responsibility for what he is.

Man's freedom and responsibility are the main sources of his anxiety. He may feel alone and isolated without some external authority to guide his behavior. This explains man's craze toward conventionality, and his tendency to "escape from freedom" (Riesman, 1950; Fromm, 1941). He also may feel abandoned when thrown into a meaningless world where he must invent purpose and projects that will confer meaning on both himself and the world of objects. Not to see possibility, not to find reason to existence, is to lose the authentic self and thus to exist in bad faith.

Anxiety and despair are the inevitable qualities of being. Man faces an uncertain future and an ultimate death. He alone must take the consequences for his choices and decisions. If he alienates himself by identifying with some corporation, organization, or system, or if he becomes "other-directed," his life is characterized by apathy, boredom, and a zombie-like existence. On the other hand, if he actualizes value, creates meaning, and takes on responsibility he suffers existential loneliness and dread. Yet this latter course of expressing his full potentiality and creativity has to be done if he is to achieve selfhood and authenticity.

PHENOMENOLOGY AND THE SUBJECT-OBJECT PROBLEM

It is evident from the preceding that both viewpoints stress the importance and significance of the individual, his capacity for growth and his freedom in realizing his own potential. Both approaches are phenomenological in that they begin with the subjective side of the subject-object relationship in examining the meaning that events have for the individual. They view the individual as active in "changing his own world" through the differentiation process of altering figure and ground. However, Rogers is concerned only with the individual's "reality," and feels that it is not necessary for the psychologist to become involved with the metaphysical question of "true" reality. "For psychological purposes, reality is basically the private world of individual perceptions" (Rogers, 1951, p. 484), and behavior is a function of this perceived reality. In contrast, the existentialists have founded their position on an attempt to resolve the epistemological dichotomy, which separates noumena from phenomena. *Being-in-the-world* implies a unity that cannot be broken down into (1) man and his sensory equipment or (2) the physical energy systems which are generally regarded as activation of this equipment. For the existentialists, existence or *Dasien* is the basic element in reality, and the polar terms *subject* and *object* are synthesized.

Rogers' approach here is phenomenological but not existential. His "reductionistic" ideas coincide with Husserl's method, which suspended judgment about real existence and stated that mental processes and ideal objects were the appropriate subject matter for science. There appears to be a subtle and indirect link between Rogers' and Husserl's brand of phenomenology. Self theory is grounded in Gestalt psychology which in turn was influenced by Husserl. This point may account for the observed similarities between self theory and existentialism, since Husserl is also regarded as one of the founding figures of existentialism (Johnson, 1966, p. 36). Thus, self theory and existentialism may have a common ancestor in Husserl.

The subject-object problem is one of long standing among the self theorists in regard to the relationship between "self-as-process" and "self-as-object" (Hall & Lindzey, 1957). Rogers makes no explanation as to how the "objective self" (the self, self-concept, self structure), is related to the "subjective self" (the organism or individual). The implications are that they are rather distinct and the self structure can become rather independent in directing experience and behavior. The existentialists, by using such concepts as *being-in-the-world*, would unify not only self and real object, but also self and perceived object. Thus, the subjective self would be in unity with the objective self, or, in Rogerian terms, the individual, or organism, would be synthesized with the self or self structure. In such a synthesis the self structure could never become an autonomous determinant of perception, but would be inseparately linked with an active, or becoming self.

SELF-ACTUALIZATION AND DETERMINISM

Both self theory and existentialism emphasize man's movement toward self-actualization. Rogers' quote from Angyal could easily have been said by an existentialist: "Life processes do not merely tend to preserve life but transcend the momentary *status quo* of the organism, expanding itself continually and imposing its autonomous determination upon an ever-increasing realm of events" (Rogers, 1951, p. 488).

The term "existence" as defined by the existentialists means to *stand out*, to emerge; it is a process of becoming rather than a state of being: "Existence is projection; it 'becomes.' With every passing moment it becomes more (or less) than it is. Existence and temporality are thus practically synonymous" (Kneller, 1958, p. 25). For Tillich, man is "asked to make himself what he is supposed to become, to fulfill his destiny. In every act of moral self-affirmation man contributes to the fulfillment of his destiny, to the actualization of what he potentially is" (1952, p. 52).

A major difference between the two viewpoints is Rogers' more deterministic treatment of this directional tendency. It appears to be a natural law that applies to all living things: "The directional trend we are endeavoring to describe is evident in the life of the individual organism from conception to maturity, at whatever level of organic complexity" (Rogers, 1951, p. 488).

The implication here is that striving is innate and based upon organic evaluation. The existentialists, on the other hand, view self-actualization as a goal toward which the person could *choose* to strive. However, it is the responsibility of the person to make of himself what he potentially is, and to shrug off this responsibility is to dwell in inauthentic existence. Plans, purposes and goals are strictly human creations, and when man makes them and acts on them his being becomes unique and quite distinct from that of the other objects and organisms in the world.

EXPERIENCED VALUES VERSUS INCORPORATED VALUES

Both Rogerian and existentialist positions agree that certain preferences and values become culturally defined and often assimilated through vicarious rather than actual experience. Some "values" are considered by society to be better than others, and, therefore, should be taught by parents and teachers. Cultural values may, however, eventually contradict real, experienced values, and thus the individual is thrown into conflict. Rogers believes that both non-experienced (incorporated) and experienced values are included in the self structure, and that the individual may be directed more by the incorporated or "false" values.

Both Kierkegaard and Heidegger fear that man is losing contact with his own concrete experience by accepting, or at least pretending to accept, non-chosen values. This leads to inauthentic existence; the person becomes an object among other objects in the world, or as Sartre puts it, a "being-in-itself" instead of a "being-for-itself." Kierkegaard viewed these unreal values as assimilated for the purpose of maintaining a false picture the individual has of himself as a result of expectations from other people. The individual is thus severed from his subjectivity and lives in pretense.

Values, according to the existentialists, are not detached and apart from the individual, but they are one and the same with his choices. A value always involves free choice without a "good" or "bad." Arbuckle (1965, p. 564), in relating existential treatment of values to counseling, states that every act that is labeled "bad" by someone is labeled "good" by someone else. Sartre implies that man has no hierarchy of values or universal ethics to guide his choices and therefore must act on his own responsibility. If universal values were valid then man would have no choice nor freedom, and, therefore, essence, a determined state, would be prior to existence.

One result of therapy, according to Rogers, is the replacement of a value *system* by a valuing *process*. Then the individual relies on his own physiological equipment for providing data for making value judgments and for continuously revising them. While this appears at first to coincide with existentialist ideas, a significant difference is involved. Rogers implies that there must be evidence upon which to make a value judgment, and that evidence comes from the individual's own sense-data. It appears that Rogers visualizes values emerging out of fact, which is the experiential evidence of the person.

According to the existentialists, notably Sartre, values are created by the free act of a human being, and they have nothing to do with facts. Existentialists believe that values are on a different realm from fact, and, unlike the pragmatists, hold that the former can never be generated out of an accumulation of the latter. Rogers, therefore, appears to be more pragmatic than existentialistic in this respect.

PHENOMENOLOGICAL SELF VERSUS EXISTENTIAL SELF

Rogers' adherence to lawfulness follows the American trend toward predictability and exactitude. His "determinism" not only rests on the assumption that the directional tendency motivates all behavior, but also upon the proposition that if behavior is "determined by the phenomenal field, then of course, he has no choice, and he can hardly be held 'responsible' for his actions" (Arbuckle, 1965, p. 560). Rogers' theory, like that of Snygg and Combs, is deterministic to the extent that the field is more important than the individual in determining behavior.

The self structure (phenomenal self) is the most influential aspect of the field in determining perceptual selectivity and defense. But the goals of client-centered therapy appear to be toward freeing the individual from these influences so that he can choose experience that had previously been denied. Rogers sees the goals of therapy, then, as a movement of the individual toward a fuller grasp of reality so that he may become less determined by inaccurate perceptions of himself. Viewed another way, this is the movement of a phenomenal self toward an existential self, or the movement from an ideal of perceived reality to one that actually exists.

The existential self has been rather well defined by Rogers' concept of the fully functioning person. Rogers states that ". . . the self and personality would emerge *from* experience, rather than experience being truncated or twisted to fit the preconceived self-structure" (1951, p. 90) and "that there would be no barriers, or inhibitions which would prevent the full experiencing of whatever was organismically present" (p. 87). The fully functioning person would be a participant in and an observer of the ongoing process of organismic experience. With this concept, Rogers shifts his emphasis from a structural and consistent self-as-object, to a self that is active, subjective, and open to reality. He appears to be less phenomenological and more existential at this point.

Braaten, working within the Rogerian theory, found that the more successful a client was rated by a therapist and a TAT diagnostician the more likely it was that he showed a movement toward greater emphasis upon an immediate, emotional experiencing of the self. These "successful" clients became more truly open to their existence "right there and then" (Braaten, 1961, p. 10). Hence, Braaten poses the following as a major theme from the viewpoint of psycotherapy: "Your own experiencing is the highest authority—be fully present in the immediacy of the moment" (1961, p. 13).

In a similar manner, Jaspers defines the goals of the therapeutic process as the increasing ability of the patient to experience his existence as real. That is, to become more fully aware of his existence and all the potentialities and possibilities that emerge from it. May says that the characteristic of the neurotic is that "his existence has become 'darkened,' blurred, easily threatened and clouded over, and gives no sanction to his acts; the task of therapy is to illuminate the existence" (May, et al., 1958, p. 398).

The existential self should be further defined by the self theorists. It is the real self, the choosing self, and the becoming self. It is the entity that creates the environment and gives meaning to existence. It differs from the phenomenal self in that it is less deterministic and it functions in the "true" reality of existence rather than in a "phenomenal" or perceived reality. To obtain this type of selfhood, the individual must not only free himself from group norms, universal ethics, and mechanistic trends, but also he must become free from a consistent self-definition. When the individual defines himself he is attempting to formulate his essence, which is detrimental to transcendence. In order to achieve existential selfhood, the individual must constantly re-define himself, revise his goals, and revive his possibilities.

SUMMARY AND CONCLUSIONS

The similarities between self theory and existentialism represent some major trends that are being renewed in psychology. For one thing the individual is growing in size and importance in relation to other factors, such as drives, urges, conditioned stimuli, etc., in determining behavior. He is viewed as being active and free in making and creating his own world, thus he has the responsibility for doing so. Also, there is a growing conclusion that all sources of values arise within the individual (Maslow, 1961, p. 53). A blind adherence to a set of values, whether external or internal, has the result of self-alienation and, thus, reduces the freedom of choice of the individual.

While self theory may be considered to be a non-deterministic personality theory, it is still built on several causal constructs. Striving toward self-actualization is viewed as an organic-biological tendency; perception is guided by a personal frame of reference; and value judgments are based on either a self structure or, in the case of the better-adjusted individual, on the facts of organic experience. Self theory is therefore existential up to a point, but insists on "explaining" much of the behavior that the existentialists would view as free actions. For the existentialists the first cause of behavior is the individual.

Also, self theory is reductionistic: it brackets off "real" reality and leaves it in metaphysical realms. Yet Rogers' theory is based upon the assumption that there is a real reality and that ultimately the individual has to approach it if he is to function properly and reach his potential. Rogers theory is caught in the same subject-object dichotomy that the phenomenologists attempt to reduce and the existentialists synthesize. The existentialists neither reduce nor deny external reality, but view it as being contained in existence. Existence is primary, so that neither pure subjectivity nor pure objectivity can be attained.

Rogers' separation of self into "self structure" and "individual" presents another problem. The self structure may come to determine the individual's experiences and behavior, but at the same time the self structure is defined and created by the individual, or organism. The reciprocal and cyclic relationship between these entities implies that they are one and the same—the individual determines the self structure and the self structure determines or restricts the individual's full functioning. An existentialist concept, existential self, may combine self-as-doer and self-as-object in one stroke. The existential self is both what the individual does, and what he is. Or put another way, selfhood is what the individual puts into action.

The use of the construct *existential self* may strengthen and enrich self theory. This holistic term would make divisions of the self, such as self-concept, self structure, individual, and organism unnecessary. Experience or perception would not have to' be *caused by* a self-definition, but would be for the *purpose of* attaining selfhood. The concept of the existential self, then, would make self theory or even more teleological and holistic and less deterministic. Self theory is unique among personality theories for its advances in these directions. If the teleological, holistic and freedom orientation have been the forte of self theory, then the existential influence should be favorable.

REFERENCES

Arbuckle, D. S. Existentialism in counseling: the humanist view. *Personnel and Guidance Journal*, 1965, *43*, 558-567.

Braaten, L. J. The main themes of "existentialism" from the viewpoint of a psychotherapist. *Mental Hygiene*, 1961, *45*, 10-17.

Fromm, E. *Escape from freedom.* New York: Holt, Rinehart & Winston, 1941.

Hall, C. S., & Lindzey, G. (Eds.) *Theories of personality.* New York: Wiley, 1957.

Johnson, E. L. Existential trends toward individual psychology. *Journal of Individual Psychology*, 1966, *22*, 33-41.

Kneller, G. F. *Existentialism and education.* New York: Philosophical Library, 1958.

Landsman, T. Discussion of the paper by Patterson, Kilpatrick, Luchins, and Jessor. *Journal of Individual Psychology*, 1961, *17*, 39-42.

Maslow, A. H. In R. May (Ed.), *Existential psychology.* New York: Random House, 1961.

May, R., et al. (Eds.) *Existence: a new dimension in psychiatry and psychology.* New York: Basic Books, 1958.

Pervin, L. A. Existentialism, psychology, and psychotherapy. *American Psychologist*, 1960, *15*, 305-309.

Riesman, D. *The lonely crowd.* New Haven, Conn.: Yale Univ. Press, 1950.

Rogers, C. R. *Client-centered therapy.* Boston: Houghton Mifflin, 1951.

Sartre, J. P. *Existentialism.* New York: Philosophical Library, 1947.

Tillich, P. *The courage to be.* New Haven, Conn.: Yale Univ. Press, 1952.

Chapter 2: Questions for Discussion

1. Glanz presents characteristics of the "free and responsible person." In which aspect do you feel that individuals in our society are typically farthest removed from being "free and responsible"? What are the major reasons or causes for this?

2. Blum traces the history of some major problems and ideas in vocational counseling. What are the chief problems which face the "career counseling" or "vocational counseling" practitioners today? What sources of relief from these problems seem probable?

3. Which of the "major models" or patterns listed by Glanz seems most prevalent in your state? What strengths does it have in terms of the present needs of your state? Could you offer reasons for moving toward another pattern or model?

4. What conflicts do you see between present practices and/or theory in counseling and the five principles offered by Zaccaria?

5. Mowrer gives several ways in which people cope with fears. Review his list, then see if you might extend it. What *positive* effects can fear and fear reactions have? Give examples.

6. Read Cribbin's last paragraph again. What are "proximate" objectives to guidance? In what way might a religiously-oriented counselor approach an agnostic or atheistic client? What special problems, if any, may arise?

7. Does Fischer's "mutual respect" differ significantly from the usual meaning of "rapport"? Which view seems most useful for counselors? for teachers?

8. Which of the philosophical problems presented by Stroup seems to you to have the most practical relationship to counselors in their daily work?

9. Maes presents several key insights on freedom and counseling. What seem to you to be the biggest obstacles to "freedom" (using the word in any of the senses in which Maes uses it) for individuals in today's society? What can counselors do to increase their clients' freedom?

10. Johnson raises some questions concerning differences between Rogerian and present-day existentialist ideas on self-concept. Which views seem closest to your own? What practical differences would such views have for your work as a counselor?

Chapter

3

The School Counselor Today

INTRODUCTION

In this chapter, men and women who are either counselors themselves or who are educating counselors speak out on matters of vital concern to counselors as they pursue their daily work. The writers have carefully considered the major trends, concerns, dangers, viewpoints, and roles which the school counselor must fulfill, and they present guidelines stemming from these endeavors. Their analyses of the problems and challenges which face school counselors are addressed to live, pertinent issues growing out of both literature and experience. Without such a presentation, the book would be incomplete. In the first edition of this book, the articles were arranged by levels, that is, elementary, secondary, and so on. While there were some advantages to that approach, we feel that philosophical-directional articles which cut across levels might be more useful and avoid the impression that the levels are isolated or totally discrete.

These writers would have all school counselors examine themselves, not only at the outset but continuously, asking, "Have I been prepared for the sort of problem before me?" "What sort of preparation would have aided me in this situation?" "What am I going to do about recurring problems and types of problems in my school?" "What is my relationship to the community? To the larger society? To parents?" "Am I genuinely making contact with the deepest hopes, fears, and aspirations of the students who bring personal problems to me, or am I merely touching their lives superficially, if at all?" "What sort of strength is this particular child before me seeking?" "When should I refer him to someone else?" "What can I do to work toward more pertinent counselor education and standards?"

The issues, views, ethical-moral outlooks, and recent directions discussed in the other chapters of this book all come to a focus in the school and in the work of the school counselor.

174

THE ROLE OF THE SCHOOL COUNSELOR

Gail F. Farwell

University of Wisconsin, Madison

Counseling is the primary function of the school counselor. In this function of counseling, the school counselor works individually with each pupil trying to help the counselee gain a meaningful perspective of his strengths and weaknesses, a clear vision of his opportunity, and a knowledge of the existing or possible interferences in his maturing and adjusting throughout life. It is not the function of the counselor to "tell" the pupil. There are enough "significant others" in each person's life committed to telling. Kahlil Gibran (1:62) in The Prophet eloquently develops a philosophy for this counseling function:

> No man can reveal to you aught but that which already lies half asleep in the dawning of your knowledge.
> The *counselor* [mine] who walks in the shadow of the temple, among his followers, gives not of his wisdom but rather of his faith and his lovingness.
> If he is indeed wise he does not bid you enter the house of his wisdom, but rather leads you to the threshold of your own mind.

The school counselor committed to assisting each pupil in the struggle for self understanding has his role defined for him. This counselor must recognize his prime commitment, the attendant functions associated with this commitment, and lastly, must have the courage to stand up and be counted in support of this commitment. Too many so-called school counselors do not have professional preparation for the task and consequently do not recognize the uniqueness of professional counseling. Rather, these school counselors (?) reflect much more vividly their experiential background as former instructor, and end up doing many things akin to this activity.

The role of the school counselor can be identified as: (1) He is a school staff member committed to education and the educational process; (2) It is his function to study human lives and the contingent environment in which they live; (3) The school counselor should devote a two-thirds majority of his time to counseling with individuals; (4) He is a consultant to teachers, administrators, and parents.

Many implications attend this role for the school counselor. School administrators should demand professionally prepared counselors. They should not select chemistry teachers for counselors but chemistry teachers to instruct in chemistry. It has always been a wonderment why counselors aren't hired in terms of their knowledge about counseling and their commitment to counseling rather than those reasons which have persisted during the past decades. In 1961, antiquated notions about the proficiency of personnel prepared as experts in instruction for implementing counseling procedures should be dissipated. I will support wholeheartedly the necessary commitment of the school

Reprinted by permission of the author and *Counselor Education and Supervision*, Vol. 1, No. 1, Fall, 1961, 40-43.

counselor to education and the purposes of the school. I will continually support the desirability of a minimal amount of teaching experience or associated experience to familiarize the school counselor with classroom realities, problems and setting. This enables the school counselor to be more accepted as a school staff member. However, those persons who demand year upon year of classroom experience are closing their eyes to the tunnel vision created. The person intensely committed to school counseling will learn more about the total curriculum, the total school situation, and a broader segment of the pupil enrollment from his vantage point of counselor than in the restricted environment of one subject matter area, in one classroom, for years ad infinitum.

With what instruments can the school counselor work? The first instrument at the disposal of the school counselor is his personality. In the instructional program at the University of Wisconsin a requirement of the course Counseling: Theory and Issues centers on a paper "My Counselor Person" which is an attempt to have potential counselors turn inward for self reflection and assessment. If you will, self-knowledge on the part of the school counselor is as important as the counselee's self-knowledge which the counselor attempts to promote. This paper is followed by interviews devoted to clarification, further expansion and self-growth — counseling if you will. Developmental counseling is a growth process — growth in self-understanding and enhancement of adjusting as a necessary construct of life. Counseling as growth is one segment of the helping relationship continuum. One end of this continuum involving a telling (advisor or instructional function) with progression to counseling (self-growth) to psychotherapy (cure and treatment). The basic instrument for implementation of the school counselor role is one's own person.

Second, many instruments developed on the measurement and human development scenes are necessary for implementation of counseling. Such items as statistical concepts, standardized tests, rating scales, anecdotes, autobiographies and others too numerous to mention in this discourse are essential for functioning in a school setting. Conceptual knowledge in career development, personality development, curriculum implementation, administrative protocol and the evolving societal scene are essential if self-growth in the school setting is to be enhanced and the base for effective adult adjusting is to be established. Research tools are an essential ingredient for the school counselor. The professional role of the school counselor demands that he be a good consumer of research studies in many fields of endeavor and that he, too, research his own activity. The best way to improvement and development of quality in school counseling is to expand the research horizons.

Where will the school counselor function? Naturally in the school and at all school levels. We have minimized the work of the school counselor, through default, in the elementary school. The trait-factor theorists in counseling took us off on a measurement binge; the Rogerians made us face up to the real importance of relationship in counseling, not that people of other points of view didn't ultimately contend with relationships. With developmental counseling focused on growth and implemented in the school setting, the importance of each pupil developing a counseling relationship and being helped to know and understand the contribution a counselor can make should receive emphasis in the elementary school. If we would do this, junior and senior high school students wouldn't approach the counselor's office with trepidation and wonder "what have I done wrong now." The pupil would have an expectancy for the contribution the counselor can make. The school counselor that will give of himself to his relationships with each counselee is in a position to help each pupil understand more meaningfully the meaning of child study (pupil appraisal) and to promote optimal performance on the assessment and evaluative instruments employed. Maturity plays an important role in all of counseling but young counselees are as open to psychological love, acceptance and understanding as the octogenarian, maybe more so. Counseling and the attendant pupil appraisal activity is important when internal placement and interferences to learning are the focus of attention. The school counselor works here to assist in greater performance in subject matter learning. At the elementary level curricular choices for pupils are few and far between. They may have a role in planning implementation but society determines much of the experiential base to be provided. The school counselor at this level will spend considerable time in direct consultation with teachers and parents to assist them in decision making on behalf of the pupil.

As the pupil matures and moves into the junior and senior high school much more emphasis is placed on self-determination, decision and choice making, and self-understanding. Effective relationships established at the elementary level promote developmental counseling at this level in contrast to much of what goes on today — "closing the barn door after the horse has escaped."

The area of social adjustment has not received much mention. Surely we're concerned with this, so are most of society's institutions. We must remember that much of social adjustment in the school still centers in settings where subject matter of the curriculum takes front seat. I want the counselor to be sensitive to total development but the school counselor continues to exist as a professional worker in this institution if his services and skills contribute to the unique characteristics of that institution.

In summary, the role of the school counselor is envisaged as a catalyst to human growth and self-understanding. He should spend a 2/3 majority of his time in one to one counseling or consulting relationships. He is expert in his knowledge of counseling theory and procedures, career development, measure and the role of the school in developmental behavior of young people. He is an educator; he is also an applied psychologist. He is a counselor because he has preparation for the role and selects this role rather than being promoted to it as a reward for good instruction. Let us recognize the unique role of the counselor in the educational setting. Let us accept, select and prepare those who want to be counselors. Let us strengthen our profession by defining the school counselor's role so that confusion ceases to exist.

BIBLIOGRAPHY

1. Gibran, Kahlil. *The Prophet.* New York: Alfred A. Knopf, 1953.

SOME NOTES TOWARD A PHILOSOPHY OF SCHOOL COUNSELING

Paul Nash
Boston University

The field of school counseling is growing at an unprecedentedly fast rate. There is a danger that many practices will perpetuate themselves simply because no one has the time to examine their worth, that theories will be accepted without rigorous examination of their assumptions because we are concentrating on satisfying urgent practical demands, that the necessity for systematic clarification of key concepts will be overlooked in favor of more immediately rewarding tasks. These dangers can be offset only by a philosophical inquiry into some of these fundamental assumptions and concepts. This article represents an exploratory consideration of some of the terms that might be included in such an inquiry. It is suggested that at the heart of a philosophy of counseling lies the problem of human freedom. Seven concepts are studied that are thought to have relevance to counseling, and to freedom: prediction, testing, conformity, efficiency, authority, values, and finitude.

School counseling is one of the fastest growing fields in education. The number of people directly and tangentially involved in it is increasing enormously. There is important financial support for the movement. Under such circumstances, certain dangers present themselves. It is particularly in a rapidly expanding and "successful" field that basic questions may easily be avoided. The very momentum of its growth and success may discourage fundamental inquiry, render efforts at clarification apparently superfluous, stifle awareness of the need for philosophical thinking.

If this is true, there would seem to be an especially pressing case for the sustained development of a philosophical inquiry into some of the fundamental assumptions and concepts of school counseling. The present paper is intended as a brief, exploratory consideration of some of the terms that might be included in such an inquiry.

An initial assumption that will be made is that at the heart of a philosophy of counseling will be found the problem of human freedom. Seven concepts will be introduced that are thought to have relevance to counseling and to freedom.

CONCEPT OF PREDICTION

Counseling is often concerned with predicting the student's future. It has in this respect been much influenced by so-called scientific psychology — positivism, behaviorism, and operationalism — which assumes that a person's past state inexorably determines his present and future states, that this process

Reprinted by permission of the author and *Personnel and Guidance Journal*, Vol. XLIII, No. 3, November 1964, 243-248.

of determination, although complex, is lawful and analyzable, and that human behavior (like animal behavior) can be accurately predicted once we know all the variables involved.

I do not propose to add to the formidable body of criticism and refutation that has been made of this behavioristic type of thinking. Instead, I should like to ask one or two questions that I think are logically antecedent to the mechanical and technical problems of prediction.

Why do we *want* to predict a student's future? Why are we so concerned with knowing what the future holds? Often the honest answer to this question will be ambivalent. On the one hand, successful prediction is associated with control, and control can enhance freedom. Through scientific prediction, for example, we have gained technological control that has partially freed us from the limitations imposed by our natural environment. No one need apologize for such a concern with prediction.

But, mixed with such worthy and respectable motives, on the other hand, are often some that are less wholesome. Why do horoscope writers still make a good living in this country? Why are insurance offices the most luxurious palaces of our day? Part of the answer must lie in our insecurity and fear concerning the future. This can be associated with a certain lack of faith that prevents us from being comfortable in the presence of *any* area of life whose future remains unpredicted. One of the attitudes we might hope maturity would bring to us is that of finding in the experience of each passing moment the confidence to trust the future to be at least as beneficent as the present. With this kind of maturity, one can afford to let aspects of the future go uncontrolled and unpredicted.

Moreover, do we have the *right* to attempt to predict a student's future? If our prediction becomes known to the student, his parents, or his teachers, what effect might it have on his decisions? And are we prepared to accept the responsibility for these effects? The *accuracy* of the prediction does not matter at this point. The mere *existence* of a prediction is an important factor when choices have to be made. Specifically, we must ask whether the act of prediction enhances or restricts the student's freedom through the external influence it adds to those factors governing his choices.

Usually, the answer to this question will depend upon the way in which the prediction is communicated to him. If it is presented as one more piece of information to fit into the matrix out of which the student must eventually make an autonomous decision, then it will probably enhance his freedom, for we become more free as we perceive more alternatives and become better informed about the probable consequences of choosing among them. But if the prediction is presented as a piece of dogmatic soothsaying, with all the spurious but impressive authority of a mysterious, scientific calculation behind it, then the student's freedom must be considered restricted. The younger and less mature he is, the less possibility will he have of rising up through the weight of the prediction to make an autonomous decision. In the extreme case, where the docile student is crushed by the prestige and certainty of the prediction, his freedom is reduced virtually to zero, for he is persuaded that in fact all alternatives save the predicted one are closed to him.

It may be argued that predictions are made in accordance with the best "scientific" techniques available and that this in some way excuses their use. This brings us to the second concept.

CONCEPT OF TESTING

Testing is frequently a major part of the technique of prediction. Particularly important in this respect are so-called aptitude and personality tests. Here again we must ask whether such tests do not restrict the freedom of the one upon whom they are perpetrated, in part because of the assumptions underlying them. Most tests have been formulated as a result of research carried out under behavioristic or psychoanalytic assumptions. Both of these outlooks put stress upon man's environment and personal history as exclusive determinants of personality they tend to ignore the pull of the future and the influence of deeply held aspirations in personality formation. Such assumptions do not enhance or encourage the individual's efforts to free himself from deterministic forces and to make his personality in part a product of his own design.

We use the tests as a *means* but there is constant danger that it will also dictate our *ends*. We tend to allow the questions we ask to be determined by the nature and limitations of the testing instrument we use. Mechanical, "objective," closed-ended testing procedures are relatively easy to score, and give a simulacrum of exactitude and pseudo-scientific objectivity. Hence, they are tempting and often employed. But we should realize the strict limits to the kind of information we can discover by such means. Moreover, the use of such tests exerts a subtle influence on us in gradually persuading us that only those things are important that can be "objectively" tested. Ultimately it leads to the belief that only such things *exist*. With the advent of machine scoring, we are increasingly tempted to limit our inquiries about man to the areas that the machine can manipulate. Eventually, we come to make man over in the image of the machine.

We must ask, in addition, whether the use of tests and other pseudo-scientific techniques does not often represent an abdication of responsibility on the part of the counselor. If we are afraid to take the responsibility of making personal, autonomous decisions, what better way is there to dodge the responsibility than to slough it off onto an "objective" test, a "scientific" technique, or a mechanical procedure? The test becomes a supposedly safe alternative to risky, conscience-pricking judgments. Not only individual decision-making but even warm, human interest on the part of the counselor may be replaced by the arid austerity of the test.

CONCEPT OF CONFORMITY

Behavioristic psychology is frankly concerned with encouraging conformity — with "behavioral engineering" — in order to bring the student's behavior into line with behavior that is valued and approved of by the culture. Counselors who are not dazzled by the promises and threats of the behavioristic outlook should constantly be estimating the potential cost of encouraging conformity. When the counselor insists upon the student's accepting social responsibility, it may merely amount to an insistence upon a conformity to the current modes of our transient and restricted society. And this may constitute a reinforcement of problems adumbrated by our mass media of communication — that is, of the advent of uniformity and the concomitant decline in originality and creativity.

Are we in danger of constantly punishing students in subtle ways for differing from hypothetical norms we set up? For example, in making criteria for the advisability of entering various professions, test makers often choose not ideals but the average of current practice. If you do not conform to this you are not considered suitable. In using these tests, counselors are in effect measuring an individual's suitability for a profession in terms of his relation to the attitudes, limitations, and prejudices of the average men who at present fill that profession.

One might mention at this point the possible dangers in the enterprise of investigating the role of the school counselor. Might not an acute consciousness of one's role as a counselor make him less effective? One cannot simultaneously concentrate on both conforming to a role and being oneself. It may be that by concentrating on our role we are less likely to achieve the unselfconscious spontaneity that is essential if we are to respond honestly to the student.

CONCEPT OF EFFICIENCY

We need to be aware that we live in a society where efficiency is worshipped. One of the dangers associated with the uncritical worship of any idol is that the nature of the idol does not receive serious examination. There is an assumption in America that education should try to help the individual to operate more efficiently. But what might this mean? Too often, efficiency is seen in terms of fitting round pegs into round holes. This is merely acceptance of a parochial concept of *short-term* efficiency. In the context of the lifetime of an individual, efficiency may involve letting him do what he most deeply *wants* to do, even if this leads to some temporary difficulties and frustrations. It may well be that *long-term* efficiency is best served by letting the individual find out by direct experience what are the implications and consequences of his desires and aspirations. Otherwise, we may achieve a measure of vocational fitness at the price of a deep undercurrent of unresolved desires, untried talents, and frustrated aspirations.

If we espouse this ideal of long-term efficiency, is there any way the counselor can help the student avoid some of the less pleasant short-term consequences? This brings us to our fifth concept.

CONCEPT OF AUTHORITY

What should be the counselor's role in making the student aware of authority? One of the paradoxes of freedom and authority is that knowledge of the limits of our freedom increases our freedom. Knowledge of the forces of authority acting upon us renders us more able to deal with those forces. We enhance our own freedom for example, as we become aware of the factors in our personal history that have affected our development, of the urges within us and the restrictions society places on those urges, of the limitations imposed on us by our membership of various groups — social, religious, racial, national, cultural, of the authority inherent in our various deficiencies and talents. He is more free who knows that his behavior is partly determined.

We can help students to gain the courage to act freely and autonomously by urging them to make their demands and aspirations personally relevant. We can encourage' the dreams and ambitions of our students and yet still encourage them to study themselves and the relationship between their talents and their dreams. Where this relationship is realistic, the student is more likely to be successful in effecting change, in exerting leverage. This success can then encourage him to further aspiration and effort. But where the relationship is drastically unrealistic, it is hard for him to escape the disillusionment that follows failure to carry out grandiose schemes, or the resentment that ensues when one refuses to accept any limits on his freedom and has them forced upon him unwillingly and uncomprehendingly. He who insists that "where there's a will there's a way," who believes that will power is the only prerequisite for successful action, who refuses to accept the intractability of nature, will be broken by nature — perhaps broken into neurosis or psychosis.

But if the individual is partly influenced by authority, he is also partly free. No man is either wholly determined or wholly free. How to exercise this modest degree of freedom most effectively is the art of life. The alcoholic is one of the least free of men, for he cannot choose whether he will drink or not: his conduct is determined by the authority of his compulsion. Such compulsions demonstrate clearly the existence of determinism in human affairs. But groups like Alcoholics Anonymous demonstrate equally clearly the existence of freedom, because here we have men who were unfree but who, through personal effort and the help of a group, have regained their freedom, albeit a knife-edge freedom maintained over an abyss of reversion to compulsive authority.

The counselor must not shirk the responsibility of helping the student to come to a realization that life represents a constant conquest of freedom in the face of internal and external forces that always wait to reduce it. This eternal task is the penalty and predicament of being human. When the student is tempted to adopt deterministic explanations, to account for his defects and failures by factors in his personal history or circumstances that have had an inexorable causal effect, he must be encouraged to resist such temptations. To be sure, such resistance will be accompanied by anxiety and guilt, but these, too, are part of the payment for freedom. The free person is not free from anxiety and guilt, but is able to live with them without being destroyed by them. Anxiety is the vertigo of freedom — an inevitable consequence of gaining height. The person who cannot stand anxiety and removes it by placing it on another person, on a leader, or on an institution, buys peace of mind at the cost of his freedom. Anxiety can be productive if it is a manifestation of thought about an unresolved conflict: it may be resolved by bringing the person to a higher and more creative level of operation.

Guilt is a concomitant of freedom because the free person is responsible, and because no one ever completely lives up to his responsibilities. The responsible person sees a gap between what he judges to be his responsibilities and his performance. Guilt — which is formed by this gap — can be a healthy force if it is accepted as an inducement to personal excellence. It is precisely when guilt is *not* accepted, *not* faced, that it becomes neurotic and hence destructive of freedom.

CONCEPT OF VALUES

What role do values play in the counseling situation? Should the counselor impose his own values on the student? Should he conceal them from the student? Clearly, if we intend to help a person toward freedom, it is not wise to try to impose our own values on him. If he should resist them, there ensues a struggle between counselor and student that ruins the relationship. If he accepts them, he has merely assumed a conforming posture that has no relevance to his unique needs and development. No growth towards autonomy has occurred.

On the other hand, extravagant and complicated attempts on the part of the counselor to *conceal* his values from the student introduce an artificiality into the situation that is again harmful to the relationship. Where there is both a genuine concern for the student and a natural warmth and spontaneity on the part of the counselor, he need not feel that the student must be protected from all expressions of opinion and judgment. Values are implicit in the counseling situation and cannot be concealed by merely refraining from saying certain words. Every glance, gesture, physical movement, pause, change of pace, reveals them. Until we sink to the level of counseling by machine, we can rest happily within this human and humane framework.

We should recognize that concealing one's own values may be the most effective way to manipulate another person. This is not to suggest that most counselors consciously *wish* to manipulate their students, but the urge to manipulate may exist below the level of conscious deliberation. Moreover, we must be aware of the tendency to conceal our true values from *ourselves*. If we deceive ourselves into believing that we accept a student's actions when they are really deeply repugnant to us, we will usually find ourselves punishing the student in some way, perhaps subtly and indirectly. If we feel condemnatory of a student, it seems that either we must admit it (to him, or at least to ourselves) or we are compelled to make him pay some penalty for his supposed offense.

Of course, our value judgments should always be made in the light of the purpose of helping the student to form himself a set of values to live by. A distinction between self-revelation and indoctrination might be helpful here. In an attitude of self-revelation the counselor might (when appropriate) say, in effect, "This has been good for *me:* you must make what use you can of this fact in the light of your own unique situation." In an attitude of indoctrination he might try to convince the student that "This will be good for *you,* and you should follow it." While the latter approach is destructive of freedom, the former may provide the kind of psychological and moral support that nurtures freedom. Moreover, a sense of timing is important in this matter. It may not be appropriate to answer all requests for our opinion directly and immediately. There will be many occasions when it may be more appropriate to reply by asking the student, "What do *you* think?" But this temporary and *ad hoc* evasion is different from a permanent and doctrinaire conspiracy never to reveal what we believe.

There is considerable contemporary support for the view that a genuine acceptance of the student necessitates a non-judgmental attitude — what Carl Rogers calls unconditional positive regard — on the part of the counselor toward the student's behavior. This does not seem to me to be a logically necessary consequence. I may accept a person in a deep and genuine way and refrain from judging him in any ultimate sense, but at the same time, I may without inconsistency make moral evaluations of his specific acts, intentions, and attitudes.

We should further recognize that a nonjudgmental, wholly accepting attitude toward a student's behavior would also be taken by a counselor who was indifferent to the student, who had no interest in what became of him. Even if this is *not* true in a particular case, it may be inferred by the student to be true, thus preventing the relationship from becoming a fruitful one.

CONCEPT OF FINITUDE

A consideration of the concept of finitude concludes this inquiry. I can think of no attitude more appropriate for a school counselor than one marked by an awareness of the finitude of his own knowledge and insight. It is appropriate on the grounds of the vastness of our own ignorance in the face of the infinite mystery of personality. It is appropriate as representing the greatest safeguard the counselor can possess against the danger of abusing his position of privilege. If we strive to enhance human freedom it is essential to carry within us an awareness of our finite limitations as students of human behavior.

Personally, I would ally the concept of finitude essentially with a sense of humor. I cannot imagine any greater gift for the counselor nor can I imagine a greater disaster than for the counselor to be devoid of one. A sense of humor is the faculty of being able to perceive the absurdity of our human situation, the oddity of events, the comic that is the other side of the tragic in life. It enables us to live with grace and serenity. It prevents us from taking ourselves too seriously. It helps us to avoid an attitude of arrogance about our powers and responsibilities. It puts our work and aspirations into the perspective of a gentle and modest finitude. It enables us to combine a genuine commitment to our present direction with a true openness to future change. It represents a gateway to truth and hence to freedom.

COUNSELING FOR AUTHENTICITY

Sidney M. Jourard
University of Florida

The first thing a school counselor must decide is his purpose. The teachers are there to teach and the administrative officials are there to see that the school functions smoothly as a social system. If the counselor is not to teach nor to administer, what is he to do?

I believe the counselor's assignment is to foster and defend the mental health of the students in all ways that he can. Unless a counselor is clear

An original article for this book.

about his commission, he will slip into myriad other roles and duties, or drop into some rut of busywork such as routine psychometric testing, that leads nowhere and contributes nothing to the school setting except bulging filing cabinets.

I have said that a counselor's job is to be a force in the direction of greater mental health among the pupils. This raises a fundamental question: What is mental health, anyway? The answer to this question is of more than academic importance, because the work of the counselor is necessarily guided by his understanding of this condition.

A VIEW OF MENTAL HEALTH

Mental health is not so much a state or a condition as a way of living![1] It used to be thought that if a person had none of the symptoms of "mental illness," he was, by definition, "mentally healthy." Now we have learned a little more, and can offer a better understanding of the connection between the way a person lives his life and the effect that it has upon his physical health, his ability to play the roles in life that are legitimately expected of him, his personal growth, and his experience of existence as free or bound, zestful or boring, going forward or standing still.

Let me define mental health, not in terms of "signs" or "symptoms" but instead as *the outcome of a way of living*. A person is mentally healthy if his ways of behaving yield certain valued consequences. The consequences I have in mind include physical wellness, some measure of social acceptability, a sense of meaning and progress in life, a feeling of being a distinct individual with intrinsic worth, some degree of creativity, and the ability to cope with challenges that society and life present to everyone.[2] These outcomes are by no means the only identifying features of mental health, but they will serve as a guiding orientation. Now the question that arises is, "How must a person *behave* in order to experience his world as one that it is feasible to live in, and worth living in, in ways that are acceptable to society? And what happens when a person does not live his life in these ways?"

EXPERIENCE AND BEHAVIOR

Let me first distinguish between *experience* and *behavior*. Everyone experiences the world in a way that is unique to him. My experience of the world is different from yours. Experience refers to our perceptions, feelings, meaning, fantasies, or more generally, to our *being in the world*.[3] This *being* changes continuously from instant to instant. What we refer to as our Self (actually, our idea of our self, or our self concept) is an inseparable part of our *being in the world*. Our concepts of things and of other people, and our perception of these phenomena are also part of our being in the world, as are our thinking, reasoning, remembering, and fantasy. We *exist* in the world; we *are* in the world. We experience the world. Nobody but me can ever have a direct glimpse of my being, that is, my experience. I am the only one to whom my experiencing happens. I cannot dictate my experience to msyelf. Experience *happens* to me. It goes on from birth to death, in waking and in sleep. It is private and personal, but I can disclose it to other people if I choose, just as they can choose to disclose their experience to me, thus enriching my experience in my world. But we are not the only entities under the sun that have a being. Animals, machines, trees, the sun and the moon, the ocean, germs — all these have a being too. These all "disclose," that is, show, their being continuously, to all and sundry, but we are not always interested in receiving their disclosures. Our phenomenal world, our world of personal experience is continuously receiving the disclosures of our own bodies, of the being of other people, and of things. If our experience is rich, full of meaning, satisfactions, and hope, if we let our world disclose itself to us, we function fully and grow. We stagnate when we shut off our disclosure to the world, and when we do not let ourselves receive the disclosure of the world. If our surrounding world, including the people in it, discloses a being to us that crushes or disconfirms our being, we shut it out to save ourselves. And if we do not want others to know our experience, we end our authentic disclosure to others. But we sicken if we have too long attempted to shut out the disclosure of the world to us and our disclosure to the world. Ultimately, our throttled experience finds a way to break through, even if it breaks us in doing so.

Now that I have discussed experience in relation to mental health, I will turn to behavior. Behavior is public; it can be seen. Behavior yields consequences in the world and in the person who behaves. Not all behavior is effective in attaining the goals for which it has been undertaken, and not all behavior is acceptable to society. People are obliged to learn ways of behaving that are deemed good, right, and proper within their society. If they will not behave in the required ways, they are punished. The patterned ways of behaving that all, to be acceptable, must learn, are called *roles*. One speaks of "the male role," "the role of the teacher," "the role of the student." Societies work, that is, function and fulfill aims only when the members do their parts, when they play their roles adequately. In a school the teachers' roles require them to present lessons to pupils. The pupils' roles entail obeying the rules of the school and mastering subject matter.

There is an aspect of behavior in roles that we must note at this point. Human beings can behave in ways that *disclose*[4] their experience, and they can also conceal their experience. We speak of a person as a phony, a liar, an actor, a pretender, a cheat, a counterfeit[5] if his words and actions do not reflect or disclose his experiencing at the time he is doing something or talking about himself. We also speak of people's "putting themselves in what they do" or "just going through the motions" as they do what they do. In the former instance, we speak of the person as enthusiastic, or involved. In the latter, we may call him dispirited, depressed, or demoralized. If a person discloses his experience in words, and intends to let another know his experience, we call him "sincere" or "authentic." If he *mis*represents himself, if his disclosures have been chosen for their "cosmetic value" or for their power to manipulate another's perception and idea of him, we call him a fake. We thus can look at behavior and speech from the standpoint of whether or not they reveal or conceal a person's experience.

The other viewpoint from which we wish to discuss behavior is that of the consequences which it yields in the world, to the world and to the behaving person. People choose their behavior to attain objectives that are important to them. If I want to be a success in my profession, there is a universe of actions that I must engage in to accomplish that end. If I wish to be well-liked and popular, there are still other actions I must undertake. If I wish to stay healthy and grow, there may be still other actions I must undertake and some kinds of behavior that I must eschew. Now, fortunately, we cannot have everything in life, much as we might like to. Every value carries a price tag. We must make choices among the many values that make life worth living, and hope that the goals we have chosen to pursue will be sufficiently satisfying that we will not mourn the other values which we have forsaken.[6] One of the values that all of us treasure, the more so when we have lost it or when it is under threat, is our health — our physical health and our mental health. When health is endangered or lost, all other values are jeopardized or lost. Now the question that we must address is, "How must a person behave in order to achieve and maintain, or regain, health?" My remarks are naturally most relevant to mental health, but they likely have some bearing as well on physical wellness.

Impasses

First I will introduce the concept of the *impasse*. Everyone encounters impasses in his existence. They are experienced as blind alleys, traps, intolerable situations, paralyses of action, "not knowing where to turn."[7] When impasses happen, the person suffers from depression, boredom, anxiety, or guilt. If he can find some way out of the bind in which he finds himself, he will get on with his existence, and indeed he will have grown as a consequence of having coped effectively with his problem. But if the impasse cannot be surmounted, time and life will seem to stand still, and he will see no future for himself beyond the unendurable present. Physical breakdown may then happen, or a refusal or inability to get on with his customary roles and activities. At this point, the person may be sent to or seek a physician or a psychotherapist in order to be "cured" so he can get back to the life he had been leading up to that point.

But here I must point out something that has frequently been overlooked. If a person sickens, and thus "checks out" of his usual round of activity, this fact itself is testimony that his way of living up to that point has not been adequate to maintain wellness. His ways of behaving may have been superb means of attaining popularity, or good grades, or the approval of authority figures, but the sickness testifies these good things have been gained at the cost of wellness. His way has led into a sickening impasse. The physician or therapist who would *heal* a person rather than merely relieve him of his symptoms must look beyond the symptoms to the way the person has been living and behaving and experiencing in the world. If the specialist falls victim to the *fallacy of symptoms,* he is in danger of ridding his client of these pains only to throw him back into the very way of existing that generated them. What is called for in any effort to help sufferers is healing, in the sense of helping the sick one to find a way of behaving in the world that will secure values without jeopardizing his wellness and integrity.

Now I would like to contrast the way of living that almost certainly leads to breakdown, or to drastically diminished existence, with the way of wellness.

Inauthenticity and Authenticity

An *inauthentic existence* leads inexorably to breakdown or diminished vitality and impoverished experience of life. What is an inauthentic existence?[8] This is a way of living one's life that is radically alienated, or separated, from one's *experience* of himself in the world. The inauthentic person is one who strives to conceal or misrepresent his experience because he finds it threatening to certain values. The values threatened by his experience include his concept of himself — the way he likes to think about himself — and also the image or concept of him that is presently held by other people. He lives in dread that he may present himself before others in ways that will jeopardize his career, his good name, the love and regard of friends and family, etc. He fears that if these other people find out what he genuinely thinks, feels, wants, believes, what he has secretly *done*, they will banish him from their lives. If this happens, if he loses his status, his job, the regard of others, he feels that his life will be over, worthless. Consequently, to avoid these dreaded outcomes, he carries on a life of concealment and "seeming." His behavior with others does not disclose his experience, his true feelings and needs. Rather, it has been chosen for its appearance.[9] He wants to *seem* to be someone whom he is not. His life is akin to that of a perpetual impersonator. He does not put "himself," that is, his being or his experience, into what he says and does. Consequently, the imaginary person whose part in life he is "playing" does not behave in ways that satisfy his authentic needs.[10]

If the inauthentic person has carried out his life of duplicity long enough, he will lose the capacity to identify his own spontaneous and authentic experiencing. Instead he will find his consciousness filled wih ideas, beliefs, attitudes, and feelings that he is "supposed" to experience. This experience does not have the "feel" of vital, vivid reality for him. If he is at all a sensitive person, he may experience himself as *lost*. Indeed, he has lost something — his sense of being. In his efforts to maintain the charade that his life has become, he has been obliged to *repress* his genuine experience of himself and the world. Eruptions of spontaneous experience would shatter the concept of himself he has so carefully constructed in his own mind and in the minds of others. Accordingly he ruthlessly roots these possibilities of experience out of his being. He has lost his soul.

When the inauthentic person is alone, he finds himself in bad company. He is in a state of emptiness, boredom, or anxiety. He cannot stand solitude. Contrariwise, he may find he *must* have people around him to distract him from introspection. He doesn't like to note his experience of himself because it is too ugly, disgusting, frightening, or unreal.

In authentic existence, the person acknowledges his experience for what it is. He does not strive to legislate what he will or won't think, what he will or won't feel, what he does or what he doesn't perceive. Rather, he lets his experience, his being, happen as it happens.[11] He lets himself *be*. He does not define himself in some fixed way, and then strive to delimit his experiencing to that range which fits the definition. He does not define the being of other people or things in a congealed way, blinding himself to all aspects of their being that do not fit his present concepts. Rather, he is capable of adopting the mode of *letting be*. He lets his experience be what it is, and he acknowledges this increasingly diversified experience. His ideas of self and world change to keep pace with the vicissitudes of his experience of self and world. Who is able to be thus open to experience? People who are *secure* and *confirmed* in their being and in their identities are able. People who have been lucky enough to have parents, friends, teachers, or just *one* significant person (it could be the school counselor) in their lives before whom they could drop all defense and pretense and "just be," having their disclosure of experience received in an honest way and confirmed are able. The confirmation that I am speaking of is not wishy-washy permissiveness or chronic agreement. Rather, it is an attitude on the part of the other person that this individual has the right to be the person he is. It is an acknowledgment that he feels what he feels, means what he says, whether or not one approves of his views.

The authentic person, secure in his being, is capable of knowing his own values and setting his own goals. He can experience his needs and behave in ways that will yield fulfillment. Moreover, since he is not defensive, he can stand on the "ground" of his own being and enter into dialogue with others. He invites them to disclose their experience honestly to him, and he responds in honesty by disclosing his experience.

Because he is capable of being open to himself, the authentic person is able to discern whether he agrees with the values and attitudes of others. The insecure person frequently finds himself assenting to others' proposals in his eagerness to please and to be liked; later he may find he has himself in an untenable and unlivable position. The secure person can say "No."

Because he acknowledges his experience no matter how pleasant or unpleasant, an authentic person is sensitive to his "all-is-not-well" signals. The inauthentic person is less so because he has alienated himself, distanced himself, from his authentic experiencing. "All-is-not-well" signals is a term I invented to describe the at first, low-intensity signs of malaise, anxiety, pain, boredom, depression that signal the fact that one is in an impasse — one's ways of behaving in the world are doing violence to one's integrity as a person. The secure, authentic person notes these signals *before* a stressing or unsatisfying way of behaving in the world has a chance to produce breakdown. When his work, his relationships with others, his relationship with himself have reached an impasse, he can introduce *changes* before he gets some physical ailment, or before he becomes vulnerable to a break-through of repressed experience that will precipitate a "nervous breakdown" or symptoms. He can disclose his dissatisfactions in a relationship with parents, friends, or others, thus providing an opportunity for adjustments to be made in those relationships, to get them back into a satisfying mode. He can change his work habits, or his play habits, to yield more satisfaction or success or leisure.

The inauthentic person handles impasses in a different way. He has closed himself off from much of his experience. It is as if he "strains" his experience through a filter, and screens off all experiencing that will not fit present concept of himself or his world. Consequently, the early warning signals of an impasse (that were received and acted upon by the more authentic person) persist unnoticed. The inauthentic person may have disturbing dreams or periods of depression or anxiety, but he passes them off, represses them, and *continues* with the way of life that has been generating "all-is-not-well" signals. The impasse persists unnoticed. He is thus actively but unwittingly behaving in a way that will lead to his eventual breakdown. The suffering that he *then* experiences cannot be ignored. He must pay attention because he cannot work, or interact with others, or believe things about himself as he had been doing. Something has to give, and it is his health and his capacity to cope.

From all that I've said, it is clear that mental health is best fostered by seeking to make it safe for a person to acknowledge his experience to himself and to other significant people who confirm him as the one he is. It is true that such freedom to disclose oneself is rare. Indeed, there are many settings where disclosure of self is downright dangerous. In authoritarian families or classrooms the ones in power may be uninterested in the children's experience. They want only *behavioral* compliance with their rules. They may punish children when they discover that the latter have been thinking thoughts or feeling feelings that are "not proper." They may invalidate the children's experience; if the children say, "We don't like our work," the adult may say, "Oh, of course you like it." In such settings, the ability to conceal and misrepresent experience can be a virtual lifesaver. One can "play the game" if it is worth it or if he cannot escape, but one can *know* that he is just playing the game and has experience that differs from what is publicly displayed in words and actions. As a counselor, sometimes I have found it necessary to help a troubled but basically secure person learn ways of faking or "going along" with the rules, because the punishment for disclosure of opposition would be disastrous.

COUNSELING FOR AUTHENTICITY

Everyone who values his well-being heeds access to some person of unimpeachable trustworthiness to whom he can confide his experience. But a receiving ear is not enough. A person in trouble needs some kind of response from his confidant, responding that will help him confirm and acknowledge his experience more fully and find his resources and courage for coping. Hopefully, the counselor will be such a confidant.

The Counseling Relationship commences with a seeker, estranged from his being, suffering pains brought on by a way of life that was obviously unfit for *him* to live, though others may have had a vested interest in his behaving as he has. Indeed, the seeker has had a vested interest in his past ways as well. He wants only to be rid of his "problems" so that he can get back to his old ways. It is for the counselor not to get "hung up" on the particular "symptoms" that the client brings to his attention, but to invite the client to reveal his past and present ways of being. The client, if he trusts the counselor, will permit him to come to know him. But as the client discloses his experience to his counselor, he will also reveal or "act out" his "way," his "way to illness" in the very relationship. To his "way" the counselor should be alert. It is from this way, to some as yet undiscovered but authentic way of being, that the counselor is seeking to invite the client. The aim of therapeutic counseling is not relief from symptoms alone, beyond that, it is to help the client find his being for himself — his identity.

It has been my experience that a client is most likely to find this way if the relationship with his counselor is one which *invites, challenges,* or *permits* the emergence of authentic being in him. I have come to the opinion that these terms, rather than technique or persuasion, best describe effective counseling. It is my task as a counselor to invite my client to take the risk of disclosing himself spontaneously, utterly, defenselessly; to run the risk of trusting me utterly. It is for me to be *worthy* of that trust. And it is my further job to respond honestly to his disclosures in the spirit of good will, that is, respond to him in any and every way that I have learned in the past, or can invent and improvise on the spot (within limits of safety and his and my integrity) that I believe has some *hope* of fostering growth in directions described. My effectiveness as a liberator from sick ways, and as inviter toward a healthier way is enhanced by my own degree of liberation. The more firmly I am committed to *my* way of wellness, the more secure I am in my being, the more conviction is carried by my invitation to the client to try finding *his* way. The more strongly I become committed to helping him find his way (this commitment to the other goes through a growth process, starting only as a formal, professional declaration of intent to be helpful, and staying at that point, diminishing, or growing to a more intense involvement and commitment), the more single-minded I become in my aim with that client, the more I create a situation in which his trust of me and gropings for his way will develop. It is as if my single-minded purposefulness creates a wake, one which carries him along, which invites him or tempts him out of his shell, naked, to take a plunge into his world which will "grow" him to the stature presently latent. I must be authentic and honest with him and with myself in this relationship. I must be honest about my degree of commitment, neither under- nor overstating it to him. He is, of course, keenly interested in the degree to which I can be trusted, and the degree to which I am interested in him and his quest for wellness, as opposed to my interest in staying on good terms with "the authorities," or in proving the superiority of my theories and techniques over those of my colleagues and competitors, etc. With commitment, freedom within myself to respond to my client in *many* ways (not just saying, "mm-hm," or "You feel . . ." or "The reason you did that was . . ."), with courage on my part to remain authentic, but with some compassion, then with these things and some luck, I may well be able to let a relationship develop in which my client can abandon his safe but strangling way of the past and seek and find a way that he can tread with dignity and hope.

ANNOTATED BIBLIOGRAPHY

1. See Jourard, S.M., *Personal Adjustment. An Approach through the Study of Healthy Personality*. New York: Macmillan, 1964 (2nd ed.). This book aims at portraying the major aspects of healthy personality, and can serve as a useful source of "signs" of mental health and the conditions which foster it.
2. See Maslow, A. H., *Toward a Psychology of Being*. Princeton: Van Nostrand, 1962. This is one of the richest sources available of ideas on human potentialities for growth.
3. This view of experience is an aspect of the phenomenological-existential approach to the study of man. See Combs, A. & Snygg, D., *Individual Behavior*. New York: Harper, 1959 (2nd ed.) for one readable statement of this approach. See also May, R. (ed.) *Existential Psychology*. New York: Random House, 1961, for an overview of the contribution existential philosophers have made to American psychologists.

4. See Jourard, S. M., *The Transparent Self. Princeton*: Van Nostrand, 1964. In this little book, I discuss the implications of self-disclosure for mental health and counseling.

5. Read Goffman, E., *The Presentation of Self in Everyday Life.* New York: Doubleday, 1959, for an excellent account of the way people "act" their way through their lives. See also his book *Stigma. The Management of Spoiled Identity.* New York: Prentice-Hall, 1963, for an account of how people handle concealed or visible faults.

6. An important book which explores the importance of finding values in life is Frankl, V. E., *Man's Search for Meaning.* New York: Washington Square Press, 1963.

7. Ronald Laing, a British existential psychiatrist, has written several books of the greatest lucidity that illumine the way in which others entrap us in untenable situations. See Laing, R. D., *The Divided Self* (1960); *The Self and Others* (1961): London: Tavistock Institute. (*The Divided Self* will appear as a Penguin paperback in 1965.)

8. The books by Mowrer are pertinent here. See Mowrer, O. H., *The Crisis in Psychiatry and Religion* (1961), and *The New Group Therapy* (1964). Princeton: Van Nostrand.

9. See Buber, M., *I and Thou.* New York: Scribners, 1958, and *Between Man and Man.* Boston: Beacon Press, 1955, for accounts of the fundamental concept of *dialogue*, which is what counseling is when it is fulfilling its purpose.

10. The many books that resemble Dale Carnegie's *How To Win Friends and Influence People* actually seek to teach people how to *seem*, or play-act, in order to get a good name. In fairness to Carnegie, he enjoins "sincerity" upon those who would benefit from his advice — but how can one turn sincerity on and off?

11. See Rogers, C. R., *On Becoming a Person.* Boston: Houghton Mifflin, 1961, for a fine portrayal of the importance of openness for healthy personality.

———————

The interested reader will find many references in the books cited if he wishes to broaden and deepen his grasp of healthy personality and the role which counseling can play in fostering it.

EPISTEMOLOGY AND SCHOOL COUNSELING

Edith Schell Daubner and Edward Daubner
Longwood College, Farmville, Virginia

Because a counselor's interactions with his clients should be an outgrowth of his philosophical commitments, he must grapple with certain epistemological questions: (a) Can human beings know the extramental world or merely their own ideas? (b) Is human knowledge a *valid* representation of the extramental world? (c) Can human beings reach agreement about the nature of extramental realities? The counselor can assume two possible stances. First, there is the "realist" position which states that there is an extramental world,

Reprinted by permission of the authors and *Personnel and Guidance Journal*, Vol. 47, No. 6, February 1969, 506-513.

we can achieve valid knowledge of it, and the knowledge of various observers can agree. Second is the "phenomenalist" position: There is an extramental world, but no one can achieve valid knowledge of it, nor can various observers easily agree regarding its nature. The realist counselor should help his client perceive his problem situation as it "really" is and as it appears to others. The phenomenalist counselor cannot do this; instead, he can only try to enter the client's subjectivity and to help him deepen and enrich his unique perception of the problem situation.

What we shall do in this paper is to demonstrate that various epistemological positions indicate varying counseling procedures: that unless the counselor is aware of, has speculated about, and has taken a position regarding the epistemological problems to be discussed here, he may be operating unknowingly from a philosophical stance that is quite at variance with the one that his counseling procedures imply.

If we are to demonstrate that the epistemological tenets which undergird the counselor's daily life may be different from the ones on which his counseling procedures rest, obviously we must begin by defining the term "epistemology," (or "theory of knowledge"), and by explaining what facets of this extensive discipline will be considered within the limited confines of this paper. What are some of the basic queries that this branch of philosophy poses that are especially pertinent to the counselor's work? Before we can answer this question, we must state an assumption made by all philosophers, i.e., that the experience of "knowing" impressions, images, ideas, or some such mental content is universal among human beings. Granting this proposition, we may set forth a fundamental question which epistemology raises: Precisely *what is it* that a human being knows? Does he know only his impressions, images, and ideas, and mental operations that produced them, e.g., his image of his dog, and that he is having the experience of having an image, or is he also capable of cognizing other things—those which presumably *caused* the impressions, images, and ideas but are separate and distinct from his mental contents and operations—in this case, a "real," actually existing dog? As another example, when a counselor examines a student's cumulative record, is he aware merely of his own impression of that record and of his act of perceiving it, or does his impression put him in touch with—constitute a bridge to— an object which exists "out there," an actual, tangible record, which would exist whether or not he was perceiving it?

A second question which epistemology asks is: If human beings are capable of knowing objects and events in an external world as well as their own mental products and operations, how *valid* is their knowledge of these extramental objects and events? Are the human cognitive abilities—the senses and reasoning powers—adequate to represent correctly the data of the extramental world, assuming, of course, that these abilities are functioning at a normal level? To refer to an example that we used above: Does the counselor's perception of the student's cumulative record put him in touch with an extramental object which is *really* a cumulative record; which *really* has the size, shape, color, and texture, and *really* has recorded on it the symbols he perceives?

A final and closely related interrogation is this: If a human being is capable of cognizing an extramental object or event, is his knowledge congruent with the knowledge that other normally functioning human beings have of this same object or event? Referring to our example again, we ask: Is the counselor's perception of the cumulative record in substantial agreement with the perceptions of other observers, such as the teacher, the principal, or another counselor? We have mentioned here perhaps the most important of the epistemological questions, and they may be summed up, rather simply, as follows: Is there a real extramental world, and am I capable of attaining knowledge of it that is truly representative of it and that is like the knowledge other people have of it?

The counselor who has never reflected on these questions may, when he first encounters them, be inclined to consider them unnecessary and even bizarre. Why, after all, should he *doubt* that there is an external world, which is separate and distinct from his perception of it? Why should he wonder if his knowledge is valid—if his cognitive abilities are adequate to inform him correctly about extramental objects and events? Why should he spend time investigating the question of whether or not his knowledge of these objects and events is congruent with that of other human beings? Probably he has never thought seriously about these problems, but even a cursory consideration of them will reveal to him the fact that he has usually given them uncritical, affirmative answers whenever they have happened to intrude upon his notice.

Even such a skeptic, however, is bound to admit that, like every other human being, he has had *some* experiences in which he was presented with incontrovertible evidence that his supposed "knowledge" was not valid at all; indeed, on these occasions, he was not able to answer any of the above questions in an affirmative way. Perhaps, for example, his visual perception had once been so distorted that an automobile accident resulted. This led to a heated disagreement with the driver of the other car, whose visual perception of the same situation had been entirely different. Or perhaps he once experienced a vivid and convincing impression of a burglar prowling on the first floor of his house at three A.M., and a few minutes later found this impression to be unsubstantiated by an actual investigation, and to be unshared by his family. As a result, he was forced to conclude, finally, that this impression had been nothing but an hallucination. Perhaps after a repeated and meticulous balancing of his checkbook, he was presented by his bank, and by his own subsequent examination, with irrefutable evidence that his original calculations had been wrong. Since such experiences as these are quite common among human beings, they constitute sufficient reason for not regarding the epistemological questions mentioned above as unnecessary and bizarre. If the knowledge furnished by our senses and reason is not valid in *some* cases, it may not be valid in *any* cases. Epistemology is rightly called the "vestibule" of philosophy and indeed of all the sciences, for until we are certain of what we *can* know, there seems to be little point in seeking any knowledge at all.

THREE SOLUTIONS

Now that we have at least intimated that the problems which epistemology poses are not outlandish but are worthy of the counselor's serious consideration, let us examine briefly some of the solutions that philosophers have proposed down through the centuries. The range of solutions is extremely broad and naturally includes numerous subtle gradations and distinctions; but for our purposes, it will be sufficient to describe in broad outline three important positions along the spectrum, one at each of the extreme ends and one in the middle.

It is possible to hold, at the one extreme, that all any person can know are the ever-changing impressions, images, and ideas of which he is aware; that he has no evidence and cannot possibly obtain any evidence that there are external objects and events corresponding to, and causing, his mental content. A person holding such a view cannot be sure that other knowing beings exist, and indeed, he cannot even be sure that *he*—an entity, a person —exists. He knows only that there are shifting impressions, images, and ideas, and that there is an awareness of them which appears to be continuously connected with what he calls "himself." For a person holding this view, the second and third epistemological questions posed previously (Is a person's knowledge of the external world valid? and Is his knowledge of the external world congruent with the knowledge which others have of it?) need not even be asked or answered. This position is, of course, one of extreme subjectivism and solipsism; the most famous example of it is found in the writings of the British philosopher, David Hume (1717-1776) (Hume, 1958).

At the opposite end of the spectrum there are philosophers who hold that in addition to knowing his own mental products and operations, a person is capable of knowing that he himself exists as an entity, and that he is capable of cognizing objects and events in an extramental world. The world "out there" is palpably, indisputably, stubbornly real. It exists independently of human cognition: It would exist whether he perceived it or not, and indeed whether *anyone* perceived it or not. Those who hold this position call themselves "realists." They admit that a person with normal cognitive powers may sometimes have distorted, even badly distorted perceptions of the extramental world. They hold, however, that such distorted perceptions may be corrected, may be made to agree more closely with the way the world out there really is. Such correction is accomplished by comparing one's own perceptions with the perceptions of other normally functioning human beings. In this way, all human beings with normal powers of cognition, i.e., with unimpaired senses and a modicum of ability to think logically, may be expected to come to know the external world in substantially the same way. This position was first presented systematically by the Greek philosopher, Aristotle, and has had many advocates through the ages, perhaps because it appeals strongly to "common sense." Two of its modern exponents are John Wild (1955) and Frederick Breed (1942). Subsequently, we shall refer to this view as the "common-to-all, knowable world" position.

Between these two poles, it is possible to discern a middle-of-the-road position. Its proponents contend that the only valid knowledge that anyone can have is of himself as an entity, of his own mental products, and of the operations which produced these products. Thus far, the position does not seem to differ from the subjectivistic and solipsistic position of Hume, except that the existence of a knower is admitted. The advocates of the middle-of-the-road view do go a step further, however, and, like the realists, postulate the existence of a real extramental world which is independent of the knower.

Such a step is regarded as necessary to account for the simultaneous reports of various observers that they are experiencing the same external object, such as the Empire State Building. The middle-of-the-roaders reason that since an event does not occur without a cause, there must be some stable entity existing independently of the various observers, which causes them to have these similar cognitions. But, unlike the realists, those who adhere to the middle-of-the-road position hold that it is impossible for anyone to know what the extramental world is *really* like; that no one can know if his impressions, images, and ideas are faithful representations of it. Some of them also contend that the knower can discover only with great difficulty if *his* perceptions of the world are substantially like the perceptions that others have of it. Why is this so? Because the knower is trapped in the "egocentric predicament." He can never escape from his own perceptions to see what the extramental world is like when it is unaffected by these perceptions, and he can never have complete access to the mental content of others.

It is as though the human knower could see the external world only through the medium of a pair of spectacles, which he could never remove, and which possibly (he is not sure if this is so or not) color and distort everything seen through them. These spectacles would, to be sure, enable him to perceive the images of objects in the external world, but he would never know for certain if the images transmitted through the lenses were accurate representations of these objects. Furthermore, because he could never look through the spectacles of others, which are similarly unremovable, and which possibly (again, no one is sure about this) color and distort the objects seen, he would never know if his perceptions were congruent with the perceptions of others. Perhaps the distortions which others experience are similar to his; perhaps they are not. He may discuss the question intelligently and exhaustively with others, but he will never really *know*, for sense impressions cannot be adequately translated into words.

We may cite as an exponent of the middle-of-the-road position the German philosopher, Immanuel Kant (1724-1804) (Kant, 1961). The belief that the "real" world exists, but is screened off to some extent from the perceptions of human beings, is clearly set forth in his work, while the view that each individual's perceptions of it are unique and private is at least suggested. More modern thinkers attempting to develop the same ideas, especially that of the privacy of each person's perceptions, are G. E. Moore (1873-1958) (Moore, 1959) and A. J. Ayer (1910-) (Ayer, 1956). Henceforth, we shall refer to this view as the "private-spectacles, unknowable world" position.

As another label for the philosopher who takes this point of view, we might use the term "phenomenalist" (to be really precise, perhaps we should say "individualistic phenomenalist"), indicating that such philosophers are concerned with *phenomena,* or things and events *only* as they present themselves in an individual person's experience, and not as these things and events exist "in themselves," or independent of and unknown to human experience. Any reality hidden from, or behind, or beyond his field of consciousness does not interest the phenomenalist, although he does not deny that such realities do exist. The world the phenomenalist knows is an experience of his mind, a "phenomenon." This phenomenon is perhaps very different from the object or event out there that provided the stimulus for it. This same extramental stimulus may possibly cause a quite different phenomenon in the mind of another person. What the original extramental stimuli are, what the "ultimate realities" are like, the phenomenalist does not know, and insists that neither he nor any other human being can know.

AN EVALUATION

Up to this point, we have attempted to explain in an unesoteric manner three of the most important problems about human knowledge which are considered in epistemology, as well as three well-known solutions to these enigmas which philosophers have proposed. The first of these solutions, however, complete subjectivism and solipsism, seems to the authors to be largely an exercise in academics. Certainly, if the speculations of philosophy are intended to provide a theoretical groundwork for the practical business of everyday life, this position is untenable. Any person who would attempt to conduct his daily affairs on the premises that the only valid knowledge he has is of his own stream of consciousness, that he cannot know that any other thing, any other person, or even that he himself exists, would be doomed to perpetual failure, frustration, and unhappiness. The world whose existence he refuses to acknowledge will regard him as schizophrenic and, unless he voluntarily seeks the solitude of the wilderness, will probably commit him to a mental institution. In particular, the counselor has nothing to gain from espousing this epistemological position. A view which negates knowledge of the external world, of other human beings, and even of one's own self, logically could not be held by a person whose major task is using himself to help others deal effectively with their life situations.

If the position described above is of no possible use to the counselor, what can we say about the two other epistemological views that we have presented here? Does either provide an adequate foundation for the counselor's work? Further, if the counselor commits himself to the common-to-all, knowable world position, should he proceed logically in his work in a different manner than would be the case if he committed himself to the private-spectacles, unknowable world position? Perhaps the answers to these questions will be forthcoming if we consider what a counselor should do with a specific situation in his daily work if he adheres to one or the other of these views.

ALICE IN COMMON SENSE LAND

Alice, a very bright eleventh grade student who was recently placed in an honors program, comes to the counselor weeping copiously and complaining vehemently that she is doing poorly in school because her mother is pressuring her to practice on the piano and to perform numerous chores around the house. If the counselor is consciously committed to the epistemology of realism, the common-to-all, knowable world position, it appears to the authors that logically his first objective should be to determine the validity of Alice's, as well as his own, knowledge of her predicament.

In view of his epistemological tenets, it is imperative for him to ask himself such questions as the following: What is the real situation which confronts us here? Is Alice's perception of this situation valid or distorted? Is my (the counselor's) perception of the situation valid or distorted? Would Alice's perception of the circumstances in her home agree with the perceptions of a jury of impartial and competent observers? Would my perception of these circumstances agree with the perceptions of other competent counselors? More specifically, the realist counselor should inquire: How much time does Alice's mother really require her to devote to piano practice? What home chores are really assigned to her, and how much of her time do they actually consume? Does Alice make effective use of her time so that her piano practice and her chores, as well as her homework, are done with dispatch? Is Alice really as bright as I and the other school personnel perceive her to be? Does she perceive herself as possessing superior ability and hence as being able to cope with the demands of the honors program if the home responsibilities were to be lessened?

Not only should the realist counselor ask these questions, but he should use every means at his disposal to answer them validly. To determine the true nature of the objects and events out there in Alice's home situation, the counselor should logically confer with her parents, older siblings, other adults in the home, and possibly even the piano teacher, in order to compare *their* perceptions of the amount of pressure being placed upon Alice with *her* perception of it and with the *actual* amount of pressure.

The same procedure should be followed in determining the level of Alice's ability and motivation. For example, the counselor's belief that she has a high degree of mental ability may be predicated upon his knowledge that at the beginning of the school term she was placed in an honors program because of previous high classroom achievement, and that she attained high scores on group intelligence tests. If so, the counselor should attempt to verify the facts on which his belief is based by conferring with Alice's past and present teachers to reassess their evaluations of her ability. In addition, he would feel impelled to have Alice retested by means of an individual rather than a group test of mental ability. He should be interested in her teachers' observations of her diligence, conscientiousness, and efficiency in performing school assignments (which information might, incidentally, throw some light on her problems in handling home chores and piano practice). He would try to discover factors in her life that might account for her apparently diminished motivation in the junior year of high school.

What is the rationale underlying the *modus operandi* of the realist counselor? Very simply, it is this: There is a set of extramental realities that can and must be known by both Alice and the counselor if Alice is to take any positive steps to cope with her unhappiness. These external realities are inexorable. They exist out there whether or not they are perceived by Alice, the counselor, or her parents. For example, the honors program requires a considerable amount of extra homework; this was and is so, even if Alice did not realize it when she enrolled in the honors program. Unfortunately, this requirement will not "go away if you do not notice it." Furthermore, the differing *ways* in which various persons perceive extramental realities do not affect the *manner* of their existence: They are not changed by anyone's distorted perceptions of them or by the emotional aura with which anyone surrounds them. For example, to Alice, the process of making her bed each morning appears to be one which is unnecessary, which consumes an inordinate amount of her time, and which is a thoroughly disagreeable experience. In reality, however, (and, incidentally, in the perception of most civilized persons), the process is necessary in any household which is run in an orderly manner, actually consumes only a few minutes, and is not really an onerous or disagreeable experience. If Alice, the counselor, and her parents have normal cognitive abilities, they can reach agreement on the real nature of this chore and the amount of stress it places on the person who must perform it—and in like manner, they can make congruent judgments about the nature of *all* the realities in the problem situation. In fact, they *must* reach a substantial agreement if a resolution of Alice's difficulty is to be accomplished. If Alice's perception of the home situation is distorted, if all her home chores actually take up only an hour of her time each day, and if she is required to practice on the piano only one hour each day, then the counselor's task becomes one of helping Alice to correct her distorted perceptions of stubborn realities which are impervious to her inaccurate perceptions of them.

To the realist counselor, the basic problem is that Alice's perception of her home situation does not correspond to the actual state of affairs in the home: Alice's understanding must be brought into better alignment with the extramental reality which she is perceiving with such distress. Hence, it is primarily the independently existing, common-to-all, knowable world reality which is the desideratum in helping Alice to deal more effectively with her environment, and secondarily, of course, it is Alice's possession of valid information concerning this reality. To be sure, the realist counselor should be concerned with Alice's perception of herself because he admits that the way she perceives herself may materially affect the way she perceives the world out there. But again, he is primarily concerned with correcting her self-perception because he believes that such a step will enable her to gain a more correct view of the realities with which she must contend. For example, if, through counseling, Alice changes her view of herself while making her bed from that of a martyr to that of a responsible member of her household performing a reasonable, necessary, and not unpleasant task, he will have accomplished this.

In a similar vein, if the counselor's or teachers' appraisals of Alice's ability are inaccurate, e.g., she really has only normal rather than superior ability, the counselor's principal task should be to ascertain her real potential and bring about an appropriate adjustment of her school program, as well as a correction of the teachers' expectations about the quality of her work. If the perceptions of the school personnel are *not* distorted, that is to say, if Alice really has very superior ability, then the counselor's task is to work with the teachers to devise ways to help Alice make the most of her potential—possibly by increasing the level of her motivation, or by showing her how to plan and use her study time more effectively.

THROUGH THE LOOKING GLASS

Now that we have seen the direction that the realist counselor logically should take when confronted with a school counseling situation of the common garden variety, we can ask next if the counselor should proceed any differently if he is consciously committed to the epistemology of phenomenalism, the private-spectacles, unknowable world position.

The answer to this inquiry seems to the authors to be a clear "Yes." Logically, he should adopt a different approach. If he adheres to the epistemological tenets of phenomenalism, he cannot possibly hope to discover what the "real" situation is like. Moreover, his task *cannot be* and *should not be* to ascertain if Alice's or anyone else's perceptions are the more correct, the more valid ones. There is no point in his attempting to persuade Alice that the perceptions of others are more valid than hers, and therefore, that she should change her perceptions to make them correspond more closely with those of others, for neither he nor Alice can ever know for certain whose perceptions *are* the correct ones.

Instead of asking such unanswerable questions as: What is the real nature of the things and events in the home with which Alice must reckon? and Are Alice's, her mother's, and my (the counselor's) perceptions of these realities valid or distorted?, the phenomenalist counselor should concentrate on understanding Alice's perceptual world. He should inquire: What view is Alice taking of the objects and events currently thrusting themselves into her awareness? and How does Alice *think* that her parents and teachers are perceiving these realities—in the same way that she does or differently?

In other words, the phenomenalist counselor's efforts should be directed toward trying to understand Alice's situation *as it looks to her*. His task should be to attempt, to whatever extent this is possible, to leave his own inner world and enter Alice's unique, private world—to view her situation as it appears to *her* through the lenses of her spectacles. Of course, it is, as we have pointed out, a tremendously difficult, almost impossible feat for one person to look out at the world through another's eyes, a feat requiring a rarely-found degree of sensitivity. It is questionable, indeed, if anyone can *completely* enter the inner world of another; yet this is the delicate task the phenomenalist counselor has set for himself. How is it to be done? By creating a counseling climate which will encourage her to freely verbalize her perceptions of her situation, and by listening most attentively and astutely to her account, the phenomenalist counselor should try to pick up every clue that will enable him to station himself at Alice's vantage point, to see the situation as it appears to her, and to understand the way in which *she believes* that others see her situation.

If Alice's view is causing her trouble and unhappiness because it appears to conflict with the views of others, then the counselor's task becomes one of helping her to examine, to explore, to inspect, to scrutinize her perceptions so that she may become more aware of their contents, may see them in fresh ways, from new perspectives—and may better understand *just how* her perceptions differ from those of others. As a result of this self-scrutiny, the phenomenalist counselor does not expect Alice to "correct" her perceptions to bring them into accord with some sort of absolutely valid perceptions, but he does think that Alice might see the advantage of restructuring her perceptual field in such a way that the conflict between her perceptions and those of others is eliminated, reduced, or dealt with in a more satisfying, less crippling and self-defeating manner.

Like the realist counselor, he thinks that her perception of herself—as bright or normal in intelligence, as a helpful member of the household or as a persecuted family drudge—has much to do with her perception of other phenomena in her life. But unlike the realist counselor, he is not interested in correcting her self-percept because he thinks that this will help her to gain a more correct view of the extramental world, but rather because he thinks that in this way, she will come to understand more fully just how her perception of herself is causing her view of the world out there to conflict with the views which others have of it—and hence is causing her discomfort.

Why should the counselor who accepts the private-spectacles, unknowable world position proceed in this fashion? Stated quite simply, the reasons are these: Although there is an extramental world, which exists independently of anyone's perception of it, it is simply not possible for any human being to know what this world is really like. There are no common-to-all, knowable realities, and there is no one "correct" way of perceiving the world, at least not for human beings, who must use senses and reasoning powers. There are only perceptions that are idiosyncratic, filtered through the lenses of each person's unremovable, private spectacles. The lenses of each person's spectacles are ground differently by reason of differences in physical make-up, mental abilities, habits, attitudes, emotions, and experiences, and thus it is hopeless to try to achieve complete congruence of perceptions.

COUNSELING THEORIES

The authors are very much aware that the epistemological positions presented here, and the conclusions drawn regarding their significance for counseling procedures, are related to the various schools or theories of counseling. Is realism the epistemological foundation upon which such theories as Williamson's (1950) clinical counseling, Ellis' (1962) rational-emotive therapy, and Wolpe's (1958) reconditioning therapy logically rest? Is phenomenalism the epistemological stance that should be assumed by the counselor who espouses Roger's (1961) client-centered paradigm of counseling, and the existentialist models of May (1958) and Van Kamm (1967)? If a counselor is consciously committed to the realist position, can he be genuinely nondirective as the term is used in reference to client-centered and existentialist counseling? Can the counselor who attempts to function congruently with the tenets of phenomenalism believe that a client has made an objectively "right" or "wrong" decision, or even a more or less favorable decision? These and other similar questions have undoubtedly occurred to the reader and are deserving of the most meticulously thought-out answers. Although such an analysis cannot possibly be undertaken in an article of this length, the enterprise is necessary if the relationship between a counselor's theory of knowledge and his theory of counseling is to be completely delineated.

REFERENCES

Ayer, A. J. The problem of knowledge. London: Macmillan Company, 1956.

Breed, F. Education and the realistic outlook. In N.B. Henry (Ed.). The forty-first yearbook of the National Society for the Study of Education. Part I. Philosophies of education. Chicago: University of Chicago Press, 1942.

Ellis, A. E. Reason and emotion in psychotherapy. New York: Lyle Stuart, 1962.

Hume, D. A treatise of human nature. (10th ed.) London: Oxford at the Clarendon Press, 1958.

Kant, I. Critique of pure reason. (Translated by N. K. Smith.) London: Macmillan Company, 1961.

May, R. Contributions of existential psychotherapy. In R. May, E. Angel, & H. F. Ellenberger (Eds.), Existence. New York: Basic Books, 1958. Pp. 37-91.

Moore, G. E. *Philosophical studies*. Patterson, New Jersey: Littlefield, Adams, and Company, 1959.

Rogers, C. R. *On becoming a person*. Boston: Houghton Mifflin, 1961.

Van Kamm, A. Counseling and psychotherapy from the viewpoint of existential psychology. In D. S. Arbuckle (Ed.), *Counseling and psychotherapy: An overview*. New York: McGraw-Hill, 1967.

Wild, J. Education and human society: A realistic view. In N. B. Henry (Ed.), *The fifty-fourth yearbook of the National Society for the Study of Education*. Part I. *Modern philosophies and education*. Chicago: University of Chicago Press, 1955.

Williamson, E. G. *Counseling adolescents*. New York: McGraw-Hill, 1950.

Wolpe, J. *Psychotherapy by reciprocal inhibition*. Stanford, Calif.: Stanford University Press, 1958.

MISAPPLICATION OF THERAPY MODELS TO SCHOOL COUNSELING

Roger F. Aubrey

Director of Guidance, Public Schools of Brookline, Massachusetts

For a considerable time professionals engaged in school counseling have borrowed heavily from psychotherapeutic models in an attempt to find a theory and techniques viable in a school context. A number of factors, however, cast doubt on the applicability of any psychotherapeutic design to this setting. Among these factors are the structure of the school, training programs for school counselors, administrative attitudes, the involuntary nature of much school counseling, the limitations of time, educational objectives, the transitoriness of school counseling, and the irregularity of counseling contacts. Many psychotherapeutic models are at odds or even totally incongruent with educational objectives. Alternatives and options for generating theory and monitoring research are examined.

For the past two decades, counselor educators have borrowed heavily from psychotherapeutic theories in an attempt to discover an adequate framework for counseling in a school context. At the same time, school counselors have significantly departed in practice from psychotherapists. In addition, the school counselor's training program has been less rigorous and demanding than that of the psychotherapist, with an orientation and perspective weighted toward that of the adequately functioning individual, rather than the neurotic and pathological one.

In a critical appraisal of the current situation, Shertzer and Stone (1968) have surveyed the field and concluded that

. . . close examination of the counseling literature reveals that its theoreticians and practitioners have done little to specify the conditions under which techniques should or should not be used, have failed to organize techniques

Reprinted by permission of the author and *Personnel and Guidance Journal*, Vol. 48, No. 4, December 1967, 273-278.

and practices into a meaningful system, and are unable to predict what behavioral results will be produced by certain techniques.

Nevertheless, the attraction of systematized, consistent, and logical psychotherapeutic models have proven too much of a lure for most counselor educators to resist. The secondary school, in particular, has increasingly been a proving ground for theories, methods, and techniques initially devised for a clinical setting. However, client-centered, psychoanalytic, and behavioral models have met with only slight success in the school context, and that evidence which has accumulated (Kehas, 1966; Krumboltz, 1965; Reed & Stefflre, 1963; Thoresen, 1969a) is so slight and sparse that it raises more questions than it answers. What the research implies, in part, is that disparate counseling philosophies are vying for ascendancy in the public schools.

DECLINE OF PERMISSIVE COUNSELING

After an initial romance with client-centered philosophy, some school counselors became disenchanted; and in recent years the behavioristic (Krumboltz, 1965, 1966; Thoresen, 1969b) and neo-Adlerian views (Dinkmeyer, 1964; Dreikurs, 1967) have received increased attention in counseling literature. School counselors have quickly attached themselves to theories which require "no necessary and sufficient conditions" in order for counseling to commence. In actuality, it would appear that many school counselors, the majority of whom are former teachers, have long awaited counseling philosophies that would allow them to return to a more comfortable authoritative position similar to that of the classroom teacher. This position was first documented in Waller's *The Sociology of Teaching* (1932), and in recent years has been described by others (Getzels & Jackson, 1963; Gordon, 1955).

This authoritative posture grants its bearer certain privileges and immunities, and it seems no exaggeration to suggest that the teaching profession has long had an attraction for persons with a strong moralistic bent. Couple that with a captive audience of young, inexperienced pupils, and the adult-child relationship is hardly optimal for counseling. Rarely is the student given an opportunity to terminate his "treatment," and seldom is he presented with viable alternatives in resolving difficulties. Problems are invariably enmeshed with institutional demands and choices are frequently limited to an area circumscribed by institutional norms. In addition, teachers and school counselors are often confronted with two dimensions psychotherapists rarely face: time and the involuntary counselee.

THE TYRANNY OF TIME

The first and most important dimension is time. The average school counselor has a yearly load of some 300 to 500 pupils. During the estimated 1,200 hours in a typical school year, he is quite often expected to see each of his counselees once for scheduling purposes, and many times if they require special assistance. This schedule alone exerts tremendous pressure on the average counselor. He values each minute and feels that any time spent building rapport, exchanging information, or actually counseling must pay off in an immediate change in counselee attitude and behavior. In an evaluative sense, it is notable that the press of the school environment seems to make for a special distinction between *counselee attitude* and *counselee behavior*. Counselee attitude is gauged more by student conduct in interpersonal relations, while counselee behavior is reflected more in changes in pupil grades, standardized test performance, and the like. The interpersonal aspect in this sense speaks to the "hidden business" of the school. On the other hand, grades, test scores, classroom performance, etc. reflect the "real curriculum" of the school.

The school counselor also has a difficult time systematizing his working day. Unlike the therapist who conducts business on an hourly or regular schedule, the school counselor must sandwich his counselees between classes, before or after school, during study hall or library period, and on days when there are no assemblies. His schedule, like his role, is of necessity flexible, changeable, and at the whim and caprice of teachers and administrators.

Thus, the counselor's schedule is dictated more by institutional limitations than the personal needs of either his clients or himself. In addition, the counselor's allegiance is constantly challenged and put to the test by the conflict between the needs of students and the institutional demands of the school. This often takes the form of legitimate requests for intervention on behalf of pupils and the expected enforcement of norms and sanctions by school administrators. This conflict is in decided contrast to what occurs in private practice, or even a clinical setting, where the institutional demands are predicated upon, and congruent with, the needs of the counselee.

RELUCTANT COUNSELEES

The second dimension the therapist rarely faces is a reluctant or involuntary counselee. The therapist outside the school setting usually works with counselees who have either been referred by another agency or who have referred themselves. Even then many therapists utilize the option of interviewing prospective counselees to determine if they wish to work with them.

Quite the reverse occurs in a school setting. Those students needing counseling or presenting serious behavioral difficulties are often given no option by teachers, administrators, or even counselors. They are referred to a specific counselor, not because he presents those skills, techniques, or personality characteristics best suited for this particular student, but merely because he is assigned to a particular grade or alphabetical unit. In many instances, both student and counselor enter an undesirable relationship because of the caprice of a teacher or administrator or the rigidity of the school structure, not because of a thoughtful and considered decision by each party.

Needless to say, involuntary counseling rarely succeeds when student and counselor are victims of a system based on expedience and tradition. Both parties are exploited although, it should be noted, the counselor is much more aware and responsible for the nature of the exploitation. On the other hand, the student usually acquiesces in the first stages of the counseling process. In time his anxiety is heightened, not only by a confrontation with a school-appointed counselor delving into his personal insecurities but also because he is given little choice or determination regarding direction, termination, or compatibility.

PSYCHOTHERAPEUTIC MODELS

Under these circumstances are any psychotherapeutic models of use to counselor educators? Is the combination of school structure, inadequate counselor preparation, lack of time and facilities, counselor load, and institutional norms too much to overcome? Perhaps, but thousands of school counselors are functioning daily in schools throughout the country, many under the assumption that their particular mode of counseling is backed by a substantial body of research and data. What, then, can be done?

First, counselor educators, psychotherapists, psychologists, and researchers must enter the schools (and stay a while) and examine the situation as it now exists. This means, among other things, that research studies not be limited to the experience of interns and practicum students. Results of counseling must be determined by how on-the-job working counselors actually function and perform. Obviously, this would meet with resistance from school officials and would require tremendous amounts of time and effort. A large number of counselors and students would have to be carefully scrutinized, evaluated, and assessed before some guidelines could be established.

In addition, longitudinal and follow-up studies would be necessary. At present, much of what passes for the effect of various counseling stances on student behavior consists of master's and doctoral dissertations with little commitment to long-term research. Reportable changes in counselee attitude and behavior are often inferred or projected upon a time dimension extending beyond the study itself, and in most instances have not been documented by evidence or follow-up studies.

The need for more research and experimentation extends beyond longitudinal and follow-up studies. If psychotherapeutic models are modified, altered, or "converted" before they are applied in a school context, then both the process and the extent to which the original theorem or method was changed must also be analyzed. Otherwise, we may be drawing conclusions about a method or technique so transformed by its adaptation from a psychotherapeutic to a school setting that it lacks any semblance of its original state.

Therefore, before any meaningful research or experimentation can begin, it is imperative that competing counseling postures be rigorously examined. In particular, it seems essential to investigate the degree of similarity between the original psychotherapeutic model and the manner in which it is carried out in the school context. It would also be desirable to establish procedures to minimize differences in levels of competence among counselors implementing these studies. Hosford and Briskin (1969) have also suggested a need for "new research designs . . . to avoid the confounding effort of selecting subjects from those who volunteer for counseling." This variation between both counselors and their assigned counselees is another crucial but neglected factor. Even when all these factors are taken into account, however, other variables can easily contaminate results. Earlier, two such crucial variables were mentioned: time, and the voluntary nature of much of what passes for school counseling.

TRANSITORINESS OF SCHOOL COUNSELING

Time, in particular, has often been ignored by investigators. Time, in this sense, refers not only to the length, duration, or number of sessions a counselor and counselee spend together; it also includes the "set" or attitude of the two parties toward this concept. It is one thing for counselor and counselee to form a contract mutually over a stipulated period of time. It is something entirely different, however, when a counselor irregularly calls a counselee to his office or when the counselee hastily asks to meet due to some pressing need.

Certainly these latter instances typify counseling as it occurs in many schools today. School counseling simply does not fit the picture of the typical research model or clinical setting with a nice, neat time sequence, uniform referral procedures, voluntary counselees, administrative support, highly skilled and supervised counselors, etc.

Time, therefore, cannot be separated from the attitude and behavior of both counselor and counselee. The majority of research efforts in school counseling has made little or no effort to control the behavior of the counselor (Wicas & Mahan, 1966). The focus has been on the pre- and post-behavior of the student, rather than on an assessment of the consistency and effectiveness of counselor technique. However, most school counselors are quite aware that their counseling stance often changes in accordance with the topic, counselee, institutional length of time one has known and press, intensity of the relationship, worked with the counselee, and a host of other factors. Therefore, differentiating or categorizing counselor behavior is an extremely tricky business, compounded by the irregularity with which a counselor sees his counselees.

To control time so that meaningful and accurate data is generated, researchers must be aware of the transitory nature of school counseling. The assumption that there is a marked degree of stability in school counseling relationships is both naive and detrimental for research purposes. This does not mean that psychotherapeutic models are inappropriate for a school context, but research designs are certainly called for approximating that which psychotherapeutic models seek to examine and improve.

The involuntary nature of much of what passes for school counseling raises a serious question as to the usefulness of any psychotherapeutic model. The ideal of having the bulk of counselees on a self-referral basis is totally unrealistic in a school context, and, when attempted, places counselors in a competitive popularity contest, vying for student favor. At the very least, counselors are frequently forced to "sell themselves" to wary and cautious students. The alternative to persuading counselees is often even more unpalatable, for it requires that the counselor assume a quasi-administrative posture whereby the client is obliged to enter a "counseling" relationship.

When this compulsory relationship is labeled counseling and results are based primarily on institutional values such as grades or test scores, the entire question of which counseling model or technique is more effective becomes ludicrous. However, this is not to deny counselors the skills and techniques they need in dealing with reluctant and involuntary students as long as school administrators base part of their evaluation of the guidance services on this criterion. Changing administrative attitudes would certainly obviate this problem to a great extent, but at present there seems to be little hope of accomplishing this feat.

WHAT THE SCHOOLS NEED

Models and techniques which speak to the on-going problems of students and counselors must be formulated, and not Pollyanna-like schemes which promise much but deliver little. Researchers and theoreticians alike would be well advised to examine the sociological structure of the school before suggesting counseling frameworks directly antithetical to institutional norms and expectations. The school is simply not a guidance clinic or mental health center, and those counseling models failing to take this into account lull counselors into entanglements beyond their expertise and institutional prerogatives. School counselors certainly are in desperate need of assistance in the area of theory and research. However, the price they now pay for attempting to operationalize impractical and unsuitable designs makes it doubly imperative that theoreticians and researchers closely scrutinize the school structure before exporting models intended for other settings and purposes.

What the schools need are theoretical models congruent with educational purposes, and/or realistic designs which will enable guidance personnel to modify or change existing educational structures and practices. Those psychotherapeutic methods and techniques which fail to take into account the counselor's training and background, the conditions under which he works, the involuntary nature of many counselees in a school setting, the limitations of time and scheduling, the institutional expectations, and the structure of the school setting should be approached with extreme caution.

The lack of theory and research in the field of school counseling has long led guidance practitioners to appropriate designs from other disciplines. Hopefully, the guidance profession and counselor educators are now at a point where they can seize the initiative and evolve corrective measures which speak to the issues with which counselors have been struggling for so many years.

REFERENCES

Dinkmeyer, D. Conceptual foundations of counseling: Adlerian theory and practice. *School Counselor*, 1964, *11*, 174-178.

Dreikurs, R. Guiding, teaching and demonstrating: an Adlerian autobiography. *Journal of Individual Psychology*, 1967, *23*, 145-157.

Getzels, J. W., & Jackson, P. W. The teacher's personality and characteristics. In N. L. Gage (Ed.), *Handbook of research on teaching*. Chicago: Rand McNally, 1963. Pp. 511-582.

Gordon, C. W. The role of the teacher in the usual structure of the high school. *Journal of Educational Sociology*, 1955, *29*, 22-29.

Hosford, R. E., & Briskin, A. S. Changes through counseling. *Review of Educational Research*, 1969, *39*, (2), 189-207.

Kehas, C. D. Theoretical formulations and related research. *Review of Educational Research*, 1966, *36* (2), 207-218.

Krumboltz, J. D. Behavioral counseling: rationale and research. *Personnel and Guidance Journal*, 1965, *44*, 383-387.

Krumboltz, J. D. (Ed.) *Revolution in counseling*. Boston: Houghton Mifflin, 1966.

Reed, H., & Stefflre, B. Elementary and secondary programs. *Review of Educational Research*, 1963, *33* (2), 152-162.

Shertzer, B., & Stone, S. C. *Fundamentals of counseling*. Boston: Houghton Mifflin, 1969.

Thoresen, C. E. Relevance and research in counseling. *Review of Educational Research*, 1969, *39* (2), 263-281. (a)

Thoresen, C. E. The counselor as an applied behavioral scientist. *Personnel and Guidance Journal*, 1969, *46*, 841-848. (b)

Waller, W. *The sociology of teaching*. New York: Wiley, 1932.

Wicas, E. A., & Mahan, T. W., Jr. Characteristics of counselors rated effective by supervisors and peers. *Counselor Education and Supervision*, 1966, *6*, 50-56.

STUDENT PROTEST AND THE COUNSELOR

Richard W. Carey

Research Psychologist, Palo Alto, California, Unified School District

The problem of student protests provides a challenge to counselors because it indicates, among other things, that guidance has been ineffective. Five trends in student attitudes are described that seem to underlie widespread student unrest against the establishment. Then the role of youth in present-day social change is defined and related to activism, and suggestions are made for counselors interested in channeling student protests into educational improvements. Finally, a more aggressive and active stance by the counselor is called for as part of a revamping of the priorities governing counselor activities.

It is painfully evident that an intense emotional furor has developed in this country concerning student protests. The purpose of this article is to provide a perspective on student unrest and to reveal its major implications for counselors.

Counselors are part of the school establishment against which students are protesting. In fact, counselors have frequently been hired to provide the very kind of educational responsiveness that students say is lacking. Student protesters claim that educators are insensitive to individual needs, that schools are bureaucratic and make unreasonable demands on students under the pretense of educating them. Supposedly, one of the major purposes of school counseling is understanding the needs of individuals and mediating between these needs and the prerogatives and programs of the school. If this is so, are not counseling programs somewhat vulnerable, and possibly even fair game, for student protests?

Beyond the limited goal of preventing additional student protests, there is a more compelling and positive reason for counselor understanding of protesters and protests. Activist students do not have to present a threat to counselors. Although they use different words, these students seem to want the same thing that counselors want. They want an education that is sensitive

Reprinted by permission of the author and *Personnel and Guidance Journal*, Vol. 48, No. 3, November 1969, 185-191.

to the individual needs of students in a modern society. If this is really the case, guidance personnel can assist in rechanneling the student protests, and at the same time achieve some of their most important educational objectives.

Before exploring this idealistic-sounding option, one other popular alternative needs to be examined. The question is often asked, Is not present unrest merely another form of the traditional youthful rebellion that will soon fade away? Why not "do nothing" and ride out the storm of protest?

There are several powerful arguments for rejecting the alternative of doing nothing. First, present student protests are more widespread and have more powerful social implications than any previous demonstrations of discontent. Bettelheim (1969) has warned of serious consequences to higher education, and possibly to the whole American society, if things do not change. Second, there is evidence to support the idea (Banks, 1969) that the attitudes underlying the protests are likely to become even more prevalent. Present-day activists may be the forerunners of tomorrow's majority. Third, the rapid movement of the protests from higher education into the secondary schools cannot be ignored. We do not yet know the impact of increasingly emotional and violent confrontations upon younger and younger people. Obviously, many protests do not provide good models for learning the negotiating skills needed in a modern democracy. Sitomer (1968) warns that the real activists, or the potential militants or revolutionaries, are now in the junior high schools. We cannot expect things to improve simply by waiting for another generation of students who will be different. In short, doing nothing is a very risky alternative.

RULES AND EDUCATION

Developing a viable perspective on student unrest is not easy. The mass media literally pour out volumes of explanations. Halleck's article (1968) illustrates the difficulty of finding even a scholarly explanation related to the "causes." It seems more productive simply to describe the attitudes and values underlying student unrest rather than to speculate on the reasons for it. Recent research on basic student attitudes (Thompson & Carr, 1966) uses the conceptualization that values are in a constant state of transition. The transition is from a set of traditional values going back many years in American culture to emergent values, derived from modern pressures. This same framework has been used to understand changes in other cultures (Gusfield, 1968). Since student protesting is an international phenomenon, its breadth can offer many points for attempting to understand it. This transitional model also has the advantage of flexibility and responsiveness to very rapid changes in values.

From a review of research and the literature, there appear to be five trends in the basic attitudes of young people that clearly contribute to their willingness to protest against the school establishment.

TREND ONE

The first trend is away from the traditional view that it is the individual's responsibility to make the education offered him relevant, or he is at fault.

The emerging view is that it is the school's responsibility to make its programs relevant, or the school is at fault. The Coleman Report (Kent, 1968) has been interpreted as redefining educational opportunity in terms of student achievement rather than in terms of the amount of money spent or the student-teacher ratio. Schools are to be judged on how well their students achieve and whether what is taught is important, not on how hard the school tries. The recent thrust of black people to have a genuinely multicultural education illustrates this trend with a slightly different focus (Olsen, 1968). Black people's demands for a curriculum that promotes respect and understanding for ethnic differences is in sharp contrast to the traditional "melting-pot" concept in which ethnic differences are viewed as undesirable. As one observer of the educational scene wryly commented, "If God had known what the schools were going to be like, I am sure he would have made children differently." Essentially, the emerging view is that the school is responsible for providing more than an opportunity; it must educate all children regardless of the kinds of differences they present.

TREND TWO

The second trend is away from the traditional belief that a rule is a rule, and right or wrong it must be obeyed. The emergent view is that in some cases it is wrong to obey an unethical or immoral rule. Two studies of student opinion (Banks, 1969; Barron, 1967) illustrate this point. Barron (1967) found only 12 out of 150 attitude items that had less than 20 percent student agreement. Two of these items were "Disobedience to the government is never justified," and "It is the duty of a citizen to support his country right or wrong" (p. 45). Barron also investigated opinions that differentiated the parents (tradition) from the students (emergence). Three opinions among less than 10 that differentiated students and their parents were these:

Students agree more frequently than either mother or father:
"If I were confronted with the necessity of betraying either my country or my best friend, I would prefer to betray my country."

Students agree more frequently than their mothers:
"The less authority the better."

Students agree more frequently than their fathers:
"It is hard to see how juvenile delinquents could have been anything else, considering the environment in which they were reared."

The Yankelovich Survey (Banks, 1969) found that as many as two-thirds of the "forerunner" students agreed that draft resistance or civil disobedience could be justified in some cases. Asked to state which attitudes were more applicable to their parents than themselves, students answered "respectful of people in positions of authority" and "likely to accept things as they are." Students saw themselves as more "likely to do something about what [they] believe to be right." Dr. Spock's support among students, as well as the frequent citation in the press of the Nuremberg trials, and the public-condoned atrocities in Germany during World War II, provide additional evidence of this emergent attitude.

TREND THREE

The third trend is away from the traditional idea that school rules were made for the purpose of insuring essential controls or for making a better educational environment. There is an emerging suspicion that many rules are made for the convenience of educators. Goodman (1968) cites the findings of the Eight-Year Study, and concludes that even when educators know better they still "act according to their imperialistic advantage and administrative status" (p. 18). Bower (1968) suggests that the primary goals of our schools become displaced. Management of group behavior—not the education of the students—beomes the primary goal. Kleiman (1967) complains that "guidance classes aimed at fitting us neatly into the system and supplying us with the prefabricated moral code are so structured as to prevent any serious discussion of relevant matters" (p. 3). The emerging questions regarding the relevance of our schools and the "real" motivations of school leaders cannot be ignored.

TREND FOUR

The fourth trend is away from the traditional view that modern young people "never had it so good" with few demands and great security. The emerging view is that laws and processes purportedly protecting or benefitting youth actually discriminate against them. Friedenberg (1967) suggests that there is both legal and social discrimination against youth. Legally, adolescents are described as "having no basic rights at all" (p. 37). In a sociological sense, Friedenberg describes adolescents as a minority group:

> The adolescent is now the only totally disenfranchised minority group in the country. In America no minority has ever gotten any respect or consistently decent treatment until it began to acquire political power. Can the status of the "teen-ager" be improved? Only, presumably, through increased political effectiveness [p. 42].

Kavanaugh (1968) paints a grim picture of today's youth and sees the student's "search for meaning and values as a major factor in student unrest" (p. 55). Kleiman (1967), in a Students for Democratic Society publication, describes high school rather bitterly: "From the moment he [the student] enters school, he is subjected to innumerable actions designed to humiliate him and remind him of his worthlessness in the face of adult authority" (p. 13).

TREND FIVE

The fifth trend is away from the traditional view that we have adequate processes available to bring about needed changes in laws and institutions. An emerging view is that riots or other less violent forms of confrontation are more effective means of bringing about these changes. In the previously cited Yankelovich Survey, students were much more likely to ascribe "faith in the democratic process" to their parents (50 to 30 percent) than to themselves (11 to 18 percent). Unfortunately, violent or threatening behavior aimed at improving the schools has been rewarded much more consistently than non-violent behavior that attempts to work through normal institutional channels. Findings in learning theory have shown that values and attitudes are developed from rewarded behaviors; thus, without meaning to, our leaders may have taught that militance is more valuable than the use of traditional channels. Even more fundamental, militants may have been created with the values and attitudes that seek violence as a means of bringing about social changes. Of all the trends, this is perhaps the most frightening and the one most needing rational action by responsible leaders. Whether this trend produces a majority of activists willing to work through evolutionary means for change, or militants bent upon revolution, is a tremendously important consideration.

These emerging views are clearly more characteristic of youth than of older people. They seem to be important components of the willingness to protest. These trends indicate the need to understand the meaning of youth and its status in our present world.

WHAT IS YOUTH?

Sanford (1967) defines youth as a stage in life when one is not irreversibly committed to social roles, such as marriage or a career. Youth is a sociological condition and not an age. A youth is free to try different kinds of roles and is in a good position to advocate what is new and emerging because he does not risk an establishment role.

Nixon (1967) provides a psychological definition of youth: It is a stage in development when the individual has completed the distinction between self and setting. As this distinction progresses, "the individual's ability to see and to define and to criticize his setting increases; at about 16 he begins to see it clearly enough to know how it might be improved upon" (p. 6).

Keniston (1968) provides a historical perspective that combines sociological and psychological elements, and he then proposes a new stage in development. He traces adolescence back to the industrial revolution when children were freed from work at a time when skills teachable only through post-childhood education were needed. Keniston hypothesizes a new stage of life that intervenes between adolescence and adulthood. This stage of post-adolescence or pre-adulthood is made possible by the post-industrial society where deferred entry into the economic system is not only possible but, according to some, highly desirable. The new stage is characterized by psychological adulthood, in which individual identity problems are solved, but the sociological role of adolescence remains. It is out of this combination of ability to perceive what is wrong with the environment and the freedom from an establishment role that our "new" youth becomes an important cutting edge or wedge for social change. The post-adolescent has the ideas and the urge to bring about change, and he is less vulnerable than adults in attempting to do so. Post-adolescents make up an increasingly large portion of the world's population. They are literally demanding relevance and a part of the decision-making power on an international scale. A not unsympathetic definition is that they have the "freedom to be idealistic." It is out of this context that we hear voices from varied and often unexpected sources suggesting that student rebellion can mean social renewal and regeneration rather than chaos (Keniston, 1968; Nixon, 1967; Rockefeller, 1968; *School Management,* 1968; Thomson, 1969).

WHITHER COUNSELORS AND GUIDANCE?

Philosophically, guidance programs have grown out of the concern of many Americans about human beings as individuals (Wrenn, 1962). Good guidance is epitomized by the individualization of education to the interests, values, needs, and concerns of students. The challenge of the student protesters is that they are saying loud and clear that this goal is not being achieved. The old ways are not good enough for counselors. We can no longer sit in our offices as "listeners" and expect to do the job of guidance in today's world. Of top priority in any new directions for guidance must be a system that feeds back vital information on student attitudes and values before students have to take some indirect way of telling us something is wrong. It is a little embarrassing to read in the popular press what the students in our schools are thinking and doing, while guidance research and professional publications are preoccupied with relatively less significant matters.

What can counselors do if they wish to become forerunners in attracting the activist and alienated students back into constructive channels?

First, they can sponsor or conduct local studies in their schools on what students are experiencing. They need to know what kind of channels now exist in their own schools for communication of student needs and concerns. They need to know how big a share in the power the students feel they do have, and what they feel they ought to have. The notion of self-study at the school level is not new. What is new is the demand that this be put into a top priority position in guidance. Sitting in offices has not kept counselors informed on what students are feeling and doing. They need to go to the students to find out. The kinds of questions asked need to be different. The counselor needs to have the courage to ask specific questions about whom students can communicate with, and where they think they should have more power, even if it may raise some new doubts. There are risks in this. For example, in the Palo Alto Unified School District in California, the preliminary findings in a survey of student participation in decision-making shows the biggest discrepancy between what "exists" and what "should be" is on "choice of counselor." In other words, the counselor, whose job is to help teach how to make decisions, is assigned to students by a system that allows the student no share of the decision. Counselors have not seen research as a high priority item. But it is very possible that counselors would do the most to help their students and their schools by doing research with groups of counselees. This could be particularly true if their study is aimed at things that prevent school from being relevant.

Second, counselors need to recognize that students want a piece of the power. More important, they should help students obtain it. There is a need to broaden the concept of decision-making. There is a need to ferret out every place within and outside the school establishment where legitimate student involvement in decision-making can be found or fostered. Guidance people need to help the school develop more opportunities for student decisions beginning in elementary school. Students are capable of handling decisions and responsibility long before they normally get the opportunity.

The counselor's role should be reviewed. Counselors should go beyond helping students choose from among existing alternatives, and actively work to create more opportunities. An aggressive program of searching for and developing new alternatives should become a top priority activity. Thomson (1969) has suggested a community counselor. The ombudsman model is receiving attention and action in many parts of the country. In some districts, the school board even has student consultants (*School Management,* 1968). Parents have also been involved in providing students with a greater share in decision-making (Gelatt & Carey, 1967).

Third, tailoring educational programs to student needs should become a central focus of guidance and not a hoped-for by-product. Thomson (1969) has suggested minicourses and flexible scheduling as ways of providing new alternatives. Variations in grading and evaluation procedures offer additional opportunities for individualizing and allowing more student decision-making. Basically, educators need a broader definition of education for today's students. For example, student tutoring, counseling, and serving in the community can be elevated to educational respectability with credits and official educational rewards. Some of these activities provide attractive opportunities for non-academic and activist students. Social recognition and respect are needed for the idea that service activities within the school or community are "education" and not just some extracurricular frosting.

Fourth, counselors should be sensitive to and fight against attempts at student involvement that are patronizing. Phony manipulations and disguised paternalism could be worse than doing nothing. Honesty is an absolute necessity in efforts aimed at student participation. If a program seems to require more "abdication of power" than the school staff is willing to relinquish, they should say so. At this stage, adults have the prime responsibility to be honest or to end up reinforcing the militant student's claim that dishonesty and hypocrisy are basic characteristics of those over 30.

Finally, which personal commitments and values can help counselors earn the title of being "relevant"? Keniston (Hall, 1968) had some personal observations that might provide a clue:

> There is no other time in the world I'd rather live. It's a terrifically exciting, terribly dangerous time to live. Many of the phenomena we see among students are consequences of extraordinary privileges of this kind of society— an abundance that lets us take our ideals seriously [p. 59].

In the preconvention presidential campaign of 1968 an interesting phenomenon occurred. One candidate well over 30, an establishment man, attracted a large, energetic following of young people including hippies, activists, and potential revolutionaries. Their early campaign success was something of a political miracle and had a powerful impact on the course of national politics. The model of this candidate at the time of his success was fairly simple. He was clearly doing his own thing regardless of political consequences. Yet, he was working very aggressively for new means of communicating and sharing power *within* the system.

While the Eugene McCarthy model may not do for all counselors, it does provide some checkpoints. Counselors who really want students to get a share of the power, and who believe in an individualized approach to human needs, ought to ask themselves whether they take their ideals seriously. Do they communicate these ideals aggressively and honestly to their students, fellow teachers, and administrators?

REFERENCES

Banks, L. (Ed.) *Youth in turmoil.* New York: Time-Life Books, 1969.

Barron, F. Crisis in belief. *California Monthly,* 1967, 77 (7), 44-49.

Bettelheim, B. The college student rebellion: explanations and answers. *Phi Delta Kappan,* 1969, 50, 511-514.

Bower, E. M. Building bridges over the River Kwai: goal displacement and constriction in human institutions. *Psychology in the Schools,* 1968, 5, 310-316.

Friedenberg, E. Z. The image of the adolescent minority. *California Monthly,* 1967, 77 (7), 37-43.

Gelatt, H. B., & Carey, R. W. Helping students learn decision-making: a parent handbook. Unpublished handbook, Instructional Materials Center, Palo Alto Unified School District, 1967.

Goodman, P. How the school establishment hoaxes the public. *Phi Delta Kappan,* 1968, 50, 18-19.

Gusfield, J. R. Tradition and modernity: conflict and congruence. *Journal of Social Issues,* 1968, 24, 1-8.

Hall, M. H. A conversation with Kenneth Keniston. *Psychology Today,* 1968, 2 (6), 16-20; 22-23; 59.

Halleck, S. Hypotheses of student unrest. *Phi Delta Kappan,* 1968, 50, 2-9.

Kavanaugh, R. E. The grim generation. *Psychology Today,* 1968, 2 (5), 51-55.

Keniston, K. *Young radicals; notes on committed youth.* New York: Harcourt, Brace and World, 1968.

Kent, J. K. The Coleman report: opening Pandora's box. *Phi Delta Kappan,* 1968, 49, 242-245.

Kleiman, M. *High school reform.* Chicago: Students for a Democratic Society, 1967.

Nixon, R. E. The anatomy of student protest. *Vassar Alumnae Magazine,* February, 1967, 4-9.

Olsen, E. G. Shall we teach ethnic differences? *Phi Delta Kappan,* 1968, 49, 533-534.

Rockefeller, J. D. In praise of young revolutionaries. *Saturday Review,* December 14, 1968, 18-20; 78.

Sanford, N. The generation gap. *California Monthly,* 1967, 77 (7), 28-36.

School Management. Special report: student unrest in public schools. 1968, 12 (11), 50-98.

Sitomer, C. J. California's master plan is floundering. *California Monthly,* 1968, 79 (2), 10-13.

Thompson, O. E., & Carr, S. G. *Values of high school students.* University of California, Davis Campus, 1966.

Thomson, S. Programs for protesters. *Highlights,* 1969, 12 (86), 1; 2; 8.

Wrenn, C. G. *The counselor in a changing world.* Washington, D. C.: American Personnel and Guidance Association, 1962.

COUNSELOR, KNOW THYSELF!

In Quest of a Viable Model of the Human Condition as a Prerequisite for Professional Effectiveness

Ronald J. Rousseve
University of Oregon, Eugene

This essay represents the attempt of a counselor-educator to examine openly the philosophic-psychological premises and related value commitments which sustain his functioning, professionally and personally. These reflections in search of a viable model of modern man are based upon the conviction that unless a counselor is aware of the ideological determinants of his own behavior, he cannot attend adequately to the client's search for values and for a sense of personal identity. The presentation is not a finished treatise, but is an honest attempt at self-examination pursuant to the dilemmas which confront inquiring men in their quest to understand the human condition.

"Okay, Doc, but how do you feel about that? We've been grappling with the contentions of these other people, now we'd like to know your position on the matter. Where do you stand?"

These are words not infrequently heard (and sometimes suppressed) in counselor education classes in which the examination of divergent values and philosophic tenets are featured. Invariably, the alert graduate student wants the professor to lay *his* soul bare so that he (the professor) can be encountered as a whole person.

Perhaps only as the counselor-educator opens himself up for full scrutiny can he serve as an effective model of the mature, integrated personality whose emotions are not at variance with the cognitive dimension of his being. As the prospective counselor gropes for a defensible professional image for himself, he *needs* to encounter the complete person of his professor in whom, ideally, one should find verbalized value commitments that mesh congruently with overt behavior patterns.

Like the client, the counselor and counselor-educator must also acknowledge the impact of their own personal values on what they do if they are to come across as genuinely open persons in their interpersonal encounters. Unless the counselor is clearly aware of the ideological determinants of *his* own behavior, how can he possibly be sensitive to the *client's* search for values and a viable sense of personal identity (Boy & Pine, 1968)?

If the counselor and counselor-educator are to function with maximum effectiveness, the periodic open scrutiny and appraisal of their own personally held convictions about man and the human adventure is an undertaking of pivotal significance—no matter how anxiety-provoking the experience may become. Moreover, it is only intellectually fair that *they* do this if, indeed, their clients and students are encouraged by them to engage in the same process.

Reprinted by permission of the author and *Personnel and Guidance Journal*, Vol. 47, No. 7, March 1969, 628-633.

The commentary which follows represents one counselor-educator's most recent attempt to assess his present posture openly with regard to value clarification. Admittedly, the formulation of a viable "emergent synthesis" attendant to the several divergent models of man discernible in the modern world is no easy task. But it is in the *process* of constantly pursuing that challenging task that we gradually sustain the cognitive needs which are certainly of no less import in our strivings as human persons than the perhaps less elusive affective components of our beings.

It should go without saying that the projections below are open-ended. Reactions which might strengthen (or weaken) the experiential validity of this evolving framework for an emergent synthesis are therefore eagerly solicited.

SCIENCE VERSUS RELIGION

Starting premises about the human condition which appear to be supported by my experience are as follows:

1. Human behavior is influenced by the phenomena of personal perception rather than exclusively by the antecedent stimulus conditions of an external, objective reality. Man thus actively engages the environmental stage upon which he is set, modifying impressions from the outside world in terms of his own felt needs and sensibilities.

While the *primary* moving forces in human action emerge from the external environment, the privately apprehended world of an active perceiver significantly influences the character of the responses which follow. It therefore appears necessary to give strong consideration to inner variables as well as to those under environmental control. Moreover, the more broadly experienced the individual and the more "pluralistic" his environment, the more likely that his conduct will show the impact of perceptual relativity.

2. The realization *that* things exist is a cognitive experience which occurs prior to the formulation of hypotheses concerning *why* they exist. Individual mortal man, therefore, must decide for himself how to answer the question, "What is life all about?"—given the many divergent answers discernible in the historical ascent of the human species. Rational man must shape his own course out of the vicissitudes of his own experience, recognizing that only a false sense of security can be gleaned from unquestioning allegiance to propositions which are incapable of validation on the basis of scientific methodology and/or logical-rational appraisal.

There may indeed be an ordered plan into which man ultimately fits, but the decisions and the choices as to where to go and what to do to find that meaningful pattern must be the lonely choice of man as an individual, whose basic challenge is to become fully conscious of the meaning of his own personal existence. The ultimate questions of life and destiny, the inevitability of death, the real nature of choice, the notion of personal responsibility—all such issues are to be resolved in the experiential encounter between individual man and circumstance in the *natural* world.

I no longer feel comfortable accepting without serious mental reservation propositions which are not scientifically verifiable, or which go against the grain of natural rational reflection, or which find no endorsement in my own personal confrontations with "reality." Accordingly, I now hold myself in a state of skeptical disbelief concerning certain tenets of traditional transcendental theology; I *do* accept the scientific validity of the *evolutionary continuity* between the powers of man and those of the lower animals.

On the other hand, I have a vague belief in some kind of "ultimate power" which many men refer to as God. This is the power behind the whole evolution of the galaxies—an intricate evolutionary progression which, my rational resources tell me, could not have been sparked into being from a void. Still, I do not accept the notion of a personalized God and now prefer to exalt the more tangible reality of *this* natural existence rather than to fix my life around some "future existence" and the ceremonial glorification of some transcendental deity about which fallible, mortal, scientific man can hardly achieve consensual certitude. Thus, beyond the findings of science and man's natural rational experience, transcendental speculation and institutionalized dogma that are empirically unverifiable more fittingly might not be accorded priority over the *behavioral science image of man*. Instead they should be relegated to that obscure void removed from natural human experience which fallible, mortal man may never be able to penetrate with complete certitude.

In short, I now endorse a modern form of rational humanism with existential overtones—a kind of positive relativism. In this perspective, *truths* are "warranted assertibilities established through man's empirical, experimental study" and what are termed *universals* are "thoughts tested by their consequences and ultimately agreed upon by a community of competent knowers" (Brigge, 1966, pp. 269-275).

3. I have confidence in the *basic trustworthiness* of the human person— were all restraints on him ever to be lifted. Harvey Jackins (1965, p. 27) puts it this way: "Vast intelligence, zestful enjoyment of living, loving, cooperative relationships with others—these seem to constitute the essential human nature." When I look in on myself I catch glimpses of these qualities once my more basic survival needs have been satisfied. It would appear defensible to assume, then, that they are also to be found in other men.

There would appear to be these basically trustworthy potentialities in man; they are, however, too frequently distorted by the antagonistic, thwarting conditions of life in a divisive social world, *preventing* the realization of his higher potential. In terms of a general social-educational philosophy, then: A responsible rational morality, the findings of science, and the altruistic values emblazoned on the democratic ethic—all colored by an evolutionary socialistic motif (as partially manifested in Sweden today)—have now captured my allegiance. Such values are permeated by what some would call the *liberal spirit*, that spirit in certain sectors of our society which can help us to reject tyranny, intolerance, selfishness, superstition, and dogmatism. Hence, in education, while acknowledging that the schools alone cannot possibly remake society, I nevertheless see them actively participating in the dynamic, dialectical process of cultural renewal and constructive social change as they forthrightly strive to increase the amount of humane and rational power in the world while supplanting the divisive "marketplace mentality." Or in the words of Beck (1968, p. 172), "The experimental liberal argues for the openness of history and the freedom of men, at least in some limited form, which grant the possibility to men of liberating themselves from conditions previously considered inevitable."

BEHAVIORISM VERSUS PHENOMENOLOGY

The following points lend themselves toward synthesizing objective and subjective models in the study of human behavior.

To build a genuine science of human behavior one might well begin with the phenomenal world, but then one must transcend it, seeking to anchor his observations to certain non-phenomenal controls. Can the problems of subjectivistic psychology (introspective experience and phenomenological-existential constructs) be resolved by means of objective, scientific methodology?

In a challenging paper published in 1964, Rogers describes an empirical investigation in which objective indices of subjective inner phenomenological events *were* devised and measured effectively, projecting an affirmative answer to the question posed.

Moreover, does the phenomenological-existential position *necessarily* negate Skinner's (1948) contention that behavior is not a function of the person stepping outside the stream of history and altering his own actions, but a function of differential reinforcement from the culture? Regarding this point, a Cornell University philosopher, Norman Malcolm (1964), has said,

> I do not see that Skinner's behaviorism commits him to denying or ignoring the existence of the inner variables which Rogers thinks are so important. . . . Skinner will agree that people have purposes, but holds that meaningful statements about purposes are reducible to statements about functional relations between independent and dependent variables . . . the fact that there *are* inner variables does not preclude their scientific study.

DETERMINISM VERSUS FREEDOM

Along with many other scientifically oriented students of the human condition, I, too, accept the world as a determined world, for the spirit of science is predicated upon the underlying notion of cause-effect sequences. And yet people do, in fact, *feel free!* How, then, can we resolve the apparent paradox occasioned by the perception of the world as a determined world on the one hand and the perception of another dimension of subjective freedom on the other (Rogers, 1964, pp. 135-136)?

Perhaps Skinner (1948) *is* essentially correct when, in *Walden II,* he asserts that what man actually experiences in a determined world is only the "illusion of freedom." Behavioral scientists who have studied Korean War POW's have found that even the most highly motivated of men will succumb eventually to isolation, disorientation, interrogation, and relentless pressure— indicating that there is a breaking point for all of us, and that perhaps those behaviorists who look *outside* of the phenomenal world of the subject for the "primary moving forces" in behavior *are* building a sound model, after all.

Moreover, might it not be that the illusion of freedom is a reflection of man's imperfection—of his still limited reservoir of knowledge about his predicament? In other words, to state that human behavior is *not completely controllable* (predictable) does not necessarily refute the contention that it is, nevertheless, *completely determined.* Accordingly, a perceptive young psychologist (Frankel, 1967, p. 29) has recently asserted, "if psychology would investigate what makes men feel free, I am convinced the findings would not contradict the view that behavior is lawful and predictable."

CORROBORATING CONSTRUCTS

In an effort to clarify some of the implications enmeshed in the reflections above, several other points of view might be briefly touched upon here. For example, I have asserted man's continuity *with* lower orders of living things. In recent years this proposition has been endorsed by a number of eminent scholars representing different disciplines. Teilhard de Chardin's *Phenomenon of Man* (1959) represents the culmination of this Jesuit scientist's thinking about evolution, its direction, its beginnings, and its ultimate end. One of Chardin's major contentions is that all characteristics which are found in the leading edge of evolution (man) have always been present in some degree in the development of evolution—a consistent but modifying line from beginning to end. Predicated upon the conviction that living matter can develop only from that which already exists in some form is the view that evolution is the modification and refinement of that which has preceded. In brief, the phenomenon of man is viewed "continuously" with the rest of the biological world. And while reason might suggest that a lone, dramatic exception to the evolutionary thesis could be represented by a "first, uncaused cause," clearly the first causes lie obscured in the phylogenetic past, and attempts to isolate them appear destined to lead to infinite regress.

A second corroborating opinion concerning the basic continuity between *homo sapiens* and the rest of animal life was recently offered by the respected philosopher Mortimer J. Adler (1967). According to Adler, the question centers on whether the power of conceptual thought can be adequately explained by reference to neurological mechanisms and processes or whether, on the contrary, it involves some "factor" in addition to the action of the brain. Adler suggests that this fundamental question may be finally resolved before much longer, and he endorses the proposition that a difference in degree and a "superficial difference in kind" (between man and other animals) are compatible with the general coherence of nature and with the special evolutionary principle of phylogenetic continuity.

In the field of psychology, a provocative reinforcing opinion has been forged by the eminent humanist and 1968 President of the American Psychological Association, Abraham H. Maslow. In his theory of "metamotivation," Maslow (1968) asserts that the great, impelling, intrinsic, or ultimate *values* of Being (truth, beauty, goodness, order, justice, perfection) are an aspect of human *biology* and are on the same continuum with the lower animal life. It is the highest part of it, but still a part of it. And while Maslow contends that this so-called spiritual life is rooted in an "instinctoid," biological base that is probably therefore species-wide or supracultural, he suggests that it must be actualized by culture in order to become operative. In this view, the value-life and the animal life are not in two separate realms as most traditional religions and philosophies have assumed.

With regard to *the question of human freedom,* it is generally assumed today that a lawful cause-and-effect world exists that is continuously more explicable and predictable. It is also commonly agreed that behavior is caused. This does not mean, however, that we must therefore deny the "existential experience" of being free. Nor is it necessary to react to an awareness of the general determinants of human behavior with a reconciled fatalism. For while behavior *is* said to be caused, to be determined, the current limited state of our knowledge of these antecedent variables continues to support a creative potential and an unpredictability to human conduct—no matter how tenuous such attributes may actually be. In short, at the present time our discovery of the probable causes of behavior may be explained only *after the fact* in many instances (Maes, 1968).

Still, man does appear to exist

as a sophisticated form of animal who has been conditioned by the society in which he lives and who experiences only that latitude within the confines of this condition which will permit a compatible relationship between the standards of his society and the morality with which he views these standards [Gutsch, 1968, p. 240].

And what if the realization that we are not fully free means also that we ourselves cannot be held fully responsible for our actions? Then, so be it. Let us acknowledge this openly and get on with the task of placing responsibility where it actually belongs—taking care to program the environmental determinants of behavior so as to induce constructive, healthy conduct characterized by both humane sensitivity and rational appraisal.

What possible justification can there be, then, for our continuing to cultivate what very probably is the mere illusion of freedom?

One response might be to acknowledge again the limited nature of our control over the variables which influence behavior, occasioning only limited predictability. But no less significant as a defense for counselors and teachers cultivating the illusion of freedom is the undeniable testimony of countless numbers of persons all around us who invariably report the subjective experience of feeling free. For it is around this perceived reality that the individual appears to structure the style of his living. So long as our society values pluralism and this kind of psychological freedom, those of us who teach and counsel will doubtlessly devote our energies to establishing the conditions necessary to expand the psychological experience of freedom in ourselves and our associates.

Thus, both operant conditioning and perceptual techniques can be viewed as strategies for increasing the subjective experience of feeling free—despite Skinner's still theoretically valid denial of objective human freedom, as inferred above.

Finally, regarding the question of how the evolution of the galaxies was generated in the first place, there are those of us who would say, "I don't know" or "I can't understand" rather than to subscribe unquestioningly to the far-fetched creeds which antedate the probings of the scientific mentality. We believe simply that the whole problem of *the* beginning is probably destined to remain a challenging enigma of major proportions, which modern man must not allow to militate against his efforts to become more humane and rational in his encounters in the realm of the here-and-now.

On with the task, then, of improving our understanding, prediction, and control of human behavior, so long as we acknowledge and accept the concomitant responsibility to attend to human values in the process.

REFERENCES

Adler, M. J. *The difference of man and the difference it makes.* New York: Holt, Rinehart and Winston, 1967.

Beck, C. E., et al. *Education for relevance—the schools and social change.* Boston: Houghton Mifflin, 1968.

Boy, A. V., & Pine, G. J. *The counselor in the schools—a reconceptualization.* Boston: Houghton Mifflin, 1968.

Brigge, M. L. Why not positive relativism? Proceedings of the 1966 Conference of the Philosophy of Education Society, St. Louis, Mo.

De Chardin, T. *The phenomenon of man.* New York: Harper, 1959.

Frankel, M. Morality in psychotherapy. *Psychology Today,* 1967, *1,* 24-29.

Gutsch, K. U. Counseling: The impact of ethics. *Counselor Education and Supervision,* 1968, *7,* 239-243.

Jackins, H. *The human side of human beings.* Seattle: Rational Island Publishers, 1965.

Maes, W. R. Human freedom and the counselor. *Personnel and Guidance Journal,* 1968, *46,* 777-781.

Malcolm, N. Behaviorism as a philosophy of psychology. In T. W. Wann (Ed.), *Behaviorism and phenomenology—contrasting bases for modern psychology.* Chicago: University of Chicago Press, 1964. Pp. 141-143.

Maslow, A. H. A theory of metamotivation: The biological rooting of the value-life. *Psychology Today,* 1968, *2,* (2), 38.

Rogers, C. R. Toward a science of the person. In T. W. Wann (Ed.), *Behaviorism and phenomenology—contrasting bases for modern psychology.* Chicago: University of Chicago Press, 1964. Pp. 124-125.

Skinner, B. F. *Walden II.* New York: Macmillan, 1948.

COUNSELOR CERTIFICATION IN PERSPECTIVE[1]

R. Wray Strowig
University of Wisconsin, Madison

Certification is of vital concern to school counselors, their employers, and to counselor educators. The purpose of this inquiry is to move toward a better understanding of the functions, trends, and problems of school counselor certification. The subject of certification is most germane at this time in the history of guidance in the United States. Professionals and laymen are acutely aware of local, state, and national developments with respect to school pupil personnel programs, as well as the preparation of counselors and other pupil personnel specialists (Wrenn, 1962).

First of all, comment is in order about the procedure used in this inquiry, because it illustrates how the subject of certification has been neglected. The method that was used in developing this paper had to be analytical, based upon apparent historical trends and one's own judgment of their value. In surveying the literature, hardly any empirical research on certification was found. As Stefflre (1965) says about the counseling field as a whole, "Research has not helped us describe the function we are talking about, the specialist who is performing the function, or the purpose for which he was

---

An original article written for this book.

[1]Revision of a position paper on school counselor certification given at the first annual conference of Wisconsin counselor educators, supervisors, and directors of guidance, sponsored by the State Department of Public Instruction, Madison, Wisconsin, March 30-31, 1965.

hired." Examination of a dozen professional books revealed mainly repetitious generalizations about certification. Perusal of five issues of the *Review of Educational Research* (1951, 1954, 1957, 1960, 1963) failed to reveal any research studies of counselor certification that went beyond norminal descriptions of status. In fact, there were very few status studies. Moreover, examination of the contents, size, and heading in those *Review* summaries that were devoted to certification leads one to believe that far less attention has been paid to this subject lately than was the case a decade ago.

The dearth of good research on certification may be corrected soon. Much concern was generated in the profession by the ASCA and ACES studies of secondary school counselor role, function, and preparation. Many careful re-examinations of certification requirements will surely follow. Almost a decade ago, Barry and Wolf (1957) pointed out that, "Certification requirements as established in some states tend to emphasize the technical and to minimize experimentation." Perhaps, it is not too much to hope that certification requirements soon will be restructured to permit needed research to be done.

PROFESSIONAL FUNCTIONS OF CERTIFICATION

Opinions differ about the contribution of certification to professional growth. Wrenn (1962) said that requirements "are generally limited, unimaginative and untied to the past." Mathewson (1962) was more supportive of certification: "At the heart of Professional advance, lies the establishment and maintenance of state standards of certification, training, and practice." According to him, counselor certification and preparation have "unquestionably up-graded the whole perspective and practice in guidance," even though there are still weaknesses to both. McCulley (1961) wondered if the school counselor's duties are perceived to be different enough from other educators' to warrant certification.

One of the pro arguments is that students, administrators, and faculty are assured that the counselor who is selected has minimal preparation. Con arguments include: "(1) administrators are hampered in making appointments, (2) since applicants for counseling jobs must still be screened for personality factors, certification does not assure suitability, (3) 'all teachers are counselors' and therefore no special guidance training is needed" (Johnson, Stefflre, and Edelfelt, 1961).

Professional licensing (*sic*) is one mark of a profession. Sociologists offer a number of criteria or characteristics that mark a profession. Byrne (1963) modified Greenwood's "attributes of a profession" in the following questions, which are answered herein in terms of counselors:

"Is there a body of theoretical knowledge?" Yes, indeed, a tremendous body of facts, theories, and skills undergirds counseling. Unfortunately not all counselors are aware of much of this knowledge.

"Is there professional authority?" Yes, to some extent, as viewed by students and staff, counselors have limited authority.

"Has counseling community sanctions?" Legally, no. No privileged communication or expert witness sanctions are guaranteed. There is the limited sanction to practice the profession in schools, which is simply an extension of the teaching sanction. This lack is a basic defeat in counseling as a profession.

"Is there an ethical code?" Yes, but there is no requirement to subscribe to it. Society would expect an ethical code as an accompaniment to community sanctions.

"Is there a professional culture?" One is developing, primarily, however, in larger schools which employ more than one counselor. In one-counselor schools, counselors apparently identify more with teachers and administrative positions than other counselors do. (Wasson and Strowig, 1965)

"Do its practicioners have occupational autonomy?" Not completely, for counselors practice in schools, which exert much control over them, and they are certified by non-counselors. Moreover, they lack the sanctions necessary for autonomy.

In general, counseling possesses many of the attributes of a profession. It would be fair to conclude, however, that counseling is only an emerging profession. It has not flowered to full maturity yet. Certification has been both a help and a hindrance. The central fact that certification of counselors does exist is a great help to the profession. The problems of certification referred to below indicate some of the hindrances that certification provides to professionalism. Viewed strictly from the outlook for the counselor, himself, certification may be said to influence the field as follows. Certification tends to:

1. Ensure a more uniform minimum quality of some practitioners, while affecting part-time and minimally trained counselors very little.

2. Upgrade the profession, mostly in terms of preparation.

3. Partially control the content of counselor education programs.

4. Restrict the size and richness of the pool of talent from which counseling may draw by restricting who may practice the profession.

5. Legitimize counseling as a para-teaching function, rather than as an independent counseling function.

6. Accrue prestige within the counseling profession, a necessary element in developing a professional sub-culture.

7. Enhance the counselor's economic status and security.

APPARENT TRENDS IN CERTIFICATION

All in all, there have been many influences on school counselor certification. The national associations, such as APGA and its divisions as well as APA division 17, have had great influence on state certification, albeit of a rather indirect nature. The U. S. Office of Education, through the several vocational education acts and NDEA has a powerful impact on counselors, counselor education, and certification. One of the strongest mutually influential interactions has been between certification and counselor education. Each helps to determine the other, and both influence counselor roles. By far the most influential, however, in determining both content and implementation of counselor certification is a group that does not belong to the counseling profession, namely, local and state administrators and teachers. Emerging from this complex of forces and developments are certain trends in the certification of school counselors. Among these are the following:

1. Certification of counselors is an example of social change at an accelerated rate. The earliest professional counselor worked in the first decade

of this century, but it was nearly a quarter of a century later before the first counselor certification regulations were established — New York State, 1924 (Barry and Wolf, 1957). By 1951, roughly another quarter-century later, twenty-one states had counselor certification requirements (McDaniel, 1956). As of 1963, only half as much time had elapsed, but over twice as many states, forty-six, had such requirements (Camp, 1963). Only Alaska, Kansas, Michigan, and Washington had none, although each of them had special NDEA eligibility requirements involving certification. We have nearly reached the peak, then, as measured by states which have certification "on the books." Conclusions about uniformly general acceptance of the concept of certification should be made cautiously: (a) Requirements vary greatly from state to state. (b) In some states they are not enforced consistently. (c) Requirements in some states tend to emphasize certain roles, e.g., educational-vocational guidance, to the exclusion of others (Barry and Wolf, 1957).

2. Emphasis on vocational guidance, as opposed to other functions, is relatively less than formerly, although it is still strong. This trend may be reversed shortly when the impact of Federal legislation during the past two years is felt on the fields of vocational education and general economic opportunity for disadvantaged youth and adults.

3. As counseling has found more financial support, and as more counselor educators and counselors have acquired preparation in the behavioral sciences, there has been an increased stress on developing psycho-social understandings and personal counseling competencies, as compared to other guidance skills.

4. Teacher certification and experience regulations remain about the same. Miller (1965) reported that about three-fourths of the 46 states require teaching experience in varying amounts.

5. Multi-level certification is popular. One reason for this is that more schools can slip in under the tent of accreditation by means of an easy entry level of counselor certification. Another reason is that top levels of certification encourage professional growth. Keeping NDEA eligibility requirements separated from, rather than integrated with, regular accreditation plans has provided comparatively weak assistance to regular certification.

6. The tendency has been to name *credits* and *courses* in spelling out certification regulations, rather than functional behaviors or competencies. *Competencies* may become increasingly popular.

7. There is no evidence that professional associations of counselors wield more than recommending power over certification, although many state associations have influenced counselor certification by means of recommendations to the real certification authorities.

8. Unilateral certification regulations that derive from unilateral counselor education programs are not integrated with other pupil personnel specialties, such as social work, psychology, and nursing except, perhaps, at the remote level of teaching certificates and experience. California is an exception (Camp, 1963). Conversely, little attention is paid to "specialty" positions such as deans, elementary consultants, and directors of pupil personnel, who are within the guidance field. There is very little differentiation among specialties, either by function or setting.

9. Discrimination in certification requirements continues to exist according to how much assigned time counselors have for counseling and related guidance duties. Counselors working less than half-time are virtually ignored

in most certification requirements. Moreover, some states appear to be certifying counselors temporarily, even though they do not meet fully qualified standards. Is the presumption here that "provisional" counselors can perform just as well as professional ones; that a "provisional" counselor cannot harm clients and other students?

10. Almost no attention is paid in certification regulations to professional codes of ethics or other personal (non-academic) qualities of counselors. Certification continues to be based almost solely on academic achievement, teaching, and other work experience.

PROBLEMS OF CERTIFICATION

From among the functions and trends in school counselor certification, there are some problems that need solving as certification continues to reflect and influence professional growth. The problems that follow are not altogether original; neither is the list exhaustive. Among the most important certification problems are the following:

To what extent should the profession determine its own standards and do its own regulating (Byrne, 1963)? Most other professions set their own standards for eligibility to practice. A profession may actually administer the licensing program, backed by legal sanctions in the several states. Counselor certification, however, is not ultimately determined by counselors, supervisors, and counselor educators. Rather, people who are typically from the ranks of school administrators and teachers, and who may be expected to make counselor certification fit the general patterns of teacher-administrator programs of certification, make final determination of regulations. In addition these people often administer the licensing program details. It is true that counseling groups are frequently consulted in planning certification requirements, but theirs is not the authority to make binding decisions. The lack of regulatory power and leadership applies even more to the failure of counseling groups to be involved in the operation of counselor certification regulations.

How can the effectiveness of each and every certification requirement be determined? Validation of regulations should be deliberately planned and continuous. There should be no "sacred cows." Highly academic abstract regulations are often justified on the basis of the most experienced, educated, consensual judgment available. It is better, however, to frame regulations in terms of performance of competency. Once each regulation is described in terms of competency, it is desirable to experiment continually with the various methods of regulating. To do this empirical validating requires an open mind as well as provisions for enough flexibility to do comparative studies of variations in certification standards. We know hardly anything about the effectiveness of certification requirements. Much work needs to be done.

How can certification requirements best avoid counselor role stereotyping, while at the same time ensuring competence and knowledge? This problem has many facets. One is that many staff members do professional counseling and guidance work, but their counseling and guidance behavior is not regulated by counselor certification. Titles proliferate, and we are still not clear on who is, or is not, covered by counselor certification. Among the confusing terms are these: deans of boys or girls, directors of guidance or pupil personnel, vocational, educational, or other counselors, guidance worker, guidance consultant, director of pupil research. Operational definitions are badly needed, as is agreement on commonalities.

Another form that this problem takes is in creating a narrow crooked tunnel through which would-be counselors must enter in order to work in schools. The tunnel is narrow in the sense that only people certified and/or experienced as teachers may enter, leaving out of consideration many people from backgrounds in other fields who may be well qualified to become counselors. The tunnel is crooked because one cannot take a direct academic route into counseling. No other profession outside of education requires that one become qualified as a professional in a different field before being able to practice in one's own. Teachers themselves are not required to become counselor's in order to understand and appreciate the work of counselors. What is so unique about formal schooling that counselors must become teachers before moving into their primary professional choice? Are not hospitals, courtrooms, and churches just as unique as schools? Do teachers really make better counselors than others?

Another aspect of role stereotyping has led to the development of separate curricula and certification requirements for counseling, social work, psychology, and nursing — all of which may be called specialized helping professions to the field of education. Granted that each has different historical origins, as well as certain unique contributions to make, it would, nevertheless, seem that foundational preparation and part of basic certification should be required of all in common. The remainder of preparation and certification should be specialized. The question of whether or not to create separate requirements for counselors according to level of setting — elementary, junior high, secondary, junior college — should be answered similarly.

How can counselor certification better ensure that there are plenty of counselors who are of a high enough quality in schools? Part of the trouble is that, until only recently, not enough professional recognition was accorded counselors. Largely, however, the difficulty is that deciding what are (1) adequate numbers of counselors and (2) standards of quality both involve making value judgments upon which it is almost impossible to get full agreement. One argument is that since something is better than nothing, we should get people into schools as counselors even if they are not well prepared. Once they get on the payroll, we can induce them to improve. The traditional argument of the older professions, however, has been to maintain high standards even though there may be too few professionals available to serve the public. There has always been a shortage of high quality counseling in schools, no matter how lenient the standards are. Besides, human beings are precious enough to require the best care. The experience of physicians is frequently cited as an example of the latter argument. Physicians are selective. Counselors, likewise, could be selective. They cannot argue, however, that quality is a matter of life and death. They can only say that the improvement of life is exceedingly important, and that properly certified counselors are more likely to improve the lives of children and youth.

Counseling is just beginning to acquire some professional authority and community sanctions. The proper policy would seem to be to stress quality more and more. Communities respect high quality. Moreover, such a policy supports the improvement of life, provided that the quantity of counselors does not diminish. The experience of other professions is that a raise in quality does not drive more people out of the profession than it attracts. Besides, the better qualified counselors are not the ones who will leave when standards are raised.

High certification standards should apply to all who are entitled to a counseling position, regardless of school size, exact title, or amount of time spent in counseling work (Byrne, 1963). It is possible and realistic, on the other hand, to differentiate among persons who perform different kinds of functions. It is also possible and realistic to set up levels of certification that encourage counselors to improve themselves beyond a minimally acceptable level.

To bring about improvements with all deliberate speed is important. Our communities are ready by and large, but improvement must be educative, not capricious or arbitrary. It is better, therefore, to invoke change gradually. Neither raising nor maintaining high quality certification standards will work without reasonable ways of enforcing them. The traditional mode of enforcement is to require a school to have certified counselors in order to be accredited or to receive state or federal funds. These status and financial incentives are sorely needed as support for counselor certification.

How can counselor certification protect and enhance the professional welfare of the individual counselor? The usual viewpoint about the professional person's welfare is that it influences the welfare of those whom he serves, i.e., what is good for the school counselor is good for his students — an example of a vague generality. More concretely, the counselor who moves from state to state will be helped if there are reciprocity agreements on certification between the states. The counselor will also be helped if the application-evaluation-certification process is efficient. Reciprocity between counselor education institutions and certification agencies should enhance efficiency. Another help to the counselor would be to guarantee him due process, i.e., provide the right and means of appeal from administrative decisions as to his certification. Among professionals, the primary source of appeal is to a board of one's peers. Finally, it will help the counselor and those he serves if certification provides ways of committing him to a professional code of ethics, as well as assuring one and all of his personal qualifications as a counselor. Like it or not, counseling is a rather personal affair which carries with it strong ethical overtones.

SELECTED RECOMMENDATIONS

No doubt current regulations on the certification of school counselors have been recommended by professional people who worked long and hard at their task. Needless to say, there have been company compromises. One of the most influential of these for many states was the idea that a modest beginning was more achievable than some ideal would be. Undoubtedly, this was true. On the other hand, it has become necessary almost at once to begin considering how the certification regulations should be upgraded. This task has been the continual concern of the state guidance supervisors and other professionals. For example, the Wisconsin Personnel and Guidance Association has an active statewide committee on revision of certification.

The recommendations that are offered below are based on current state regulations as viewed in the light of the foregoing analysis. Following the recommendations there is a concluding section on implementation. Neither list is exhaustive. Rather, those stipulations that appeared to be most vital at this time were selected for mention. This is as it should be, for a complete proposal for a revised code will be the work of many hearts and minds in each particular state.

Recommendation "A"

The certification of a counselor is not just a matter of being assured that he passed certain courses or even whole curricula. Certification by course and credit should be eschewed. Rather, the code should be geared to the man — what he is and does. More specifically, it is recommended that certification be based partially on skills and undertandings that grow out of predominantly graduate (professional) level preparation. The ASCA report (1964) lists these as "Professional Competencies." These competencies are minimal requirements for the certification level called Professional Counselor below. Lesser or greater levels of certification would involve modifications of the ASCA list.

Recommendation "B"

Professional Competencies are primarily a product of academic preparation, but Professional Responsibilities are acquired in field and laboratory settings. Both facets of professional development may be under the supervision of counselor education institution, and both are closely related (hopefully!). Responsibilities, however, are qualitatively different from Competencies as portrayed in the ASCA report (1964). Hence, it is recommended that state counselor certification requirements include recognition of the determination of Professional Responsibilities at the same level as Competencies described in the ASCA report cited in "A" above. Endorsement of the applicant for certification by laboratory and field supervisors should be mandatory.

Recommendation "C"

Counselors seeking certification should be required to swear or affirm their commitment to a professional code of ethics for school counselors. The code of APGA, or a state version thereof, may be appropriate, although a briefer, more general, Hippocratic-type statement is preferable. The writer is aware of the dangers of loyalty oaths, the reluctance of some people to swear to anything, and the futility of legislating beliefs. On the other hand, a profession is a voluntary association, not open to anyone without meeting prerequisites. Counselors must stand together on their commitments to their practice. There is presently little to compel them to do so. To affirm one's ethics may help to live up to them, and it may assist in building a professional culture.

Recommendation "D"

The applicant should be required to furnish evidence that character and personality are not inimical to the practice of counseling at the time of application. Usually, the evidence would be in the form of opinions from people who know the person and who know counseling well. This recommendation is stated negatively because there is little agreement on the positive attributes of successful counselors. It is geared to opinions of the applicant at the time of application because no one should be asked to evaluate another person for all time. This recommendation forces recognition of the importance of personality in counseling that goes beyond academic and practical preparation.

Recommendation "E"

It is necessary to provide for different levels of certification, both in order to recognize and upgrade professional advancement and to supervise the work of people who are doing related guidance tasks but who are not qualified counselors. Therefore, it is recommended that there be three levels of certification.

The main level may be called "Professional Counselor." It is this level that is the guideline for other recommendations in this paper. It may be the entry level of certification for many counselors, although there is a lower level of certification. The professional level, however, is the lowest one that uses the title, counselor. The Professional Counselor's academic preparation should be the equivalent of a master's degree in counseling, assuming that the Competencies referred to above are covered in the preparation program. (Let counselor educators worry about one vs. two-year master's degrees.)

It is further recommended that the lowest level of certification be called "Guidance Worker" or some similar title that does not include the term, counselor. Guidance Workers would be paraprofessionals in a sense, although they might or might not be teachers, e.g., housewives who had taken a short term intensive institute in guidance techniques. A school might employ such people temporarily, but after a period of, say, five years the school would be expected to employ a Professional Counselor. For the individual, however, this level of certification would be as permanent as any other (see below).

The third level of certification could be entitled "Specialist in ———," and would designate the competency and responsibility of a Professional Counselor who had secured advanced preparation and/or significant experience in an area of specialization. A master's degree in counseling, plus approximately one academic year of preparation in specialized competency areas would be minimal. Requirements for scholarly and practical advancement could vary in quantity and type according to the specialty. Among these specialties might be: advanced counseling, pupil personnel administration, research, psychometrics, admissions and placement, elementary school guidance consultant, vocational counseling. One person might specialize in several areas. Suitable certificates should be issued for each specialty, and schools should be induced to reward advancements tangibly.

Recommendation "F"

No certificate should be permanent. All three certificates should be renewable indefinitely, provided that evidence of professional growth is presented in the form of further studies and experience that is relevant to the certificate. Ordinary on-the-job experience, presumably, would not count, since that accumulates for everyone.

IMPLEMENTATION

It is important to consider carefully how changes can be made best. Many a good program has failed because it was not well executed. Here are a few suggestions. The last one is the most important, perhaps.

1. Allow a period of three to five years for transition from the present plan to a new one. School, counselors, and counselor education institutions should be well informed at an early date. There should be no grandfather clause that lasts beyond ten years after the new plan begins, although currently employed counselors should be given ample time to meet the new certification requirements.

2. Begin work on defining the scope of certification in terms of various job titles used in schools (see above). At the same time, commence explorations with fellow professions — social work, nursing, and school psychology — in search of common bases for preparation and certification.

3. Develop interstate reciprocity agreements, especially at the approximate level of Professional Counselor. In doing this, work with certification stipulations, not titles, and provide for meeting requirements by examination or other suitable means in emergencies.

4. Build into the certification code definite provisions for doing research studies to improve certification. This will involve granting authority to persons or groups to deviate from regulations for a stated time period in order to accomplish the research.

5. Get the colleges and universities that prepare most of the state's counselors to indicate in detail how they prepare people to meet particular standards. The certification agency and each institution should publicize this information. There is no intention here of forcing institutions to have identical programs of preparation. Institutions could continue, of course, to endorse an individual en bloc if he had successfully completed their entire program, and if that program met standards of certification in all of the competencies and responsibilities.

6. Put teeth into certification by recognizing the levels as special classes of membership in the professional association and by having the state apply the sanctions of school accreditation and financial aids to schools that employ certified guidance personnel.

7. The chief state school officer and the leaders of the state counselor associations should support the administration of counselor certification by the state as follows: Jointly appoint a Counselor Certification Board composed of school counselors, pupil personnel administrators, counselor educators, and state supervisors of guidance, the latter serving as executive secretaries to the Board. Terms of office for other Board members should be rotated at different times to provide continuity. The state association should help pay for necessary expenses. The Board would make policy and would execute certain tasks. Its functions would be to: (a) conduct a program of regular and systematic evaluation of counselor certification; (b) encourage and conduct research studies designed to test new ideas in certification; (c) keep counselors and the public informed about counselor certification; (d) receive communications from laymen and professionals about certification problems; (e) explore ways of cooperating with other professional groups; (f) determine acceptable kinds of "irregular" preparation and experience for certification,

e.g., conferences, workshops, contribution to a research project in counseling; (g) conduct hearings and written examinations of applicants for certification whose cases cannot be decided through routine procedures; (h) demonstrate the efficacy of cooperation between a professional group and state school authorities in ways that enhance the dignity, creativity, and growth of school counselors everywhere.

References

(Page numbers are listed in the order of mention in text.)

American School Counselor Association. STATEMENT OF POLICY FOR SECONDARY SCHOOL COUNSELORS. American Personnel and Guidance Association, 1964. 11 pp.

Barry, Ruth and Beverly Wolf. MODERN ISSUES IN GUIDANCE-PERSONNEL WORK. New York: Bureau of Publications, Teachers College, Columbia University, 1957. Pp. 94, 83, 134.

Byrne, Richard Hill. THE SCHOOL COUNSELOR. Boston: Houghton Mifflin, 1963. Pp. 274-282, 256.

Camp, Dolph. GUIDANCE WORKERS CERTIFICATION REQUIREMENTS. (rev.) Washington: U. S. Dept of Health, Education, and Welfare. 1963 (OE-25005A). 107 pp.

"Guidance and Counseling." REVIEW OF EDUCATIONAL RESEARCH. 21 (1951) 159-166.

"Guidance, Counseling and Pupil Personnel." REVIEW OF EDUCATIONAL RESEARCH. 24 (1954) 109-112.

"Guidance and Counseling." REVIEW OF EDUCATIONAL RESEARCH. 27 (1957) 174-185.

"Guidance and Counseling." REVIEW OF EDUCATIONAL RESEARCH. 30 (1960) 115-130.

"Guidance, Counseling, and Personnel Services." REVIEW OF EDUCATIONAL RESEARCH. 33 (1963) 171-178.

Johnson, Walter F., Buford Stefflre, and Roy A. Edelfelt. PUPIL PERSONNEL AND GUIDANCE SERVICES. New York: McGraw-Hill, 1961. Pp. 208.

McCully, C. Harold. "A Rationale for Counselor Certification," COUNSELOR EDUCATION AND SUPERVISION. 1 (1961) 3-9.

McDaniel, Henry B. GUIDANCE IN THE MODERN SCHOOL. New York: Dryden, 1956. Pp. 446.

Mathewson, Robert Hendry. GUIDANCE POLICY AND PRACTICE (3rd. ed.). New York: Harper and Row. 1962. Pp. 181, 95.

Miller, Carroll H. GUIDANCE SERVICES. New York: Harper and Row. 1965. Pp. 229.

Stefflre, Buford. (ed.) THEORIES OF COUNSELING. New York: McGraw-Hill, 1965. Pp. 269.

Wasson, Robert M. and R. Wray Strowig. "Professional Isolation and Counselor Role." PERSONNEL AND GUIDANCE JOURNAL. 43 (1965) 457-460.

Wrenn, C. Gilbert. COUNSELOR IN A CHANGING WORLD. Washington: American Personnel and Guidance Association, 1962. Pp. 176.

(31)

CONTRIBUTIONS OF TELEOANALYTIC THEORY AND TECHNIQUES TO SCHOOL COUNSELING

Don Dinkmeyer

DePaul University, Chicago

Counselor educators should be concerned with presenting varied theoretical approaches to school counseling. This article develops the teleoanalytic position and acquaints the reader with Adlerian concepts and procedures. 10 assumptions for understanding personality are set forth. Unique counseling procedures that develop from this rationale, such as Early Recollections, Family Constellation, and "The Hidden Reason," are described.

School counseling demands competency in a variety of psychological areas in the dimensions of educational, vocational, and personal-social problems, and in the area of consulting teachers and parents.

The most noticeable deficiency in some counselor-education experiences is the lack of familiarity with a theory demonstrated to be effective in school counseling. The purpose of this paper is to present the contributions of Adlerian psychology to school counseling.

AN OVERVIEW OF PERSONALITY THEORY AS RELATED TO COUNSELING

Adlerians perceive man as an indivisible, social, decision-making being whose psychological movement and actions have a purpose. The fundamental assumptions for understanding personality are:

1. *Human personality is best understood in its unity or pattern.* This is the holistic approach, which views man as a unified organism, a unity moving by definite life patterns toward a goal. He is seen as a total unit and regarded as an irreducible whole. From this vantage point, we do not add to our understanding by fragmentary analysis, but instead are required to see the pattern and relationship between the data.

2. *Behavioral is goal-directed and purposive.* A contrast is apparent here. There are theorists who adhere to the view that behavior is caused, and can always be explained in mechanical terms. From this point of view, motivation can be understood in the light of its goal-directed nature; such goals give direction to man's striving which becomes the final cause or final explanation. In contradistinction, Adlerians look forward to determine the cause; they comprehend the goal as the cause.

   Furthermore, the goals are recognized and treated as subjective, creative, and unconscious goals, that may be only dimly perceived by the individual. It is recognized that they direct the person's selective responses

Reprinted by permission of the author and *Personnel and Guidance Journal*, Vol. 47, No. 7, March 1969, 628-633.

in two areas: in the cognitive life (revealing his private logic) and in the emotional life wherein emotions may be employed as social tools.

3. *Motivation can be understood as the striving for significance or the movement to enhance self-esteem.* Striving for significance receives its direction from the individual's unique, subjectively conceived goal of success (self-ideal). This search for significance emerges when man experiences the subjective feeling of being less than others and then engages in various attempts to compensate. His inferiority feelings are often due to a faulty self-evaluation. This situation suggests that we seek a master motive, a concept common in organismic psychology. It has sometimes been called self-actualization, self-expansion, or competence (Dreikurs, 1950; Rogers, 1951; Maslow, 1954; Combs & Snygg, 1959; White, 1959).

4. *All behavior has social meaning.* Man is primarily a social being, and his behavior is understood in terms of its social context. The significance of behavior really lies in our interaction and transaction with others. Social striving, from this point of view, is primary, not secondary. Behavior is highly influenced by the consequences of the reactions of other persons. Behavior often makes sense in terms of an ironic social regard, e.g., a child's bothering the teacher and forcing her to deal with him so that he can have a special place among the peers of the class and the school.

5. *Each individual has the creative power to make biased interpretations.* Biased apperception influences our every process. Behavior is not only reactive, it is creative. The individual has the power of choice. His uniqueness ultimately rests in this creative power. Behavior is thus understood not only within the purview of stimulus and response, but also in terms of the intervening variable of the organism or person who makes a creative decision about that stimulus (S-O-R).

6. *The individual is understood in terms of his phenomenological field.* The individual, being always understood in terms of his subjective point of view, impels us to be concerned with the meaning that a given event possesses for him.

7. *Belonging is a basic need.* Man has the desire to belong to someone or something. His social significance derives from belonging. He is not actualized without belonging. Many of man's fears and anxieties arise out of the fear of not belonging or of not being acceptable.

8. *The emphasis is on idiographic, not nomothetic laws.* There is a greater concern with finding laws that apply characteristically to the individual in relation to his style of life (idiographic) than in the development of nomothetic laws that apply generally but include many exceptions.

9. *The Psychology of Use has priority over the Psychology of Possession.* We are concerned with determining the conclusions the person has drawn from his experiences. The individual at any moment does that which is most useful or best accomplishes his purposes and strivings at that moment. That which interferes with his goals is not done. This principle is noted in the varying ways in which individuals make use of their heredity or their environment.

10. *The development of social interest is crucial for mental health.* Social interest is based on our capacity to give and take. It is demonstrated by a readiness to demand less than one is able to offer and in the desire to cooperate. Social interest becomes a criterion of mental health. This

method of counseling places as much emphasis on cognitive change as it does on affective change.

COUNSELING PROCEDURES

The foregoing assumptions, fundamental to Adlerian psychology, lead naturally into a set of procedures.

Counseling is seen as a learning process that provides a re-educative bridge for solving the tasks of life. Counseling involves communications for the purpose of modifying concepts, convictions, and attitudes.

The counseling process is divided into four parts: (1) the relationship; (2) the investigation of dynamics and motives; (3) insight; and (4) the reorientation phase.

The Relationship

There is an emphasis upon an alignment of the goals of counselor and counselee. Effective counseling cannot take place unless the counselor and the counselee are working within a framework of similar purpose. This type of relationship transcends rapport.

Since school counseling often involves contact with children who are not self-referred, the aspect of goal alignment becomes crucial to the relationship from the very start. A bridge to such alignment can be found, more often than not, through the development of intermediate goals. The counselor may ask, for example, "Would you like to find out why you feel that way?" Or he may choose to work with the counselee on a current problem which may lead to the major concern.

Indispensable to the relationship is mutual trust and respect. The child is treated with respect even when his ideas are diverse and opposed. It is axiomatic that one of the functions of the counselor is to listen and to understand. A child seldom has situations in which adults show that they really care about what he says. It is this unique understanding that leads to and provides a therapeutic relationship. Empathy in this relationship is the result of being understood. Stated another way, when the child is in contact with an adult who shows he understands how that child feels and can guess his private logic, the highest form of empathy is achieved. It becomes important, through motivation, to win the child and gain his confidence, revealing enough to convince the child that the counselor does understand, anticipates success, and that the child has found an individual with whom he can align his goals.

The Investigation

The counselor begins by exploring the current situation and the way in which the child approaches social relationships and responsibilities as they appear, first in the home and then at school. The counselor might systematically raise certain questions and investigate them further by listening attentively to what is said and what is not said. It is seen that the investigation begins with "here" and "now" problems, and always with focus on determining "for what purpose?"

The family constellations and the relationship between siblings are important in this system also. The individual's ordinal position in the family can show how he uses his situation to create his style of life, while a systematic study of the relationship between the siblings is made to derive the psychological position of the child in the family.

Early recollections provide another method of understanding individual goals and mistaken assumptions about life. The first incidents in life that a person can recall are consistent with the pattern of life as seen by the individual (Mosak, 1958; Ferguson, 1964). Adlerian clinicians using early recollections can develop a type of diagnosis that might be made by a clinical team. Therefore, early recollections are used as an aid in comprehending individual life style (Hedvig, 1965).

Adler placed emphasis on utilization of hunches and the ability to guess correctly the psychological movement of the individual. Dreikurs developed a technique that he calls the "hidden reason." This technique is effective in understanding what transpires in a person's private logic. It is used when the person does something out of the ordinary that is puzzling. Thereafter, when he is quizzed about it, he does not seem to understand why he did it. The person is really not aware of the reason. The "hidden reason" technique attempts to determine the individual's rationale for his behavior; it involves guessing what he is thinking. The counselor attempts to determine under what circumstances certain behaviors make sense. The counselor asks the individual if he wants to change, and then asks him to cooperate by telling what goes on in his mind. If one can get the exact words that were on his mind at the time, then he immediately will acknowledge it (Dreikurs, 1966).

Techniques such as these are devised to assist the counselor to understand how the client thinks and how he came to hold these convictions. The understanding, in this procedure, often exists in the counselor first and then is transferred to the counselee's awareness so that he ultimately develops self-understanding. These techniques are concerned with understanding the life style and self-image.

Insight

During this phase the counselor should be concerned with making the individual aware of why he chooses to function in the manner he does.

Interpretation, when used within this frame of reference, places emphasis upon the goals and purposes of the symptoms that are seen. It is usually based on a tentative hypothesis, e.g., "Could it be. . . ?" or "Is it possible. . . ?" In this way the individual is actually confronted with his goals. The private logic which he may not see for himself is mirrored for him. During the confrontations the child will often produce a "recognition reflex." This reflex has been described by Dreikurs (1957, p. 47):

> This automatic reaction consists of a roguish smile and a peculiar twinkle of the eye, a so-called "recognition reflex." The child need not say one word or he may even say "no" but his facial expression gives him away.

The proper sequence in disclosure involves: (1) asking "Do you know why you are doing this?" "Would you like to know why you are doing this?" (2) If there is a willingness for such discussion, interpretation in a tentative manner is also involved, such as: "Could it be. . . ?" or "I have the impression. . . ."

This procedure is referred to as the "mirror technique." The individual is confronted with his goals and his intentions.

Empathy in this form of counseling involves making the individual aware of his private logic and showing interest in helping him change. Little time is spent in description of feelings or straight reflection of feelings. The emphasis is focused on the purpose of the feelings.

It is important to find one point or place where the counselee may want to change. If the counselor cannot find the place, as in the case of a difficult child, then in all probability the counselor cannot change him at all. In some instances the child has been referred to counseling because of a conflict with a teacher or parents; perhaps the child really does not choose to change. However, in a case wherein the child would like to get along better with his peers, this may be the proper point or place to begin the attempts toward change.

Reorientation

In this phase of counseling the counselor and counselee think the situation through together. The counselor's basic responsibility is to help the individual see the alternatives in attitude and behavior. But mere awareness of alternatives is not enough. It still is necessary to develop the courage to try to change. Encouragement restores the individual's faith in himself (Dinkmeyer & Dreikurs, 1963). Encouragement helps one to realize his own strengths and abilities and develops a belief in his dignity and worth. If a person is discouraged, neither insight nor change is possible.

It is in the reorientation aspect of counseling that the counselor strives to help the counselee become aware he is functioning in a way that inevitably will cause problems of his own choosing. Eventually he is confronted with choice, one of the most important therapeutic agents of all. He can then decide the way in which he will choose to function.

There is an investigation of values involved in these premises. It is vital to the counseling relationship that the counselor does not moralize. The "oughts" and "shoulds" are to be discreetly avoided. Most certainly the therapeutic experience can help to provide some success experiences within and external to the counseling process.

In other situations the counselee will be helped by a setting of tasks. If he does not get along well with his peers, for example, perhaps he can learn to deal effectively with just one child. In some instances children have been helped by learning to act as if they were aggressive, as if they were happy, etc.

Adlerian psychology contributes to school counseling theory by establishing certain assumptions about personality and providing unique procedures in the counseling process. The "compleat" counselor will want to become well acquainted with Adlerian theory and practice as he develops his personal theory of counseling.

REFERENCES

Combs, A. W., & Syngg, D. *Individual behavior.* New York: Harper & Row, 1959.
Dinkmeyer, D., & Dreikurs, R. *Encouraging children to learn: the encouragement process.* Englewood Cliffs, N. J.: Prentice-Hall, 1963.
Dreikurs, R. *Fundamentals of Adlerian psychology.* Chicago: Alfred Adler Institute, 1950.

Dreikurs, R. *Psychology in the classroom.* New York: Harper & Row, 1957.
Dreikurs, R. The holistic approach: two points of a line. In *Education, guidance, psychodynamics.* Chicago: Alfred Adler Institute, 1966. Pp. 21-22.
Ferguson, E. D. The use of early recollections for assessing life style and diagnosing psychopathology. *Journal of Projective Techniques,* 1964, *28,* 403-412.
Hedvig, E. Children's early recollections as basis for diagnosis. *Journal of Individual Psychology,* 1965, *21* (2), 187-188.
Maslow, A. *Motivation and personality.* New York: Harper & Row, 1954.
Mosak, H. Early recollections as a projective technique. *Journal of Projective Techniques,* 1958, *22,* 302-311.
Rogers, C. R. *Client-centered therapy.* Boston: Houghton Mifflin, 1951.
White, R. Motivation reconsidered: the concept of competence. *Psychological Review,* 1959, *66,* 297-333.

CHAPTER 3: QUESTIONS FOR DISCUSSION

1. Farwell raises the question of whether counselors must have had teaching experience. How do you feel about this matter? What are your reasons? Have you read any statements in the literature which tend to support your stand?
2. Nash presents a number of concepts which he deems as potentially dangerous in counseling today. Which of these do you feel poses the most serious danger?
3. For what reasons might a person keep leading an "inauthentic existence" as Jourard describes it?
4. Daubner and Daubner draw a distinction between "realist" and "phenomenalist" counselors. Which position seems closest to your views? How do you *differ* from that position?
5. Can you think of factors other than the ones presented by Aubrey either to support or refute his strong indictment of the irrelevance of much therapy-oriented theory to the school situation?
6. Carey proposes an active, ombudsman type of role for counselors today. How do you feel about this? What practical problems do you see if counselors do/do not accept such a role?
7. Rousseve offers a personal statement dealing with important aspects of man. If you were to cover the same topics, how would your views on man and his other key topics differ from his? On what experiences have most of your own views been based?
8. Strowig's recommendations on certification depart significantly from present practices in many states. Which of his recommendations do you feel would create the most serious problems in your state? Which do you feel might do the most to improve counselor preparation in your state? Give reasons for your answers.
9. What questions come to mind concerning Dinkmeyer's ten fundamental assumptions?

Chapter

4

Ethical and Moral Outlooks

INTRODUCTION

Any time that one person enters deeply into the world of meanings of another, the question of values and value conflicts arises. The counseling relationship, and indeed the whole idea of guidance itself, brings into question the legitimacy of such relationships as well as how they might most effectively be carried out. The age-old philosophical question, "What is man's proper relationship to his fellow men?" now arises with new urgency. The writers who have contributed to this chapter offer clarifications, viewpoints, and experiences to the counselor-candidate and to others. Perhaps no area of counselor education is so vital as this. Ethical problems arise even at the outset: does the counselor feel he has a reasonable chance of possessing strengths necessary to aid the client?

Since the majority of those reading this book will likely be school counselors, two Codes of Ethics have been presented instead of the usual code for counselors. The second code is that of the National Education Association, intended for the teaching profession. It becomes necessary for the counselor, who often serves a dual role in schools (or at least functions in a school setting) to be cognizant of the principles by which both professions operate. He must examine them carefully for possible conflicts or needed clarifications. Further, he must ask himself whether the pooled professional judgments of his peers and predecessors are acceptable to him in his deepest life commitments. If they are not, then he is faced with vital decisions indeed. Is he then to believe the old quotation, "One man with courage is a majority" or is he to heed the words of Mowrer that if one is functioning in any given social system, he must either play by the rules of the system or withdraw honestly and openly from it? At various points the counselor will ponder this again and again, and will realize that no one else can make such judgments for any given case. In many ways counseling is a lonely task, one in which the existential statement comes home to the counselor with awe-inspiring heaviness: Man is alone with his fellows in a hostile world; he defines himself by his actions; he has no one to blame but himself, no one to turn to except his fellow men; whatever meaning is to be found, he himself must find. It is to the counselor as meaning-seeker that this chapter is addressed.

ETHICS AND COUNSELING DECISIONS

Edward V. Daubner and Edith Schell Daubner

Longwood College, Farmville, Virginia

Although some behavioral scientists and practitioners contend that man has no genuine moral choices to make, common sense and philosophical reflection ineluctably affirm the moral nature of man. When young people are faced with moral decisions, they often seek the assistance of a counselor. Although such counselors are routinely expected to aid clients in making decisions about their education and their careers, there is considerably less agreement about their responsibility for helping students to make moral choices. The central thesis of this article is that a knowledge of ethical theories, the practical principles which flow from them, and the method of decision-making which they indicate will enable the counselor to assist his clients with their moral problems.

Although the literature on ethics and counseling is quite extensive, practically all of it is concerned with the "rightness" of the counselor's professional behavior. For example, should the counselor respect the confidences of his client even if the client reveals that he is engaged in activities which are unlawful? The importance of such an ethical question for counseling is beyond cavil. The purpose of this article, however, is to explore another kind of nexus between the two disciplines. Specifically, we will attempt to demonstrate that a knowledge of that branch of philosophy known as *ethics* or *ethical theory* could help a counselor in an educational setting to assist clients in making moral decisions.

Ethics is a philosophical discipline concerned with the conduct of human beings as they make moral decisions. A moral decision is a judgment usually leading to action and involving the use of one of that group of words known as the moral predicates: "ought," "should," "right," "good," and their opposites, when applied to human conduct (Brandt, 1959). A down-to-earth example of a moral decision which might confront a high school or college student is: "Should I inform the school authorities about one of my peers who is pushing dope as a means of earning money to pay his college expenses?"

Ethics, unlike a discipline such as psychology, is normative rather than factual. It is concerned with the principles or norms that *ought* to govern human conduct rather than with those that *do* govern it. A fundamental and necessary postulate of ethics is that human beings are capable of self-determination, i.e., that at least some human decisions are free ones. Ethics, therefore, is concerned only with volitional behavior, and not with such behavior as reflex actions. Ethics also excludes from its province the conduct of those persons who by common consent are not considered to be responsible agents, such as idiots and psychotics. Finally, it should be noted that there is wide disagreement among ethicists about *which* specific human actions are right

Reprinted by permission of the authors and *Personnel and Guidance Journal*, Vol. 48, No. 6, February 1970, 433-442.

and wrong, as well as *what it is* that causes them to be so. (We must except here such philosophers as the non-cognitivists, e.g., C. L. Stevenson, 1944.) As a consequence of this divergence of views, there is no one ethical theory about which all philosophers are in agreement, no one generally accepted body of principles. Instead, there is only a plethora of ethical theories.

ETHICAL KNOWLEDGE IN COUNSELING

This lack of agreement among ethicists has tremendous practical significance for anyone who consciously attempts to use ethical theory in making a moral choice, and this is especially true in counseling. In searching for a principle that will enable a person to distinguish between right and wrong, and in finding cogent reasons why *this* particular principle should be used rather than another, he who looks to the discipline of ethics is confronted with numerous solutions, more than one of which may seem sufficiently impelling to warrant his assent. To analyze and evaluate these answers for the purpose of choosing an ethical theory that will consistently govern his own moral decisions is a formidable task, even for an intelligent, well-informed adult. For the adolescent, whose ideas of right and wrong may be largely the result of uncritical introjections from the significant persons in his life, the task is even more arduous; yet it is one that he must accomplish if he is to attain full moral development. The difficulty as well as the importance of the task seem to indicate the adolescent's need for help in coping with it.

To illustrate the desirability of the counselor's knowledge of ethical theory, we intend here to use a rather common problem faced by many clients, which will indicate how knowledge of one particular ethical theory may be brought to bear on the decision-making process. Before presenting the illustrative example, however, it is necessary to meet the objections that some may raise to the task being attempted.

OBJECTIONS

Some counseling authorities contend that the moral choices students bring to counselors are not really moral in nature, but are only guises or facades for other problems, often ones involving intrapersonal conflicts. Some even maintain that man is an amoral being, and thus *has* no genuine moral choices to make. "Should I smoke pot?" may really mean "I want to belong to the in-group at my school" or "I feel terribly guilty about smoking pot, and I'm afraid of being found out." Hence, it is contended that the counselor should focus his attention on the underlying and *real* conflict, e.g., the guilt feeling, rather than the "moral decision" that the client used as a disguise when he first broached the subject.

We freely admit that the client's requests for help with many so-called moral choices are really only veils for other problems that are basically nonmoral in nature, but we do not believe that this is always and necessarily true. Furthermore, no matter how sophisticated it may be considered in certain circles to regard man as an amoral being, the vast majority of students of human nature in all ages have affirmed man's moral nature. In addition, the world of everyday affairs, which impinges inexorably upon the client's life, literally demands that he look upon himself and others as moral beings, under the pain of being severely maladjusted to the very milieu in which he must exist. Unless we as counselors are willing to face the consequences of ignoring this obvious fact of life and of imposing an amoral view of man on our clients, we must conclude that our clients, at times, *do* have genuine moral choices to make, and when this happens, they frequently turn to a counselor for help.

Interwoven Problems

A second objection that may be raised is that even if clients *do* have genuine moral choices, these choices are seldom uncomplicated, but rather are often interwoven with other factors, e.g., a feeling of guilt. In a situation of this kind, so the argument runs, the counselor should not deal with the moral aspects of the situation. Instead, his only task is to help the client understand and resolve the emotional component of his difficulty, while referring him for help with his moral choice to someone who is supposedly an expert in such matters, such as a clergyman.

Undoubtedly, moral choices are frequently complicated by emotional and attitudinal factors, but even if this is true in *every* instance, what happens when the client say, in effect, "I understand that there are some emotional aspects of my problem that I need to work out, but I would still like your help in thinking through the moral choice that I am facing." Should we deny him the assistance for which he is asking? Should we subject him at this point to a type of professional schizophrenia by informing him that we are willing to help with his emotional conflict, but that we are *not* prepared to render him assistance when he makes his moral decision? If human lives and human problems are all of a piece, it seems more plausible to believe that the client would profit more from working with a counselor who is prepared and competent to help him with both aspects of his difficulty than with one who shunts him to someone else when matters take a moral turn.

We hasten to add that we are not opposed to referrals. At times, for example, if some religious tenet of the client is involved, the counselor may do well to refer the client to a clergyman, who may be better qualified to give information on religious doctrines bearing on the client's moral decision. On the other hand, if the counselor makes it a practice to refer every client who asks for help in making a moral decision, he comes perilously close to shirking the responsibilities of his profession.

In dealing with this second objection, it is not our intent to delve deeply into the reasons why a counselor may be reluctant to work with a client on a moral problem; this is more properly a subject for empirical investigation. Still, we suggest that the counselor's reluctance may arise from his own lack of knowledge of ethical theory, and hence he may feel threatened and uncomfortable when the discussion moves into this domain. Also, it may be that the counselor's reluctance to help stems from the fact that he has not come to grips with, and does not know how to handle, his own moral problems. In such a case, an avoidance or defensive response on the part of the counselor would not be surprising.

Imposing Counselor's Views

A third objection is that if a counselor accepts the responsibility for aiding a client with a moral decision, he is courting the danger of foisting his own moral principles on the client. That such a danger exists can scarcely be denied. That it is impossible to avoid seems to us to be an overstatement. If the counselor is genuinely committed to the client's potentiality for and right to self-determination, it should not be any more difficult for him to avoid imposing his moral views on the client than it is for him to avoid imposing his views about which vocation the client should choose.

Certainly, it is not the counselor's business to provide the client with "patent medicine" solutions to his problems, including a set of ready-made moral principles, whether they be the counselor's own or those of some ethicist. But, if it is apparent (a) that the client's moral development has not progressed beyond the stage at which he resolves moral issues on the basis of unthinking habit or blind impulse; (b) that he is operating without the moral principles he needs for decision-making; and (c) that he recognizes this inadequacy and indicates that he wishes to rectify it, then the counselor should be able to set before the client some of the ethical principles that mature persons use as bases for making moral decisions (Brammer & Shostrom, 1960). Following this, he can further assist the client to understand just how a particular ethical principle can be used to decide the concrete moral question that confronts him. In order to render this kind of assistance, it is not necessary for the counselor to impose his own ethical principles on the client; it *is* necessary, however, for the counselor to have a working knowledge of various ethical theories and the principles which flow from them.

The Place of Information

A final objection to the use of ethical theory in counseling is that this process may involve the giving of information about theories and principles, and there are some counseling authorities who believe that it is ineffectual, if not actually detrimental, for a counselor to supply a client with information.

We agree emphatically that the counselor should not be perceived by the client basically as a *source* of information, but rather as one who can help the client *use* information in an intelligent manner (Arbuckle, 1965). At the same time, we are completely in accord with the view that, "If a client needs information in order to think soundly about something that concerns him, he should be helped to obtain it" (Tyler, 1961, p. 179).

Counselors who operate in an educational setting must be particularly concerned with the question of whether or not to impart information to their clients.

> Our educational institutions are essentially the tools society uses in its efforts to acculturate its members. Any social system of acculturation will have weak spots; the individual may fail to acquire, or lack the opportunity of acquiring, particular kinds of information or skills necessary to his function as a member of his social group. The counselor, through his individualized contact with the student, is able to discern these blanks in understanding *and should be in a position to help the student fill them* [Bordin, 1968, p. 25, emphasis added].

It would be extremely naive to pretend that a knowledge of ethics is not one of those "blanks in understanding" that the counselor in an educational setting often discerns in his clients. Clearly, in order to make a rational decision, a person needs *knowledge* of the ethical principle which will govern his choice. Surely the client has not made his decision in an intelligent manner if he chooses on the basis of whim, impulse, or habit, rather than on the strength of some consciously held and rationally determined principle.

TWO ETHICAL TASKS OF THE CLIENT

The moral question we will use to illustrate the use of ethical theories in counseling is, "Should I ask for information about a test from a student who has taken the same test previously?" In order to understand how the counselor could help his client arrive at an answer to this question through the use of ethical theory, we must distinguish three processes which are involved, only the second two of which are ethical in nature.

First, the counselor must help the client discern any relevant *non-moral* questions that may affect the client's practical decision. In the case under consideration, these might be: What penalties does the teacher impose on those who ask for advance information on tests? What sanctions does the school administration place on those who engage in this practice? What is the attitude of the client's peer group toward this practice?

Second, the counselor must search with the client for some moral principle that the latter can use as a rational basis for his moral choice.

Third, and most difficult of all, the counselor must help the client ascertain if the moral principle he has chosen is justifiable.

Let us consider these points in greater detail. We purposely chose the question dealing with advance information about tests because the first task, i.e., examining the non-moral facts in the case, does not appear to be excessively troublesome. The teacher's penalties, the sanctions that the administration imposes, and the attitude of the client's peer group are undoubtedly as well known to the client as to the counselor. If, for example, the client knows that the faculty, the administration, and his peer group all frown upon this practice, he is likely to answer "No" to the question, and this answer is dictated by fear, prudence, or perhaps a desire to please rather than by ethical considerations. For the purpose of this discussion, we shall assume that although the client has considered the relevant non-moral facts, he is not satisfied to let the matter rest here but wishes to pursue it further, thus advancing onto ethical ground. (We shall also assume that any emotional element in the situation has been resolved, such as the student's distress over the possible disapproval of his peers or of other significant persons in his life.)

If these assumptions are granted, the remaining tasks that confront the client and the counselor are (a) to select a principle that the client can use as a basis for making a rational moral decision; and (b) to determine how the moral principle that the client chooses can be logically defended or justified. Both tasks are purely ethical in nature, and are much more readily dealt with if the counselor has a knowledge of the pro's and con's of various ethical theories.

SELECTING THE PRINCIPLE

Let us examine more closely the first point: Recent literature on ethics (Hare, 1962; Niblett, 1963) emphasizes that it is impossible to make a defensible moral decision without appealing, consciously or unconsciously, to some generally applicable moral principle. Perhaps one might have to decide between two rival principles, or even develop a new principle, but there is always a general moral principle involved. The only alternative to appealing to a principle in making a moral decision is to use some irrational basis such as a whim or impulse. If this premise is granted, the answer to the question, "Should I ask for information about a test from a student who has taken the test previously?" must rest on some general ethical principle, such as: Whatever action I *feel* to be right is right; or, I should always do that which results in the greatest *happiness* for me as well as for all concerned; or, I should always perform those actions which are *intrinsically* right rather than those which are *intrinsically* wrong. All these are general ethical principles that have been suggested by well-known philosophers.

But a principle that is freely asserted is just as freely denied. Anyone who asserts such principles can be challenged and must be ready to meet the challenge. Thus, the counselor must be prepared to help the client justify the principle he has chosen. This means exploring the answers to such questions as: Why are my *feelings* a reliable criterion of right and wrong? Why is *happiness* the ultimate norm in judging the rightness or wrongness of an act? If it is true that some actions are intrinsically right and others are intrinsically wrong, *what element* in these actions makes them so?

This task of justifying ethical principles is an extremely difficult one. It is impossible to appeal to empirical data, as one could if he tried to discern what principles other people do follow and have followed. Such data would be of no use in trying to *justify* the use of a particular principle. After all, ethical principles involve "ought-ness," and one cannot derive a statement about how things *ought to* be from empirical evidence about how they *are*.

How, then, do ethical philosophers justify their principles? In some cases, they may appeal to a chain of *a priori* reasoning, and in others to their private intuitions. Both these methods of justification have serious drawbacks. A given chain of reasoning may not be cogent to some students of the theory and, in the case of intuition, some persons may be absolutely unable to comprehend and accept the private intuitions of the theory's proponent. Still, a way of justifying ethical principles must be found. At this point, we will say merely that the justification of a principle is accomplished according to the particular ethical theory that a person embraces. We cannot identify one universal method. Later, we will deal with the baffling problem of how to justify the principle used by the client in the example used here. For the present, let us consider how a counselor could, in the light of a particular ethical theory, assist a client to make the moral decision mentioned in our example.

A PRACTICAL EXAMPLE

Let us suppose that the client has said, "I'm not clear in my own mind about why I shouldn't get advance information about this exam if I feel like it, and if I can get away with it." The counselor might respond with, "It's important for you to know *why* you should or shouldn't do this."

Client: Right! I'm not a kid anymore, and I ought to have good reasons for doing things.

Counselor: At your age, you no longer think that doing something just because you *feel* like doing it, or because you won't get *caught,* are good enough reasons for thinking it's right.

Client: No, I don't. That's kid stuff. There've been lots of times that I've *felt* like doing things that I knew were wrong when I stopped to *think* about them. As for getting caught—oh, I know that lots of my friends think anything's OK as long as you can get away with it, but this doesn't make much sense to me anymore either.

Counselor: That "kid stuff" doesn't seem to satisfy you any longer when it comes to deciding what's right.

Client: No, it doesn't. But, the thing that's really bothering me now is that when I talk about this with my friends, they say, "OK, so just because you feel like doing something, or just because you won't get caught doesn't prove that it's the right thing to do, but, then, how do you know what *is* the right thing to do?" This is where I get stuck. I don't know what to say.

Counselor: You think there *might* be an answer to this, but you aren't sure just what it is.

Client: Well, I do have some ideas, but—(*Pauses, hesitantly*)

Counselor: Perhaps you would like to explore them.

Client: Well, take this Golden Rule bit. I've been doing some thinking about that, and it seems to make some sense. I learned it first in Sunday School, but I've also heard that some philosopher used it as a guide. I'd really like to know more about how the philosopher explained it, and why he believed in it, since I'm not too interested in the religious reasons any longer.

Counselor: Yes, Immanuel Kant, an 18th century German philosopher, used a similar idea as the keystone of a whole system of ethics. Kant stated it this way: "Act only on that maxim whereby thou canst at the same time will that it should become a universal law" (Kant, 1957, p. 302). I know that sounds complicated, but in simple words it just means, "Do only those things that you would be willing for all others to do." I can give you the names of some books to read which explain this theory if you are interested. This isn't the only ethical theory, by any means, nor am I saying that it is the right one, but many people have used it in the past, and it is still being used by many today. Well, would you care to try this particular theory on for size?

Client: Why not? What do I have to lose?

[*After doing some reading about Kant's theory, the client might return to the counselor with these observations and questions.*]

Client: I think that Kant's rule, "Do only those things that you are willing for all others to do," is a good one, but I'm not sure I go along with him when he says that *everyone* knows about this rule. I know lots of people who act as if they never heard of it.

Counselor: You just don't buy the idea that everyone knows about this rule, because obviously everyone doesn't follow it.

Client: No, I don't, but maybe I don't know exactly what Kant means, either.

Counselor: Would it make any more sense to you if you thought of it this way? We are all sort of born with this rule in our minds. It's not something that we have to learn. It's just there, but it's dormant.

Client: You mean, it's there but you are not aware of it and if no one ever brings it to your attention, or if you never happen to think about it, you'd go through life never knowing about this rule? Is that the way it is?

Counselor: That's just about what Kant means. He also means that if your attention is called to the rule, or if you think it out on your own, you understand right away that this is the rule you should follow to guide your actions.

In a similar manner, i.e., by thinking *with* the client and not *for* him, by helping him to clarify concepts and relationships that he only dimly understands, by occasionally filling some hiatus in his knowledge or some lacuna in his reasoning, the counselor can help the client think his way through a number of other puzzling points that would confront anyone trying to understand Kant's theory sufficiently to use it as a guide for practical action.

He would help the client understand that anyone who was serious about using the theory as a guide could scarcely act in a selfish way in making moral decisions because he himself, if his maxim were universalized, would become the victim of such treatment, and no normal human being could will that everyone should treat *him* in a selfish manner.

The counselor would help the client perceive, too, that a person should not judge the rightness or wrongness of an action entirely, or even primarily, by its results. Instead of asking whether the contemplated action will have favorable or unfavorable consequences, the client should focus his attention on his motive. He should say, "I will act according to the *only* correct motive —my willingness that everyone in similar circumstances should act in the way I am acting." Of course, Kant probably does not mean that the consequences of an action should be completely ignored. For example, if a person wanted to move a severely injured man from a busy street to a comfortable bed in a nearby house to await medical help, but at the same time he knew that this might cause the man to receive further injuries, he should avoid this act. The person's motive is kindly, to be sure, but the results may be disastrous. In such a case, it seems very likely that Kant would advise him to take consequences into consideration.

The client would gradually come to understand that Kant seems to hold that all reasonable men, acting according to correct motives, in similar circumstances, would make the *same* moral choices. Citing examples such as the rightness of almsgiving for any wealthy man confronted with a person in poverty, Kant indicates that some acts are intrinsically right and some are intrinsically wrong, and hence that there are objective and universal norms of morality.

Another point that would need clarification is that Kant holds that it is not necessary for a right act to coincide with one's natural inclinations; in fact, an act is more praiseworthy if it does *not* coincide with a person's natural inclinations than if it *does*. It would be more meritorious for the client to visit a bereaved friend if the experience saddened him than if it gave him satisfaction. According to Kant, the important element in this act is simply that the client act according to the correct motive, i.e., his desire to have everyone in the world render comfort to bereaved persons in their distress.

As the client and the counselor think aloud together about the various facets of Kant's theory, the client begins to perceive how the theory could be used in resolving his own dilemma. He realizes that the maxim that he is following when he asks for advance information on tests is: It is right to take advantage of the mental labor of others to pass a test for which I supposedly prepared by my own efforts. He perceives also that if he universalized this maxim, he should be willing for every student to pass off as his own the scholarly work that others have performed. If the client is not willing that every student should act in this manner, he has gained a fairly clear negative answer to his original question, and every point that he is likely to have thought through with the counselor would tend to reinforce this answer.

A purely selfish course of action would be ruled out because no one would wish all his peers to "use" him in this manner. The consequences of asking for advance information would probably be favorable to the client in that he might, as a result, receive a higher grade. But, the client has learned that according to Kant, the desideratum in judging the rightness of an act is not a favorable consequence, but a correct motive. The act that he has been pondering about is either intrinsically and universally right, or wrong; and if he entertains the correct motive, he will perform a right act. Doing the work for himself rather than "cribbing" may be contrary to his natural inclinations, but a concern about his natural inclinations is not important to a follower of Kant's theory; indeed, he may often have to go against his natural inclinations.

REACHING A DECISION

Could the client's consideration of these facets of Kant's theory help him reach a decision about this particular moral problem? We think that probably it could.

We do not wish, however, to give the erroneous impression that difficulties may not arise as the client and the counselor think together. Some of them cannot be resolved or, at least, so it seems. One particularly troublesome point is that the client may be puzzled about whether he should ask the moral question in broad outline or in all its specific details. A specific or "narrow" manner of asking the question might be: Should I press my best friend who has just taken the test for the information I need (and only a bare minimum of the information—just a general idea of what the test covers), in strictest privacy, with the understanding that I am in dire need of the information because my college entrance depends upon it, and I have been too ill to study for the test; and that my friend emphatically states that he must modify his principles about divulging such information, and that he will do so only out of compassion for me; and that both of us swear never to reveal to anyone that we have engaged in this transaction? On the other hand, a "broad" way of asking the question might be: Should I make a regular practice of publicly asking as many students as possible, when they have just taken a test, for the information I need (a maximum of the information—as many details as possible about which specific questions the test contains)?

Obviously, the way in which the client states the question will affect the way he states and universalizes the maxim that he intends to use as a guide; and the way in which he states and universalizes the maxim will affect the decision at which he arrives. For example, the narrow way of asking the question given above may lead the client to a "Yes" answer, for even a morally sensitive person might modify his principles out of compassion in a situation where there are many mitigating factors, or might urge another to modify his out of sympathy. This is especially true if the parties to such a transaction are convinced that they will not give a bad example to others, that is, that their action is secret or private. On the contrary, the broad way of asking the question would probably lead to a "No" answer, at least for the morally sensitive person, for the act certainly appears to be dishonest behavior, publicly and consistently practiced. We do not pretend to know how to solve this problem at present, and Kant himself does not offer much help with the matter. The problem is only one of several loopholes in Kant's theory, and it has been the subject of much discussion by his philosophical critics.

JUSTIFICATION OF KANT'S THEORY

Up to this point, we have not concerned ourselves with the question of how the counselor can help the client *justify* the theory that the latter has chosen to use as a rational basis for making moral decisions. In this particular case, the client happened to choose the theory because he had had an early encounter with a similar theory in Sunday School. But *why* should he decide to adhere to the Kantian ethic as he explores its ramifications?

One way in which the counselor can help the client justify his use of Kant's theory is by relating Kant's moral imperative to the strong sense of justice that is characteristic of the adolescent period. Once the client grasps the relationship between the theory and his own feelings, it seems likely that he would be willing to render to others that same consideration and esteem that he wants to receive from them.

When the client perceives clearly that the Kantian theory fosters a noble regard for the dignity and worth of each human personality, the awareness that the feelings of others are as significant and vivid to them as his are to himself, the understanding that human beings should interact as "persons" or "thou's," and not as "things" or "it's," he may be likely to respect the theory and think that his continued use of it as a basis for setting moral questions is amply justified. Like the Golden Rule, which guided the client toward the theory in the first place, the Kantian ethic appeals to the sensitive and thoughtful person's empathy for others in the human condition.

The process of helping the client think through Kant's theory and use it as a basis for making this particular moral decision might well terminate in an exchange somewhat similar to the following:

Counselor: Well, how do you feel now about using Kant's theory to help you decide whether to get advance information about tests?

Client: I guess now that I've thought about it and we've talked it over, it's pretty clear that if I use this theory as a guide, I'd have to be willing for everybody else to get this kind of a jump. I'm not sure that I . . . (*Lapses into a thoughtful silence*).

Counselor: You have some doubts about whether you are willing for every other student to act in this way.

Client: Well, it just seems to me it would be terribly unfair. Everybody would be trying to get information from somebody else who had taken the exam before him. The guys who had to take the test first would have to work hard and study, but their grades wouldn't be any better—maybe not even as good—as those who took the test later and didn't do much studying. It all seems so unfair.

Counselor: When you look at it that way, it seems to be a pretty mean and shabby way to treat people.

Client: Yes, it does.

Counselor: Well, then, would you say that Kant's theory has helped you to answer the question you started with?

Client: I think so. I don't see how I could possibly be willing to "universalize my maxim," as Kant says. I don't see how I could go along with the idea that everybody should try to get the dope on the test from those who took it first. If I were one of those in the earlier classes, I'd be pretty mad if I were the victim of this kind of treatment! I certainly don't want to treat other people this way, and I don't want to have students in general act this way.

Although it is possible that the client who is determined to avoid preparing for the test may turn to some other ethical theory in the hope of finding some justification for getting advance information on the test, one point is clear: The use of Kant's theory has enabled him to reach on rational grounds an answer to his moral question. Hence, we believe that our main thesis is substantiated. The counselor's knowledge of ethical theory can be a valuable asset in helping the adolescent client satisfy his need for answers to the moral questions that constantly confront a developing human being.

REFERENCES

Arbuckle, D. S. *Counseling: philosophy, theory, and practice.* Boston: Allyn and Bacon, 1965.

Bordin, E. S. *Psychological counseling.* (2nd ed.) New York: Appleton-Century-Crofts, 1968.

Brammer, L. M., & Shostrom, E. L. *Therapeutic psychology.* Englewood Cliffs, N. J.: Prentice-Hall, 1960.

Brandt, R. *Ethical theory.* Englewood Cliffs, N. J.: Prentice-Hall, 1959.

Hare, R. M. *The language of morals.* London: Clarendon Press, 1962.

Kant, I. Selections in T. Greene (Ed.), *Fundamental principles of the metaphysic of morals.* New York: Scribner's, 1957.

Niblett, W. R. (Ed.) *Moral education in a changing society.* London: Faber and Faber, 1963.

Stevenson, C. L. *Ethics and language.* New Haven: Yale University Press, 1944.

Tyler, L. E. *The work of the counselor.* (2nd ed.) New York: Appleton-Century-Crofts, 1968.

THE PLACE OF VALUES IN COUNSELING AND PSYCHOTHERAPY

C. H. Patterson

University of Illinois

The place of values in psychotherapy has been receiving increasing attention recently. The accepted point of view has been that the therapist's values should be kept out of the therapeutic relationship. Wilder, (in 7) commenting upon a paper by Ginsburg puts it as follows: "It has been taken for granted that the analyst must not try to impose his value systems on the patient," and he adds: "and I still think this to be true." In line with this "hands off" approach, therapists have been exhorted to become aware of their value systems, for the purpose of keeping their own values out of the therapy and to avoid deliberate or unconscious indoctrination of the client (7).

Perhaps few therapists feel that values should not be *dealt* with in psychotherapy. As Green (8) has pointed out, therapists *must* deal with values, since they are part of the personality of the patient, and the source of many of his problems. That some therapists still are uncomfortable in doing so seems to be indicated by Zilboorg's (35) defense of subjectivity.

Recently there has been developing the realization that the therapist's own values cannot be kept out of the therapeutic relationship.

HOW VALUES AFFECT COUNSELING AND PSYCHOTHERAPY

Besides the fact that many of the client's problems involve values and value conflicts, there are other ways in which values affect the therapeutic relationship.

Values and Counseling Ethics

Values and ethics are related; the ethics of individuals and groups reflect their values. In fact, ethics might be considered as an expression of a group's values, an attempt to represent or express them in a systematized form. This is no doubt why Sutich (28) became involved in values in his discussion of ethics. Bixler and Seeman (3) state that "ethics are principles of action based on a commonly accepted system of values," thus relating professional ethics to social values. The APA code of ethics (1, p. 49) states that a cardinal obligation of the psychologist "is to respect the integrity and protect the welfare of the person with whom he is working." This is clearly an expression of the value of the individual in our society, as is recognized in Principle 1.13: "The psychologist should express in his professional behavior a firm commitment to those values which lie at the foundation of a democratic society, such as freedom of speech, freedom of research, and respect for the integrity of the individual" (1, p. 10).

Reprinted by permission of the author and the *Journal of Counseling Psychology*, Vol. 5, No. 3, 1958, 216-223.

Philosophy of Counseling

From ethics and values to philosophy is only a short step. A philosophy is an integration of values, usually resulting in statements of postulates and assumptions, or principles.

It is only natural, and to be expected, that philosophies of counseling and psychotherapy should reflect the philosophies of the societies in which these activities operate. The prevailing philosophy of our society is a democratic one. This is more than a political term, although Meehl and McClosky (15) would make it primarily such. Democratic principles and values have permeated our economic, social, educational and occupational institutions and relationships. And as Sutich (28) points out, "It is evident that modern therapeutic and analytical principles have their roots in democratic principles. And it is equally evident that most American psychologists are committed to the support of democratic principles throughout the entire range of human behavior."

What are the democratic principles which are accepted by counselors and psychotherapists? Bixler and Seeman (3), in their discussion of counseling ethics, present the postulates of Hand (10), which succinctly express these principles:

1. The belief that human life, happiness and well-being are to be valued above all else.

2. The assertion that man is master of his own destiny, with the right to control it in his own interests in his own way.

3. The determination that the dignity and worth of each person shall be respected at all times and under all conditions.

4. The assumption of the right of individual freedom; the recognition of the right of each person to think his own thoughts and speak his own mind.

The philosophy of the client-centered approach to counseling appears to many counselors to be an expression of this democratic philosophy in the counseling relationship. Rogers (21, p. 5), speaking of the development of client-centered therapy, writes that "some of its roots stretch out . . . into the educational and political philosophy which is at the heart of our American culture." Green (8) feels that client-centered therapy is supported by the "democratic-liberalistic idealogy."

The philosophy of client-centered counseling is expressed in the attitudes which the client-centered counselor holds and expresses toward his clients. These basic attitudes may be stated simply. The client-centered approach to counseling and psychotherapy is based on the following attitudes toward others, whether as clients or persons in other relationships with the counselor:

1. Each person is a person of worth in himself, and is therefore to be respected as such.

2. Each individual has the right to self-direction, to choose or select his own values and goals, to make his own decisions.

These, as simple as they seem, express the philosophy of client-centered counseling. They would probably not be disagreed with by most counselors today. Nevertheless, the extent to which these attitudes are implemented in counseling varies tremendously.

Goals of Counseling and Psychotherapy

Goals are influenced by our values, and therapeutic goals are no exception. The therapist has goals, either specific or general, and these are influenced by his values. Since no complete cure is possible, according to most therapists, what constitutes "tolerable conflict" is a matter of the therapist's values (6).

Concepts of mental health vary. Adjustment has often been conceived as the goal of counseling and psychotherapy. However, there has been increasing dissatisfaction with this concept. The question must be raised, "adjustment to what?" It is evident that adjustment to certain situations is undesirable — the conditions should be changed. And if everyone were adjusted, change and progress would cease. Therapeutic progress or even success can be achieved while the client remains unadjusted to his environment, or to some aspects of it. The concept of adjustment is static. It leads to a subjective interpretation, influenced by the bias of the evaluator, or to a mass, statistical interpretation leading to the definition of adjustment as non-disturbing behavior.

Integration is another concept applied to the goals of psychotherapy. This places the stress on the internal state of the client, rather than on his adjustment to a particular environment. Presumably an individual can be integrated as a person and at the same time be in conflict with his environment. But it has been pointed out that a paranoiac may be integrated but yet not be mentally healthy.

Realizing the inadequacy of adjustment and integration, alone or in combination, as criteria of mental health, Jahoda (12, 13) and Smith (26) have added to them a third, which they call "cognitive adequacy," or the perceptual adequacy for testing reality, thus proposing a triple criterion. Jahoda (12, p. 213) examined five criteria of mental health: absence of mental disorder of symptoms, normality of behavior, adjustment to the environment, unity of the personality, and the correct perception of reality. The first two were discarded, since symptoms are normal or abnormal depending on the cultural context, and it is difficult to define what is normal. Also, recognizing that adjustment may be "passive acceptance of social conditions to the detriment of . . . mental health," she proposes a criterion of active adjustment, or "mastery of the environment, involving a choice of what one adjusts to, and a deliberate modification of environmental conditions" (12, p. 216). Integration, or self-consistency, is not acceptable alone, since it doesn't imply freedom from conflicts with the environment. Correct perception of reality, both of the world and of oneself, while difficult to establish, since the majority judgment is not necessarily correct, is still useful as a criterion. No one criterion is adequate by itself.

While it is thus difficult to define mental health, counselors and psychotherapists have stated various goals of psychotherapy. Adjustment, integration, and an adequate perception of reality usually are included in these goals. One of the most extensive lists of the goals of therapy is that of Maslow (14, Chap. 12) in his study of the characteristics of normal, healthy, "self-actualizing people." This list includes most of the goals mentioned by other authors. Included is the goal of adequate interpersonal relations stressed by

Sullivan, who writes that "One achieves mental health to the extent that one becomes aware of one's interpersonal relations" (27, p. 102).

There has been concern on the part of some regarding such goals as independence, spontaneity, and self-actualization. These goals seem to emphasize the individual to the detriment of society, and to encourage anti-social or asocial behavior. Mowrer (16, 17) has criticized psychoanalysis for its emphasis on freeing the id from the rule of the superego, and suggests that psychotherapy should strengthen the superego. Actually, self-actualization depends on other people. The individual is dependent on the esteem and regard of others for his own self-esteem — for his mental health. He is thus dependent on satisfactory interpersonal relations. This means that mature, responsible behavior is essential. In the goals listed by Maslow there is this concept of responsibility, as well as independence. Mowrer (16, 17) also has emphasized responsibility. Shoben (25) has suggested the "development of responsible individuals capable of maintaining and advancing a democratic society" as the goal of student personnel work, involving the "dual commitment to the worth of the individual and the furtherance of democracy."

The goal of psychotherapy might well be thought of as the development of a responsible independence. Counseling and psychotherapy thus would attempt to facilitate the development of individual independence in a client who takes responsibility for himself, his behavior, his choices and decisions, and his values and goals. This would be consistent with the democratic concept of the freedom of the individual, and also with the concept of the responsibility which accompanies freedom. Such a goal is clearly an expression of the value of a democratic society.

There may seem to be the possibility of a conflict between the attitudes and goals of the counselor and the desires or wishes of the client. Should the counselor be committed, as Meehl and McClosky (15) state "to help the client achieve the client's end," whatever it is? Most counselors would say no. Almost every therapist, and not only the client-centered counselor, is prepared "to thwart the momentary motivations of his client, apparently in terms of long-time goals, which are assumed to be mutually acceptable" (15). The counselor's ethics, values, and philosophy determine his goals in counseling, and he should not be required to compromise these if he does not choose to do so. The client who does not wish to work under these conditions is not compelled to do so. He has the freedom to accept or reject any counselor and his services. To the charge that the counselor is putting himself in the position of thinking he knows best what the goals of counseling should be, the answer can only be one of "Guilty" — the counselor must be free to choose his own goals for the counseling process. Actually, counselors and therapists have always done so. Psychoanalysts have insisted on the goal of personality reorganization as opposed to symptom relief.

Therapeutic Methods

It should be obvious that if values influence, or even determine, the goals of therapy, they also influence methods and techniques, which are means toward the goals. The APA code of ethics recognizes that "the psychologist's ethical standards and his professional techniques are inseparable" (1, p. 37). Methods and techniques will not be dealt with here; it is sufficient to point out their relationship to therapeutic goals. Techniques are not chosen primarily on the pragmatic basis of whether they provide relief to the client, but in terms of their appropriateness to the ultimate goal of therapy. If this goal is client responsibility and independence, then it would appear to follow that all techniques should be consistent with this goal. The client learns responsibility by practicing it, and this should begin in psychotherapy, not at its conclusion.

Influence of the Counselor's Values on the Client

We indicated earlier that the generally accepted point of view has been that the counselor's values should be kept out of the counseling relationship. In addition to Wilder, others have stressed this avoidance of influencing the values of the client (5, 33). Therapists have been exhorted to become aware of their value systems, and those of the society and culture in which they work, to better avoid impressing them upon the patient. Some writers have insisted that the client's value system cannot be influenced by psychotherapy, or that only those values which are consistent with his existing value system will be accepted by him.

But is it possible for the therapist to avoid influencing his client? There is growing opinion, and some evidence, that he cannot. Ingham and Love (11, pp. 75-76) express this conviction. Wolberg (in 7), commenting on Ginsburg's paper, states that "No matter how passive the therapist may believe himself to be, and no matter how objective he remains in an attempt to permit the patient to develop his own sense of values, there is an inevitable incorporation within the patient of a new superego patterned after the character of the therapist as he is perceived by the patient. There is almost inevitably an acceptance by the patient of many of the values of the therapist as they are communicated in the interpretation or through direct suggestion, or as they are deduced by the patient from his association with the therapist." Parloff (19) states that "The disclosure of many of the therapist's values is inevitable," and "such disclosure and communication may occur without the therapist being aware of it." It might be expected that the therapist, by reason of his position and prestige, would become an example to the client, and that the client would tend to imitate him, consciously or unconsciously, in terms of his perception of the therapist. The APA statement quoted earlier continues by saying that "the attitudes, values, and ethical concepts of the psychologist are expressed in his clinical relationships and very directly influence the directions taken by his client" (1, p. 37).

There is some evidence that what these writers claim happens actually does. Rosenthal (23) studied 12 patients presenting a wide variety of diagnoses, and ranging in age from 18 to 46, who had from three weeks to one year of psychotherapy. It was found that, in general, patients' scores on a moral values test changed during therapy, with those patients rated as improved becoming more like their therapists; while those rated as unimproved tended to become less like their therapists.

In another study, Parloff and his associates (20) had observers list topics discussed during therapy by two schizophrenic patients. The patients and the therapist then ranked the topics from most to least important. While both patients differed from the therapist's values, as indicated by agreement in their rankings of topics, at the beginning of therapy, they came closer to the therapist's values as therapy progressed, though one patient came no closer after the first six weeks of treatment.

There is also some clinical evidence that the therapist influences the patient's values without consciously attempting it or being aware of it. Parloff (19) refers to the well-known fact that patients conform in their verbalizations to the terminology and theories of the therapist. If therapists value dreams, patients dream; if the therapists value sexual material, patients produce it, etc. "The literature is replete with examples of patients unwittingly adapting their productions and even use of symbols to the particular psychodynamic theories and preferences of their therapist" (19).

The mechanism of such influence is suggested by some interesting experiments of Greenspoon (9) and Verplanck (30, 31). In these studies it was found possible to control the subjects' verbal behavior by means of operant conditioning, without awareness on the part of the subjects. In the case of psychotherapy, it is easy to imagine the effect on the client of such responses of the therapist to the patient's verbalization as a trace of a smile or a pleased look, an incipient nod of the head, or other mannerisms indicating his attitude, favorable or unfavorable, toward the patient's productions. And all this may be unknown to the therapist and the patient. Parloff (19) presents some evidence that the therapist's responses may be classed by observers as "approving" or "disapproving," and that these responses were related to the therapist's ranking of the topics responded to in terms of their importance. This occurred without the therapist being aware of the differential nature of his responses as "approving" or "disapproving."

CONSCIOUS INFLUENCE OF THE CLIENT'S VALUES

As has been indicated above, it has been generally agreed that the therapist should not consciously attempt to manipulate the patient's values. Recently, however, there have been what Wilder (in 7) refers to as "rising voices to the effect that the analyst not only does but should transmit his own value system to the patient." Taylor (29), in a letter to the editor taking issue with the writer of an article making a plea for the abandonment of guidance in counseling, suggests that there are common, general patterns of human conduct which are ethically "good," and that counselors are justified in introducing them in guidance. Weisskopf-Joelson (34) proposes that the inculcation of a philosophy of life be considered as one of the objectives of psychotherapy.

Gardner Murphy (18) has recently asked: "Shall personnel and guidance work . . . attempt to impart a philosophy of life?" While admitting that "no one knows enough to construct an adequate philosophy of life," he suggests that "it is not true that the wise man's sharing of a philosophy of life is an arrogant imposition upon a defenseless client." He feels that the young need help and advice from those who have thought things through. But he warns counselors not to "attempt the arrogant and self-defeating task of guiding men and women without a rich, flexible, and ever-growing system of values of your own."

There is some slight evidence, in the studies of Rosenthal and Parloff (23, 19, 20) that those clients who improved, or improved most, tended to approach most closely to their therapists in values. This, if true and borne out by other studies, might appear to be an argument for direct intervention toward influencing the values and philosophies of clients. However, it must be remembered that this result occurred where no overt or direct attempt was made to influence the client. It might not hold where direct influence was attempted. Indeed, every counselor well knows the resistance that often develops where direct influence is attempted, and the resistance that often follows the attempt to fulfill a direct request of the client for advice or other help.

Granted that the counselor will influence the client, whether he desires or directly attempts to do so, is it therefore justifiable to attempt conscious, direct manipulation? The present writer believes not. There are a number of reasons for this.

First, while there are no doubt some generally, or even almost universally, accepted principles or ethical rules, these do not constitute a philosophy of life. One may even question how much agreement there is on ethical principles or rules of behavior. Each individual's philosophy is different, unique, and something which is probably not adequate for any other individual.

Second, it is too much to expect all counselors to have a fully developed, adequate philosophy of life ready to be impressed on the client. All counselors are not, to use Murphy's term, wise men.

Third, the counseling relationship is not, in the opinion of the writer, the appropriate place for instruction in ethics and a philosophy of life. The home, the church, and the school are more appropriate sources for such instruction.

Fourth, an individual does not develop a system or code of ethics, or a philosophy of life, from one source, or in a short interval of time. It is a product of a long period of time and many influences.

Fifth, it would appear to be best for each individual to develop his own unique philosophy, and not be deprived of the experience of doing so. Such a philosophy will probably be more meaningful and effective than one adopted from someone else, no matter how wise a man he be.

Sixth, we must still accept the right of the client to refuse to accept any system of ethics, or any philosophy of life.

Now this does not mean that the counselor refuses to discuss ethics, values, or philosophy. It does not mean that he is not concerned about the influence he has on the client in these areas. He recognizes this, and attempts to be a constructive influence. But he does this not by attempting to manipulate the client in the counseling process. He does it by being himself. As Murphy suggests (18), "A great deal of what you communicate to your client is not what you say but what you are." Further than this, the counselor on some occasions must express his own values. He may do so on the request of the client. But he carefully identifies these expressions as his own, perhaps only opinions, and avoids imposing them on the client, or implying that the client ought to feel the same way.

There may also be times when the counselor, whether on the request of the client or not, feels it necessary or desirable to inform the client of the attitudes, standards, or values of society, or the ordinary or generally accepted rules of ethics and morality.

The counselor should not strive to be an amoral, ethically neutral individual. Such a goal would be impossible of achievement — all of us have values, merely by being living human beings. Nor should the counselor attempt to pretend that he is amoral. It is unlikely that he could successfully give this impression to his clients, but it is also undesirable that the counselor attempt to appear to be other than he actually is. Further, the attempt to appear to be neutral as regards social and ethical standards may lead to the danger of appearing not only to accept the client's unethical or immoral behavior, but of approving or condoning it. Counselors are not indifferent to social and moral standards, and should not attempt to appear to be so.

Biestek (2) presents an excellent discussion of the behavior of the counselor in the area of ethics and standards. He points out that while the counselor may judge the attitudes, standards, or actions of the client in terms of his own or prevailing standards, he does not judge the client himself. He further states that "this judgment is preferably made non-verbally; the client usually is able to make such appraisals of himself in the security of an accepting relationship." He suggests that the counselor cannot be indifferent to social, legal, or moral wrong, and must favor the good: "In the non-judgmental attitude the (counselor) does not relinquish his own sense of values, his personal and social ethics. He cannot remain interiorly indifferent to standards contrary to his own if he is to maintain the integrity of his own personality. He must remain true to them. He does not become moralistic, but he has a right to his own sense of social, moral, and spiritual values, personally and professionally" (2).

Ingham and Love (11, p. 77) add a second reason for avoiding indoctrination of moral standards to the usual one. This reason is that the therapist might fail. "And trying to impress moral values in psychotherapy without success interferes with the freedom of the participants' communication and the strength of their relationship."

The point of view expressed above may appear to be a departure from the client-centered framework. Like many other therapists, the client-centered counselor has professed neutrality, and has in many cases at least felt that he has achieved this. But, actually, he has perhaps been no more successful than have other therapists. De Grazia (4. pp. 152-158) gives examples of the expression of counselor moral attitudes and values from published typescripts of client-centered interviews.

The proposal that the counselor not only should be aware of, and has a right to have, his own moral attitudes and values, but should sometimes express them in the counseling relationship, is consistent with recent developments in client-centered thinking. Stressing that the therapist should be himself in the relationship between himself and the client, Rogers (22) suggests that he should express his own feelings as he experiences them.

SUMMARY

The approach to values in counseling as outlined in this paper appears to have several advantages. By recognizing that the counselor's moral attitudes and values do enter into counseling, it prevents the counselor from erroneously believing that he is neutral. Freed from this belief, and the feeling that it is necessary or desirable to be neutral, the counselor is better able to recognize and accept his own values. He then can be aware of them in the counseling relationship, and, when he feels that the counseling relationship would be improved or furthered by his expressing his own attitudes and feelings, he can do so. That is, he can freely be himself, without guilt about doing so, or without feeling that he should not have any feelings. Finally, this approach contributes to the openness of the counseling relationship, without violating its client-centeredness. In fact, the relationship is probably more client-centered. That is, where the counselor's attitudes and feelings are unexpressed, even unrecognized by the counselor, they may, and apparently do, have a pressuring influence on the client. Where they are expressed by the counselor and labeled as representing his own values, feelings, attitudes or point of view, or identified as those of others, or society in general, there is less coerciveness about them. While there are some who would sanction the counselor acting as a representative of society in prescribing moral or ethical values or standards (4), the majority of therapies, including client-centered therapy, still insist that the client must freely accept or reject such values, and develop or construct his own ethical system or philosophy of life. Some apparently fear that the client when given such freedom will choose wrongly or adopt an unethical or immoral course of behavior. The client-centered counselor would respect the client's right to do so. He would not feel that the counseling relationship is the place to teach moral or ethical standards, or a philosophy of life. He is confident, as apparently some are not, that the client in the therapeutic relationship will be aware of and influenced by social realities. He will leave to the family, the church and the school, as institutions representing the moral and ethical standards of society, the teaching of such standards.

REFERENCES

1. American Psychological Association. *Ethical standards of psychologists.* Washington, Author: 1953.
2. Biestek, F. P. The non-judgmental attitude. *Soc. Casework*, 1953, 34, 235-239.
3. Bixler, R. H., & Seeman, J. Suggestions for a code of ethics for consulting psychologists. *J. abnorm. soc. Psychol.*, 1946, 41, 486-490.
4. De Grazia, S. *Errors of psychotherapy.* Garden City, New York: Doubleday, 1952.
5. Deutsch, F., & Murphy, W. F. *The clinical interview.* New York: International Universities Press, 1955.
6. Ginsburg, S. W. Values of the psychiatrist. *Amer. J. Orthopsychiat.*, 1950, 20, 466-478.
7. Ginsburg, S. W., & Herma, J. L. Values and their relationship to psychiatric principles and practice. *Amer. J. Psychother.*, 1953, 7, 546-573.
8. Green, A. W. Social values and psychotherapy. *J. Personality*, 1946, 14, 199-228.
9. Greenspoon, J. The effect of two non-verbal stimuli on the frequency of two verbal response classes. *Amer. Psychologist*, 1954, 9, 384. (Abstract)
10. Hand, H. C. America must have generally democratic high schools. In *General Education in the American High School*. Chicago: Scott Foresman, 1942. Chapter 1.

11. Ingham, H. V., & Love, Leonore R. *The process of psychotherapy.* New York: McGraw-Hill, 1954.

12. Jahoda, Marie. Toward a social psychology of mental health. In Senn, M. J. E. (Ed.), *Symposium on the healthy personality. Supplement II: Problems of infancy and childhood.* New York: Josiah Macy Foundation, 1950.

13. Jahoda, Marie. The meaning of psychological health. *Soc. Casework,* 1953, *34,* 349-354.

14. Maslow, A. H. *Motivation and personality.* New York: Harper, 1954.

15. Meehl, P. E., & McClosky, H. Ethical and political aspects of applied psychology. *J. abnorm. soc. Psychol.,* 1947, *42,* 91-98.

16. Mowrer, O. H. Motivation and neurosis. In Brown, J. S., *et al., Current theory and research in motivation.* Lincoln, Nebraska: Univ. of Nebraska Press, 1953.

17. Mowrer, O. H. Some philosophical problems in mental disorder and its treatment. *Harvard educ. Rev.,* 1953, *23,* 117-127.

18. Murphy, G. The cultural context of guidance. *Personnel guid. J.,* 1955, *34,* 4-9.

19. Parloff, M. B. Communication of values and therapeutic change. Paper read at symposium on "Evaluation of Process and Results of Therapies: I. General Problems of Methods and Theory." American Psychological Association, New York, N. Y., August 31, 1957.

20. Parloff, M. B., Iflund, B., & Goldstein, N. Communication of "therapy values" between therapist and schizophrenic patients. Paper read at American Psychiatric Association annual meeting, Chicago, Ill., May 13-17, 1957.

21. Rogers, C. R. *Client-centered therapy.* Boston: Houghton Mifflin, 1951.

22. Rogers, C. R. *A theory of therapy, personality, nad interpersonal relationships, as developed in the client-centered framework.* Chicago: Author, 1956. Mimeo.

23. Rosenthal, D. Changes in some moral values following psychotherapy. *J. consult. Psychol.,* 1955, *19,* 431-436.

24. Seeley, J. R. Guidance: A plea for abandonment. *Personnel guid. J.,* 1956, *34,* 528-535.

25. Shoben, E. J. New frontiers in theory. *Personnel guid. J.,* 1953, *32,* 80-83.

26. Smith, M. B. Optima of mental health; a general frame of reference. *Psychiatry,* 1950, *13,* 503-510.

27. Sullivan, H. S. *Conceptions of modern psychiatry.* Washington: William Alanson White Psychiatric Foundation, 1947.

28. Sutich, A. Toward a professional code of ethics for counseling psychologists. *J. abnorm. soc. Psychol.,* 1944, *39,* 329-350.

29. Taylor, Charlotte P. Social and moral aspects of counseling. (Letter to the Editor.) *Personnel guid. J.,* 1956, *35,* 180.

30. Verplanck, W. S. The control of the content of conversation: reinforcement of statements of opinion. *J. abnorm. soc. Psychol.,* 1955, *51,* 668-676.

31. Verplanck, W. S. The operant conditioning of human motor behavior. *Psychol. Bull.,* 1956, *53,* 70-83.

32. Walker, D. E., & Peiffer, H. C. The goals of counseling. *J. couns. Psychol.,* 1957, *4,* 204-209.

33. Weiss, F. Psychoanalysis and moral values. *Amer. J. Psychoanal.,* 1952, *12,* 39-49.

34. Weisskopf-Joelson, Edith. Some suggestions concerning Weltanschauung, and psychotherapy. *J. abnorm. soc. Psychol.,* 1953, *48,* 601-604.

35. Zilboorg, G. Clinical variants of moral values. *Amer .J. Psychiat.,* 1950, *106,* 744-747.

SCIENCE AND ETHICAL BEHAVIOR

Nicholas Hobbs

George Peabody College for Teachers

Some years ago I got interested in professional ethics while serving on the Committee on Ethical Standards for Psychologists. Although the objective of this committee was to develop some guidelines for professional conduct, the empirical operations involved in the process, focusing on behavior more than on abstract ethical principals, constantly invited thinking about the behavior of psychologists as a psychologist thinks about behavior. In other words, interest in ethics refused to stay put at the professional level; I kept wondering about the relationships between ethical behavior and behavior theory. I think it was Gordon Allport who suggested to the Institute of Humanistic Studies for Executives at the University of Pennsylvania that I might talk to its interesting group of young officers of the Bell Telephone Companies on the topic, "Psychology and Ethics." I am grateful to him for this recommendation because the subsequent invitation precipitated me into an inquiry that I have enjoyed very much. I think other psychologists might be interested in the outcome, for the issues involved seem timeless. I must admit being both surprised and a bit daunted to find that a number of eminent psychologists have written on ethical problems, among them Wundt, Galton, James, Münsterberg, McDougall, Dewey, Kohler, Hollingsworth, Gordon Allport, and R. B. Cattell. The paper growing out of three annual lectures at the institute has been written a dozen times, added to, cut, and rearranged. It seemingly will not get finished, yet I think the time has come to see if other psychologists will find the problem as engaging as I have. I should like to add that I feel more tentative about some of the ideas than the formal style of writing might suggest (in the last revision I recast the whole business in the third person to see if it would give me more distance and better perspective). The paper might be thought of as a highly tentative effort to identify some of the parameters of an important human problem by examining the point of intersection of the trajectories of professional and scientific psychology. I hope interested readers will share their thoughts with me, for I am thoroughly caught up in the problem and only hope to understand it well enough some day to be able to let it alone.

Some writers claim that science is ethically neutral (Lundberg, 1950), but ethics clearly cannot be neutral about science. Ethical thought cannot escape the insistent implications of scientific findings. Indeed traditional modes of thought about ethics have been shaken to their foundations, and there have emerged the polar reactions of (a) rejecting science in ethics altogether and of (b) turning to science to find an entirely new basis for ethical theory.

IMPACT OF SCIENCE

Three conceptions related to science have made trouble for traditional, revealed, or rationally self-evident ethical theories. One of these is the con-

Reprinted by permission of the author and *The American Psychologist,* Vol. 14, 1959, 217-225.

cept of probability. Probability theory is a central tool of all contemporary science. Its use generates an habitual mode of thought leading to skepticism of any conceptual system based on absolutes, as many ethical systems are. For the scientist, imperatives give way to probabilities, and ethical relativism is the consequence. A second source of disturbance in ethical thought comes from the findings of cultural anthropologists. Behavior strictly tabooed in one culture may be encouraged in another with no apparent ill effects. Ethical systems appear then to be, at least partly, the expression of a particular culture and to have no necessary pervasive validity. John Locke pointed out that "self-evident" values are simply reflections of early childhood indoctrination, and psychoanalysis lends confirmation to his observation. In the words of one writer on psychoanalysis: "The moral faculty is often the unconscious residue of our nursemaid's admonitions" (Feuer, 1955). Finally with increasing knowledge, science has, paradoxically, become increasingly tentative about what is known. One criterion of a good theory is that it be precise enough to be disproven. Traditional ethical theories are not thought of as time limited, whereas scientific theories are regarded by scientists as expendable. A scientific theory is simply the best formulation of which scientists are capable at a given point in time, and constant revision of theories is the expected order of things. Conant (1952), for instance, has suggested that it would be more accurate to call scientific theories "policies" to denote their tentative working relationship to an ongoing process of inquiry. Though Dewey and others have incorporated the notion of constant reconstruction in ethical thought, it nonetheless would be quite disturbing to apply Conant's suggestion to the field of ethics and talk not of ethics but of "ethical policies." Like Alice reciting "Father William," the words do not seem to come out right at all.

One reaction to the disturbance caused by science is to exclude it entirely from ethical thinking. This position has been taken by both scientists and ethical theorists. Thus, Bertrand Russell (1935): "Science cannot decide questions of value, that is because they cannot be intellectually decided at all and lie outside the realm of truth and falsehood." It is said that science has to do with means but not with ends, that science can perhaps increase our understanding of human behavior but cannot help us judge whether a particular act is good or bad.

Another reaction to the disturbance caused by science is to recognize its potency in problem solving and to turn to it as a source of authority for ethical systems. New developments in science have repeatedly freshened ethical thought, as may be seen from several examples.

Evolution and Ethics

The scientific theory which has had the most profound influence on the construction of ethical theories is evolution. The discoveries of Darwin and Wallace were immediately perceived as offering a new foundation for ethics. Evolution with its biological and ecological emphasis appeared to offer sources of value rooted in the nature of man and independent of the influence of man-made cultures.

It is a point both of interest and of warning to note that one of the first efforts to derive an ethical system from Darwinian theory fell forthwith into the trap of cultural bias. Spencer found in evolution, by placing central emphasis on the idea of survival of the fittest, biological justification for *laissez-faire* capitalism! The economically strong survive and the economically weak perish, and this is not only good business but it is morally right, a manifestation of the natural order of things. "Nature red in tooth and claw" implied a positive good and sanctioned unregulated economic competition. The fact that England was then in a most favorable competitive position does not seem to have been weighed in the formulation, at least not consciously. As we move on to examine contemporary efforts to derive ethics from science, the example of Spencer should alert us to similar confusions of what science warrants believing and what man wants to believe.

The growing sophistication of ethical systems based on evolutionary concepts may be seen in two fascinating papers written 50 years apart and delivered from the same platform — one by Thomas Henry Huxley and the other by his grandson, Julian Huxley (1947). Although T. H. Huxley based his ideas on the science of his day, he still subscribed to intuition as the ultimate asserter of right and wrong. "Cosmic evolution may teach us how the good and the evil tendencies of many may have come about; but, in itself, it is incompetent to furnish any better reason why what we call good is preferable to what we call evil than we had before." T. H. Huxley concluded that man must reach beyond the implications of evolutionary theory of his times. The cosmic processes of struggle and survival at a physical level must be combated by dedication to a higher ethical sense.

Fifty years later Julian Huxley was able to interpret the implications of evolutionary theory in a different light and reach conclusions quite at variance with those of his grandfather. He identifies three emergent stages of evolution: the inorganic level, which encompasses the eons of interplay of vast physical forces which made possible the appearance of life; the level of life, where the main mechanism of change is "natural selection between competing variants"; and the level of social organization, which is mediated primarily by the acquisition and dissemination of knowledge serving the end of more and more effective organization. "There is one direction within the multifariousness of evolution which we can legitimately call progress. It consists in the capacity to attain a higher degree of organization, but without closing the door to further advance." Ethics is a consequence of social evolution and a main contributor to further social development. Relativity in ethics is still very much present, but the situation is not chaotic. "Ethics are relative to a process which is both meaningful and of indefinitely long duration — that of evolutionary progress."

At this point, Huxley takes a huge and unnerving leap; he cannot resist a grand extrapolation. He finds that emerging ethical theory demands a one-world government. "This is the major ethical problem of our time [1953] — to achieve global unity for man. . . . Present-day men and nations will be judged by history as moral or immoral according to whether they have helped or hindered that unification." One is reminded of Spencer justifying *laissez-faire* capitalism. The possibility of world government is intriguing but seems more required by Huxley's personal convictions than by his evolutionary theory.

George Gaylord Simpson (1950), the eminent Curator of Fossil Mammals and Birds in the American Museum of National History, also finds in evolution the basis for a most admirable ethical theory. He argues that many people have simply tried to substitute evolution for God or for His revelation as authority for absolute ethical principles and thus avoid responsibility for decision making. Such an endeavor he thinks is doomed to failure: "There is no real evidence whatever that evolution has had a goal, and there is overwhelming evidence that it has not. . . . Evolution has no purpose; man must supply it for himself." He argues that there is nothing in organic evolution that can serve as a guide in the fashioning of ethical principles but that such principles must be derived from social evolution. "The old evolution was and is essentially amoral. The new evolution involves knowledge, including the knowledge of good and evil."

Thus Simpson finds ethically good those acts which tend to serve the process of social evolution, and ethically bad those acts which warp or thwart this process. What kinds of specific propositions are derived from this viewpoint? His first ethical principle is that the "promotion of knowledge is essentially good." This includes not only the development of new knowledge but also the dissemination of knowledge so that it "may then be turned by human choice and responsible action for either good or evil." Here is his stirring appeal:

> Human responsibility requires, in each individual as well as in society as a whole, that the search for knowledge be a search for truth, as unbiased as is possible to human beings; that probable truths as discovered be tested by every means that can be devised, that these truths be communicated in such a way as is most likely to ensure their right utilization and incorporation into the general body of human knowledge, and that those who should receive this knowledge seek it, share in its communication, and in their turn examine and test with as little prejudice as possible whatever is submitted as truth.

From the observation of an important evolutionary characteristic of man — that of high individualization — Simpson draws his second major ethical principle:

> It is good, right and moral to recognize the integrity and dignity of the individual and to promote the realization of fulfillment of individual capacities. It is bad, wrong, and immoral to fail in such recognition or to impede such fulfillment.

The psychologist will find both of these statements appealing; but their very appeal, both in their endorsement of the methods of science for the solutions of the problems of every man and in their concern for the integrity of the individual, should make him wary of accepting the ideas as ethically required. The ideas are those of a good man who devotes his life to the pursuit of truth. They are an expression of the finest aspects of our scientific and humanitarian culture. But are they more securely bound to the nature of man and of society than are ethical principles with a higher intuitive component such as would be associated with a commitment to a life not of action but of contemplation, not of pursuit of knowledge but pursuit of inner peace? Helpful here as a check on personal dedications is F. S. C. Northrop's (1946) analysis of how prior assumptions shape our evaluations of the moral commitments of people of our own and other cultures.

The effort to build an ethical system on the foundation of evolutionary theory has not been too fruitful. The situation is well summarized by Dobzhansky (1955): "Evolutionary ethics have not been formulated yet, and one may reasonably doubt that they can be made scientifically convincing or esthetically satisfying."

Psychoanalysis and Ethics

Next to evolution in its impact on ethical theory is psychoanalysis, with results that are equally open to varied interpretations. Just as evolution shook traditional ethical systems and then provided a basis for new but narrowly conceived systems, so it is with psychoanalysis. For some, psychoanalytic thinking has led to "ethical nihilism," to a "sphincter ethics" no more valid than the toilet training prejudice of a particular culture. But a much more positive construction is possible as can be seen in the work of Erich Fromm (1947) and others. For the purposes of this paper, I would cite the positive interpretation of psychoanalysis provided by Lewis Samuel Feuer (1955). He argues that:

> Freud's methods are a tremendous contribution to ethics as an applied social science. He provided the techniques for determining the extent to which attitudes are imposed or are the expression of autonomous choice, for the decision, in other words, as to whether values are authentic or inauthentic, expressive or repressive.

Feuer argues that psychoanalysis has provided a tool which can be used to uncover deeper layers of experiencing, closer to the true nature of the individual, at which levels one can find ultimate criteria for values in the "underlying realities of human personality." For instance, the ascetic is shown on deeper analysis to long for comfort, the passive individual to long for self-assertion, the Nietzschean superman to long for simple affection and acceptance. Monolithic ultimate values, such as the will-to-power, are seen as desperate and ever-unsuccessful efforts at allaying neurotic anxiety. Authentic values, on the other hand, reflect the "primal drives of the organism."

Many ethical precepts, embodying such symbols as "good" and "duty," are loaded with anxious promptings from childhood learnings in which values of parents are taken over by the child in order to avoid the catastrophic withdrawal of parental affection and support; such secondhand values have never been tested by the child against his own experience. Through analysis, one gains insight into the operation of these hand-me-down values, and they lose their control over behavior, to be replaced by personally authenticated values. A similar concept, without direct concern for ethics, is developed by Rogers (1951, Proposition X, p. 498).

The rejection of anxiety as an appropriate source of motivation for human behavior is an appealing notion, but it generates about as many problems as it solves. The fact that neurotic behavior is whipped on by anxiety (as revealed for instance in studies which show that the extreme authoritarian has deep disturbance in many areas of functioning) does not permit the conclusion that normal behavior is anxiety-free behavior. On the other hand there must be many deeply anxious people who lead exemplary lives from an ethical point of view. We must also allow for the possibility that Kierkegaard is right when he maintains that to be fully human is to experience and courageously deal with anxiety. Furthermore, human motivation is more complex than Feuer seems to assume. Apply his system of analysis, for instance, to the behavior of the conscientious objectors who volunteered to participate in the Minnesota starvation studies undertaken to provide a basis for planning the rehabilitation of victims of Nazi concentration camps. Their phantasy life was filled with longing for food, while the continuation in the experiment, doubtlessly conditioned by early acquired concepts of duty, required a denial of this fundamental need. It would be hard indeed to say that their behavior was neurotic and unethical, regardless of the extent it denied the primal drives of the organism.

Perhaps a more basic objection to the position taken by Feuer and Rogers is the discontinuity of the person implied in establishing a "wisdom of the body" criterion for the healthiness of behavior — not to mention Feuer's assumption that what feels healthy will be ethical.

It would be unfair to question the validity of Feuer's psychoanalytic method as an instrument for validating ethics without describing at least briefly the positive ethical commitments which are suggested.

The recommendations for ethical conduct are admirable, even though not clearly required by the antecedent analysis. What emerges is a liberal utilitarianism, substituting "happiness" for "good" in Bentham's famous equation: "The greatest happiness for the greatest number." The picture is of an individual who has shaken the incubus of a punishing superego and substituted therefor an ego vastly strengthened by a personal experiencing of the organically good, a person who knows happiness for himself and can freely seek it for others, a person who is spontaneous and free, who can give and receive affection with joy. That this happy picture is tempered by the recognition that such a fortunate individual would still live in a far from perfect world only adds to the honesty of the argument.

Other contradictory formulations could be added to this list. Ashley Montagu (1955), for instance, says that man by nature is cooperative and that he must move ever toward more cooperative patterns of living. Not so, says R. B. Cattell (1948). Cooperation within limited groups is good, but intergroup competition is essential to the emergence of new and more adaptable forms of behavior. Thus Spencer, the Huxleys, Simpson, Feuer, Montagu, and Cattell offer their diverse and often contradictory interpretations of the scientific bases of ethical theory.

ETHICAL IMPLICATIONS OF PSYCHOLOGY

Simpson (1950) has made the pertinent observation that many people today turn to science for ethical revelations, science being the twentieth century Mt. Sinai from whose heights might be brought down a new moral decalogue. Such a set of commandments, carrying all the persuasion of scientific authority, would bring new certitude and confidence to an anxious world and would relieve the individual of some sense of responsibility for the consequences of his behavior. But such a dispensation cannot come from science; science can never provide us with ethical imperatives. This is not to say that science has nothing to offer to us in our efforts to improve our ethics, or, more pertinently, to improve our behavior. Let us then turn to a consideration of some of the ethical implications of science, and particularly of psychological science.

Freedom of Choice

To talk about psychology and ethics intelligibly one must first come to grips with an age-old and possibly insoluble problem: that of freedom of choice of the individual. It is a problem that psychologists would often prefer to ignore but cannot let alone. In 1880, William James (1954) wrote: "A common opinion prevails that the juice has ages ago been pressed out of the free-will controversy, and that no new champion can do more than warm up stale arguments which everyone has heard." James goes on to say, "This is a radical mistake," and one is inclined to agree with him today for the issue is quickened every time psychologists get close to contemporary man and his problems.

Experimental psychologists generally seem less bothered by the problem than personality theorists and clinicians, though hewing the deterministic line is not always easy. In his book on the logic of problem solving in psychology, Benton Underwood (1957) says simply and persuasively: "Determinism is a necessary assumption for the scientific enterprise." B. F. Skinner (1953) is equally explicit: "If we are to use methods of science in the field of human affairs, we must assume that behavior is lawful and determined." From this point on, as though to provide a firsthand illustration of the complexity of the problem, Skinner gives the impression that the one person who is exempt from this rule is the psychologist himself. "Who's conditioning whom?" is not just a good joke; it is an unanswered question as well. While Skinner is too knowledgeable to claim such exemption, he has a hard time keeping in mind, for example, that Frazier is anything but a free agent in planning for the well being of the good people of *Walden Two* (1948).

George Kelly and Gordon Allport, as personality theorists interested in moving psychology closer to man, cannot easily accept the axiom of determinism that seems so simple to the experimentalist. Common sense makes trouble.

Kelly's position (1955) is a puzzler. He maintains ingeniously that freedom and determinism are two sides of the same coin. The behavior of a person is strictly determined by the constructs he uses to define the choice-demanding situation. However, the person does not have to accept these constraints; he may simply redefine his constructs. When he moves from lower order to higher order constructs, man gains freedom. Once a person adopts a construct, his behavior in the domain of the construct is determined by the construct; however, he remains free to redefine his constructs. Kelly does not specify what determines the choice of a superordinate construct. If Kelly means simply that the adoption of a superordinate construct system increases the person's response repertory, his degrees of freedom, all would be well within Underwood's postulate of determinism as a necessary assumption of psychological science. But Kelly is talking about human freedom in the classical sense. Saint Ambrose was a fourth century advocate of constructive alternativism. He observed: "A wise man, though he be a slave, is at liberty." Boethius, Epictetus, Marcus Aurelius, and others have endorsed a similar "let's rise above it" attitude. Does Kelly's constructive alternativism offer more than this today? The answer is unclear. In any event, it would appear that Kelly works three concepts of freedom interchangeably: (a) the classical freedom-determinism type, from which he would like to extricate man, at least partially; (b) the degrees of freedom type, which refers simply to richness of response repertory; and (c) the semantic construct type, or the north-south argument, which maintains that the construct determinism requires the existence of freedom. Kelly solves the dilemmas of type a freedom by type b and c arguments.

Allport (1955), on the other hand, chafes under the restraints of science without really abandoning them. He first observes:

> It is customary for the psychologist, as for other scientists, to proceed within the framework of strict determinism, and to build barriers between himself and common sense lest common sense infect psychology with its belief in freedom.

But the kinds of alternatives that Allport describes do not join the issue. He first argues that, from the point of view of the actor, choice is "a paramount fact." Underwood and Skinner would not be discomfited by this. He then makes three additional points bearing not upon "freedom of choice" but rather on "degree of freedom." Allport is not at all sure that he has settled the matter: "These considerations fall short of solving the problem of freedom. They urge us, however, to forego naive solutions."

Anatol Rapaport (1954) argues persuasively that, without freedom of choice, ethics is meaningless. If man is not free to choose between right and wrong, between the better and the worse part, what good is it even to talk about ethics at all? This requirement of free choice as a postulate puts the psychologist in a difficult spot, unless one is willing to accept his definition of choice. The act of choice is the primary datum for nearly all of psychlogical science, but the psychologist has his own definition of choice which can cause difficulty unless one understands what the psychologist is trying to do.

The psychologist is concerned with understanding and explaining behavior, mostly human behavior. One of the ways in which a psychologist tests the validity of his explanation is to make predictions derived from some explanatory system. If a particular prediction is confirmed, as through an experiment, his confidence in the system is increased. If the prediction is not confirmed, and if he is confident of the adequacy of his experiment, he must go back and rework his explanations. Psychologists, like other scientists, work to advance understandings by testing specific "if — then" equations and working the results into more general formulations. The ground rules of science say that these equations cannot contain variables which are nonrandom in their operation but which at the same time are considered to be unavailable for any possible quantitative assessment. This does not mean that science maintains that all phenomena can be measured, since technical limitations (including those subsumed under Heisenberg's principle of indeterminacy) obviously limit what can be achieved in the way of mensuration. On the other hand, no scientific equation can contain an "X" variable which turns out to be the influence of any demon, pixie, gremlin, fate, entelechy, god, or spontaneous individual will. Now there is nothing in science that can disprove the existence and effective operation of demons, pixies, gremlins, fates, entelechies, gods, or undetermined individual choices. It is just that science is not set up to deal with these kinds of problems. There is no way for the scientist ever to write an equation incorporating such variables. The famous equation $E = mc^2$ does not suggest that engineers should build into an atom bomb a little man to decide whether or not the bomb is to explode. The psychologist cannot write such an elegant equation as this one of the physicist, but he too must write his equations without benefit of little men. Insofar as psychological science is concerned the notion of free choice is a homunculus. Psychology cannot prove that the behavior of the individual is determined, but for purposes of inquiry he must assume so and be content to live with whatever limitation this assumption may (or may not) make on his activities as a scientist.

But, one may protest, has not physics, the most advanced of sciences, had to admit ultimate indeterminancy? What about Heisenberg's principle after all? Surely psychology does not pretend to be more rigorous than physics! No, not at all. Indeterminancy in physics means something quite different from the freedom of choice involved in human behavior. Heisenberg's principle says that in certain restricted areas of physics an event cannot be measured because the process of measurement alters the nature of the event. This is a phenomenon very familiar to the psychologist, in whose work this kind of indeterminancy operates with a vengeance. The psychologist cannot give a person an intelligence test without altering his intelligence. But the effect is trivial, and no great harm is done by ignoring it.

And one may argue further that modern atomic physics has become a statistical science, dealing in probabilities and not in absolute predictions. The pathway of a particular molecule cannot be predicted and is random. Actually this development in physics has been comforting to psychologists, who are accustomed to dealing in probabilities. But it should be noted that there is nothing in physics that implies that a molecule chooses by an act of will to go in any particular direction. There is nothing in the probabilities and indeterminancies of atomic physics to establish the freedom of man or the existence of paraphysical influence in human affairs, as some writers fervidly assert (see, for example, A. H. Compton (1957) in a recent issue of the *Atlantic Monthly*).

What we need to keep in mind is that science is one system which has been invented by man for the purpose of finding order in events which often appear to be more or less randomly organized with reference to his existence. Man has invented other construct systems to achieve the same grand purpose or to permit orderly transactions in some more limited sphere. Each of these construct systems may have its own unique validity. While it would be esthetically satisfying (and possibly, though not necessarily, more efficient) to have one overarching construct system, there is little to be gained from forcing consonance where little or none exists. The criterion for the validity of a construct system is not its consonance with another system but its utility in giving order and meaning to human experience. Within a scientific construct system, the assumption of determinism (plus randomness, perhaps) is required.

There are other construct systems where different assumptions rule. For example, the individual scientist, getting up in the morning, chooses to shave or not to shave; he construes the world with the assumption of almost complete freedom of choice. The legal system for construing the world assumes a middle position on determinism and individual freedom; the criminal behavior of the young person or of the psychotic is considered to be determined by circumstance, while the sane adult is construed as being responsible for his behavior. A religious system for construing the world obviously has to assume the effective functioning of some supra-individual influence. And a poetic system might make even other assumptions. It is when we attempt to shift from one construct system to another, without explicit recognition of what we are doing, that we get into trouble.

The Process of Choice. Earlier it was suggested that psychology might offer a description of choice with more limited meaning than the popular definition with its implication of freedom of will. Here is the way many psychologists would see the situation. An individual is confronted with a situation requiring one of a given number of possible responses. The individual brings to the situation as he perceives it a collection of hypotheses (behavior potentials, habits, personal constructs, as you like) about what he should do based on past experience, including experiences in simliar situations. Within the limitations of the situation (a man in jail cannot choose to take a stroll in the park), of time available, of the individual's repertory of more or less appropriate responses, and from his habits of problem solving, the individual scans the situation and tries out various responses symbolically until there emerges into prominence (or until time runs out) a response that fits into his expectancies of establishing a more satisfactory state of affairs. He makes the response, or better, the response is made which is most prominent at the time when the response is required. The psychologist's incredibly complex task is to build a regression equation that will permit him to predict the relative prominence of various potential responses at any particular time. If this description of choice is acceptable, the psychologist can get about his business. The problem will still give him plenty of trouble, but it will not defeat him by erecting insurmountable theoretical barriers.

There are inescapable facts, however, that make it difficult to accept the description of determined choice just offered: the introspective realness of the experience of choice itself and the insistence of feelings of responsibility for the consequences of one's own behavior. People, including psychologists, act in the assumption of freedom of choice, and no amount of talk about the ground rules of science is going to change much this primary assumption. That people are going to behave as though they have freedom of choice is an important datum that must be included in a scientific system which says they do not in fact have such freedom. There may be some comfort in face of this contradiction in noting that science not infrequently can get ahead with its business only when it does adopt a formulation at variance with daily experience.

The process of choice or of choosing is not complete with the occurrence of a particular determined event. The event itself becomes a part of the past experience of the individual, and it is also likely to alter future circumstances either for the individual himself or for others. Behavior is a product of interaction of the individual and his environment. Psychology is concerned with the nature of this interaction. Interactions that involve the welfare of individuals and of man may be described as ethical behavior, and psychology is not only interested in such interactions but has contributed significantly to their development. Thus the individual and his world are engaged in a process of continuous reconstruction of each other. Man remakes the world, and the world remakes man in an ongoing process.

The extent to which psychological science can contribute to this process of interaction valid observations about the nature of man, to this extent psychology can make a contribution to ethical behavior and then, secondarily, to ethical theory itself by supplying the philosopher with more data to work into his ethical systems.

But more pertinent, and intriguing, are the direct contributions that psychological science can make to the ethical behavior of the individual. Psychology makes its most distinctive contribution to ethical behavior by altering both the kind and the number of hypotheses that the individual brings to any given choice situation involving the welfare of others.

Psychology can (or better, will) alter the ultimately determined process of choice in a number of ways. Suppose for instance that psychology could demonstrate, what many have asserted, that the probability of a satisfactory choice occurring will be partly a function of the amount of time devoted to the symbolic manipulation of alternative courses of action. Common sense says that this is true, and the late Thomas Watson of IBM promoted the idea with his ubiquitous signs. But we really do not have much precise knowledge about what goes on when we think. If psychology can add to our understanding of the mechanisms of thought, it will make a contribution to ethical behavior.

Psychology may also increase the probability of the occurrence of ethically good responses by freeing a person to act on ethically good hypotheses that he already has but cannot use. This is what the psychologist attempts to do in psychotherapy. People may often not be able to use the knowledge they have about what is ethically good because of debilitating anxiety evoked by the anticipated consequences of efforts at constructive behavior. A common expression of this dilemma may be seen in the plight of the person who cannot risk loving for fear of getting hurt. There is the intriguing possibility that man may already know all that he needs to know to achieve fullest self-realization for himself and others. A simple factoring out of common elements in the major revealed or intuitive and rational developed ethical systems of the world might yield say 90% of the ethical ideas that are important to have. If this commonality be found, then all the energies that go into efforts at refinements of ethical theories on the basis of new knowledge might well go into investigations of why man cannot act on available hypotheses as to what is good. Such incapacities, of course, are a primary concern of research in clinical psychology.

Regardless of the adequacy (or inadequacy) of available hypotheses about human behavior, good or bad, psychology must and will go on testing old hypotheses and generating new ones to be tested. Such is the nature of psychological science. If psychology can make widely available to people the results of a number of verified "if – then" statements about the behavior of people in relationship one with the other, the required consequence will be an improvement in ethical choices, if the description of the process of choice, given earlier, is accurate. For good to ensue from an increase in knowledge requires the assumption that we live in an orderly universe of which individual expressions of choice are an integral part. To the extent that choices are in harmony with whatever universal order there is, to that extent they should be ethically good. The incompleteness of our knowledge of the universe and of man possibly accounts in part for the large number of disparate criteria that have been suggested as bases for ethical systems. Psychology has no such confident solutions to offer. It can only accept some responsibility for continuous enquiry into man's changing behavior in an evolving world.

So far it has been suggested that psychological knowledge should result in more ethical behavior: (a) by clarifying the process of decision making; (b) by divesting repressed responses already in the individual's repertory of their anxiety-producing potential, thus making them useful in problem solving; and (c) by adding to the response repertory of the individual a number of alternative ways of behaving. All of this appears to be to the good.

Control of Behavior

But if the psychologist at this point in the process of scanning the problem situation shifts construct systems and speculates on his personal responsibility as a scientist and a citizen, there emerges a much less sanguine view of the consequences of a constantly growing body of verified knowledge about human behavior.

As psychological knowledge grows, the possibility of more effective control over human behavior increases, with profound consequences for ethics. The very process of enquiry that promises to improve decision making also adds to the gravity of the decisions made.

Increasingly man will be able to employ the results of psychological science to manipulate his fellow man often without his victim knowing that he is being controlled.

Developing psychological knowledge presents the same conjunction of good and evil that we have all felt so keenly in the development of atomic energy. Atomic energy can ease man of drudgery and disease, and it can also annihilate him. Psychological knowledge can bring man increased certitude, dignity, and joy, and it can also enslave him. These antinomies are among the most exiciting and demanding developments of our time. They have within them the seeds of ultimate tragedy or triumph. The stakes seem to be getting even higher, and the rules of the game, embodied in ethics, ever more important.

References

Allport, G. W. *Becoming*. New Haven: Yale Univ. Press, 1955.

Cattell, R. B. Ethics and social sciences. *Amer. Psychologist*, 1948, 3, 193-198.

Compton, A. H. Science and man's freedom. *Atlantic Monthly*, 1957, 200(4), 71-74.

Conant, J. B. *Modern science and modern man*. New York: Columbia Univer. Press, 1952.

Dobzhansky, Th. G. *Evolution, genetics, and man*. New York: Wiley, 1955.

Feuer, L. S. *Psychoanalyses and ethics*. Springfield, Ill.: Thomas, 1955.

Fromm, E. *Man for himself, an inquiry into the psychology of ethics*. New York: Rinehart, 1947.

Huxley, T. H., & Huxley, J. *Touchstone for ethics, 1893-1943*. New York: Harper, 1947.

James, W. *Essays in pragmatism.* New York: Hafner, 1954.
Kelly, G. A. *The psychology of personal constructs.* New York: Norton, 1955.
Lundberg, G. A. Can science validate ethics? *Bull. Amer. Assn. Univer. Professors,* 1950, *36,* 262-275.
Melden, A. I. *Ethical theories.* New York: Prentice-Hall, 1955.
Montagu, A. *The direction of human development.* New York: Harper, 1955.
Northrop, F. S. C. *The meeting of east and west.* New York: Macmillan, 1946.
Rapaport, A. *Operational philosophy.* New York: Harper, 1954.
Rogers, C. R. *Client-centered therapy.* New York: Houghton-Mifflin, 1951.
Russell, B. *Religion and science.* New York: Holt, 1935.
Simpson, G. G. *The meaning of evolution.* New Haven: Yale Univ. Press, 1950.
Skinner, B. F. *Walden two.* New York: Macmillan, 1948.
Skinner, B. F. *Science and human behavior.* New York: Macmillan, 1953.
Underwood, B. J. *Psychological research.* New York: Appleton-Century-Crofts, 1957.

SOME ETHICAL AND SCIENTIFIC VALUES IN THE COUNSELING PSYCHOTHERAPEUTIC PROCESS

Charles A. Curran

Loyola University, Chicago Illinois

The English essayist, G. K. Chesterton [1], once described a young man who left England on a journey of discovery. He was determined to discover by himself a perfect country and there settle and raise a family. He went from city to city, from civilization to civilization, from the most primitive to the most developed, in a difficult and thorough search. Finally, across a sea he came to an unknown shore and found there if not a perfect setting, one that was the most satisfying. And as he explored, in delight, his newly found land, he climbed a hill to look at a new landscape and there off in a distance, the gleaming towers of the cathedrals and buildings of London. He had found by long and arduous pursuit, what he had, in a way, always known and loved.

The counseling psychotherapeutic process is, as I have seen it, a search for values but not in the usual sense of this phrase. It is rather, an adventurous and thrilling personal pursuit, in an independent and sometimes seemingly dangerous way, of values which are uniquely new and personal for the client. As the therapeutic process moves forward, one of the most consistent things I have observed is the increasing anxiety of the client, particularly the younger client, to safeguard his newly acquired cache of self-determined values and to resist forcibly the counselor or anyone else trying to impose, even surreptitiously, values from the outside.

But the astonishing thing here is, as Chesterton's analogy suggests, that this intensely jealous and often fiercely independent pursuit does not necessarily produce social rebellion or philosophical and theological anarchy. Rather, the opposite seems most often to happen. When the client, with deep personal integrity and security, probes himself in the searching and sincere pro-

Reprinted by permission of the author and the *Personnel and Guidance Journal,* September 1960, 15-20.

fundity of his relationship with the counselor, he retraces the basic steps by which civilization and society itself has, in some way, been formed. Or to put it another way, he surprisingly finds, in this absolutely personal pursuit, many of the basic values that are most fundamental to our whole Western Civilization and often shared in varying forms by all civilized societies if these societies are really understood. Here, it seems to me, with a strange twist and in a way G. Stanley Hall and others of his time would perhaps never have dreamed, we have "ontogeny recapitulates phylogeny."

In this paper, therefore, I would like to discuss (1) the client's personal pursuit of values in client-centered therapy particularly as I have observed it in clients, and some things this seems to imply, and (2) how this is related in some ways to the philosophical and theological value systems of Western Civilization.

A GREATER RATIONALITY

Rogers has recently said, describing his observations of this same therapeutic process, the following:

> I have little sympathy with the rather prevalent concept that man is basically irrational, and that his impulses, if not controlled, will lead to destruction of others and self. Man's behavior is exquisitely rational, moving with subtle and ordered complexity toward the goals his organism is endeavoring to achieve. The tragedy for most of us is that our defenses keep us from being aware of this rationality, so that consciously we are moving in one direction while organismically we are moving in another [5, p. 202].

A major factor in personal conflict and unhappiness, as Aristotle pointed out, is this fact: that a person can seek an apparent good which satisfies one or the other of his needs but which is actually contrary to the over-all reasonable good of his whole person. Problems arise apparently because an individual's craving for particular personal, emotional, or sensual satisfactions are leading him away from the reasonable goals which he ultimately seeks. A man is, therefore, capable of a most complex self-deception. He can allow himself to be misled by particular urges to objects and goals which he knows will not really satisfy him nor ultimately be good for him.

For a number of years now we have been doing research on this process of the shifting perception of motivating personal values in the client's counseling awareness. It invariably involves a shift in focus and an increasingly broader realization of all the factors involved in a situation or personal relationship. This in turn results in a changing perception of what is really good and thus his choices and actions change. We have discussed this research elsewhere [3] but to illustrate this, may we consider excerpts from a second interview and contrast it with the insight stage of the tenth interview with the same person [3].

These data were drawn from a series of interviews of a married woman in a serious infatuation with another man. In the second interview the only thing she considers beyond herself and John is one brief phrase: "I've got people that I don't want to hurt either." In the whole of the first and second interviews the above statement represents the only expression of consideration for any factors or persons except herself and John. However, if we contrast this limited viewpoint with the insight stage of the tenth interview, we have a striking change in perception. The superimposed image of John and herself has given away to quite a different picture of the whole situation.

> When John and I were together it just sorta pushed everything into the background . . . But you just can't turn aside and say, "Well, I'm going back to where I was" — even though I, if I really wanted to — I couldn't do that. It's hard to give up John after all the good times we've had and the things we've done, but when you stop and think what could have happened why you see things different. (Long pause) . . . but I know even now, just by not seeing John, I'm better physically and spiritually too . . . Yes, the way it was before I wasn't really happy, it was just a state of conflict and misery and fear of being found out and thinking of the kids and all — no, it really wasn't happy, even when it seemed most enjoyable . . . There's no happiness in it. You're always under a constant strain. (Pause) I'll lose a lot in a worldly way but I'll gain too. I would gain more than I would lose spiritually.

Observe here the perceptual language in the phrase, "When John and I were together it just sorta pushed everything into the background," suggesting the superimposed image of "John and I" blocked out the over-all awareness of her responsibilities to her husband, family, and God. The second phrase, "But when you stop and think what could have happened why you see things different," suggests that the thinking process of the counseling interviews also brought about a different self-perception. When we analyze what is the difference in these perceptions, it seems to be the removal of the superimposed, narrowed focus on "John and I" for the broad reality awareness of the responsibilities to husband, children, and God. Now, even though giving up John is a severe sacrifice when she focuses on the pleasure that John brought her, she sees herself to be better off physically and spiritually, when her perceptions are clearly on the total field of responsibilities, as distinct from John [3].

Stated in goal-directed language, this viewpoint would suggest that the superimposed image is itself an apparent good and that the self tends to move towards this apparent good until its perceptions are broadened and the reasoning and insightful process of the personality, in this case brought about through counseling, brings out from the background the real good, the total perceptual field. This puts into its proper perceptual organization the immediate good, which in this case, came from the relationship with John. When the immediate good is measured against the total perceptual field of all values involved, the self chooses and moves towards the relationship of husband, children, and God in the total perceptual field, as the real good, and rejects the apparent good which previously was a narrow focus on "John and I."

TOWARD INNER VALUES

We see too in these insight excerpts and this description of the therapy process, a goal directed and self-responsible morality. That is to say, we are not dealing here with some type of built-in Kantian "categorical imperative"

which can be variously explained by the effects of social mores or early conditioning and learning of cultural attitudes or the imposition of family attitude
or some other type of code. All these things may in fact be operating in the
client in the counseling relationship and probably are operating, but the peculiar quality that the therapeutic process seems to reveal is an inner capacity
where, by holding up inadequate and ultimately unsatisfactory goals, I can
stimulate myself to want these goals and to project on them much more
meaning than they really have. Evil, then comes in the degree to which I am
responsible for such self-deception and for the impulsive yielding to emotions
or basic drives which cause me to seek these disproportionate goals.

Obviously, there is a wide variety of degrees of responsibility in such
matters and while certain objective factors — such as legal or theological codes
may determine — doubtless enter here, there is at the same time almost always
a strong factor which only the person himself at the deepest level of his self-
understanding — best acquired through counseling — would only know and
be able to reveal.

We see in the therapy process therefore, an inner value system which is
yet objectively effective in producing a better operational fulfillment and
achievement. Operational reality, by implication, has apparently some kind of
reasonable substructure, granting all its apparent disorder, into which the
client's own reasonable process penetrates. The therapy process, as we see
it, ultimately facilitates not only a more reasonable integration and control of
the personality but also somehow a better, more adequate way of living. This
pursuit of a basic reasonableness in the midst of widespread disorder, which
the counseling therapy process implies, is what joins its implications to our
whole legal, social, philosophical, and theological tradition in one of its most
ancient Judaeo-Greek-Christian forms.

Let us pursue further what happens philosophically in the client's therapeutic process. It seems to me one way of illustrating what happens might
be symbolized by a triangle. The client begins at the point, with unique and
personal events, situations, feelings, and reactions that seem peculiarly to
happen only to him. Slowly he moves down to the discovery that others share
many of these things — that he is not as different or unique as he thought.
He begins to adapt himself to others and to learn from others but in a way
most interestingly personal and self-determined. In counseling, where the
counselor struggles to understand him and thus he is helped to understand
himself, he studies and investigates himself in an intense search which the
counselor's responses keep objective and in a sense impersonal.

THE DISCERNING LISTENER

In our focus on the release and emotional oneness and commitment of
the counseling relationship, we have perhaps somewhat overlooked the degree
of value that the counselor's accurate understanding and verbalization adds
to the client's clarification and objectification of himself. In a recent research
project we have been having clients comment on their reactions to the interview a few minutes after it is over. One of the most consistent comments is
the way the counselor's response helped them to understand what, in a complex and often emotionally involved way, they had just said. The following
illustrates this:

I've never been listened to so well — no one before ever cared so much about what I was saying. I have confidence in speaking. Even if what I say is stupid or foolish, I am not made to feel stupid or foolish myself. I trust the counselor to hold what I say and not to let it slip or become blurred. In such a situation I can react to myself and my own thoughts and feelings much as I might react to those of someone else. There is an objectivity about the counselor's responses that is freeing.

Another person said:

When I finished last time I thought I was too confused to say anything more. Then, as I heard your responses, I somehow understood what I had said and it seemed very easy to say something further. I didn't sound really as foolish or stupid as I thought. I began to become understandable to myself.

But this reasonable objectivity about oneself in counseling is the exact opposite of a cold analysis. On the contrary, it is only possible to a maximum degree in a profound relationship of mutually deep commitment. It is a commitment made possible by a love on the counselor's part which Greek and Medieval philosophers called *amor benevolentiae* — a love that concerns only the other and his good. This they contrasted with *amor concupiscentiae* where the person was seeking some self-determined return from the other. But in the commitment of mutual love of *amor benevolentiae*, the counselor is not only a catalytic agent of emotions, he is at the same time and even more essentially a warm, understanding, auxiliary reasoning power.

TOWARD ULTIMATE VALUES

Where does this mutual process of client reasonable self-search lead? It leads, it seems to me, down the triangle to issues and values that are increasingly more universal and more ultimate. It can lead — it does not always — to the most ultimate question of all, the meaning of life itself and to a struggle with all these final anxieties which in the traditional language of Western civilization one would have to call philosophically metaphysical and theological.

But even when the basic and most universal issues of life, symbolized by the broad base of the triangle, are not questioned by the client, they seem contained and implied in the values by which he questions and changes more immediate personal situations. Some years ago Rogers wrote, discussing a case, that insight tends to move through the "difficult and painful . . . not for its immediate but for its longtime satisfaction" [4, p. 210].

This awareness might be carried to ultimate conclusions. The analysis of the counseling process demonstrates that increased insight and a broader understanding of his personal values, aims, and purposes enable a person to direct himself towards and eventually to reach, more ultimate goals that are more permanently satisfying. But no transient, material thing can, upon analysis, produce the permanent security, peace, and lasting happiness that each one seeks. The fear of loss is the other side of every human possession and security. This kind of evaluation should logically lead a person to seek a final and ultimate Good, which will be a permanent source of happiness.

Each man seems therefore to be in a state of both being and becoming for which no transient goal or value — however immediately satisfying — can offer any final longtime fulfillment. We seem to have implied here a profound core existential anxiety in man — an essential dissatisfaction to which Augustine's famous remark was applied: "Oh God, Thou has made us for Thyself Alone and our hearts are ever restless until they rest in Thee." This being and becoming would be then, something both unique and yet shared by all mankind and, I believe, by God.

A TASK IN FREEDOM

But it is not only this pursuit of values that are ultimately the most universal and perduringly rewarding that relate the counseling psychotherapeutic process to the pursuit of values well-known in the tradition of Western Civilization. It is also in the more immediate values which the process of change in itself contains.

The counseling psychotherapeutic process at its best facilitates a person's own reasonableness, literally frees him to be more reasonable when he is enslaved by conflicting, emotional, instinctive, or somatic urges. This greater state of reasonableness not only enables him to study himself in an unthreatened and non-defensive way and to accept and use all he learns about himself, but it also makes him capable of a more adequate judgment of his own immediate or ultimate life goals and better means to them. Finally, this counseling psychotherapeutic process seems to do a third thing. It integrates the person's whole psychosomatic self so that he is now also able — often to his amazement — to do with surprising ease, what he now knows he should do and wants to do.

We have here an illustration in which a client discusses deep positive changes in himself:

> . . . and yet, frankly, it hasn't been at the expense of much consciousness on my part. Does this happen? I just don't know . . . I just don't want to be naive and say that this change has to be due to what we have done at this table. But I know that it is the *greatest* cause for the change. There may be other factors like my work, a change in Marie, and so on, that help to make me more agreeable, too. I'm not perfect or a new person but my temperament has been of fewer moods and less apartness. The changes have been obvious to Marie, too, and she tells me so . . .
>
> Yep, that's it. The same personality with greater control and more integrated function . . .
>
> And the role that you played did it.
>
> If you said to me to quit browbeating my wife, or to stop this, or to stop that, it would have been a useless attempt, I think that technique would have completely failed. Instead I've brought these things out time and again, time and again. The fruits of these discussions are that I'm better and that the cure has been effortless on my part. I'm not perfect or anything, but I've been so much better, and it's noticeable to others especially Marie [6, *pp.* 243-262].

This, perhaps surprisingly, is very similar to, if not the exact process that Aristotle and many of the ancients and medievalists considered the prudential process. Prudence was considered an incommunicable ability that could be acquired ultimately only by oneself. It could not as such, be taught. The first stage of this prudential process was the self-investigation and inquiry which was called counsel. But this is not seeking counsel from another, as it later implied, but rather taking counsel with oneself, sometimes with the help of another. From this concept apparently came our modern word, "counseling."

This first stage led then to the second prudential stage which involved a double judgment — the rejection of past reactions, operations, and plans and the development of new and more adequate personal solutions. The third prudential stage followed from this and was the self-command stage which brought order and integration into the emotions, impulses, and bodily functions so that a prudent man could carry out what he judged to be according to his own reasonableness.

VALUES REDISCOVERED

What I mean to say here in this discussion of the values of the therapeutic process as they relate to our civilization might be best illustrated by an incident reported in the Korean War. There was great difficulty in the soft mucky terrain and the huge modern tanks were bogging down in the mud. But in one section the soldiers found a path, overgrown with bushes and not used for many years apparently, which actually held up even the largest tanks and trucks and immeasurably facilitated their movements. When they investigated the history of this valuable passageway they learned it was at least a thousand years old, constructed by hand in some very ancient, now forgotten dynasty.

This exactly illustrates something of my astonishment in the dawning realization that many of the things this counseling process is revealing about human nature in a fresh and dramatic way, are yet not so completely new but that some of the ancient philosophical conceptions of Aristotle's Ethics and what used to be called the Cardinal Virtues can yet hold this powerful modern and new psychological movement. To be sure, much underbrush and debris have gathered here, that must be swept away. Much misunderstanding, confusion, and misinterpretation of ancient ethical and characterological terms like prudence, temperance, fortitude, and humility must be carefully clarified and adapted to all that we now profoundly know of the therapeutic process. But I am convinced that there is yet much that could be helpful to us, even now, like the ancient road in Korea. There is evidence, I believe, that would join these new psychotherapeutic discoveries to the ancient ethical tradition and value scheme of our Western Civilization, without in any sense warping the meaning and usefulness of either. But we must be willing to drop our own historical stereotypes and, perhaps, even ancient prejudices and seek to understand these conceptions with something of the freshness and clarity they really had for the men of much earlier times. By this I do not mean necessarily any return to some basic theological or philosophical unity, however desirable this may or may not be. I rather mean the common ethical concepts which in fact we all more or less accept by implicit observation in Western democratic society and which most of us want to preserve for ourselves and our children. But we accept these values too implicitly perhaps, and we are in danger of chopping at the roots of the tree or letting someone else chop at these roots and eventually jeopardize the tree, while we yet enjoy and treasure its fruits. We need to seek, perhaps, not only personal integration but to see that this can also be in some way an integration with the whole civilization that produced us. We need to know not only our relationship to our parents, family, and immediate environment but also to those older peoples whose thoughts and values have affected us with equal, if unknown, potency.

What then, finally, would be the personal values involved for us if we could do this — as the ancient Korean road proved so valuable to the movement of the modern tanks? Basically, I think it would do two things. It would free us from the more recent, probably Kantian, ethical concept that all personal values must be imposed from without which has come not to mean either by parents, society, or even more threatening and dangerous, by the state. It would restore again the possibility of starting out, like Chesterton's traveler, on a thrilling personal pursuit of oneself in a fierce and independent search for reasonable self-values and yet allow that one would ultimately come by this process, not to violent rebellion and anarchy, but to ancient and secure traditional values. These values have helped to carry through many centuries the burden of human hearts and, I think, can still help this burden.

Secondly, this would restore our own sense of belonging to the civilization that produced most of us and is basically responsible for our whole democratic tradition. It would make a place for education in values which in no way would impinge on a man's freedom to be unsparingly honest and sincere with himself and his own self-determined pursuit, through counseling psychotherapy, or by other educational and social means. This kind of personal pursuit the Greeks and Medievalists would have called, with a meaning strange to our modern ears, the seeking of humility. But by this word they would not have meant a fawning, inferior, "Uriah Heep" sort of thing, the "umble" man, but something very clean, dignified, and positive. This concept of humility has been defined as "the reasonable pursuit of one's own excellence." Such a definition, it seems to me, gives in one phrase about as good a statement as anything we have to delineate a core therapeutic concept and basic value scheme. This could be equally applicable to counseling, psychotherapy, education, and society itself without in any way doing violence to society and the rights of others and yet at the same time without distorting or warping the person's profound and deep need of personal integrity, responsibility, and basic independence.

REFERENCES

1. Chesterton, G. K. *Orthodoxy*. New York: Lane, 1918.
2. Curran, C. A. The counseling relationship and some religious factors. *J. Counsel. Psychol.*, 1959, *6*, No. 4, 266-270.
3. Curran, C. A. Some preliminary perception experiments related to insight in counseling therapy. In Bier, William (Ed.). *Perception*. New York: Fordham University, 1957.
4. Rogers, C. R. *Counseling and psychotherapy*. Boston: Houghton Mifflin, 1942.
5. Rogers, C. R. A note on "The Nature of Man." *J. Counsel. Psychol.*, 1957, *4*, No. 3, 202.
6. Snyder, W. U. *Casebook of non-directive counseling*. New York: Houghton Mifflin, 1947.

(36)

ETHICAL RESPONSIBILITIES OF THE COUNSELOR

James F. Adams

Department of Psychology, Temple University

One of the marks of the professional status of counseling is an increasing concern with ethical problems. This old adage about an ounce of prevention being worth a pound of cure is particularly apropos in this area. Many of the ethical problems which arise in counseling could have been either avoided or settled with a minimum of concern if the counselor had considered them in advance or had been aware of his ethical responsibilities (12). Hence the need for some general guidelines and considerations.

COUNSELOR'S LEGAL STATUS

Wrenn (16) has pointed out that the counselor actually has more legal protection, in a broad sense, than he may realize. A counselor does not have to release confidential information, personnel or counseling records, upon the *request* of a police officer, an officer of the court, or any other court official. Quite the contrary, the counselor should probably not release such information, for the counselee would then have every right to bring legal action against him. An exception to this statement may be found in those states, e.g., California, where the counselor may legally release information to certain public agencies and is protected under the law in such release. However, in general, the only legal way in which a court can gain access to a counselor's records is by serving a warrant for release of the records. Further, if the counselor keeps personal records which are not a part of the official records of the institution which he serves, these records do not have to be released when the official records are taken into custody. They would need to be mentioned specifically in the original subpoena or subpoenaed separately.

Schmidt (11) discusses the problems of the counseling and clinical psychologist with respect to professional recognition, privileged communication, libel, slander, the right of privacy, malpractice, and criminal liability. Gradually psychologists are gaining certification in a number of states. This certification usually affords the psychologist the same rights for "privileged communication" as is given to ministers, lawyers, and physicians. Insofar as counselors meet the requirements for certification, they would of course have the same protection under the law. However, for those counselors who are not certified or do not reside in states which have certification, the problem remains.

The last comprehensive survey of the counselor's right to "privileged communication" was conducted by Smith (14). At that time Michigan was the only state in which the counselor was protected under the law. A California attorney general's opinion suggests that confidential communication,

Reprinted by permission of the author and *The School Counselor*, May 1965, 197-205.

since it is information not required by law, *might be privileged*. While this
is hardly a satisfactory state of affairs, it does suggest the possibility that in
California, if the issue were to arise, counselors would have legal protection.
Montana specifies privilege in civil proceedings only for any information
obtained "in the study and observation of child mentality." Oklahoma makes
it a misdemeanor for a teacher to reveal any information concerning a child,
"except as may be required in the performance of his contractual duties."
It would seem that Oklahoma counselors, if they are also considered teachers,
should take a close look at their "contractual duties." Seven states empower
the local board of education to rule on the disposition of information as long
as there is no legislation to the contrary. Thirty seven states have no laws or
rulings which are of any help to a counselor in the withholding of confidential information. Information on this problem was not available for Hawaii
or Alaska.

Counselors should note that where they do not have privileged communication, they do not have an obligation to reveal confidential information unless
they are under oath before a court of law. The mere request for the information on the part of an office or court official does not obligate a counselor
to reveal the information. If under oath a counselor refused to reveal confidential information, he could be cited for contempt of court. It would be-
hoove counselors to be very certain that they are justified in withholding such
information. It is likely that if the counselor's case for the withholding of such
information were very strong, his professional societies, such as the American
Psychological Association or the American Personnel and Guidance Association, would come to his aid. However, the counselor should make his decision
to withhold legally requested information on the basis of his own personal
and professional ethics and should not count on receiving aid from an outside source. It will take a number of favorable court decisions to establish
precedent, and it is the writer's opinion that tests of a counselor's right to
privileged communication should very clearly concern a violation of counseling ethics since unfavorable decisions will not strengthen the counseling profession's position (4).

Another point to consider is the possession of "hearsay evidence" (16).
When a counselor possesses information that a counselee has broken a law
and this information has been gained in a counseling session, it is likely to
be considered as "hearsay evidence." This type of evidence is not generally
admissible in a court of law. Certainly an objection by an attorney as to the
admissibility of the evidence would rule out the information in most cases.
As much of what is gained in a counseling interview is "hearsay evidence,"
the possession of such information will not normally be a legal problem, although it may be an ethical problem for the counselor. Further, the possession
of such information, while an ethical problem, is not a legal problem *until*
the counselor is under oath. Many problems of this nature can be readily
solved by encouraging the counselee to go to the proper authorities himself.
The fact that a counselee reveals something of this nature to his counselor
frequently indicates that he is asking for support and encouragement in
making restitution.

In a juvenile court case, "hearsay evidence" may carry more weight.
Attorneys are usually not present and the admissibility of evidence is left to
the discretion of the judge. In an instance of this nature the counselor will

have to decide for himself whether or not his testimony is a violation of counseling ethics and in the best interest of the counselee and society.

None of the foregoing should be interpreted to mean that the counselor will not cooperate with any agent of society. The intent of what has been said is only to point out that counselors may have more protection under the law than they realize and the counselor is not under an obligation to "reveal all" upon request but should use caution and discretion.

ETHICAL PRINCIPLES IN COUNSELING

Ethical standards which are of importance for counselors have been proposed from a number of sources and discussed in many more (7, 16, 5, 8, 14, 6, 1). Many of these standards are equally applicable to all of those who are in the helping professions. Some of the more pertinent of these standards will be discussed within this section.

Counselors in all areas of work should clearly recognize the limits of their competence and should not offer services which fail to meet the professional standards of recognized specialists in the fields in question. Furthermore, a counselor should not attempt to diagnose, treat, or advise a counselee with reference to problems which are not within the counseling domain. There are times when it is very difficult or impossible to obtain the aid which is necessary for the counselee. To be realistic, there are also situations which occur when there are mandatory professional referral sources available which, in the counselor's opinion, may do more harm than good, i.e., there are "professionals" in all fields who are incompetent in their profession but who are "available." There are then, two separate problems, the first one that of no available referral source. Tyler (15) states that there are some individuals whom the counselor, by virtue of his training, cannot help and that good intentions do not guarantee good results. While this is quite true, this writer cannot help but feel that the *skilled* counselor has the responsibility in this situation to act in a supportive role i.e., be aware that he is *not* conducting therapy but at the same time realizing that by being an empathic listener he may give the individual the time he needs to resolve his own problems. It would be quite easy to become diverted into a discussion of whether or not, in fact, this isn't therapy and, perhaps, the best type of therapy (10). In any case, the counselor will need to carefully weigh the pros and cons for continuing the relationship, and if there is any question of his being able to conduct the type of support necessary, he should follow Tyler's advice and terminate the relationship.

The second problem, i.e., referring, when in the counselor's opinion there is substantial evidence that a mandatory referral source is not a good one, is not an easy one to resolve. However, it occurs frequently enough that the issue is one which must be faced, although the writer does so with some trepidation. As an opinion which is neither supported nor negated from other sources, it would seem that the ethical thing to do would be to continue to refer individuals to this "professional" when absolutely necessary, even though in the counselor's opinion little of a beneficial nature for the counselee may be accomplished. At the same time, the counselor has a very real responsibility to sensitize his administrators and fellow counselors to the problem. Incompetency is much more difficult to document than unethical behavior; yet the counselor should do everything he can to remedy a situation of this type through documentation and through enlisting the aid of other professionals if possible.

A counselor should not normally accept a counselee who is receiving psychological assistance from another professional worker unless an agreement has been reached as to the respective areas of help being offered or unless the counselee's former professional relationship has been terminated. This principle has both ethical and practical implications. Counselors should work in cooperation with other agencies and professional workers far more than they do at the present time (9, 13). Without this cooperation there can be much duplication of effort as well as a loss of valuable information. If counselors wish to consider themselves as professional people, they will need to develop professional relationships.

The counselor should also insist on ethical standards with respect to his associates. As a general rule, the counselee's permission should be gained before communicating any information to another person or agency. A counselor in a school setting should assume, until proved wrong, that other school personnel are capable of maintaining confidences. He should be quite sure that they are aware of the need and the reasons for maintaining this confidence. It is the counselor's responsibility to help develop this awareness. Many problems in this area could have been avoided if counselors had assumed this responsibility, or educative function, prior to expecting its automatic occurrence. If the counselor finds that his professional colleagues are not able to act in a professional manner, he should withhold confidences even though their knowledge of the counselee's problem might benefit the counselee. Many times a counselor can sensitize teachers to the fact that a child has a problem without being specific about what has been told the counselor in confidence. The welfare of the counselee is a primary consideration, and considerable thought should be given to this before a confidence is revealed (without the counselee's permission) to teachers or other professional people.

The counselor should guard confidences which are extended to him in respect to a counselee. When information is gained from other professional workers or parents, it is not wise in most instances to inform the counselee that the information has been obtained. This is not to say that the counselee should be unaware of the fact that the counselor has contacted and is working with the pertinent outside agencies (although it is desirable to get the counselee's permission to make this contact); but rather that by telling the counselee of the information obtained, the counselor may be destroying another very essential relationship. As a rule, the only time a counselor should reveal a confidence received from another professional or, for that matter, a confidence received from counselee or his parents, is when it is quite clear that there is imminent danger to the counselee or to society. Of course, if permission is given to release the confidence, it ceases to be an ethical problem and becomes one of wisdom.

A counselor should present or report his findings with respect to a counselee accurately and simply to facilitate understanding. It should not be assumed that the referral source or the recipient of the report understands complicated psychological jargon unless this is known to be true. In many instances the counselor does not have the professional training to make a diagnostic judgment (e.g., schizophrenic behavior), and typing a counselee with such a term can have deleterious effects. If the counselor feels that the counselee has an emotional problem, he can state it just as simply as that, i.e., "I feel that the counselee has an emotional problem which needs attention." Psychological nomenclature which is misused, and even sometimes when correctly used, can be harmful. The rule is that any communication concerning a client should promote the welfare of the client. It should be insured that any recipient of a communication (or possible future recipient) concerning a counselee can understand and profit from that communication. With respect to this, the professional training and experience of the recipient, if known, should be considered.

The counselor should refuse to suggest or support unwarranted assumptions, invalid applications, or unjustified conclusions with respect to psychological instruments or techniques. This is frequently done with the individual intelligence test when questionable clinical conclusions are drawn from very meager evidence. Many counselors have had an introductory course in the use of projective techniques. While this experience is valuable in sensitizing the counselor to an area of personality evaluation, the use of these same tests for diagnosis, without much more extensive training, is most unethical and may be harmful to the counselee.

Occasionally a counselor is found who has been oversold on a personality theory. Psychoanalytic personality theory seems to produce this result quite frequently. It should be remembered that there is *no* personality theory to the present time which has been sufficiently validated to warrant unrestrained enthusiasm. In any case, diagnosis of this type is seldom a function of the school counselor, and it seems to this writer that many counselors verge on being unethical in their diagnoses which are based on personality theory and which are largely unsupported from objective evidence.

As a member of a helping profession a counselor should be willing to devote part of his services to work not included in his duties or for which he will receive little, if any, financial return. School counselors occasionally will have students come back to them after they have graduated from school. Within limits the school counselor and other counselors have a continuing responsibility for past counselees. The problem of performing counseling without financial remuneration when the counselee is unable to afford a fee is not as simple as it seems. In our society a premium is placed on that for which we pay financially. Frequently services which are offered for nothing are evaluated at the same level. Consequently the counselor should be very sure that the counselee cannot pay at least a token fee if this is the customary practice.

A cardinal obligation of the counselor is to respect the integrity and to protect the welfare of the counselee. A counselor's ultimate responsibility is to society, and his professional behavior should reflect his awareness of this. The welfare of the counseling profession and of the counselor are clearly subordinate to the welfare of society. In most instances the welfare of society can be best served by protecting the welfare of the counselee. Only when it is quite clear that either society or the counselee is in imminent danger should a counselor consider breaking a counseling confidence.

Bordin (3) notes four areas of counselor responsibility to be considered in ethical decisions: to society, to his sponsoring unit, to his client, and to his profession. Another source for ethical consideration is the counselor himself. Most certainly a counselor's values will enter into his ethical decisions. It is impossible to state precisely what personal ethical standards a counselor should hold, particularly in a constantly shifting environment and society. About all that can be said is that a counselor should be aware of his values and his reasons for holding them. A counselor should not insist that all individuals hold the same standards that he personally holds. This is not to imply that a counselor must compromise his personal standards, but it should be remembered that they are *personal* standards. A statement from Ethical Standards of Psychologists (5) is worthy of note as it applies equally well to counselors.

> "Very often the resolution of ethical problems requires that the psychologist choose between two or more interests that are in conflict. Are the psychologist's obligations primarily to the social group, or to his individual client, or to his profession, or to himself? There is, of course, no simple answer to this question. Most situations where ethical decisions are necessary involve an implicit hierarchy of values, and this hierarchy has to be redefined for each situation. The equation of ethical responsibility is a complex one: weights for the variables must be computed anew as each new ethical problem is solved."

HOW DO COUNSELORS FEEL ABOUT ETHICAL PROBLEMS

A study by Smith (14) will be considered in some detail because of its pertinence to this topic and because of the large number of counselors found in the secondary schools. In this study professional members of the National Vocational Guidance Association submitted critical incidents in which ethical decisions were involved. From these incidents an ethical questionnaire was constructed. This, in turn, was sent to 1,225 professional members of NVGA. Six hundred questionnaires, or approximately 50 per cent, were returned. The questionnaire was scored to indicate the degree to which the respondents would favor revealing confidential information to some authorized agency or person. A near normal distribution of scores was found. A high score on the questionnaire indicated that the respondent favored revealing confidential information to an authorized agency or person; a low score indicated the converse. In other words, a high score indicated that the respondent's major loyalty was to society; a low score indicated that the respondent's major loyalty, or feeling of responsibility, was to the counselee. The group most closely associated with secondary school counseling showed the greatest preference for social obligation choices. Public school employees emphasized civic responsibility more than did any other occupational field. All educational counselors below the college level were significantly higher in social obligation choices than were college counselors. The greater the amount of public school teaching experience the respondent had, the greater was his degree of loyalty to society, and the lesser was his feeling of loyalty to the counselee.

One hopeful sign found was that the more graduate units in guidance, psychology, and related subjects, the greater was the loyalty of the respondent to the counselee. Respondents with the doctorate had the lowest mean scores on the questionnaire or were the highest counselee-centered group. Neither amount of counseling experience nor amount of time devoted to counseling proved to be a significant factor when comparing responses to the questionnaire.

A comparison of related items concerning access to cumulative records ranked administrators, other counselors, parents, teachers, social welfare agencies, law enforcement agencies, and employers — in decreasing order — for accessibility to records. Availability of records to the latter two groups was considered extremely debatable. Respondents tended to agree that personal problem information should not be available, but they tended to disagree as to whether administrators, other counselors, welfare agencies, or the counselee himself should have access to this information. Three fourths of the respondents agreed that when information was received directly from the counselee, the counselor had a responsibility to maintain the confidence.

Smith concludes that, with the exception of imminent harm to the counselee or others, respondents tended to place loyalty to the counselee above loyalty to society, although there was a tendency for public secondary school counselors not to share this direction of loyalty. Based upon the concurrence of at least 70 per cent of the respondents, Smith proposes that the following ethical standards be considered by counselors:

1. The counselee commands the primary loyalty of the counselor under ordinary conditions.
2. A counselor is justified in revealing confidential information to selected individuals when the counselee or others are in imminent physical danger.
3. A counselor should not voluntarily, nor upon request of the police, reveal counselee information of any offense short of guilt of a major crime.
4. A counselor should not voluntarily, nor upon request of administrators or parents, reveal any information about a counselee or former counselee received in confidence.
5. A counselor is not released from maintaining a confidence because others have the same knowledge.
6. A counselor is released from maintaining a confidence if he gains the counselee's consent to reveal such information.
7. When two counselees are seeking help on a mutual problem, a counselor should not reveal either counselee's confidence to the other.
8. When two counselors are working with the same counselee, it is ethical for them to share confidential information.
9. Confidential information may be revealed to another counselor if the counselee's anonymity is maintained.

Smith also proposes the following standards relating to the confidentiality of cumulative records:

1. Cumulative records should contain a counselee's transcript of grades, achievement test results, mental ability and other aptitude test results, interest inventories, personal problem information, and discipline records.
2. Teachers and other counselors who are directly concerned should have routine access to all cumulative record data except discipline and personal problem information.
3. All data concerning a Counselee except personal problem information should be available to school administrators.

4. Parents and social welfare agencies should have access to achievement test results, interest inventories, and transcripts of grades.
5. A counselee should have access to his own transcript of grades and all test data except mental ability test results.

It might be said, as a practical criticism of these cumulative record proposals, that most schools have extremely lax filing systems. It is possible for almost any determined person to obtain access to cumulative record files with little difficulty. Furthermore, withholding materials from the files before handing them to a responsible person seems a little like questioning a person's patriotism. A more practical proposal might be for the counselor to keep two sets of records. In one set of files would be kept materials on the student to which authorized personnel would have access. In the counselor's personal file would be kept the confidential materials on the counselee.

Lastly, Smith proposes several standards relating to other aspects of counseling:

1. A counselor should not intervene in a counselee's curriculum choice despite predictive evidence of academic or emotional outcomes.
2. A parent who has given information about a counselee's problem should be promised confidence.
3. A counselor's record of a counselee's psychotic behavior should be made available to other schools.
4. It is ethical for a counselor to gather information about a counselee from other schools without the counselee's consent.

It will be noted that almost all of Smith's proposals can be subsumed under the heading of counseling in a manner which will do the most to promote the counselee's welfare. It is also apparent from her study that there is a further need for school counselors to consider their ethical responsibilities with respect to their own school and their personal professional status. Lack of agreement of these counselors on many ethical problems highlights the need for continuing thought in this area. Perhaps the school counselor could sensitize his administrative and teaching colleagues by an open discussion of ethical problems and communicate his ethical responsibilities to those with whom he works.

CONCLUSION

Schwebel (12) believes that the causes of unethical behavior can be categorized into three areas: "The overpowering self-interest of the professional worker as expressed in personal profit, self-enhancement, and the maintenance of security and status poor judgment, due in part at least to inexperience in problem solving in counseling; ignorance of technical knowledge and of one's own values." It may be that not much can be done to help the counselor in the first of Schwebel's categories; however, by being familiar with the problems which are likely to arise in the ethical area and by being adequately trained in counseling, the counselor should have little excuse for violations of ethical principles because of the last two categories.

Many of the considerations which have been discussed here are common problems for counselors. The theme running through almost every ethical consideration is that the goals and purposes of society can be best served by keeping the welfare of the individual counselee as the paramount concern.

REFERENCES

1. Adams, J. F. *Problems in Counseling: A Case Study Approach.* New York: Macmillan Co., 1962.
2. American Personnel and Guidance Association. Ethical Standards. *Personnel guid. J.,* 1961, *40,* 206-209.
3. Bordin, E. S. *Psychological Counseling.* New York: Appleton-Century-Crofts, Inc., 1955.
4. Carter, T. M. Professional immunity for guidance counselors. *Personnel guid. J.,* 1954, *33,* 130-135.
5. Committee on Ethical Standards for Psychologists. *Ethical Standards of Psychologists.* Washington, D. C.: The American Psychological Association, 1953.
6. Committee on the Preparation of Ethical Standards. A proposed code of ethics for A.P.G.A. *Personnel guid. J.,* 1959, *38,* 168-170.
7. Gluck, S. et al. A proposed code of ethics for counselors. *Occupations,* 1952. *30,* 484-490.
8. Hahn, M. E. and MacLean, M. S. *Counseling Psychology.* New York: McGraw-Hill Book Co., 1955.
9. Mitchell, H. E. A brief history of an interdisciplinary relationship. *J. couns. Psychol.,* 1955, *2,* 201-204.
10. Rogers, C. R. The characteristics of a helping relationship. *Personnel guid J.,* 1958, *37,* 6-16.
11. Schmidt, L. D. Some legal considerations for counseling and clinical psychologists. *J. couns. Psychol.,* 1962, *9,* 35-44.
12. Schwebel, M. Why? unethical practice. *J. couns. Psychol.,* 1955, *2,* 122-128.
13. Shoben, E. J., Jr. Some thoughts on interprofessional relationships, *J. couns. Psychol.,* 1955, *2,* 196-201.
14. Smith, Carol E. *Development of Ethical Standards in the Secondary School Counseling Relationship for the Use of Counseling Information.* Unpublished Doctoral Dissertation, University of Southern California, 1956.
15. Tyler, Leona E. *The Work of the Counselor.* New York: Appleton-Century-Crofts, Inc., 1961.
16. Wrenn, C. G. The ethics of counseling. *Educ. psychol. Measmt.,* 1952, *12,* 161-177.

HELP-GIVING AND MORALITY

Joann Chenault

Southern Illinois University, Edwardsville

A model for the counselor's definition of help is presented as an aid to the exploration of questions of morality. Morality as a professional issue raises questions of counselor control as it relates to the meaning of help.

Reprinted by permission of the author and *Personnel and Guidance Journal,* October 1969, 89-96.

Questions of morality which apply to all aspects of life are not generally asked of the professional help-giver regarding his behavior with his client. Help-giving is regarded by some as an amoral activity. And perhaps the professional status of help-giving has mistakenly suggested to others that professional competence assures morality. The offering of professional help may seem to be an inherently moral act.

This article proposes (a) that counseling is not inherently moral; (b) that the counselor's professional status, implying expertise, places him in a peculiar position of psychological power over his client; and (c) that a responsible profession giving help must examine the morality of its use of power over the individuals it serves.

The particular aspect of morality suggested here as being most relevant to the counselor's behavior concerns control of another's existence. Questions are raised regarding the nature of one's influence and the degree to which it is controlling. Such questions are questions of morality.

A model for counselors' definitions of help is proposed because the moral behavior of the professional and his definition of help are inseparable issues. It will be seen that the problem of definition has concomitant implications for research in the area of counseling effectiveness.

The contributions of Pepinsky (1966, 1969) and Pepinsky and Schmidt (1969) to the issue of professional help-giving have stimulated the author's interest in this subject. Pepinsky states (1966) that "conditions within the superorganization of help-giving are such that much of its visible output must be interpreted by the spectator as productivity in search of a criterion." This paper is an effort to focus attention upon those criterion questions which should precede productivity.

INFLUENCE AND CONTROL

Influence is an inescapable result of any interpersonal relationship. It is not undesirable, for without it there can be no community among men. In a sense, choosing to remain alive is a commitment to influence others. Counselors would have no reason for being if their purpose were not to influence.

But the issue of control cannot be dismissed in a cavalier way on the grounds that influence exists. The words *influence* and *control* are not synonyms. It may be unwise to dichotomize their meanings as absolutes, thereby assuming no similar components. We can speak of differences in terms of the degree rather than the presence or absence of influence or control. Still, degree alone is not an adequate differentiation of meaning. The major distinction lies in the psychological freedom provided the client—freedom to discover and develop his own values, freedom to accept an action, idea, or value as desirable, or reject it. Such freedom is inversely related to control.

Some argue that control is not a serious problem because clients are free to reject control. This freedom of the client is inherent but is not an actualized absolute. It is a potentiality subject to varying degrees of psychological control by the counselor. The degree to which the counselor's influence prevents the client from exercising his own abilities to differentiate, judge, and decide is the degree to which the counselor's behavior is controlling. The degree to which this condition prevails is the degree to which the counselor's behavior fails to meet the condition of morality.

The question of the nature of our influence is of vital importance in a culture where professional words are associated with wisdom and truth. The words of an oracle have a greater potentiality for controlling those who seek his advice than do the same words from a peer.

In spite of our protestations that the client always retains the ultimate responsibility for his own decisions, we must question the degree to which we, intentionally or not, usurp that responsibility through the nature of our influence. Psychological control can be exerted in subtle, unconscious ways.

THE QUESTION STATED

There can be no universal or consensual differentiation between moral and immoral acts. This relativity of morality applies to it as a generalizable concept. But the propositions in this article refer to morality as it is judged by a person, morality as a matter of individual value and decision.

Given the issue of control, the individual counselor's moral question becomes: Where is the line between brotherhood and the colossal presumption to control another's destiny? What is the distinction between altruism and professional chauvinism? At what point does service become disservice? Is my client's need for help the need for control?

DEFINING HELP

It can be seen that the moral questions raised above can only be answered in terms of one's definition of help. While such a definition refers here to the issue of morality, one's definition of help is the most basic and essential question for all professional issues in this field. It is, consciously or unconsciously, the ultimate source of the professional's directions, whether he deals with questions of theory, practice, or research. For this reason, the benefits of a thoughtful development of one's definition of help will extend beyond the issue of morality.

What is help? Certainly it is more than altruism. In Steinbeck's *Sweet Thursday*, Hazel, in his effort to help a wounded gull, chases it into the sea to drown.

In stating one's definition of help, it may be profitable to distinguish between help as goal (H-g), help as process (H-p), and help as consequence (H-c). We must first determine what we feel should happen, what we are there for. It is only after we have determined what we want to occur (what is helped) that we can begin to determine the operations (H-p) for attaining the goal and that we can determine whether "helped" actually occurs.

It should be obvious that, because help can be defined only by the individual, an absolute definition cannot be supplied here. However, guidelines for remaining within the bounds of one's own morality can be suggested.

Help as Goal

Help as goal refers to the philosophical or value bases of what we do. One of the attractions of eclecticism has been that one is not required to suffer the difficult task of defining help (making value assumptions explicit). How easy it is to dismiss the question of morality by saying "different things help different people." The model proposed here requires eclectics to supply some rationale or value basis for their services to clients because individual differences can be accounted for in one's theory or rationale. Counselors who have made their intentions explicit will be better able to satisfy questions about the morality of their counseling.

Those counselors who have not developed a theoretical framework or rationale of their own and who wish their practice to rest upon more consistent bases than eclecticism may accept the goals set down by a respected psychological theory. When this happens counselors often assume that their goals come previously endowed with morality. Perhaps it is not too shocking to suggest that the morality of an individual's goals is not assured by the respectability of the theory to which the goals belong. Questions of morality must be asked individually by each counselor in terms of his own values. Individual morality requires individual definition of help.

The only restriction which morality places upon the counselor's goals (his definition of help) is that of protecting the client's freedom to determine his own destiny. Following the earlier premise that control is a negative criterion of morality in professional help-giving, the definition of H-g would not include control as an underlying value assumption. The closer a counselor comes to determining goals for the client or deciding the acceptability of goals which the client chooses, the closer he approaches the immorality of controlling another's life.

To those who have equated help with control, the elimination of control as part of H-g may seem to be eliminating the very possibility of help. They may assume that the absence of control means the absence of help. But there are many kinds of degrees of influence which are relatively noncontrolling, as defined here. Of course, the choice of morality is not the absurd choice between controlling and doing nothing. It is the choice of defining the nature of one's influence.

For those who may be inclined to transpose the client's goals into the counselor's definition of help, a further explanation may be helpful. While the client's own goals for himself are important variables in the counseling process, they should not determine the counselor's definition of help. That is, the counselor's definition is made independently of an individual client's particular problems or goals. Such counselor goals represent the professional reason why counselor's meet with clients. The goals are the rationale for the existence of the counseling relationship offered to clients.

It may be well to examine this contention more closely. Counselors often assume mistakenly that the client's freedom is best protected by defining help individually for each client in terms of the client's own goals. On the contrary, the counselor's separate delineation of goals for each client is the most severe limit to the client's freedom.

Unless the counselor feels that anything and everything "helps" his clients, he cannot in good conscience automatically accept as his own any and all client goals. (He may accept them as the client's goals but not as his own.) And when he is selective about his adoption of only certain acceptable goals, he is at the same time making value decisions which properly belong to the client. Thus, the adoption of different goals for each client is a selective and consequently a limiting and controlling decision on the part of the counselor.

Those who maintain that help must be defined differently for each client may have been trapped by the fallacious assumption that help must mean the implementation of specific client behaviors. It may help to place these remarks in perspective if one keeps in mind that goals may be broad and general or specific and behavioral. It can be seen that the counselor's adoption of different behavioral goals for each client is more likely to be limiting than his adoption of broad enabling goals which apply to all.

When help is defined as the mutual accomplishment of client goals, the client and counselor are both participants in the client's acts of accomplishment, thereby diminishing the client's responsibility or ownership of his own behavior. A noncontrolling definition of H-g refers to enabling the client to decide for himself and does not refer to the counselor's deciding for him as an expert or even with him as a partner. The partnership refers to *making things possible for the client*, not to *doing the possible things*.

The counselor best protects his client's freedom by allowing him to own completely his own thoughts, feelings, and behavior, rather than to own them conjointly with the counselor. The client's goals belong to the client. The counselor's goals are his definition of help.

H-g as an enabling goal refers not to the accomplishment of specific desired behaviors but to the enablement of the client to think for himself, decide for himself, and to assume the responsibility for his actions and inactions. The difference between controlling and enabling goals is the difference between helping a client to make decisions and helping a client to be *able* to make decisions.

Because they do not refer to specific behaviors, enabling goals are equally applicable to all clients. One way to provide the foundation for a moral definition of help is to build into one's definition the protection of each client's freedom. A protection of freedom prevents the encroachment of control.

Help as Process

Help as process can be defined in relation to H-g and H-c but it is not the same thing as either one. In defining help as process, we must differentiate between change (consequence) and chang*ing*. Change describes a point in time, but changing is a moving description. Most studies which purport to be concerned with process actually refer to outcomes. They tell what happened (H-c). In order to avoid confusing H-p with H-c, we cannot focus upon conditions in any way except periodically over the time between, and not including, H-g and H-c.

Process must refer to a series of connected descriptions or a description referring to the act and not to the condition of change. Thus, a time continuum showing what you wish to happen, the happening, and what happened illustrates how H-p is connected to but does not include H-g and H-c.

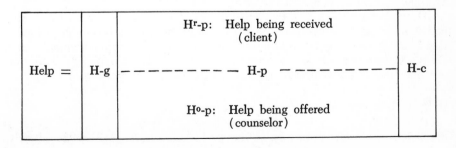

		H^r-p: Help being received (client)	
Help =	H-g	— — — — — — — — H-p — — — — — — — —	H-c
		H^o-p: Help being offered (counselor)	

H-p refers both to what the counselor is doing (H°-p) and what the client is experiencing (H^r-p). It is important not to confuse intentionality with the transitive meaning of the verb to help. Help requires that the verb's object actually be affected by the act. Helping does not mean trying to help; it means the actual success of the effort, and help does not occur unless the object of the act is actually its recipient.

Therefore the two aspects of H-p are not equal dimensions, not equally necessary nor equally sufficient. H-p can occur even when H°-p does not occur. (The originator of the act may be someone or some condition outside the counseling relationship.) But H-p can never occur when H^r-p does not occur. (If the client does not experience help, the counselor cannot be said to be helping, but only trying to.) The meaning of the verb is transitive and requires that the object receive the action.

The distinction between H°-p and H^r-p is useful in that it keeps one from assuming the presence of both from the presence of one. For example, counselors who define H-p as the providing of facilitating conditions will be required to determine whether their verb (H-p) is, in fact, transitive. Facilitating conditions are not facilitating unless it can be shown that the client is experiencing help. Without this relationship to H^r-p, the concept of facilitating conditions belongs more properly in the H-g definition.

Conditions, general and specific (e.g., atmosphere, relationship, emphathy, rapport), may be proposed as necessary for the process of help to occur. But we cannot speak of these terms as process without introducing into their definition the experiencing of the client. That is, the H-p model suggests that client experiencing (H^r-p) be a part of the definition of the counseling process. Each of the common adjectives which might be used to describe process—understanding, clarifying, differentiating, interpreting, accepting, to mention only a few—can be examined in this context.

Let me illustrate with two of the above-mentioned terms. Empathy is often defined as though it exists somewhere in space between client and counselor. In this sense, it is a conceptual abstraction used to explain a feeling you have that something exists apart from you. Empathy as process lives inside persons; it is a continually changing feeling which is experienced. The feeling that this experience transcends you or is space. People, not space, have feelings.

Understanding as process would mean more than the counselor's "taking in" what his client says. The counselor's confidence that he understands is not evidence that he does. Counselor understanding cannot properly be labeled understanding until it has been tested or confirmed by the client. And counselor understanding as process requires that the client experience it (H^r-p). Thus, the introduction of confirmation into the definition of H-p provides assurance of both requirements for understanding.

Until the counselor has examined the intricacies of his definition of H-p, he has not completed his test of morality. Morality refers primarily to behavior. H-p is the primary test. Moral intentions (H-g) do not justify immoral means (H-p). Controlling methods to free the client are not justifiable. By definition, psychological freedom occurs only through choice, not coercion.

Help as Consequence

One's definition of help as consequence will describe what the client is like if what you wished to happen did, in fact, occur. Those who do not wish to specify particular behavioral or attitudinal outcomes may use descriptions such as "the client had the experience of . . . ," "the client had the opportunity to . . . ," or "the client felt free to . . . ." A noncontrolling definition of H-c is not likely to specify that the client make particular decisions (decide to decide), only that he be able to choose between making them or not (decide or decide not to decide), only that he be freed of the psychological controls which make him feel simultaneously that he must choose, yet cannot choose.

As with H-p, it is easy to confuse intentionality (H-g) with effect (H-c). For example, some counselors justify their control by assuring themselves that it is better to control intentionally than to suffer under the illusion that one is not controlling. Help (H-c) is seen by them as more likely to result if we plan to control than if we control unknowingly.

This reasoning is equivalent to proposing that murder with malice aforethought is morally superior to manslaughter. Intentional control does not guarantee more helpful effects than unintentional control. Nor does it guarantee more helpful effects than an intentional freeing influence. Proof of helpful effects depends upon one's choice of a definition of help as consequence. When we say, "By intentionally controlling I caused him to make better grades," we have not proved that help occurred except in terms of our own value definitions of help. We have said we think making better grades is a good thing. Another counselor might consider making better grades irrelevant or even antithetical to what he considers help (H-c).

There is no reason why some definitions of help may not blend combinations or aspects of the three-part model. The value of the model lies not in its use as a molder of definition but as a malleable framework from which one can examine his understanding of help-giving.

QUESTIONS OF CONTROL

Questions of control as they apply to the issue of morality will, of course, differ according to the individual asking them. However, the nature of such an examination of one's position can be illustrated by the following examples of arguments one might have with oneself.

An H-c Issue

Perhaps control is quite as moral as noncontrol as long as it works.

But a behavior that works cannot automatically be moral simply because it works. Chloroforming a child "works" if your purpose is to keep him quiet.

H-c can have no moral justification if it rests upon immoral means (H-p). Nor can it be justified without a value base (H-g). Verbal conditioning and other behavior therapies implicitly rest upon the "it works" assumption. The model for help proposed in this paper reminds us that "what works" has value only in terms of what we feel should work (H-g). To discover that a counselor can cause certain behavior changes is meaningless until we have morally justified the assumption that these changes *should* occur.

An H-p Issue

Well, then, control is quite as moral as noncontrol as long as it *helps*.

But the morality of the act (H-p) is dependent upon one's definition of help. Lobotomies have been justified on the grounds that they help. Routine daily tranquilizing on alcoholic wards is rationalized on the same grounds. Certainly the morality of these implicit definitions of H-p is a moot question.

In justifying control as help, the definer has often unwittingly substituted someone other than his client as the object of his help, e.g., a distraught family or a harassed hospital staff. For counselors, a moral definition of H-p requires that the object of the verb be the client.

An H-g Issue

An act is not immoral simply because of its consequences. If I reach out my hand to help a person and inadvertently cause him bodily injury, the consequences were not helpful but the act was not immoral because my intention (H-g) was to help.

But the same argument does not sound so reasonable when applied to different examples. Many Nazi guards who led the Jews to the gas chambers have been said to have acted from a true sense of patriotism, respect for their country's laws and leaders. The dropping of the Hiroshima bomb is said to have been a moral act because it was done with moral intentions.

The power of the counselor over the client may be motivated by altruistic intention. (John Adams observed that power always thinks it has a great soul.) But it can be seen that H-g morality does not guarantee H-p or H-c morality. The purpose of the three-part model is to ensure that each aspect of one's definition meets the requirements of morality.

The issue is not an easy one. The superiority of one argument over another is not a simple truth, and there are other facets of the questions which have not been raised here. At least we can say that morality is a professional issue. It is the basis of the professional issue of help.

THE ISSUE OF HARM

There is no doubt about it: Some counselors help, some hurt, some are relatively ineffectual. Neither can there be much doubt that the first and last of these possibilities are safer on moral grounds than the middle one.

Patterson (1968) has brought to the attention of counselor educators studies reporting deterioration in clients (Barron & Leary, 1955; Bergin, 1963; Cartwright, 1956; Cartwright & Vogel, 1960; Fairweather, et al., 1960; Mink, 1959; Powers & Witmer, 1951; Rogers, 1961; Rogers & Dymond, 1954; Truax, 1963; Truax & Wargo, 1966).

If a counselor assumes that vulnerability is a characteristic which clients do not possess, that assumption must be challenged. The capacity to be influenced or helped cannot exist without vulnerability. If a counselor believes that help for a number of clients morally balances the harm of a few, that value must be challenged.

How can one answer such a difficult question as the justification for psychological harm without knowing first the nature of help and the nature of harm, the many qualities and degrees of both, and especially their meanings for the particular individuals involved? Does the relative psychological comfort of 10 John Does justify the "pain" of one John Smith? Whatever the answer, it is not in numbers.

Although we can never have complete assurance that no harm will result from counseling, that conclusion does not justify dismissal of the question. Certainly the only moral position to take is to require of oneself serious and thoughtful attention not only to what help is but also to what harm is. Harm and help are not always dichotomous. It is a professionally irresponsible position to assume without having defined harm, that one's counseling does not seriously harm his clients.

RESEARCH IMPLICATIONS

Research results supporting the presence of counseling effectiveness do not assure the absence of harm. The occurrence of X (help) can be accompanied by the occurrence of Y (harm). As with the issue of influence, we are not concerned with presence or absence but with nature and degree. It is possible for the effects of harm to outweigh the values of help. Unless one's research seeks also the answers to Y questions, conclusions of help may be doubtful.

There are reasons for this doubt. In spite of the legitimacy of one's study of a particular criterion or criteria, the presence of help must eventually and ultimately be determined by total effects. A researcher cannot morally duck the issue by pronouncing himself immune to total questions. His selected criteria are legitimate units of study. But the meaning of his study may be of limited value for the field of counseling if it is not placed somewhere within the broader context of total or ultimate effects.

We know that questions of help and harm when dealt with statistically can refer only to specific criteria. Even the most global concepts of counseling effectiveness can be dealt with empirically only when they are fractionated into discrete, operationally definable, measurable factors or aspects. But the answers to these separate questions refer only to those aspects of help which were measured and do not deal with total effects. The total effect may more properly include a comparative weighing in the balance of positive against negative effects.

A profession's justification for being depends upon its ability to bring together its findings in some general total conclusion that what it does "helps." Surely it is imperative that our researchers' definitions of help be explicitly stated. Our journal literature indicates that this practice has not been followed. Definitions of criteria rarely represent a complete definition of help.

The model presented in this paper suggests that a meaningful research study of counseling process or effectiveness requires the explicit defining of H-g and H-p in addition to the usual attention to H-c.

As has been said before (Chenault, 1965) our research questions cannot continue to be isolated from their value bases. Perhaps it is not too strong to say that no research study on counseling outcomes or process is professionally meaningful until its relationship to the researcher's definition of help has been clearly established. In this way, not only will the value bases of our research become more explicit but the morality of our individual endeavors can be more thoughtfully examined by ourselves and by others.

REFERENCES

Barron, F., & Leary, T. Changes in psychoneurotic patients with and without psychotherapy. *Journal of Consulting Psychology*, 1955, *19*, 239-245.

Bergin, A. E. The effects of psychotherapy: negative results revisited. *Journal of Counseling Psychology*, 1963, *10*, 244-250.

Cartwright, D. S. Note on "changes" in psychoneurotic patients with and without psychotherapy. *Journal of Consulting Psychology*, 1956, *20*, 403-404.

Cartwright, R. D., & Vogel, J. L. A comparison of changes in patients during matched periods of therapy and no-therapy. *Journal of Consulting Psychology*, 1960, *24*, 121-127.

Chenault, J. Research and the monolithic tradition. *Personnel and Guidance Journal*, 1965, *44*, 6-10.

Fairweather, G., et al. Relative effectiveness of psychotherapeutic programs. *Psychological Monographs*, 1960, *74*, 1-26.

Mink, D. C. A comparison of effectiveness of non-directive therapy and clinical counseling in a junior high school. *School Counselor*, 1959, *6*, 12-14.

Patterson, C. H. The counseling practicum: an ethical problem. *Counselor Education and Supervision*, 1968, 7 (3), 64.

Pepinsky, H. B. Help-giving in search of a criterion. In E. Landy and A. M. Kroll (Eds.), *Guidance in American education III: needs and influencing forces*. Cambridge, Mass.: Harvard Graduate School of Education, 1966.

Pepinsky, H. B. *Psychological help-giving*, 1969, in press.

Pepinsky, H. B., & Schmidt, L. D. *People and information*, 1969, in press.

Powers, E., & Witmer, H. *An experiment in the prevention of delinquency*. New York: Columbia University Press, 1951.

Rogers, C. R. A theory of psychotherapy with schizophrenics: a proposal for its empirical investigation. In J. G. Dawson and N. P. Dellis (Eds.), *Psychotherapy with schizophrenics*. Baton Rouge, La.: Louisiana State University Press, 1961.

Rogers, C. R., & Dymond, R. F. (Eds.) *Psychotherapy and personality change*. Chicago: University of Chicago Press, 1954.

Truax, C. B. Effective ingredients of psychotherapy. *Journal of Counseling Psychology*, 1963, *10*, 256-263.

Truax, C. B., & Wargo, D. Psychotherapeutic encounters that change behavior; for better or worse. *American Journal of Psychology*, 1966, *20*, 499-520.

METAPHYSICS, RELIGION, AND PSYCHOTHERAPY

Orville S. Walters[1,2]

University of Illinois

In the physical sciences, the swing from a thesis of prescientific speculation to the antithesis of a cocksure empiricism has been followed by a

Reprinted by permission of the author and the *Journal of Counseling Psychology*, Vol. 5, No. 4, 1958, 243-252.

[1]Part of a symposium presented September 1, 1958 at the annual meeting of the American Psychological Association, Washington, D. C. In an earlier form this paper was presented at the 1957 Conference of Administrators of College and University Counseling Services, University of Illinois, November 5, 1957.

[2]The author is Director of Health Services at the University of Illinois. *Ed.*

wholesome heuristic humility in search of a synthesis. The resurgence of an attitude that is willing to acknowledge aspects of reality beyond the reach of science has been recognized both by its opponents and its advocates.

Hook (19), in describing this trend, comments: "In the schools, the churches, and in the literary arts the tom-tom of theology and the bagpipes of transcendental metaphysics are growing more insistent and shrill." He contends that "the refurbishing of theological and metaphysical dogmas about the infinite as necessary presuppositions of knowledge about the finite" indicates a latter-day "failure of nerve."

Flewelling (13), on the other hand, declares that "the traditional abrogation of metaphysics by science has been brought to sudden pause." Citing the philosophical implications of relativity, indeterminacy and the new significance of the observer in physical phenomena, he concludes, "The positivistic philosophies, in faithful obedience to the dogmas of a discarded science, still 'hold the sack' waiting for the materialistic rabbit, while contemporary science approaches a new personalism."

METAPHYSICS AND THE SCIENCE OF MAN

The sciences of man have been slow in reflecting this change. The pendulum has swung from psychology's early identification with metaphysical philosophy to an extreme empiricism. As Borow (7) has expressed it, "When psychology joined the company of the experimental sciences, it embraced empiricism with a vengeance." There is increasing conviction that an ultimate synthesis will require recovery of some of the elements that were rejected by psychology in the process of achieving recognition as a science.

Psychology becomes most deeply involved in metaphysical issues when it turns to the treatment of personality ills. Contemporary psychotherapy is confronted by a question that has far-reaching theoretical and practical implications: What is to be the place of metaphysics in psychotherapy? At opposite poles are those who are trying to "exorcise the metaphysical gremlin," (7) and those who hold that "at the bottom of every neurosis there is a metaphysical problem" (2).

Some of psychology's reluctance to modify an empiricistic rigidity is traceable to the influence of Freud. In his lecture, "A Philosophy of Life," Freud (15, p. 203) asserts the adequacy of science to achieve a full understanding of personality. While acknowledging that the world view of science is incomplete, he disdains and disparages the constructs of philosophy that would offer a more complete tentative picture of the universe. He denies any validity to philosophy and religion, and stakes out "the whole field of human activity" as the exclusive province of science.

Much of the psychotherapy now being taught and practiced has its roots in the Freudian system. Freud's personal philosophy has often been tacitly regarded as a part of psychoanalysis, although there is evidence that he himself acknowledged the separability of the two (26). Because they are frequently interwoven, Freud's reductive naturalism and the principles of psychoanalysis have had widespread influence upon American psychology and psychiatry.

Some of the present-day protests against this influence are voiced by Stern (41) and Maritain (22), who see Freud's reductionism currently producing a devaluation of man, contempt for the spirit and a loss of the meta-physical sense. Stern states that when divested of its Freudian positivism, psychoanalysis contains a movement toward personalism.

Freud's renunciation of metaphysics in favor of science has been continued and reinforced by some contemporary theoreticians. Feigl (12) lumps theology and metaphysics with magic, animism and mythology and describes them as "remnants of and regressions to . . . prescientific thought patterns." He con-demns the "something more" philosophy as a "seductive fallacy" and rejects the assertions of transcendent theology and metaphysics as "largely emotive."

PSYCHOTHERAPY AS APPLIED SCIENCE

The practice of psychotherapy plunges psychology into metaphysical issues. There is general agreement that science cannot determine values. The function of science is to observe, describe and classify what *is*, but not to decide what *ought to be*. Psychology, as long as it remains a pure science, does not make judgment of value. It is when turning to treat maladjustments of human personality that psychology moves away from the canons of scien-tific precision and ventures into the realm of values.

The transition from a pure to an applied science involves a value judgment of major consequence. Such a judgment presumes to differentiate between illness and health, and proposes to use scientific knowledge to displace the one the servant of the ethical judgments and, in some measure, the value system in favor of the other. In psychotherapy, psychology as a science thus becomes the servant of the ethical judgments and, in some measure, the value system of the therapist. As a healer, he seeks the recovery of his patient, sacrificing the neutrality and objectivity of the scientist for a stake in the outcome.

The application of psychological knowledge by one person to modify the attitudes and ideas of another involves the formation of further value judg-ments as to the need, the goal and the method of therapy. The counselor may be called upon, for example, to assist a person who is troubled by con-science. Is this illness or health? Is *any* trouble with conscience compatible with health? If so, how much? And if too much is present, how is the pres-sure of conscience to be abated? How much sensitivity of conscience should be left when the end-point of treatment has been reached?

In an effort to stay close to its scientific base, psychotherapy has concen-trated upon technics of uncovering the patient's conflicts, upon analysis of interviews and upon theories of personality organization. The patient, on the other hand, is struggling with metaphysical concerns: What is the good life? Where does it lead? How much freedom does man have? Are the claims of religion illusion or are they insight into transcendent reality? Before these questions science stands silent, claiming no competence in matters of ethical discrimination, moral responsibility, and ultimate destiny.

Not everyone is willing to concede this inherent limitation in the nature of science. There is confidence that science will ultimately be able to pro-vide a full explanation of the phenomena of the universe, including human behavior. This faith is responsible for most of the opposition toward permit-ting metaphysics to complement the incomplete world view that science now offers.

Freud proclaimed his loyalty to "the scientific *Weltanschauung*," not only staking out "the spirit and the mind" as proper objects of scientific investigation, but specifically rejecting religion and philosophy as collaborators in truth-finding. In this broad repudiation of philosophy, Freud was merely electing a different metaphysical viewpoint and enunciating an impassioned *credo* in the philosophy of scientism.

Feigl (12) similarly scorns "the sham completeness metaphysicians procure for their world pictures by verbal magic" and declares that it is a sign of maturity to be able to live with an unfinished world view. To proclaim such an affirmation of faith in the ultimate adequacy of science is to close the gaps in a science-centered *Weltanschauung* by philosophical scaffolding and to crystallize a unique value system. The unfinished world view is an abstraction. Commitment to something is necessary to existence. Even to repudiate metaphysics is to affirm a significant metaphysical position.

There are many who doubt that science will ever be able to offer a complete world view. Conant (10) expresses this viewpoint:

> As to the unifying, materialistic World Hypothesis, my doubt stems from its manifest inadequacy. As a conceptual scheme attempting to account for everything in the whole universe, it seems to me unsatisfactory because it is incomplete. It fails to provide for the altruistic and idealistic side of human nature.

Freud declared that since psychoanalysis is a part of science, it has no concern with judgments of value. It is no less valid to say that psychoanalysis, psychotherapy and counseling cannot be purely scientific, even though they are grounded in an empirical psychology, since they inescapably involve human values. The limitations of science are apparent wherever human autonomy becomes a variable in a problem.

Zilboorg (49) recognizes that the therapist cannot avoid encounter with philosophical, ethical and moral issues:

> Suffused with anxiety . . . man again is forced to contemplate what it is that he is, what it is that he wants, what it is that he ought to want, and what his place is in relation to his fellow man individually, to society, to himself as an autonomic person. These are ontological, metaphysical and fundamentally religious questions. A psychoanalyst, more than any other professional man, must cultivate a philosophy of values.

NEUROSIS AND WELTANSCHAUUNG

The scientific framework in which any exploration of neurosis and anxiety begins is soon found to be inadequate to encompass all the phenomena, implicating as they do the values and the world view of the patient.

Masserman, who has produced what he calls "experimental neurosis" in animals, cautions against the drawing of sweeping identities between his experiments and "the almost incomparably more complex dynamics of clinical psychotherapy" (23, p. 458). In the treatment of neurosis, Masserman departs widely from the experimental approach to recommend that the therapist enter into the patient's "personal universe of desires, meaning, values and actions" (23, p. 488).

Rioch (34), in a review of "experimental neurosis" acknowledges that the degree of complexity, modifiability and variability of human behavior is of a different order of magnitude than that in lower forms and refers to Harry Stack Sullivan's contention that anxiety is limited to human beings.

Efforts to understand neurosis apart from an ontology of anxiety have been disappointing. Even after the creation and unrestricted manipulation of his metapsychological constructs, Freud (16, p. 92) concedes:

> We find ourselves abruptly confronted, once again by the oft-repeated riddle: What is the source of neurosis, what is its specific, underlying principle? After decades of analytic effort this problem rises up before us, as untouched as at the beginning.

Shoben (37) formulates a theory of neurosis based upon experimental findings and learning theory. His view of neurosis as a consequence of defective social learning fails to deal with the concept of conscience and superego, and identifies guilt with anxiety.

Mowrer (25, p. 483) draws upon both learning theory and Freudian concepts to elaborate his concept of neurosis, concluding that neurotic persons suffer because they have repudiated their own moral strivings. This makes the undoing of repressions preeminently a moral enterprise.

A similar view was advanced by Pfister (28):

> . . . The repressed conscience plays a still more troublesome role than the known conscience . . . There consequently remains nothing but to purify the known, and, very often, too, the unknown conscience. In every psychoanalytic transaction deserving of the name, it is of great importance to replace the ill-advised with a clear and noble-piercing voice of conscience.

Stekel (39), another of Freud's early pupils, described neurosis as "the disease of a bad conscience" and recognized that somatic complaints could have a similar origin:

> Important is the fact that the voice of conscience may find bodily expression, this being what we call somatization. . . . The psychotherapeutist, taking his patients by the hand, must help them to restore the ideals which, deliberately, or under compulsion, they have destroyed (40).

May, after a detailed examination of the various concepts of anxiety offered by Freud and by the deviant schools of psychoanalysis, formulates a broad definition of anxiety as "the apprehension cued off by a threat to some value which the individual holds essential to his existence as a personality" (24, p. 191). He concludes, "The system of value on the basis of which one confronts normal anxiety . . . broadly speaking . . . is the person's religious attitude toward life" (24, p. 230).

Winkler (44) argues the inadequacy of the leading psychological doctrines of man. Freud saw man as a natural organism, Adler viewed him as a social being and Jung emphasizes him as an individual. "In addition to this," Winkler continues, "he is also a person in the philosophic and theologic sense, and he relates as an individual to the transcendental reality. He can also fail in this regard, producing that which may be labelled 'existential neurosis.'"

Frankl (14) believes that every man has a will-to-meaning, the frustration of which produces existential neurosis. His logotherapy aims to revise the defective world view in terms of meaning and value. "Patients themselves bring us philosophical problems," Frankl writes. ". . . The proper diagnosis can be made only by someone who can see the spiritual side of man."

Progoff (30) traces the progressive emergence of this recognition through Freud, Adler, Jung and Rank. He writes,

> Their psychological investigations led them to a realization of the funda-
> mentally spiritual nature of man. . . . They came in other words, to the
> metaphysical foundation of life that underlies psychology. . . . Psychological
> work fulfills itself only when it goes beyond psychology.

While psychological theory is moving to recognize the necessity of active encounter with the patient's value system, a parallel current is influencing the practice of psychotherapy. Pumpian-Mindlin (31) traces the ten-year evolution of practice in a mental hygiene clinic through various stages during which different emphases were found inadequate and dropped, one after another. The expression of hostility by the patient, the giving of love and affection by the therapist, the offering of psychodynamic interpretations and, finally, attempts at ego-integration, were all pronounced "not enough." In the continuing search for a more adequate approach, Pumpian-Mindlin concludes, "We must examine our culture and our values and those of our patients. We must see how these affect the 'self,' the total person."

A similar awareness is apparent on a social scale. Schindler (36) holds that many personality disturbances are caused by "confusion on a spiritual level," growing out of cataclysmic events in the past few decades that have brought the fundamental questions of human existence to the psychiatrist's attention. May (24, p. 109), in applying Mowrer's concept of neurosis, observes: "The repression of guilt feelings, with its concomitant generation of neurotic anxiety . . . in some ways is pervasive of our culture as a whole." This view is supported by Riesman (33) who comments:

> Increasingly today, this new type of analytic work with people who are
> not obviously ill — whose "symptom" is their malaise, their whole way of
> life — people who are troubled about moral issues, or who ought to be
> troubled about them, forces analysts to become concerned with problems of
> casuistry, of values, as part of the very task of therapy.

Tillich (43) finds that the common denominator in all theories of anxiety is the awareness of conflict between structural elements of the personality. Only in the light of an ontological understanding of human nature, he believes, can a consistent and comprehensive theory of anxiety be formulated. In the interpretation of human existence, the psychotherapist can benefit by collaboration with the philosopher and the theologian. Tillich views existential anxiety as basic, growing out of the threefold ontological threat of death, meaninglessness and guilt. These belong to existence and cannot be eliminated. Existential anxiety is properly the object of priestly concern, while pathologic anxiety is the concern of the psychotherapist. The goal of both professions is to help the patient achieve full self-affirmation. They may collaborate fruitfully, but neither should try to replace the other.

FREUD, PSYCHOTHERAPY, AND RELIGION

Although he emphatically denies its validity, Freud (15, p. 206) acknowledges that religion possesses a philosophy of incomparable strength and consistency, that has successfully resisted severe criticism. Religion, he concedes, exerts power over the strongest human emotions. A religious view of the universe adds strength and stability to personality, Freud acknowledges, even while he is trying to refute religion's claim to truth by arguments from psychoanalysis.

Freud's attacks have undoubtedly contributed strongly to the reluctance of psychotherapy to appropriate and apply the insights of religion. This unwillingness to deal with religion is discussed by Gordon Allport (4). Noting that "psychologists write with the frankness of Freud or Kinsey on the sexual passions of mankind but blush and grow silent when the religious passions come into view," Allport argues that the phychologist has no right to retire from the field, since two-thirds of the adults in this country regard themselves as religious people and nine-tenths affirm belief in God. Seventy per cent of the 500 college students questioned by Allport felt that they needed some form of religious orientation or belief in order to achieve a mature philosophy of life. Seventy-five per cent of the women and 65 per cent of the men acknowledged praying, many every day.

In spite of Freud's professional atheism and his violently anti-religious writings, Zilboorg (50) believes that he had "unconscious, intense, positive religious leanings." There is a note of wistfulness in one of his letters to Oskar Pfister, a Swiss Protestant clergyman who was one of the earliest practitioners of psychoanalysis. In the letter, Freud complained about the kind of patients who came for analysis, describing them as "often very poor material." "You, on the other hand," he wrote, "have young people with recent conflicts who are attached to you personally, and who are in a suitable state for sublimation and indeed for its most convenient form — religious sublimation . . . You are in the fortunate position of leading them on to God and reconstructing the conditions of earlier times, fortunate at least in the one respect that religious piety stifles neurosis" (20).

Freud's observation that religion can give strength and stability to personality and can "stifle neurosis" is not bound to the hypothesis that he devised to explain the fact. By "genetic analysis" he arrived at the conclusion that "the religious *Weltanschauung* is determined by the situation that subsisted in our childhood" (15, p. 210). Religion provides ethical precepts and a sense of protection, Freud decided, by preserving childhood attitudes.

This explanation has two flaws: Freud's defective understanding of religion, and his neglect of one of the most significant aspects of personality, purposive striving.

Freud's anti-religious writings indicate a lack of any real acquaintance with religion. Immediately after the appearance of *The Future of an Illusion*, Pfister (29) replied with a paper giving effective answer to Freud's criticisms of religion. Dalbiez (11) has offered a comprehensive criticism of the logic and philosophy inherent in Freud's position. In biographies and critiques, friend and foe alike have referred to the evidence for unconscious bias in Freud's anti-religious pronouncements.

Allport (3, p. 92) warns against "the trivial view that holds adult religion to be merely a repetition of the experiences of the child," adding, "The most comprehensive units in personality are broad intentional dispositions, future-pointed." This aspect of universal human experience, largely unrecognized by an empiricism that sees man as a passive being responding only to forces outside himself, is illuminated by the insights of religion. "While religion certainly fortifies the individual against the inroads of anxiety, doubt and despair," Allport continues, "it also provides the forward intention that enables him at each stage of his becoming to relate himself meaningfully to the totality of Being."

The stability of personality and resistance to neurosis that Freud observed and acknowledged in religious people thus has an alternative explanation more inclusive than Freud's hypothesis, because it articulates with major aspects of personality that he failed to include. Poverty in representing the future, in Allport's opinion, is the chief shortcoming of American psychology. Leo Alexander (1) also comments, "The concepts of ego and superego must be widened to include the will and the purpose as the key to responsibility. There is undeniable historical and social evidence for the existence of will and purpose in human affairs." Limitations set by the canons of scientific method and by the philosophies derivative from science have prevented psychology from recognizing or adequately studying these facets of personality.

THE THERAPIST'S VALUE SYSTEM

Every psychotherapist is a philosopher of sorts. When the psychologist turns away from his measurements and statistics to deal with troubled individuals on a one-to-one basis, he leaves pure science behind. Becoming a participant in the healing process draws him inescapably into the realm of values. At this point, as Allport (5) has pointed out, "Whether he knows it or not, every psychologist gravitates toward an ontological position. Like a satellite he slips into the orbit of positivism, naturalism, idealism, personalism." Refusing, as Freud did, to acknowledge commitment to a basic philosophy, is to defend it less effectively than if it were consciously avowed.

Furthermore, the therapist's own value system is deeply involved in the process of psychotherapy. Developments in ego psychology have not abated metaphysical involvement. The therapeutic goal of psychoanalysis is described by Gill (18) in these terms:

> A progressive analysis from the surface to the depth; analysis of the defenses and the motives for defense; the development and analysis of the transference neurosis; a resolution of symptoms, and as complete a "structural" alternation of the neurotic aspects of the personality as possible.

The process is further elaborated with the statement, "The gross major decision is whether the defenses of the ego are to be strengthened or broken through as a preliminary toward a reintegration of the ego."

This view of psychotherapy makes it a prerogative of the therapist to decide what aspects of personality shall be dismantled, as well as the form and content of the restorative process. Here the personal philosophy of the psychotherapist may determine the pattern of reconstruction. Reorganization of his patient's personality cannot help but implicate the therapist's own value system.

Even apart from active intervention in the reintegrative process the therapist's value system exerts its influence. Wolff (46) in his survey found some therapists contending that treatment should consist of reshaping distorted value concepts, while others advocated exclusion of the therapist's values from psychotherapy as far as possible. Wolff (47) also reported that while only 6 per cent of 43 therapists regarded change of values as a goal of therapy, 48 per cent believed that therapy does in fact directly transmit or develop value concepts in the patient. An additional 24 per cent thought that values have an indirect effect in therapy.

Rosenthal (35) commented after his study upon the changing of moral values in psychotherapy:

> It may be that the therapist communicates his values to the patient in many unintended, subtle ways, even when trying to avoid doing so. The patient, who is often sensitized to the therapist's every word and inflection, may be able to receive these communications, and because of his trust, admiration and respect for the therapist, may permit himself to be influenced by them.

The world view of the counselor apparently exerts its influence in ways unrecognized by either the patient or the therapist himself — in the selection of subject matter for response or discussion, in nonverbal cues if not by verbal expression. This was true even of Freud in the analytic situation. The account of Wortis (48) describes frequent manifestations of his misanthropy and pessimism. If only in subtle, inadvertent expression, the therapist's value system appears to be a constant factor in the relationship.

The therapist usually conceives of himself and is often represented as the detached, dispassionate scientist. A more realistic view would see him as an involved participant with an interest in the outcome, following a sectarian psychotherapeutic doctrine or combination of doctrines, the selection and practice of which are tinctured by his own basic philosophy of life.

THE THERAPIST AND RELIGION

Recognition of the role of the therapist's philosophy of life raises questions fundamental to the success of therapy. Can a therapist that denies the importance of supra-empirical factors in neurosis achieve an empathic relationship with a patient who is burdened with a sense of sinfulness? To reassure such a patient that "this is not a moral problem but can be understood only with impersonal, objective, scientific attitudes" (42) may lead in a direction opposite to improvement and insight.

If metaphysical concerns are at the bottom of many neuroses, to avoid the discussion of religion in psychotherapy as Wolberg (45) recommends, may be to bypass the most significant area of conflict. Masserman (23, p. 494) advises assuring the patient that his philosophic or theological faith will not be challenged, confessing that "only in the early years of his inexperience and defensive dogmatism did he think it necessary to explore, let alone attack, the patient's religious beliefs or practices." This calculated inattention to an area of frequent personality conflict may easily overlook a greater difficulty for a lesser.

To ignore or minimize the field of metaphysical concern in favor of sexual conflict or any other predetermined framework may leave untouched the most important cause of difficulty. Reider (32), for example, tells how a patient called him ten months after treatment had ended to say, "I just wanted you to tell me that there is no such thing as hell where people go for their sins." He complied with a pontifical negative, giving no recognition that the patient's request expressed anxiety growing out of a metaphysical concern that had been presented at the beginning of treatment, and that had obviously remained unresolved.

The responsibility for determining what religious attitudes are healthy or neurotic is a crucial one, certain to be colored by the therapist's own basic orientation toward religion. This is well illustrated by Casey's (9) citation of an analyst whose own unconscious resistance to religious appeal led to his opposing any religious adjustment by his patient. In the presence of such an attitude, the question of Arnold (6) is pertinent, "whether the therapist can correctly evaluate the resistance of a patient with whose philosophy of life he cannot agree."

Many psychoanalysts believe that religious beliefs and practices have a sexual origin and represent infantile emotions. Others regard religious concepts as benign but delusional. Can a therapist with such views enter into the personal universe of a religious patient's meanings and values to establish emphathy on any other basis than as the discerning possessor of truth communicating with the naive victim of error?

The frequent concern of the religious-minded patient and his family over the therapist's attitude toward religion is not without relevance. The naturalistic orientation not only includes certain beliefs, but excludes others. In providing himself with one variety of philosophical stuffing "to stop up the gaps in the universe," (17) the naturalistic psychotherapist at the same time rejects those philosophies that are open-ended toward a reality beyond science. The patient's concern is whether such a counselor can be tolerant toward a world view that he regards as error, and can leave such faith undisturbed during treatment. How many therapists will recognize and acknowledge the error of attacking the patient's religious beliefs, as Knight (21) did in his analysis of a minister?

DOCTRINES OF MAN

The inability of science to provide a complete view of the universe is most apparent in its apprehension of the nature of human personality. There is no mature science of man; there are only doctrines of man. Science at its best provides a truncated view of man. Every doctrine of man includes a substantial body of theoretical assumptions. These doctrines vary from the biological emphasis of Freud with its destructive death instinct, through the deviant psychoanalytic schools that stress social and cultural factors, to those that postulate an inherent upward drive in man toward self-enhancement.

Somewhere between these extremes is the Jewish-Christian doctrine of man that recognizes both the potential for good and the tendency to evil in man's nature. In contrast to the relatively scant empirical data and unilateral focus characterizing most of the neonate doctrines of man, the insights provided by religion are supported by centuries of observation and experience, and deal with the full sweep of human existence.

The psychotherapist is not offered a choice between a scientific and an unscientific doctrine of man. Rather, the choice is among different views of man that are corollary to various philosophies. Most of today's psychotherapy is set in a context of naturalism or positivism. The empirical findings of scientific psychology are not bound inseparably to either of these basic faiths. Such a context is a psychology-plus-philosophy; there are other philosophies equally compatible with the science of man that may lead to a clearer understanding of the patient who is troubled by metaphysical concern. To quote Outler (27), for example:

> The Christian faith is at least an equal option for the thoughtful man. . . . It is at least as intelligible a faith, resting on at least as much experimental evidence and exhibiting a capacity to interpret the inescapable issues of human life in a fashion both more meaningful and truly profound. The truth claims of the Christian faith cannot be "proved". . . . But they can be tested by those who place themselves inside the circle of faith. . . . Moreover, the Christian faith can be an ample and hospitable context for the scientific enterprise, in all its proper dimensions and concerns.

The Thomistic affirmation is similar: "A truly comprehensible and tenable view of man is achievable within the Christian ideology" (8).

Among others, two factors have contributed to the growing congeniality between psychotherapy and religion. The first is an increasing insistence on the part of religionists that "psychiatry cannot adequately perceive the whole man without taking into account the contributions religion has made available for the search" (38). Coupled with some acceptance of this claim by psychotherapy is a measure of recognition that the synoptic view of man offered by religion is both comprehensive and penetrating, its validity being supported by an impressive empirical background and maturity. As a consequence, the offices of the minister are being more widely utilized to augment the skill of the psychotherapist in the recognition of metaphysical concern as contributory to neurosis, and in the resolution of that concern through the resources of religion.

References

1. Alexander, L. Moralism and morality from the viewpoint of the psychiatrist. In I. Galdston (Ed.), *Ministry and medicine in human relations.* New York: International Universities Press, 1955. P. 97.
2. Allers, R. Psychiatry and the role of personal belief. In F. J. Braceland (Ed.), *Faith, reason and modern psychiatry.* New York: P. J. Kenedy & Sons, 1955.
3. Allport, G. *Becoming.* New Haven, Conn.: Yale Univer. Press, 1955.
4. Allport, G. *The individual and his religion.* New York: Macmillan, 1950.
5. Allport, G. The psychological nature of personality. *Personalist,* 1953, *34,* 347.
6. Arnold, M. B. The theory of psychotherapy. In M. B. Arnold & J. A. Gasson (Eds.), *The human person.* New York: Ronald Press, 1954. P. 529.
7. Borow, H. The logic of counseling research. *J. counsel. Psychol.,* 1956, *3,* 292.

8. Braceland, F. J. Clinical psychiatry — today and tomorrow. In *Faith, reason and modern psychiatry*. New York: P. J. Kenedy & Sons, 1955. P. 27.
9. Casey, R. P. Religion and psychoanalysis, *Psychiatry*, 1943, 6, 291.
10. Conant, J. B. *Modern science and modern man*. New York: Doubleday Anchor, 1955.
11. Dalbiez, R. *Psychoanalytical method and the doctrine of Freud*. New York: Longmans Green, 1941.
12. Feigl, H. The scientific outlook: naturalism and humanism. In H. Feigl & M. Brodbeck (Eds.), *Readings in the philosophy of science*. New York: Appleton-Century-Crofts, 1953.
13. Flewelling, R. T. The metaphysical predicament of science. *Personalist*, 1953, 34, 117.
14. Frankl, V. *The doctor and the soul*. New York: Knopf, 1955.
15. Freud, S. A philosophy of life. In *New introductory lectures on psycho-analysis*. London: Hogarth Press, 1933.
16. Freud, S. *The problem of anxiety*. New York: Norton, 1936.
17. Freud, S. Letter to Jung in Ernest Jones, *Sigmund Freud life and work vol. II*. London: Hogarth Press, 1955. P. 488.
18. Gill, M. M. Ego psychology and psychotherapy. In R. P. Knight (Ed.), *Psychoanalytic psychiatry and psychology*. New York: International Universities Press, 1954. P. 77.
19. Hook, S. The new failure of nerve. *Partisan Review*, 1943, 10, 2.
20. Jones, E. *Sigmund Freud, life and work, vol. 2*. London: Hogarth Press, 1955. P. 489.
21. Knight, R. P. Practical and theoretical considerations in the analysis of a minister. *Psychoanal. Rev.*, 1937, 24, 350.
22. Maritain, J. Freudianism and psychoanalysis — a thomist view. In Benjamin Nelson (Ed.), *Freud and the 20th century*. New York: Meridian Books, 1957.
23. Masserman, J. H. *The practice of dynamic psychiatry*. Philadelphia: Saunders, 1955.
24. May, R. *The meaning of anxiety*. New York: Ronald Press, 1950.
25. Mowrer, O. H. *Learning theory and personality dynamics*. New York: Ronald Press, 1950.
26. Ostow, M. Review of *The third revolution*. *Psychoanal. Quar.*, 1955, 24, 448.
27. Outler, A. C. *Psychotherapy and the christian message*. New York: Harper, 1954. P. 255.
28. Pfister, O. What transformations does psychoanalysis require in ethics and moral education? *Psychiatric Quar.*, 1931, 5, 407.
29. Pfister, O. Die illusion einer zukunft. *Imago*, 1928, 14, 149.
30. Progoff, I. *The death and rebirth of psychology*. New York: Julian Press, 1956. P. 250.
31. Pumpian-Mindlin, E. Changing concepts of therapy in a veterans administration mental hygiene clinic. *Am. J. Psychiat.*, 1957, 113, 1095.
32. Reider, N. Psychotherapy based on psychoanalytic principles. In J. L. McCary & D. E. Sheer (Eds.), *six approaches to psychotherapy*. New York: Dryden Press, 1955.
33. Riesman, D. *Individualism reconsidered*. New York: Doubleday, 1954.
34. Rioch, D. McK. Experimental aspects of anxiety. In J. H. Masserman & J. L. Moreno (Eds.), *Progress in psychotherapy, Vol. II Anxiety and therapy*. New York: Grune & Stratton, 1957.
35. Rosenthal, D. Changes in some moral values following psychotherapy. *J. consult. Psychol.*, 1955, 19, 431.
36. Schindler, R. The development of psychotherapy in Austria since 1945. In F. Fromm-Reichmann & J. L. Moreno (Eds.), *Progress in psychotherapy 1956*. New York: Grune & Stratton, 1956. P. 267.

37. Shoben, E. J. Some observation on psychotherapy and the learning process. In O. H. Mowrer, *Psychotherapy theory and research.* New York: Ronald Press, 1953.

38. Steinbach, A. A. Can psychiatry and religion meet? In Simon Noveck (Ed.), *Judaism and psychiatry.* New York: Basic Books, 1956. P. 174.

39. Stekel, W. *Conditions of nervous anxiety and their treatment.* New York: Liveright, 1950. P. 22.

40. Stekel, W. *Technique of analytical psychotherapy.* New York: Norton, 1940.

41. Stern, K. *The third revolution.* New York: Harcourt Brace, 1954.

42. Thorne, F. Directive and eclectic personality counseling. In J. L. McCary & D. E. Sheer (Eds.), *Six approaches to psychotherapy,* New York: Dryden Press, 1955.

43. Tillich, P. *The courage to be.* New Haven, Conn.: Yale Univer. Press, 1952. P. 70.

44. Winkler, W. T. The present status of psychotherapy in Germany. In F. Fromm-Reichmann & J. L. Moreno (Eds.), *Progress in psychotherapy 1956.* New York: Grune & Stratton, 1956. P. 288.

45. Wolberg, L. R. *The technique of psychotherapy.* New York: Grune & Stratton, 1954. P. 333.

46. Wolff, W. *Contemporary psychotherapists examine themselves.* Springfield, Ill.: C. C. Thomas, 1956.

47. Wolff, W. Facts and value in psychotherapy, *Am. J. Psychotherapy,* 1954, *8,* 466.

48. Wortis, J. *Fragments of an analysis with Freud.* New York: Simon & Schuster, 1954.

49. Zilboorg, G. Psychoanalytic borderlines. *Am. J. Psychiat.,* 1956, *112,* 706.

50. Zilboorg, G. Some denials and affirmations of religious faith. In F. J. Braceland (Ed.), *Faith, reason and modern psychiatry.* New York: P. J. Kenedy & Sons, 1955. P. 99.

COUNSELING, CULTURE AND VALUE

Cornelius L. Golightly
Professor of Philosophy, Wayne State University

I

The rapid migration to urban centers of vast numbers of rural and semi-rural underprivileged people who experience difficulties in adjusting to urban life has created major social and educational problems for the larger society. Counseling is a valuable social instrument for dealing with these problems because it enlists the energies of the people from whom the problems emanate. Hopefully, not only can the problems be eliminated with the help of the underprivileged but these persons also may become positive assets to the society.

However, a practical difficulty intervenes. The theory and practice of counseling apparently were shaped by middle-class practitioners for middle-class clients. Unlike medicine and surgery which work equally well for rich

An original article for this book.

and poor, counseling has not worked as well for the poor as for the rich. For example, psychiatrists have been notably unsuccessful in the treatment of underprivileged individuals.[1] In order to meet this difficulty some writers like Frank Riessman[2] and Georgene Seward[3] have offered practical suggestions to teachers, social workers, psychologists, and psychiatrists on how best to counsel and deal with the lower classes. The difficulties of counseling the underprivileged and their *ad hoc* solutions raise the perennial question of the place of values in the social sciences. This paper examines the current problems of counseling the broad background of philosophical and methodological discussions of knowledge and valuation. A major presupposition is that the current counseling problems have implications for the older philosophical issues and that the insights of the latter may be useful in resolving present difficulties. The modest aim is that intellectual perspective may be reaffirmed in an area which under pressure for immediate results leans dangerously toward a narrow pragmatic professionalism.

Counseling is an activity in which a professional individual or social practitioner through face-to-face or personal contacts attempts to help individuals who are maladjusted, perplexed, failing or delinquent. Generally, the aim is to assist the individual to grow or achieve greater personality integration so that he can handle present and future problems more independently and responsibly in less confused and better organized ways.

In terms of a distinction which has been much debated since the time of Aristotle, counseling is a practical rather than a theoretical science. Aristotle used the distinction to draw a sharp line between the natural sciences which included both biology and psychology as well as physics and the sciences of ethics and politics. For Aristotle, the crucial differences lay in their purposes. The practical sciences, unlike the theoretical sciences, are for the sake of doing or making something, not for the sake of contemplating, defining, or knowing it. However, Aristotle also recognized differences as to the types of phenomena studied and the role of moral ends in the phenomena under observation. The subject matters of the practical sciences are not limited to things or natures, but involve the habits and skills of man as he seeks to achieve practical social and political ends. Man is a moral agent and however precise biological or psychological definitions may be, man's behavior varies according to environmental determination, educational background, and the influences of social and economic position. Aristotle's conclusion was that problems of political association cannot be separated from problems of morality. Accordingly, he did not develop separate sciences in the *Nicomachean Ethics* and the *Politics* but let them supplement each other by treating a common field according to different aspects. Furthermore, Aristotle repeatedly warned that because of differences in purposes, subject matters, and methods of accumulating and interpreting materials, the practical sciences are incapable of the exactness of the theoretical sciences.[4]

Perhaps a word of caution is necessary here about the Aristotelian distinction between theoretical and practical sciences. We have used it primarily as an heuristic device to place the problem of values in counseling in perspective. If the distinction is interpreted literally to mean the difference between pure and applied science, we should remember that these two terms do not necessarily draw a real distinction.[5] Pure or basic research, familiarly known as pure science, is usually conceived as the disinterested search for knowledge.

Knowledge consists of facts and interpretation and inference. The latter are formulated in probability laws that tell us what happens under what conditions. Facts are propositional statements about empirical observations. Both facts and the interpretation and inference which compose "theory" are subject to the verification procedures of the empirical methodology commonly called "the scientific method."

Applied science is somewhat ambiguous. Herbert Feigl has drawn attention to at least two distinct meanings of the term applied science. "It may refer to such *activities* as the constructing of buildings, the making of drugs, or the enacting of measures of social or political reform. It may also refer to the *cognitive* content of such disciplines as mechanical engineering, industrial chemistry, medicine, or social work. 'Applied science' interpreted in this second sense consists in a body of knowledge selected from pure science and focused for application in the first sense."[6]

In addition to Feigl's two distinctions we may add a third meaning of applied science, one which is frequently used in social science research. It is research undertaken specifically to guide practice, that is, research for application. Kurt Lewin coined the term "action-in-research" to denote the activity of applying research methodology to the diagnosis and solution of practical problems of taking action. Typically, it is research designed to help solve pressing practical problems. Such scientific activity is the focusing of pure science research on a limited area to insure the relevance of the cognitive products of the research for this selected problem at hand.

Now we can see that despite the frequent use of the terms basic or pure research and applied research or research for action, the terms do not draw a real distinction between the knowledge and methods of scientific research. The difference between the two seems to be not a question of subject matter or method but rather a question of motivation and intention on the part of the researcher. If the motivation is sheer intellectual curiosity and the intention is to advance the horizons of knowledge with fact and theory, then the research activity is considered basic or pure. If the motivation is pressure of a practical problem and the intention is to solve the problem then the research is called applied or action-research.

Now if motivation and intention are ignored and we look at the end products of the two research activities we find that they are the same. The end products of research, basic or applied, are collected facts and their explanation, which is theory. A fairly simple way of supporting the argument that pure science and applied science are not intrinsically different is to point out that their results overlap. The results of pure science may have fruitful application and the results of applied science may make important contributions to the wider horizons of scientific theory. Further, at any given moment of time, there may be no clear distinction between what is pure and what is applied.

Ronald Lippitt has compared the results of basic research and action-research as follows: "It is quite probable that the methodological sophistication . . . in these action-research projects, and the genotypic generalization range of the data, will be inferior to the work . . in more highly controlled experimental settings where our problem springs from previous theoretical development and represents a planned step in the stepwise development of a field of knowledge. On the other hand, there are certain areas of needed basic knowledge which are most accessible for clinical observation and systematic research if one gets immersed in this process of intense interaction between values, decision situations, and action."[7]

While the distinction between the practical and theoretical sciences poses a family of knotty problems as the history of the philosophy of science attests, our discussion of counseling will focus mainly upon the place of values in counseling. Generally, values may be examined in the social sciences under three headings: (a) as public objects of description and classification as they occur in studies of personality or culture (b) as hidden valuations, bias, or subjectivity as they are discussed in the literature called the "sociology of knowledge"; and (c) as deliberate intentional choices of means and ends, methods and goals.

Obviously, the last is of central importance in all counseling as a practical science. The first serves as a bridge between the facts and theory of the so-called pure behavioral sciences and the applied science of counseling. The important connection between the two, as Feigl has intimated, is that theoretic knowledge about values can be focused for application in the practical science of counseling. The second focuses upon a major source of weakness or error in counseling. All three of these topics have special significance for the current difficulties in counseling underprivileged or socially disadvantaged persons.

II

Maladjustment, because of its negative and hence value connotations, is at best an unfortunate scientific concept. It is also ambiguous and imperfectly understood. We may delineate two logically distinct but perhaps factually overlapping types of maladjusted behavior. The first logically distinct type of maladjustment is behavior which is primarily a problem for society because it lacks social integration. For convenience let us use the familiar term of *social disorganization* for this type of maladjustment. The second logically distinct type is behavior which is primarily a problem for the individual himself because it lacks personality integration. For convenience, this type of maladjustment may be designated by this familiar term of *personality disorganization*.

As David Riesman has pointed out, behavior in any society, or class within the society, may be adjusted, anomic or autonomous. The adjusted respond in their character structure to the demands of their society. The anomic are the genuinely maladjusted, the rule-less or ungoverned who do not conform to the characterological pattern of the adjusted because they are socio-psychologically unfit. "The 'autonomous' are those who on the whole are capable of conforming to the behavioral norms of their society — a capacity the anomics usually lack — but are free to choose whether to conform or not."[8]

The nonconforming behavior of the autonomous individual sabotages society and thus is primarily a case of social disorganization. The nonconforming behavior of the anomic individual sabotages himself and perhaps society as well and thus is primarily a case of personality disorganization.

Now let us apply these distinctions to a counseling situation where the counselor is typically a middle-class professional reflecting the values of his middle-class culture and the client is typically deprived and segregated and reflects the values of his lower-class subculture. Negroes, Indians, Spanish-

Americans, Appalachian poor whites, migratory workers, slum-dwellers — the twenty per cent of our population who live on the outskirts of poverty — constitute a distinct subculture with values different from the prevailing values of the majority middle-class culture. Three-fourths of all Negroes, some fifteen million persons, and perhaps a tenth or more of all whites, an additional twenty million persons, constitute America's lower class. These are the people who are the perpetual concern of middle-class social workers, educators, legislators, and law-enforcement officials.

The most basic differences in middle-class and lower-class behavior are those between the habit formations of the lower class and the adjacent lower-middle class. "The patterns of behavior in these two groups, in either the white or the Negro population, are so widely different that it is common practice, even of sociologists, to speak of the lower class as 'unsocialized,' from their middle-class point of view. The social expectations and available goal responses of lower-class and lower-middle-class people are separated by a virtual chasm which is maintained by taboos on participation across class lives."[9]

The crucial value differences between the middle-class and the lower-class cultures are in their different habits of aggression, sexual behavior, education, recreation, and etiquette. Aggression and sexual behavior are the most important of these differences because from the middle-class point of view they involve first order moral values which are sanctioned by legal prescriptions and prohibitions. Education, recreation, and etiquette, while sanctioned by numerous cultural rewards and punishments, generally fall within the category of legal choice or permisison.

From the point of view of lower-class culture, extra-marital partnerships, sexual promiscuity and illegitimacy, fighting with fists and knives, and gambling are normal behavioral adjustments. However, depending on character or personality involvement, the individual may be described as adjusted, anomic or autonomous. From the point of view of middle-class culture, these habits of aggression and sexual behavior are never considered normal behavioral adjustments. Depending on character or personality involvement the individual may be either anomic or autonomous. He is never described as adjusted, however, because his behavior obviously is nonconforming.

If our exposition has been clear thus far, we can see in sharp outline the problems facing the middle-class counselor whose clients are from the deprived and segregated lower-class culture. Because of their recalcitrant, impulsive, physically aggressive and sexually promiscuous behavior which lacks social integration in the larger middle-class society, all lower-class clients from the point of view of the middle-class counselor are maladjusted or socially disorganized. In terms of personality integration or characterological response to the demands of the lower-class culture, however, the lower-class clients fall into three distinct groups: the adjusted, the anomic, and the autonomous. The adjusted, tautologically, are simply adjusted and hence are presumed to be free of hidden affect or feeling. The autonomous are nonconforming out of free choice and hence are presumed to have a measure of insight. The anomic individuals, because of their personality disorganization, are obviously ill. In terms of their relationship to the subculture, however, adjusted and autonomous cannot be maladjusted or socially disorganized. They are simply outside the conceptual framework within which the middle-class counselor is operating.

In a different sense, namely as an artifact of the ways psychiatrists respond to different classes, the anomic lower-class persons also probably fall outside the conceptual framework of the prevailing scientific discipline of counseling with its middle-class orientation. Initial treatment by a perceptive psychiatrist of their neuroses and psychoses may consist in attempting to bring them into adjustment with the norms of the lower-class culture. Since the anomic are demonstrably ill and especially if they are very ill, however, the counselor most often will recommend hospitalization. The expensive individual psychotherapy, which can be purchased privately or secured at clinics which provide largely for the middle class, is rarely available to the lower class. Thus the poor are usually sent to hospitals and, once there, receive the less humane treatment of electric shock or drugs.[10]

E. Franklin Frazier's studies of the folk culture of the simple Negro peasant of the rural south indicate that extra-marital sex relations and illegitimacy may be combined with well-adjusted, morally responsible behavior.

> "The attitudes of these women indicate that they regard sex relations as normal behavior during courtship which may or may not lead to marriage. When it results in the birth of a child, certain obligations are thereby imposed upon the mother. These obligations are the obligations which every mother should feel toward her offspring. The unmarried mother is as sensitive as the legally married mother to what is expected of the woman who is a mother. A certain distinction attaches to being fruitful. To say that a woman 'never did find anything,' meaning that she has never had a child, may imply disparagement as well as commiseration. Motherhood signifies maturity and the fulfilment of one's function as a woman. But marriage holds no such place in the esteem of many of these women. If they marry the father of their illegitimate offspring, it is not due to the fact that the woman regards it as an obligation on the part of the man . . . in many of these rural communities where relationships are sympathetic and informal and marriage and the family do not have an institutional character, the father of the girl's child is not guilty in the eyes either of her family or of the community of any offense against the integrity of her family . . illegitimate children have the same status as those born in wedlock."[11]

Some of the sex delinquency and illegitimacy of recent migrants represents the persistence in the urban environment of folkways that were relatively harmless in the rural community. In such cases where the behavior is simple and naive, individual character is uncorrupted and personality is well adjusted. The persons involved are problems for society but they are not problems for themselves. Inevitably, however, these simple folkways of the subculture conflict with the ideals and standards of the larger middle-class world. Further, the cohesiveness and sympathetic character of the simple community are lost. Then genuine social disorganization and personality deterioration set in. Ironically, social workers and other counselors often speed the process of making the individual a problem for himself without succeeding in changing his status as a problem for society.

Basically, as intimated earlier, the real problem lies outside the framework of counseling. Stated in its simplest terms, the real problem is the incorporation of the lower class into the middle class with the resultant elimination of the lower-class subculture with its behavior problems. The behavior of the lower-class adult, especially his freedom in sex and the expression of aggression, constitutes the cultural rewards, satisfaction and compensations of his lower-class status. Increased education, income, and respect are the cultural rewards, satisfactions and compensations of the middle-class. Upward mobility from the lower class into the middle class indicates that some adjusted and autonomous lower-class persons are *willing to trade* lower-class behavior for middle-class respectable behavior provided they receive in return the economic, educational, and status rewards of the middle class. But this is possible only when the opportunities are *genuine* and the larger society is politically and economically *open*. Always it is a risky business, for the individual may be suspended indefinitely between two worlds, the old and the hoped-for, and he may be literally a man without a culture.

III

Counseling as a practical science involves the making of decisions about values in a way that is never necessary in the theoretic sciences. Yet it is the theoretic sciences that provide the important knowledge about values which make wise decisions possible. The counselor probably will be predisposed to reject delinquency and illegitimacy under any circumstances. The same is true of other subcultural traits like intolerance, anti-intellectualism, illiberalism, prejudice, and aggression.[12] However, he can deal with them effectively only if he knows whether they are innocently based in a subculture or are the results of genuine social and personality disorganization. The crux of this is that despite being immersed in a process of intense interaction between values, decision situations, and actions, the counselor *qua* professional scientist should never confuse valuation and knowledge about values. Valuation occurs when knowledge about values is put to use but this is extraneous to the scientific activity of knowing, without prejudice or bias, what values are and how they operate in human behavior.

REFERENCES

1. A. B. Hollingshead and F. C. Redlich, *Social Class and Mental Illness*. New York: John Wiley and Sons, 1958.
2. Frank Riessman, *The Culturally Deprived Child*. New York: Harper and Row, 1962.
3. Georgene Seward, *Psychotherapy and Culture Conflict*. New York: The Ronald Press Company, 1956.
4. Richard McKeon, ed.: *The Basic Works of Aristotle*. New York: Random House, 1941. See especially McKeon's "Introduction: The Philosophy of Aristotle," p. XXVI.
5. *Cf.* Raymond L. Wilder, "The Nature of Modern Mathematics," *Michigan Alumnus Quarterly Review*, LXV (1959), pp. 302-312.
6. Herbert Feigl, "The Difference Between Knowledge and Valuation," *Journal of Social Issues* VI (1950), p. 40.
7. Ronald Lippit, "Action Research and the Values of the Social Scientist," *Journal of Social Issues*, VI (1950), pp. 54-55.
8. David Riesman, *et al.*, *The Lonely Crowd*, abridged edition. New York: Doubleday Anchor Books, 1955, p. 278.

9. A. Davis and J. Dollard, *Children of Bondage*, Washington, D. C.: American Council on Education, 1940, pp. 264-265.
10. Robert Coles, "Psychiatrists and the Poor," *Atlantic Monthly*, 214 (July, 1964) pp. 102-106.
11. E. Franklin Frazier, *The Negro Family in the United States*, Chicago: The University of Chicago Press, 1940, pp. 115-117.
12. See Frank Riessman, *op. cit.*, pp. 26-30, for a concise catalog of cultural traits of the underprivileged.

CODE OF ETHICS OF THE EDUCATION PROFESSION

Adopted by the NEA Representative Assembly, July, 1970

PREAMBLE

The educator believes in the worth and dignity of man. He recognizes the supreme importance of the pursuit of truth, devotion to excellence, and the nurture of democratic citizenship. He regards as essential to these goals the protection of freedom to learn and to teach and the guarantee of equal educational opportunity for all. The educator accepts his responsibility to practice his profession according to the highest ethical standards.

The educator recognizes the magnitude of the responsibility he has accepted in choosing a career in education, and engages himself, individually and collectively with other educators, to judge his colleagues, and to be judged by them, in accordance with the provisions of this code.

PRINCIPLE I
Commitment to the Student

The educator measures his success by the progress of each student toward realization of his potential as a worthy and effective citizen. The educator therefore works to stimulate the spirit of inquiry, the acquisition of knowledge and understanding, and the thoughtful formulation of worthy goals.

In *fulfilling his obligations to the student, the educator—*
1. Shall not without just cause restrain the student from independent action in his pursuit of learning, and shall not without just cause deny the student access to varying points of view.
2. Shall not deliberately suppress or distort subject matter for which he bears responsibility.
3. Shall make reasonable effort to protect the student from conditions harmful to learning or to health and safety.

Reprinted by permission of the NEA Commission on Professional Ethics.

4. Shall conduct professional business in such a way that he does not expose the student to unnecessary embarrassment or disparagement.
5. Shall not on the ground of race, color, creed, or national origin exclude any student from participation in or deny him benefits under any program, nor grant any discriminatory consideration or advantage.
6. Shall not use professional relationships with students for private advantage.
7. Shall keep in confidence information that has been obtained in the course of professional service, unless disclosure serves professional purposes or is required by law.
8. Shall not tutor for remuneration students assigned to his classes, unless no other qualified teacher is reasonably available.

PRINCIPLE II
Commitment to the Public

The educator believes that patriotism in its highest form requires dedication to the principles of our democratic heritage. He shares with all other citizens the responsibility for the development of sound public policy and assumes full political and citizenship responsibilities. The educator bears particular responsibility for the development of policy relating to the extension of educational opportunities for all and for interpreting educational programs and policies to the public.

In fulfilling his obligation to the public, the educator—

1. Shall not misrepresent an institution or organization with which he is affiliated, and shall take adequate precautions to distinguish between his personal and institutional or organizational views.
2. Shall not knowingly distort or misrepresent the facts concerning educational matters in direct and indirect public expressions.
3. Shall not interfere with a colleague's exercise of political and citizenship rights and responsibilities.
4. Shall not use institutional privileges for private gain or to promote political candidates or partisan political activities.
5. Shall accept no gratuities, gifts, or favors that might impair or appear to impair professional judgment, nor offer any favor, service, or thing of value to obtain special advantage.

PRINCIPLE III
Commitment to the Profession

The educator believes that the quality of the services of the education profession directly influences the nation and its citizens. He therefore exerts every effort to raise professional standards, to improve his service, to promote a climate in which the exercise of professional judgment is encouraged, and to achieve conditions which attract persons worthy of the trust to careers in education. Aware of the value of united effort, he contributes actively to the support, planning, and programs of professional organizations.

In fulfilling his obligation to the profession, the educator—

1. Shall not discriminate on the ground of race, color, creed, or national origin for membership in professional organizations, nor interfere with the free participation of colleagues in the affairs of their association.
2. Shall accord just and equitable treatment to all members of the profession in the exercise of their professional rights and responsibilities.
3. Shall not use coercive means or promise special treatment in order to influence professional decisions of colleagues.
4. Shall withhold and safeguard information acquired about colleagues in the course of employment, unless disclosure serves professional purposes.
5. Shall not refuse to participate in a professional inquiry when requested by an appropriate professional association.
6. Shall provide upon the request of the aggrieved party a written statement of specific reason for recommendations that lead to the denial of increments, significant changes in employment, or termination of employment.
7. Shall not misrepresent his professional qualifications.
8. Shall not knowingly distort evaluations of colleagues.

PRINCIPLE IV
Commitment to Professional Employment Practices

The educator regards the employment agreement as a pledge to be executed both in spirit and in fact in a manner consistent with the highest ideals of professional service. He believes that sound professional personnel relationships with governing boards are built upon personal integrity, dignity, and mutual respect. The educator discourages the practice of his profession by unqualified persons.

In fulfilling his obligation to professional employment practices, the educator—

1. Shall apply for, accept, offer, or assign a position or responsibility on the basis of professional preparation and legal qualifications.
2. Shall apply for a specific position only when it is known to be vacant, and shall refrain from underbidding or commenting adversely about other candidates.
3. Shall not knowingly withhold information regarding a position from an applicant or misrepresent an assignment or conditions of employment.
4. Shall give prompt notice to the employing agency of any change in availability of service, and the employing agent shall give prompt notice of change in availability or nature of a position.
5. Shall adhere to the terms of a contract or appointment, unless these terms have been legally terminated, falsely represented, or substantially altered by unilateral action of the employing agency.
6. Shall conduct professional business through channels, when available, that have been jointly approved by the professional organization and the employing agency.
7. Shall not delegate assigned tasks to unqualified personnel.

8. Shall permit no commercial exploitation of his professional position.
9. Shall use time granted for the purpose for which it is intended.

BYLAWS, NATIONAL EDUCATION ASSOCIATION

ARTICLE I, SECTION 12. Adherence to the Code of Ethics adopted by the Association shall be a condition of membership. The Committee on Professional Ethics shall after due notice and hearing have power to censure, suspend, or expel any member for violation of the Code subject to review by the Executive Committee. A member may within sixty days after a decision by the Ethics Committee file an appeal of the decision with the Executive Secretary.

PROVISIONS FOR NATIONAL ENFORCEMENT

CODE DEVELOPMENT—It shall be the duty of the Committee to maintain a continuous review of the *Code of Ethics of the Education Profession*. Amendments or revision of the Code shall be presented for approval to the Representative Assembly.

INTERPRETATIONS OF THE CODE OF ETHICS OF THE EDUCATION PROFESSION —A request for interpretation of the Code shall be in writing and shall describe the matter to be interpreted in sufficient detail to enable the members of the Committee on Professional Ethics to evaluate the request in all its aspects.

DISCIPLINARY ACTION—In addition to the provisions of Article I, Section 12, the Committee on Professional Ethics will consider disciplinary action against a member when written charges are preferred by the official governing body of the NEA affiliated state or local education association or NEA Department of which the person in question is a member.

If charges are based on a hearing held by any of the groups authorized to prefer charges, a record of the hearing shall be submitted to the Committee on Professional Ethics. Disciplinary action will only be considered as resulting from a fair hearing or a proper hearing record. A member will have an opportunity to show cause why such action should not be taken.

ETHICAL ASPECTS OF CHANGE IN COUNSELOR EDUCATION

Carlton E. Beck
University of Wisconsin—Milwaukee

One of the most perplexing problems facing modern man is the rapidly changing world. Old formulae no longer can be trusted, exceptions to time-

Reprinted by permission of the author and *Counselor Education and Supervision*, Vol. 6, No. 3 SP, Spring 1967, 216-221.

cherished rules multiply, and problems unique to given areas of endeavor arise because of progress in other areas. Such is the often-overwhelming effect of change. Adjusting to a world which is rapidly changing, one in which most of man's activities are subtly interrelated with all others, is a never-ending process of "act, revise, act, revise again."

The field of counseling, which deals in adjustment to and development of persons living in dynamic conditions, must either strive to understand change or become irrelevant.

EXPECTATIONS OF COUNSELOR CANDIDATES

In any profession the novices look to their predecessors for guidelines. Their assumptions are that their predecessors (a) have special skills useful in dealing with the *usual* problems, (b) have had experiences which can provide "patterns of approach" for investigating and acting upon *unusual* or exceptionally serious problems, (c) know the limits within which their expertise applies, (d) are searching for ways to improve their services, and, finally, (e) can pass on to others what they know and do.

These are reasonable expectations and should be viewed by the leaders in any field as a challenge to their professionalism. The ethical codes of all professions, including counseling, in some manner give not only *sanction* but *obligation* to their members to meet all of these expectations. Counselor education can ignore these expectations only at its professional peril. Titus (3, p. 363), although not speaking specifically to counselor educators, has provided perhaps the most useful statement concerning these expectations written by any contemporary philosopher. If we substitute the word *counselor* for the words *mature person*, the wisdom of Titus' observations for counselor education becomes clear.

> When a mature person faces a question of right or wrong for which his past training and experience give him little or no immediate guidance, he seeks to discover all the relevant factors in the situation. Then, in the light of his evaluation of the total situation, he makes his decision. The essence of reflective morality is the ability and the willingness to weigh all the facts in a situation and to base one's choice on the results of such reflection. Reflective morality consists not only in making personal decisions but also in making clear the reasons for one's decisions.

All major counseling theories approve the development of the "mature person." Titus' description of a mature person's approach to ethical problems sounds familiar to all serious students of counseling, since it embodies the prime requisites of the leading schools of thought in counseling. By way of summary, he describes (a) reliance on past training and experience, (b) examining all relevant factors, (c) decision making, and (d) making clear the reasons for the decisions. As we can see, the listing of what the novice counselor expects of the counselor educator comes very close to what the philosopher describes as attributes of the mature person. If the counselor educator wishes to discharge his own ethical responsibility to his students, he must strive to provide for the strengths discussed in both lists above.

Before considering the individual points above as they relate to change, it is necessary to make clear our terms. Both "ethics" and "morals" derive from words in Greek and Latin, respectively, which meant "the custom" or "the way of living." While both terms are used interchangeably in normal discourse today, the term "moral" is usually applied to acts or conduct while "ethical" tends to bring to mind codified or systemized outlooks. While acts and outlooks on "right" actions can never be totally divorced, we shall consider *ethics* (meaning here a codified, unified way of viewing counseling and counselor education) as of prime concern here.

BEHAVIORAL CODES AND CHANGE

Ethical codes and morality itself have grown out of man's experience. Certain ways of behaving have stood the test of time for given societies or smaller social units and have been almost reified. Other ways of behaving seem misguided, strange, wrong, or repugnant. After a mode of behavior (custom, law, or long-standing "preference") has served well the goals of a social group for many years, it is rarely seriously questioned or defied, except by the few but ever-present "rebels" who are then ignored, ridiculed, punished, or put to death. The burden of proof is placed on the rebel, not on the social group. Ethical and moral guidelines must be re-evaluated under certain conditions. Among these would be included the following guidelines: (a) When *more* than occasional rebellions arise, whether covertly or overtly, it is an indication that the comfort, security, effectiveness or other originally-commending factors in the mode of behavior have been lessened seriously, and that changes in other segments of the society have come about to initiate the reversal of loyalties to the ways of the past. (b) When a law is passed which exceeds the limits of custom, social conflict is inevitable. The value of the law may be worth the strife, but a price must be paid in conflicts (e.g., the May, 1954 school integration decision). (c) When a way of behaving is imposed upon a social group, social conflict is inevitable (e.g., enemy occupation, declared war, epidemics); old relationships undergo conflict.

This listing is, of course, not all-inclusive regarding conditions which challenge established ways of behaving. They do serve, however, to point up a note of *imposition* or *intrusion* into the daily life of the individual by factors outside his control. Such is the lot of modern man. He is caught up in changes not of his own creation and he feels powerless to repel them—automation, wars, religious changes, family role changes, fashions and fads, taxes, laws.

Young people are especially vulnerable to the confusion brought about by change. They have warily sensed that the advice and morality preached by their elders seemed "phony" or at best irrelevant in today's world, yet they must continue to live in this world of change, and must somehow come to grips with it. Here the school counselor often enters the picture. He is expected to provide the synthesizing force, the explanations, the guidelines or points of reference. He is willing to do what he is prepared to do. We have now come full circle to the relationship of the counselor educator with his counseling candidates.

RESULTANT QUESTIONS

If the foregoing analysis of what the counselor-to-be reasonably expects and what the philosopher describes as desirable in all mature persons, including counselors, is substantially correct, a serious consideration of the counselor educator's task in a world of change is in order.

If the counselor educator sees legitimacy in the "expectations" listed previously, he must ask himself these questions, and ask them often:

1. Have I kept myself informed on new skills and new uses of older ones for dealing with the "normal range" of human problems? Have I made clear to my students just what constitutes the "normal range" of problems to which these skills and techniques apply? Is the "normal range" of problems substantially the same as when I last seriously reviewed them?

2. Have I tried to build into my students "patterns of approach," critical thinking, and cautions against gross errors in deciding what constitutes an *unusual* problem in counseling? Have I recently rethought the matter of what is *now* "unsual" myself?

3. Have I tried to define, and in behavioral terms whenever possible, the reasonable limits of expertise for my students as they enter their first position as counselors? How long has it been since I checked employers' perceptions of what expertise my graduates possess, and consequently what they designate as counselor responsibility? What lines of communication have I set up to prevent breaches of ethics along these lines? What recent developments (social, technological) have rendered counselor roles and functions different from what they were?

4. Have I tried to "stay current" on legislation, information retrieval, new theories of counseling, socio-economic developments, industrial developments, race problems, important research, now-disproven assumptions, and new research techniques? Have I expanded myself as a person through new and different experiences, reading in fields other than my own, exploring literature, travel—and perhaps through quiet reflection and contemplation?

5. Have I sincerely tried to improve my classroom presentation? Have I imposed too much and consulted too little with my students? Have I used the best-proven evidence on human learning in passing on to others the skills and understandings of counseling? Have I encouraged my students to explore modern man as he is portrayed in literature and plays as well as in textbooks?

A cursory review of the APGA Code of Ethics, the NEA Code, or the APA Code, as well as others, will reveal by specific statements or by implication all of these "expectations" of the counselor-in-training, and more. No one can fulfill all of these obligations perfectly, but then no candidate reasonably expects this, either. The point here is that the counselor educator is a leader in his field and must come *closer* to the ideal than his charges. If ethical behavior and morality do emerge from the "tried and true" experience of human beings in their relations with one another, counselor educators must know these experiences. But we must not lull ourselves into believing that there is *only one* code of ethics, only one morality in our world, our nation, our city, and even our school or agency. This has been our shame in years past. Let us be honest about it: of course we *knew* there were other cultures and moral patterns—but we didn't seriously try to *investigate* them more than superficially, let alone *understand them*. Acceptance? This implies either *understanding* or a *genuine attempt* to understand. Many have accepted the *existence* of more than one moral and ethical outlook, but have not truly accepted the fact that it is worthy of our time to consider them as serious possibilities in our marketplace of values.

ON DECISION-MAKING

To the rather humbling and onerous "expectations" of candidates might well be added questions based on the philosopher's views previously discussed.

Have I, in addition to imparting and providing a wide range of training and experience, made my students aware of all the factors in society which are involved in producing change? Have I required my students to be familiar with the nature of decision-making? Have they had to make decisions which have then been evaluated? Have they been required to *make clear* their reasons for decisions made in difficult situations?

Counselor educators, however, cannot be held responsible for the total preparation of their students. It must be said that there is no place in counseling for the lazy counselor candidate. He cannot hide behind the omissions or "dated" teachings of his busy mentors. Man defines himself by his actions. The counselor candidate cannot expect the counselor educator to "spoon-feed" to him the nature of change and its implications for counseling. If these considerations are deemed important enough to be included in his program, the candidate must take upon himself the responsibility for exploring more widely and deeply the meanings, sources, and counterforces of change in our modern world.

Finally, the counselor educator must be aware of the full import of the previously-listed fifth "expectation" of counselor candidates, namely, that they (counselor educators) can pass on to others what they know and do. Let it be understood that this is *not* to say that counselor educators can pass on to *all* others what they know and do. There will be, as every counselor educator knows, candidates who will be so rigid, so personally threatened, or so ingenuous that a counselor's certificate in their hands would negate all that we deem essential. It is perhaps the greatest ethical obligation of the counselor educator either to steer these persons out of the field, or to delay their entry until they show more openness or breadth of life experiences, because one who has not been able to cope with change in his own life seems a poor risk to understand or to adjust to the vast changes in society which will impinge on his prospective clients.

SUMMARY

Change has made necessary a frequent re-evaluation of counselor education. To fail to ask certain relevant questions about our goals, procedures, and professional pertinence, is to fall short of our ethical obligations as counselor educators.

We can no longer be in the position of the fabled dachshund in the anonymous poem:

> There once was a dachshund quite so long
> 　　He hadn't any notion
> The time it took to notify
> 　　His tail of an emotion.
> And so it happened while his eyes
> 　　Were filled with woe and sadness
> His little tail went wagging on
> 　　Because of *previous* gladness!

If we can stretch this "doggerel" just a bit, we can see change rendering incomplete, inaccurate, or inapplicable much of what we "knew" yesterday. A re-reading of the goals of counseling written only a few years ago, for example, gives one the feeling of walking through a musty museum. We can ill-afford the cultural lag—or is it "wag"?

REFERENCES

1. Beck, Carlton E. *Guidelines for Guidance.* Dubuque, Ia.: Wm. C. Brown Company Publishers, 1966.
2. Beck, Carlton E. *Philosophical Foundations of Guidance.* Englewood Cliffs, N. J.: Prentice-Hall, 1963.
3. Titus, Harold. *Living Issues in Philosophy.* New York: American Book Co., 1959.

AN EXAMINATION OF CLIENT STRENGTH AND COUNSELOR RESPONSIBILITY

Joseph Samler[1]
Vocational Rehabilitation and Education Service, The Veterans Administration

A central motif runs through our present approaches in psychotherapy and counseling. The client has a history which makes his problems under-

Reprinted by permission of the author and the *Journal of Counseling Psychology,* Vol. 9, No. 1, 1962, 5-11.

[1]This paper was presented in preliminary form at the NDEA Guidance Institute at the University of Florida, in November 1960. The writer is indebted to Louis S. Levine, Donald E. Super, and Leona Tyler, as well as to his long-suffering colleagues at work for reviewing the manuscript. This does not mean that the points made or progression in thinking necessarily is shared by the reviewers, but rather that their criticisms and evaluation were most useful to the writer.

standable, if not inevitable. He is not to be held responsible for past difficulties or present unhappy life patterns. It is as if he were acted upon rather than acting, neutral and imprinted upon rather than an agent in his own right.[2] There are other views but the extent of their influence seems a moot question. Thorne's first edition was published in 1950. Rosen's particular therapy in psychiatry is well known. Williamson's writings over the years have emphasized client responsibility. In vocational counseling at least, Super continuously has urged the need to work to and from existing client strengths and assets. Yet with the possible exception of the effect on vocational and rehabilitation counseling, it is questionable how much counseling practice has been affected. It is not that client strength is lacking as a firm concept. Client strength and responsibility for self is a central issue in Rogers' work, for instance, but it is a goal to be achieved as a result of counseling, not a resource to be immediately utilized.

The literature reflects our enormous commitment to the client's history in our attempt to understand him. Perhaps it is a price we have paid in order to simplify what cannot be simplified; to seek lawful relationship with variables that can be identified, leaving out factors so variable, e.g., self-awareness, that they would make our quest for science, or at any rate for a science as we know it, quite impossible. To put it quite badly, the client in our counseling approaches is never at fault. He is the present product of circumstance — a possessive mother, a cold and distant father, lack of love in infancy, a hostile environment, or other inimical circumstance. The world in which he lives is one he was in effect forced to inhabit. His low self-esteem, his filled cup of unhappiness, his distress and discomfort are, so to speak, supplied to him. His guilt is pointless, and useful only for examination.

We seem to have neglected aspects of the human being that are central to his humanity: his cognitive character, his essential autonomy, the possibility within him for self-direction and determination of choices, the planful and purposive aspects of his living, his symbolic activity, and his great capacity for ideation. Our philosophies and our procedures seem based upon a view of the human being as almost totally a feeling organism. We are all ready to attest that behavior has both cognitive and affective components, but we do not act that way in the consulting room.

There are probably many reasons for neglect of given cognitive resources in the human personality. For example, the extant personality theories set before us as models do not, generally, provide for man's strength, his self-awareness, his ability to pull himself into the future, his self-determining capacities. It seems no great exaggeration to posit a kind of combined model in which the individual is moved by unconscious motives, deflected from self-awareness by anxiety, and perceives anything but objectively. Not infrequently he is misled by our symbols of communication. His interests are determined for him by early childhood experiences, and he is caught up in the inevitability of response to cultural expectations he had no part in establishing. The import of the discussion thus far is that this is an insufficient model and a misleading one.

The central point about presumed client passivity is reflected in current literature. In addressing himself to this problem Shoben (1961) points out

---

[2]The emphasis on personal history in psychoanalysis is well known. It is apparent that classical behaviorism also contributed to our present problem. In denying consciousness to the individual, a premium is put on his passivity.

that we have exchanged the devil of which the demented once was possessed for the modern devil of the disturbed client's parents. The client himself remains a neutral and acted upon figure. He goes to the root of the problem in noting that the clear result of looking for lawful relationship between unhappy history and personality problems is to ignore the idea of individual responsibility.

In a framework much more threatening to the counselor committed to present counseling philosophy, Mowrer (1960) urges that: "The unassailable, brute fact is that personality disorder is the most pervasive and baffling problem of our time; and if it should turn out that persons so afflicted regularly display (or rather hide) a life of too little, rather than too much, moral restraint and self-discipline, the problem would take on an empirical urgency that would require no fine-spun argument."

We come to terms with the central problem in a thoughtful proposal presenting a new descriptive framework for categorizing individuals with respect to many behaviors and qualities. Levine and Kantor (1960) urge that:

> The impulse-ridden, id-driven image of man utilized by psychologists for some years has recently been challenged by personality theorists and clinicians. The validity of the old image has been questioned. Is man only a hapless and hopeless organism, a servant to his surroundings and a prisoner of his inhibited passions? From such questioning and from clinical observation and theory, a new image is gradually taking shape, one in which the developmental, integrative and ongoing aspects of life are alluded to by concepts such as Allport's 'becoming.' This new image includes the 'soft voice of intellect'; it includes man's productivity as well as his passion, his creativity as well as his conflicts, and his resourcefulness and resilience as well as his repressions and rigidities.

The emphasis on what at best can only be a corrective must not be mistaken as an invitation radically to change our orientation. It is not intended that counseling would offer only a prescription of limits and a set of demands on the individual. The problem of self-direction is in any case as old as is man's awareness of himself. It is as persistent as are his questions about the reasons for and purpose of his being, and quite likely will remain with us as a central problem. The emphasis on an available element of choice to each individual is offered as a corrective to the prevalent practice which views the person as being acted upon, with none or most limited volition, intent, and freedom of his own.

The idea that a degree of self-determination is available and should be called upon is central to what I am trying to say. The immediate problem which we will not resolve but must consider, deals inescapably with the problem of determinism. Unless there is at least hope of forcing this closed door we cannot refer to elements of responsibility for self in our perception of and expectations from the people who come to us for help.

THE PROBLEM (STILL) OF DETERMINISM

The philosophy of science, including the science of human behavior, hews to determinism as its basic principle. It is perfectly clear why this should be so. If given events are to be predicted and controlled, then the lawful relationships between effect and cause must at least be postulated and hopefully identified and found.

It is possible to take courage from a great and imaginative soul. Writing in 1884, the opening sentences of William James' "The Dilemma of Determinism" are:

A common opinion prevails that the juice has ages ago been pressed out of the free-will controversy, and that no new champion can do more than warm up stale arguments which everyone has heard. This is a radical mistake. I know of no subject less worn out . . . (1948).

Hobbs in his consideration of this problem (1959), says he is inclined to agree with James because, Hobbs says, "The issue is quickened every time psychologists get close to contemporary man and his problems."

The issue has always been keen but it is persuasive to think that it is more troublesome now than it has been before. Not only are we in psychology becoming more self-conscious but there is currently a wave of worry in human behavior about values, ethics, sin, guilt, morality. Here we are up against it for it is clear that without choice between one course of action and another, without some measure of free will, there is no sense in talking about values and ethics. This of course only identifies a possible motivation for a belief in free will; it does not provide an answer.

If determinism is an inescapable fact in science, an equally hard nut to crack is the common conviction every day that man has a certain amount of freedom of choice in his behavior.

There is no way out of complexity here because we talk of human behavior. Perhaps the outline of a possible answer, not yet properly taken into account, is in James' definition of *in*determinism. "The parts," he felt, "have a certain amount of loose play with one another . . . . Of two alternative futures which we conceive, both may now be really possible; and the one becomes impossible only at the very moment when the other excludes it by becoming real itself." James' thinking in this remarkable essay is seemingly as pertinent now as it was three quarters of a century ago. His grand affirmation, basic to his thinking, is that man is a rational organism and that it is given him to work toward his conception of the "good." Determinism he says ". . . virtually defines the universe as a place in which what ought to be is impossible."

We have still to take into account an assumption which has built into it human intention and commitment to a given way, self-selected. To some it may seem presumptuous, but to others the only possible definition of our humanity. It is completely understandable that science as we know it has not as yet been able to come to grips with so subjective, so seemingly capricious a force. I believe that we must require that science suit itself to our needs, and our needs require as a first condition an affirmation of our rationality and ethical nature. Wheelis puts it into a nutshell when he says "we have gained determinism, but have lost determination."

The critical question is whether in the study of man we have carried over the postulates of a science that may not be applicable to organisms that have self-awareness and self-understanding. The "if-then" paradigm of classical science seems to fall quite short in considering the organized complexity of the human being. For here each part stands in interrelationship to the other.

We become greatly uncomfortable with personality theory based upon white rat experiments, for instance. The plain fact is that a rat is not a man. And it may be that our difficulty with learning theory, and the fact that none really is satisfactory, is that we cannot really account in present models for motivation, self-scrutiny, the nuances of need, and so on, especially in their complex interrelationships. It is not enough to call them "intervening variables." If this is true, our urgent requirement must be that a science be brought into being that will take the human condition into account.

BEHAVIOR AS A CRITERION

This is our assumption, then, that there is a measure of basic freedom of choice available to the individual, and that within limits he can move in given directions. The central point in this discussion is that the nurturing atmosphere of the consulting room, the incredible investment of one person in another, the almost total address to the client's emotional life, these are not the only necessary conditions of change. Indeed it is a startling truism that all therapies, deep, superficial, rationalized or not, honest or not, have their successes.

In therapy at least, we do not seem to capitalize on the individual's *present* strengths. In all counseling we have the theoretical signposts for working to existing strength and this seems to be the development of greatest promise for differentiating therapy from counseling and the clinical psychologist from his colleague in counseling. The contrast is the emphasis on pathology as against an emphasis on the individual's abilities. As counselors in rehabilitation probably know best, the orientation is vastly different and the results vary remarkably with the orientation.

It seems a safe statement that practice in vocational counseling relative to the basic orientation is quite varied. As against Super's differentiating and healthy emphasis is the continued force of analytically-oriented' psychology with its interest in the profound search and major restructuring of personality.

Nevertheless there is greatest hope for productive change here. The necessary directions have been brought to attention by a number of counseling and vocational psychologists. Brayfield (1960) presented a map of the country to travel in a recent paper. Leona Tyler (1960) in her excellent treatment of minimum change therapy underscores the possible positive aspects of the personality defenses. In addressing themselves to the foundation task of a descriptive framework for behavior, Levine and Kantor (1960) urge that "some 'defensive' behavior enables the individual to attain psychological objectives other than those involved in guarding against overwhelming anxiety experiences." Actually, much of the short-term therapy may be considered as approaching a different orientation, provided it is not considered "second-best." The emphasis on ego-psychology is of course for consideration, although its analytic orientation relates it basically to personality restructuring.

In the paper already referred to, Levine and Kantor urge "effectiveness"[3] as the keystone of a new descriptive framework for behavior. The central

[3]Levine and Kantor state that: "The generic term of 'effectiveness' can be defined nominally as the fullest utilization of ability and the commitment of energy to goals valued by the individual and congruent with the social expectation for the roles he assumes. The utilization of his ability and energy is to be considered relative to the opportunities available to him as set by his imposed social position."

ideas in the present paper are congruent with Levine and Kantor's development. The point is that it is an aspect of the individual's strength to respond to the need put before him to behave, to perform, in other than destructive ways. The point is, further, that it is appropriate, at least in given types of problems, to require such change, and to put force and emphasis on such requirement.

This is in no way startling with certain types of cases, e.g., acting out, manipulative clients. The need for the imposition of limits is clearly set forth, for instance, by Murphy & Guze (1960). Ford, Robles & Harlow (1960) affirm the position that permitting or condoning diffuse and uncontrolled acting out of instinctual drives, whether libidinal or aggressive, is the antithesis of psychotherapy.

The question is whether the approach of the counselor in requiring certain behavior, e.g., setting limits, may not be extended. A few not too hypothetical case instances may be useful.

THE SPECIFIC INSTANCE IN CONTEXT

The requirement for particular behavior, the urgent proposal for change in behavior, cannot be made by an up-stage, moralistic counselor, separated from and emotionally distant from his client. A requirement made in this atmosphere carries its own negation. The communication must be embedded in the same kind of deep concern for the client that characterizes present relationship therapy. *It should in fact arise out of the concern.* The basic message is one of understanding of and feeling for the unhappy person but it is accompanied by the involvement of aspects of his being other than his defenses.

Here is a person suffering from a condition we might call deep prejudice. The reasons for his disability are available from the literature and may relate to his early childhood experience, great hostility in his makeup, rigidity, and so on. Let us assume that possibly he may want to change but finds himself helpless because the nucleus of his disability is in the basic structure of his personality. Given, say, three years of therapy it is not impossible to assume that something can be done with his problems. But for many reasons this may not be feasible, and yet we have one more recourse. We can say to such a person, "Look, however you feel is your business, and whether or not you change is your business, but *act* differently. You don't have to spit when you pass a Jew or a Scandinavian, or a Hottentot in the street." "Keep your feelings if you must but change your behavior!"

Let us consider the case of a person with a real full-blown "poor me" operation. When such a person has an itch it is the worst itch any one ever had, when there is any pain, the whole world knows about it, and so on. Confident of the unreality of such feelings we are justified in saying, "Look, be as terribly sorry for yourself as you please, drown in your own tears if you must, but keep it to yourself, don't keep pushing it on your family or your friends." Again a change of behavior is strongly urged, without, at the moment anyway, working for basic examination of personality needs and defenses.

A third illustration, but out of the consulting room, may also be familiar. Here is a worker in industry, government or the schools. He is unhappy for whatever reason and doing his work badly. The supervisor, let us assume a competent psychologist, has a choice of a sort. He can play a therapeutic role and help the worker achieve insight and understanding, hopefully leading to better work. It seems to me that this is not warranted, and that what should be required is the kind of work behavior which will help achieve necessary performance. The key question here is whether in going along with unsatisfactory work we are not in fact dealing quite disrespectfully with the worker.

It is to be hoped that the reinforcement of the results of acceptable behavior may in itself be curative. Thus the "poor me" boy cited before may find that behavioral control of his great sorrow results in enough comfort so that he will be moved to greater inhibition of his self-sorrow on his own.

But the necessary disclaimers are obviously in point: It is critically important that requirement for changed behavior which says in effect, "control yourself" can work only in particular situations and under given circumstances. It would be useless to instruct a paranoid person to stop being suspicious of all around him, and probably equally unproductive to say to the man desperately searching for a semblance of intimacy to stop seducing every woman he meets. Only the general proposal can be made here. We have still to find out, following accepted procedure, under what conditions and in what manner the requirement for change in behavior can work.

It should provide thoughtful material for us that life in fact sets constant limits to behavior and that learning takes place quite frequently in what seems like desirable directions. The need for establishing limits in helping children grow and adjust is nowhere questioned, quite the contrary. It is not so clearly seen that in our working world we are nearly all confronted with quite firm demands to which nearly all of us respond quite well.

Similarly, although it seems very odd to call it to attention, learning takes place as a result of cognition. We seem not to build on the examples before us of the salutary, quite didactic communication that suddenly gives insight. The counselor says "What I do not understand is why you are so intolerant of hypocrisy," or to the protesting mother: "The worst thing you can do to a child is to be indifferent to him."

We tend to identify the counseling session as a learning situation, but, granted the profound emotional involvement in many personality problems, we are not ready to carry over to counseling what we take for granted in other learning and teaching settings.

THE PROBLEM OF COUNSELOR RESPONSIBILITY

Implicit in the requirement for change in behavior, in setting limits, in urgent statement of counselor belief, in firm cognitive formulations, is the idea of counselor responsibility.

The dicta are well known: we cannot assume responsibility for the client; we are not and cannot be so knowledgeable; we simply cannot foretell the future well enough; our science at best deals in probabilities. The very issue urged in this paper argues against it because *self* determination cannot be someone else's.

I must dismiss out of hand the issue of respect for the client. The acknowledgment of his integrity is not in question. It is out of concern for him and in his own interest that we do what we do. Similarly the application of the concept of democracy must be viewed quite sceptically. As Meehl and McClosky (1947) have clearly demonstrated, the term is meaningful in politics but has no pertinence in helping people in trouble.

Perhaps as is not uncommon, the answer we get depends on the questions we ask. The question of acceptance of responsibility totally, must be answered in only one way; but a question whether in given instances and in particular circumstances it is improper for the counselor to accept responsibility is capable of different answers. Indeed it is already answered. In whole classes of conditions it is perfectly clear that responsibility is assumed by the worker. This is apparent in working with the suicidal, in dealing with the abnegation of responsibility of the schizophrenic, with the dangers offered by the paranoid, the hazards of the impulse ridden, or in dealing with the desperate retardate reflecting insistent parent need for considerable education.

The principle of nonacceptance of responsibility, therefore, is by no means absolute. It follows logically then that the problem is not one of taking over but rather of the specific and individual instance in which specified assumption of responsibility by the counselor is warranted, its desirability in terms of the client's interest, and its feasibility. Presently no more than the theoretical point can be made; we lack the instances and examples to specify where and in what manner the counselor properly can play a role as here postulated. What cannot be dismissed, however, is the reiteration of concerned therapists and counselors that as the occasion warrants, dogma or not, they *do* step into such roles.

The instance of the brilliant student who attended college only as a result of the table pounding, home visits, and urgent insistance of the counselor, is a typical enough case in point. Involvement of the police and the law on the counselor's initiative, positive environmental changes — these are all in the counselor's repertory. This is reality and we cannot ignore it.

The assumption of counselor responsibility even though safeguarded and made specific to the particular instance leads inevitably to the question of values. Or perhaps it is much more correct to say that counselor responsibility flows out of a particular view of the nature of values and of the counselor's role in the promulgation of given values. The problem is too complex to be treated in limited space. But it makes sense that thinking on the problem should start with what seems to be clear, that whether the counselor wills it or not, he affects in his client value derivation, commitment, and integration. There is reason to think that the professed neutrality of counselor and therapist is more a professional stance than it is reality. If these points are admitted, the problem seems to be either to work toward an impossible neutrality or to determine which values to support, under what conditions, and with how much force.

It ought not to be irreligious to propose that if value commitment and promulgation work in bringing about lasting client change in desirable directions then it provides its own justification. It is not inconceivable that there are means other than the acceptant, nurturing relationship in helping people to change.

CONCLUSION

A final and critical point remains to be made but it can be made best in the context of a quick recapitulation.

The counseling client is too often regarded as remarkably passive, neutral, acted upon, nonresponsible. Emphasis is placed upon his history or his situation as the unhappy factors leading to his ills. The discussion urged that in so regarding the client we have lost sight of his available strengths, his cognitive ability, planfulness, ideation, drive to autonomy and his freedom to an extent to choose, that is, his aspects of self-determination.

Inevitably we have had to consider the age-old question of determinism and free-will. The basic intention in that part of the discussion was to show that determinism does not so foreclose the argument as to make it idle to talk of a measure of self-determination.

With this hope in mind, the possibility was offered of working to the individual's strengths in terms of his cognition, the planful and purposive aspects of his being, and the possibility within him presently for self-direction. This is a broad highway, however, to the critical problem of the frank assumption of responsibility by the worker and in turn this led to involvement in values and to the proposal that the counselor accept responsibility for the promulgation of values with his clients.

An important point may now be made. It is clear that the higher the abstraction, the more universal is agreement and so everyone is against sin and for motherhood. The difficulty makes itself evident in the particular situation, but this is why a presumably skilled, experienced, and feeling person is on the other side of the desk. At the risk of sounding quite stuffy, it must be stated that the proposal made in these pages is not for the ill-trained but well meaning. It requires not an exercise in safety, and in using techniques that are difficult to abuse. It requires the utmost in understanding and the greatest possible concern for the client; relative ease in going beyond surface behavior; and a level of sophistication that can come only with arduous work and commitment to this most difficult task.

Received February 20, 1961.

REFERENCES

Brayfield, A. H. In symposium honoring Donald G. Paterson: Vocational counseling — past, present, and future. *American Psychological Association Convention,* 1960.

Ford, E. S. C., Robles, C., & Harlow, R. G. Psychotherapy with child psychotics. *Amer. J. Psychother.,* 1960, *14,* 705-718.

Hobbs, N. Science and ethical behavior. *Amer. Psychol.,* 1959, *14,* 217-225.

James, W. *Essay in pragmatism.* (Castell Alburay, Ed.). New York: Hafner, 1948.

Levine, L. S. & Kantor, R. E. Psychological effectiveness and imposed social position. *Personnel guid. J.,* 1962, *40,* 418-425.

Meehl, P. E., & McClosky, H. Ethical and political aspects of applied psychology. *J. abnorm. soc. Psychol.,* 1947, *42,* 91-98.

Mowrer, O. Some constructive features of the concept of sin. In symposium, The role of the concept of sin, in psychotherapy. *J. counsel. Psychol.,* 1960, *7,* 185-188.

Murphy, G. E., & Guze, S. B. Setting limits: the management of the manipulative patient. *Amer. J. Psychother.*, 1960, *14*, 30-47.

Shoben, E. J., Jr. Personal responsibility, determinism, and the burden of understanding. *Personnel guid. J.*, 1961, *39*, 342-348.

Tyler, Leona E. Minimum change therapy. *Personnel guid. J.*, 1960, *38* 475-479.

ETHICAL STANDARDS

American Personnel and Guidance Association

PREAMBLE

The American Personnel and Guidance Association is an educational, scientific, and professional organization dedicated to service to society. This service is committed to profound faith in the worth, dignity, and great potentiality of the individual human being.

The marks of a profession, and therefore of a professional organization, can be stated as follows:

1. Possession of a body of specialized knowledge, skills, and attitudes known and practiced by its members.

2. This body of specialized knowledge, skills, and attitudes is derived through scientific inquiry and scholarly learning.

3. This body of specialized knowledge, skills, and attitudes is acquired through professional preparation, preferably on the graduate level, in a college or university as well as through continuous in-service training and personal growth after completion of formal education.

4. This body of specialized knowledge, skills, and attitudes, is constantly tested and extended through research and scholarly inquiry.

5. A profession has a literature of its own, even though it may, and indeed must, draw portions of its contents from other areas of knowledge.

6. A profession exalts service to the individual and society; above personal gain. It possesses a philosophy and a code of ethics.

7. A profession through the voluntary association of its members constantly examines and improves the quality of its professional preparation and services to the individual and society.

8. Membership in the professional organization and the practice of the profession must be limited to persons meeting stated standards of preparation and competencies.

9. The profession affords a life career and permanent membership as long as services meet professional standards.

10. The public recognizes, has confidence in, and is willing to compensate the members of the profession for their services.

The Association recognizes that the vocational roles and settings of its members are identified with a wide variety of academic disciplines and levels of academic preparation. This diversity reflects the pervasiveness of the Asso-

Reprinted by permission of *American Personnel and Guidance Association*.

ciation's interest and influence. It also poses challenging complexities in efforts to conceptualize:

    a. the characteristics of members;
    b. desired or requisite preparation or practice; and
    c. supporting social, legal and/or ethical controls.

The specification of ethical standards enables the Association to clarify to members, future members, and to those served by members the nature of ethical responsibilities held in common by its members.

The introduction of such standards will inevitably stimulate greater concern by members for practice and preparation for practice. It will also stimulate a general growth and identification with and appreciation for both the common and diverse characteristics of the definable roles within the world of work of Association members.

There are six major areas of professional activity which encompass the work of members of APGA. For each of these areas certain general principles are listed below to serve as guide lines for ethical practice. These are preceded by a general section which includes certain principles germain to the six areas and common to the entire work of the Association members.

Section A

GENERAL

1. The member exerts what influence he can to foster the development and improvement of the profession and continues his professional growth throughout his career.

2. The member has a responsibility to the institution within which he serves. His acceptance of employment by the institution implies that he is in substantial agreement with the general policies and principles of the institution. Therefore, his professional activities are also in accord with the objectives of the institution. Within the member's own work setting, if, despite his efforts, he cannot reach agreement as to acceptable ethical standards of conduct with his superiors, he should end his affiliation with them.

3. The member must expect ethical behavior among his professional associates in APGA at all times. He is obligated, in situations where he possesses information raising serious doubt as to the ethical behavior of other members, to attempt to rectify such conditions.

4. The member is obligated to concern himself with the degree to which the personnel functions of non-members with whose work he is acquainted represent competent and ethical performance. Where his information raises serious doubt as to the ethical behavior of such persons, it is his responsibility to attempt to rectify such conditions.

5. The member must not seek self-enhancement through expressing evaluations or comparisons damaging to other ethical professional workers.

6. The member should not claim or imply professional qualifications exceeding those possessed and is responsible for correcting any misrepresentations of his qualifications by others.

7. The member providing services for personal remuneration shall, in establishing fees for such services, take careful account of the charges made for comparable services by other professional persons.

8. The member who provides information to the public or to his subordinates, peers, or superiors has a clear responsibility to see that both the content and the manner of presentation are accurate and appropriate to the situation.

9. The member has an obligation to ensure that evaluative information about such persons as clients, students, and applicants shall be shared only with those persons who will use such information for professional purposes.

10. The member shall offer professional services only, through the context of a professional relationship. Thus testing, counseling, and other services are not to be provided through the mail by means of newspaper or magazine articles, radio or television programs, or public performances.

Section B

COUNSELING

This section refers to practices involving a counseling relationship with a counselee or client and is not intended to be applicable to practices involving administrative relationships with the persons being helped. A counseling relationship denotes that the person seeking help retain full freedom of choice and decision and that the helping person has no authority or responsibility to approve or disapprove of the choices or decisions of the counselee or client. "Counselee" or "client" is used here to indicate the person (or persons) for whom the member has assumed a professional responsibility. Typically the counselee or client is the individual with whom the member has direct and primary contact. However, at times, "client" may include another person(s) when the other person(s) exercise significant control and direction over the individual being helped in connection with the decisions and plans being considered in counseling.

1. The member's *primary* obligation is to respect the integrity and promote the welfare of the counselee or client with whom he is working.

2. The counseling relationship and information resulting therefrom must be kept confidential consistent with the obligations of the member as a professional person.

3. Records of the counseling relationship including interview notes, test data, correspondence, tape recordings, and other documents are to be considered professional information for use in counseling, research, and teaching of counselors but always with full protection of the identity of the client and with precaution so that no harm will come to him.

4. The counselee or client should be informed of the conditions under which he may receive counseling assistance at or before the time he enters the counseling relationship. This is particularly true in the event that there exist conditions of which the counselee or client would not likely be aware.

5. The member reserves the right to consult with any other professionally competent person about his counselee client. In choosing his professional consultant the member must avoid placing the consultant in a conflict of interest situation, *i.e.*, the consultant must be free of any other obligatory

relation to the member's client that would preclude the consultant being a proper party to the member's efforts to help the counselee or client.

6. The member shall decline to initiate or shall terminate a counseling relationship when he cannot be of professional assistance to the counselee or client either because of lack of competence or personal limitation. In such instances the member shall refer his counselee or client to an appropriate specialist. In the event the counselee or client declines the suggested referral, the member is not obligated to continue the counseling relationship.

7. When the member learns from counseling relationships of conditions which are likely to harm others over whom his institution or agency has responsibility, he is expected to report *the condition* to the appropriate responsible authority, but in such a manner as not to reveal the identity of his counselee or clients.

8. In the event that the counelee or client's condition is such as to require others to assume responsibility for him, or when there is clear and imminent danger to the counselee or client or to others, the member is expected to report this fact to an appropriate responsible authority, and/or take such other emergency measures as the situation demands.

9. Should the member be engaged in a work setting which calls for any variation from the above statements, the member is obligated to ascertain that such variations are justifiable under the conditions and that such variations are clearly specified and made known to all concerned with such counseling services.

Section C

TESTING

1. The primary purpose of psychological testing is to provide objective and comparative measures for use in self-evaluation or evaluation by others of general or specific attributes.

2. Generally, test results constitute only one of a variety of pertinent data for personnel and guidance decisions. It is the member's responsibility to provide adequate orientation or information to the examinee(s) so that the results of testing may be placed in proper perspective with other relevant factors.

3. When making any statements to the public about tests and testing care must be taken to give accurate information and to avoid any false claims or misconceptions.

4. Different tests demand different levels of competence for administration, scoring, and interpretation. It is therefore the responsibility of the member to recognize the limits of his competence and to perform only those functions which fall within his preparation and competence.

5. In selecting tests for use in a given situation or with a particular client the member must consider not only general but also specific validity, reliability, and appropriateness of the test(s).

6. Tests should be administered under the same conditions which were established in their standardization. Except for research purposes explicitly stated, any departures from these conditions, as well as unusual behavior or irregularities during the testing session which may affect the interpretation of the tests results, must be fully noted and reported. In this connection, un-

supervised test-taking or the use of tests through the mails are of questionable value.

7. The value of psychological tests depends in part on the novelty to persons taking them. Any prior information, coaching, or reproduction of test materials tends to invalidate test results. Therefore, test security is one of the professional obligations of the member.

8. The member has the responsibility to inform the examinee(s) as to the purpose of testing. The criteria of examinee's welfare and/or explicit prior understanding with him should determine who the recipients of the test results may be.

9. The member should guard against the appropriation, reproduction, or modifications of published tests or parts thereof without express permission and adequate recognition of the original author or publisher.

Regarding the preparation, publication, and distribution of tests reference should be made to:

"Tests and Diagnostic Techniques" — Report of the Joint Committee of the American Psychological Association, American Educational Research Association, and National Council of Measurements used in Education. Supplement to *Psychological Bulletin*, 1954, 2, 1-38.

Section D

RESEARCH AND PUBLICATION

1. In the performance of any research on human subjects, the member must avoid causing any injurious effects or after-effects of the experiment upon his subjects.

2. The member may withhold information or provide misinformation to subjects only when it is essential to the investigation and where he assumes responsibility for corrective action following the investigation.

3. In reporting research results, explicit mention must be made of all variables and conditions known to the investigator which might affect interpretation of the data.

4. The member is responsible for conducting and reporting his investigations so as to minimize the possibility that his findings will be misleadng.

5. The member has an obligation to make available original research data to qualified others who may wish to replicate or verify the study.

6. In reporting research results or in making original data available, due care must be taken to disguise the identity of the subjects, in the absence of specific permission from such subjects to do otherwise.

7. In conducting and reporting research, the member should be familiar with, and give recognition to, previous work on the topic.

8. The member has the obligation to give due credit to those who have contributed significantly to his research, in accordance with their contributions.

9. The member has the obligation to honor commitments made to subjects of research in return for their cooperation.

10. The member is expected to communicate to other members the results of any research he judges to be of professional or scientific value.

Section E

CONSULTING AND PRIVATE PRACTICE

Consulting refers to a voluntary relationship between a professional helper and help-needing social unit (industry, business, school, college, etc.) in which the consultant is attempting to give help to the client in the solving of some current or potential problem.[1]

1. The member acting as a consultant must have a high degree of self-awareness of his own values and needs in entering a helping relationship which involves change in a social unit.

2. There should be understanding and agreement between consultant and client as to directions or goals of the attempted change.

3. The consultant must be reasonably certain that he or his organization have the necessary skills and resources for giving the kind of help which is needed now or that may develop later.

4. The consulting relationship must be one in which client adaptability and growth toward self-direction are encouraged and cultivated. The consultant must consistently maintain his role as a consultant and not become a decision maker for the client.

5. The consultant in announcing his availability for service as a consultant follows professional rather than commercial standards in describing his services with accuracy, dignity, and caution.

6. For private practice in testing, counseling, or consulting the ethical principles stated in all previous sections of this document are pertinent. In addition, any individual, agency, or institution offering educational and vocational counseling to the public should meet the standards of the American Board on Professional Standards in Vocational Counseling, Inc.

Section F

PERSONNEL ADMINISTRATION

1. The member is responsible for establishing working agreements with supervisors and with subordinates especially regarding counseling or clinical relationships, confidentiality, distinction between public and private material, and a mutual respect for the positions of parties involved in such issues.

2. Such working agreements may vary from one institutional setting to another. What should be the case in each instance, however, is that agreements have been specified, made known to those concerned, and whenever possible the agreements reflect institutional policy rather than personal judgment.

3. The member's responsibility to his superiors requires that he keep them aware of conditions affecting the institution, particularly those which may be potentially disrupting or damaging to the institution.

4. The member has a responsibility to select competent persons for assigned responsibilities and to see that his personnel are used maximally for the skills and experience they possess.

---

[1]This definition is adapted from "Dimensions of the Consultant's Job" by Ronald Lippitt, *The Journal of Social Issues*, Vol. XV, No. 2, 1959.

5. The member has responsibility for constantly stimulating his staff for their and his own continued growth and improvement. He must see that staff members are adequately supervised as to the quality of their functioning and for purposes of professional development.

6. The member is responsible for seeing that his staff is informed of policies, goals, and programs toward which the department's operations are oriented.

Section G

PREPARATION FOR PERSONNEL WORK

1. The member in charge of training sets up a strong program of academic study and supervised practice in order to prepare the trainees for their future responsibilities.

2. The training program should aim to develop in the trainee not only skills and knowledge, but also self-understanding.

3. The member should be aware of any manifestations of personal limitations in a student trainee which may influence the latter's provision of competent services and has an obligation to offer assistance to the trainee in securing professional remedial help.

4. The training program should include preparation in research and stimulation for the future personnel worker to do research and add to the knowledge in his field.

5. The training program should make the trainee aware of the ethical responsibilities and standards of the profession he is entering.

6. The program of preparation should aim at inculcating among the trainees, who will later become the practitioners of our profession, the ideal of service to individual and society above personal gain.

CHAPTER 4: QUESTIONS FOR DISCUSSION

1. Daubner and Daubner present certain important aspects of Kantian ethics. Could you operate comfortably and effectively as a counselor, basing your choices on that system? What problems would you as a person have with it? What other systems of choice-making or ethical behavior have you read about which might be more appealing? Why?

2. Read again the summary of Patterson's essay on values in counseling. What are his major points? If any of them disturb you, give your reasoning on them.

3. Hobbs raises the question of whether free choice (or free will) does in fact exist. Philosophers generally state that "Ought implies *can*" (i.e., it is meaningless to say that someone "ought" to do something which he is *unable* to do. If free will does not exist, what differences take place in law, human relationships, and guidance? Can you find some "middle ground" for the extreme positions on this matter?

4. Curran quotes the old philosophical principle that "ontogeny recapitulates phylogeny." What does this *mean?* What evidences do you see of this in counseling and guidance?

5. Adams quotes Smith's study of how information should be used in counseling. Do any of the findings trouble you? What alternative ways of viewing the use of such information do you feel might be better?

6. Chenault presents an argument for making clear what we mean by help. What alternative ways of defining "helping" can you think of in a counseling situation? Which seems most sensible to you? Why?

7. After reading Walters' article, consider the often-made statement that "A clergyman must stop being a clergyman before he can counsel anyone." Do you believe this? Discuss the statement for all of its possible meanings in counseling.

8. Golightly raises the question of middle-class counselors' attempting to function with underprivileged clients. What are the major social class differences, according to sociologists? If Golightly's analysis is valid, what measures must we take to improve services to the underprivileged client?

9. Compare the APGA Ethical Standards with the NEA Code of Ethics. Since the counselor is generally regarded as a member of both the counseling and teaching professions, he might well examine both codes. Do you see any fundamental conflicts between the two codes? Are there points with which you cannot agree, or which need clarification?

10. Bring to the attention of the class a situation which is not covered or not clearly covered by the codes of ethics. Discuss possible approaches, and the problems involved in each of them. What "guiding principle" seems to emerge?

11. Beck sets forth "reasonable expectations" which a novice has for those who are preparing him for a profession. Are there other expectations for the preparation of counselors which he has not mentioned? Which of those he has listed seems the most important to you? the least important to you? Why?

12. Samler states that there are times when a counselor simply must step in and accept responsibility for the client. How might a counselor defend himself against critics in such cases? What sorts of instances might warrant such assumption of responsibility by the counselor? What are some of the problems arising from such actions?

Chapter

5

New Directions

This group of essays may prove to be the most controversial of all the chapters in this book. The essays express viewpoints which in many ways do not coincide with the thinking of many thoughtful and well-established men in the fields of counseling, guidance, and therapy. They raise a host of questions about "usual" procedures, value orientations, emphases in research, and order-of-importance in helping relationships.

The counselor must ask himself, "How do these ideas square with what I have read about helping relationships, techniques, and viewpoints on objectives?" He must then ask himself, even if he rejects the major emphases proposed, "What can I learn from each of them?" From the standpoint of the philosopher, of course, his major question might well be, "**On what grounds** do I reject or accept their major premises and recommendations?"

Regretfully, not all "recent directions" can be included in any single book, nor can any new thought current be elaborated in great detail. One of the most widely-discussed new viewpoints in counseling and therapy today is existentialism and counseling. The rapprochement between this brand of philosophy and counseling offers promising and exciting times ahead in the formulation of guidance theory and practice. Those interested in this way of viewing the human condition might survey several journals which have provided thought-provoking essays about existentialism and helping relationships in the past few years: APGA *Journal, Journal of Counseling Psychology, Journal of Humanistic Psychology, Review of Existential Psychology and Psychiatry, Existential Inquiries, The American Psychologist* and others. The works of Rollo May, Adrian Van Kaam, Abraham Maslow, Viktor Frankl, O. H. Mowrer, recent writings of Carl Rogers, and shorter works by Edward Dreyfus and others also bring into focus the major contentions of existential philosophy. In particular those who wish further reading might investigate Rollo May's *Existence*, Jean-Paul Sartre's *Existentialism*, and Carlton Beck's *Philosophical Foundations of Guidance*.

The counselor should ask himself, "What can I learn from all of these writers about the human condition and human aspirations? What differences in emphases do they demand?"

(44)

A PROPOSED MODEL FOR A HUMANISTIC COUNSELOR EDUCATION PROGRAM

Joann Chenault
Southern Illinois University, Edwardsville

Many counselor educators across the nation are in the process of revising their present counselor education programs or building new ones. A major difficulty in the accomplishment of these tasks lies in the relating of philosophical bases to the more definitive aspects of operations. To say it another way, the things we do often conflict with our stated beliefs.

This proposed model for a counselor education program attends to this problem by illustrating the evolvement of operations out of philosophy and by offering a kind of working paper which might be used as a frame of reference in the development of programs valuing a humanistic orientation. It should be clear that there is no intent to convert those having other theoretical or philosophical preferences.

Although the master's, six-year, and doctoral programs ideally follow one model, it may be well to regard this proposal specifically as a model for doctoral programs.

RATIONALE

The rationale or philosophical premises underlying any program of education are the most important factors to be made explicit. Because all aspects of the program, from planning to implementation to evaluation to revision, necessarily have a value base, it is considered imperative to state explicitly those assumptions out of which the entire program evolves. Ensuring that these assumptions are clearly understood brings the additional reward of a basic consistency which would not underlie the program were its value premises only implicit.

The form of this proposal, then, will follow in four stages from the general to the specific. Those stages will be statements of: (a) a general frame of reference for the term humanistic; (b) illustrations of some of the more significant value premises which define humanism; (c) further value assumptions stated in terms of their application to education, that is, presenting directions which might lead to specific operational structure of a program; and (d) illustrations or examples of curricular practices which may grow out of the previous three sets of assumptions. The last examples will be on a more operational and structural level.

Reprinted by permission of the author and *Counselor Education and Supervision,* Vol. 8, No. 1, Fall 1969, 4-11.

THE HUMANISTIC BASIS

The general premises underlying this proposal do not follow a specific psychological or educational theory. They do, however, represent a general point of view or "attitude" referred to as humanistic psychology. These premises are broader than learning theory, broader than personality theory, broader than educational theory. To further clarify the basis of the proposed model, the views of the following persons in psychology and education may be considered to be representative:

Allport	Angyal	Jung	Gendlin
Goldstein	Maslow	Fromm	Watts
Rogers	Moustakas	May	Harper
Lewin	Bugental	Frankl	Morris

It would, of course, be absurd to assume that all of these persons would agree with every statement of this proposal. Because there are different interpretations of humanistic psychology, the assumptions which follow are stated broadly enough to be representative of the various aspects of the humanistic framework, yet specific enough to differentiate clearly these premises from behavioristic or other premises. Some of the assumptions are stated in the negative with the specific intention of pointing up differences from other points of view.

VALUE PREMISES

The following assumptions illustrate some of the more basic values which may underlie a humanistic counselor education program. It is expected that users of this model will alter, delete, or augment these points, depending upon their individual preferences.

GROWTH

1. *The goal for the education of students in counselor education is growth, as differentiated from learning.*

The model for growth is organic. Growth in persons, as in all aspects of nature, is inside-out, not outside-in. Concepts which require a "doing to" the student more appropriately apply to a mechanistic model.

Learning may be an internalizing of externally presented stimuli. One can learn nonsense syllables. Growth is a happening that one cannot "make." It happens best in the absence of outside-in pressures and forces.

There is no man-made, outside-in action which is as potent, as effective, as healthy, as strong, as real, or as self-perpetuating as the organic phenomenon of psychological growth. The growth potential is an awesome phenomenon to be passionately respected and valued. It works.

2. *Growth is a creative process.*

The process of creativity is subjective. It originates in the student, is expressed from within the student, and is altered in relationship to the total person. This is not to say that external conditions have no effect upon creativity; it does say that the energizing forces, the act, and the process of creativity are an organic part of the person. The meaning of external stimuli is created by the person. Dualism, or the separation of subject and object, is rejected.

Creativity is not a process of selecting among alternatives. It is a process of original and new choices, not a mechanistic repetition of learned responses to problem situations.

Holism

3. *A humanistic counselor education program focuses upon the person as an organic entity rather than as a receptacle for learning.*

Its goal is to nourish potentialities. As a creative process, growth is not an accumulation of intellectual or content knowledge, learned behaviors, or interpersonal skills (outside-in learning). The learner is not a passive recipient or internalizer of information. He actively reaches out, seeks, searches, examines and creates.

Content knowledge has no inherent value in itself. Its only meaning or importance lies in the meaning which is created by the student in terms of his total development.

4. *The highest form of morality (personal and professional) is the encouragement of the individual's growing his own values.*

The lowest form of morality is the subjection of the individual to standards or principles which have been preordained. Each student should "grow" his own way of looking at himself, at life, as his professional and personal choices and responsibilities. Behavioral and personal skills are not taught. The behavior of each student should be a *consequence* of his total growth, not a mechanistic essential ingredient in the "making" of a counselor. Counselor education is not an acquisition of skills or learning of behaviors to be performed.

5. *Counseling effectiveness is not a function of technique.*

A teacher or supervisor cannot observe methodology and performed behaviors and discover the effects or meaning of any human experience like counseling. The relationship of technique to counseling is one of consequence. The counselor uses the methods he does as a consequence of who he is. It is not true that the person he becomes should be a consequence of the techniques he masters. The methods of any one individual are not generalizable to others, but are meaningful only in terms of his own uniqueness.

The holistic and organismic views underlying this model require the rejection of such concepts as "training" of counselors, making of "products," and the fractionation of growth into mechanistic parts. One's personhood or self is not a combination of learned skills.

SUBJECTIVE INVOLVEMENT

6. *A necessary condition for growth is the subjective involvement of the student.*

This involvement is best understood in terms of responsibility; that is, the student's experiencing of his private, personal responsibility for determining his own values, directions, and destiny. The professional status of counseling

does not nullify the above condition; it emphasizes its importance. It is especially in a helping profession that it becomes necessary for the professional to
be a product of the self he becomes.

7. *The highest educational goal is the student's search for meaning, his
search for himself.*

His professional self is not a separate entity. The student's quest for meaning is basic to growth in a humanistic program. Any competencies, skills, or
knowledge which have meaning for the student are consequences of this basic
search. That knowledge which is cognitively adopted out of a need for social
(professional or academic) survival holds no intrinsic value.

PROCESS

8. *The purpose of a humanistic counselor education program is to facilitate growth as a process.*

It is a contradiction of values to speak of growth as process and then to
spell out the finished product which we hope to create. At graduation the
student does not carry out a bag of answers but a bag of questions that were
born inside him, not handed to him via the establishment of performance
criteria by which he will be judged. Growth as process must not imply completion, but embarkation.

INDIVIDUALITY

9. *The nature of the growth potential is and should be different for each
student.*

A humanistic program does not seek identical products. The differences
among graduates must be *individual* differences, not program differences.
Alternate programs accounting for differences in job functions or roles do not
provide for individual differences as well as a single program allowing students
to define their own paths.

GENERAL PROGRAM ASSUMPTIONS

The following assumptions will attempt to draw general value premises
closer to educational specifics.

EVALUATIVE CRITERIA

10. *Since there is no identical finished product (graduate) required or
desired, one cannot define the product except in the very broadest terms.*

One can describe the nature of the experiences which the student encounters. One can define, loosely, the process of growth. One can make judge-
ments about the degree to which the student has developed his own way
of thinking, has been responsible for his decisions, opinions, and behaviors,
has been subjectively involved in creating meaning, and similar criteria. One

can make judgments about the student's respect for the dignity of his clients, about his ability to understand them, and other criteria relating to his counseling practices.

These are not operationally convenient criteria to measure by any objective instrument. However, there are three major arguments in favor of such relatively general and subjective criteria over more operationally defined behaviors:

a. A program's goals should be determined by one's values (what one believes in and desires), not by the ease with which the goals may be measured.
b. There is no scientific evidence to support the assumption that objective measures of subjective criteria are more valid than subjective judgments of the same criteria.
c. Neither is there evidence to support the assumption that such subjective criteria should be "turned into" measurable traits. The more operationally love is defined, the more one is removed from its essence.

11. *The question of evaluation places the act and experience of evaluation in the student.*

The unit in which all criteria lie is the person. The unit is not in performance or behavior defined publicly. Consequently, each student will develop his own criteria in preference to the acceptance of those predetermined for him by the faculty.

12. *Decision-making is a creative process.*

Decision-making is inhibited, not enhanced, by the use of learned techniques of problem-solving. A technician chooses among alternative performance skills. The "natural" counselor never selects from a bag of tricks, but responds with his total self in a fresh new way to each individual client. He *creates* alternatives; he does not select from a finite source of learned techniques. It is the absence of technique sources which facilitates creative thinking and decision-making. It is the *seeker* of new understandings which we value, not the *user* of mastered methodologies.

It should not be assumed the above value leaves no professional basis for the counselor's behavior. The student's meaningful picture of his own values, understandings, and questions will provide a most professionally consistent and effective basis for his behavior.

CURRICULUM

13. *The program is geared to facilitate individual growth, not to teach for a position, role, or particular job setting.*

If the student becomes a particular kind of person of his own choosing, he is free to move into a variety of positions. This model proposes working toward personal growth rather than toward specialized competencies. A person who is confident in creating his own meaning from job situations and who continues to question and grow is valued over the graduate possessing the answers of specialization. The medical model of specialization is rejected.

This means that our graduates on the job would be expected to *create* roles manifesting their own understandings and values in helping others.

Rather than fitting themselves into previously defined positions, they would create individual roles for themselves deriving from their own responsibility, not from the acceptance of roles learned in school. The degree to which skills are seen as specialized functions is evidence that the student has not examined critically the question of the meaning of help. The open student is more sensitive to the expectations of his employer and to the limitations which he encounters on the job than one who has a predetermined knowledge of his specific role and function.

IMPLICATIONS FOR CURRICULUM

The following assumptions are offered as illustrations of curricular practices which may evolve from the model. A curriculum model would, of course, be more comprehensive in structure. These are merely glimpses of a few operational consequences of the previously stated value assumptions.

CORE AND SPECIALIZATION

1. *Since counseling competence is not regarded as an accumulation of specialized skills, there will be a major core program for all students.*

The concept of core refers to certain experiences which are considered essential for each student. As an illustration, these experiences might be represented in (a) philosophical and social foundations, (b) psychological foundations, and (c) counseling experience.

The concept of core in this program presupposes that there is a basic preparation for counselors of all specializations. Although the idea of specialization requires minimal emphasis in curricular scheduling, this does not prevent any student from pursuing specialized interests. However, it is assumed that minimal course requirements in any given specialization will be adequate (indeed, that additional course requirements would be superfluous). Many, if not most, of the important experiences and learning in the nature of specialization in counseling occur on the job.

CURRICULAR SCHEDULING

2. *Since growth and the actualization of self occur best in a setting free of predetermined goals, curricular experiences ensuring this opportunity will be provided.*

Experiential gains in terms of personal growth can occur in pursuit of academic knowledge (subject matter). But they do not often occur in the absence of complementary experiences free of academic, external goals. The first purpose is realized through traditional and non-traditional courses. The second is realized through the addition of new experiences in the curriculum.

One aspect of such a program may be integrative seminars where students can pursue questions relating to all of their courses and counseling experiences in a group which will have non-academic goals and no grade evaluation. These seminars, or interaction groups, will be the vehicle for the development of individual values through the expression of moral, ethical, personal, and professional questions, these questions being a primary source of motivation and personal involvement.

Because "sensitivity" and T Groups have acquired a traditional methodology and purpose which is antithetical to the humanistic model premises, the interaction groups offered in a humanistic program will reflect major differences from such traditional groups. For example, the interaction groups of this program would have no externally imposed purpose other than the facilitation of growth as defined earlier. (Specific descriptions of this process are available in an unpublished paper.)

PRACTICUM

3. *Since an organic model values experiencing as a necessary concomitant to cognitive searching, practicum is not a "course."*

Counseling experiences will occur continuously throughout the student's program.

4. *Since a humanistic model encourages the development of responsibility and individuality, the practicum experience will create a "working out of" umbilical relationships with the faculty and an increase of independence.*

A guidance practicum has little more value than observation without the characteristic of complete responsibility of the student in his job. There is little value in going through the motions of guidance work at any particular school. The motions at another school will be different ones, and we do not want our students to learn a set of motions but to learn how to respond to any situation and to be responsible for setting their own motions.

Counseling practicum may, but need not, occur in a school setting. Counseling experiences with persons of varying age groups and settings help the counselor learn to adapt to varying conditions. They also help him to regard his client as a person rather than as an "adolescent," "a student," "culturally deprived," or "Negro."

PERSONAL GROWTH

5. *Individual counseling and/or group therapy may be planned as a part of the curriculum as an elective.*

However, it should be emphasized that the value of this experience depends upon its nature. That is, minimal threat procedures are considered helpful; "confrontation" practices are considered harmful, even immoral.

POSTSCRIPT

A humanistic program model does not require that all of its faculty hold humanistic views. Indeed, diversity and pluralism are highly valued. Just as faculty members holding humanistic views have complemented traditional programs for the past few decades, so may humanistic programs build a faculty representing a variety of theoretical and philosophical positions.

（ 45 ）

THE LOGIC OF COUNSELING RESEARCH

Henry Borow

University of Minnesota

It took psychology a long time to divest itself of the intuitive and speculative trappings which marked its pre-twentieth century identification with
metaphysical philosophy. When it finally joined the company of the experimental sciences it embraced empiricism with a vengeance. The discovery that
man's behavior was not after all inscrutable, that it was orderly and potentially predictable within the sphere of natural law, produced the exhilaration
of a heady wine. Radical behaviorism of the 1920's and its applied counterpart, trait-measurement psychology, made common cause in their zeal to (1)
measure and (2) correlate anything which breathed and moved. This was a
free-wheeling period in psychology's history, in America if not in Europe,
during which the connections between controlled observation and behavior
theory troubled few workers. For many psychologists, building a body of
knowledge about man's behavior rested on the strategy of formulating an
expanding list of response-response laws (e.g. correlations between two trait
tests).

With scientific maturity has come a tempering sobriety. We are no longer
so supremely confident about the explanatory powers of our instruments. Two
insistent interdependent questions disturb us: (1) *What* is being measured?
(2) What does it *signify*? In research in psychotherapy and counseling psychology these questions are caught up in the enigmatic criterion issue. Contemporary clinicians and counselors seem to sense that a descriptive language
which includes only sense data (i.e. observation) terms is too impoverished
to permit them to talk in a satisfactory way about their clients' behavior.
They use hypothetical constructs freely in behavior description and explanation. Yet about this state of affairs many of them seem most unhappy and
apologetic. Their statements leave the impression, and in this feeling I believe
they are wrong, that they will not have exorcised the metaphysical gremlin
until they recast all constructs in language referring to the observable. If they
are merely insisting that we need to locate proper indicator variables for our
hypothetical constructs for purposes of research, there is no quarrel. Such
indicators are the empirical referents which we must use to formulate and
test laws which we then hope to connect with theory. But I fear they propose
ultimately to supplant the terms of theory by those of observation. Like the
radical behaviorists (e.g. Skinner) they want to build a reduction language
by translating the hypothetical terms of behavior science as purely operational
terms. Operationism, they seem to be saying, will lead us out of our conceptual wilderness.

Reprinted by permission of the author and the *Journal of Counseling Psychology*,
Vol. 3, No. 4, 1956, 292-296.

OPERATIONISM IN QUESTION

This is perhaps not the place for a critique of operationism. Since, however, the strategy of much current research design in counseling and psychotherapy is rooted in operationism, a few dissenting comments may not be inappropriate. In a private communication, Vernon Dolphin, a former Minnesota colleague, points to an abortive attempt to frame operational definitions in psychology which frequently occurs but is seldom challenged. Dolphin notes that it is dispositional terms (e.g. compliant, manic, anxious) for which operational definitions are commonly contrived. He contends, and I believe correctly, that dispositional terms are logically distinct from operational terms. Unlike the latter, they "carry implications of an indeterminate kind and number" and cannot be adequately defined by single, specific acts or discrete behavioral items. They cannot in consequence, Dolphin writes, be made over into operational terms. I would add that neither can clearly theoretical terms be operationally defined. Such constructs as the unconscious, guilt and over-compensation, like the term electro-magnetic action in physical science, are essentially non-instantial variables. They do not exist in the data language even though we may come to some agreement about their indicators in the world of observation. Operational terms tend to be descriptive in character; theoretical terms are explanatory. The two proceed from different logical bases and cannot be strictly equated. How, for example, is the lavish theoretical language of psychoanalysis to be cast in operational terms? Those readers who have inspected the valiant but unconvincing attempt by Albert Ellis (1) will doubt that this trick can be carried off. Even if it were possible to reduce terms of theory to the data language, one would still have to decide whether the result would be salvation or disaster.

Herbert Feigl and Michael Scriven of the Minnesota Center for Philosophy of Science at the University of Minnesota have noted the limitations of operationism in this connection. Scriven's (6) recent paper "A Study of Radical Behaviorism" is a detailed and systematic attack on Skinnerian psychology partly on the ground that it attempts to strip the science of behavior bare of theory and partly on the ground that it often makes use of theory while denying that it does. Ernest Nagel of Columbia University, in an invited address at the University of Minnesota, forcefully contended that theoretical (non-operational) terms are essential to science, that with the help of theory one can make a wider range of deductions than from laws alone. Proper statements of theory, Nagel believes, allow us to establish a better relationship between the other statements in science.

Where does all of this leave us in counseling psychology? Does it mean a return to untestable metaphysical speculation in talking about our procedures and our clients' behavior? I do not think so. The language of theoretical science and that of metaphysics are not equivalent and the use of one does not require that we lapse into the other. When we say there are hypothetical constructs (as well as operational terms) in the language of psychodynamics, we are admitting only that certain statements in our science which tend to be explanatory in character are not directly testable. It is no different in the other sciences. They have theories and they have laws. So does psychology.

Laws, which have an observation base, can be confirmed or disconfirmed on the strength of the experimental evidence. Strictly speaking, theories are never confirmed in this manner. Because they cannot be put to test of direct observation, they must be accepted,, modified, extended or rejected according to their ability to unify the known facts and laws of our science. A theory which logically connects a large number of laws, which helps us "explain" the laws and the causal relations between them, and from which the laws themselves may be deduced and accurate predictions made is a sound theory. It is this type of theory we seek for the counseling process. We shall never get it by precipitously rewriting all the statements of counselor and client behavior into alleged operational terms.

THE CHARACTER OF FUTURE RESEARCH

Three rather general proposals might be made regarding the direction research in counseling should take if it is to be fruitful.

(1) High priority should be given to research which tries to bring a semblance of order and standardization to the descriptive language of counseling psychology. It is saying nothing new to assert that terms in science must be used with precision and rigor. It may, however, surprise some counselors to learn how inconsistent and inefficient the terminological fabric of their field is. A few years ago Vernon Dolphin and I essayed an informal survey and analysis of the language of adjustment. We found for some common terms, e.g., adjustment, a variety of conflicting and disjointed definitions. Conversely, some concepts (e.g. sound mental health) were represented in the literature by a host of verbal labels. Some readers will recall the attempt of Rotter (4) to come to grips with the problem in his recently published book. Here Rotter confronts questions such as "The problem of labeling and categorizing," "The problem of an inadequate language of description," and "Criteria for an ideal language of description." In a yet unpublished symposium paper, "Toward a Concept of the Normal Personality," delivered before the 1956 Convention of the American College Personnel Association, E. J. Shoben of Columbia University attacked what he called the "lack of conceptual clarity concerning the nature of psychological normality." Shoben called into serious question the concepts of conformity and statistical normality as criteria by which the normal personality is identified. In an eloquent and thoughtful explication of the concept of integrative adjustment, he proposed four distinguishing characteristics of the person to whom the label is to be applied. These were self-control, acceptance of personal responsibility, social interest, and ideals. Shoben freely admitted that this was but a first approximation to the reformulation of the concept of integrative adjustment.

The four descriptive terms are, of course, themselves global in character and require delimitation and clarification. Even if they were to prove acceptable to the body of counselors, sets of factual referents would have to be evolved by which counseling researchers might make repeatable observations and classify their findings. Lest the reader be puzzled, there is no contradition between this last statement of mine and what I said earlier about the inordinate use of operational definitions. As I understand him, Shoben is using the term "integrative adjustment" as a summary descriptive term rather than as an explanatory one and as such it will require observation-based indicators to be useful. Incidentally, Shoben wisely notes that one cannot hope to avoid questions of ethical values in defining something which brushes the social code as broadly as does this one. He says, "At this point the behavioral sciences and ethics meet and merge — (it) seems unlikely that any conception of normality can be developed apart from some general considerations that are fundamentally moral." Meehl (2) has also raised the issue of psychotherapy's convergence on ethics. He writes, "A rigorous, sophisticated consideration of the ethics of therapeutic 'guidance' — by workers competent in axiology and casuistry is long overdue. Current thinking on this topic is almost wholly confined to cliches."

(2) More evidence, much more, is urgently needed on precisely what occurs during the counseling process. Except for the Rogerians and to a far lesser degree some schools of psychoanalysis, moment-to-moment factual reports of the counselor's and client's operations are absent from the experimental literature. To feed into a counseling-outcomes experiment an assortment of unanalyzed "homogeneous" counselors loosely categorized as "eclectic," for example, is to obscure forever the specific inter-counselor behavior differences which contribute to variance in momentary and long-range client behavior. Tedious as it may be to compile and to analyze, we need to know what a large assortment of counselors do with a large assortment of persons who come for help. If this suggests to the reader that we invite the risk of forcing the description of counseling into an ideographic mold, it is a risk we shall have to take. Should the nature of counseling and its net effect turn out to be functions of the *particular* counselor, the *particular* client and the *particular* problem set, this is something we had better discover sooner than late.

The principal point then, I think, is that we need a much more nearly exhaustive report on what counseling is as actually practiced. The editor of this section of the *Journal*, Harold Pepinsky (3), comes close to expressing the same concern. He argues that the counselor must be explicit in telling what he does with a client. In enumerating two requirements of the counselor as a theory builder, Pepinsky says the counselor must specify "the kinds of responses he wants the client to make as an end-product of counseling and (he must specify) the decisions by which he makes it maximally likely that such client responses will occur." One certainly would not wish to quarrel with these laudable proposals with which Pepinsky exhorts counselors. I would, moreover, agree with him that counselors are not now doing these things. That they are not is attributable, I believe, to personal and situational conditions quite different from those which Pepinsky invokes as an explanation. That is another matter. My thesis here is that if we are to talk to one another univocally in this field we need desperately to know what counselors are now doing in counseling. This is a straightforward research problem in factual description. It is not an alternative to Pepinsky's proposals in which the counselor functions both as a practitioner and as a theorist testing his hypotheses. Both research emphases are needed. If they were adopted, we might get somewhere with counseling.

(3) My last proposal takes the form of an admonition. It is that research on the overall evaluation of outcomes is likely to furnish a spare yield until

more basic questions about personality formation, the nature of counseling and the counselor-client interaction are given better answers. Is Pepinsky (3) right when he asserts that it is premature to speak about a general theory of the counseling process? Is Meehl (2) right when he contends that "the state of theory (in psychotherapy) and its relation to technique is obviously chaotic whatever our pretentions?" The evidence is on their side. What we need then is analytic research that will feed back to theory and nourish it. I have been struck with how many attempts have been made to assess counseling "in the mass" and how little all of this has taught us. Where does it lead? Even when results have been positive (i.e. in the predicted direction), and the frequency of such occurrences has been depressingly small, the cause of scientific explanation has not been well served. The antecedent conditions of client "improvement" in such global attacks on counseling have not been convincingly teased out and too often the nature of the "improvement" itself has not been formally (logically) analyzed.

Of course, the most important question we ask about counseling in the long haul is "does it work?" Yet we are hardly in a position currently to make a rigorous formulation of the issue. Research attempts in this domain have often been immodest to the times and logically over-extended. Before we can get intelligible information on this jackpot question we will have to raise and frame answers to a number of others. I conceive of these prior questions as concerned with the clarification of terms and with the establishment of the lower-order causal connections of the therapeutic process. How are the descriptive terms in the language of mental health to be formulated? What counselor dispositions and behaviors and what assigned therapy tasks accompany what client movements in counseling? Which are the stable and non-subjective criterion variables which may best serve as unambiguous referents for the client constructs we wish to manipulate through the therapeutic strategy? The state of our knowledge about therapy and counseling being what it is, experimental attacks on the problem must continue to be pressed on many fronts. I do not wish to propose a moratorium on all research on counseling outcomes. My plea is rather for a redress of balance in our total research program.

References

1. Ellis, Albert. An operational reformulation of some of the basic principles of psychoanalysis. In H. Feigl and M. Scriven (Eds.), *The foundations of science and the concepts of psychology and psychoanalysis.* Minneapolis: University of Minnesota Press, 1956. Pp. 131-154.
2. Meehl, Paul E. Psychotherapy. In Stone, C. P. (Ed.), *Annual Review of psychology, volume 6.* Stanford, California: Annual Reviews, Inc., 1955. Pp. 357-78.
3. Pepinsky, Harold B. Research notes from here and there. *J. counsel. Psychol.,* 1956, *3,* 222-28.
4. Rotter, Julian B. *Social learning and clinical psychology.* New York: Prentice-Hall, 1954.
5. Schrier, Harvey. The significance of identification in therapy. *Amer. J. Orthopsychiat.,* 1953, *23,* 585-604.
6. Scriven, Michael. A study of radical behaviorism. In H. Feigl and M. Scriven (Eds.), *The foundations of science and the concepts of psychology and psychoanalysis.* Minneapolis: University of Minnesota Press, 1956. Pp. 88-130.

46

PHILOSOPHERS, COUNSELOR EDUCATORS, AND RELEVANT QUESTIONS

Glenn R. Dey

Wichita State University

Counselor educators are constantly seeking to extend or clarify existing definitions of human nature and the human condition. Increased application of the scientific method with an assist from modern technology has extended our knowledge of human behavior and actions beyond our greatest expectations. However, the dilemmas facing counselor educators, as they seek to assist their students and clients, remain as numerous as ever. This condition suggests the need for continued evaluation of assumptions about individual man and his society. How can counselor educators advance professional approaches and understandings which will be functional for future man and his emerging societal relationships?

Questions of this scope evade resolution through immediate answers. While more easily answerable questions presently command our attention, counselor educators must examine their role in establishing the target questions which will consume our endeavors in the future, a future in which the uninformed and possibly unindoctrinated consumers of our product will increasingly ask the question, how does this advance society?

The thesis of this article is (a) that a need exists today for counselor educators to examine their singular and cumulative efforts as these affect the form and essence of life in our society, and (b) in examination of these efforts, other specialists, such as philosophers, can be of assistance in examining present assumptions about human nature and resulting societal orientations.

As man increases his specialization in work and professional roles he becomes increasingly vulnerable to societal institutions, particularly those institutions whose efforts promulgate myths which function as societal cannons sustaining the institution's pattern—a pattern which often becomes increasingly dysfunctional in responding to individual needs of people.

An example of the effects of a dominant belief system or myths may be found in that institution with which counselor educators should have frequent contact, the school. This institution usually reflects to its members and consumers certain concepts, values, and attitudes which reflect the currently held values of dominant powers on the local or national level. School personnel consecutively mirror the currently held industrial view of man, running the gamut from "mechanistic man," "economic man," "emotional man" to "instrumental man," the unattached, uncommitted expert. In short, rarely does the school provide a condition where adequately functioning individuals are allowed to explore the behavioral forms which are manifestations of, to use

Reprinted by permission of the author and *Counselor Education and Supervision*, Vol. 8, No. 2, Winter 1969, 135-142.

Broudy's definition, "rules for eligibility for membership in the human family" (Broudy, 1967, p. 116).

Seemingly, the emerging societal power utilizes, directs, and propounds those myths and needs of human nature that serve its purposes. It does this with an awareness that the stronger the belief in myths the easier it is to shape human behavior, and the myths of mankind about human nature are the most serviceable. For as Herzberg states, "since man is the indivisible unit of society, no society can exist without an implicit conception of what people are like" (Herzberg, 1966, p. 13).

The probability of new understandings and knowledge about factors producing the human condition being used to enhance the climate for the individual person is low as institutions find it easier to adapt or adopt myths than to engage in a searching examination of current conditions.

THE CHALLENGE

Counselor educators perform as specialized men in a world of work serving institutions within a society characterized by a hegemony of historical and emergent forces struggling for a dominant role. Counselor educators may well pause to ask themselves what their role is, or should be, in order to advance present understandings of the nature of man and the human condition which effect change, or the illusion of change, in man as a functional or dysfunctional member of his society and species.

Are professionals aiding and abetting the perpetuation of myths which are aggravating the individual condition in a mass society? To plead ignorance of sources of power presently or potentially exploitative in their effect upon a majority of the populace will not absolve professionals of their responsibility to their society and times. To reflect upon, or reflect to the society, individual views, while helpful, seemingly falls short of the reflection or freeing effect which specialized man such as counselor educators might have on the "business as usual" syndrome.

Beck has admonished the profession to "understand change or become irrelevant" (Beck, 1967, p. 216). Counselor educators must understand the varying modes of practice which are dictated by self needs as specialized men. They also need to understand the antecedent conditions and current effects of these practices upon the varying themes of life of individual and mass man. For both use many themes and modalities for verifying and validating experience and behavior which enhances the achievement of ultimate goals. If counselor educators assume this task, the aid of others, especially philosophers, is crucial in examining the political nature of their efforts. These efforts as they affect every man, therefore public in nature, suggest that the request to other specialists embodies a demand that they function not only as consultants, but that they also participate in the dialogue. The motives concerning the meaning of life and purpose for being which sustained the development of philosophy in early man are still present today. Behavioral scientists as well as philosophers have largely ignored this legitimate request.

Is it possible that counselor educators may be too concerned with the advancement of technique? Beset by a multiplicity of modes of practice, desirous of stature within the larger academy of scholars, counselor educators may be seduced into reliance upon a select body of critics, critics who sustain the biases rather than assist in the examination of these encapsulating attitudes and myths. Reliance upon such a body of critics will encourage a professional deformation which may render us dysfunctional to the larger society.

In counselor education, as well as other specialties concerned with the helping relationship, two families of players are contesting for the spotlight on the theoretical stage. Their manner suggests self-avowed hopes of ultimately being the only participants on stage. This interaction may give on-stage players the opportunity to view the validity, efficiency, and vulnerability of each theoretical approach to currently understood conditions and problems. However, the understandings for counselor educators, gained through observation of this interaction, have only limited usefulness. As London states:

> approaching therapy by a description of such technical systems serves clarity, but it is not quite sufficient for comprehension; techniques must finally be seen in the context of their application and related both to the assumptions from which they are deduced and to the goals to which they are addressed (London, 1964, p. 40).

If, as players, counselor educators are to comprehend the entire performance, the view from off-stage becomes imperative.

The need for discourse between specialized man, mass man, and individual man represents a condition which is public in nature. Arendt suggests that such discourses and decisions are too great to be left to the pure scientist and professional politician. For they "move in a world where speech has lost its power, and whatever men do or experience can make sense only to the extent that it can be spoken" (Arendt, 1958, p. 4). She continues, "Men in the plural, that is men in so far as they live and move and act in this world, can experience meaningfulness only because they can talk with and make sense to each other and themselves!" (Arendt, 1958, p. 5). In present attempts to validate individual efforts of counselors as specialists, who will speak for individual and mass man? Can other specialists serve as *Omsbudmen* or *Amicus Curiae* as counselors attempt to understand and produce change?

AN INVITATION

Counselor educators should consider ways of inviting others, especially philosophers, to join in a dialogue to communicate their perceptions and experiencing of the movement on the human stage. Their understanding as specialists could enhance the communication that individual and mass man would like to convey to the specialty of counseling about their nature and condition.

Counselor educators ought to hope that participating individuals, particularly philosophers, would reject that "curiously remote position to which modern society has relegated philosophy and which philosophers themselves have been content to accept" (Barrett, 1962, p. 3). Dare philosophers philosophize and in the process communicate their perception of relevant vital questions which face men and ultimately the individual specialized man? Such action by philosophers would be helpful to counselor educators in the search for meaning voiced by people, clients, counselors, and counselor educators.

ESTABLISHING THE AUTHENTIC QUESTIONS

There is a possibility that individuals tend to be overly concerned with static answers. The determination of humanly relevant questions may be far more significant. How does, and will, man determine the authentic questions related to contemporary existence?

Do men seek the authentic questions relative to their time and experience? Or can it be argued that they only seek to authenticate the questions of which they are presently aware? The authentic expression of current existence as a person, as well as the planning of change for effectiveness as a productive, specialized member of modern society, demands a lucid definition of basic questions which man must seek to answer.

In the social sciences both *homo humanus* and *homo faber* are seekers of truth. The need for a claim upon truth and knowledge is quite evident. Boring (1964) suggests that models can be substituted for theory. In this way the emphasis upon the question of truth is reduced. He suggests that "causality is only the form of a model, and freedom is also a model, and we can use our models at will without letting them dominate us" (Boring, 1964, p. 17). Are counselor educators in a position to shift their emphasis from these models and what they represent?

Can one use theories and/or models to create new, more useful and illustrative models? Or are counselor educators in the similar position of the artist, who as product of an age can only project the currently held image of man? Can we build models utilizing most creatively those forces within man and within contemporary society. Specialized man's departure from the office at day's end allows him to leave his models behind, useful curiosities to pursue another day. But what of the man in the street for whom labor represents the primary way of validating his existence?

FUNDAMENTAL HUMAN ACTIVITIES[1]

The organization of daily lives and the variety of activities which constitute the experiential world of behavior reflect dominant themes by which individuals arrive at meaning. One of these themes centers about one's role as a productive member of a technological society. The adequacy of one's production, in light of the product's utility for the society, determines the subsequent rewards.

Man's society has at times varied in its recognition of the individual's contribution through labor. This labor varied from production to maintain individual existence to that production which benefited the society as a whole. Making a living by producing through one's labor is threatened by rapid automation and specialization. The meaning which one attached to individual daily endeavor is in danger of being lost. These endeavors enabled men to present

---

[1]Hanna Arendt in *The Human Condition* proposes "three fundamental human activities: labor, work, and action." She suggests that labor represents the vital necessities which produce and feed the life process; work is the activity which provides an "artificial" world of things which transcend each individual life; and action refers to that activity that goes on between men, and corresponds to the condition of plurality, that men, not Man, inhabit the world.

themselves before others as worthwhile individuals and in addition provided a means for sustaining their biological existence. The machine in striking the chains of toil from man is also reducing the possibilities for labor and work which have been meaningful activities. What activities are left?

Since the Middle Ages, scientific knowledge and the objective view have stripped religion of much of its meaning for Western man. Certainly organized religion has been dislodged from a central place in the affairs of men. Automation and the modern technological organization with its emphasis on consumable products are removing the significance of much individual labor. The modern meaning of work as a central aspect of self-affirmation is threatened. What can or will replace these ways of establishing one's identity?

FUNDAMENTAL ETHICAL RULES

Philosophers are uniquely prepared to discuss the question of ethics as it relates to individual man as well as to the counseling relationship. As men ruminate on the clouded shape of the future, the dilemmas regarding individual choice of ethical rules remain a problem of the "here and now." The selection of a style or strategy by which one can give continuity to one's interaction with others becomes increasingly complex.

There is a need for focusing more attention upon the arena of personal decision-making. An area in which individual self-affirmation, reflecting personhood for self and others, is sorely in need of a viable ethic. An ethic, reflecting "not only *sanction* but *obligation*" (Beck, 1967, p. 216) for the decision-maker. The understanding of others with respect to the attendant meaning of the ethic as represented in a specific action is vital. Wolff has written that "to be true to one's principles" is either a metaphor or else an elliptical way of describing loyalty to other men who share those principles and are relying upon you to observe them" (Wolff, 1966, p. 224). Can an increased awareness of ethics increase our expectation that men will focus not only on the act but also upon "Why?" and the ethical rules involved in the decision.

The individual taste of the ethical decision as well as the public consequences suggests the importance of group size upon the individual decision or set of rules. Does the size and psychological proximity of the referent group shape the response and modify the strategy utilized? Buchanan (1965) in a theoretical paper examining the economic utility of ethical rules suggests that it does. Utilizing the concepts of private maxim and moral law he suggests six social states which change the utility of the decision rule if one wishes to maximize his benefits. Do these social states indicate the utility of returning to a tribal way of life as some suggest?

In what way can men understand the individual basis of an ethical choice? "Here I stand;—I can do no other"—Martin Luther's bold defiance is asserted in the first person singular. It is an assumed obligation, not a claim to rights or an assertion of freedom and certainly not, as is true with criminals, an attempt to evade the law. In this context, can actions within the civil rights movement be evaluated (Walzen, 1967)?

A characteristic of those societies to which men and specialized man have belonged has been the evolvement of code ethics. Such codes have rules reflecting traditions and other evolved methods of behaving which are useful to the society in enjoining the individual from acts which injure the society or the picture of that society. Often such codes are characterized by an *always* or *never* series of pronouncements for the individual societal member.

Arranged against the traditional ethics was an individual expedient ethic which suggests that "I do what I do," an ethic depending upon varying measures of utility for the individual as the criterion of choice. Often it took an anti-law or anti-institution form.

More recently, a new theme has been articulated by such individuals as James Pike (1967). He suggests the usefulness of situational or existential ethics. That is, individual decisions must be made in the context of the situation for all parties with no *a priori* answer possible. He indicates that this entails, among other considerations, a responsible approach to all decisions, a rating of persons above things, and an awareness of pertinent factors to be weighed on the scales.

What place does the above consideration of useful ethical rules for clients and other members of society who indirectly are influenced by the contribution of counselors have as the review of efforts and the setting of goals are undertaken by educators and practitioners of counseling?

SUMMARY

The purpose of this discussion has been to suggest possible topics which could serve as a basis for a dialogue with philosophers regarding current practices and goals of counselor educators, philosophers being representative of but one of the areas with whom such discussions might be entertained. In this way counselor education would continue to evolve as a socially efficient and socially responsive profession.

REFERENCES

Arendt, Hanna. *The human condition.* Chicago: University of Chicago Press, 1958.
Barrett, W. *Irrational man.* New York: Anchor Books, 1962.
Beck, C. E. Ethical aspects of change in counselor education, *Counselor Education and Supervision,* Spring, 1967, 6, 216-21.
Buchanan, J. J. Ethical rules, expected values and large numbers, *Ethics,* October, 1965, 76, 1-13.
Boring, E. G. When is behavior predetermined? In Russell, R. E. (Ed.) *Frontiers In psychology.* Chicago: Scott-Foresman, 1964.
Broudy, R. C. Art, science and new values, *Phi Delta Kappan,* November, 1967, 49, 115-19.
Herzberg, F. *Work and the nature of man.* New York: World Publishing Co., 1966.
London, P. *The modes and moral of psychotherapy.* New York: Holt, Rinehart, and Winston, 1964.
Pike, J. *You and the new morality.* New York: Harper & Brothers, 1967.
Walzen, M. The obligation to disobey, *Ethics,* April 1967, 77 163-75.
Wolff, R. P. An analysis of the concept of political loyalty, In Wolff, R. P. (Ed.) *Political man and social man.* New York: Random House, 1966.

MINIMUM CHANGE THERAPY

Leona E. Tyler

Professor of Psychology, University of Oregon, Eugene

I have some misgivings about the problem we are considering today. Any attempt we make to limit the duration of counseling, though we may think of it as a purely quantitative change, may turn out to have large qualitative effects. One of our ground rules, so basic that we seldom even state it explicitly, is that a person is *worth* whatever amount of time and trouble it takes to help him. We do not measure concern and kindness in hours or dollars. It would be as though a mother should say to herself: "Let's see. I can afford to devote 10 years of my life primarily to the nurture of these children. That means that the total amount of time that each of them can claim is 10,000 hours." Instead of thinking in this fashion, a mother naturally assumes that she must give whatever the task demands, without rationing it. An increasing mass of evidence is showing that the optimal growth of a human being requires just this kind of unlimited commitment on somebody's part. Under favorable circumstances, a person has had enormous amounts of love and care devoted to him by the time he reaches maturity.

The experience of having someone really care about him is such an indispensable part of what counseling means for a client that we must be especially careful never to jeopardize it. It is for this reason that I am inclined to doubt the wisdom of setting arbitrary time limits. If what the client understands by the arrangements we make is: "You are worth spending 10 hours on, but no more," an experience he might otherwise have had simply will not occur. It has always seemed to me that there is a big difference psychologically, between limits that are inevitable and obviously necessary, such as those resulting from the end of a school term or the illness of the therapist and those that are arbitrary or unexplained.

However, after all this has been said, the fact remains that to prolong counseling contacts unnecessarily does not do a client any good and may even hamper his further development. And our own full schedules make it imperative that we try to avoid this type of error. Thus we do need to give some thought to the matter of how this can best be done.

CHANGE OR UTILIZATION

My own approach to this and other counseling problems has been to attempt to clarify the nature of the task itself. Elsewhere during the last year

Reprinted by permission of the author and the *Personnel and Guidance Journal,* February 1960, 475-479.

This article was delivered at a symposium on Considerations in Controlling the Duration of Counseling Contacts held by the American Psychological Association in Washington, D. C., August 30, 1958.

I have tried to distinguish between two kinds of helping process. Therapy generally has as its goal personality *change;* counseling attempts to bring about the best possible *utilization* of what the person already has. It is a distinction similar to the one Tolman years ago introduced into learning theory, the difference between learning and performance.

The only trouble with simple, clear-cut classifications like this is that they don't seem to fit a lot of the tasks and situations with which we are confronted. Certainly most of the work we do in facilitating occupational choices and educational decisions can be classified as *utilization* rather than as *change*. But what of the client with major or minor personality problems? Is the treatment we offer in such cases therapy or counseling? Is it perhaps really therapy, but called counseling in order to make it more palatable to him or to the community? It would not be so important what label we used, except that the ambiguity spreads out over our own thinking about what we call therapeutic counseling. And because we are not at all sure what we are trying to accomplish, we never know just when we are through.

What I have been questioning in my own mind more and more is the assumption that therapy should attempt to bring about as much personality change as possible. Could it be largely because of the enormous prestige psychoanalysis has acquired that we tend to assume that personality reorganization is the goal toward which we should strive? Is it really true that the therapy that produces the most changes is the best therapy? Would it not be possible to make the opposite assumption and deliberately set as our goal "minimum-change" therapy? This would be a kind of undertaking that would fit in well with the rest of the activities that go on under the name of counseling. We would try in each case to help the person discover some unblocked path in which he could move forward, develop his unique personality, and thus transcend rather than delve into the anxieties and conflicts in which he is now enmeshed.

I picture this process in terms of a change of *direction* rather than in terms of distances or amounts. The difficulties a client is experiencing can be thought of as indications that he is headed in a direction that is wrong for him or that he has at some former time made a wrong turn into a blind alley. All of this may have occurred without conscious awareness, of course, Counseling can create a situation in which a person may become aware of the directional shifts that are possible for him and in which he can be sure someone will see him through what may be a difficult "rotation of his axis." In pursuing the implications of this geometric analogy a little further I calculated that a directional shift of only 10 degrees makes a difference of 170 miles in where one comes out if his journey is 1,000 miles long — enough to make a considerable difference in terrain and landscape. Similarly, a relatively minor shift in the psychological direction in which a person is moving may well change his life considerably over a long period of years.

This is what I mean by *minimum-change* therapy. It has made it possible for me to see how in principle therapeutic counseling could be shortened considerably without making it any less valuable. It involves no great change in the procedures we use, but some aspects of the complex counseling situation need to be emphasized or even modified to some extent.

Emphasis on Strength

In the first place, it implies that more emphasis than one ordinarily finds be placed on *positive* diagnosis. By and large, our diagnostic thinking rests on concepts taken over from psychopathology. We try to ascertain where a person's weak spots are. Many psychologists, especially in recent years, have criticized this approach and advocated the diagnosis of strengths. In minimum-change therapy we pay no attention to personality weaknesses that are adequately controlled or neutralized. We all have areas like this. It is only the difficulties that are actually blocking the person's forward movement that we must attempt to deal with. And as suggested in the previous section, it is quite possible that these may be by-passed rather than attacked. A person who knows his real strengths and is clear about his basic values may be able to turn away from anxieties about aspects of his life that would be very difficult to change.

Though there is a widespread current interest in ego processes and positive personality traits, we do not as yet have tests we can count on for this sort of diagnostic task. We are more likely to become aware of a person's strengths by observing things he does than by asking him questions. Some of this meaningful behavior occurs in the interview situation itself. For example, when Mary Hart flashes a sudden smile as she is struck with the amusing aspects of a particularly humiliating social experience she is recounting, we know that she possesses an asset that may be of considerable use to her. Call it a defense if you will, but in social situations and in personal emotional adaptation to the vicissitudes of life her ability to laugh at her own predicament will be a valuable asset. Other assets frequently showing up even in interviews where hostility, doubt, guilt, and anxiety are the main themes include moral principles of which the person is absolutely certain, demonstrated courage in the face of adversities, loyalty to those he loves. Whether or not it is advisable for the counselor to reflect or interpret such expressions at the time they occur is another question. But he can make a mental note of them.

We are more likely to become aware of a client's personality assets if we have some knowledge of his life outside the counseling room. In small or moderate-sized colleges, the counselor is likely to encounter his clients here or there — on the street, in the student union, at concerts, plays, or games. The growing practice of placing psychologists on the wards in mental hospitals serves the same purpose of permitting the kind of observation that positive diagnosis is based on. Conversations with a client's family or friends is another resource, but I am strongly of the opinion that it should not be used without the person's knowledge or permission. It is the characteristics he *knows* you have had a chance to observe — the things you can talk over together — that are grist for counseling's mill. In the last analysis, it is the client himself who must make the positive diagnosis we have been talking about if it is to be effective in his life.

Counseling Structure

A second point of emphasis in minimum-change therapy is the way in which the situation is structured for the client. We must take into account *his* expectations and goals as well as our own. To a person profoundly dissatisfied with the way his life has been going, the only thing that really looks good is change — complete change. What he may have read about psychotherapy in popular magazines or seen in movies leads him to expect or at least hope that some fundamental change will occur. True, the experience of countless therapists has shown that such a person will hang on to his unconscious defenses and fight every sort of change at every step of the way. But if anyone *tells* him at the beginning that small shifts of direction rather than larger changes in total pattern are to be expected he is likely to reject the whole undertaking. He thinks he wants to be made over.

It is in this connection that some explicit verbal distinction between counseling and therapy may be useful. Instead of trying to fight the person's wishful dreams about miraculous effects of therapy, I can simply explain that I am a counselor rather than a psychoanalyst and that my job is to help a person find out what his personality is like and decide how he can use the assets he has and get rid of the obstacles that are blocking his progress. If he accepts the situation on these terms, therapeutic counseling can proceed within the framework of the very broad general question "What kind of person are you?" Anything the person wishes to bring up can be considered but we have not committed ourselves to an analysis of all his problems and innumerable childhood experiences out of which they may have arisen.

Necessary Support

A third essential feature of minimum-change therapy is the use of the counseling relationship to reduce the client's anxiety enough to allow him freedom to consider new possibilities. This, of course, is nothing new or at all peculiar to therapy of this type. It seems to be the one common denominator linking together all sorts of diverse procedures. I suppose many workers in the psychotherapeutic vineyard would classify the approach I have been presenting as just another variety of *supportive* therapy. I would have no quarrel at all with that idea were it not that we are so prone to discredit support and to think of it as a superficial palliative measure to be used when more powerful methods are impractical. The idea of support should not be devalued in this way. Obviously by support I do not mean inspirational pep talks, shallow reassurance, or the encouragement of dependence. What I do mean is the act of lending one's own strength to the client for the period during which he needs it, so that he can be certain that his world is not going to fall apart if he moves. I have an idea that this is by far the most important thing we do for our clients, whatever our special theoretical predilections are. It is the crucial factor that enables his own development processes to operate.

I suspect that it would be possible in many cases to furnish this firm support much more economically than we now do if we are willing to use it without working for insight or drastic re-structuring of self-concepts. Once a client has established a new direction for himself, it may well be that regularly scheduled interview hours a month apart may be enough to maintain his courage and confidence. It is the quality of the relationship rather than the amount of time spent in the counselor's presence that constitutes support.

The Closing Phase

This brings us to the last point I wish to make about minimum-change therapy. Its intensive phase is brought to a close as soon as a clear direction has been established in the client's life, even though there are many emotional complexes still unexplored, many interpersonal problems still unsolved. Here again, as in the preliminary diagnosis, evidence from outside the interview room can be combined with what comes up during therapy sessions in judging whether a change of direction has been stabilized. A client may mention casually, without apparently attaching any importance to the remark, something that marks such a significant movement. Mr. Elridge, for example, may speak of having had a long talk with his wife the night before, an action unprecedented in his previous experience. Gwen Riley, who has always been an anxious, perfectionistic procrastinator, may say that she has handed in, on time, an assigned paper for a course she is taking. Or the counselor may note the change in the incidental observation we discussed earlier. When he sees Bill Laraway having a coke with a girl, he knows that Bill has taken the first step toward overcoming the paralyzing shyness of which he has been complaining. A newspaper item stating that Mr. Bellingham has given a talk before the Active Club indicates to the counselor that this client's inferiority feelings are being surmounted. I know that, taken alone, such examples sound trivial. But remember, it is these ten-degree or even five-degree changes in direction that we are trying to facilitate. A small change in the direction of closer emotional ties with one's family or greater willingness to assume responsibility is the kind of shift that has a profound effect on later development. When it is clear that this shift has occurred it is time to think about the termination of formal therapy interviews.

One way of characterizing this kind of therapeutic counseling is to say that its basic premises come from the psychology of development and individual differences rather than from the psychology of adjustment. Its most fundamental assumption is that there are many different ways of living an individual life richly and well, and that it is natural for a person to continue to develop throughout his life in his own unique way. We work with nature instead of fighting or ignoring it.

I have often been struck by the fact that almost any personality trait one can think of may be either an asset or a liability, depending on how it is used. Touchy oversensitiveness to slights and insults is not really basically different from tact and social awareness. Aggression can lead to high achievement as well as murderous rage. Timidity and reasonable caution, compulsiveness and constructive orderliness are opposite sides of the same coins. Instead of bewailing our heredity and the mistakes that were made in bringing us up, perhaps we can learn to turn what we have to good account.

I have been thinking a good deal about the way in which therapeutic counseling of this sort might be evaluated. It is an intriguing thought that the very failure to obtain clear evidence for personality change as a result of therapy may be construed as success rather than failure if we reverse our basic assumption — namely, that maximum change is what we are after. It may even be that Eysenck is right and that no kind of therapy produces change that is greater than that which time and the processes of nature would ultimately have brought about by themselves. The therapist may make a contribution only to the extent that he facilitates or speeds up this natural process. The kind of evaluation I should like to see would be designed to show whether our therapeutic efforts do in fact accomplish this facilitation, so that individuals find their way with less suffering and wasted time with therapy than without. And if so, we need to know what aspects of the help we give contribute most toward this end.

To come back at the end to the topic of this symposium, the point I have been trying to make is that we can best control the duration of counseling contacts by adopting consistently an attitude of respect for what each individual client now is and lending him support and understanding while he comes to terms with this unique self of his. Whether it takes him two hours or two hundred, if he succeeds the effort will have been very much worth while.

$$48$$

REALITY THERAPY AND COUNSELING

William Glasser, M.D.
Los Angeles, California

Reality Therapy is an effective method of psychiatric treatment for people's psychological problems. Although to date its principal applications have been in the treatment of office patients, mental hospital patients, and adult and juvenile lawbreakers, it has been practiced with some success in California schools, especially in the Sacramento area. It has the advantage that it can be taught in a relatively short period of time to teachers, administrators, school nurses, guidance counselors, and psychologists, whether or not they have any previous training in psychology. All that will be possible in this brief account will be a general description of the theory and practice but a book[1] is now available for those who wish to pursue this subject further.

THE THEORY

In order to understand the underlying theory we must assume that everyone has two constant psychological needs. First there is the need to love and to be loved, second there is the need for achievement or self-worth, the feeling that you are worthwhile as a person both to yourself and to others. In each instance these are two-way needs. It is not enough only to feel worthwhile to oneself or to feel worthwhile to other people; both aspects of worth must be satisfied. Similarly, to fulfill the need for love we need not only love others but also to have others love us. In order to satisfy the need to love, therefore,

An original article for this book.
[1]*Reality Therapy — A New Approach to Psychiatry*, William Glasser, M.D.; Harper & Row; New York, 1965.

there must be at least one other person in this world we love and he or someone else must love us. Ordinarily, there are several people who love us and whom we love and, in the case of self-worth, the feeling that we are worthwhile to at least a few people, hopefully many.

With this in mind, what happens if we do not satisfactorily fulfill these two basic needs? Under these conditions we will suffer and our suffering will be manifested either directly, by causing others to suffer, or most often by a combination of these two common conditions. From a treatment standpoint, and Reality Therapy is treatment, it should be emphasized that the way we suffer when we are unable to fulfill our needs is relatively unimportant. In psychological or psychiatric terms, this suffering is manifested as the "symptoms" from which "diagnosis" of the person who has the problem is derived. For example, a person who is unable to fulfill his needs might become psychotic, that is he might withdraw from the real world and try to establish a world of his own, hoping that in his self-created world he might better fulfill his needs. All psychoses, which include schizophrenia, autism, dementia praecox, and other common, but meaningless, psychiatric terms, can be understood as the behavior and thought processes that reflect the suffering of a person unable to fulfill his needs. Why he becomes psychotic is yet unknown but it is a common and not illogical choice for people who are unable to fulfill their needs. In the elementary, junior and senior high schools and in college, we see many evidences of psychotic behavior but we must not be misled by the extremeness of this particular expression of the inability to fulfill one's needs. With this, as well as all other psychological problems, we must understand that psychosis was, or is, the best the person is able to do at the time, but that if we can help him to fulfill his needs, the psychotic behavior will disappear. Psychosis is only one of the many psychological results of inability to fulfill needs. Far more common than psychosis in the school situation are the acting out problems or character problems, exemplified by students who seem to have no regard for the rights and feelings of others or normal social values. They behave irrationally, erratically, and with hostility for seemingly unexplainable reasons. If we examine this behavior in terms of need fulfillment, however, we can discover that the purpose of their behavior is either to gain recognition or attention or is an angry reaction to their inability to gain recognition through socially acceptable pathways. Most often it is a combination of these conditions. Rather than withdraw into a psychosis, the child with character problems fights the world in an attempt to wrest his need fulfillment from it forcibly. The fact that his antisocial methods fail only causes him to increase his unsuccessful struggles; character and behavior problems therefore tend to intensify as the needs are more and more unsatisfied.

In addition to these two main psychiatric catagories or ways in which people suffer, there are many neurotics, people who, unable to fulfill their needs, develop extreme anxiety about this inability. In an effort to free themselves from the anxiety they develop neurotic patterns of behavior — phobias, hysteria, obsessions, compulsions, hypochondriases — all examples of major neuroses. The last major group of people who suffer because they cannot fulfill their needs are those who either become severely depressed or have psychosomatic problems such as stomach ulcers, asthma, migraine headaches, or eczema. Although these kinds of suffering are indirect and difficult to understand, the depressed and psychosomatic sufferer uses these expressions to get attention, recognition and care, as well as to express hostility to the world because he is unable to fulfill his needs. Why one person chooses depression and psychosomatic illness, another psychosis, a third a behavior disorder, and a fourth neurotic behavior is not well known at present and, from the standpoint of Reality Therapy, is unimportant. What is important is to understand that none of these people is able to fulfill his needs. The form of suffering they exhibit, whatever their symptom or diagnostic category, will disappear once we can help them fulfill their needs.

Reality Therapy is a psychiatric treatment which attempts to solve this basic lack for those who are unsuccessful in fulfilling their needs, but it has been derived from careful observation of people who are essentially successful in fulfilling their needs. From this observation one important element has been found which is essential to need fulfillment — people. In order to fulfill our needs we always need someone whom we feel cares about us and thinks we are worthwhile. It is through this person and persons that we gain human involvement, closeness, psychological warmth and emotional ties which are necessary to fulfilling our needs. We assume, therefore, and this may seem to be a drastic assumption to some, that when the person is unable to fulfill his needs, when he is suffering in his own particular way, he does not have anyone close enough to him or involved enough with him emotionally so that he can fulfill his needs. Unless we, whatever our capacity may be, school teacher or psychiatrist, can provide this person, there will be no therapy.

It therefore follows that people who are unable to fulfill their needs and suffer psychologically are isolated, alienated, or separated from people at the time we become aware of their suffering. Further, we may assume that in the majority of cases this isolation from people has been going on for a long time. We will find in using Reality Therapy that intensive review of this misery, commonly referred to as the case history, is unnecessary. No matter how long the isolation has been, what is important to us as therapists is that the individual is isolated now. To help him fulfill his needs we must get enough peronally involved with him to break down his isolation. Whether the therapist is a psychiatrist, psychologist, social worker, school teacher, school psychologist, or administrator, he therefore must, fundamental to Reality Therapy as soon as possible get humanly involved with this suffering person. As limited as the therapist's time may be, he must develop a warm emotional involvement through which the person who is suffering can begin to feel "here is someone who cares enough about me so that I can begin to work toward the fulfillment of my needs, first through him and then through others."

Axiomatic to this process is the concept that the behavior which the suffering person exhibits is always unrealistic. He never engages reality in an adequate way but always distorts it, runs from it, escapes from a portion of it, or suffers at the hands of reality in a way which is always unrealistic. The job of the therapist therefore is not only to get involved with the person but to get involved with him in a way that he is able to present reality to the patient; only if the patient can learn to fulfill his needs within the bounds of reality will he successfully surmount his suffering. What we do is called Reality Therapy because the therapist's primary task, together with his involvement, is to be completely honest in every aspect of his relationship to the patient. Only through behaving within realistic social standards can the patient learn to fulfill his needs, and only after he fulfills his needs will he be able to be relieved of his suffering.

This brief discussion of the theory outlines the therapist's approach which we call Reality Therapy. Theory, however, is worthless unless it can be applied in a reproducible way to various problems. So far this theory has been used successfully in the treatment of adolescent delinquents in institutions, psychotic persons in mental hospitals, patients who come to a psychiatrist in private practice, and children in school situations by teachers, administrators, school nurses, and psychologists. As this theory becomes more well known it will be applicable to other problems, but its application has been successful enough so there is reason to believe it can be applied more widely in schools as one way to cope with the increasing number of school children who present serious problems.

Before explaining the specific application of this theory, I must emphasize that no theory will solve many specific and serious school problems. Children will continue to behave in ways which will baffle the best psychologists and psychiatrists and defy the most intensive work by classroom teachers and administrators. What needs to be established first, and has proven successful in institutions for delinquents and mental patients is a set of principles for working with pupils, principles which if applied through a school system will substantially reduce the number of children who manifest serious psychological problems. The writer therefore emphasizes Reality Therapy as a total approach to the whole school system as much or more than as a specific approach for problem children. If this is utilized, fewer requests will be made of the guidance counselor for individual help, freeing him to assist the classroom teacher in working out solutions for those children who require a more specific application of Reality Therapy to help them to fulfill their needs.

THE APPLICATION OF REALITY THERAPY — THE PROCESS

First and most important the teacher must attempt to get involved with his pupils so that they feel he genuinely cares about them. So that the child understands that his teacher cares, his principal cares, his nurse cares and others in the school really care about him, these people must be personal in their approach to him. This means that in their everyday dealings with children the personal "I" must be substituted for the impersonal "we," "they," "the school," or "It is good for you." As much as possible these impersonal phrases, should be eliminated from the school vocabulary. The teacher's approach should be, "I am interested in you," "I want to teach you," "I want to explain to you what you are doing," "I want to point out to you the things that you might do that are better," "I would like you to behave better for me," "I would like you to do your homework for me," "It is important to me that you are here everyday." These phrases emphasize the personal; they lead to involvement with the child not only as a teacher but as a person who cares about him, who teaches him important things which he needs to know. With this personal approach there is the obvious danger that the teacher, who becomes personally involved as the writer has advocated here, can also be hurt much more than the teacher who remains objective and from the child's point of view, detached. Objectivity, a poor approach to any child, is useless with problem children. They have had too much objectivity. They need personal interest, an immediate involvement with someone so that they can begin to fulfill their needs. Without this, they are helpless to change their behavior.

Although subjectivity is essential in the process of relating to the child, the teacher must take an objective and realistic approach to the child's behavior. Without neglecting his personal interest in the child, the teacher must stress that he cares about what the child does, his school work and his conduct. The behavior of the child must be emphasized more than the child's feelings; the completion of homework, for example, is more important than the fact the child may be upset. Reality Therapy emphasizes behavior and de-emphasizes the feelings or emotions that accompany deviant behavior. Teachers should learn that they can do nothing directly to make a child happy unless they condone bad behavior which is unrealistic — short-lived at best. If the teacher believes that the child behaves badly because he is emotionally disturbed, and that first he must work with the child's feelings, he will fail. Instead he must show little interest in the child's emotional upset and guide his counseling toward behavior by saying, "What is important to me is what you do; if you feel badly, I can't help you but I do know that if you do better you will feel better." This statement, stressing the personal interest of the teacher and the reality of the child's behavior, is the backbone of Reality Therapy. We believe very firmly that bad behavior leads to bad feelings, and that bad feelings can best be corrected by better behavior. We have been unable to correct bad behavior by changing bad feelings into good feelings because we have never been able to do this, even though it is a part of the psychiatry we learned. It just can't be done. Even if it could be done or if, as some may assume, this were a "chicken-and-egg" situation, we have been unable to help children unless the behavioral approach is used.

A further factor in the application of Reality Therapy (in practice these are all interwoven) is the necessity to accept the child as he is now, regardless of his past. In contrast to the teaching of most courses in guidance and counseling, as well as what is ordinarily taught in psychology and psychiatry, we believe that the patient's history, what has happened to him prior to our seeing him, is unimportant for therapy. The statement that our job is to help him, not to understand why he became the way he is, is not facetious. Why he becomes the way he is is important to sociologists and research psychologists who wish to change social patterns, but to help individuals fulfill their needs, the less we know about their history the better. If we can accept that he is doing the best he can do, regardless of how badly he is behaving, then we must accept him as he is. Reality Therapy therefore accepts the child as he is with the understanding that we believe that he can do better. Our emphasis is on what he is doing, on his behavior, and that better behavior will lead to better feelings and further better behavior.

Further, our acceptance of him does not mean we accept any excuse for present bad behavior. The child must understand that no one in the school, above all his teacher, will excuse him for doing something that is wrong. There must be no excuses for the child who disrupts the class, who doesn't do his homework, who doesn't come to school on time, who cuts school classes — any of the common behavior problems. With this approach consistently applied the child will learn that he can do better, that we are interested enough in him personally not to excuse or condone behavior which does not lead to need fulfillment. We never encourage him to look for the reason that he behaves the way he does. We are uninterested in discussing why he has not done his homework, why he disrupts the other children, why he fights, steals, lies, cheats or cuts school. On the other hand, we are extremely interested that we know and he knows what he is doing that is unsatisfactory. All of our discussions with him, brief as they may be, must point out to him what he is doing and ask, "How can this help you?" and "Do you feel that what you are doing is right?" Our job is not to look for excuses but to point out the reality of his behavior and further (this is essential to Reality Therapy) ask him to make a value judgment of his behavior in terms of right or wrong or good and bad.

In our work with patients, school children included, we emphasize the importance of right and wrong. In order to avoid confusion, however, we are careful to derive the definition of right and wrong from the basic needs. By this we mean that any behavior which leads to the fulfillment of the two basic needs, love and self-worth, is right, good, moral, or correct behavior. Any behavior which does not lead to the fulfillment of these basic needs — which necessarily must lead to separation from people, to lack of self-worth or self-demeaning behavior — we classify under the category of wrong behavior. The child must be helped to make this judgment himself (and we find he almost always can), to understand that when he does something right it benefits him because he fulfills his needs and he feels better. As we work with him, therefore, the child quickly discovers that we genuinely care about him and that our care is strong enough that we will not accept excuses for bad behavior. We care because we emphasize what he is doing now, that there are better courses open to him, that the behavior which is disrupting the class is irresponsible, unrealistic and, above all, that it is wrong. Further, he learns that we want to help him find better ways than he has been able to up to now.

Therefore, the last and the most important part of Reality Therapy is to make a plan through which the child can improve his behavior. This plan may take only a few seconds to evoke or it may take up to an hour (more than that is very unusual). The plan must always lead to behavior which will allow the pupil to get some recognition, to gain some satisfaction and to move toward a position where he is able to give and receive more love than before. A hypothetical plan for an elementary school child who is disrupting the class with bad behavior is to talk with him briefly, say that his behavior is not good and that he could do better, and then ask him to do something through which he gains an added sense of self-worth. For instance, he could become a playground monitor, take care of the classroom animals, wash off the blackboards or do any one of innumerable jobs around the school. More than this, to fulfill his need for love he might be asked to help direct other children to do these jobs. A simple plan carried out consistently over a period of time always succeeds in alleviating the less serious behavior disturbances. A more complex plan is necessary for more serious problems, but it usually can be worked out. The plan demonstrates that the teacher cares about him, doesn't accept the bad behavior, but is willing to help him toward doing something definite which will lead in the direction of the fulfillment of his needs.

For each child who fails to adjust, the teacher or the teacher and the administrator together must make some plan and then adhere rigidly to it. The plan always involves the nonacceptance of excuses and much positive reinforcement for what the person can do which is good. As emphasized in the beginning of this section, planning for children who are in serious difficulty in school is always difficult, and the best plan may not work as well once the child is in serious trouble as it might have earlier. We therefore feel it is important to apply these principles to the class situation from kindergarten to prevent serious problems later. Few plans are complex but putting them into action requires strength and a working knowledge of these principles. One public school, the Pershing Elementary School of the San Juan Unified District of suburban Sacramento, has attempted to utilize these concepts as part of a total school program. The following excerpt is contributed by Richard Hawes, Psychologist for the District.

> Donald O'Donnell, Principal of the Pershing Elementary School and I were first introduced to Reality Theory during the early part of the 1963-64 school year. After consulting the school staff, we decided to try to apply the concepts to the Pershing Elementary School, and I also attempted to use these ideas in secondary school counseling. We wondered if the first phase of this therapeutic process, establishing personal relationships, would be possible in a classroom with thirty-five or more pupils and if the achievement of the first phase would actually minimize irresponsible behavior. We wondered whether we could develop specific techniques from these general principles which could be effectively applied in the typical school environment. We hoped to affect the classroom environment so that the pupils' ego development would be enhanced without distracting from the academic responsibilities of the school.
>
> At this time (early 1965) the entire Pershing Staff is engaged in an experimental effort to improve their understanding of the concepts and to develop specific techniques within the classroom. Aside from encouraging an exciting experimental mood throughout the school, and of course, helping individual pupils, the most significant observation so far is the confidence and strength the individual teachers seem to be gaining as their ability to handle classroom behavior problems (which heretofore seemed impossible with the pupil's only hope lying in that elusive phantom — "outside professional help") improves.
>
> Reality Therapy seems to offer a set of psychological concepts relatively conducive to application in the typical school situation by psychologically untrained people. It offers a way to operate with behavior problems immediately in the classroom or school situation. The process of establishing a personal relationship, not allowing irresponsible behavior, and learning new ways to operate or behave is designed to strengthen the function of the ego. As this process is applied by the teacher, it not only affects the pupil but also seems to strengthen the teacher's ego functioning significantly. Herein lies some of its greatest strength and potential. One of the Pershing teachers explained it this way when asked to comment on Reality Therapy: "It is hard to pin down isolated cases because the methods really changed my entire attitude and approach to discipline. It's impossible to isolate one event because one leads to another."
>
> The first case concerns a ten-year-old fifth grade pupil who was originally referred to me as a candidate for the special education program for mentally retarded pupils because of consistently poor grades and his lack of pro-

duction and participation in school. Surprisingly, individual testing showed that this healthy, well-built boy not only had bright-normal intelligence but had mastered the basic academic skills (reading, arithmetic, writing, etc.). His referral to the school psychologist was due to his attitude toward class assignments and almost total lack of achievement. He always seemed to find something else to do instead of the assigned class activity. The teacher's problem was to somehow get this reluctant pupil to experience that feeling of worthwhileness that comes with responsible achievement. This is how she did it: One day during class, Joe (as we will call him) was sitting sprawled at his desk tossing a paper clip into the air when he was supposed to be writing ten spelling words for his homework assignment. Mrs. B. approached Joe at his desk, placed her hand on his shoulder (the personal touch), and gently but with just the right amount of curiosity asked, "What are you doing?" Joe's reaction, and one we've experienced many times with this particular classroom technique, was bewilderment, mainly because teachers frequently say, "Stop doing that," or "Get going on your assignment," or "You'd better go to the principal, young man."[2] He did not know how to respond or what to say. At this time Mrs. B. encouraged him by saying something like: "Joe, tell me what you're doing? Describe it. Tell me and show me what you're doing — put it into words." To this Joe remarked, as he demonstrated tossing the paper clip, "Well, I'm throwing up the paper clip." To which Mrs. B. responded with an enthusiastic smile, "That's right, you are." Joe smiled spontaneously, and at this moment is demonstrated a very solid interpersonal experience which took no more time to transpire than some of the more typical procedures and remarks mentioned above which tend to discourage positive personal relationships and rob the pupil of the opportunity to accept and demonstrate individual responsibility.

At this point Mrs. B. simply asked: "Does that help you do the homework assignment?" Which was followed by Joe's equally simple response, "No." With that, Mrs. B. smiled knowingly at Joe, turned, and went on to another classroom activity leaving Joe with the decision to continue his paper clip tossing or to copy the list of ten words for his homework assignment. In Joe's case, as in many others where we have tried this particular technique, the results were encouraging. As the personal relationship between Joe and Mrs. B. became stronger through similar experiences, his irresponsible behavior began to disappear.

Throughout this episode, Joe was treated with dignity and respect as any person should be. The teacher felt he was worthwhile, and she expressed it by her actions. This not only fulfilled part of one of her basic psychological needs but also helped Joe fill his. A curious thing about this whole process is when one becomes more personally involved and consciously tries to make another feel worthwhile, it's very difficult not to feel more fulfilled yourself. This led another teacher to exclaim, as he became more involved in trying to apply these concepts to the classroom situation, "I don't know if these things I'm trying are doing the kids any good . . . (pause) . . . Yes! I know it's helping them, but man, is it helping me!" This statement reflects the significant insight we have discovered through the application of reality concepts: One important way to help another is to help yourself in terms of ego fulfillment. Feeling worthwhile as a result of engaging in activities which encourage the development of one's own ego

---

[2]These responses by the teacher suggest that she has decided to exercise responsibility over the pupil rather than having the pupil accept and demonstrate responsibility for himself. The statements also do not encourage a positive personal relationship.

in turn puts you in a better position to help another less fortunate with a significantly weaker ego.

Another illustration comes from a high school in the San Juan District and deals with the typical situation of an extremely angry teacher who has had considerable trouble with the student he sent to the administrator. Jane, the student, has had a long-term problem of disrupting classes — usually talking — and not producing in class commensurate with her ability. Her parents are quite upset because she has received several failing notices, and they are pressing her to do better. She is not too happy with school and threatens to drop out when she gets old enough.

Instead of holding a counseling or lecture session to point out why the pupil shouldn't behave as she has (she has been told this a hundred times), Mr. T., the dean, asks, "What happened?" To which Jane replies vaguely, "Oh we just don't get along well." "I know that," Mr. T. says, "but what I want you to tell me now is exactly what happened this period. I want you to tell me what you did, and what you said, and what he did and said." Again, Jane answered vaguely, "Well, I made a little noise and he blew his top. . ." At this point, Mr. T. interrupted, "Hold it, Jane, that's not what I want. I want you to tell me exactly what you did and said, and exactly what Mr. R. (the teacher) did and said."

"Oh, you mean exactly?" Jane queried.

"Yes, exactly," was the reply from Mr. T.

Jane began, "Well, Mary and I were talking in class, making plans for a date when he (Mr. R.) yelled clear across the room to shut up." "What were his words, Jane?" Mr. T. interrupted. To which Jane, mimicking Mr. R., replied: "All right you two, knock it off and get busy."

"What did you say?" asked Mr. T.

"O.K., already," Jane said with a rather sarcastic inflection and loud voice.

"And what did he say to that?"

"He said, 'all right, young lady, that's it for you. We're going to the dean!'"

At this point, Mr. T. (the dean) asks in a low-keyed and nonjudgmental way: "How do you feel it worked out?" (The manner in which this is said is critical. It must be said in a nonjudgmental or nonpunitive way. The main point is that you want the pupil to think critically about what happened.) To which Jane hesitates, then rather indignantly said, "O.K.!" Mr. T. re-responds, "O.K. Have a seat in the outer office and I'll see you a little later." (It is important at this point that the dean does not argue with the pupil. This approach would tend to defeat the build-up of a personal relationship. Isolating Jane at this time gives her a chance to work it over in her own mind without outside interference. The previous short discussion should encourage her to think about the recent class episode.)

At the end of the period she is sent to her next class with the comment, "I enjoyed talking with you, Jane, and I want to talk with you again. I'll call you in a couple of days." In the meantime, the dean meets with the teacher in order to give him a chance to express himself about the pupil which, hopefully, will somewhat relieve the teacher's anxiety. The dean then calls Jane to his office and encourages discussion about anything except the situation which just occurred. The sole purpose is to establish a solid personal relationship and not to focus on the irresponsible act. This is sometimes very difficult for school people to do, especially administrators, counselors and teachers, who feel they need to express their power rather than allow the student to express his feelings. The assumption is, if we are able to successfully develop a personal relationship, the irresponsible behavior which caused the classroom disturbances will tend to disappear. (Assuming, of course, that the pupil has been the irresponsible one and not the teacher.) The sessions are kept brief (between 5 and 15 minutes) because time is a factor in our district when a counselor, for example, is responsible for 500 or more pupils. It is becoming our opinion that if one has an hour to spend with one pupil during one month in order to establish a personal relationship, it is usually better to spend it in six 10-minute or four 15-minute sessions over a period of time rather than one 1-hour session once a month.

We're particularly encouraged at Pershing School, where Daniel O'Donnell and his staff are attempting to learn and apply reality concepts throughout the school's entire environment. We're learning that it is not easy to do this, and that one successful application of the reality procedure does not necessarily guarantee general responsible behavior thereafter by a pupil. However, we are beginning to realize that each situation where these concepts are applied encourages later positive behavior better than the more traditional ways of handling these problems. Mr. O'Donnell put it well when he said, ". . . The process of establishing a personal relationship tends to eliminate the irresponsible behavior and, in the interim, seems to reinforce the teacher's ability to deal with the specific situation and help set the tone for the entire class. Our experiences to date show that teachers can deal effectively with individual pupils with these concepts if the teachers can withstand temporary setbacks of individual unresponsible behavior."

It remains a question of taking the time and effort to think of new techniques and the strength to put them into practice, even though immediate results are at times discouraging. We welcome inquiries from interested school personnel and would be glad to share our experiences as we learn more about this approach to working with people.

(For further explanation of applied Reality Therapy, see "Reality Therapy: A Realistic Approach to the Young Offender" in *Crime and Delinquency,* April, 1964.)

AN OVERVIEW OF THE BEHAVIORAL APPROACH

Patricia Jakubowski-Spector
Washington University, St. Louis

The behavioral field is composed of a wide variety of techniques and therapeutic approaches. The diversity is so great that it has led one leader in the field to remark that he knew of no behavior therapist who would accept as true everything every other behavior therapist suggested (Ullmann, 1967). The field has been known by a variety of names and each label has a somewhat specialized meaning: behavior therapy, behavioral counseling, reinforcement therapy, behavior modification, contingency management, etc. In this overview of the behavioral field, the term *Behavioral Approach* will be used to refer to these diverse therapeutic approaches. This presentation will focus on the major features of the Behavioral Approach.

An original article for this book.

In the last fifteen years the Behavioral Approach has undergone a considerable amount of change and development. The earlier picture of a highly experimental and limited approach is no longer accurate. This overview will focus on some of the latest developments in the field which have relevance for school counseling. Thus, this picture of the Behavioral Approach may be dissimilar to others presented in the literature.

MAJOR FEATURES

The Behavioral Approach has frequently been identified solely with its particular techniques. This has led counselors to view inaccurately the Behavioral Approach as simply a bag of interesting gimmicks. The Behavioral Approach involves a great deal more than a collection of techniques. It also involves two other important aspects: *A particular way of thinking about behavior* and a body of principles drawn from psychological experiments. Of these, the way of thinking about behavior is the most important. When the way of thinking about behavior is grasped, a counselor can use the body of psychological principles to tailor-make techniques to suit the individual needs of clients. When a counselor tries to use the techniques without understanding the Behavioral Approach, he is apt to apply them incorrectly or crudely; for example, trying to extinguish a client's crying before assessing whether the crying is an operant, that is, behavior which is maintained by its consequences, or a respondent, that is, behavior which is in response to a preceding stimulus.

What does the term *behavior* mean? *Behavior is what an organism does* (Schaeffer and Martin, 1969). This includes a person's thinking and feeling behaviors as well as acting behaviors. A growing number of behaviorists advocate this viewpoint (Lazarus, 1969; Ullmann and Krasner, 1969), although there are still some who adhere to the older, more narrow view which is restricted to acting behaviors. Neither view of behavior includes such phenomena as ideal-real self discrepancies, inferiority complexes, and unconscious conflicts, which are thought of as constructs rather than behaviors. The Behavioral Approach deals with those behaviors which are observable (by either the individual himself or another person), definable, and measurable. Behavior is assumed to be learned, lawful, and orderly: an appropriate and reasonable outcome of past and continuing learning experiences and biological processes (Ullmann and Krasner, 1969).

When a behavioral counselor deals with client behaviors, he asks *what* rather than *why* questions. What is the person doing rather than why is he doing it.[1] *Why* questions are typically designed to discover a person's motivations for engaging in a particular behavior, or the original "cause" of the behavior. In contrast, *what* questions are designed to clarify the nature of the behavior and to determine the independent variables which currently control or "cause" the behavior. This is one of the crucial differences between the

---

[1]Other *what* questions which may be posited are—Under what conditions does the person engage in the behavior? What are the consequences of these acts? What precedes the emission of the behavior? What other behaviors could the person emit? What reinforcers are available to the individual? What behaviors will be the focus of counseling efforts? What are the goals of counseling?

Behavioral Approach and insight-oriented approaches. An example may serve to clarify this important distinction.

An Example of *What* versus *Why* Questions

Client Problem

Inability to study

Why can't the person study?

Feels inadequate, insecure. Poor impulse control. Poor self image.

What can the counselor do?

Provide optimum conditions of empathy, positive regard, and genuineness. Help client to realize inner potentialities and reduce blocks to inner growth. Deal with the client's feelings. Work towards insight. Etc.

What is the person doing?

Does attend class and take notes. Is behind in history, reading, and in English papers. Lets studying go until night before exam and then is too nervous to concentrate.

What maintains this behavior?

Has not learned how to organize time. Little reinforcement for studying given by friends. Has learned to feel anxious in certain study situations which leads to avoidance behaviors. Does not know how to organize a paper.

What can the counselor do?

In addition to maintaining a relationship, build a study schedule with the client which gradually shapes increasing amounts of study time. The schedule includes self-administered reinforcements. Teach client how to organize a paper. Teach client relaxation skills to be used when studying. Teach client techniques for studying for exams. Etc.

As can be seen in this example, the client's initial problem (inability to study) is put into behavioral terms before the counselor attempts to deal with it. Behavioral terms mean that the initial problem is defined in terms of specific, clearly identified behaviors (the client is behind in history, reading, and in English papers). A behavioral counselor uses *what* questions to arrive at a behavioral assessment of (1) the current variables which maintain the particular behavior, (2) the individual's potential strengths and limitations for changing the behavior or instituting new behaviors, and (3) the procedures or techniques which may be the most viable and efficient to change the behavior or institute new behaviors.

The Behaviors Approach uses *direct* rather than indirect means to change behavior. This means focusing counseling efforts on the problematic behavior itself, rather than attempting to change the problematic behavior through changing an inner personality construct or dynamic. As illustrated in the example, changing the client's self-concept which, in turn, theoretically changes the person's study behavior is an example of an indirect method. Focusing on the study behavior itself and teaching relaxation skills to be used in study situations is an example of a direct method. In this example the difference between direct and indirect methods is clear. However, sometimes the distinction is not so clear-cut. For example, there may be occasions when a behavioral assessment reveals that the variable which controls the inability to study is worrying about an unwanted pregnancy, or parents' consideration of divorce, or possibility of cancer, and so on. In these situations a counselor may describe the inability to study as a kind of "symptom," which means that he will treat the presenting behavioral complaint (inability to study) by treating some other behavior (fear of pregnancy) (Goldiamond and Dyrud, 1968). This behavioral view of "symptom" does not have the surplus meaning of an underlying pathological process which erupts in symptoms.

An important feature of the Behavioral Approach is using techniques which are based on various psychological principles derived from learning theory research and other psychologically-based research. This may be contrasted with most other counseling approaches which use techniques based on personality theory and research. Insight is not a major counseling tool in the Behavioral Approach. When insight is used it is generally for the purpose of helping the client become *aware* of events which control or influence his behavior so that he can better control or change his behavior. It is in this sense that insight is used and not in the sense of providing an understanding of the pathological process which produces an individual's "symptoms." Insight may also follow rather than precede behavior change in some cases.

In order to use behavioral techniques most skillfully a counselor needs to understand learning theories and psychological research findings. Fortunately there are many good books which can help a counselor supplement his background in this area (Bandura, 1969; Ullmann and Krasner, 1969; Goldstein, Heller, and Sechrest, 1966). In addition there are several articles which review the various principles and techniques (Hosford, 1969A; Grossberg, 1964; Bandura, 1961). It is beyond the scope of this paper to deal with the principles which are used in the Behavioral Approach. However, some of the major techniques which have relevance for school counseling will be reviewed in a later section.

Another important element in the Behavioral Approach is tailor-making techniques and procedures to suit the individual's needs. Beltz (1969) has called the individualizing of specific procedures the *sine qua non* of the Behavioral Approach. Thus, a behavioral counselor would not routinely use techniques, regardless of how effective a technique may have proven to be. Techniques are specified for each individual and are derived after a careful assessment of the individual's problem.

In a summary, the Behavioral Approach to counseling involves a particular view of behavior and a set of procedures that are intended to alter a person's behavior directly through the application of general psychological principles which are derived from learning theories and psychologically-based research.

RELEVANT TECHNIQUES

In this section various behavioral techniques will be discussed in terms of their research supports and possible use by school counselors. Systematic desensitization and relaxation procedures are usually thought of as being in the reciprocal inhibition framework. Wolpe (1958) developed the reciprocal inhibition principle: *If a response which inhibits anxiety (e.g. relaxation) can be made to occur in the presence of anxiety-evoking stimuli (e.g. tests), that response (relaxation) will weaken the bond between these stimuli (tests) and the anxiety responses.* According to this principle, the response which inhibits anxiety and the anxiety cannot simultaneously occur because they are incompatible. Theoretically, one cannot be relaxed and anxious at the same time.

Systematic Desensitization

In a conventional systematic desensitization procedure, the counselor and the client work together to construct a hierarchical list of anxiety-evoking situations in a graduated sequence from barely to intensely anxiety-evoking: seeing a girl, walking toward the girl, asking for a date, and others. (For a more complete illustration of this technique see Paul, 1966.) The client is taught how to relax his body, and he practices these relaxation skills at home. When the hierarchy is constructed and the client has learned how to relax, the systematic desensitization procedures are undertaken. The client is instructed to imagine an anxiety-evoking scene *while he is relaxed.* When he feels anxious, he stops imagining the scene and relaxes those parts of his body which became tense. After he is relaxed, he again imagines the scene. In successive desensitization sessions the client gradually imagines greater anxiety-evoking scenes. According to the reciprocal inhibition principle, the scenes will gradually lose their ability to evoke anxiety. This theoretically generalizes to the actual situations in the client's life.

Wolpe (1958) published the first statistical study regarding the efficacy of nine years of behavior therapy, based on the reciprocal inhibition principle. He reported that eighty-nine per cent of the 210 clients he had seen had either apparently recovered or were much improved in nearly thirty sessions. In a recent review, Paul (1969B) examined seventy-five papers which covered the application of systematic desensitization to nearly 1,000 different clients by over ninety different therapists and concluded:

> The findings were overwhelmingly positive, and for the first time in the history of psychological treatments, a specific therapeutic package reliably produced measurable benefits for clients across a broad range of distressing problems in which anxiety was of fundamental importance. "Relapse" and

"symptom substitution" were notably lacking, although the majority of authors were attuned to these problems. (p. 159)

Paul (1966) provides the most adequate comparative evaluation of systematic desensitization with insight-oriented counseling to date. College students who had severe fears of speaking in public each received five sessions of either systematic desensitization, insight-oriented counseling, or attention-placebo. The results showed significantly superior effectiveness for systematic desensitization on a variety of measures. Eighty-six per cent of the clients treated by systematic desensitization were much improved and fourteen per cent were improved. This compared with twenty per cent much improved and twenty-seven per cent improved for the insight-oriented group. In the attention-placebo group none were much improved and forty-seven per cent were improved.

Some of the problems for which systematic desensitization procedures have been successfully employed include anxieties about tests (Emery, 1969; Weinstein, 1969), public speaking (Paul, 1966, 1968), and school (Garvey and Hegrenes, 1966). Additional cases are reported in Paul (1969B), Bandura (1969), and Krumboltz and Thoresen (1969).

Although Paul (1969B) gave systematic desensitization a highly favorable review, other writers have not been so enthusiastic. Lazarus (1969) contends that conventional systematic desensitization is not very effective in reducing phobias and anxieties, but he still has hope that "improved results can be obtained by modifying conventional desensitization techniques." This position actually helps school counselors who, by virtue of inadequate training or disinterest, would probably find little use in conventional systematic desensitization procedures. Lazarus (1969) believes that techniques like behavioral rehearsal (Lazarus, 1966) and direct instruction in rational and assertive behavior (Ellis, 1962) produce rapid and longer-lasting results than conventional systematic desensitization. Lazarus and Abramovitz (1962) have used a variation of systematic desensitization which involved emotive imagery, in which the child imagines pleasant scenes which arouse feelings of self-assertion, pride, and affection. As these anxiety-inhibiting feelings are aroused, the child imagines the anxiety-evoking stimulus (dogs). Emotive imagery may be a useful technique for elementary school counselors. Hosford (1969B) used role-playing situations instead of visualized scenes to desensitize a child to anxiety in certain school situations.

In summary the systematic desensitization procedure appears to be highly effective, particularly if some modifications are made in its conventional use. Systematic desensitization seems to work even though there is much controversy regarding how it works (Murray and Jacobson, in press). School counselors would be able to make the most use of variants of systematic desensitization, rather than the conventional systematic desensitization procedure, which requires additional training and is often time-consuming and exceedingly boring. Elementary school counselors in particular may be able to use emotive imagery procedures in the context of traditional play therapy.

Relaxation Training

In relaxation training, the counselor teaches a client how to relax his body through a set of exercises which successively tense and release gross muscle groups, with accompanying sensations of relaxation, warmth, and calmness. The relaxation training is often a shortened version of Jacobson's (1938) "progressive relaxation training" and may resemble some of the warming-up techniques that are sometimes used in sensitivity groups.

Relaxation training has typically been used in conjunction with systematic desensitization rather than as a procedure in itself. When relaxation training alone has been compared with systematic desensitization, relaxation alone does not seem to significantly reduce phobic behavior (Lang, Lazovik, and Reynolds, 1965). In these studies relaxation was not coupled with any instructions in how to use it when dealing with feared situations. Graziano and Kean (1967) found that relaxation training alone significantly reduced autistic children's high excitement behaviors. The relative calmness also generalized beyond the original training situation. Laxer *et al.* (1969) found that relaxation training was more effective in reducing *general* anxiety for test-anxious secondary school students than systematic desensitization. Zeisset (1968) presents evidence that relaxation training plus discussion and instructions on how to use relaxation in specific stressful interpersonal situations was as effective as desensitization with male psychiatric patients who complained of interview anxiety. Zeisset (1968) concludes that relaxation plus application training could be useful in many situations where systematic desensitization is not practical or possible. In addition it provides the client with a procedure he can use by himself when counseling is terminated. Zeisset's study suggests that relaxation training coupled with instructions may produce some specific effects.

The author knows of school counselors who have successfully used relaxation training coupled with instructions for test anxiety, stuttering, and insomnia. Cautela (1969) contends that

> Relaxation . . . can be considered a self-control technique in its own right: first, when it is used to reduce the overall anxiety level, and second, as a means of decreasing anxiety or tension whenever the patient is either involved in a readily identifiable anxiety-provoking situation, or is experiencing anxiety without being able to discern the antecedent conditions. (p. 328)

In addition, relaxation training may also help an individual to feel in greater control of his own behavior and thus increase his self-esteem and self-confidence.

In summary, although the use of relaxation as a procedure in itself has not been extensively researched, the available research supports its use when it is coupled with specific instructions in how to use relaxation in specific situations. Relaxation training looks like a promising counseling technique, although little is known about its strengths and limitations at this time. Counselors who are not familiar with the relaxation training procedure can consult Emery (1969), Wolpe and Lazarus (1966, Appendix 4), or Paul (1966) for a detailed description of the relaxation exercises. It is a technique that school counselors could easily add to their armamentarium.

Operant Procedures

Operant procedures involve modifying behavior through changing the incidence and sometimes the nature of the reinforcing consequences that the

behavior produces by providing positive consequences for desired behavior
and no consequences or aversive consequences for undesired behavior (Bandura, 1969). When a behavior occurs and is followed by positive consequences
(reinforced), the likelihood that it will occur again in a similar situation is
increased (Skinner, 1953, 1969).

The use of positive consequences or reinforcement *per se* is not new. What
is new is knowing when and how to use reinforcement. In the operant procedure, a reinforcer is given only on a contingent basis, which means that
the desired behavior must occur *before* a reinforcer is given. Four elements
are necessary in any change program which employs operant procedures: (1)
The reinforcers which are used must be potent enough to increase the probability that the behavior will be repeated; (2) The reinforcers must be
applied systematically; (3) The reinforcers must be made contingent upon
the emission of the desired behavior; and (4) The behavior which is to be
reinforced must be able to be elicited (Hosford, 1969A).

Operant procedures have been extensively employed in the modification
of diverse maladaptive behaviors like autism (Wolf, Risley, and Mees, 1964),
anoxeria nervosa (Bachrach, Erwin, and Mohr, 1965), and school phobias
(Patterson, 1965). A number of studies which have utilized positive consequences for modifying maladaptive behaviors have been collected in several
case studies books (Krumboltz and Thoresen, 1969; Ulrich, Stachnik, and
Mabry, 1966; Ullmann and Krasner, 1965; Eysenck, 1964).

In most of these cases the counselor has had control over the reinforcements the clients received from significant others in his environment. However, many school counselors do not have such control, particularly when the
sessions are conducted almost entirely in the counselor's office. In these cases,
the counselor can help a client learn how to alter his own contingencies and
reinforce himself when he has performed in desired ways. Of course, throughout the sessions the counselor would be using reinforcement to encourage the
student to discuss his problematic behaviors, etc. Most school counseling
probably bears little resemblance to the published research studies, which use
reinforcement to modify extreme maladaptive behaviors, for two reasons: (1)
School counseling is typically focused on client behaviors which are not clear-
cut, such as inability to study or make friends, as opposed to the clear maladaptive behaviors, like psychotic verbalizations, which are the focus of much
of the published counseling studies in the literature; and (2) The reinforcers
which are used in school counseling are usually verbal and embedded in the
nature of the counseling itself, as opposed to the clear-cut reinforcers (food,
tokens) which are used to modify grossly maladaptive behaviors like autism.
Goldiamond and Dryud (1968) wisely point out that what may be a critical
reinforcer in counseling is change in the problematic behaviors outside of the
office. "Events in the session which are related to such change may thereby
become linked to them as reinforcers themselves" (p. 74). If this is true, most
counseling involves a great deal of reinforcement which is not easily discernible. So, although the use of reinforcement to alter behavior has been
widely researched and found to be extremely effective, this procedure is one
that a school counselor may have difficulty in clearly implementing in his
counseling. Perhaps the most valuable thing he can do is be very aware of
the importance of reinforcement and attempt to make judicious use of this
technique even though he may seldom be sure that client change is due to

his use of reinforcement. Perhaps school counselors can make the most use of operant-reinforcement procedures for developing client self-control.

Operant Procedures for Developing Self-Control

An operant-based self-control program may be concerned with decreasing undesired behaviors such as stealing, or increasing desired behaviors such as studying.

Behavior that is immediately self-reinforcing, such as overeating, tends to occur in a wide variety of situations. One way of developing client self-control is to alter the stimulus conditions under which the behavior usually occurs and progressively limit these situations until the behavior is brought under the control of a specific set of stimulus conditions. Ferster *et al.* (1962) employed this method with people who overate. He instructed them to eat only in highly restricted situations, for example, at a dining room table covered with a purple cloth. Similarly, effortful behavior (studying) that is initially under weak situational control can be gradually brought into control by the individual. Fox (1962) instructed students who could not study to use one specific place (a desk) to study, from which all potentially distracting stimuli were removed. Fox (1962) and Goldiamond (1965) use essentially the same procedures for developing self-control for studying.

A second operant-based method for self-control involves the individual's interrupting the chain of behaviors which lead to the emission of an undesired behavior (Ferster *et al.*, 1962). When a counselor works with a client who wants to control his food intake, the counselor can instruct his client to interrupt the chain of food-ingestion behaviors by writing in a notebook, at the time the food-ingestion impulse is experienced, how much he intends to eat, what is happening at the time, and his thoughts and feelings. This may achieve three purposes: (1) When the student has completed his notes, he may decide not to eat; (2) The notes provide the counselor and client with added information which may be useful for constructing other self-control procedures; and (3) The notes provide a clearer picture of the nature of the overeating habit. A similar procedure may be followed when a student frequently fails to come to school. The counselor and the client can examine the chain of behaviors which start with waking in the morning and end at walking into the school door to determine where the chain breaks down. Self-control measures may be instituted at that point, for example, if friends on the bus dissuade the student from going to school, the student could possibly arrange to take another bus at a different time, or the student may be taught how to be more assertive with his friends.

A potentially valuable operant self-control technique utilizes self-administered reinforcements.[2] This procedure may be particularly helpful for increasing desired behaviors. Homme (1965) has utilized a self-reinforcing procedure based on Premack's (1959) differential probability hypothesis, "For any pair of responses, the more probable one will reinforce the less probable one." If a client wants to increase his studying behaviors, the counselor and the client determine the behaviors the client engages in frequently, such as watching

---

[2]Skinner (1953, p. 237) comments that "The place of operant reinforcement in self-control is not clear."

TV, talking with friends, daydreaming, and others. Then these so-called high-probability behaviors are made contingent upon the client's studying (a low-probability behavior). A system is devised in which the student studies a certain amount of material and then administers a reinforcement to himself, that is, a high-probability behavior like daydreaming or talking with a friend. The amount of studying is gradually increased (shaped). In this way the individual can gradually bring the studying behavior under control until, hope-fully, studying in itself becomes self-rewarding. The valuable contribution that Homme and Premack have made is conceptualizing reinforcers in terms of high-probability behaviors rather than behaviors which are enjoyable, although, to be sure, many high-probability behaviors are pleasant. So instead of asking a client what he finds *pleasurable,* a counselor asks what he *does frequently.*

Homme (1965) believes that the same procedure can bring covert behavior (thoughts) under control. For example, by making drinking coke (high-probability behavior) contingent upon thinking, "I am a worthwhile person" (low-probability behavior), the thought will theoretically increase in fre-quency. The assumption is made that "symbolic covert events obey the same psychological laws as overt behavior" (Bandura, 1969, p. 239). There is some evidence that self-administered reinforcement can maintain behavior (Cautela, 1970; Bandura and Perloff, 1967). Cautela (1970) recently presented an exciting approach in which the reinforcer is presented by the individual him-self in imagination. In this procedure the counselor has the individual imagine himself engaging in a desired behavior after which he imagines a reinforcing stimulus occurring. Cautela (1970) reports on various cases in which he used this covert reinforcement procedure for modifying avoidance behaviors and obsessive-compulsive behaviors. He also reports on the unpublished research of Cautela, Steffan, and Wish (1969) who found strong support for the hypothesis that reinforcement in imagination can increase the probability of behavior's occurring.

In another operant-based self-control method, Ferster *et al.* (1962) used an imaginary aversive consequence to reduce undesired behaviors. The indi-vidual selects an ultimate consequence (UAC) of the undesired behavior which can be used as a covert negative reinforcer. For example, when the individual smokes, he immediately imagines an ultimate aversive consequence of smoking, as being told he has incurable cancer. To the extent that suf-ficiently aversive consequences of the behavior can be created, the undesired behavior may be significantly reduced. This procedure may be very valuable in those cases in which a person typically does not consider any aversive consequences of the behavior at the time he engages in the behavior. This employment of ultimate aversive consequences (UAC) is very similar to a covert sensitization procedure.

In a covert sensitization procedure a client imagines an aversive or anxiety-producing stimulus (becoming nauseated and vomiting) as he is about to commit the problem behavior (take an alcoholic drink). In the UAC pro-cedure the individual uses an aversive consequence which realistically could occur if he engaged in the undesired behavior for a long period of time. In contrast, in the covert sensitization procedure the individual uses any stimulus which is aversive or anxiety-producing. In addition, each procedure is ex-plained by different learning principles. The UAC procedure is thought to be in an operant paradigm, while reciprocal inhibition or counterconditioning is thought to be operating in covert sensitization. Because these two procedures are so extremely similar, the author has viewed them as being essentially the same for all practical purposes.

A number of studies indicate that covert sensitization has been effective in successfully modifying such behaviors as alcoholism (Ashem and Donner, 1968), overeating (Stuart, 1967), sadistic fantasy (Davison, 1968), compulsive behavior (Cautela, 1966), and misbehavior at home (Davison, 1969). In addition, Paul's (1969A) research provides some experimental support for covert sensitization. For a more specific description of the covert sensitization procedure, a counselor can consult Cautela (1969, 1967) and Davison (1969).

There is ample anecdotal evidence indicating that these operant-based self-control procedures are effective in modifying behavior. However, lacking is the experimental evidence which is needed to determine precisely how these procedures work and how self-control procedures will affect the future probability of a particular maladaptive behavior. It is not known how self-control procedures will affect an individual's life over a long period of time.

In the meantime, school counselors could make good use of these methods, which are relatively easy to employ and are desirable ways of teaching clients how to rely upon their own resources for dealing with problems. Additionally, self-control methods may have far-reaching consequences for the individual who knows that he can control his own behavior. There is some support for this in the literature. Rehm and Marston (1968) found a reduction in social anxiety and an increase in social adaptation as a result of self-reinforcement procedures.

Operant Token Economies

A token economy is a system which sets the rules for giving tokens or points contingent upon the emission of predetermined desired behaviors; tokens may be later exchanged for a variety of reinforcers.

Token economies have been widely applied in a variety of situations, such as for school dropouts (Clark, Lackowicz, and Wolf, 1968; Wolf, Giles, and Hall, 1968), pre-delinquent boys (Phillips, 1968), classroom disorders (O'Leary and Becker, 1967; Barrish, Saunders, and Wolf, 1969), and study behaviors (Hall, Lund, and Jackson, 1968), with such creative innovations as using free time as a reinforcer in the management of classroom behavior (Osborne, 1969). The aim of Cohen's (1968) token economy for juvenile delinquents was having the adolescents engage in various academic behaviors and thereby improve their academic performances. Points could be earned for high achievement scores in programmed instruction courses and related academic activities. These points could then be exchanged for a variety of reinforcers, such as privacy, access to a game room, merchandise, and others.

The research literature strongly supports the use of token economies. Counselors who are interested in working with teachers could make good use of this procedure. The strength of a token system is that it can produce changes in a relatively short period of time and can be effectively used for either an entire class or a few individuals within a class. This procedure would also extend the counselor's influence to larger groups of people. Counselors who wish to know more about token economies should read the *Journal of Experimental Analysis of Behavior* and Madsen and Madsen's (1970) book which contains anecdotal reports of various types of reinforcement systems that have been used successfully by teachers. Cantrell *et al.*'s (1969) contingency contracting work would also be a useful resource.

Modeling

Social modeling procedures involve the provision of a live or symbolic model who demonstrates particular behaviors to an observer, and the observer's behavior changes vicariously through observation of the model's behavior and its consequences for the model (Bandura, 1969).

One aspect of the modeling literature has been concerned with the use of models to effect changes in an individual's verbal behavior. Heller (1968) has reported on the unpublished papers of Marlatt *et al.* and Zerfas which deal with modeling. Marlatt, Jacobson, Johnson, and Morrice (1966) found that college volunteers, who had prior exposure to a model who disclosed personal problems, exhibited similar problem-admitting behavior in their own personal interviews, when consequences to the model's behavior were either passive acceptance or active encouragement. Psychotic patients increased their participation in group therapy sessions after exposure to modeling procedures (Zerfas, 1965). Similarly, exposure to a talkative model significantly increased verbalizations of chronic schizophrenics (Wilson and Walters, 1966). Institutionalized patients who heard a tape of "good" client behavior showed significantly higher levels of interpersonal exploration in group psychotherapy (Truax, 1963). More recently Truax and Wargo (1969) used their tape of "good" client behavior as a "vicarious therapy pretraining" with neurotic outpatients and found that the group which has prior exposure to the client model showed significantly greater improvement on a number of MMPI scales. Myrick (1969) presented a client who modeled self-reference statements on audio and video tape to eighth-grade students. Those who heard the model tended to increase self-references in a subsequent counseling interview. Although exposure to models tends to influence the nature of the verbal behaviors which occur in subsequent interviews, there are indications that the model's sex, the nature of the setting, and the way the model is presented affects observers in ways which are not yet clearly understood (Whalen, 1969; Heller, 1969; Thoresen, 1969).

For some types of clients and problems it may be desirable to use modeling procedures to modify the client's verbal behaviors in the counseling session. However, more importantly, counseling efforts should be directed to using modeling procedures to change the client's behavior *outside* of the office rather than within the counseling hour.

Krumboltz and his associates (Krumboltz and Schroeder, 1965; Krumboltz and Thoresen, 1964; Krumboltz, Varenhorst and Thoresen, 1967) have focused their efforts on using modeling procedures to change behavior outside of the office. They have found modeling procedures to be effective in increasing high school students' vocational information-seeking behavior. Bandura and his associates (Bandura, Grusec, and Menlove, 1967; Bandura and Menlove, 1968) used modeling procedures to help nursery school children overcome their fear of dogs. They used peers as models who interacted with dogs in a variety of ways. Modeling procedures have been used to teach psychotic children to perform a variety of self-care and social behaviors (Lovaas, Freitas,

Nelson, and Whalen, 1967; Metz, 1965). Modeling has also been used with hyperactive children who were exposed to films of child models studying and attending in classroom situations (Nixon, 1966). Heller (1969) reports on encounter group films that are being used to facilitate interpersonal openness in sensitivity groups. Sarason and Ganzer (1969) used modeling procedures to prepare unemployed juveniles for job application interviews.

In summary, the research has indicated that modeling procedures have generally been effective for developing a variety of new patterns of behavior and for modifying existing behaviors. (See Bandura, 1969; Bandura and Walters, 1963, for excellent summary reviews of modeling research.) Unfortunately, much of the modeling research has been with children in special laboratory situations. There is a paucity of research dealing with modeling procedures which have been employed in therapy-like situations. (A notable exception is the recent work by Hansen *et al.*, 1969.) There is a danger of extrapolating directly from laboratory research to the therapy situation without benefit of some intervening studies (Heller, 1969). Little is known about the factors that facilitate modeling effects in counseling settings, particularly for adults and adolescents, as well as for what types of clients and problems modeling approaches may be particularly useful. As the literature now stands, the elementary school counselor may be able to make the most use of modeling procedures since the majority of research has been directed to children.

At this time high school counselors will have to rely on the modeling literature which is predominately anecdotal. The literature on role-playing is an example of such anecdotal material. Role-playing is a kind of dramatization in which an individual play-acts a particular role or a set of particular behaviors. A client may role-play those behaviors he wishes to adopt such as being more assertive in asking a girl for a date, asking for the family car, and so on. The counselor typically plays the role of the other person involved in the interaction. The counselor may also change roles with the client and demonstrate more effective behaviors or alternative ways of handling situations. It seems obvious that role-playing extensively involves modeling procedures. Role-playing is an integral part of assertive training (Wolpe, 1969; Wolpe and Lazarus, 1966) and behavior rehearsal (Lazarus, 1966). Unfortunately, there is a paucity of experimental research on role-playing even though this is a procedure which many behavioral counselors often use.

The current literature on modeling procedures appears to be a wealthy resource for school counselors to consider, especially elementary school counselors. Modeling, however, needs more additional research in therapy-like situations before it can be readily incorporated into the school counselor's armamentarium of counseling techniques.

ISSUES

The Behavioral Approach has received a variety of criticisms, the most important of which seem to revolve around three main issues: What is the role of learning theory in the Behavioral Approach? How important is the counseling relationship in this approach? What are the ethical implications of this approach?

Regarding the Learning Theory Base

It has been pointed out that not only is there no learning theory which is accepted by all theorists but also that such key concepts as stimulus and response do not carry the same meaning when applied in a counseling setting as when they are applied in a laboratory setting (Breger and McGaugh, 1965). In addition it has been noted that the Behavioral Approach makes use of concepts other than learning theory concepts as a basis for some of its techniques, for example, using white noise to reduce stuttering (Yates, 1970B).

These criticisms are essentially true. Behaviorists are lately beginning to agree that the Behavioral Approach does not rest on learning theory *per se* but rather on learning theory research and other psychologically-based research (Yates, 1970A). Unfortunately, there are still some who talk about the Behavioral Approach in terms of its being based on "modern learning theory" (Eysenck, 1970), which thus propagates this misunderstanding about the position of learning theory in the Behavioral Approach.

It must be pointed out that just because there is no single universally agreed upon learning theory, this does not mean that the Behavioral Approach is invalid. The techniques which the approach makes use of have been found to be generally effective even if they are subject to conflicting learning theory explanations, or have no relationship to learning theory as currently developed. So although this criticism is accurate, it does not necessarily constitute a very great threat because the foundations generally rest on research findings rather than theory *per se*.

Regarding the Counseling Relationship

It has been said that the counseling relationship is responsible for client changes rather than the behavioral techniques which are employed (Patterson, 1969), that the counseling relationship is a necessary and sufficient condition for change to occur.

As far as I know, behaviorists have always viewed the counseling relationship as an important aspect of most counseling efforts, although it has not been until recently that this has been explicitly stated in the literature (Klein, Dittman, Parloff and Gill, 1969). Behaviorists view the counseling relationship as usually necessary but often insufficient to effect changes.

The Behavioral Approach uses relationship factors in its counseling. Indeed many of its techniques are so confounded with these factors that it is difficult to separate the effects of the techniques from the effects of the relationship. Even when the desensitization procedure is presented to a client on audio tape, one might argue that the human voice on the tape has an element of an interpersonal relationship (Patterson, 1969)! One might also argue that the behavioral techniques which are used by a counselor could be viewed as ways of establishing the relationship and helping it to grow deeper and more meaningful.[3] Techniques may even be necessary in order for the relationship to develop!

Conversely, the relationship-oriented approaches also appear to have behavioristic elements embedded in their counseling. The genuineness, empathy,

---

[3]My appreciation is extended to Dr. Robert Easton for bringing this point to my attention.

and warmth in the relationship may function as general potent reinforcers (Truax and Carkhuff, 1967). Truax (1966) has found that Rogers uses selective positive reinforcement in his counseling. The relationship itself may hinge on the counselor's ability to establish himself as a positive social reinforcer for his clients! It may be that both approaches are looking at the same phenomena with different perspectives. Perhaps when the smoke clears we may discover that in some respects the behaviorists and the relationship-oriented people are not so terribly far apart after all.

It is true that there are clients who seem to thrive on the relationship itself, who can easily translate insights into changed behaviors. For these clients, it may well be that they have the needed behaviors in their repertoire and that the relationship itself may be sufficient to unlock the door to these behaviors which are already present. But there are many more clients who are not in this position, who need additional help in strengthening the behaviors they already possess, to build in new behavior patterns. For these clients, the relationship itself is not sufficient and specific techniques are mandatory to effect the desired changes.

Ethical Implications

Any approach which effects behavior change involves ethical issues. Two main ethical implications of the Behavioral Approach will be discussed: the behavioral view of man and the behavioral use of influence.

Image of Man

In the Behavioral Approach, man is viewed as an experiencing organism with a potential to learn a variety of behaviors which our society variously labels as good, bad, and so forth. He generally has no predisposition to emit good, bad, or conflicted behaviors. His behavior is viewed as being lawful and as being a function of biological factors and environmental consequences. In practice this view usually inspires a certain optimism because learned unadaptive behaviors theoretically can be unlearned and man can learn more effective and potentially meaningful ways of living.

Since this image of man emphasizes the specific behaviors that man emits, it has been suggested that this image may promote a fragmented picture of man, which is of concern in today's increasingly fragmented and alienated society (Maes, 1969). This *is* of concern *if* this view of man becomes disseminated to the lay public, because this view may exacerbate the already present feelings of fragmentation.

This emphasis on specific behaviors rather than on the wholeness of behavior is a mixed blessing. On the one hand it may promote a fragmentation of man, while on the other hand it is precisely this emphasis on specific behaviors which enables a counselor to define a client's problem in workable terms. For instance, defining insecurity in terms of specific behaviors may mean that a client fails to make decisions, or cannot be assertive with friends, or avoids taking risks in social situations, or compares himself unfavorably with a sibling. This specifying of particular behaviors often enables a client to see himself more clearly as a generally adequate person who has some specific areas or behaviors that are problematic. To change this focus on the specificity of behaviors gains wholeness and lessens productivity of counseling efforts. It is clear that seeing man as an eco-person, a whole person in relationship to his environment, and seeing man in terms of specific behavior patterns that are maintained by particular environmental consequences are both needed for maximum counseling effectiveness and minimum negative effects.

Of greater ethical concern than the possible fragmentation of man is promoting depersonalization and the treatment of others as objects. In the Behavioral Approach a greater emphasis is placed upon change and devising methods to promote change, and a lesser emphasis is placed on the people involved in the relationship itself. This greater emphasis on behavior change may lend itself to depersonalization. There is some support for this concern in the literature. Stuart (1969) reports using an operant-interpersonal treatment for severe marital problems, where counseling was the last resort. A token system was employed for four couples in which the wife gave her husband tokens for engaging in conversation with her, which he could later exchange for sexual favors. In this case there is an ethical concern that the people may view each other as objects to be manipulated for self-gratification and view their marriage as a kind of barter. It is also generally known that Wolpe and Lazarus (1966) feel it is entirely proper to encourage a husband to seek out a more responsive woman when his wife fails to provide him with the physical and affectional relationship that is necessary to help him overcome an impotency problem. Although it might be argued that these two situations are not examples of depersonalization, at the least they do raise ethical concerns. There may be a certain danger of training clients to react to others as objects to be manipulated. The counselor who uses powerful techniques for inducing behavior change will need to be ever careful that the use of power does not corrupt him.

Another ethical implication of the Behavioral view of man is that a client may depersonalize himself and learn to view himself as a kind of object which he manipulates. This kind of ethical concern is, of course, most relevant when the various self-control techniques are utilized and should be taken into consideration when these techniques are employed. However, I do not think that this ethical problem will frequently occur.

If it is true as Wolfe (1968) suggests that a person's image of man is actually identical with his sense of self and that there is a direct relationship between man's image of himself and his behavior, then the image of man as presented thus far by the Behavioral Approach is clearly of ethical concern.

The Use of Influence

Any approach that changes behavior raises ethical questions about using that influence justly, and whenever influence is used, behavior control inevitably exists (London, 1969; Kelman, 1968). Some influence and behavior control are not only desirable but also necessary for the maintenance of our society and culture. An important ethical question is whether influence will be used to limit man's freedom, freedom being

> . . . the individual's capacity *to know that he is the determined one,* to pause between stimulus and response and thus to throw his weight, however slight it may be, on the side of one particular response among several possible ones. (May, 1967, p. 175)

Freedom is also "man's capacity to be conscious of himself as the experiencing individual" (May, 1967, p. 174). Kemp (1967) also sees freedom as awareness of the self. But freedom means more than conscious understanding; it also means the ability to control one's self, one's behavior. If I can only understand *why* I procrastinate but cannot control my procrastination, then I am not very free. Similarly, if I can only respond in one way to a situation, to withdraw as an angry person, then I am not very free. I am not free to engage in a variety of behaviors.

The Behavioral Approach can help man to increase both kinds of freedom, the ability to understand and control one's own behavior and the ability to respond in a variety of ways to situations. By using *what* questions (In *what* situations does your behavior change? *What* environmental consequences follow your behavior?), the client can become more conscious of the forces which act upon his life. Self-control procedures can also help a person learn how to control his behavior in desired ways and thus expand his sense of personal freedom. This is extremely important. London (1969, p. 212) points out, "If behavior technology endangers freedom by giving refined power to controllers, then the antidote which promotes freedom is to give more refined power over their own behavior to those who are endangered." It is in this way that the behavioral influence is utilized to increase human freedom.

Of course, influence can also be used to limit freedom, for example, using the token system in a classroom of normal youngsters to keep them quiet all day. Whether token systems or other behavioral techniques will be used to promote conformity will depend on the values of the counselor and the society. If the counselor defines mental health as a strict conformity to the prevailing societal mores and folkways, any deviance from the established and accepted patterns of behavior will be viewed as indications of mental aberration. These nonconforming behaviors may then become the legitimate targets of behavior-change programs. The counselor needs to have a clear understanding of his values as subjective judgments.

The Behavioral Approach has made a major contribution in that it has clearly indicated it does deal with values and exerts influence (Ullmann and Krasner, 1965, 1969).

It is clear that safeguards are needed to insure that the values of the client may generally preempt the values of the counselor. One such protection that has been built into the Behavioral Approach is the behavioral contract, which is an agreement between the counselor and client about the problems which will be the focus of counseling. An additional safeguard which could easily be implemented in the Behavioral Approach is insuring that clients maximally participate in the decisions regarding the therapeutic procedures that will be employed to effect behavior change.

SUMMARY

This overview of the Behavioral Approach attempted to focus on the major features of this approach and on some of the latest developments which have relevance for school counseling. It was noted that the Behavioral Approach utilizes a *particular way of thinking about behavior* as well as a body of principles drawn from psychological experiments. The behavioral counselor focuses on *what* questions and makes a behavioral assessment *before* instituting change programs. He uses direct means to change behavior and individualizes techniques to suit the needs of each person.

Systematic desensitization was seen as being highly effective. It was suggested that school counselors would probably make the most use of variants of systematic desensitization. Although relaxation training has not been extensively researched, it appeared to be an extremely promising counseling technique which could be easily added to a school counselor's armamentarium of techniques. Various operant-based self-control procedures were presented which were supported by anecdotal evidence. It was suggested that counselors could make effective use of these easily employed techniques. Token economies were presented as being potentially helpful in the counselor's work with teachers. It was suggested that elementary school counselors in particular may be able to make the most effective use of modeling research, while high school counselors would need to rely on the anecdotal evidence for modeling effectiveness.

The place of learning theory in the Behavioral Approach, the counseling relationships, and various ethical implications of this approach were also discussed in this overview.

REFERENCES

Ashem, B., and Donner, L. "Covert Sensitization with Alcoholics: A Controlled Replication." *Behaviour Research and Therapy* (1968) 6, 7-12.

Bachrach, A. J.; Erwin, W. J.; and Mohr, J. P. "The Control of Eating Behavior in an Anorexic by Operant Conditioning Techniques." In *Case Studies in Behavior Modification*, edited by L. P. Ullmann and L. Krasner. New York: Holt, Rinehart & Winston, 1965, 153-163.

Bandura, A. "Psychotherapay as a Learning Process." *Psychological Bulletin* (1961) 58, 143-159.

——. *Principles of Behavior Modification.* New York: Holt, Rinehart & Winston, 1969.

——; Grusec, J. E.; and Menlove, F. L. "Vicarious Extinction of Avoidance Behavior." *Journal of Personality and Social Psychology* (1967) 5, 16-23.

——, and Menlove, F. L. "Factors Determining Vicarious Extinction of Avoidance Behavior Through Symbolic Modeling." *Journal of Personality and Social Psychology* (1968) 8, 99-108.

——, and Perloff, B. "Relative Efficacy of Self-Monitored and Externally Imposed Reinforcement Systems." *Journal of Personality and Social Psychology* (1967) 7, 111-116.

——, and Walters, R. *Social Imitation and Personality Development.* New York: Holt, Rinehart & Winston, 1963.

Barrish, H. H.; Saunders, M.; and Wolf, M. M. "Good Behavior Game: Effects of Individual Contingencies for Group Consequences on Disruptive Behavior in a Classroom." *Journal of Applied Behavior Analysis* (1969) 2, 119-124.

Beltz, Stephen E. "Some Gentle Comments on Dr. Hosford's Review of Behavioral Counseling." *The Counseling Psychologist* (1969) 1, 40-44.

Breger, L., and McGaugh, J. L. "Critique and Reformulation of Learning Theory Approaches to Psychotherapy and Neuroses." *Psychological Bulletin* (1965) 63, 338-358.

Cantrell, R. P.; Cantrell, M. L.; Huddlestron, C. M.; and Wooldridge, R. L. "Contingency Contracting with School Problems." *Journal of Applied Behavior Analysis* (1969) 2, 215-220.

Cautela, J. R. "Treatment of Compulsive Behavior by Covert Sensitization." *Psychological Record* (1966) 16, 33-41.

——. "Covert Sensitization." *Psychological Record* (1967) 20, 459-468.

——. "Behavior Therapy and Self-Control: Techniques and Implications." In *Behavior Therapy: Appraisal and Status,* edited by C. M. Franks. New York: McGraw-Hill, Inc., 1969, 323-341.

——. "Covert Reinforcement." *Behavior Therapy* (1970) 1, 33-50.

——; Steffan, J.; and Wish, P. "Covert Reinforcement: An Experimental Test." Unpublished data, Boston College, 1969. Cited by J. R. Cautela, 1970.

Clark, M.; Lackowicz, I.; and Wolf, M. "A Pilot Basic Education Program for School Dropouts Incorporating a Token Reinforcement System." *Behavior Research and Therapy* (1968) 6, 183-188.

Cohen, H. L. "Educational Therapy: The Design of Learning Environments." In *Research in Psychotherapy,* Vol. 3, edited by J. M. Shlien. Washington, D. C.: American Psychological Association, 1968, 21-53.

Davison, G. C. "Elimination of a Sadistic Fantasy by a Client-Controlled Counter-Conditioning Technique: A Case Study." *Journal of Abnormal Psychology* (1968) 73, 84-90.

Davison, G. C. "Self-Control Through Imaginal Aversive Contingency and One-Downsmanship Enabling the Powerless to Accommodate Unreasonableness." In *Behavioral Counseling: Cases and Techniques,* edited by J. D. Krumboltz and C. E. Thoresen. New York: Holt, Rinehart & Winston, 1969, 319-328.

Ellis, A. *Reason and Emotion in Psychotherapy.* New York: Lyle Stuart, 1962.

Emery, J. R. "Systematic Desensitization: Reducing Test Anxiety." In *Behavioral Counseling: Cases and Techniques,* edited by J. D. Krumboltz and C. E. Thoresen. New York: Holt, Rinehart & Winston, 1969, 267-288.

Eysenck, H. J., ed. *Experiments in Behaviour Therapy.* New York: The Macmillan Company, 1964.

——. "Behavior Therapy and Its Critics." *Journal of Behavior Therapy and Experimental Psychiatry* (1970) 1, 5-15.

Ferster, C. B.; Nurnberger, J. I.; and Levitt, E. B. "The Control of Eating." *Journal of Mathematics* (1962) 1, 87-110.

Fox, L. "Effecting the Use of Efficient Study Habits." *Journal of Mathematics* 1 (1962): 75-86. Also in *Control of Human Behavior,* edited by R. Ulrich, T. Stachnik, and J. Mabry. Glenview, Ill.: Scott, Foresman, and Company, 1966, 85-90.

Garvey, W. P., and Hegrenes, J. R. "Desensitization Techniques in the Treatment of School Phobia." *American Journal of Orthopsychiatry* (1966) 36, 147-152.

Goldiamond, I. "Self-Control Procedures in Personal Behavior Problems." *Psychological Reports* 17 (1965): 851-868. Also in *Control of Human Behavior,* edited by R. Ulrich, T. Stachnik, and J. Mabry. Glenview, Ill.: Scott, Foresman and Company, 1966, 115-127.

——, and Dyrud, J. E. "Some Applications and Implications of Behavior Analysis for Psychotherapy." In *Research in Psychotherapy,* Vol. 3, edited by J. M. Shlien. Washington, D. C.: American Psychological Association, 1968, 54-90.

Goldstein, A. P.; Heller, K.; and Sechrest, L. B. *Psychotherapy and the Psychology of Behavior Change.* New York: John Wiley & Sons, Inc., 1966.

Graziano, A. M., and Kean, J. E. "Programmed Relaxation and Reciprocal Inhibition with Psychotic Children." *Proceedings of the 75th Annual Meeting of the American Psychological Association.* Washington, D. C. (1967) 3, 253-254.

Grossberg, J. M. Behavior Therapy: a review. *Psychological Bulletin* (1964) 62, 73-88.

Hall, R. V.; Lund, D.; and Jackson, D. "Effects of Teacher Attention on Study Behavior." *Journal of Applied Behavior Analysis* (1968) 1, 1-12.

Hansen, J. C.; Niland, T. M.; and Zani, L. P. "Model Reinforcement in Group Counseling with Elementary School Children." *Personnel and Guidance Journal* (1969) 47, 741-744.

Heller, K. "Ambiguity in the Interview Interaction." In *Research in Psychotherapy*, Vol. 3, edited by J. M. Shlien. Washington, D. C.: American Psychological Association, 1968, 242-259.

———. "Effects of Modeling Procedures in Helping Relationships." *Journal of Consulting and Clinical Psychology* (1969) 33, 522-526.

Homme, L. E. "Perspectives in Psychology—XXIV: Control of Coverants, the Operants of the Mind." *Psychological Record* (1965) 15, 501-511.

Hosford, R. E. "Behavioral Counseling—A Contemporary Overview. *The Counseling Psychologist* 1 (1969A) 1-33.

———. "Teaching Teachers to Reinforce Student Participation." In *Behavioral Counseling: Cases and Techniques*, edited by J. D. Krumboltz and C. E. Thoresen. New York: Holt, Rinehart & Winston, 1969B, 152-154.

Jacobson, E. *Progressive Relaxation*. Chicago: University of Chicago Press, 1938.

Kelman, H. C. *A Time to Speak: On Human Values and Social Research*. San Francisco: Jossey-Bass, 1968.

Kemp, C. G. *Intangibles in Counseling*. Boston: Houghton Mifflin, 1967.

Klein, M.; Dittman, A. J.; Parloff, M. P.; and Gill, M. M. "Behavior Therapy: Observations and Reflections." *Journal of Consulting and Clinical Psychology* (1969) 33, 259-266.

Krumboltz, J. D., and Schroeder, W. W. "Promoting Career Exploration Through Reinforcement." *Personnel and Guidance Journal* (1965) 55, 19-26.

———, and Thoresen, C. E. "The Effect of Behavioral Counseling in Group and Individual Settings on Information-Seeking Behavior." *Journal of Counseling Psychology* (1964) 11, 324-333.

———, and Thoresen, C. E. *Behavioral Counseling: Cases and Techniques*. New York: Holt, Rinehart & Winston, 1969.

———; Varenhorst, B. B.; and Thoresen, C. E. "Non-Verbal Factors in the Effectiveness of Models in Counseling." *Journal of Counseling Psychology* (1967) 14, 412-418.

Lang, P. J.; Lazovik, A. D.; and Reynolds, D. J. "Desensitization, Suggestability, and Pseudotherapy." *Journal of Abnormal Psychology* (1965) 70, 395-402.

Laxer, R. M.; Quarter, J.; Kooman, A.; and Walker, K. "Systematic Desensitization and Relaxation of High-Test Anxious Secondary School Students." *Journal of Counseling Psychology* (1969) 16, 446-451.

Lazarus, A. A. "Behavior Rehearsal vs. Non-Directive Therapy vs. Advice in Effecting Behaviour Change. *Behaviour Research and Therapy* (1966) 4, 209-212.

———. "Behavioral Counseling: Some Pros and Cons." *The Counseling Psychologist* (1969) 1, 60-61.

———, and Abramovitz, A. "The Use of Emotive Imagery in the Treatment of Children's Phobias." *Journal of Mental Science,* (1962) 108, 191-195. Also in *Case Studies in Behavior Modification*, edited by L. P. Ullmann and L. Krasner. New York: Holt, Rinehart & Winston, 1965, 300-304.

London, Perry. *Behavior Control*. New York: Harper & Row, 1969.

Lovaas, O. I.; Freitas, L.; Nelson, K.; and Whalen, C. "The Establishment of Imitation and Its Use for the Development of Complex Behavior in Schizophrenic Children." *Behaviour Research and Therapy* (1967) 5, 171-181.

Madsen, C. H., and Madsen, C. K. *Teaching/Discipline*. Boston: Allyn & Bacon, 1970.

Maes, J. L. "A Reconstructed Rogerian with a Psychoanalytic Bias Views Behavior Therapy." Paper presented at American Personnel and Guidance Association, Las Vegas, 1969.

Marlatt, G. A.; Jacobson, E. A.; Johnson, D. L.; and Morrice, D. J. "Effects of Exposure to a Model Receiving Varied Informational Feedback upon Consequent Behavior in an Interview." Paper presented at Midwestern Psychological Association, Chicago, 1966.

May, R. *Psychology and the Human Dilemma*. Princeton, N. J.: D. Van Nostrand Company, 1967.

Metz, J. R. "Conditioning Generalized Imitation in Autistic Children." *Journal of Experimental Child Psychology* (1965) 2, 389-399.

Murray, E. D., and Jacobson, L. T. "The Nature of Learning in Traditional and Behavioral Psychotherapy. In *Handbook of Psychotherapy and Behavior Change*, edited by A. E. Bergin and S. L. Garfield. New York: John Wiley & Sons, Inc., in press.

Myrick, R. D. "Effect of a Model on Verbal Behavior in Counseling. *Journal of Counseling Psychology* (1969) 16, 185-190.

Nixon, S. B. "Ways by Which Overly Active Students Can Be Taught to Concentrate on Study Activity." Cooperation Reach Project No. S-379, Office of Education, US Department of Health, Education & Welfare, 1966.

O'Leary, K. D., and Becker, W. "Behavior Modification of an Adjustment Class: A Token Reinforcement Program." *Exceptional Children* (1967) 33, 637-642.

Osborne, J. G. "Free-Time as a Reinforcer in the Management of Classroom Behavior." *Journal of Applied Behavior Analysis* (1969) 2, 113-118.

Patterson, C. H. "Some Notes on Behavior Theory, Behavior Therapy, and Behavioral Counseling." *The Counseling Psychologist* (1969) 1, 44-56.

Patterson, G. R. "A Learning Theory Approach to the Treatment of the School Phobic Child." In *Case Studies in Behavior Modification*, edited by L. P. Ullmann and L. Krasner. New York: Holt, Rinehart & Winston, 1965, 279-285.

Paul, G. L. *Insight vs. Desensitization in Psychotherapy: An Experiment in Anxiety Reduction*. Stanford, California: Stanford University Press, 1966.

———. "A Two Year Follow-up of Systematic Desensitization in Therapy Groups." *Journal of Abnormal Psychology* (1968) 73, 119-130.

———. "Inhibition of Physiological Response to Stressful Imagery by Relaxation Training and Hypnotically Suggested Relaxation." *Behaviour Research and Therapy* (1969A) 7, 249-257.

———. "Outcome of Systematic Desensitization." In *Behavior Therapy: Appraisal and Status*, edited by C. M. Franks. New York: McGraw-Hill, Inc., 1969B, 63-160.

Phillips, E. L. "Achievement Place: Token Reinforcement Procedures in a Home-Style Rehabilitation Setting for Pre-Delinquent Boys." *Journal of Applied Behavior Analysis* (1968) 1, 213-224.

Premack, D. "Toward Empirical Behavior Laws: I. Positive Reinforcement." *Psychological Review* (1959) 66, 219-233.

Rehm, L., and Marston, A. "Reduction of Social Anxiety Through Modification of Self-Reinforcement: An Investigative Therapy Technique." *Journal of Consulting and Clinical Psychology* (1968) 32, 565-574.

Sarason, I., and Ganzer, V. J. "Developing Appropriate Social Behaviors of Juvenile Delinquents." In *Behavioral Counseling: Cases and Techniques*, edited by J. D. Krumboltz and C. E. Thoresen. New York: Holt, Rinehart & Winston, 1969, 178-193.

Schaeffer, H. H., and Martin, P. L. *Behavioral Therapy*. New York: McGraw-Hill, Inc., 1969.

Skinner, B. F. *Science and Human Behavior*. New York: The Macmillan Company, 1953.

———. *Contingencies of Reinforcement: A Theoretical Analysis*. New York: Appleton-Century-Crofts, 1969.

Stuart, R. B. "Behavioral Control of Overeating." *Behaviour Research and Therapy* (1967) 5, 357-365.

———. "Operant-Interpersonal Treatment for Marital Discord." *Journal of Counseling and Clinical Psychology* (1969) 33, 675-682.

Thoresen, C. E. "The Counselor as an Applied Behavioral Scientist." *Personnel and Guidance Journal* (1969) 47, 841-848.

Truax, C. B. "Depth of Intrapersonal Exploration on Therapeutic Process in Group Psychotherapy With and Without Vicarious Therapy Pretraining." Mimeographed. Wisconsin Psychiatric Institute, 1963.

———. "Reinforcement and Non-Reinforcement in Rogerian Psychotherapy." *Journal of Abnormal Psychology* (1966) 71, 1-9.

———, and Carkhuff, R. R. *Toward Effective Counseling and Psychotherapy.* Chicago: Aldine Publishing Company, 1967.

———, and Wargo, D. G. "Effects of Vicarious Therapy Pretraining and Alternate Sessions on Outcome in Group Psychotherapy with Outpatients." *Journal of Consulting and Clinical Psychology* (1969) 33, 440-447.

Ullmann, L. P. "The Major Concepts Taught to Behavior Therapy Trainees." Paper presented at American Psychological Association, Washington, D. C., 1967.

———, and Krasner, L., eds. *Case Studies in Behavior Modification.* New York: Holt, Rinehart & Winston, 1965.

———. *A Psychological Approach to Abnormal Behavior.* Englewood Cliffs, N. J.: Prentice-Hall, 1969.

Ulrich, R.; Stachnik, T.; and Mabry, J., eds. *Control of Human Behavior.* Chicago: Scott, Foresman and Company, 1966.

Weinstein, F. "Reducing Test Anxiety." In *Behavioral Counseling: Cases and Techniques,* edited by J. D. Krumboltz and C. E. Thoresen. New York: Holt, Rinehart & Winston, 1969, 471-485.

Whalen, C. "Effects of a Model and Instructions on Group Verbal Behaviors." *Journal of Consulting and Clinical Psychology* (1969) 33, 509-521.

Wilson, F. S., and Walters, R. H. "Modification of Speech Output of Near Mute Schizophrenics Through Social Learning Procedures." *Behaviour Research and Therapy* 1 (1966) 4, 59-67.

Wolf, M. M.; Giles, D. K.; and Hall, R. V. "Experiments with Token Reinforcement in a Remedial Classroom." *Behaviour Research and Therapy* (1968) 6, 51-64.

———; Risley, T.; and Mees, H. "Application of Operant Conditioning Procedures to the Behavior Problems of an Autistic Child." In *Case Studies in Behavior Modification,* edited by L. P. Ullmann and L. Krasner. New York: Holt, Rinehart & Winston, 1965, 138-145. Also in *Behaviour Research and Therapy* (1964) 1, 305-312.

Wolfe, B. E. "Behavior Therapy and the Image of Man." Unpublished manuscript. University of Florida, Gainesville, Florida, 1968.

Wolpe, J. *Psychotherapy by Reciprocal Inhibition.* Stanford, Calif.: Stanford University Press, 1958.

———. *The Practice of Behavior Therapy.* New York: Pergamon Press, 1969.

———, and Lazarus, A. A. *Behavior Therapy Techniques.* Oxford: Pergamon Press, 1966.

Yates, A. J. "Misconceptions about Behavior Therapy: A Point of View." *Behavior Therapy* (1970A) 1, 92-107.

———. "Misconceptions about Behavior Therapy: A Rejoinder to Meyer." *Behavior Therapy* (1970B) 1, 113-114.

Zeisset, R. M. "Desensitization and Relaxation in the Modification of Psychiatric Patients' Interview Behaviors." *Journal of Abnormal Psychology* (1968) 73, 18-24.

Zerfas, P. G. "Effects of Induced Expectancies and Therapist Activity upon Patient Behavior in Group Psychotherapy." Unpublished doctoral dissertation, Indiana University, 1965.

A Suggested Reading List for the Interested Reader

Bandura, A. "Psychotherapy as a Learning Process." *Psychological Bulletin* (1961) 58, 143-159.

————. *Principles of Behavior Modification*. New York: Holt, Rinehart & Winston, 1969.

Cantrell, R. P.; Cantrell, M. L.; Huddlestron, C. M.; and Wooldridge, R. L. "Contingency Contracting with School Problems." *Journal of Applied Behavior Analysis* (1969) 2, 215-220.

Cautela, J. R. "Covert Sensitization." *Psychological Record* (1967) 20, 459-468.

————. "Covert Reinforcement." *Behavior Therapy* (1970) 1, 33-50.

Goldstein, A. P.; Heller, K.; and Sechrest, L. B. *Psychotherapy and the Psychology of Behavior Change*. New York: John Wiley and Sons, Inc., 1966.

Kelman, Herbert C. *A Time to Speak: On Human Values and Social Research*. San Francisco: Jossey-Bass, 1968.

Krasner, L., and Ullmann, L. P., eds. *Research in Behavior Modification*. New York: Holt, Rinehart & Winston, 1965.

Krumboltz, J. D., ed. *Revolution in Counseling: Implications of Behavioral Science*. Boston: Houghton Mifflin, 1966.

————, and Thoresen, C. E. *Behavioral Counseling: Cases and Techniques*. New York: Holt, Rinehart & Winston, 1969.

London, P. *The Modes and Morals of Psychotherapy*. New York: Holt, Rinehart & Winston, 1964.

————. *Behavior Control*. New York: Harper & Row, 1969.

Madsen, C. H., and Madsen, C. K. *Teaching/Discipline*. Boston: Allyn & Bacon, 1970.

Rubin, R. R., and Franks, C. M., eds. *Advances in Behavior Therapy, 1968*. New York: Academic Press, 1969.

Shlien, J. M., ed. *Research in Psychotherapy*, Vol. 3. Washington, D. C.: American Psychological Association, 1968.

Skinner, B. F. *Science and Human Behavior*. New York: The Macmillan Company, 1953.

Ullman, L. P., and Krasner, L., eds. *Case Studies in Behavior Modification*. New York: Holt, Rinehart & Winston, 1965.

————. *A Psychological Approach to Abnormal Behavior*. Englewood Cliffs, New Jersey: Prentice-Hall, 1969.

Ulrich, R.; Stachnik, T.; and Mabry, J., eds. *Control of Human Behavior*. Chicago: Scott, Foresman and Company, 1966.

Wolpe, J. *The Practice of Behavior Therapy*. New York: Pergamon Press, 1969.

————, and Lazarus, A. A. *Behavior Therapy Techniques*. Oxford: Pergamon Press, 1966.

JOURNALS

Behavior Therapy
The Counseling Psychologist, No. 4, "Behavioral Counseling"
Journal of Applied Behavior Analysis

$$\boxed{50}$$

COUNSELING FROM THE VIEWPOINT OF
EXISTENTIAL PSYCHOLOGY

Adrian van Kaam

Duquesne University

Counseling is essentially a process of making-free, a humanizing of the person who has lost his freedom in sectors of his existence where he can no longer transcend his life situation by freely giving meaning to it. He behaves there more or less as a lower form of being, as a dehumanized, determined existence. It is the aim of counseling to assist the person in regaining his freedom in these areas by creating insight into the meanings he attributes to these situations, by starting the extinction of the responses which the counselee — after gaining insight — no longer likes to retain, and by the conditioning of other responses corresponding to his new free evaluation of reality. In order to make the counselee free we have to make the counseling session an existential situation where he can be present with his whole being spontaneously and pre-reflexively.

We know the person from his phenomenal universe, not from his isolated and interior world. Therefore from the very beginning the attention of the client is oriented towards himself as moving in a vivid universe of events and encounters. He moves in the present, in the "here and now" of his actual world as a human existence — as "consciousness that is involved." The counselee is not encouraged to escape his present by a flight into a past, where there are no decisions to make and where there is no necessity to shape freely a world of "here and now," where existence seems determined and explained by inescapable needs. Instead of forcing the client to revise the fixed history of his past, the counselor invites him to face his situation today, not to excuse himself but to return to his world in a new mode of being, to accept its challenges.

The aim of existential counseling is to make the client feel at home in his real world by reshaping his phenomenal world, to make his real situation bearable by making it bearable phenomenologically. The counselee reconditions his behavior in his real world by reconditioning his behavior in his phenomenal universe.

The counselee who transcends his barriers and who learns to conquer the regions at the other side will know how to move with a new freedom in his world of everyday reality. Only he can cope with anxiety who calls the real world his dwelling place, the whole world from high to low and from right to left, not only the bright side of the world but its shady side as well; the mature person says yes to the whole universe.

Reprinted by permission of the author and the *Harvard Educational Review*, Vol. 32, No. 4, Fall 1962.

THE EMBODIMENT OF OBJECTIVES IN ATTITUDES
AND BEHAVIOR

The counselor translates these objectives of existential counseling into attitudes which he in turn embodies in word, posture, facial expression and movement.

The attitudes of the counselor are determined not only by his purpose but also by the situation of his client. He must clarify the existence or modes of standing-out of the counselee who exists in a personal world, which has to be explored and expressed by means of the therapeutic relationship. In order thus to understand the attitudes in which we must embody our objectives we should first of all gain an insight into the existential world and into the kind of relationship which can induce the counselee to explore and express the realms of his existence. The insight gained in these considerations will enable us to describe some desirable attitudes which may embody the objectives so that they are communicated to the counselee within this relationship.

THE EXISTENTIAL WORLD OF THE CLIENT

The main characteristic of the human existent is that he exists, literally stands out in a world of meaning. Subject and world, self and world are correlatives. When we know the world in which a person lives we know *him;* the counselee is best understood from his personally lived and experienced universe. His feelings, desires, hopes and ideas are embedded in a world of meaning, and consequently every experience explored by him has somewhere a place in this system of meanings. This structure as a differentiated whole explains partly the meaning of every single experience which belongs to it. Each single experience in turn colors all meanings which make up the world of the counselee as a whole. When he is able gradually to express the main lines of his existential world, the counselee will be able to understand the precise meaning of his problem within this system.

RELATIONSHIP AND EXPRESSION OF EXISTENTIAL WORLD

Relationship is the principal means for bringing to expression the world of meaning in which the client lives. The quality of the relationship determines to what degree the personal existential world will find genuine expression. The first task of the counselor is, therefore, to establish a relationship which leads to optimal communication. People learn to hide the personal world in which they live in order to protect themselves from being misunderstood, humiliated, condemned or abused. To reveal my personal world is in a sense to surrender my very being, to expose my sensitivity, my project of life, and to unveil my vulnerability when certain meanings which I cherish are at odds with the values appreciated by my environment. This fear of disapproval limits the free admission not only of base inclinations but also of sublime aspirations. It is difficult for many to verbalize their finer sentiments. They fear that the communication of refined feeling would sound ridiculous in the world of functional meaning which they share with contemporary man. This repression of the personal world under the pressure of the shared social world may be so effective that the client himself is not aware of the deepest meanings which constitute his personal existence. The counselor may make himself mistakenly the ally of this social world by lightly joking about noble sentiments in order to give the client the reassurance that counselors are regular fellows like the rest of the population. If he does so he can be sure that the personal world of experience of the counselee will remain a closed book. Some counselors may cherish the illusion that such "open-mindedness" may break barriers forgetting that an exclusive open-mindedness for the cultural-social scene may mean a closed-mindedness for the personal world of the individual in its unique, most revealing features.

THE IMPOSITION OF ONE'S OWN EXISTENCE

Every one of us has his own project of existence which implies among other things the style in which we embody our strivings in daily behavior. Such a style of existence has been formed in the light of individual experiences of the attitudes of the surrounding culture in which we are inserted by birth and education. This cultural component of our style of behavior and perception is mediated by the image of "ideal" behavior as held by the people of our home, neighborhood and society. This ideal style of life permeates our human relationships, being particularly pervasive in the meetings between us as counselors and the counselee who presents himself to us with his problems. The secret influence of this personal and cultural norm may be harmful. Existence as embodiment in space and time necessitates that we be present to others in some style of life. However, our personal embodiment of existence is not the only possible or desirable one for everybody else. The unconscious identification of our personal way of life with "the" way may limit our therapeutic relevance to that part of the population which is spontaneously in touch with our style of being while it averts others.

Therefore, the counselor should grow daily in the awareness of his pre-reflexive attitudes. Of course he cannot do away with a personal style of existence; as a human being he must embody his mode of being in concrete behavior, which is always limited in space and time and therefore necessarily onesided. But he can increasingly free himself from the identification of existence as such with his personal-cultural style of being. This inner freedom will enable him to sense the unique potentialities in those counselees who differ from him in expression and perception. When the counselor is deeply aware that his own modes are incidental and transient, he will distinguish what is essential from that which is accidental. This self-awareness will enable him to transcend the temporal to become aware of his cultural and subcultural stereotypes, of his antipathies and sympathies his emotional blocks will become manifest to him in this maturity. He may discover, for instance, that he *a priori* does not like people with esthetic inclinations because the good farmers at home confused artistry with frivolity. Or he may realize that he one-sidedly prefers "regular guys" because as a high school or college student he disliked some pale companions who were delighted more by books than by baseball. Another may find that he is unconsciously enamored with scholarly types because he is fed up with his more pragmatic colleagues who make great fun of him. Or a counselor may discover during this process of growing up that he unconsciously favors a certain compulsiveness because he has identified the compulsive mode of being with sound strictness and consequently distrusts spontaneity in himself and others.

The counselee in turn may be tempted to identify the counselor with his parents, teachers, administrators, supervisors or school friends. These identifications may harm the effectiveness of counseling, for such daily relationships usually imply some withholding of one's personal world in order to function smoothly within the frame of daily life. The counselor is usually an unknown alien for the candidate. He seems different from the people in authority whom he meets in school, family and society. His function is vague and unusual; he comes from a strange faraway world. This relative strangeness can be an advantage. If the counselor were identified with the authorities in the environment of the candidate, the client's daily mode of existence towards those people would be immediately adopted towards him. The interview would then structure itself in terms of this mode of existence; the formal, casual, dependent or superficially friendly features which characterize daily interactions would determine this new relationship and keep it on a level which may generate pleasantries, polite caution or formal respect but no experience in depth.

When the client, however, cannot experience the counselor as he does his daily associates, then no stereotyped mode of existence toward him is available. Moreover, the candidate faces this ambiguous situation alone and not in the company of his friends or classmates. Therefore he cannot fall back on a mode of existence which he could share with others towards this new person; he has to handle this interaction all by himself. Such a situation is conducive to responses which will reveal his unique way of being in the world and which are less contaminated by socially shared modes of existence.

On the other hand, if the ambiguity is too much to bear it will evoke too much anxiety in the client and paralyze communication. The effective counselor, therefore, should not make himself known too much by being too friendly and jovial and by removing all social distance. For in that case he and the client will act out superficial social roles which usually prevent communication on a deeper and more personal level. Neither should he be so distant, alien and withdrawn that his counselee freezes in anxiety. The counselor should not maneuver himself into a situation in which he will be forced to do most of the talking; yet he must avoid sitting there like a sphinx which would prevent the possibility of spontaneous communication. This attitude of professional composure and serenity may be inspired by an unauthentic, false image of the "wise," "mature" man without emotion, which is a neurotic imitation of real wisdom and maturity.

Ideally the counselor should be experienced by the counselee as a deeply interested, wise friend whose only interest is to help me in finding myself in relation to my possible project of existence. However, the counselor may have his own unconscious needs which may make it difficult for him to establish such an interested and at the same time detached relationship. Therefore he should explore his motivations after every session. Does he need to sound like an oracle, is he in love with his sonorous voice or clever verbalizations, does he feel that he "knows" people already through and through, is he authoritarian, domineering, does he need to be popular, to be liked or exalted as a "nice chap" by his counselee, is he afraid of depth in himself and others, does he repress his own feelings and paralyze his spontaneity, is he afraid to verbalize or to hear the verbalization of certain experiences? This list could be expanded indefinitely. It is only after a period of growth and experience that a counselor is able to approximate the ideal attitude which makes the relationship itself his most efficient instrument. A mature and experienced counselor is indeed a precious gift for a community.

THE STRUCTURE OF THE RELATIONSHIP

The relationship itself which should be established by the counselor — from the first moment of the initial meeting — differs from the structure of other relationships. First it is different because of its objectives, which we have discussed earlier, and second, it is different from other relationships because of the specific attitudes of the counselor.

The attitudes of the counselor aim at the expression of the personal existential world of the counselee. At the base of these attitudes is a genuine unconditional acceptance of the client regardless of what world of meaning he will reveal. Any trace of explicit or implicit disapproval diminishes the ability of the counselee to unveil his personal existence. On the other hand, the expression of this personal world can also be arrested by too great a personal involvement of the counselor in one or another aspect mentioned by the client. Such emotional concentration on one aspect prevents the narration of other dimensions of the world of meaning which may be just as important for full understanding. The counselor must encourage the client by his patient and accepting attitude to express spontaneously all vague and confused feelings, attitudes and motives which he may have in regard to his project of existence.

The counselor should be emotionally involved to the extent necessary to keep the client interested and alive in the exploration of his world. But this interest should be tempered with a distance which enables him to accept all aspects of existence expressed by the counselee without reacting to them favorably or unfavorably. Either reaction may encourage a positive or negative concentration on some particular aspect of the counselee's world at the expense of the revelation of other ones. The counselor must be a participant in the existential world of the client while being at the same time its respectful observer.

ATTITUDES OF THE COUNSELOR IN THIS EXISTENTIAL RELATIONSHIP

The description of the counseling relationship implies the desirability of certain attitudes.

Creativity

The counselor should be creative. His counseling should not be a rigid application of rules which he has learned from books or formed for himself on the basis of experience with former clients. On the contrary, he should be convinced that every world of meaning is unique. Everything that the counselor says and does should be the creative outgrowth of his participation in this individual existence. This presupposes that the counselor is a mature person free from threat and therefore free from rigidity. Rigid behavior is a defense against the possible challenge of an unexpected world, a world which is communicated to us and which may expose us to our own repressed regions of being. The counselor who is not at home in his own existential world is unable to risk the full revelation of another world of meaning. There are two main forms of rigidity; one leading to a stiff formal attitude in order to escape communication in depth, the other leading to a compulsively "jolly good fellow" attitude which may be an even more effective defense against a truly existential encounter. Both defenses may be based on some neurotic insecurity in the counselor. Sometimes we find a curious combination of both defenses in the same insecure, anxious person; in the fulfillment of functional and administrative obligations he may be formal and rigid, while in his personal relations compulsively joking, gay, and funny. The mature person can be serious, gay, or detached according to the challenge of the situation. He adopts none of these attitudes compulsively; his behavior is not identical in different situations. Existential creativity implies flexibility of attitude, feeling, and behavior in authentic response to the real situation.

Acceptance

Another fundamental attitude in this relationship is acceptance, an attitude which generates in the counselee an experience of really feeling understood in his own existential world. The counselee feels that he really shares this personal world with the counselor, and this feeling enables him to explore this world further and to communicate the outcome of this exploration with less embarrassment. When the candidate perceives that the counselor co-experiences what things mean to him and still accepts him, he gradually feels a safe experiential communion with the counselor and with the world which the counselor represents.

That the counselor co-experiences what people and things mean to the client does not imply that he agrees with this meaning or that he approves of it. Acceptance of a person does not imply personal agreement with his thought or feeling as such. The co-experience and acceptance of the counselor implies only a non-judgmental attitude. His whole attitude communicates to the person: I do not judge at this moment whether or not your feelings and attitudes prove that you are personally guilty for maintaining them; I leave that to your own conscience for this moment. My special function here is not to judge how far you personally are responsible for those attitudes and feelings but to understand what region of your existence they reveal. Basically I respect and like you because deep down your nature is a gift of being; this gift is fundamentally good, and therefore, lovable no matter how it may be overgrown and veiled by attitudes, feelings, and opinions with which I could not agree personally.

The attitude acceptance is so fundamental for effective counseling and at the same time so different from our usual mode of encounter that it may be fruitful to go somewhat deeper into this matter. The views, feelings, and behavior of the counselee can be accepted under various aspects. For example, the counselor might consider expressed views, feelings, and behavior as isolated abstract norms of human conduct, in which case he can accept or reject them as such. When a client mentions, for instance, that he thinks that certain races should be exterminated, the counselor cannot accept this personally as a highly commendable norm for human existence. Or, he might consider those views, feelings, and behavior under the aspect of their usefulness for the counselee himself. For instance, the counselor may personally dislike poetry and would not accept and cultivate this interest in his own life; he may sense, however, that the poetical mode of existence may be very important for this specific person and he may accept it under this aspect. At the same time, he would reject under this aspect a suicidal interest of the counselee. However, he does not openly express the acceptance or rejection of those judgments as isolated judgments. For, regardless of his acceptance or rejection of those particular views, feelings, or behavior as isolated absolute expressions, the counselor always accepts and respects the client himself as a worthwhile human person dynamically present in those communications. For the same attitudes are not only categories of socially or personally acceptable or rejectable behavior but are also manifestations of a fellow human being. They manifest that the client is not an animal or an inanimate being; their specific content reveals that this human being has adopted certain modes of existence in the world.

The counselor *as counselor* experiences primarily in all these views, feelings, and behavior a wrestling, suffering, sometimes victorious, sometimes defeated human being who tries desperately to find his existential position within this world. It is in this last way that the understanding counselor experiences and accepts the views, feelings, and behavior of the client, namely, under the aspect of their being manifestations of the coping human person, desperately looking for a meaningful project of existence. He shows, therefore, deep genuine interest in those communications. It is this acceptance which opens up the client who becomes actively involved in the process of self discovery and its expression when he senses that the counselor really cares about what he thinks and feels; a climate is created in which the flow of communication is not halted by the anxious expectation of disapproval, rejection, criticism or other negative responses which the counselee expects on the basis of his past experience in family, school or society. Acceptance lessens considerably defensiveness and therewith the compulsion to rationalize, deny, or distort existential attitudes and inclinations in order to prevent disapproval.

If the counselor himself has deeply buried in himself some aspects of his personal existence he should become aware of it. The same anxiety which made him bury the awareness of regions of his own existence may close him when he senses the slightest indication of the same threatening reality in another. The implicit communication of this anxiety will prevent the free exploration of this specific area of existence. This danger points to the necessity for the counselor to evaluate himself continuously and thoroughly. Every session with a candidate should be a source of self reflection. What did I say? How did I respond? What did I feel? How did this communication affect me? Was I uneasy, excited, threatened, at ease, uncomfortable? Why was I so? The personal existence of the counselor is his main tool. In order to keep it refined and sensitive he should work through his inhibitions, anxieties, and insecurities with a therapist whom he trusts. He should keep refining this instrument that he himself is. For, no amount of literature, study, or oratory can replace the impact of his very being upon the relationship with the counselee.

Gentleness

The counselor should maintain mildness in his approach. We do not mean anything sentimental, effeminate, or soft. Gentleness reveals itself in sensitive, considerate, and tolerant modes of existence. The counselor should be able to manifest this amenity spontaneously; it will be difficult for the counselee to express himself fully if this atmopshere of gentle consideration is absent. For some counselors it may seem nearly repulsive to be gentle. Sometimes a male counselor in a high school may believe that he should ideally give the boy he is counseling the impression that he himself is just another boy, one who is bigger, taller, heavier, and more muscular, yet a boy, an enlarged version of an adolescent who speaks and acts big, very big. This attitude was perhaps deeply rewarded by his friends in college or high school who looked up towards him as the real tough guy. For some it may take time to realize that the same behavior will be ineffective in their new adult role when they like to go beyond the peripheral and reach the core of human existence. Others may not have worked through their anxious concern about being a real man and the unconscious occupation with their manliness may paralyze their gentility. Others again have not worked through the loneliness of existence and remain unconsciously in search of a tenderness which fulfills sentimental needs. Their gentility lacks spine and strength; it has a sticky, slimy quality which repels certain people. Some counselors may develop unauthentic friendliness which does not originate in the depth of existence but is calculated and carefully added to behavior in those situations in which the good counselor should be pleasant. It is practiced as a tour de force, a feat of strength, a stunt of psychology. Such a forced gentility remains superficial and will not open up the deeper layers of existence.

Sincerity

Finally the attitude of the counselor should be straightforward, honest, and sincere. The counselor should be aware that he has been compelled in daily life to develop a social facade in order to protect himself against obliteration by the demands of the crowd. He cannot get involved in everyone's problems. He has had to develop a smooth, easy way of dealing with large numbers of people who accost the counselor with their questions, neuroses and venerations. Moreover, the population at large demands from him that he be "nice" regardless of his mood, his toothache or the troubles with his principal. The effective functioning and the serenity of the school community to which he belongs requires a smooth interaction between faculty and counselor which implies certain social niceties. How tempting it is to fall back on these habits when meeting the counselee. However, such habits, no matter how useful in the community at large, if introduced into the counseling session will prevent effectively that deeper communication which is the aim of this encounter.

EXISTENTIAL COUNSELING AND THEORIES OF PSYCHOLOGY

We described the openness of the existential counselor, and considered attitudes of his that foster optimal communication with the counselee. The final question to be dealt with is that of the relationship between existential counseling and theories of psychology. Does the openness of the existential counselor imply that psychological theory is superfluous; if not, what is its role?

The Avoidance of a Premature Use of Theoretical Concepts

Existential counseling fosters a self-understanding in the counselee, which is free from subjectivistic influences; it attempts to uncover the real structures and meanings of experience; it means a purification of the naive knowledge of self by a search for real self-experience beyond the subjectivistic explanations of everyday life. If the counselor, however, brings uncritically theoretical categories to naively experienced behavior he may be caught in another sophisticated form of subjectivism, which might distort the given phenomena. He may unwittingly substitute for the experience of daily life an artificially made up "scientific experience." He immediately "perceives," for example, in the counselee inferiority feelings, projections, archetypes, repressions, reinforcements, resistances, Oedipus-complexes, transferences, sublimations and the like. This artificial scientific *experience* is the abortive result of two sources: one is the naive experience of everyday life, the other the immediate interpretation of this naive natural experience by established scientific theories. Such an interpretation — when prematurely indulged in — prevents a respectful attention for the inner structure and meaning of experience itself in this unique situation. Consequently, established intersubjectivistic theoretical influences are substituted for or added to the subjectivistic distortions which are already present in the naive experience itself. This impoverished, made-over experience is then considerd as *the* full real experience, substituting for the experience in everyday life. This scientific experience is called fact and this fact is then hailed as the first primary original experience of the counselee. Out of the collection or enumeration of these facts one should come by induction to the establishment of laws which should govern the activities of counselors and clients alike. This process leads to a system of counseling autonomous and closed in itself, an empty game with splendid ideas irrelevant to real experience of people in vital situations, a mythology of behavior which claims to explain everything while it explains nothing.

Obviously much harm can be done by a counselor when his perception is distorted by the premature introduction of theoretical explanations. The existential counselor will penetrate first into behavior as it manifests itself and only then ponder how existing scientific theories may illuminate this behavior without distortion, or how scientific theories should be corrected, expanded, or renewed in order to keep in touch with behavior as given in reality today. Theories of personality and psychotherapy should supplement rather than supplant existential understanding. The existential counselor should draw on the rich fund of insight called science of psychology which is a collection of intellectual contributions by numerous enlightened theorists of behavior. But, his prudent selection from this treasure-trove of theoretical explanations should be illuminated by real behavior as it manifests itself in his clients. His primary commitment is to existence, not to a theory about existence, even an existential theory. His existential openness for the communications of his counselee will enable him not only to spot the relevant theoretical explanation but also to adapt it to the concrete situation or even to improve it on the basis of his observation. In the last case he may possibly enrich the treasury of psychology so that others after him may have more knowledge available. It should be his wish, however, that his successors will neither abuse his ideas for the distortion of data or substitute his observation for their own existential perception. It should be his hope that they may be more sensitive to behavior than to his explanations about behavior, that their ears may not be deafened by the noise of theories, and that their eyes may not be blinded by expositions in journals, books, and papers, even if they happen to be his own.

Language Habit

Language habit in this context refers to the embodiment in our language of psychological theories. The language may be scientific or pre-scientific; likewise psychological theories embedded in the language may be scientific and pre-scientific. English, for instance, is a pre-scientific language; the psychoanalytic idiom is a scientific language. Language is not the experience itself of the counselee but an expression of this experience. Many words may communicate more than the pure experience of the client. They express, for example, also the pre-scientific view of his experience, which he has received from his culture in the package of his language. In that case the language habit implies not only the expression of experience but also the pre-scientific view which created this biased and selective expression. By the same token it conceals other real aspects of experience which fall outside the scope of the pre-scientific theory, which dominates the mood of his civilization, and therewith the cast of its language.

An example of the influence of theory on language is the term "experience." The German word for experience is "Erlebnis"; the Dutch word is "beleving." The German "Erlebnis" is derived from "erleben" which literally means "to live an event," for, "erleben" connotes "leben" which means "to live." "Experience" denotes thus in both languages the actuality of a lively presence of the subject to a reality here and now. The term experience in the English language, however, has lost this meaning under the impact of empiricism. "Experience" instead of indicating an awareness in the present points to an awareness in the past. Consequently, this language habit may obscure or falsify the perception of the counselor and of the client. They may — misled by the language — overlook or misinterpret behavior which embodies an actual "lived" presence of the subject to reality without reflection. An open perception, however, that momentarily suspends the language habit may rediscover this reality of behavior which was lost in the language. The rediscovery of such a reality may force the counselor or counselee to enrich the language with a new expression which covers the forgotten phenomenon. They may speak, for instance, of "lived" experience, or "lived" awareness. Language is thus the treasure-trove of accumulated theories, insights and observations uncovered by a people in the current of its history; the fascinating history of a-standing-out-together in certain ways toward reality. This shared ex-sistence towards reality reveals itself in peculiar ways to the cultural co-existents. The resulting insights are conserved in the constituted language of a people. This constituted language should be a help, not a hindrance, towards further discovery of reality; it should not suppress but support living language, not fossilize but foster vision, not limit but expand perception.

Constituted *scientific* language presents a similar problem. Psychoanalytic, behavioristic, or organismic terminology should not paralyze but nurture the openness of observation, should not limit but expand perception and vision. The counselor might profit fully from the treasure of scientific language if he frees himself temporarily from its influence on perception. For perception unadulterated by theoretical tenets prepares him for a new appreciation of what other theorists have seen before him. Yet, his previous open perception of "behavior-as-it-is" liberates him from the limitations inherent in the position of every theorist.

The existential openness with its attitudes of suspension and vigilance is fundamental in the counselor who should encounter people beyond theory and classification. Only afterwards may he see in what sense and to what degree he may characterize their behavior by constructs *about* behavior. Theoretical psychology becomes then a light that enlightens, not a veil that dims, the perception of the counselor.

SELECTED REFERENCES

1. Buytendijk, F. J. J. "The Phenomenological Approach to the Problem of Feelings and Emotions." In M. L. Reymert (ed.), *Feelings and Emotions, Mooseheart Symposium.* New York: McGraw-Hill, 1950. Pp. 127-141.
2. Dondeyne, A. *Contemporary European Thought and Christian Faith.* Pittsburgh: Duquesne University Press, 1958.
3. ———. *Geloof en Wereld.* Antwerpen: Patmos, 1961.
4. Frankl, V. E. *From Death-Camp to Existentialism: a Psychiatrist's Path to a New Therapy.* Boston: Beacon Press, 1959.
5. Kwant, R. C. *Encounter.* Pittsburgh: Duquesne University Press, 1960.
6. Lopez, Ibor, Juan. "The Existential Crisis." In J. Braceland (ed.), *Faith, Reason and Modern Psychiatry.* New York: P. J. Kenedy and Sons, 1955.
7. Luijpen, W. *Existential Phenomenology.* Pittsburgh: Duquesne University Press, 1960.
8. May, R. *Freedom and Responsibility Re-examined.* Unpublished paper read at the 1962 meeting of the American College Personnel Association, Chicago, April 18, 1962.
9. ———. "The Meaning of the Oedipus Myth," *Review of Existential Psychology and Psychiatry,* I, 1 (1961), pp. 44-52.
10. Perquin, N. *Paedagogiek,* Roermond-Maaseik: J. J. Romen & Zonen, 1952.
11. Rogers, Carl R. "The Loneliness of Contemporary Man," *Review of Existential Psychology and Psychiatry,* I, 1 (1961), pp. 94-101.
12. ———. *On Becoming a Person.* Boston: Houghton Mifflin Company, 1961.
13. Van Kaam, A. "The Nurse in the Patient's World," *The American Journal of Nursing,* LIX (1959), pp. 1708-1710.
14. ———. "Freud and Anthropological Psychology," *The Justice* (Brandeis University), May, 1959.
15. ———. *The Third Force in European Psychology.* Greenville, Delaware: Psychosynthesis Research Foundation, 1960.
16. ———, "Assumptions in Psychology," *Journal of Individual Psychology,* XIV, 1 (1958), pp. 22-28.
17. ———. "Phenomenal Analysis: Exemplified by a Study of the Experience of 'Really Feeling Understood'," *Journal of Individual Psychology,* XV, 1 (1959), pp. 66-72.
18. ———. "The Impact of Existential Phenomenology on the Psychological Literature of Western Europe," *Review of Existential Psychology and Psychiatry,* I, 1 (1961), pp. 63-92.

19. ———. "Clinical Implications of Heidegger's Concepts of Will, Decision and Responsibility," *Review of Existential Psychology and Psychiatry*, 1, 2 (1961), pp. 205-216.

20. ———. "Psychology and Psychopathology of the Religious Mode of Existence." To be published in 1963 by Temple University Press, Philadelphia, Pa., in the book *Psychopathology: a Collection of Essays on Psychopathology by Various Experts of American Universities.*

21. ———. "Humanistic Psychology and Culture," *Journal of Humanistic Psychology*, I, 1 (1961), pp. 94-110.

22. ———. "The Fantasy of Romantic Love." In *Modern Myths and Popular Fancies.* A series of lectures given at the community college, sponsored by the Duquesne University Alumni Association, Oct. 6 to Oct. 27, 1960. Pittsburgh: Duquesne University Press, 1961.

23. ———. "Will and Religion," *Academy Newsletter of Religion and Mental Health*, Summer, 1962.

EXISTENTIAL ANALYTIC PSYCHOTHERAPY

Wilson Van Dusen

Mendocino State Hospital, Talmadge, California

Existential analysis is an example of a theoretical advancement which has far outstripped the development of actual techniques adapted to the new theory. There is no accepted technique of psychotherapy in existential analysis.[1] The technique varies with the analyst. What remains the same is the general program as to how the patient should be regarded and understood. All such analysts will begin with an attempt to understand the phenomenological world of the other person. Beyond that there are wide differences in practice. In part these differences are fruitful since they represent a continued exploration unhampered by a dogma of technique.

Two points will be made here. The first is that there is such an organic unity between the phenomenological approach and existential theory that the theory can and will be derived here from the basic phenomenological frame of reference. The second point is that there is a psychotherapeutic approach which most closely fits the theory. In fact a close adherence to the theory demands a particular approach. The approach has been called gestalt therapy, and considerable credit for it is due to Dr. Frederick S. Perls.[2, 3] So, in addition to redriving existential analytic theory from its phenomenological foundations, we will show a psychotherapeutic approach which fits this theory.

The door into existential analysis is through phenomenology and in this case the structure of the door implies much of the house. In the phenomenological approach to another person, one attempts to understand his mode of being-in-the-world. There are a number of immediate and important impli-

Reprinted by permission of the author and *The American Journal of Psychoanalysis*, Vol. XX, No. 1, 1960, 35-40.

cations. One is not coming to his world with objective yardsticks or categories. One cannot translate his world into oral and genital, id, ego or superego terms unless the patient spontaneously sees these as real characteristics of his world. There is no objective, outside-of-him system into which one can fit his world. One must be ready to discover worlds radically different from one's own. The patient's world may be a hole-like one out of which one crawls laboriously to look momentarily at daylight. His may be the seething restless world of the hipster,[4] where one swings from orgasm to orgasm in an attempt to break out of all boundaries. In every classificatory system our worlds differ relatively little, but in a phenomenological approach one encounters strange and radically different worlds. In therapy my own criterion as to whether I have understood the world of the other is whether or not he can recognize his world in my description.

The other day I examined a chronic schizophrenic patient of a colleague in an effort to get him more information about the patient. He told the patient I felt he was psychotic and the patient became angry and launched into a disturbed denial. Actually, I agree with the patient. He is not psychotic (the external-objective classification of him). Rather, he lived on the surface in his eyes and his tongue because his brain and heart were paralyzed. Of course, the patient is technically psychotic, but in a phenomenological approach I don't wish to be technical. I told the patient that I really saw him as living in his eyes with a paralyzed brain, and he accepted this. Someone understood him. He felt my colleague so misunderstood him as to be psychotic himself.

This is the effect of the phenomenological approach. Insofar as one can describe the world of the other person as he finds it, the other person feels understood. Then one can work with him in full communication and interchange. From the paralyzed brain and heart we go to other aspects of his world. He feels safe. He is understood. Any sort of judgment or technical approach to his world leaves him with the justified feeling that the therapist is bending him to the therapist's own ends. One discovers the being-in-the-world of the other, with even the terms and all the subtle qualities of the world of the other. This does not imply I am in his world. At the end of the hour he goes back to his hospital ward or his home and I return to my other professional duties. He knows I do. He knows mine is a different world. But as he leaves the door he feels someone is beginning to understand how he feels. I don't need to pretend to be in his world. When he says he is being poisoned I can quite seriously accept that he feels poisoned and even explore the qualities and circumstances of this poisoning without pretending I feel that material poison is being slipped into his food. Usually he doesn't mean poison *qua* poison. Even if he does, our exploring his poisoned world should open up other and more psychic aspects of poisoning.

So far we have said that the door into existential analysis is through an attempt to understand (not judge or value) the being-in-the-world of the other. This understanding is in his terms, with his qualities. It is the opposite of any sort of objective or technical approach to him, such as a diagnosis implies, for instance. He feels understood and not apprehended and bent by the other person. In this one need not pretend to have a world exactly like his. One remains an individual with a different world. He doesn't feel he is with an expert with mysterious powers. He is with another person who is attempting laboriously and slowly to understand him. Nor is he with the lover who cries when he cries. The transference is less than in classical analysis. As one meets and learns to describe the patient as he is here, one is also uncovering transference reactions. They too are described as part of his present being-in-the-world. They are discovered as they form and described so that they won't have a hidden effect on the relationship. If you wish, one could say there is a continuous analysis of transference. This phenomenological entering into the being-in-the-world of the other is the foundation of existential analysis. It is so fundamental that the therapist who learns how to do this alone is very likely to discover spontaneously for himself all the other aspects of existential analysis.

There are a number of collateral discoveries once one has entered the phenomenological door. Most of science is an attempt to find static law. One finds the world of the other is fluid and changing. The schizophrenic living in his eyes will be found to have a far richer and complex world than appears at first sight. Also it changes as we come to understand it. In one schizophrenic we are exploring a gesture as simple as rubbing his nose. It was at first a filling up of the hole of nothingness.[5] As we looked further it took on many and varied meanings. Not only is the therapist learning, but the patient is recalling in a gesture aspects of himself he had lost. We explore his style of movement, the changing emotional qualities in his voice and his experiences here. Whereas he may have appeared simple to himself, he grows more complex, varied, and subtle in this exploration. A simple symptom takes on layers of emotional and interpersonal meaning. As we explore, his awareness expands. He is not the same person from moment to moment. Nothing has been done to him. He hasn't been interpreted. He has simply participated in a discovery of himself here.

Another implication is that one will not want to discard any part of his being-in-the-world. One will not look exclusively at the outer world as he sees it, or at the internal. Both are his world. He may live more in one or another sphere (the introvert-extrovert dichotomy). If the solidity and resistance of material things engages him then we will look at this. If a fantasy plagues him, then it is an important part of his world.

Dreams[6] can be used as an important part of this discovery. Boss[6] makes the important point that dreams are not, strictly speaking, symbolic. They speak in a purely existential language. They tell what is currently critical in one's life by describing it in terms of dramatic events. Dr. Perls goes after the meaning of dreams by having the patient play-act all aspects of the dream until the patient is caught up in the events and thereby finds their meaning.

Also, one will not grasp the patient solely by his words (a tendency in many overly logical therapists). Features of his world are his bodily sensations, his use of his musculature, his gestures, his choice and use of clothes, and even the inflections of voice underlying the words. Such a small matter as where he puts his gaze is quite important. Does he communicate eye-to-eye with the therapist or is he talking to a potted plant in the corner? No part of his world is so small as to be meaningless. This approach to patients implies a much richer and more subtle understanding than the simple grabbing another by his words. I would hope to be able to fully understand another person without having heard a single word of his. It would please me immensely to be able to imitate his movements and the sound of his uniqueness.

In the exploration of the world of another person one tends to center on the critical. In the past, experimental psychologists centered on unimportant aspects of the worlds of others. Look, for instance, on the vast number of studies of the two-point sensory threshold and similar works. They did this to grasp what could be translated into the modes of exact science. Because the psychotherapist is not attempting to catch what is measurable by science, he can afford to look at the critical. There is a most simple reason why the existential analyst centers on the critical. The patient insists on it. The patient's life and destiny are at stake. He cannot help but present the critical, even though what he presents may look very peripheral to the therapist. The term existential has come to be nearly equivalent to the term critical. How does one find the critical? By exploring all the aspects of the being-in-the-world of the other.

The space-time aspects of the world of the other person are found to be important. In classical Freudian psychoanalysis, the analyst shifts the patient back into an exploration of the patient's history. In exploring the being-in-the-world of the other, one explores the world here, now. Only insofar as past or future are tangled in the world here-now do these become of consequence. After all, his world is here-now. It's not back in toilet training in childhood or forward in after-life. He sits here before me and demonstrates his world. The centering in the here-now is a modern tendency coming into most therapies. Practically speaking, it causes an intensification and speeding up of therapy. There isn't the long escape into what mamma, papa, or sister did. "We are here. What are you doing now?" One need not wander for years examining aspects of the person projected in remote historical events. The person is here. We can study what he does here. In the hereness he shows how he chooses space, time, and the qualities of his world. One patient occasionally rubbed his hand across the bridge of his nose. It was perhaps two weeks before we began to understand this. The meaning was something like this. "I become anxious under your close regard (or anyone else's). In the anxiety, time and space suddenly develop a frightening hole. In the hole is nothing. I can't even remember. Nothingness. By touching my nose I am physically active and fill up the hole. Also I touch physical reality (my body) and come back to reality that way. Incidentally, my hand covers my eyes for a moment and your (analyst's) gaze is shut off for a moment." Here we begin to discover his problem in a palpable way. It is with us here. It is not in the historical past. It is so palpable we can study it together now.

With the basic phenomenological approach I believe many others will discover that to some extent all study of past or future is a subtle abrogation of present responsibility. One cannot exclusively steer the patient into the present, either. If the past or future intrudes into the session it says something about how the patient is present. In the existential-analytic approach one doesn't steer the patient into past, present, or future. One discovers where the patient is now in his present being-in-the-world. It is a simple discovery in this approach that all psychopathology involves some degree of escape from the here and now into the spatially or temporally there, into otherness. The well-integrated person looks at the therapist, eye-to-eye, with security and composure, and chooses his being-in-the-world now. He is content to be here.

In his approach one will undo projections as fast as they form. The patient may ask, with some feeling, "Do you think therapy should go on indefinitely?" The patient is bothered and is projecting responsibility onto the analyst. The analyst can help bring the projection back to the patient by simply asking: "Would you make that into a statement?" The patient says, "You feel therapy should be interminable." There is a little more emotion in the voice and actions. Can the patient say it again clearer and more forcefully? "You feel therapy should go on forever!" After a moment the analyst can ask how the patient feels now. What was projected into the other is then discovered as arising from one's own emotions. Usually the patient reacts after such an exchange as though he had been restored to power. The projection was not interpreted as a defect in the patient. The affect underlying it was recovered and the patient was restored to power.

There is no unconscious in this approach.[7] Nothing is totally outside the realm of his present being-in-the-world when that world is examined in considerable respect. One finds himself dealing with varying degrees of awareness from what is easily verbalized to not quite understood gestures to vague feelings that are not at first verbalized. Nothing is totally outside of his present being here, hence the term dasein ("being here") analyses. There are a great many ways of exploring the present. While the patient talks, something of an emotion may show in the eyes, or voice, or a gesture appears. When the emotion is strong enough to grip the person, then a simple noting of its presence by the analyst may help bring it to the fore. With a little help its expression becomes clearer. Something has been discovered in the testing ground of the present relationship. He finds and determines himself, rather than finds himself interpreted by another person. Well-handled, one can tell from moment to moment whether gains are being made because the pathology and the choices around it are here.

In this I am dealing with findings from the phenomenological approach which others may not have experienced yet. I am so secure in these findings, though, that I would be inclined to say that anyone who has learned to understand the being-in-the-world of others and is involved in their care in psychotherapy will of himself enter into existential analysis. At this point I would like to clarify what differentiates between the phenomenological entrance and the inside of the house of existential analysis. In a few words, the entrance is phenomenological, the inside of the house is ontological, the essential nature of man.[8] This was touched upon when we examined the critical and found it in the here and now. In the other (there, in time and space) it is hidden. One can enter on the ontological, the critical, and the here and now by exploring the patient's choosing.

All the productions of the patient (words, actions, dreams, etc.) are, so to speak, puppets. By examining his choosing here and now with me, I deal directly with the puppeteer. This is the existential engagement. He is caught. All avenues of escape are sealed. As he grows in awarenss of the size and qualities of his world, his area of choice expands. In the beginning of therapy it appears he had no choice. He was caught as an actor in a repetitive, unpleasant drama. As awareness of his world expands he comes to deal with the playwriter — his forgotten choices. The drama changes. It appears more and more that he writes the drama. Therapy ends without any massive transference, because the therapist was no all-wise magician. He only permitted the patient to discover and choose himself.

In case it is not clear that this is relatively different from most other forms of psychotherapy, the difference will be underlined. Here there is no need to explore, or even to know, a patient's history. One could fully explore what is wrong here and what is chosen here without a history. In this approach there is no unconscious. His world is here. There are varying degrees of awareness in that world. There is no resistance or defense. This may be difficult to see, but both resistance and defense imply one is outside the world of the other and makes an outsider's judgment of their world. There is no denial. To say the patient is denying is to say that the analyst has a conception of the world of the patient that does not match with the patient's world. The patient doesn't deny. He states what he knows of himself at the moment. In this form of therapy both transferences should never become intense and burdensome. If you want, it is because this therapy is almost a constant analysis of transference, though even the term "analysis" is out of place here. One doesn't come to analyze (take apart) the world of the other. One comes to understand it. These few examples of differences from ordinary psychotherapy should suggest that this form of existential analytic therapy is relatively new. It has historical roots in the work of Adler, Rank, gestalt therapy, and the work of Freud, but in itself it is a major shift in what is seen in psychotherapy.

SUMMARY

Existential analysis is not yet identified with a particular therapeutic approach. By beginning with a phenomenological foundation one can rederive the structure of existential analysis, and by so doing one discovers a technique that is particularly close to the theory of existential analysis. From phenomenology one learns to enter the present being-in-the-world of the patient without overlooking any of the qualities of that world. By centering in the present world one discovers the critical and the role of the patient's choosing. By this the patient feels understood and not interpreted, and discovers that he changes as the horizon of his present experiences expands. Starting from a phenomenological foundation one rediscovers existential analysis and discovers that this analysis is a significant departure from classical therapies in several respects.

REFERENCES

1. May, R. *et al.*: Existence, A New Dimension in Psychiatry and Psychology, New York, Basic Books, 1958, 77.
2. Perls, F. S.: Ego, Hunger and Aggression, London, Allen & Unwin, 1957.
3. Perls, L.: Two Instances of Gestalt Therapy, Case Reports in Clinical Psychology, 3: 139-146, 1956.
4. Mailer, N.: "The White Negro," In, The Beat Generation and the Angry Young Men, G. Feldman and M. Gartenberg (Eds.), New York, Citadel Press, 1958, 342-363.
5. Van Dusen, W.: Wu Wei, No-Mind and the Fertile Void in Psychotherapy. Psychologia, 1: 253-256, 1958.

6. Boss, M.: The Analysis of Dreams, London, Rider, 1957.
7. Van Dusen, W.: The Theory and Practice of Existential Analysis, American Journal of Psychotherapy, 11: 310-322, 1957.
8. Van Dusen, W.: The Ontology of Adlerian Psychodynamics, Journal of Individual Psychology, 15: 143-156, 1959.

AN EXISTENTIAL APPROACH TO COUNSELING

Edward A. Dreyfus

University of California, Los Angeles

There are many approaches to counseling and psychotherapy[1] which legitimately may be termed existential, e.g., Boss (1963), Binswanger (1963), May (1958), to name a few. Each of these approaches, including the present one, has as its prime focus the nature of man's existence and how he experiences the world. The existential approach is not a system of techniques, but rather an underlying attitude which transcends all techniques.

It has been my experience that many students of counseling enter the counseling situation with the erroneous notion that if they know a series of techniques which have been employed by experienced counselors then they too are counselors. It is as though these novitiate counselors reason: "Dr. Jones is a counselor. He uses a particular technique. I use that technique. Therefore, I am a counselor." It is obvious that this is not a valid argument. These students fail to realize that Dr. Jones has spent many hours with clients developing his particular technique. More importantly, these techniques are firmly rooted in a theory of man and a philosophy of counseling. It is my belief that a counselor, armed with a myriad of techniques but with no theory of man or philosophy of counseling, would be like a surgeon entering the operating room with all of the standard techniques but with no understanding of anatomy or physiology.

Technique emerges from theory. Techniques alone are of little value without a more basic understanding of the subject with which one is working. Thus the counselor's approach during the therapy hour must be governed by his underlying philosophy of counseling. The philosophy of counseling, in turn, emerges from and in many ways is symbiotic with the theory of man. The way in which a person perceives man's existence will govern his philosophy of counseling. One cannot adopt a technique which is alien to his underlying philosophy and expect to be an effective counselor.

The existential counselor is concerned with an approach to counseling. He allows whatever technique that emerges during the counseling session to occur. These techniques will then be an expression of the philosophy. It may happen that the techniques which emerge will be phenotypically similar or identical to techniques which emerge from different philosophies. Such is the case with some of the psychoanalytic techniques. Boss (1963), for example,

---

An original article for this book.
[1]These terms are considered to be synonymous and will be used interchangeably as will counselor and therapist, patient and client.

contends that the psychoanalytic *techniques* (e.g., free association and dream interpretation) are acceptable, but psychoanalytic *theory* is not. Benda (1960) extends this notion by saying that there are no essential differences in the techniques of the existential therapist and the psychoanalytic therapist, but the underlying attitude and framework in which interpretation of the material thereby obtained is different. In counseling, technique in and of itself does little regarding change within the client. It is only what one does with and how one views the material evoked via the technique that allows change to occur. Thus I would maintain that when the existential counselor employs the technique of dream interpretation or free association (see Boss, 1958) it is quite different than when the psychoanalyst uses it.

To be concerned with technique and its development is the antithesis to what the existential approach stands for. The existential point of view maintains that man is not a machine to be operated upon in order to gain a particular effect. Technique implies manipulation; one manipulates objects, not people.

Existential counseling, then, is not a system of techniques but an underlying attitude toward counseling. It is concerned with the uniqueness of man. More specifically, it is concerned with the uniqueness of that particular man seated before the counselor during the therapeutic hour. It is concerned with the client as he presents himself in his particular world — in the world of the here and now.

The method employed by the existentially oriented counselor is called the phenomenological method. That is to say, the counselor is concerned with the immediate, existing world of the client at the moment. He is concerned with the raw data offered by the client. Hence the approach is ahistorical in the sense that the counselor does not attempt to actively delve into the client's past. The past is important only insofar as the client introduces it into the present. One of the main tenets of existentialism is that man is free; he is free to choose his way of being. Likewise he is free to explore with the counselor those areas of his existence that he, the client, feels important. This is quite in contrast to those schools of thought in which the client discusses those areas which the therapist judges to be important. The point of departure during the counseling hour is the conflict which brought the client to the counselor, not that which led up to 'the conflict.

The existentially oriented counselors, of course, are not the only group of therapists who use the phenomenological method. Carl Rogers (1951), among others, has been using this method in his nondirective counseling for years. In many respects, especially within recent years, his approach is very much akin to the existential position.[2] However, in his early works Rogers placed a great deal of emphasis on technique, particularly the technique of reflection. It seems that while Rogers has always been a proponent of the phenomenological method, it is only within recent years that he has adopted the existential position.

The existential position, as already mentioned, argues that counseling is a real life process and as such allows whatever "technique" that emerges during the counseling process to occur. The counselor does not passively

---

[2]A comparison of the two approaches has been made more explicit elsewhere (Dreyfus, 1962).

reflect the feeling tone and words of the client, but rather is actively involved in the world-experiences of the client. Benda (1960) characterizes the process as being similar to the obstetrician who gently guides the newborn baby from the womb, though it is the patient who is doing most of the work. As such there is active participation of the therapist in the emerging of the client into the world.

As I have indicated earlier, the existential counselor will even utilize the techniques of the psychoanalytically oriented therapist. Rogers, on the other hand, excludes such techniques. By doing so it would seem that he is not allowing the client to express himself and his experiences in all of the possible ways open to him. Hence the client is not entirely free during the therapeutic hour. We must admit that lying down on a couch, dreaming, and free associating are human modes of experiencing; not permitting them to occur binds freedom.

Now that I have stated an existential position regarding psychotherapeutic techniques, I would like to present a theory of man, draw from it a philosophy of counseling, and subsequently attempt to delineate some ground rules governing the counselor's role in the counseling process. It should be understood that this is only one of the many approaches which could be classified as existential in orientation.

A THEORY OF MAN

Man is born into an unknown world. From the moment of his birth he is continuously experiencing his world. He does not know what lies ahead, nor does he know what his potential for being in this world is. Despite this uncertainty, in the face of it, or even because of it, man moves forward. Hence, by virtue of the uncertainty of his existence, man is born anxious. It is this existential anxiety — the anxiety of being — that makes man a dynamic, emergent being. To explore the unknown is part of man's ontological make-up.

Man is a feeling, thinking, acting being. He feels a world, thinks about a world, and acts in a world. His actions are based on how he feels and thinks and are therefore outer representations of his inner world. Furthermore, man is basically authentic. That is to say, he is honest with himself and with the world. His actions are held to be genuine manifestations of how he experiences the world. It is through these four attributes — feeling, thinking, acting, and authenticity — that man explores his world and emerges a unique being. It is through these modes that man actualizes his potential.

Affect

When the infant is born he experiences the world solely through his senses and his body in general. He reacts to the world with his entire body. All he is aware of is that which he feels. He feels, he responds. He is happy, sad, hungry, content. Whatever the feeling, his response to the world is immediate. There is no past nor future only the moment exists. The infant does not think about being hungry, he simply experiences hunger and reacts. One can say that the infant's world is composed solely of feeling — he is all effect. He expresses his feelings through action; it is through action that he makes his presence in the world known. As the child grows older, another process comes to bear on his actions. The process of cognition intervenes between feeling and action. He becomes capable of thinking about his feelings.

Cognition

Thinking allows one the opportunity to reflect upon his world and upon his feelings. One becomes alert to his environment and capable of choosing between alternative actions. One can choose to express affect or to inhibit it. One can choose to act or not to act. With cognition, choice or intentionality emerges as part of man's existence. Intentionality is ontologically given. Before cognition affect determined action. With intentionality man's fate and actions are determined by man. He can now reflect on his past and determine his future rather than live only in the immediate.

Man is essentially a conscious being, forever making choices regarding his own existence. There is no single choice which is predetermined, over which man has no control. When he perceives a limited array of choices of the many possibilities, it is because he chooses to limit the choices.

Action

In order for men to emerge into the world extending himself beyond his physical confines, he must act. His actions are determined by how he thinks and feels about his world. He can choose to act on his feelings without thinking, or he can choose to disregard his feelings and act solely on the basis of his thoughts. For the most part, however, man acts with respect to both modes. Furthermore, it seems that the more one thinks the less one feels, and hence the less one acts. It is the balance of these modes which will, in part, determine the unique being-in-the-world of the person.

With the development of cognition, and hence with control of action and freedom of choice, man emerges as a responsible being. While man has freedom of choice and action, he is also responsible for his actions. At birth, without cognition, the child is not responsible. The potential for being responsible, however, is ontologically given. When man chooses a course of action he has made a commitment — he is responsible. He stands alone as he determines his own existence.

Authenticity

Man responds to the world in a way which reflects his feelings and thoughts. There is little doubt that the child, as an infant, is genuinely hungry or uncomfortable when he cries. When man behaves in a way which runs counter to his feelings or thoughts he is being dishonest or inauthentic. While man is a social being, he need not be governed by the crowd. He can stand alone. He can look the other in the eye without trepidation. He can look himself in the eye when he is authentic. He can accept responsibility without shifting blame. Such authenticity is ontologically given.

It is only through the "socialization" process or "dehumanization" process that man becomes inauthentic. It is through such a process that the existential honesty is lost. To be sure, not being honest is a choice and one must accept the responsibility. But since it is alien to man's essential way of being, he experiences guilt. Likewise, one is inauthentic when he chooses to not-act, or when he fails to move in the face of anxiety, and thus he experiences guilt. This is existential guilt, or the guilt of not-being.

In summarizing this point of view, man is seen as born anxious in an unknown world. He moves into the world in the face of this existential anxiety. Each time he moves into the unknown he experiences anxiety. As he moves he is constantly emerging into a unique being. At first he reacts to the world in terms of his feelings. With the development of cognition he becomes conscious of his feelings and is capable of choosing a course of action. He is free to choose among many action-possibilities as his consciousness expands. While he has freedom of choice, he is also responsible for these choices. He is responsible for his behavior and hence his own existence. The combined interplay of affect and cognition will, in part, determine his uniqueness. When he commits himself to a choice, man stands alone, singularly responsible for the choice. He moves into the unknown continuously making choices. Failure to move, acting contrary to his feelings or thoughts, precluding choice, all leave man experiencing guilt for being inauthentic. When man realizes that he is being inauthentic, when he has so limited his choices, when he feels uncomfortable enough to the extent that he is unable to realize his potential, he seeks help.

A PHILOSOPHY OF COUNSELING

In developing a philosophy of counseling once one has some theory of man, two important questions must be answered. First, why does a person seek counseling? Second, what is counseling?

I began to answer the first question in the first part of this paper. A person seeks help because he feels uncomfortable; he feels unable to solve his problems alone. It is assumed that when a person enters the counselor's office his world-view — his perception of himself and himself-in-the-world — is somewhat clouded. He has difficulty seeing the action-possibilities open to him. He experiences disabling anxiety as opposed to existential anxiety. He feels inauthentic, not being able to realize his potentialities.

Most problems which bring a person to seek help concern one or a combination of the modes we have discussed, namely affect, cognition, action, and authenticity. He has difficulty experiencing, expressing, recognizing, or coping with affect. He may be depressed, angry, fearful, etc., but cannot deal with the feeling effectively. He may have difficulty in the cognitive sphere, such as not being able to concentrate, make decisions, or feeling so much that he cannot think. He may have difficulty acting upon his choices, or he may see only limited possibilities or none at all, or he may think so much that he cannot feel. A major source of difficulty centers about authenticity. The person has difficulty with intrapersonal and/or interpersonal relations. He cannot face himself or others; he feels inauthentic and guilt — he feels not himself.

At this point one may ask the question: How does a person come to be in need of counseling? The answer to this question will vary with the individual and can be understood only in terms of the person's unique being-in-the-world. It may be that he was taught to view the world as a place where the expression of affect is forbidden. In lieu of this, it may have been that his integrity was violated to the point where he could not exercise his freedom of choice or responsibility was usurped. Perhaps external control was placed upon him so that action was limited. Whatever the circumstances, however, the main concern is with the client's present world-view, clouded or distorted though it may be. How he came to be what he is will be elucidated in the light of the understanding which occurs during the counseling process.

Now let us turn to the second question; what is counseling? First and foremost, counseling is a process. It is not a series of techniques. Being a process, it flows, it develops, and like man, it is dynamic. Counseling entails a relationship between two or more people — a collaborative effort — the purpose of which is to illuminate a world which is, for some reason, clouded. Through this collaborative effort it is presumed that an elucidation of the client's world will occur and the understanding gleaned through such an elucidation will permit the client to perceive increased action-possibilities.

It should be clear that from this point of view, one does not *do* counseling; one lives it during the interpersonal encounter. One does not make change; change happens when the client feels that he is understood. In essence, counseling occurs when at least two people are engaged in a mutual relationship, each making an effort to understand the world of at least one of these persons who is finding it difficult to realize his potential. It is assumed that through such understanding an expanding of consciousness will occur, allowing for an increase in the possibilities for effective action.

To many counselors this approach may appear somewhat mystical. Many of these counselors have long believed that without a set of techniques they would not be counselors. Perhaps such an aura of mysticism stems from a reluctance on these counselors' part to engage in a truly interpersonal encounter. Thus their techniques serve to maintain some degree of distance from their clients.

In the proposed philosophy of counseling there is no correct method or technique. There is no expert in the sense of the counselor's knowing what to do in order to alleviate the client's problem. Both the counselor and the client are engaged in a human task, and to be human[3] does not require a technique. More will be said about the counselor's role in this approach in the next section of this paper.

In the form of counseling advocated here, one must believe that the goal of each person is to realize, to the best of his ability, his human potential. One must believe that solutions to problems in living lie within the individual, but for some reason or reasons the solutions cannot be recognized or acted upon. No counselor can know his client better than he knows himself. Counseling can be only as effective as the client wants it to be.

It may sound as though counseling must always involve very complex problems and must always be quite intense. This is not so. The approach, however, remains the same regardless of the complexity of the problem. For example, if a client comes into the counselor's office with a question regarding the courses that the client should take during the following semester, it would

---

[3]A discussion of what it means to be human can be found in a paper by Dreyfus and Mackler (1964).

be a violation of the client's integrity for the counselor simply to give him an answer (if such an answer could be offered). One must assume that the client has given the problem considerable thought even before thinking about asking for help. Often the client knows beforehand what he wants to do and is seeking confirmation. If the client is to actualize his potential, he has to assume responsibility for his actions. Thus if the counselor supplies an answer he is assuming responsibility for the client. To be sure, there are times when a simple answer will suffice. Too many counselors all too often feel, however, that when a client enters the office the counselor must *do* something. In many cases he should listen. Hearing is not necessarily listening. While a client may present what appears to be a simple problem, as in the example of the student trying to plan a program, it may well turn out to be an acceptable way of seeking help. The counselor must listen to what the client is trying to say and help him elucidate his world. Before the counselor can offer assistance he must first understand the client's immediate, existing world as the client experiences it at the moment.

This point of view assumes that each person is unique. The counselor operating from the existential viewpoint recognizes that the only similarity between one client and another is that they both enter the counseling situation with a somewhat clouded world-view. From there on the similarity ceases. The client is viewed as a figure standing out from the ground of other people, animals, and things. The goal of counseling is the illumination of this world and the elucidation of this client's existential uniqueness.

AN APPROACH TO COUNSELING

I have stated earlier that the existential approach is a way of looking at and understanding the world of the client as he sits before the counselor. I have also said the counseling involves a relationship between two or more people. Thus far I have dealt with only the client's world. Now I would like to focus on the counselor.[4] It is hoped that such a discussion will serve as a guide for counselors who may make the point of view put forth in the preceding pages compatible with their own theory of man and philosophy of counseling. The discussion will center about two concepts: encounter and confrontation. One might consider these concepts as the basic "tools" of the existential counselor.

Encounter

The encounter refers to the genuinely personal interaction between counselor and client; it is a truly human experience. In order for the counselor to feel comfortable with the feelings of his client, he must feel comfortable with his own feelings. He must recognize that there is no essential difference between himself and the client. He must be willing to engage in a relationship where his feelings may be exposed. The counselor is quite different than the physical scientist insofar as his role is concerned. The physical scientist works *on* his subject matter; the counselor works *with* his client. The counselor's

---

[4]A further discussion of the counselor's role within the existential approach can be found elsewhere (Dreyfus, 1964).

function is not to change the client but to allow change to occur. He cannot view the client as an object to be explored, manipulated, or exploited. The counselor's role as a counselor must be transcended by his role as a human being. He must respond to the client with the essence of his own humanness. While the counselor may be hoping that the existential authenticity of the client will emerge during the encounter, he too must be authentic.

During the encounter the counselor and the client are free to express their feelings. In such an atmosphere of freedom each is open to the other. Openness permits understanding and a growing awareness of self. The counselor must allow the client's world to unfold. Probing into the past is unnecessary and offers little to the client when his problems are in the here and now. Only as the past emerges into the moment will its exploration be of value. The client will allow his world to unfold to the extent that he feels understood. The counselor must feel and demonstrate a genuine respect for the client as a human being. Such respect requires that the counselor not force the client to reveal part of his world which he is not ready to reveal. To force such a revelation would be to violate the client's integrity. The client is not to be exposed because the counselor wants a specific piece of information. Counseling is for the client.

The counselor gleans a picture of the client's world as it is illuminated in the mutual sharing between counselor and client during the encounter. The counselor is being permitted by the client to share in the client's world. He is therefore obligated to share that which he sees with the client. Moreno (1960) has said of the encounter: "A meeting of two: eye to eye, face to face. And when you are near I will tear your eyes out and place them instead of mine, and you will tear my eyes out and place them instead of yours, then I will look at you with your eyes and you will look at me with mine" (p. 144). Such openness and mutuality as exists between counselor and client is the encounter.

While each relationship need not be a very intense one, it can be an existential one. It is existential in that two beings are meeting for the purpose, expressed or implied, of gaining a greater awareness of the existence of the other. The relationship is a human one where the other is free to explore and the two explore together. In the light of the existential encounter the client is free to explore his attitudes, his feelings, his thoughts, his actions, and his authenticity. The counselor is always with him during the exploration. The humanness of the encounter allows the client to become aware of his own humanness and the uniqueness of his own existence.

Confrontation

"Every confrontation is an encounter, but not every encounter is a confrontation. The encounter may not involve a dispute or controversy whereas the confrontation always contains some conflict" (Moustakas, 1962, p. 281). As used in this context, conflict refers to the client's being faced with a choice regarding his own existence. The counselor confronts the client with an aspect of the client's world and the client must choose how he will respond to it, what he will do about it, or whether he accepts or rejects the implications of the confrontation.

In counseling, as opposed to the courtroom situation where confrontation implies an "I caught you" attitude, confrontation implies a direct meeting of the counselor and the client on the issue of the client's existence. The counselor's concern for the integrity of the client which underlies the encounter is always present during the confrontation. The client is faced with a decision and is respected regardless of the choice he makes; integrity is not at stake, the issue is. The mutual respect is maintained.

The therapist actively engages in the confrontation and remains with the client throughout; he does not attempt to expose the client. During the confrontation the counselor and client may argue violently, but the argument is with regard to the issue and not with regard to the personal worth of the other as a person. The resolution of the conflict often brings the two people even closer. The client struggled and the counselor stayed with him during the struggle. In many respects the confrontation deepens the encounter; the counselor must be himself as a human being, fully committed to the client.

I am reminded of a movie in which the main character, a Negro war hero, had suffered hysterical paralysis of his legs as a result of a traumatic incident during battle. While in the hospital he met a white psychiatrist with whom he related in a meaningful encounter. The relationship continued for some time, but the soldier was still unable to walk. Then at one point during the therapy the psychiatrist stated in a very harsh tone "You are nothing but a lazy nigger!" The soldier's eyes met the therapist's in a blaze of fury. The soldier cursed his psychiatrist-friend, and as he crossed the room to attack the therapist for his cruel words he realized that he had walked — he cried.

The confrontation is quite well illustrated in this example. Two men had met in a meaningful encounter. They had displayed mutual respect and admiration. Meeting in the confrontation each pitted his own existence against the other. It was obvious the therapist had maintained his respect for the soldier as he remained with the patient during his struggle with the implied conflict. The anger of the therapist was not directed toward the patient as a person, but rather toward the issue of walking and the patient's giving up. The anger showed the therapist's human concern — that he really *cared* for the patient. The therapist stood fully committed to the soldier, exposing his humanness. At first the soldier thought he was being betrayed by his therapist and had to choose whether he was going to react and how. It wasn't until after the confrontation and after he had made a choice that he understood the confrontation.

Lest the foregoing example be construed as implying that existential counseling is applicable only to more severe forms of emotional disturbance, I should like to make some final comments regarding this approach and the kinds of problems faced when working within a school guidance setting.

Existentialism is concerned with the human condition. As such it is concerned with all forms of human experiencing. It is concerned with the bizarre as well as the normal. Its focus is on the unique experience of the client and how he perceives his world. Whether the problem presented by the client appears to the counselor as minor or major is of little import so long as the client feels it is important. The concern of the counselor is for the immediate existing person seated before him.

A student enters the guidance bureau and states that he is uncertain as to what course of study he should pursue. For him this problem is just as important as the problem of being dropped out of school is for another student, or the problem of being chased by the FBI is for the paranoid schizophrenic. Our imaginary student states that he would like to take some tests in order to learn for what field he is best suited. The counselor has a choice to make: namely, should he assign interest tests to the student or should he explore the uncertainty with the client, and then decide whether to assign tests. The existentially oriented counselor chooses the latter course. His position is that psychometric testing should be used to expand the psychological world of the client by opening more possibilities for action which may remain undisclosed. Psychometric testing is for the client *not* for the counselor. The client stated that he was uncertain as to a course of study which implies that he has some ideas or even that he knows what course he wants but desires confirmation of his choice. Perhaps it is making decisions in general which is difficult or making a commitment which is a problem. The counselor must be open to the client's world and allow it to unfold before he issues tests. To be sure it is often easier to assign tests, interpret the results, and give advice; however, the easy way may not be the best way. The counselor should be willing to engage in a human encounter with his client and be with the client as he, the client, elucidates his world. It is only against the background of the client's unique existence that psychometric tests can be of real value to him.

One does not have to spend many hours with each client before he makes the decision regarding the tests or pondering an answer to a student's question. Rather he should spend just enough time to be relatively certain that both he and the client understand the question. An encounter need not be more than a few moments. With some persons the encounter comes in a flash at the moment of meeting; with other persons it may take considerably longer. The need for confrontation may never arise.

The counselor should be prepared not only to hear what the client says but to listen to him saying it. He should recognize the world of the client for what it is at the moment without trying to classify, categorize, or in any other way violate the uniqueness of the client. He must be ready to engage the client, no matter how briefly, and stay with the client in whatever path he chooses to take along the road to self-actualization.

SUMMARY

Counseling is more than a series of techniques. It requires that a person develop a theory of man — a way of looking at and understanding the nature of man. From this theory one can develop a philosophy of counseling. This philosophy sets the stage for the interaction which will take place during the counseling session. It defines the roles of both the client and counselor. The techniques emerge from the philosophy. In this context some remarks regarding technique in existential counseling, psychoanalysis, and nondirective counseling were made.

I was concerned with developing an existential approach to counseling. The approach centers about the uniqueness of man and the nature of his being-in-the-world. It is concerned with the client as he presents himself in the here and now. In essence, the existential approach is an attitude toward man. It views man as responsible, free to choose his way of being, and as a constantly emerging being. Man is born into an unknown world and thus he is anxious. He moves in the face of this existential anxiety. Failure to move leaves him experiencing guilt — the guilt of not-being.

Within this framework four attributes of being human were discussed: affect, cognition, action, and authenticity. The additional concepts of freedom, choice, and responsibility were also discussed. Through these aspects of man's existence a theory of man and a philosophy of counseling were developed which led to an approach to counseling. Two important aspects of counseling emerged: the encounter and confrontation. The former refers to the inter-human relationship between counselor and client and the latter to the facing of an issue. Each confrontation is an encounter, but each encounter need not be a confrontation.

Finally some remarks regarding counseling in the schools were offered.

REFERENCES

Benda, C. E. The existential approach in psychiatry. *Journal of Existential Psychiatry*, 1960, 1, 24-40.

Binswanger, L. *Being-in-the-World* (Jacob Needleman, Translator), New York: Basic Books, 1963.

Boss, M. *Analysis of Dreams*, New York: Philosophical Library, 1958.

———. *Psychoanalysis and Daseinanalysis*, New York: Basic Books, 1963.

Dreyfus, E. A. Counseling and existentialism. *Journal of Counseling Psychology*, 1962, 9, 128-132.

———. The counselor and existentialism. *Personnel and Guidance Journal*, 1964, 43, 114-117.

Dreyfus, E. A. and Mackler, B. On being human. *Journal of Existentialism*, 1964, 5, 67-76.

May, R. et al. *Existence: A New Dimension in Psychology and Psychiatry*, New York: Basic Books, 1958.

Moreno, J. L. Concept of the encounter. *Journal of Existential Psychiatry*, 1960, 1, 144-154.

Moustakas, C. E. Confrontation and encounter. *Journal of Existential Psychiatry*, 1962, 2, 263-290.

Rogers, C. R. *Client-Centered Therapy*, Boston: Houghton-Mifflin, 1951.

EXISTENTIALISM IN COUNSELING: THE HUMANIST VIEW

Dugald S. Arbuckle

Professor of Education, Boston University, Boston, Massachusetts

Certain philosophical issues which appear to be of paramount importance to the counselor are discussed. Particular attention is paid to the humanism of existentialism and client-centered counseling as compared with the determinism of the behavioral sciences. Phenomenology is considered to be potentially either existential or deterministic. Other aspects of existentialism and determinism that are closely examined are reality, freedom, religion, and values. Both reality and values are viewed in a phenomenal sense, and as a

Reprinted by permission of the author and the *Personnel and Guidance Journal*, February 1965, 558-567.

This paper was part of a symposium, "Existentialism: What it Means to Counseling," held at the American Personnel and Guidance Association Convention, San Francisco, March 25, 1964.

part of the perceptual field of the individual; they are thus relative and dependent on each individual's particular perception. Freedom of the individual is considered to be the basic thread which permeates all views of
existentialism. Some doubt is expressed as to the future of the freedom of
man if man must see himself as a determined person living in a determined
world. The relationship between existentialism and psychotherapy is examined.

There is general agreement today, in the field of counseling and psychotherapy, that the counselor, in his relationship with a client, is sharing of his
self in a personal and human relationship with a fellow human. If we accept
this general premise, then it would seem more logical, in any discussion of
counseling, to move away from the more technique-oriented arguments about
directive or non-directive, client-centered, or counselor-centered, diagnostic
or acceptant. These, after all, are primarily symptomatic indications of one's
basic philosophical concepts regarding man. The purpose of this paper is to
examine certain of these concepts, with particular attention to humanism of
existentialism, the empiricism of determinism and phenomenology, and the
relationship that each of these bears to the others.

DETERMINISM AND EXISTENTIALISM

Determinism and empiricism are close companions, and Skinner, as one
of the most prominent determinists of the day, feels that if we are to use the
methods of science in human affairs, then we must assume that behavior is
lawful and determined. He feels that in the long run man is determined by
the state, and that the only scientific logical conclusion that one can come
to is that man's behavior is a product of his environment (Skinner, 1948,
p. 273). The determinist's version of a counselor's function is given by Michael
and Meyerson (1962): "The phenomena with which counselors deal, then is
behavior, and the independent variable which controls behavior must be the
environment."

Hobbs (1959) is another who accepts a psychological version of man's
limited, and determined, "choice," and while he appears to be somewhat uneasy about this concept, he clearly feels that within a scientific construct
system, the assumption of determinism is required.

Freud would certainly appear to have been deterministic, at least from
the point of view of his scientific theories about man and his behavior, in
which man appeared to be pretty much a victim of forces beyond his control,
forces which he spent his life striving to suppress and direct. On the other
hand, one has only to read Freud to sense the humaneness of the man above
and beyond his theories, a feeling which is borne out by Binswanger, a contemporary of Freud.

Some writers have adopted an in-between attitude on determinism. Samler
(1962), for example, wonders whether in the study of man we may have
carried over the postulates of science that may not be applicable to organisms
that have self-awareness and self-understanding, and he feels that there is a
measure of basic freedom of choice available to the individual, and that within
limits he can move in a given direction.

Combs and Snygg (1959, p. 17) would also appear to be deterministic
in their phenomenological approach to human behavior, although their means

of determinism would not be the same as those of empiricist Skinner or therapist Freud. They see lawfulness and determinism in our behavior at any
moment of behaving. However, while phenomenologists Combs and Snygg
would apparently feel that what one does, and what one sees, and what one
chooses, and where one goes — in fact, all human behavior — is determined
by the phenomenal or perceptual field, they do not see man as a hapless and
hopeless organism, a creature who is the victim of his surroundings. They see
man as part controlled by and in part controlling of his destiny (Combs &
Snygg, 1959, p. 310). In this regard they agree with Shoben, who is critical
of what he feels to be an oversimplification of determinism into a fatalism
of events, and a neglect of the self-determining quality of human character
(Shoben, 1953).

Sharply different in its concept of man is a humanistic existentialism,
although existentialism by no means see eye to eye on all matters. Certainly
the differences among such figures as Heidegger, and Kierkegaard, and
Sartre, and Jaspers are quite apparent. Nevertheless, the existentialist is anti-
deterministic in that he sees the person transcending both himself and his
culture. Existentialism centers on the existing person, and it places priority on
the existing man (existence) rather than on truth and laws and principles
(essence). It sees a man as *being*. It also sees man with decision and will
and choice, and there is the element of freedom and choice even in the seeing
and the exploring, and the challenging, if necessary, of the determined world
around him (May, 1961a; May 1961b).

For Sartre, one of the European stalwarts of existentialism, man is free,
man *is* freedom, and if we accept the concept that existence does precede
essence, then there can be no determinism. Man can be what he will (Sartre,
1947). Jaspers, too, would tend to see the true authentic "transcendental"
self as being the source of meaning in life. This self is free, and it makes
choice possible, and this self is not subject to study (Titus, 1959, p. 301).

Thus this self, this person-in-being as seen by the existentialist, is one who
is not subject to empirical prediction and control. Ostow (1958) expresses
this anti-deterministic concept when he indicates that the failure of religion,
if failure it is, to obtain complete control over human behavior is because of
the ultimate independence of the human spirit and the essential autonomy
of the instinctual apparatus. Frankl (1958), too, feels that a real human person is not subject to rigid prediction, and that existence can neither be reduced
to a system or deduced from it.

Thus, it would appear that one cannot be both deterministic and existential, but at the same time neither can be considered as absolute terms. Skinner
might be considered to represent the extreme at the deterministic end of a
continuum, where man would appear to be little more than a hapless thing,
to be measured and manipulated and controlled for the furtherance of some
unknown ends of some faceless "group," and Sartre might represent the other
end of the continuum which would see man as supreme, answerable only to
himself, responsible for his own actions. He may live in a world in which
things and events have not been "determined" by him, but the human self
is the determiner of the manner and mode and way in which he will grow
and live and die in this somewhat "determined" outside. Enculturation is *not*
the automatic fate of the true, of the existential, of the authentic person. He
transcends both himself and his culture, and as Maslow (1961, p. 55) puts it,

he becomes ". . . a little more a member of his species and a little less a member of his local group." Man is the maker and the master of his culture. The culture is his; he is not the culture's, but the attempt to suppress the existential self, while bound to fail, has a long history. Michael and Meyerson (1962) give a frighteningly accurate picture of the modern scientific version of suppression as they calmly accept the concept that the function of the "guidance" person is to influence and induce people to behave the way society thinks they should behave, and his major problem is to discover ways of getting people to behave the way we think they should behave. There is, apparently, little or no difference between the school counselor and the Chinese brainwasher!

This is the view of the behaviorist, the positivist, the determinist. Whatever the name might be, it would seem to spell autocracy, and whether it be the autocracy of the church, or of the state, or of science, the end result is the suppression of the individual, the degradation of man.

Any "government" which is "of the people" obviously cannot consider democracy to be the suppression of the rights of the minority by the majority. This is nothing more than a slightly broader version of autocracy, in which more than one half of the people suppress the less than one half. If freedom is to go with democracy then we must think of the existing living human being, rather than the "law." When we accept as immutable and fixed a "law," democratic or not, which in effect says to a human, "You cannot be what you are — you cannot *be*," then we have indeed become encrusted and encultured. We then become the ones who are no longer free, we are the serfs and the slaves, and what may happen, as what has happened, is that the man we suppress or jail or torture or kill — he is the man who is free. The man lives within the laws of his culture, if he lives in a relatively "free" culture, but he is not bound by them. They do not control him, but, rather, his self transcends them.

PHENOMENOLOGY, DETERMINISM, AND EXISTENTIALISM

We have noted that the phenomenological approach and existentialism have often been apparently linked in the literature, but it is important to note that the existentialist self and the phenomenal field are not one and the same. The phenomenological approach seeks to understand the behavior of the individual from his *own* point of view. It attempts to observe people, not as they seem to outsiders, but as they seem to themselves (Combs & Snygg, 1959, p. 11). One can be phenomenological in his approach and still be deterministic, whereas one cannot be deterministic and existential. There would seem, however, to be little difference between the concept of the phenomenal self and that of the existential self, since both operate within the perceptual field. Combs (1959, p. 146) indicates his own feeling of the primacy of the *self* over the *field*, which is, of course, the opposite of the deterministic point of view, when he says, ". . . the perceptual field is usually organized with reference to the behaver's own phenomenal self," and ". . . the phenomenal self is both product of the individual's experience and product of whatever new experiences he is capable of." The degree of determinism, however, depends on the primacy of the field over the self. If one feels that one's actions are determined by the phenomenal field, then, of course, he has no choice, and he can hardly be held "responsible" for his actions. Combs would seem to at least be somewhat acceptant of this deterministic concept when he describes the term "conflict" as a term of external description. It is an outsider's description of what he observes and the behaver himself does not experience conflict (Combs & Snygg, p. 185).

May (1961a, p. 26) apparently feels no necessity of a phenomenological concept also being deterministic, and thinks of phenomenology, the first stage in the existential psychotherapeutic movement, as being the endeavor to take the phenomena as given. Nor does Rogers (1951, p. 532), who sees a goal of human development as being a basic congruence between the phenomenal field of experience and the conceptual structure of the self.

Again, however, it is important to note that unconditional acceptance is not *dependent* on the identity of the value system of the self with the value system of some other "well-adjusted" members of the human race. This *may* or *may* not happen, but it is the self, the transcendent self, the self-in-being, that is the determiner of the congruence.

Thus we might even say that it may be that an acceptance of the phenomenological field theory of human behavior might make it easier to see determinism as the fate of mankind, yet, on the other hand, the existentialist accepts the phenomenological concept without in any manner feeling that this means the dominance of the field in which the self operates over the self. In fact, one could hardly hold to an existential concept without being acceptant of the basic phenomenological approach to reality and to the self.

REALITY AND FREEDOM

The phenomenologist, the existentialist, and the client-centered counselor see reality in much the same way. When May (1961a, pp. 17-18) says "There is no such thing as truth or reality for a living human being except as he particulates in it, is conscious of it, has some relationship to it," and "The more absolutely and completely you formulate the forces and drives, the more you are talking about abstractions, and not the existing, living human being," he is expressing the phenomenological concept that reality lies in the individual's experience of the event, rather than in the isolated event. One might also say that there is, "really," no "event" without the human individual. Hatreds and bogey men and chairs exist only as they appear to the individual as they become a part of his experiencing, his living. Thus, we may say, with the determinist, that there *is* a world of reality, but it cannot be "reality" apart from the people who are the basic part of it. This is a problem faced by all student counselors, and many of even the more sophisticated and experienced counselors and therapists still appear to feel strongly that "reality," for them, must somehow, be reality for their client. Rather than accepting him, and thus his reality, and living through it and experiencing it with him, they sit on the outside, subtly or directly imposing their concepts upon him. They thus impede and make more difficult his growth toward greater freedom and self-actualization. It is difficult to modify or change one's reality if one is never allowed to deeply experience just what that reality might be.

Actually this ability to live another's reality with him might be considered as a description of empathy. This also means that the counselor is one who can live certainly in a world of uncertainty, one who accepts the probability in living with security. All too frequently in counseling, it really is "cases" that we are discussing, and with which we are working, whether we are in a staff conference "case" discussion, or involved in an actual counseling session. We operate with events, and problems, and questions and supposed meanings, and the real-life, experiencing person, either represented (and nothing more) on a piece of paper, or the flesh-and-blood person in front of us, is ignored and unseen, and we give him little help in the struggle to see who he is, because it is not "him" with whom we are relating.

In a different way, Barry and Wolf (1962, pp. 90-91) said much the same thing when they described realism as essentially a mask for the value judgments about the practicality and practicability of an idea, a feeling, a plan. It is a judgment dependent upon time and the point of view of the person making it.

Alas, how many thousands of students throughout the United States, have sat, today, in hundreds of schools, listening to their "counselor" as he said, among other things, ". . . Now Joe, let's be realistic about this, and. . ." The counselor is indeed making a value judgment, and even worse, in the name of an absolute reality (his), he is imposing this reality upon his unfortunate victim.

The existential concept of reality is closely related to freedom, which is the core of existential thought. This may be expressed as Sartre's consciousness as freedom, Jasper's existence as freedom, Kierkegaard's self as freedom, or Tillich's concept of man as freedom. To this unsophisticated individual they are all saying the same thing in somewhat complicated philosophical language —that I am free, that where I go and what I do depends on me, not on the forces outside of me, or even on the forces which I may have internalized as a part of me. I, and I alone, always have the ultimate choice, and this choice I am free to make. The very fact that one is alive means that he has the potential to be free, but one is never free to live, of course, until he is free to die.

Effectively expressing this point of view is Rogers (unpublished) when he talks of freedom as essentially an inner thing, something which exists in the living person, quite aside from any of the outward choice of alternatives which we so often think of as constituting freedom. So, too, Frankl, (1955, p. 65) and Buber (1937, p. 53), and May (1961a, p. 41) all stress the *inner* concept of freedom, and with it one can determine the ultimate direction, and make, when necessary, his final choice.

This movement toward freedom is also the core of the therapeutic process, and as one moves toward freedom — and responsibility — he becomes more aware of the deterministic forces pressing in on him (Michael & Meyerson, 1962). While determinism may be a fact of the physical world, it is man who completes that world, and it is man who makes of the world whatever reality he may wish it to become. Thus the growth that occurs in counseling might be considered to be the process, the experience, the learning to be free.

Freedom may not be the opposite of determinism, but one does not find the concept of freedom in a deterministic society. The existentialist would feel that the individual may live in a physical world which is, in a sense, determined, but the human individual, the existential self, the spirit of man, is not bound by any set of determined chains. Man basically *is* free, and any man can come to learn and to grow and to become the free person he is. This is the purpose of counseling — to help the individual to loosen himself from his deterministic shackles, and to come to realize and to see what he has always had — choice and freedom.

Being free is difficult, and one cannot be free without continually running the risk of losing one's person. The struggle to be free, too, is often much more intense and complicated, at the inner-self level, than is the struggle against overt and obvious forces of oppression. If education results in real understanding, then it can widen one's horizon of freedom, and the counselor must be concerned about the extent to which the educational experience helps to free each child.

RELIGION, VALUES, AND EXISTENTIALISM

The existentialist camp is dotted with religious figures such as Jaspers, Tillich, Marcel, Maritain, Kierkegaard, Buber, and May who outnumber the atheistic speakers such as Sartre and Heidegger. While theistic and atheistic existentialists would not agree on the question of the existence of a God, of some supreme all-knowing Being, some supernatural Deity, they would agree that man must live alone, that his living-now is all he can know, that man *is* only what he does and what he lives. Sartre would add that existence must precede essence. Neither would they see any ordered plan into which man must fit, and in this way the religious existentialists would likely differ from most of their more-dogma-and-less-philosophy-oriented colleagues. The religious existentialist would likely feel that there *is* meaning, but the decisions and the choices as to where to go and what to do to find that meaning must be the lonely choice of man, and his choice may be wrong. The atheistic existentialist would likely feel that there is no "meaning" that one seeks, but rather man evolves his own "meanings" as he moves and lives. Man *is*, and he creates his meanings. He does not seek *the* meaning.

Thus both would probably agree that determinism may be a part of the world in which man exists, but determinism does not apply to man. In this regard the theistic existentialist would probably not be very acceptable to most theologians who tend to see the world as a pre-determined place, operating on some Grand Plan under some Divine Order, in which man only exists, but does not actually live, since his life is determined and he thus cannot be free. To many theologians, possibly to most, God is some outer external force which controls and directs man to do its bidding. This is why it may be easier for many of them, for many "religious" individuals, to see God in a magnificent church, or in some symbol of power and might, rather than in some ordinary, insignificant man, even though surprisingly enough, the man that most "Christians" would say they try to emulate was a very ordinary, simple, loving, compassionate individual!

Religion is generally deterministic, and it sees man not only as living in a deterministic world, but very much a determined part of this deterministic world. If one holds the view that life is ultimately determined by Divine

Will, then he is expressing a deterministic point of view. Both the non-religious and the theistic existentialist would feel that man *is* not *one* important determinant, but that man *is* the creator. He does not live in a "created" world; he creates it as he lives. This is the only world he can know.

The existentialist does not see a value as something which is apart from a person. Values are human products, and they exist only in a human community. Usually, a "value" implies a judgment, but the same act may have as many different values placed upon it as there are people who are involved in it. A generally accepted cultural concept is that certain "values" are better than others, and an equally acceptable concept is that values can, and should, be taught. The questionable assumption here is that the teacher somehow is the possessor of a value which is not possessed by the learner, and that it is the function of the teacher to teach this better value (his), to the learner, who either does not have this value, or has a "wrong" one. This concept detaches the value from the person, so that, just as one can be taught how to drive, one can be "taught" morality, virtue, and courage. This concept also makes possible the widely accepted tenet in counseling that "I like him but I don't like what he is doing." It obviously implies that the counselor should, and must, have as part of his value system a feeling of the rightness of his ways *for others*, an obligation to impose this rightness on others, and an assumption that this rightness can be imposed (taught) to others. While these assumptions are questionable from an existential point of view, they are, nevertheless, widely held.

Mueller (1958), for example, has indicated her feeling that not only can one teach ethics, but that the "counselor" must teach ethics as he "counsels." There would appear here, again, to be the concept of a detachment of a human act from a person, the idea that values are some form of appendices that one "learns" by being taught. There is an absence of the feeling that values, being a part of the person, can only come through an experiencing and a living and a human relationship. Close human contact with a patient and compassionate person may help another person to free himself so that he, too, may move in the direction of patience and compassion. He may thus "learn," from a counselor, from a teacher, from a friend, but he has not been taught. History would surely bear witness to the futility of the attempt of one person to "teach" another his value system.

Williamson (1958) also expresses a deterministic feeling of human limitations when he appears to view the counselor as one whose outside-of-me values control him, rather than one whose inner self is expressed in terms of his values. This concept also implies a striving by the counselor to achieve for the client something, some answer, some right path or goal which is external to the client, and possibly to the counselor. This is almost like the counselor who cheats on his income tax returns striving to convince the client who has been cheating on exams that the virtue of "no cheating" is something which he really should practice. Actually, this "virtue" is real for neither client nor counselor, and it is unlikely that any change is going to take place in either one. On the other hand, we might hypothesize that if the counselor is a "noncheating" sort of fellow, in his living-being, regardless of any words, then he will see no point in trying to press this on to the client, who, in turn, might possibly internalize, or at least let stir around inside him the idea that this might be something worth incorporating so that it becomes a part of his being. People who believe, feel no particular pressure to convince others that they should believe the same way too. It is likely that the evangelist is actually very concerned about who he is and where he is going, and this is why he continually tries to convince others that they should follow him. He neither respects nor trusts the other fellow to find his right way, and, if his "religion" includes compassion and gentleness and love toward his fellows, he spends his time preaching it rather than practicing it.

The concept that one can separate a person from his values is a very common one in counseling. It is almost as if one can view a human act and the person who commits it as two separate entities. One might feel that the act of robbery, the taking away from one person of his belongings so that I can further my own interests, is questionable. But when a counselor is relating with another fellow human who has committed the act of robbery, he cannot now divorce the person from the act. Part of the person is the fact that he has committed a robbery, and since we accept the client as he is, the un-related fact of robbery, or what the counselor may think about it, has no relationship to the therapeutic interaction whatsoever. It is the person, all of him, with whom we are concerned, and the various bits and pieces, by themselves, mean nothing. The existential counselor, however, would not view acts at any time as being detached from humans, so that a question such as "Well, do you mean that you don't think that robbery is bad?" really isn't a question because robbery, per se, *really* doesn't mean anything. It is only when it becomes a part of an individual human's behavior that it means something, and the counselor, being concerned with the person, is not par-ticularly aware of the "goods" or "bads" of the individual's actions.

This is likely why, too, practically every act that is labeled "bad" by some-one, is labeled "good" by someone else. Robin Hood's thieving was considered wonderful by those who were the recipients of his loot, but not by those from whom he stole. Americans think affectionately of the "robber barons" who were the ancestors of some of our most illustrious current figures, po-litical and otherwise!

Shoben (1953) expresses the "doing something to somebody" attitude when he comments that the field is committed to the development of respon-sible individuals capable of maintaining and advancing a democratic society. The existentialist would be more concerned with helping the individual to come to be able to release and use the potential that he has, and he would have little concern about whither the "inner man" would go. He would help the person to grow to freedom, and while a product might be a "democratic society," this would be somewhat meaningless, since in today's world we have earnest people who are sure they have "democratic societies" in such countries as China, Jugoslavia, Ghana, and Russia. Shoben, of course, means *his* concept of a democratic society, and while doubtless many of us would share this concept very closely with him, can we not, at least in a counseling relationship, operate on the assumption that the client who has learned to be free will help to develop a society in which all may live their life to the ut-most, with respect for the rights and the integrity of their fellows, since they respect the rights and the integrity of their self.

While we could agree that the counselor might as well admit that he has his own values, but that there is no reason that these will be most meaningful for the client (May, 1962), it is important to distinguish between those values which are a part of the make-up of the inner self of the counselor, and are shown in his patience, his compassion, and his acceptance of the client, and values of judgment and evaluation. The counselor who feels that "robbery," *per se*, is "bad," is not actually too far removed from the counselor who feels that the client who has robbed is "bad," who in turn is not too far removed from the individual who feels that the person who has robbed is bad, and should therefore be punished. While such individuals may be being existential in the sense that they are saying "You, and you alone must be responsible for your deeds," they are not existential in the sense that they are not getting close to, or being understanding of, the existential self. They may be observing it, but they are not living with it.

Curran (1960) expresses more of a trust in the person-in-being when he indicates that we should seek a personal integration which is also an integration with the whole civilization which has produced us. This might then free us from the concept that all personal values must be imposed from without and restore again the possibility of starting out on a personal pursuit of oneself in a search for reasonable self-values.

This might represent a somewhat theistic existential point of view, in that while Curran trusts the individual to determine for himself how he will move and when and where he will move, he believes that there are, somehow, already established answers and values which the individual will come to find. The individual does not develop and create his own answers, but he moves toward pre-established answers. In this case, in Curran's mind, these are likely established by some Deity or God. Curran also indicates the interesting concept that somehow the ancient values are more secure, and, we can assume, somehow better, than more recent values. Were the ancient and traditional values of the Romans more secure, and better, than some of the values that were being advanced by a heretic named Christ? Were the ancient and traditional values of the Greeks more secure than those of the heretic Socrates? The non-theistic existentialist would likely feel, with Curran, that the individual must find his own way, and, with Curran, he would have faith that the individual could find his own way, but he would differ with Curran in that he would have no pre-conceived concept of where the individual might end, or what his values might become. They might be like those of yesterday, or they might be like those of tomorrow, but man lives his life, and he creates his values. He never goes back, to what once was, although he may become like what once was.

In a sense, Curran would seem to have his "man" attempting to discover pre-existent truths and values, to somehow become congruent with what already is, and in this sense, of course, he is expressing the view of determinism. For him, what is, was, but for the existentialist, what is, is. Life is today, now, not yesterday, and we move away from yesterday, not toward it even though we may yearn for this return to the womb.

One cannot discuss values and freedom and living, without also taking into consideration that closely allied experience that eventually comes to all — death. The free man of the existentialist, the human who is never merely a victim of a predetermined culture, the person-in-being who is the maker of his values, this man, being free to live, is also free to die, and it would seem that no person can really be free to live if he is afraid to die. Feifel (1961, p. 71) expresses this feeling when he comments that we "are not altogether free in any deed as long as we are commanded by an inescapable will to live." Sartre (1947, p. 545) relates freedom with death when he says "The very act of freedom is therefore the assumption and creation of finitudes: If I make myself, I make myself finite and hence my life is unique."

It is ironic, and sad, that one of the basic feelings that many individuals learn from their "religion" is fear, and particularly fear of death. Feifel (1961, p. 68), for example, found, in a study of his patients, that the religious person, as compared with the non-religious person, was personally more afraid of death. There must be untold millions of Christians who spend much of their life trying to guarantee their entry into Heaven, but since they feel that they are not the ones who control their destiny, they are never quite sure whether their Deity is approving or disapproving. They thus seek as much as they can in the way of assurances that there is a Heaven, and that they, and a few of their chosen fellows, will be the ones who will be there. The old and hoary joke about each group in Heaven having to live their segregated lives behind walls for fear that they might discover there are other peoples in Heaven too, is not a joke to many. Equally shocking to some white, male Christians is the story of the angel, who, on being asked to describe God, said, "She is a Negro." Many "devout" Christians cannot accept doubt and uncertainty as part of their religion. They must know, particularly about the rewards and punishments of the hereafter, and this might logically tend to make them somewhat self-centered in their actions toward others. The one who does not know about the future, and will, with certainty, face this uncertainty, even to the point of dying to defend a fellow human, is indeed showing a far higher level of altruism and compassion.

The existential man would live his life of freedom and responsibility, and would not have to "know" about what happens after death. If his reason conflicted with some religious fairy stories, he would not be too disturbed, since his life is now, and he would live this the best he could. The rest he could accept, without fear, as the unknown. For him, the person is as he is, satisfaction must come from within, man is able to be free, man is able to choose, and so, to himself, become tolerable to behold. Whether he is tolerable to others is of secondary importance. He must first be tolerable to himself, and it would surely seem that most people who are intolerable of their self, are the ones who find others intolerable. One person becomes a heretic to another person because that person has not yet learned the life of the free man, and is thus afraid.

EXISTENTIALISM AND PSYCHOTHERAPY

It is unfortunate, but probably unavoidable that psychotherapy has come to have certain tags and handles, and these carry with them the obvious implication of a "method" of psychotherapy. It is probably just as safe to assume that Rogers was not thinking of a method of counseling when he used the term "non-directive" and later, "client-centered," as it is to assume that there is really only one Rogerian, namely Carl Rogers, as there was only one Freudian, Sigmund Freud. What is too often missed is that "client-centered" means literally, not just figuratively, what it says: it refers to a human relationship which is centered on one of the two people involved, the client. And the client-centered concept of man, and of the counseling relationship, is very much an existential point of view. This, it might be pointed out, is not the traditional doctor-patient relationship of medicine, nor is it the somewhat similar doctor-patient relationship as it is carried over into much of the traditional pre-Rogers psychotherapy. In much of this, as in much of counseling today, at best only lip-service is paid to the concept that the client must be the central figure, and the deciding agent as far as any choice or decision is concerned.

It would seem that at least the client-centered counselor and the existential therapist are talking pretty much the same language when they discuss man, the person-in-being, and the counseling relationship, the process of becoming. It should be noted too, that existentialism is primarily a product of European philosophers, rather than psychotherapists. The earlier existentialists, Kierkegaard (some would add Marx and Nietzsche), Sartre, Heidegger, Marcel, Jaspers, Maritain and Buber were, and are, tremendous beings, and while they lived fully, and wrote extensively about man, they wrote from a philosophical and theistic or atheistic point of view. It may be, in a living and experiencing way, they knew more about man than they knew man. Their modern American counterpart might be Tillich, while May would appear to be an American therapist who has an existential approach to man. This might be one reason why the older non-therapist existentialist had a somewhat more pessimistic and deterministic viewpoint of man, and the more optimistic point of view of client-centered therapist Rogers would appear to be shared more by therapist May than by theologian Tillich. Again, we note here that religion, at least in a formal and doctrinaire sense, would appear to be more a part of the make-up of Tillich, somewhat less of May, and still less of Rogers. On the other hand, Rogers, at least in the sense of his deep respect for the integrity of others, and his sense of responsibility that he shares living with others, is surely a deeply "religious" person.

Thus it would seem that client-centered therapy, as it views man, and the human counseling relationship of man with man, is very much existential. It is not as pessimistic as existential philosophy would appear at times to be. It is phenomenological in the sense of the phenomenological world of the individual as being the world of reality for the individual, but it is not phenomenological in a deterministic sense.

REFERENCES

Barry, Ruth, & Wolf, Beverly. *An epitaph for vocational guidance.* New York: Teachers College, Columbia University, 1962.

Buber, M. *I and thou.* Translated by R. G. Smith. Edinburgh: T. Clark, 1937.

Combs, Arthur W., & Snygg, Donald. *Individual behavior.* New York: Harper, 1959.

Curran, Charles A. Some ethical and scientific values in the counseling therapeutic process. *Personnel guid. J.,* 1960, 39, 15-20.

Feifel, Herman. In May, Rollo, *Existential psychology.* New York: Random House, 1961.

Frankl, V. E. On logotherapy and existential analysis. *Amer. J. Psychoanal.,* 1958, 18 (1), 28-37.

Frankl, V. E. *From death camp to existentialism.* (Translated by I. Lasch) Boston: Beacon Press, 1955.

Hobbs, Nicholas. Science and ethical behavior. *Amer. Psychologist,* 1959, 14, 217-225.

Maslow, A. H. In May, Rollo, *Existential psychology*. New York: Random House, 1961.

May, Rollo. *Existential psychology*. New York: Random House, 1961a.

May, Rollo. *Existence*. New York: Basic Books, 1961b.

May, Rollo. Freedom and responsibility re-examined. Unpublished paper given at Chicago, 1962 APGA Convention.

Michael, Jack, & Meyerson, Lee. A behavioral approach to counseling and guidance. *Harvard Educ. Rev.*, 1962, 32, 383-402.

Mueller, Kate H. Theory for campus decline. *Personnel guid. J.*, 1958, 36, 302-309.

Ostow, Mortimer. The nature of religious controls. *Amer. Psychologist*, 1958, 13, 571-74.

Rogers, Carl R. *Client-centered psychotherapy*. Boston: Houghton-Mifflin, 1951.

Rogers, Carl R. Learning to be free, an unpublished paper.

Samler, Joseph. An examination of client strength nad counselor responsibility. *J. counsel. Psychol.* 1962, 9, 5-11.

Sartre, Jean-Paul. *Existentialism*. (Translated by B. Freeman) New York: Philosophical library, 1947.

Shoben, E. J. New frontiers in theory. *Personnel guid. J.*, 1953, 32, 80-83.

Skinner, B. F. *Walden two*. New York: Macmillan, 1948.

Titus, Harold H. *Living issues in philosophy*. New York: American Book Co., 1959.

Williamson, Edmund G. Value orientation in counseling. *Personnel guid. J.*, 1958, 36, 520-528.

CHAPTER 5: QUESTIONS FOR DISCUSSION

1. Would Chenault's proposed model for humanistic counselor education programs seem more or less desirable than your present one? In what respects? If such a program were adopted, would anything be conspicuously missing? gained?

2. Borow recommends a "redress of balance" in counseling research. The article was first published in 1956. Do you see any encouraging "redress in balance" in the types of research and theoretical writings in the literature?

3. Dey has suggested a modification in the role of counselor educators. What factors may stand in the way of instituting such changes? Would the possible gains be worth confronting these factors? Why, in your opinion?

4. In what ways are Tyler's ideas on minimum change therapy different from common ideas and practices in school counseling? What recent developments have tended to support her position, as indicated by the literature?

5. Glasser places great emphasis on "good and bad" behavior, "right" and "wrong" actions. Read his essay carefully to be sure you understand how he is using these terms. Then, what long-held beliefs does Reality Therapy seem to violate or play down?

6. Jakubowski-Spector has described the major operating assumptions and some possible ethical questions related to behavioral counseling. Which assumptions seem to run counter to other approaches found in your readings? Can you reconcile them?

7. Many counselor educators view Van Kaam's existential outlook in counseling as a welcome corrective to recent "objective" ways of viewing people. What do you find appealing in his outlook? What criticisms might be made of the views?

8. Van Dusen has addressed himself to psychoanalysis, but has given interesting insights into perceptions of clients. What can the school counselor learn from his essay which may be helpful in working with the so-called "normal range" of clients with whom he has most of his contacts?

9. How do the views of Dreyfus differ from older positions and beliefs in counseling? Dreyfus uses the example of a baby's reacting honestly and authentically as a whole organism in expressing feelings. What factors tend to move

man away from such "authentic" ways of responding as he grows into adult-hood? In what instances do we see "authentic" behavior among adults?

10. What similarities and differences do you see between the Rogerian counseling concepts and the main concepts of existentialism?

SUMMARY

The philosophical aspects of guidance, counseling, and therapy have been the "dark area" of helping relationships. This book has brought together major articles which have dealt thoughtfully with these aspects of guidance and counseling. The new articles written especially for this book in order to fill gaps in the literature, the previously-published articles synthesizing important trends and viewpoints, and other articles have been addressed here toward providing guidelines for the new generation of counselors. We know in advance that much of our thinking will become dated and will be discarded in favor of the "new voices" even now taking their places in the field. But it is the task of every profession to pass on the best of past and present thinking to the novice, that he might examine it, think about it, and build on it.

It is my firm belief that the task of the philosopher is not merely to write for other philosophers: that is too safe, too remote from life as it is lived. It is, rather, his task to involve his best efforts in any area of education, of help-ing relationships, or other areas vital to human welfare whenever he is con-versant with the literature and the issues. The rapprochement between philoso-phy and counseling cannot do other than benefit both. Since most philosophers are not conversant with the issues and literature of counseling, it falls to the counselors themselves to serve as their own "physicians," so to speak, until and if aid is forthcoming from the philosopher. Indeed, the leaders in the field of counseling have done an admirable job of pinning down the basic issues and addressing themselves to their resolution, consonant with present goals. It is now the task of the "new wave" to pursue an ever more intense study of philosophy and counseling, and to communicate the need for such examination to their own students. We can never know in advance who, sit-ting quietly perhaps, in our classes may be able to tie the loose end, turn the proper phrase, raise the synthesizing question, or bring forth, haltingly, a needed concept. They must raise questions frequently, and eyebrows oc-casionally, with their thinking.

Some of the articles in this book have indeed raised questions *and* eye-brows, but this is necessary before eventual refinements of new views can filter into the field. The philosopher William James once said, "A difference, to *be* a difference, must *make* a difference." This seems a sensible attitude to take in evaluating our literature, especially the theoretical-philosophical aspects of it. We must ask ourselves, "If we accept the views put forth by this writer, what seems indefensible or undesirable in present practice? What must be approached differently? How can we implement the change? How can we defend it, if it be a sweeping change involving many people? What are the alternatives? How can we best evaluate the changes we make in terms of chosen goals?"

We have tinkered with the machinery of helping relationships for a long time. Perhaps the time has come for a new design, based on what most of us have seen as design-weakness in older models. We do not wish to discard everything about the whole mechanism, but rather to help it fulfill better its intended purposes. We must also periodically examine those purposes, as our society changes. All of us who have participated in the present book hope that we have made a step in some of these directions.